Typhoons

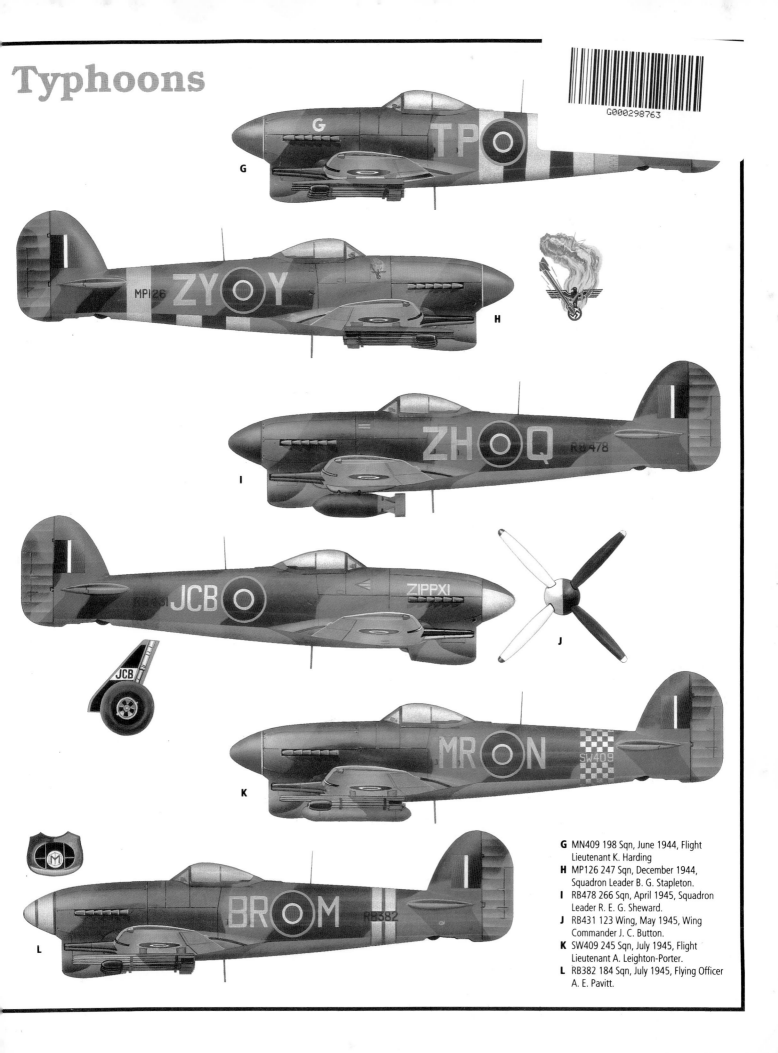

G MN409 198 Sqn, June 1944, Flight
Lieutenant K. Harding

H MP126 247 Sqn, December 1944,
Squadron Leader B. G. Stapleton.

I RB478 266 Sqn, April 1945, Squadron
Leader R. E. G. Sheward.

J RB431 123 Wing, May 1945, Wing
Commander J. C. Button.

K SW409 245 Sqn, July 1945, Flight
Lieutenant A. Leighton-Porter.

L RB382 184 Sqn, July 1945, Flying Officer
A. E. Pavitt.

G000298763

The Typhoon & Tempest Story

181 Squadron Typhoon 1Bs flying from Hurn in April 1944.
Unlike the others, the lead aircraft is not equipped with
rockets. (Bill Grey)

Rocket Typhoon 1Bs of 175 Squadron dispersed on their first
German base, B.100 Goch. (Public Archives of Canada)

The Typhoon & Tempest Story

Chris Thomas and Christopher Shores

ARMS AND ARMOUR PRESS
LONDON NEW YORK SYDNEY

First published in Great Britain in 1988 by Arms and Armour Press, Artillery House, Artillery Row, London SW1P 1RT.

Distributed in the USA by Sterling Publishing Co. Inc., 2 Park Avenue, New York, NY 10016.

Distributed in Australia by Capricorn Link (Australia) Pty. Ltd., P.O. Box 665, Lane Cove, New South Wales 2066, Australia.

British Library Cataloguing in Publication Data:
Thomas, Christopher
Typhoon and Tempest story.
1. Tempest (Fighter plane) – History
2. Typhoon (Fighter plane) – History
I. Title II. Shores, Christopher
623.74'64 TL686.H32

ISBN 0-85368-878-6

Edited and designed by DAG Publications Ltd. Designed by David Gibbons; layout by Anthony A. Evans; edited by Michael Boxall; typeset by Typesetters (Birmingham) Ltd., camerawork by M & E Graphics, North Fambridge, Essex; printed and bound in Great Britain by Butler & Tanner Ltd, Frome and London.

Contents

174 Squadron, August 1943

152 Squadron, 1946

438 Squadron, January 1945

175 Squadron, May 1945

197 Squadron, late 1944

263 Squadron, November 1944

Foreword

by Group Captain D. E. Gillam DSO✫✫, DFC✫, AFC

WHEN the authors said they were writing a book about the Typhoon and Tempest, I was delighted, because I have long felt that insufficient credit has been given to the operations by these aircraft.

Having flown Spitfires and Hurricanes in the Battle of Britain, and throughout 1941, I was posted on a lecture tour of the USA. When I returned I received the exciting news that I had been promoted and posted as Wing Leader to the first Typhoon Wing, then being formed at Duxford. I flew my first Typhoon on 26 March 1942.

In those early days, we were greatly troubled by engine failures, and somewhat later by structural failures, but in June 1942 we commenced limited operations, mostly patrols. We were involved in the Dieppe action but suffered from bad recognition, being attacked by Spitfires and shot at by the Navy. Operations continued, however, and the teething troubles were eventually overcome.

In April 1943 I formed the Special Low Attack Instructors School at Milfield, which gave me the opportunity to see the development of the low-level bombing techniques, and the new RP weapons, which would be the strength of 2nd TAF after the Invasion.

The next task was to form 16 Wing, consisting of 121 and 124 Airfields – the first mobile Typhoon Wings in 83 Group. These large Wings proved unwieldy, and the constituent Airfields eventually became Wings in their own right. Operations were stepped up in anticipation of the Invasion; by this time I was leading 146 Wing at Tangmere and, like the other Typhoon Wings, we were heavily involved in attacking German radars along the French coast. Although this was expensive, as we lost a number of pilots, especially Squadron Leaders, we achieved our object and denied the Germans effective radar cover during the vital stages of the Invasion.

By July 1944 we were operating in France, giving direct support to the Canadian Army. The German counter-attack at Mortain and the battle for the Falaise 'gap' were memorable actions, when the Typhoon squadrons used bombs, rockets and 20mm cannon to devastating effect. The Typhoon was proving an excellent weapon platform and could take a lot of punishment. While the Spitfires kept the Focke-Wulfs away, the Typhoons virtually stopped German transport movements. Later the Spitfire's role was partly taken over by that most splendid development of the Typhoon, the Tempest, which had already played an outstanding part in the battle against the V-1s. We would see these aircraft with increasing frequency in the last months of the war, and they did

much to ensure that the Luftwaffe rarely interfered with our operations.

When the Wing moved into Belgium, in addition to the continuous support for the Army, a limited number of special targets, including Wehrmacht and Gestapo HQs, were successfully attacked. At the end of February I was posted to 84 Group HQ, but managed to fly occasional operations until the end of the war.

So, having been involved with the Typhoon throughout its operational life, I can verify that after those initial teething troubles it became a very successful ground-attack aircraft indeed. In fact, had it not been developed, the war on the ground would have lasted much longer and been very much more expensive for the Army. The aircraft was fast by the standards of the day and carried extremely effective armament which it could deliver with accuracy. None of which would have been much use if we had not had the pilots who, despite casualties well above the average for fighter pilots, pressed home their attacks with great courage, and were always looking for more action. These pilots I particularly salute, and the groundcrews who kept us flying in such difficult conditions. I hope that this book will bring back the memories of the good and the bad times we shared.

Authors' note: Denys Gillam saw service as a Spitfire pilot with 616 Squadron during the fighting over Dunkirk and the Battle of Britain in 1940, during which period he was credited with seven and two shared aerial victories. In the later part of the Battle he helped to form 312, the second Czech squadron in the RAF, and then took command of 306 Squadron, one of the Polish fighter units then being formed. Commanding 615 Squadron in 1941, he led this unit's four-cannon Hurricanes on a series of daring and costly anti-shipping operations throughout that summer, at the culmination of which he was forced to bale out into the English Channel when his fighter was hit by Flak. During his subsequent long association with the Typhoon he became known as the 'Father of the RAF's Ground Attack Wings', and was the only British fighter pilot to receive three awards of the prestigious Distinguished Service Order. Indeed, in congratulating him upon the last of these, his Air Officer Commanding assured him that, 'had it been the First World War it would have been a Victoria Cross'. By the end of the war he had amassed an incredible total of 2,000 fighter and ground-attack sorties.

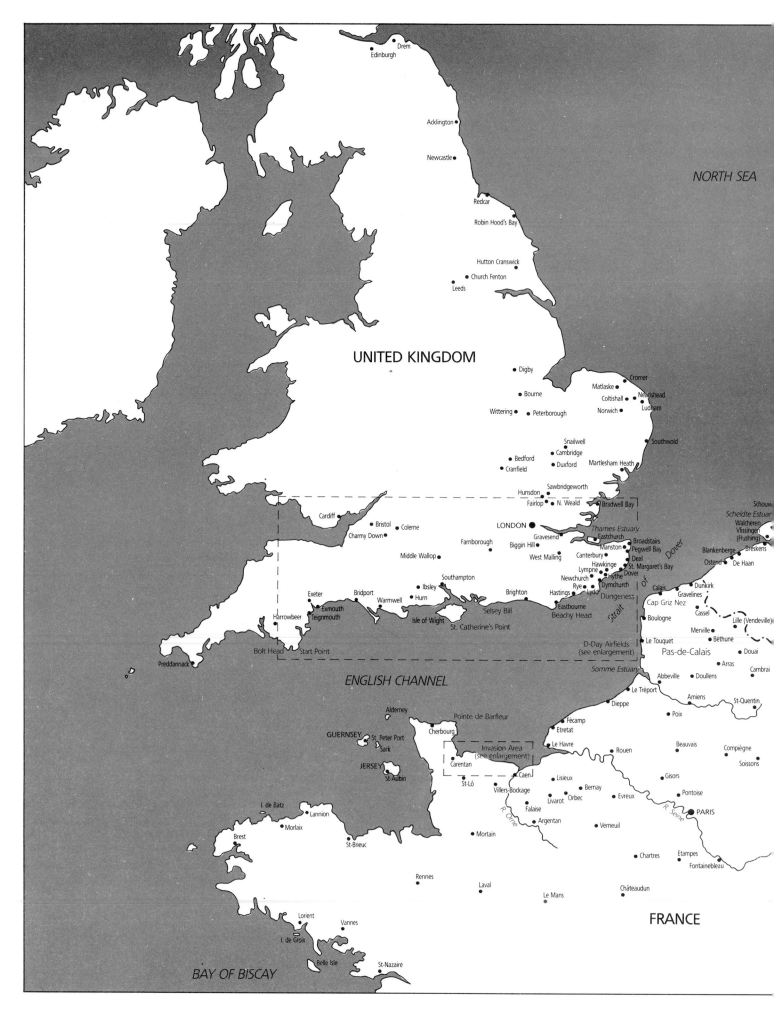

NORTH SEA

UNITED KINGDOM

Drem
Edinburgh

Acklington

Newcastle

Redcar

Robin Hood's Bay

Hutton Cranswick
Church Fenton
Leeds

Digby

Matlaske · Cromer
Bourne · Coltishall · Neatishead
Ludham
Wittering · Peterborough · Norwich

Snailwell
Cambridge · Southwold
Bedford · Duxford · Martlesham Heath
Cranfield

Sawbridgeworth
Hunsdon
Fairlop · N. Weald · Bradwell Bay

Cardiff

Scheldte Estuar
Walcheren
Vlissingen
(Flushing)
Schouv

Bristol · Colerne
Charmy Down
LONDON
Thames Estuary
Gravesend
Farnborough · Eastchurch · Broadstairs
Biggin Hill · Manston · Pegwell Bay
West Malling · Canterbury · Deal
Middle Wallop · Hawkinge · St. Margaret's Bay
Lympne · Dover
Newchurch · Hythe · Dover
Southampton · Rye · Lydd · Dymchurch
Ibsley · Hastings · Dungeness
Exeter · Bridport · Brighton · Eastbourne
Warmwell · Hurn · Beachy Head
Exmouth · Selsey Bill
Harrowbeer · Teignmouth · Isle of Wight
St. Catherine's Point
Bolt Head · Start Point
D-Day Airfields
(see enlargement)
Preddannack

Dover
Strait of Dover
Calais
Blankenberge · Breskens
Ostend · De Haan
Dunkirk
Gravelines
Cap Griz Nez · Cassel · Lille (Vendeville)
Boulogne · Merville · Béthune
Le Touquet · Douai
Pas-de-Calais · Arras · Cambrai
Somme Estuary · Abbeville · Doullens
Le Tréport · Amiens · St-Quentin
Dieppe · Poix
Fécamp
Etretat
Le Havre · Rouen · Beauvais · Compiègne
Soissons
Gisors · Pontoise
Lisieux · Bernay · Evreux · PARIS
Villers-Bockage · Livarot · Orbec · Verneuil
Falaise · Argentan
Mortain · Chartres · Etampes
Fontainebleau
Châteaudun

ENGLISH CHANNEL

Alderney
Pointe de Barfleur
GUERNSEY · St. Peter Port
Sark
Cherbourg
Invasion Area
(see enlargement)
JERSEY
St-Aubin
Carentan
Caen
St-Lô

I. de Batz · Lannion
Morlaix
Brest
St-Brieuc

Rennes
Laval
Le Mans

Lorient
Vannes
I. de Groix
Belle Isle · St-Nazaire

BAY OF BISCAY

R. Orne
R. Seine

FRANCE

Areas of Operations and Bases of Royal Air Force Typhoon and Tempest Units, 1942–5

1 Squadron, May 1943

257 Squadron, June 1944

54 Squadron, November 1945

247 Squadron, 1944

164 Squadron, July 1944

137 Squadron, May 1944

80 Squadron, Spring 1945

26 Squadron

Introduction
and Acknowledgements

AT the time of writing, more than forty years have passed since a Typhoon was last seen in flight, and more than thirty years since the Tempest disappeared from European skies. Yet, during that time, no comprehensive survey of these two closely related aircraft has appeared in print. Many of the Typhoon and Tempest pilots interviewed during our research bewailed the lack of such a history. We sincerely hope that this book goes a long way towards filling that gap.

The Typhoon's service career has always been controversial, and in recent years the controversy has focused on the efficiency of the Typhoon/rocket combination, particularly in a 'tank-busting' role. We believe that the true value of the aircraft lay in its successful close support of the Allied armies – whatever the target – which was such a feature of the campaign in north-west Europe, and that the results speak for themselves.

We have endeavoured to encompass, both in the text and the illustrations, the full spectrum of both types' operations. This would not have been possible without the enthusiastic help and trust of many pilots and ground-crew, who have lent treasured logs and photographs, and given freely of their hospitality and time in recording recollections of those stirring times. Rather than list their names here, we felt it more appropriate that they be found where they belong – within the story itself. Such a wealth of material has been forthcoming that it has not been possible to utilize it in full; nevertheless, our sincere thanks go to all who helped in any way.

Prominent among the most enthusiastic contributors have been those from the Commonwealth. There were Canadian and Rhodesian Typhoon units, and a New Zealand Typhoon and Tempest squadron, but in addition to the pilots in these formations there were many more from these nations, plus large numbers of Australians and South Africans, who flew both types in RAF squadrons. Some of them (with justification) feel that their part has been overlooked; we trust that we have restored the balance in some measure.

No work of this nature is compiled without the help of friends and fellow enthusiasts, and in particular we should like to thank Trevor Stone for his compilation of production contract details; Brian Cull for valuable assistance with pilot details in the loss lists; Bruce Lander and Russell Guest for other practical help. The following have also been most helpful in the search for fresh material and photographs: Chris Ashworth, Mike Cookman, Regis Decobeck, Norman Franks, George Jenks, Richard King, Simon Parry, Ken Rimell, Douglas Rough, Andy Saunders, Mike Schoeman, Paul Sortehaug, Bill Smith, Dave Smith, Ray Sturtivant, Andy Thomas, Piet Truren, Dick Ward and Gerrie Zwanenberg. The staffs of the Air Historical Branch, Imperial War Museum, Public Record Office and the RAF Museum have been ever-helpful, but the generous assistance from Evelyn Boyd, Peter Murton and Richard Simpson has been especially appreciated, as has the long-standing practical aid and encouragement from Mike Stroud of British Aerospace, Kingston. Finally we should like to record our appreciation of the support of our wives and families during the years of research, especially in the last months of intensive effort.

We should draw the reader's attention to the comprehensive appendices which follow the main text; these contain the essential details of losses, claims, units and commanders, etc., and their presence has enabled the authors to exclude confusing detail from the main text. Pilots' initials are not quoted in the narrative when there is an equivalent entry in an appendix. In the main, decorations have also been excluded from the text, because of the difficulty in establishing the awards applicable to an individual at any given time; they have, however, been included in the lists of unit commanders.

It has not been possible to name all those who appear in photographs throughout the book; generally the policy has been to mention those who also figure in the text.

The well-read enthusiast will detect differences between previously published information and that given here; despite the forty years elapsed, research continues and this book represents the most recent findings. We should also point out that many of the aircraft serial numbers in the tables of losses differ from those quoted in the Squadron Operations Record Books (Forms 540 and 541). These 'diaries' were often compiled in the field, in (sometimes distant) retrospect; serial numbers were not only liable to errors in transcription, but replacement aircraft serials were often quoted for earlier losses, and vice versa. After very careful research, and cross-checking with all available sources, we are confident that the serials we have given for losses are correct; those quoted in the claims tables are subject to a note at the head of that appendix.

C. H. Thomas and C. F. Shores,
April 1987

5 Squadron, 1946

CHAPTER ONE

Typhoon versus Tornado

HAWKER Aircraft Limited, successors to the Sopwith Aviation Company Limited, were responsible for a line of single-engined fighter aircraft including the beautiful Fury and, by 1937, the RAF's first monoplane fighter with a retractable undercarriage, the Hurricane. While this aircraft was still only on the verge of entering RAF service, Sydney Camm, Hawker's Chief Designer, aware of the rapidly increasing tempo of fighter design, was already working on its successor. He based his preliminary designs around two engines which promised to provide twice the power of the current 1,030hp Rolls-Royce Merlin employed in the Hurricane. Both these 24-cylinder engines were unorthodox: a Rolls-Royce design, the Vulture, was based on the combination of two Peregrine 'V' engines into an 'X' layout, while its Napier rival, the Sabre, favoured an 'H' configuration – four banks of cylinders driving two crankshafts. Hawker submitted their ideas to the Air Ministry in July 1937, but were advised to await the issue of a new specification for an advanced fighter, which appeared in January of the following year.

This specification, F.18/37, called for a replacement for the Spitfire and Hurricane and its outstanding requirement was that the new aircraft should have the greatest possible speed margin over the contemporary bomber. It was expected therefore that the successful type would have a top speed in excess of 400mph at 15,000 feet. Armament was to be 'not less than twelve Browning guns (0.303in) and the aircraft must be a steady platform for them at its maximum speed'.

As both the new power plants considered by Camm were in the very early stages of their development, his proposal to meet the specification featured versions for each engine, as an insurance against failure of either one of them. The Rolls-Royce version was known as the 'R-type' and the Napier-engined design as the 'N-type'. The Air Ministry responded quickly with a contract for four prototypes, two of each variant.

Construction of the first two prototypes, which shared very similar airframes, began at Hawker's Kingston-on-Thames factory in March 1938. Centre and forward fuselage featured Hawker's patented tubular construction, steel and duralumin tubes forming a box-like structure, which was entirely covered by close-fitting detachable panels to facilitate maintenance. Aft of the cockpit the fuselage was a monocoque skinned with flush-riveted light alloy. Each wing was built separately and fixed to the fuselage by four bolts, two to each of the main spars. The wings were cranked; the inner section anhedral was just over 1° while the outer section had a dihedral of 5½°. The inner section housed a sturdy, inward retracting undercarriage, and self-sealing fuel tanks in the leading edge; the outer section housed the gun bay, and landing lights were set in its leading edge. Ailerons, split flaps and elevators were metal-covered, the rudder being the only fabric-covered structure. The major difference between the two types, which were soon named Tornado (with the Vulture) and Typhoon (with the Sabre), apart from the engine mountings, was in the positioning of the radiator: on the Tornado this was located beneath the fuselage midway between the wings, while the Typhoon's was beneath the nose, immediately aft of the airscrew. A less obvious difference was in the mounting of the wings on the fuselage – three inches lower on the Tornado because the Vulture could not be mounted over the front wing spar in the same way as the Sabre.

The engine for the Tornado, a Vulture II, was received from Rolls-Royce in December 1938, but the Napier Sabre was already experiencing development problems, so work on the Tornado, which had been given the serial number P5219, raced ahead. At the end of July 1939 it was taken by road to Hawker's new factory at Langley, near Slough, for final assembly and testing. The all-up weight of P5219 was 9,520lb (compared with 5,416lb for the Hurricane prototype) and its Vulture II was rated at 1,760hp. Although provision was made for twelve machine-guns, it was unarmed. On 6 October 1939 the Tornado took to the air for the first time, at the hands of experimental test-pilot, P. G. Lucas. The first flights were successful, but when the test programme reached high-speed runs approaching 400mph it was apparent that the ventral radiator position was causing reversal of the air flow round the rear of the fairing, leading to an unacceptably high rise in drag. Testing was halted while the radiator was re-positioned in the same location as on the Typhoon. Flying recommenced on 6 December 1939 and the new radiator position was found to be satisfactory. Meanwhile work on the Sabre had progressed to the stage where Napier were able to deliver a Sabre I, for installation in the Typhoon prototype, at the end of December 1939. The Typhoon (P5212) was quickly prepared for test flying and Lucas took it up for the first time on 24 February 1940, at Langley.

Impressed by the potential of both fighters, the Air Ministry had already given Hawker an 'Instruction To Proceed' for the produc-

tion of one thousand aircraft. As the Vulture seemed to be the more promising engine, 500 of these aircraft were to be Tornadoes, 250 to be Typhoons, and the remaining 250 to be decided when the definitive production types could be compared. At this time Hawker were overwhelmed by increasing demands for Hurricane production, so it was decided that the new types would be built by other members of the Hawker-Siddeley Group. A. V. Roe would be responsible for the Tornado, with a production line at their new factory at Yeadon, near Leeds, while the Gloster Aircraft Company would built the Typhoons at their factory at Hucclecote, near Gloucester.

Test flying of both types continued throughout the spring of 1940, although the Typhoon narrowly avoided a major setback, thanks to some courageous flying by Philip Lucas. On 9 May 1940, P5212 suffered a failure of the rear fuselage monocoque at the point where it joined the centre fuselage section, just aft of the cockpit. Lucas could see daylight through a huge split down the starboard side, but refused to abandon the aircraft, and for saving the valuable prototype he was awarded the George Medal. Just six days later the Minister of Aircraft Production, Lord Beaverbrook, decided that resources must be concentrated on the production of five existing types (Spitfire, Hurricane, Whitley, Wellington and Blenheim) until the war situation improved.

Left: The Typhoon prototype, P5212, nearing completion in 1939. Note the six machine-gun ports in the leading edge of the wing. (BAe)

Above: First into the air was the Tornado prototype, P5219. The Hurricane-style radiator evident here (October 1939), was

soon repositioned under the nose. (BAe)

Below: The Typhoon prototype, P5212, seen at Langley at about the time of its first flight. It features the original small rudder and triple exhaust stubs; there were no wheel covers at this time. (BAe)

Left: Typhoon P5212 after minor changes, including wheel covers hinged on the main undercarriage fairings, and small windows in the canopy fairing. (BAe)

Right: Tornado HG641 played a vital role in Centaurus engine development and is seen here at Langley in its original configuration; the engine cowling and exhaust system were later extensively redesigned. (BAe)

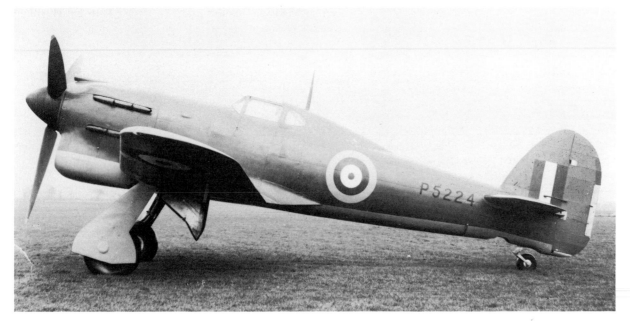

Left: P5224, the second Tornado prototype, illustrates the final radiator position for the Vulture-engined Tornado. (BAe)

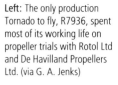

Left: The only production Tornado to fly, R7936, spent most of its working life on propeller trials with Rotol Ltd and De Havilland Propellers Ltd. (via G. A. Jenks)

Right: The second Typhoon prototype, P5216, was the first to be fitted with the eventual standard armament of four 20mm Hispano cannon. All subsequent Typhoons with this armament were designated 'IB' whereas those with 12 × 0.303in machine-guns were designated 'IA'. (BAe)

Consequently production plans for the Tornado and Typhoon were postponed and development flying continued at a reduced rate.

During 1940 minor changes were made to the Typhoon prototype. These included the addition of hinged wheel covers on the undercarriage leg fairings; tail-wheel doors; small windows in the rear of the canopy fairing; and an enlarged rudder (the latter being the only modification retained on subsequent Typhoons). In this configuration P5212 was flown to Boscombe Down for assessment by the Aeroplane and Armament Experimental Establishment (A&AEE). Their tests revealed that the Typhoon met the specified top speed, achieving 410mph at 20,000 feet, but performance above that level, and climb rate, were disappointing. Doubts were also expressed about the adequacy of the view to the rear, but the aircraft's stability, especially at high speed, promised a good gun platform. Fully loaded it weighed in at 10,990lb.

The second Tornado prototype, P5224, eventually flew on 5 December 1940 and also featured the new windows and rudder; although no armament was carried, there was provision for four 20mm cannon which, in the light of Battle of Britain experience, was now the RAF's preferred armament for its next generation of interceptors. In March 1941 both this aircraft and the first Tornado were fitted with improved Vultures (the Mark V, rated at 1,980hp). Towards the end of the year, P5224 underwent performance and handling trials at the A&AEE where maximum speed was measured at 398mph at 23,300 feet. Handling was generally similar to the Typhoon although it was more longitudinally stable and stalled at slightly slower speeds; the view over the nose was marginally better. By this time, however, the Vulture engine programme was in serious

trouble. The Vulture had been selected by Avro to power their new bomber, the Manchester, and this aircraft, after a disastrous record of engine failures, eventually had to be taken off operations. Although the Vulture in the Tornado had given little trouble, it was decided to terminate production of the engine, and cancellation of the Tornado production contracts followed. Before this occurred the first production Tornado (R7936) had already flown, at Woodford on 29 August 1941, and four more were nearing completion from the 100 sets of detail parts already manufactured by the Yeadon factory. One airframe (R7938) was allocated to Rolls-Royce for engine trials, but never flew. Both Tornado prototypes continued flying until 1943, undertaking a variety of trials with the manufacturers, Rolls-Royce, and the Royal Aircraft Establishment (RAE) at Farnborough. After

similar trials, R7936 went to De Havilland and Rotol for propeller testing, including the fitting of a 6-bladed contra-rotating unit; it was eventually scrapped in April 1944.

Before the Tornado project was cancelled, an order had been placed for a third prototype, to be powered by another new engine, a 2,210hp, 18-cylinder, air-cooled radial, the Bristol Centaurus. This aircraft, HG641, did not fly until 23 October 1941, and it utilized surplus Tornado wings and rear fuselage with a newly built front fuselage. It showed enough promise for a small pre-production order, for six similar aircraft, to be placed early in 1942. In February of that year the exhaust arrangement was comprehensively redesigned and when, after the installation of the new system, it flew again in November 1942, it achieved 402mph at 18,000 feet. Again the Tornado was unfortunate, for the pre-production batch had

Above: The third production Typhoon, R7578, photographed at Hucclecote, circa August 1941, prior to delivery to Langley as a trials aircraft. In common with several other early production aircraft, it was delivered in the Dark Green/Dark Earth and Sky camouflage scheme, with black spinner. In service this was soon replaced by the Dark Green/Ocean Grey and Medium Sea Grey scheme, with Sky rear fuselage band and spinner. (Gloster Aircraft)

already been cancelled because installation of the Centaurus in the Typhoon II was considered to hold greater promise. The sole Centaurus Tornado gave valuable service as a test-bed, paving the way for the use of this engine in the Tempest II and Sea Fury. It was to be the last surviving Tornado, finally going to the breakers in August 1944.

Returning to 1941, the Typhoon programme was now running into problems. The Sabre was proving to be temperamental and did not give the power required at altitudes above 20,000 feet; manoeuvrability was below current standards, particularly in respect of roll-rate. Attempts were made during 1941 to improve the performance in the suspect areas; extended and clipped wings were both test flown, but as the improvements gained were at the expense of performance loss in other areas, both schemes were abandoned. A 6-cannon in-

stallation, which reached mock-up stage, and an exhaust-driven supercharger were two other projects which failed to find favour. Other major improvements under consideration would lead to the Typhoon II, development of which is dealt with in a subsequent chapter.

The second Typhoon prototype (P5216) flew on 3 May 1941. It carried four 20mm Hispano cannon, two in each outer wing section; they were belt-fed and there was room for 140 rounds per gun. The small windows in the canopy fairing had been found to be of little use and were deleted, and the hinged wheel covers were replaced by 'D' doors hinged on the fuselage/wing joint, since they had been prone to damage in their original position.

Gloster had made good progress and the first production Typhoon (R7576) flew just a few weeks after the second prototype, on 27 May 1941. This aircraft was very similar to P5216 except that it reverted to the machine-gun armament – not because of any change in the military requirement, but simply owing to a shortage of the Châtellerault cannon feed mechanisms. This machine-gun armed variant was designated the Mark IA and the cannon armed version would become the Mark IB. Initially all deliveries were of IAs, but as the cannon

feed supply problems eased they were replaced in increasing numbers on the production line by IBs. Total production of the Typhoon IA was 110 aircraft, some of which were later converted to IB standard.

Reservations about the Typhoon's suitability for service were put aside when, in the autumn of 1941, it became apparent that the Luftwaffe had a new fighter which could outrun and outroll Fighter Command's current best, the Spitfire V, with ease – the Focke-Wulf Fw 190. With the first four aircraft involved in trials with the manufacturers, and with A&AEE and RAE, the fifth and sixth off the line were delivered to the Air Fighting Development Unit (AFDU) at Duxford for brief tactical trials prior to entering squadron service. In comparative tests with the Spitfire V the Typhoon proved to be 40mph faster at all levels above 14,000 feet and even faster below that level. It was no surprise to find that the Typhoon was less manoeuvrable than the nimble Spitfire, but the AFDU's report concluded that it would be possible to use the Typhoon's high speed to good advantage. Plans to equip the first squadron with the aircraft went ahead. The recipient of this dubious honour was to be 56 Squadron; the full extent of the Typhoon's problems were about to become evident!

Right: Contrasting engine installations on the Typhoon (top), Vulture Tornado (middle) and Centaurus Tornado (bottom). (BAe)

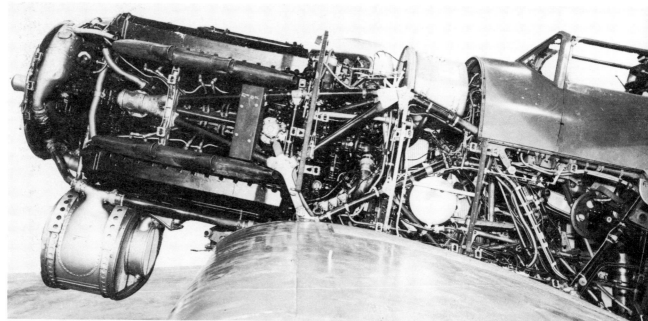

CHAPTER TWO

Typhoon Developments

REALIZING that the Typhoon I's thick wing section was a limiting factor on the aircraft's maximum speed, Camm set about a complete redesign of the wing, using a much thinner section and a semi-elliptical plan form. In November 1941 the company received a contract for two prototypes of the Typhoon II, which featured the new wing and was to be powered by a developed Sabre, the Mk IV. The following month the official specification (F.10/41) was issued, detailing the requirements of the new design. Early in 1942 continuing Sabre problems led to the consideration of other engines, namely Rolls-Royce's Griffon II, the two-stage Griffon 61, and the Bristol Centaurus; by August of that year, these designs had progressed so far from the original Typhoon that they were renamed 'Tempest'. The development of this charismatic aircraft is covered in a later chapter.

Typhoon I's were now pouring off the production line at Hucclecote, with the RAF still undecided about a suitable role for the aircraft, and the manufacturers trying desperately to develop engine and airframe into a reliable combination. The first problem to be encountered after service entry was that of carbon monoxide fumes in the cockpit (see Chapter 3). Although never completely eliminated, at least the effects could be avoided by the use of an oxygen mask. The next serious problem was less tractable.

On 29 July 1942 one of 257 Squadron's newly received Typhoons shed its complete tail unit during a turn in a shallow dive. The pilot, who had been familiarizing himself with the aerobatic qualities of his new mount, was killed. Barely two weeks later Hawker test-pilot, Ken Seth-Smith (a 7-victory fighter pilot with 70 Squadron during the First World War), was carrying out spinning trials with the canopy roof removed (part of a programme to improve vision at night); his Typhoon also shed its tail and he was unable to escape. The following week a 56 Squadron aircraft disintegrated in mid-formation and a third pilot died.

Immediately suspicion fell on the rear transport joint – the point where the tail assembly could be separated from the rear fuselage – and by the beginning of September an externally fitted steel strap to provide local strengthening had been designed, and a modification programme was initiated. This was a temporary measure and two months later 'Mod 286' was introduced. It involved the riveting of twenty 'fish plates' across the suspect joint, one at each stringer station, together with internal strengthening frames. In a huge priority programme all the Typhoons were modified in this way, 13 Maintenance Unit (MU) at Henlow alone handling more than 300 aircraft from December 1942 until March 1943. On the production line the modification was fitted as standard from the 820th aircraft.

While this treatment of the symptom was taking place, Hawker and the RAE carried out investigations to discover the cause. Detailed examination of the wreckage yielded no definite clues, although weakening of the rear fuselage by the stresses of aerobatic manoeuvres, particularly pulling out of high-speed dives, was suspected. Suitably instrumented Typhoons were subjected to hair-raising trials, such as inducing vicious yaw at 500mph; fortunately for the intrepid pilots (for there was little chance of escape if tail failure ensued) no aircraft were lost, but then no conclusive evidence was forthcoming either. Buckling of the rear fuselage near the joint was noted on some of these aircraft, and on some aircraft of 181 and 182 Squadrons (which, as the first dive-bombers, were particularly at risk) when they were examined in February 1943. However, structural tests revealed that the rear fuselage and tailplane were more than capable of accepting the loads imposed by dive recovery or sudden yawing in the dive.

Left: This close-up of Flak damage on DN489 'US-F' of 56 Squadron also gives a clear view of the plates riveted over the fuselage/tail assembly joint (Mod. 286) in an effort to cure the structural failures. (BAe)

Top right: Typhoon IB R7646 was the first aircraft to have the transparent fairing aft of the cockpit. It was retained by Hawker for a variety of trials and was also used for evaluations at Boscombe Down. (BAe)

Right: Typhoon EK122 shows the production standard in the spring of 1943. The cannon barrels are now faired, a rear-view mirror is housed in the small blister on the canopy, and the external rudder balance has been replaced by an internal one. EK122 never reached the RAF, being retained for trials by Hawker, including high-speed dives during the investigation into tail failures. It survived and was later used by Napier for engine development. (BAe)

The catalogue of disasters continued and by the end of May 1943 thirteen Typhoons were known for certain to have been victims of structural failure. Only one pilot had survived – Pilot Officer Kilpatrick of 193 Squadron, whose Typhoon had shed its tail in a turn at 27,000 feet. Badly bruised about the head from the battering he received in the tumbling aircraft, he had managed to fight his way out at 10,000 feet. Although Mod Z86 had reduced the accident rate (in relation to the rapidly increasing numbers of Typhoon hours being flown), five of the victims had been strengthened in this way, so it was obviously no ultimate cure.

Suspicion now switched to the elevator mass balance – a weight on the end of a rod protruding from the leading edge of the elevator, inside the rear fuselage. Harmonic vibrations could lead to the failure of this unit, with dire results, and much effort was expended in perfecting the system. Eventually a completely redesigned balance was incorporated in existing Typhoons and on the production line.

In September 1943 Flight Sergeant Waddington of 183 Squadron returned from a dive-bombing sortie over Poulmic airfield, having experienced elevator flutter as he began to pull out of his 535mph dive. The disturbance had been sufficient to elongate the elevator control rod holes. Could flutter be the long-sought answer? Early in 1944 the original tailplane design was replaced by a larger unit, as fitted to the Tempest, and in August of that year the final modifications to

the elevator mass balance weights were made. This was confidentally expected to see the end of the failures.

Indeed, the rate of failures did slow, but they still occurred. In the last three accidents, in 1945, the character of the failures seemed to have changed. Undercarriage doors or legs had apparently dropped in flight, initiating events which led to the aircraft breaking up. But by now the Typhoon was rapidly leaving service and the accident file was closed without an entirely satisfactory solution to the enigma which had cost at least 25 Typhoons and the lives of 23 pilots.

Despite these tribulations, Sabre engine production (or rather lack of it) and unreliability had a far greater effect on the Typhoon programme. By April 1942 airframe production was exceeding engine production and with no suitable alternative power plant available, large numbers of engine-less Typhoons were stored at maintainance units having been ferried to them using 'slave' engines which were then removed and taken back to Glosters for re-installation in another new Typhoon! The shortage of engines was exacerbated by the unreliability of the Sabre in service. Frequent failures, usually caused by seizure of the sleeve valves, demanded inordinately short periods between major inspections (which necessitated engine changes). At the end of 1942 this period was only 25 hours, and by May 1943 although it had risen to 30 hours, the Sabre supply situation was

critical, leading to a restriction on hours flown by the squadrons – 300 hours per month for the fighter squadrons and only 200 hours per month for the fighter-bomber units. The shortage had been made even worse during this period because large numbers of Sabres were being returned to the manufacturers for essential modifications – Napier had at last found the answer to the sleeve valve problem. After consulting the Bristol Aeroplane Company, whose engine division had much experience of sleeve valves on their air-cooled radials, Napier found the solution lay in the selection of the correct materials (18 different ones were tried), plus nitriding and 'lapping' the valves before assembly. Sabre serviceability reached acceptable levels almost overnight.

During the course of Sabre development in 1943, Napier fitted Typhoon R8694 with the Sabre IV, utilizing an annular radiator and dispensing with the Typhoon's characteristic 'chin'. A maximum speed in level flight of 452mph was claimed by Napier, but with Tempest development proceeding well, it was not considered worthwhile to disrupt the Typhoon production line with the major changes necessary to the airframe.

Meanwhile, committed to receiving large numbers of Typhoons, Fighter Command had to find a role for the newcomer to its ranks. There was a body of opinion within the Command which wanted the Typhoon withdrawn from service. There were even tentative plans to divert all deliveries to the

USSR, but the advent of the 'hit-and-run' raids and the realization that the Typhoon was the best counter available ensured that the aircraft remained in service, and during this period, late 1942/early 1943, much effort was expended to improve the airframe and develop it for other roles.

First priority was to improve the pilot's view. Soon after their introduction into service, early production aircraft had been modified by the replacement of their 'solid' canopy fairings with a transparent structure. Even so, the view to the rear was still restricted and the heavy framing to the windscreen and canopy reduced all-round visibility. Hawkers began work on a new, lightly framed windscreen but this was overtaken by the development of a totally new canopy – a new windscreen allied to a one-piece sliding 'bubble' hood – which afforded a magnificent all-round view. Although the trial installation on R8809 was complete by January 1943 and received enthusiastic comments from service pilots when flown to Northolt on 2 February, for their evaluation, it was not introduced on the production line until November 1943. A further attempt to improve the rear view until the new canopy was available, involved the fitting of a rear-view mirror in a small perspex blister on the canopy roof. In service this was found to be of little use as the mirror was prone to vibration; frequent failures of the canopy roof led eventually to its abandonment. Many older Typhoons were retrospectively fitted with the new canopy and it was some of these that were the first to reach the squadrons in September 1943. Typhoons with the old framed canopy were not totally replaced in front-line service until shortly after D-Day, by which time Typhoons so encumbered were known as 'coffin-hood jobs'. Small numbers were still in service with training units at the end of the war.

One characteristic of the Typhoon which caused the pilots concern was the high-frequency vibration of the airframe in flight. This was said to cause sterility, although subsequent events seem to have disproved

Left: Despite its successful installation, and a claimed top speed of 452mph, the annular radiator tested on R8694, seen here on the flight line at Luton, was not adopted for production. (Napier)

Top right: The heavily framed 'car-door' canopy was standard on production Typhoons from early 1942 to late 1943. Note the identification light aft of the aerial mast; the square panel below the cockpit gave access to radio equipment and the first aid kit. (BAe)

Right: A similar view of the trial installation of the sliding hood on R8809, early in 1943. Also visible, the whip aerial which replaced the large mast and, just aft of the roundel, the IFF aerial which ran from both sides of the fuselage to the tips of the tailplane. This latter aerial was later replaced by a 'bayonet' type protruding from the bottom of the fuselage. The identification light under the canopy was not present on production sliding-hood Typhoons. (BAe)

that theory! However it was discomforting, so a specially sprung seat was designed to insulate the pilot from the worst of the trouble. Even so, some pilots reported that their noses tickled, and that touching the cockpit walls gave a sensation like a small electric shock. The vibration was somewhat reduced by the introduction of the 4-bladed propeller early in 1944. This had been under consideration as early as 1941, 56 Squadron conducting trials in November of that year. Handling, however, was unacceptable, despite further development, until the introduction of the enlarged Tempest tailplane in February 1944. Then the improved take-off performance conferred by the 4-blader came in very useful. This was especially so for the bomber squadrons which had to struggle to get their Typhoons, laden with two 1,000lb bombs, airborne from rough strips; they were given priority in re-equipment with 4-bladed Typhoons.

Other small improvements to the airframe were the introduction of fairings for the cannon barrels; replacement of the aerial mast protruding from the canopy by a neat 'whip' aerial; and the fitting of exhaust-stub fairings. The latter, proving unpopular in service and not particularly beneficial, were eventually discarded.

Further changes to the Typhoon airframe were mainly concerned with different roles and the following were considered:

Top left: The first production Typhoon with the new canopy, JR333, seen at Langley, prior to assessment at A&AEE Boscombe Down. (BAe)

Left: The only Typhoon NF.IB, R7881. The transmitter and receiver aerials of the AI Mk VI radar can be seen on the leading edges and tips of the wings. Long-range tanks were permanently carried, as one internal wing tank had been removed to make room for the radar equipment. (BAe)

Below: DN340 spent most of its life on armament and propeller trials and is seen here with a 4-bladed propeller and two 1,000lb bombs at A&AEE Boscombe Down in April 1943. (RAF Museum)

Night-Fighter

In June 1942 R7651 was delivered to the Fighter Interception Unit (FIU) at Ford for night-flying trials. Perhaps surprisingly for such a fast and heavy aircraft, the Typhoon proved easy to fly at night, the FIU's report remarking that it was easier to fly on instruments than either the Hurricane or Spitfire. The report recommended the Typhoon as a night-fighter, with the following provisos:

(a) a sliding hood to be provided (to facilitate upward search)
(b) cockpit lighting redesigned
(c) brakes improved.

In August, Typhoon R7630 was flown by the FIU in a series of trials with a Turbinlite Boston (an AI radar-equipped aircraft which, when it located its target, would illuminate it with the beam from a huge searchlight carried in the specially modified nose, for its satellite fighter to attack). Although the Typhoon's speed proved useful in latching on to the target when illuminated, it also proved a handicap as the Boston's normal cruising speed was only just above the Typhoon's minimum, which made formation-keeping in the dark very difficult. However it was felt that with the provision of a pilot-operated AI radar, improved field of vision, extra endurance and other minor alterations, the Typhoon would make the ideal front-gun night-fighter.

In view of the fact that the highly successful Mosquito night-fighter was in service, already with several victories to its credit, and with the advantage of a two-man crew, greater endurance, and a top speed not far removed from that of the Typhoon, it is difficult to see why the decision was made to proceed. Hawker took a standard aircraft, R7881, and modified it as the prototype Typhoon NF.IB. This entailed removal of the main port wing fuel tank to make room for the AI Mk VI transmitter and receiver, installation of aerials in the leading edges of

both wings, and provision of a small radar display in the cockpit. Loss of the 40-gallon wing tank was more than compensated by the permanent carriage of two 45-gallon underwing tanks. The completed aircraft was delivered to the RAE Farnborough for assessment of the radar installation in April 1943, after which R7881 was passed to the FIU for flying trials, carrying out several uneventful night patrols over London, in November 1943. In all, the FIU were impressed – the speed of the aircraft allowed quick interceptions to be made, and its manoeuvrability, allied to good AI radar coverage (maximum range 9,000 feet, minimum range 500 feet) allowed quick recovery in the case of overshoots. Adequate tail warning was given by rearward cover, and by making a quick turn it was possible to intercept the interceptor. Despite its successful development, no requirement for the Typhoon night-fighter materialized and R7881 remained the only one built. Stripped of its radar equipment, it was pensioned-off to 3 TEU at Honiley in July 1944.

Fighter-Bomber

Following the success of the Typhoon's predecessor, the Hurricane, as a fighter-bomber, it was logical that the Typhoon should be considered for the same role.

In August 1942, R7646 was fitted with a faired bomb rack under each wing and a series of test flights were made, with 500lb bombs, at the A&AEE at Boscombe Down. These trials were promising, showing that the bombs and fairings had little effect on the handling of the aircraft although increasing buffeting was experienced in dives over 350mph(IAS) effectively limiting dive speed to 400mph(IAS). Change of trim on releasing the bombs was negligible. In October the same aircraft, now fitted with small extensions to the cannon shell case ejector slots beneath the wings (so that the empty cases were ejected clear of the bombs), was used to measure the effect of bombs and racks on the Typhoon's maximum speed in level flight at 8,000 feet. The clean aircraft was capable of 372mph(TAS), and with the two 500lb bombs attached, 336mph(TAS). Meanwhile Hawker had begun fitting some Typhoons with bomb-carrying equipment and the first examples reached 181 Squadron in mid-October. Initially production was split between fighter and bomber variants, but by mid-1943 all Typhoons coming off the line were capable of carrying bombs. To make the heavily laden Typhoons more manageable on the ground, 'anti-shimmy' tyres were fitted to the tail wheels; following service trials in March 1943 they were introduced on the production line from the 1,001st aircraft.

The Typhoon's load-carrying capability had, however, not yet been fully exploited.

In April 1943, DN340 (with a 4-blade propeller) was successfully flown by the A&AEE with a 1,000lb bomb under each wing. Fully loaded the Typhoon scaled 13,250lb! Earlier trials had shown that bomb-carrying Typhoons tended to 'buck' when taking off from grass runways so the tests were carried out using nearby Thruxton's concrete runways. With 15° flap, take-off was similar to a normal Typhoon without bombs (i.e., with full left trim, left rudder was still required to hold the powerful swing to the right) and though longer, not unduly so considering the extra weight. As earlier trials with 500lb bombs had been limited to 400mph(IAS) in the dive, DN340 was not pushed to its maximum, 390mph (IAS) being the highest dive speed recorded. Service clearance was delayed by a series of problems including handling with the 4-blade propeller (see earlier) and faulty release mechanisms, and it was not until 24 April 1944 that the Canadians of 143 Wing were the first to use the 1,000lb bomb in action. From then on, 500lb or 1,000lb bombs were used, depending on the range or type of target. Further trials in June 1944, utilizing a Typhoon with the larger Tempest-style tailplane, showed handling with two 1,000lb bombs to be satisfactory up to 450mph(IAS). All these speeds would regularly be exceeded on operations.

During the last months of the war a 520lb (in 26 × 20lb segments) anti-personnel bomb was also carried on operations.

Tropical Variant

In November 1942, at the instigation of Prime Minister Winston Churchill, three standard Typhoons were taken from the Gloster production line and modified by Hawker for trials in the Middle East. The original aircraft were R8889, R8891 and R8925, but accidents to R8889 and R8925, before they left the UK, led to their replacement by DN323 and EJ906. The major modification was the fitting of an air-cleaning filter in a fairing beneath the fuselage to the rear of the radiator. Air for the engine could then be drawn in via the normal inlet (in the centre of the radiator) or via this filter; selection was controlled by a lever on the right side of the cockpit. The filter was to be used for ground running, taxiing, take-off and landing, switching to the normal inlet in flight.

Shipping priorities further delayed the three Typhoons' departure for the Middle East, but they eventually arrived at Casablanca on 25 April 1943. After erection and testing the Typhoons were flown to Idku, Egypt for protracted trials with 451 Squadron, a Royal Australian Air Force Hurricane fighter-bomber unit. The Typhoons were mainly flown from Landing Ground 106, El Daba, and by the time the trials were completed in October 1943, they had been flown

Top: DN323, one of the three Typhoons shipped to North Africa for tropical trials. (H. Holmes Collection via G. A. Jenks).

Centre: The three 'tropical' Typhoons were operated by 451 Squadron RAAF, and here one of them 'beats up' the Hurricane dispersal, probably at Idku or El Daba, Egypt. (via D. Howley/R. L. Ward)

Bottom: With commitment of the Typhoon to the ground-attack role, additional armour plate was fitted to the radiator, cockpit floor and sides; trial installation of the latter is seen here. (BAe)

Above: EK497, the first Typhoon fitted with rocket rails, photographed during trials at A&AEE Boscombe Down in August 1943. (MoD)

by 19 different pilots, who, according to the Squadron diary, 'all expressed their admiration of the capabilities of the aircraft'.

Although the feasibility of the Tropical Typhoon was proven, build-up of the 2nd TAF in the UK was the main priority and none could be spared for the Desert Air Force; no further Typhoons reached the Middle East (with the exception of MN290 for trials with a modified cooling system).

Long-Range Tanks

Drop-tanks had been developed for use by the Hurricane, and a pair of these (each of 45-gallon capacity) were flown on Typhoon R8762 in December 1942. Normally the Typhoon's range was approximately 600 nautical miles, depending on engine settings and altitude, but with the long-range tanks this was increased by more than 50 per cent. During the trials, R8762 showed that 1,090 miles could be achieved at 5,000 feet (provided that the tanks were dropped when empty). Despite the reduction in top speed (about 30mph), the long-range tanks enabled the Typhoons to penetrate areas of France, the Netherlands, and even Germany, previously out of reach, and to score some notable successes.

After the Invasion, when the Typhoons were operating from dusty Normandy airfields, replacement aircraft were often ferried in with 90 gallons of beer inside steam-cleaned long-range tanks. It did not taste quite the same as beer from the barrel, but was none the less most welcome.

Later the tanks were again very useful when the rapidly advancing Allied armies left the Typhoons' bases at the limits of their range. A pair of rockets could still be carried outboard of each tank; asymmetric loads of six RP and one tank, or one tank and one bomb, were also utilized.

Rockets

Rocket projectiles (RP) had been in operational use on Swordfish aircraft since 1942 and on Hurricanes since June 1943. In the same month Hawker fitted Typhoon EK497 with a set of Mk I rails for eight 3in RP and the combination that would ensure the Typhoon's place in the history of warfare was born. During the following months trials at the A&AEE and AFDU showed the new combination's potential and by October 1943 the first Typhoon RP squadron, 181, was equipped. A massive modification and training programme (for rocket firing involved the mastery of new techniques) allowed the 2nd TAF to field eleven RP Typhoon squadrons alongside seven Typhoon bomber squadrons by D-Day.

The weapon itself was a simple 3in diameter tube filled with cordite, having cruciform fins at one end and a warhead at the other; on Typhoons this was normally a 60lb High-Explosive/Semi-Armour Piercing round, although from December 1944 a 60lb High-Explosive/Fragmentation head was used against personnel and thin-skinned vehicles. A smoke-producing warhead for use on special operations (target marking) was also available. Concrete heads were used for practice firings.

Fitting of RP equipment had little effect on the handling, although a slight shift forward of the centre of gravity made the aircraft more stable than a normal Typhoon. EK497 was dived successfully to 480mph (IAS), with no buffeting, but acceleration from 450 to 480mph was much slower than for a clean aircraft. Top speed of the Typhoon in level flight was reduced by 38mph.

The original Mk I rails were made of steel; total weight of the installation was an unwieldy 408lb. In the summer of 1944, Mk III rails, constructed of aluminium, were test flown and by December 1944 the Typhoon Squadrons of the 2nd TAF began receiving aircraft so fitted. Total weight of the rails was now reduced to 240lb, conferring an extra 15mph on an RP Typhoon. Rails had been necessary to guide the rockets during their initial acceleration from the slow-flying Swordfish, but with the high attack speed of the Typhoon they were found to be unnecessary. Unfortunately this was not discovered until 1945 and the 'zero-length' launchers then developed were too late to see service during the European war.

Attempts were made to increase the fire power of the rocket-Typhoon by double-banking rockets on each rail. In its initial form two rockets were linked by a 'Duplex No. 2 saddle' and remained linked when fired. Later a 'Duplex No. 3 saddle' was developed which enabled the lower rank of rockets to be fired independently of the upper rank, but this was too late to see operational use.

The 16-rocket installation was flown on MN861 at Boscombe Down in August 1944 and the A&AEE found handling characteristics satisfactory, including dives to 450mph(IAS), while take-off from grass was 'not unduly long'. During the same month

Right: The 16-rocket installation on Typhoon MN861 at Boscombe Down in August 1944. These rockets were fired in linked pairs, but early in 1945 the same aircraft was used for trials of a 16-rocket installation which allowed the bottom row to be fired independently of the top row. (MoD)

the installation was evaluated by the AFDU at Wittering on Typhoon EK290, but their pilot's opinion was somewhat different. He found take-off and landing runs considerably longer, initial climb very poor, and maximum speed at 3,000 feet only 310mph. The difficulties of operating 16-rocket Typhoons from 2nd TAF strips ensured that it never saw operational use, but the 12-rocket configuration (double rockets on the inner pairs of rails) did see some small use, and a total of 590 double rockets had been fired on operations by the end of the war.

The AFDU carried out many other RP trials, mostly aimed at improving aiming technique and accuracy, but including 'screaming' rockets and a 5in American version.

Fighter-Reconnaissance

During 1943 this role was adequately filled by the Allison-engined North American Mustang I, but by the end of the year this had been replaced on the production line by the Merlin-engined Mustang III. Although this version could carry out the fighter-reconnaissance role, it was more urgently required as a long-range escort fighter, and stocks of the Mustang I were inadequate to sustain the prolonged campaign expected following the invasion of north-west Europe. A decision was made to equip five squadrons with specially modified Typhoons, and JR207 with a trial installation of cameras was assessed by 400 Squadron in January 1944. The following month MN315 became the production prototype for what would be known as the Typhoon FR.IB, with one 14in and two 5in cameras mounted in the port wing, replacing the port inner cannon. Hawker Aircraft undertook the production of 200 modification sets for the conversion of existing airframes (there were still many in storage from the days of the Sabre shortages), but in July 1944 the 2nd TAF decided it had more urgent use for its Typhoons in the ground-attack role; the aircraft was not in any case considered to be ideal for fighter-reconnaissance duties. Suitably modified Spitfire IXs and later Mk XIVs would take over the role, but as an interim measure, in July 1944, 268 Squadron was partially re-equipped with the Typhoon FR.IB. The CO of this unit was Squadron Leader 'Bertie' Mann, DFC, and he recalls the addition of this makeshift variant to the complement of his Squadron.

'The first Typhoons arrived in July, and we used them on suitable operations from then onwards. I would agree with anyone who says that the Typhoon was an absolutely splendid aeroplane bearing in mind the purpose for which it was designed. Nevertheless it was a bad choice as a Mustang I replacement in the "fighter-recce" role. The reasons were plain enough in practical terms, but some subjective comparisons with the Mustang coloured pilots' opinions. This was surely because they were all trained and were mostly very experienced on the Mustang, to which they owed a great sense of loyalty, confidence and affection. As a low-level reconnaissance aeroplane the Mustang IA had a good turn of speed near the ground, and excellent downhill acceleration (very useful for camera runs past heavily defended targets), it was fairly light and responsible when manoeuvring to observe or photograph movement on the ground; it also had effective armament (4 × 20mm cannon) which could be used to keep enemy heads down, or to attack any attractive targets. The camera installation was trouble-free, and the oblique sighting angles through the canopy were familiar to all operational pilots in the role. The Typhoon FR.IB was an ungainly beast in comparison. On the plus side it was well armoured and with the enormous Sabre engine in front one felt very secure; but I remember feeling also that I was doing my "TacR" [Tactical Reconnaissance] from the top of a double-decker bus! Perhaps the worst drawback was the vibration; this aeroplane was not a good camera platform, and the camera installation was inadequate. Detail on the ground was blurred, both in photographic and visual terms! The armament could not be used effectively, as the missing cannon*

*Some Typhoon FR.IBs had the starboard inner cannon removed in order to resolve this problem.

caused a slight but unhelpful yaw, and the act of firing interfered with the forward-facing camera. When we moved to France in early August 1944 we had eleven serviceable Mustangs and seven Typhoons, and the ratio between the types remained at this level. We were, therefore, able to fly the Mustangs on all sorties for which this was best. Generally speaking, the Typhoon became our second string.'

268 Squadron continued using their Typhoons until mid-November 1944, by which time reorganization and re-equipment of other FR squadrons freed Mustang IIs to replace them. In the previous month 268 had lent some of their Typhoons to 4 Squadron, a Spitfire XI squadron in 84 Group, and this unit used them for low-level work, particularly over the by-passed Channel ports. They suffered the only loss of an FR.IB to enemy action – one hit by flak in November – before phasing out the type in January 1945.

The Typhoon FR.IB story was not quite over. Three of the surplus aircraft were acquired by 146 Wing at B.70, at the instigation of Group Captain Gillam. He was anxious to have results of the Wing's pin-point attacks available for assessment as soon as possible, and not to have to wait for a follow-up PR sortie. There were several Tac/R trained pilots in the Wing, but to make this specialist task possible for the uninitiated the existing cameras were removed and replaced by a forward-facing F.24 camera of long focal length, synchronized with the gun-sight. Photographs could now be taken on a shallow dive towards the target, and the opposition sprayed with cannon-fire if necessary. The system was an immediate success and yielded excellent results.

'Abdullah'

Scientists at the Telecommunications Research Establishment, Malvern, developed a radar homing device, code-named

Left: The underside of the port wing of a Typhoon FR.IB showing the apertures for the three cameras which replaced the inboard cannon (BAe)....

Right:

1. .... and the camera installation in the inner port gun bay. (BAe)

2. A three-cannon Typhoon FR.IB, possibly EK324, showing the problematic asymmetric cannon arrangement. (via D. J. Smith)

3. One of the Typhoon FR.IBs operated by 146 Wing in 1945. EK372 'B' has the reduced armament of two cannon and has been locally modified to carry a forward-facing camera (note the 'window' in the leading edge above the port undercarriage leg). (D. H. G. Ince)

4. 'DP-E', the Typhoon used by Flight Lieutenant David Ince for his napalm demonstrations in September 1945. A 193 Squadron badge is visible below the windscreen and, in common with other aircraft of the unit at this time, it had red cannon fairings and spinner. (D. H. G. Ince)

△1

△2

△3   ▽4

'Abdullah', designed specifically to locate German 'Wurzburg' radars. During April 1944, fitted in a Typhoon, it was tested against a captured 'Wurzburg' by the FIU and was found capable of detecting and homing on to the target from a range of 50 miles, provided that the approach was made over the sea. When, prior to the invasion, the campaign against the German coastal radars was in full swing, 1320 Flight was formed, using FIU pilots and 'Abdullah' Typhoons, in order to carry out operational trials. Their operations are described later.

Napalm

During the autumn of 1944 initial trials of this emotive weapon were undertaken by the AFDU. First drops took place on the Holbeach range and later against dummy slit trenches and bunkers at Collyweston. These were made by Typhoons and Mustangs, each using their own distinctive long-range tanks filled with napalm gel, ignited by white phosphorous grenades. The trials were completed by January 1945 and as results had been disappointing, a larger, 1,000lb container was developed which underwent operational trials with 193 Squadron. Flight Lieutenant David Ince was closely involved. 'On 1 April 1945 I accompanied a Typhoon carrying two 1,000lb Napalm bombs from our airfield at Mill to the 's-Hertogenbosch ranges in order to photograph the results. The photographs were good but both bombs failed to explode! Later on 9 April, as part of Operation "Jap", I dropped two similar bombs which spread their flaming petroleum jelly very satisfactorily over the top of and into a replica Japanese bunker. Actually we were pretty apprehensive about Napalm – the containers were large, barrel-shaped and painted bright red with very visible external pistols. Their aerodynamics were nil, the aircraft handling was very noticeably affected – much more so than with 1,000lb bombs – and they tumbled immediately on release. As a result Napalm had to be dropped at a very low altitude and the sight of a shower of flaming liquid chasing one's tailplane, immediately after release, was really quite something!

On 12 April, 193 Squadron with eight aircraft delivered a Napalm attack on a German strongpoint south-east of Arnhem – this was followed up later in the day by a conventional low-level bombing and strafing attack. Although the Napalm attack could have been better – there was thick artificial smoke and some aircraft bombed from too high – we understood that the Germans manning the strongpoint were still very shaken and that it was overrun by our ground troops, with less difficulty than expected, shortly after the second sortie. After the war I gave a Napalm demonstration to British army units south of Hilde-

△1

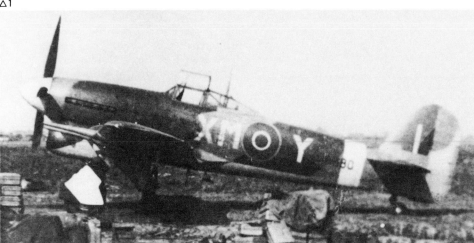

△2

△3   ▽4

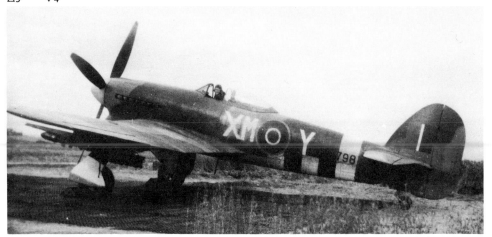

sheim on 5 September, and in my personal final curtain to the Typhoon, dropped Napalm at the 84 Group Battle of Britain display at The Hague on 15 September 1945.'

Other Stores

The Typhoon's speed and load-carrying ability made it a natural choice for trials with other underwing loads. Perhaps the most unusual were the M10 smoke tanks successfully tested on JR307 at Boscombe Down early in 1944. Some of the bomber squadrons were equipped with these tanks and took part in several exercises and demonstrations prior to D-Day, showing their ability to lay an effective smoke-screen at high speed. In the event, the Typhoons were needed for more aggressive roles on D-Day and the smoke-laying was carried out by Boston aircraft.

During August 1944, and on subsequent occasions, the bomber squadrons dropped 'bumph bombs' – canisters packed with leaflets urging surrender – on the retreating German forces. Another change from the usual bombs were the supply containers dropped by 193 Squadron in April 1945 to SAS troops operating behind German lines. The pilots reported that when the pin-point for the drop was reached 'bearded scare-crows' appeared from nowhere, cleared the containers, and disappeared with a wave.

Smoke bombs, Mk VIII mines and practice bombs (four under each wing) were all assessed by the A&AEE, the latter seeing use with the Typhoon training units.

Despite all the refinements to the Typhoon airframe, including the major changes to the canopy and tailplane, the basic designation, Typhoon I, remained unchanged. As the machine-gun armed Typhoon IAs were soon removed from service, all the remaining Typhoons in service were Mk IBs, even though a 'coffin-hood', 3-bladed propeller Tiffie with un-faired cannon could present quite a different appearance from a late-war 'bubble'-canopied, 4-blader fitted with a Tempest tailplane and rockets!

Left:
1. Among the more unusual underwing stores tested on Typhoons at Boscombe Down were these M10 smoke tanks, fitted to JR307 in February 1944. This aircraft, together with its pilot, was one of the victims of structural failure, crashing at Crichel Down on 26 March 1944. (MoD)

2, 3 and 4. Three successive 'XM-Y's flown by Flight Sergeant (later Flying Officer) Douglas Coxhead of 182 Squadron illustrate the changing appearance of operational Typhoons from mid-1943 to mid-1944. JP380, in use from June 1943 to February 1944 and photographed at New Romney, has the framed canopy, aerial mast and bomb racks. JR255 saw service from March 1944 to June 1944 and is seen at Merston, featuring a whip aerial, exhaust fairings and long-range tanks. MN798 in its dispersal at B.6, Coulombs, in July 1944, has a sliding hood, rockets, a 4-blade propeller and the larger (Tempest) tailplane; the exhaust fairings have gone. (D. J. Coxhead)

CHAPTER THREE

Into Service with Fighter Command

THE first delivery of a Typhoon to a front-line RAF squadron was made to 56 Squadron, at Duxford, on 11 September 1941, more arriving throughout that and the following month so that by the end of October they had sixteen Typhoons on charge.

Initially the Typhoon was seen as a high-performance addition to Fighter Command's main fighter force, and a full wing of three squadrons was to take its place at an early date in cross-Channel operations such as the 'Circus' and 'Ramrod'. Squadron Leader Peter Prosser Hanks and his pilots in 56 Squadron had been involved in such operations with their Hurricanes prior to the arrival of the Typhoons, but their initial experience with the new aircraft soon indicated that there would be no early introduction of it to such duties. The aircraft suffered from many failings which the rapid introduction to service had not given sufficient time to eradicate during development. Much of the trouble was caused by the virtually untried Sabre engine which had a distressing tendency to fail at inopportune moments. But the airframe too had faults, some of which could be cured, but others

were inherent and ineradicable. These have been described in detail in the preceding chapters.

With its great, thick wing section, the Typhoon exhibited a disappointing fall-off in performance as altitude increased – and in the European theatre altitude was the key to success. The aircraft also proved to be less manoeuvrable than the Spitfire or Hurricane, although its stability in the air made it an excellent gun platform for accurate aerial firing. These shortcomings were no surprise to Fighter Command, the AOC having prophetically remarked as early as July 1940 that the Typhoon was expected to be 'good in the defensive role, a good low-altitude strafer and probably a good night-fighter, but lacks the manoeuvrability for dogfighting'.

The early production aircraft featured a heavily framed windscreen and cockpit canopy with side doors; windows operated by hand-winders (often likened to those on an Austin Seven), and hinged roof for access. Behind the pilot's headrest was a sheet of armour and a completely metal-skinned fairing. The pilot's view to the front and side was just about adequate, but to the

rear it was non-existent. Coupled with the poor altitude performance and indifferent manoeuvrability, the Typhoon's suitability as a pure fighter was questionable to say the least. The only advantages it offered over the then-current Spitfire V was its heavy armament (in the cannon version), remarkable acceleration in the dive, its steadiness as a gun platform, and above all, a remarkable turn of speed at low altitude. This last factor would eventually play a large part in keeping the Typhoon in service.

Duxford had been chosen as the first home for the Typhoon because it allowed the squadrons to prepare for action relatively peacefully, the base being beyond the normal range of intruding German fighters and fighter-bombers. Despite the obvious shortcomings of the early Mk IAs, 56 Squadron continued its familiarization with the new equipment until 1 November 1941. On that date tragedy struck for the first time

Below: An early Typhoon IA, possibly R7594 'US-B', in service with 56 Squadron at Duxford late in 1941 or early 1942. The machine-gun ports in the leading edges have been covered by doped patches to exclude dust – standard RAF practice. (Public Archives of Canada)

when one of its aircraft dived into the ground without obvious reason, the pilot being killed. The cause was traced by investigators to carbon monoxide poisoning resulting from exhaust leakage into the cockpit. At once the aircraft were grounded and, but for essential tests flights, remained so for more than a month. After fitting extended exhaust stubs and improving the cockpit sealing (the port cockpit doors were sealed permanently) training recommenced on 8 December. In fact, the carbon monoxide problem was never to be entirely solved and as a precaution pilots wore their oxygen masks from start up to shut down for the rest of the Typhoon's service life.

With this problem at least under control, if not resolved, the re-equipment of a second squadron began; 266 (Rhodesian) Squadron moving to Duxford in January 1942 to exchange its Spitfires for Typhoons. At this stage Squadron Leader Denys Gillam was promoted to Wing Leader of the Duxford Typhoon Wing – when it was complete. Gillam's squadron commanders, 'Cocky' Dundas, who had taken over 56 Squadron from Prosser Hanks in January, and Charles L. Green, the Rhodesian commander of 266 Squadron, continued to work hard to get their units ready for operations – although at this stage both would have preferred Spitfires.

As a result of 56 Squadron's experiences, improvements were being incorporated on the production line, and after the 163rd aircraft the cockpit canopy was modified by replacing the solid rear fairing with a completely transparent one, and the pilot's head armour was reduced to a triangular section flanked by armoured glass windows. This greatly improved rearward vision and all the earlier aircraft were withdrawn and modified to the new standard. By the middle of April 1942 56 Squadron was fully equipped with eighteen of the modified aircraft, and had moved to nearby Snailwell which was to be their new operational base. At about this time the first cannon-armed Mk IBs reached the squadrons and began to replace the Mk IAs.

△1

△2

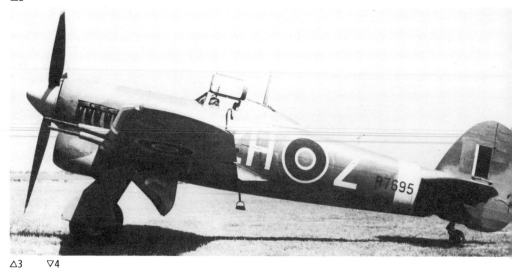

△3   ▽4

Right:

1. Squadron Leader 'Cocky' Dundas in the cockpit of his 'US-A' watched by Flying Officer Haabjoern and Flight Lieutenant Piltingsrud, two Norwegians serving with 56 Squadron, who would later become wing and squadron commanders respectively. (Group Captain D. E. Gillam)

2. A still from film taken in June 1942, showing R7694 'US-R' of 56 Squadron after canopy modifications. (IWM)

3. One of 266 Squadron's early Typhoons, R7695 'ZH-Z', was also one of the first to suffer structural failure, crashing in Dorset and killing its pilot. (RAF Museum)

4. R7698 was Denys Gillam's Typhoon in the autumn of 1942; as Duxford Wing Leader he was entitled to mark his aircraft with his own initials, but instead chose the anonymous but distinctive 'Z-Z' (Group Captain D. E. Gillam)

Much has been written of the high loss rate of Typhoons to non-operational causes during this working-up period, but this appears to have been at least partly popular myth, fuelled by losses to such causes suffered later in the year. One of 266 Squadron's aircraft crash-landed during February 1942, one spun into the ground in March, and a third flew out of cloud into the ground in April but, in fact, this was the sum of total losses during the first four months of the year. It is true, however, to say that there were many less serious accidents during this period, many due to engine failure or mishandling, but these were non-fatal and the Typhoons involved were repaired.

On 10 April, 609 Squadron, which had brought its Spitfires from Digby to Duxford, received its first Typhoon IAs. By early May their conversion was complete, bringing the Typhoon Wing to full strength at last. 609 Squadron was led by another experienced fighter pilot, Squadron Leader 'Sheep' Gilroy, who would hand over a month later to Squadron Leader Paul Richey, a pilot on his second tour of operations.*

At last, on 28 May 1942, the Typhoon became operational, when a 266 Squadron aircraft was scrambled to investigate an intruder; this turned out to be a Spitfire. Two days later 56 Squadron detached four aircraft of 'A' Flight and a similar number of 'B' Flight to Manston and Tangmere respectively. Patrols were begun immediately in the hope that they might be able to utilize the Typhoon's high speed to intercept the 'Jabo'† Messerschmitt Bf 109s and Focke-Wulf Fw 190s from Jagdgeschwadern 2 and 26, which were now making frequent 'hit-and-run' nuisance attacks all along the south and south-east coasts, either at low level, or by diving at high speed from altitude over France, making good their escape at sea level. There was little the Spitfire Vs could do against such attacks so it was hoped that the Typhoon might prove the answer; initial results were to prove far from encouraging. On the third day of operations a pair of 56 Squadron's Typhoons from Manston were vectored on to a suspected raider off Dover. Unfortunately two Canadian Spitfires from Gravesend were after the same target and the two pairs met at 17,000 feet over the Channel. The Spits had the height advantage and circled above the Typhoons before misidentifying the two 56 Squadron machines as Fw 190s. Diving down suddenly the Spitfires opened fire and both Typhoons plunged into the sea. Sergeant Stuart-Turner was killed, while Pilot Officer Deugo (RCAF) managed to bale out and was

picked up by an ASR launch, suffering from burns. Although two further interceptions were attempted, no raiders were located and the detachments returned to Norfolk on 7 July having seen no action against the enemy.

During its working-up period, 609 Squadron had suffered the loss of five aircraft. Pilot Officer De Selys became the first pilot to bale out of a Typhoon successfully (after an engine failure), another was lost to an undercarriage malfunction, two more in a collision when Flight Lieutenant De Spirlet was killed. His Typhoon swung violently when a tyre burst on take-off and rammed Pilot Officer Lallemant's Typhoon, losing its tail and crashing in flames. The last of the five was lost on 30 July, the day 609 became operational, when Pilot Officer Gilbert* force-landed following yet another engine failure. During this period 266 Squadron also lost three more, two in forced landings following engine failures. Nevertheless the re-equipment programme was now getting into its stride. During July, 1 Squadron at Acklington, 257 Squadron at High Ercall and 486 (New Zealand) Squadron at Wittering all began replacing their Hurricanes with Typhoons; all three would be operational by early September. Originally, following reports from the AFDU regarding the Typhoon's suitability for night operations, it was intended that these three units would utilize their new mounts in similar roles to their Hurricanes, i.e., as night intruders and 'Turbinlite' satellites. However, as already related, further trials in August between an FIU-flown Typhoon and a Turbinlite Boston III of 1455 Flight, showed that the Typhoon was too fast to formate comfortably on the Boston and the scheme was dropped. Strange to relate, another AFDU report dating from this period assessed the Typhoon (and other current types) in the 'army support' role – and it came equal fourth with the Spitfire, being judged inferior to the Mustang, Hurricane and Whirlwind!

Operations were now getting well under way, and on 20 June Group Captain John Grandy (OC Duxford) and Wing Commander Gillam had led 56 and 266 Squadrons on the first sweep by the Duxford Wing over enemy territory. In support of 'Circus 193' the Typhoons flew down the occupied coast from Mardyck to Boulogne but no opposition appeared. Success still eluded the Typhoons, and the cloud of ill-fortune apparently hanging over the aircraft was again accentuated on 30 July when ten of 56 Squadron's aircraft escorted six Bostons from Bomber Command's 2 Group to attack Abbeville airfield. A Norwegian pilot, Flying Officer Erik Haabjoern, suffered engine trouble and returned early. Off Dover he

was intercepted by Spitfires, and once more a Typhoon was identified as an Fw 190 and shot down into the sea; fortunately Haabjoern was able to extricate himself and was rescued unhurt; it was the first of three involuntary dips in the Channel for him.

Success was not far off, however. A few days later, on 9 August 1942, two of 266 Squadron's aircraft caught a Ju 88 over the North Sea, some fifty miles off Cromer; this was shot down by Pilot Officers Munro and Lucas for the Typhoon's first victory. Within four days Flight Lieutenant Johnson, also of 266, had added a second of these bombers (at first thought to be an Me 210) in the same area.

At this time all operations by Typhoons over enemy territory had to have prior approval from 12 Group HQ and in order to prevent a Typhoon falling into enemy hands pilots were ordered to abandon the aircraft in mid air rather than attempt a forced landing. The first major action for the Wing occurred during the Dieppe landings – Operation 'Jubilee'. In Fighter Command's biggest single day of operations throughout the war, an 'umbrella' of fighters was maintained over the invasion fleet and battle area throughout the day, the Luftwaffe turning out in force to give battle. For the first time the Wing operated at full three-squadron strength, taking off from Duxford at 1100 hours. The Typhoons rendezvoused with nine 'calibration Defiants'* over Orfordness for a diversionary feint to within ten miles of the enemy coast and kept ahead of them, hoping to catch any intercepting Luftwaffe aircraft. These did not put in an appearance and the Wing continued with an uneventful sweep down the coast to Ostend before returning to West Malling, somewhat short of fuel. After refuelling, the Wing was airborne again at 1400 hours; with 609 leading at 15,000 feet and 56 and 266 as top cover 2,000 feet higher, the sector Le Touquet to Le Tréport was patrolled. Among the 609 Squadron pilots was a flight lieutenant who had recently joined them following a spell testing Typhoons at Hawker's – R. P. Beamont:

'The Wing dived round behind Dieppe, through the cloud, coming out about 4,000 feet, continuing with a high speed pass right round the town and back out over the coast. A number of '190s were seen but 609, in the lead never really got near enough to them.' One Fw 190 miraculously appeared in the middle of 609's rear section but rapidly peeled off after a burst from Sergeant de Saxce. Meanwhile 266 Squadron had spotted some Do 217s of Kampfgeschwader 2 inland from Le Tréport and three of their number were detached to attack these.

*Squadron Leader Paul Richey had fought with 1 Squadron in the Battle of France and subsequently wrote the aviation classic, *Fighter Pilot*, about his experiences.
†'Jabo', a contraction of 'Jagdbomber', was German slang for 'fighter-bomber'.

*The late H. L. Gilbert was well known to TV viewers of the fifties by his first two names – Humphrey Lestoq.

*The 'calibration Defiants' were probably aircraft of the Defiant Flight (later 515 Squadron) which carried 'Moonshine' – a device which re-transmitted German radar signals, giving the resultant 'echo' the appearance of a much larger force.

Flight Lieutenant Dawson downed one and a second was claimed as a probable by Pilot Officer Munro, but the third member of the trio, Pilot Officer Smithyson was not seen again; it has been suggested that his aircraft was a victim of the structural failure which would plague the Typhoon over the coming months. Meanwhile the rest of 266 tangled with some Fw 190s, claiming one probable, and the Wing Leader knocked pieces off another but could only claim one damaged. Remaining at high altitude, 56 Squadron had sparred with more 190s without result. The drama was not over, for on the way home, the victorious Flight Lieutenant Dawson was attacked by Norwegian Spitfires whose pilots, almost head-on, failed to recognize the Typhoon; he was hit by the first burst, half rolling up to 1,000 feet before plunging into the Channel. Other Typhoons of 266 and 609 were also attacked by Spitfires but escaped without damage. Later in the afternoon a third sortie was carried out by the Wing, but cloud cover had increased and this trip was uneventful.

There were many lessons to be learnt both from the Dieppe action and other Typhoon operations to date, and early in September Squadron Leader Richey compiled a report summarizing the problems and advantages of the Typhoon and suggesting how best the aircraft might be used. His idea, which had the support of the other Typhoon squadron commanders, was that Typhoon squadrons should be relocated in the Coltishall, Tangmere and Exeter sectors, with their aircraft further dispersed at advanced landing grounds to maintain an advanced state of readiness. The plan found favour with Fighter Command and consequently on 18 September 1942 the Duxford Wing was disbanded, and the various squadrons now operational on the aircraft were spread about the southern part of the country. 609 Squadron moved to Biggin Hill in Kent, 486 Squadron to North Weald in Essex, 266 Squadron to Warmwell in Dorset, 257 Squadron to Exeter in Devon to defend the south-west, while 56 Squadron remained at Matlaske in Norfolk, where it had moved at the end of August; from there it could cover the North Sea coast. While these moves were taking place, two new squadrons were forming with Typhoons as their initial equipment. 181 Squadron came into existence at Duxford on 7 September; 182 Squadron was formed five days later at Martlesham Heath. These two units were commanded by Squadron Leaders Dennis Crowley-Milling and Pugh, experienced squadron commanders previously on Spitfires and Whirlwinds respectively. These two units were scheduled to be the first Typhoon fighter-bomber squadrons, but initially they were equipped with a motley selection of Typhoons, including many Mk IAs donated by other squadrons. Meanwhile Hawker were working with all speed to produce forty sets of bomb racks for the new aircraft which the units would receive when they were fully worked-up.

Another lesson learned was that the Typhoon must be more easily identified by other Allied pilots. To aid this a 1-foot wide yellow band was painted around each wing, in line with the inner cannon; this was to prove inadequate. Another and greater problem, however, was now casting further doubts on the Typhoon's continued service life, namely the structural failure of the rear fuselage. The technical aspects of this malady and its attempted cures have been detailed in Chapter Two, but an account of some of its effects on the squadrons is not amiss here. As most of the accidents seemed to occur in high-speed dives or recovery from them, some restriction on diving speed was considered. This was thought impracticable and instead manoeuvres likely to cause black-out were to be avoided. By September at least three and possibly four (see Dieppe above) Typhoons had been lost, but the first of the 'cures' was ready – a steel strap around the rear fuselage joint. Hardly had this modification programme got under way when it was superseded by 'Mod.286'. From November 1942 until well into 1943 Typhoons were systematically withdrawn from service for this tail strengthening modification, each aircraft spending about a week away from its squadron. As stated earlier, the modification was ineffective; when normal flying was resumed and further squadrons equipped in 1943, losses from structural failure continued at the rate of one or two per month. Perhaps 'Mod.286's greatest effect was in boosting pilot morale; many Typhoon pilots today are still under the illusion that it solved the problem.

Returning to September 1942, there had been some bright spots amid the gloom. At Acklington, 1 Squadron had completed conversion from Hurricanes and were declared operational on 4 September. Just two days later a pair of their Typhoons were vectored on to two 'bogys'. These were intercepted at 28,500 feet off Redcar and identified as Ju 88s or Me 210s; both enemy aircraft turned and dived, each with a

Right: Some of 181 Squadron's first pilots gathered in front of R8877 'EL-X', the CO's aircraft. Left to right: Sergeants 'Vin' Vincent, 'Jimmy' Bryant, Hugh Collins, 'Billy' Grey, Flying Officer 'Paddy' King, Squadron Leader Denis Crowley-Milling, Flight Lieutenant Tony Zweigbergk. (W. Grey)

Below: Although 182 Squadron was formed as a Typhoon bomber unit, its first equipment included several 'second-hand' Typhoon IAs, one of which is seen here in a blast pen at Martlesham Heath in September 1942. The first attempt at Typhoon identity markings – a yellow chordwise band – can just be discerned inboard of the machine-gun ports. (D. J. Coxhead)

Typhoon rapidly closing on its tail. The raiders, subsequently confirmed from their wreckage as Me 210s, were shot down, although the RAF pilots both blacked-out in the dive or the recovery. One of them saw 520mph IAS 'on the clock' before his vision went!

Later in the month, one year and three days after receiving their first aircraft, 56 Squadron at last got their name on the Typhoon scoreboard. The victim was a Ju 88 on a reconnaissance flight over the North Sea; intercepting was a pair of Typhoons led by Flight Lieutenant Mike Ingle-Finch. 'We caught him about 40 miles out to sea, under the guidance of Coltishall. It was the interception of his radio reports by the 'Y' Service which revealed his position and it worked fantastically well. The way we used to do these patrols was the No. 2 "on the deck" and the No. 1 above him at 1,000 or 1,500 feet. This way it was easier for the No. 2 to spot anything low down while the No. 1 could keep an eye on him and a more distant horizon.' Just how well the system worked on this occasion is revealed by the combat report.

Mike Ingle-Finch was flying a Typhoon IB, but his Canadian No. 2 was in a machine-gun armed Mk IA: 'Controller told "Green section", before leaving the ground to fly on a course of 110 degrees for eleven minutes and on 090 degrees for four minutes. After which they were put onto 270 degrees, which was accurately flown for two minutes, when they were told to watch out to the north-west, at approximately 1710 hours. No. 2 was then flying at zero feet and No. 1 at 1,000 feet, but later dropped down to 800 feet to get below cloud. Just then No. 2 sighted a Ju 88 flying underneath (the cloud). No. 1 had not seen it, so No. 2 called to him to follow as he was going in to attack. The Ju was evading hard and there was black smoke coming from his exhausts. No. 2 kept ahead, closing in until he was able to make an attack with 12 machine-guns from about 170 yards, closing to 80, experiencing return fire, and then broke away to let No. 1 get in a burst with cannon. No. 1 went in on a beam quarter attack and pressed the button at 300 yards closing to 150 yards; he slowed down (so as) not to overshoot. From this range he started firing another 3 or 4 bursts, totalling 8 seconds, and had to break away to avoid collision with the e/a. He saw large pieces fly off the fuselage and starboard wing and also saw hits on the starboard engine, from which large pieces fell away and thick black smoke emerged.' After a further attack the Ju 88 turned on its side and disappeared into cloud. The Typhoons followed and found a large patch of oil on the water.

The problem of mis-identification continued, and spread to the light AA defences along the south coast. From 1 October 1942,

as part of the measures against the troublesome 'Jabos', the trigger-happy gunners had been given licence to open fire on any aircraft approaching without prior warning from seaward below 1,000 feet. On the last day of the month, stirred up by Fw 190s attacking Canterbury, they opened fire on patrolling Typhoons of 609 Squadron and Flying Officer Roy Payne was lucky to survive a forced landing in the shallows of Pegwell Bay. The yellow wing bands had proved barely adequate for distinguishing the Typhoon from enemy fighters, but now something more obvious was needed to provide instant identification for anti-aircraft gunners. From 19 November 1942 the noses of the aircraft were painted white ahead of the wing leading edges, and four 12-inch wide black stripes were painted beneath each wing, 24 inches apart, the first stripe being at the wing root. The white noses were instantly unpopular, and following the pilots' violent objections they were deleted by an order dated 5 December; the original nose colours were restored and the under-wing area between each black band was painted white instead. Many aircraft retained the yellow band on the upper wing for several more months, but these were eventually eliminated. The black-and-white striping was to remain the Typhoon's specific recognition feature until February 1944, when they were removed, no longer being considered necessary. They should not be confused with the equal-width black-and-white 'invasion stripes' which would be applied to the wings and fuselage of most Allied aircraft in June 1944.

While efforts were being made to deal with the structural and engine problems, increasing production flows were enabling more units to be formed. During the last two months of 1942 five more new squadrons came into existence:
183 Squadron at Church Fenton on 1 November; 195 Squadron at Hutton Cranswick on 27 November; 197 Squadron at Drem on 28 November; 198 Squadron at Digby on 8 December; 193 Squadron at Harrowbeer on 18 December; and on 30 December, 245 Squadron at Charmy Down exchanged its night-fighting Hurricanes IICs for Typhoons, becoming a day unit once more.

The new duties were at last bringing some solid success. By the end of September 257 Squadron had added another Ju 88 to the Typhoon's sparse 'scoreboard', but on 17 October the New Zealanders of 486 Squadron, having just moved again to West Malling airfield, managed to intercept one of the elusive 'hit-and-run' raiders, when Pilot Officer Thomas and Sergeant Sames caught an Fw 190 from 10(Jabostaffel)/JG 26 flown by Feldwebel Klaus Niesel, and shot it down into the sea off Hastings. On 3 November 257 Squadron compounded this success by

bringing down two more of the fast, low-flying Focke-Wulfs west of Guernsey. These aircraft had been attacking Teignmouth and were caught by two Typhoons from Bolt Head, in use as an ALG for Exeter. When first spotted the 190s were three or four miles ahead; this distance had been closed in six minutes flying at 360mph IAS, an overtaking speed of 30mph or more. Of those units in the south, only 609 Squadron now remained 'unblooded'.

Squadron Leader Roland Beamont had taken over 609 Squadron in October when Paul Richey was rested. Beamont, having spent a 'rest tour' with Hawker, was a firm believer in the aircraft and under his leadership the unit was about to leap into the forefront of Typhoon operations. While at Biggin Hill 609 was regarded very much as an interloper by the resident Spitfire Wing; not allowed to join in with Spitfire operations, 609's flying was restricted to standing patrols along the Kent coast, and these had so far been fruitless. An appeal to 11 Group HQ resulted in a move to Manston on 2 November and from here three days later Flight Sergeant Haddon made the first interception, claiming an Fw 190 probably shot down off Dover. Ten days later Haddon was credited with the first confirmed claim against a Focke-Wulf for the squadron in the same area, claiming a second damaged, but the Germans fought back on this occasion, and Pilot Officer Amor was shot down. Another section also intercepted and one more Fw 190 was claimed damaged by Flying Officer 'Johnny' Baldwin, later to become the most successful of all Typhoon pilots in air combat. A further aircraft destroyed and one damaged were claimed next day, 16 November.

Squadron Leader Beamont had obtained permission to investigate the Typhoon's potential in other areas. He had substantial experience of night intruder operations on Hurricanes with 87 Squadron so what more natural than to exploit its big brother's speed, firepower and known night-flying ability in this role? On the moonlit night of 17 November Beamont flew the first Typhoon night 'Rhubarb' (the code-name for small-scale fighter operations seeking targets of opportunity, and using the cover of cloud or darkness), attacking a train near Abbeville. This was the first of many similar sorties over the coming winter months; other pilots were given a night-training programme and were soon active with marked success. On the same day that 609 had begun night operations, 56 Squadron had flown their first day 'Rhubarb', crossing the North Sea to Walcheren and strafing Bf 109s on an airfield near Vlissingen. Flight Lieutenant Piltingsrud, another Norwegian with 56, destroyed one 109 on the ground and damaged another, while Flying Officer Deugo, the survivor of the Spitfire attack on

1 June, flew so low in his attack that he hit a German soldier with his wing as the latter scrambled out of a flak position. He returned with grim evidence of this encounter on the leading edge of his Typhoon's wing.

December was to prove a most profitable month for the Typhoons in south-east England, a total of eleven confirmed, three probables and four damaged being claimed by 486 and 609 Squadrons for the loss of three Typhoons, only two of them to enemy action. The New Zealanders had claimed two Bf 109s on 17th, and on the 18th, a Do 217 was intercepted by Flying Officer Thomas and Flight Sergeant Penny off Shoreham. This was shot down by Thomas, but not before the rear gunner had hit Penny's Typhoon which also went down into the sea. 486 Squadron was to add one more Do 217 on 22nd and another two Bf 109s on 24th, as well as a couple of Fw 190s, ending the year as top-scoring squadron. Sergeant Turek of 609 Squadron claimed two Fw 190s during the month, the second

Right:
1, 2 and 3. Squadron Leader Paul Richey in R7752 'PR-G' (he had always chosen 'G' as his personal code-letter since France in 1940) whose serial has been partly obscured by the first tail-strengthening 'mods'. A squadron leader's pennant and 609's white rose and hunting-horns badge were displayed beneath the windscreen. When Squadron Leader 'Bee' Beamont took over 609 he inherited 'G' which he further personalized with his 'scoreboard' and cannon barrel fairings (adapted from those of a Spitfire); the latter were painted yellow, together with the spinner. By the time the lower photographs were taken, early in 1943, 'G' had also acquired identity stripes and 609's unique white 'chin' stripe. (1. RAF Museum; 2. Wing Commander R. P. Beamont)

△1

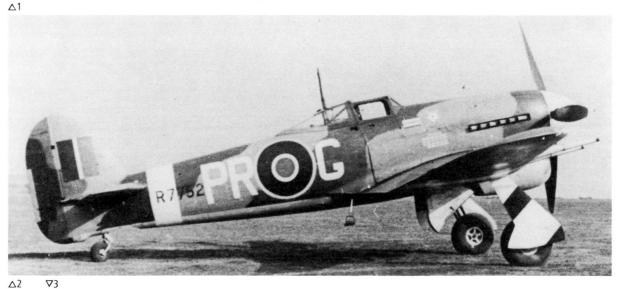

△2   ▽3

off Dungeness on the 20th, when he also claimed a probable. This time his opponent was not one of the specialist fighter-bombers from the Jabostaffeln, but was a fighter aircraft of I/JG 26, the pilot being a seven-victory 'ace', Leutnant Heinz-Gunther Adam, who was killed.

These successes were timely, for forces within Fighter Command were lobbying against the Typhoon. Attrition during the increased flying undertaken in the course of the last four months of the year had been heavy, some 36 Typhoons being written off to causes other than enemy action. Landing accidents and forced-landings occasioned by engine trouble accounted for most, but 1 Squadron had lost two in rather mysterious circumstances, one of the pilots being Gloster's Chief Test-Pilot, P. E. G. Sayer. The pair disappeared off the Northumberland coast, probably due to a mid-air collision, although one aircraft was seen coming

down minus its tail – whether due to a collision or structural failure remains a matter for surmise. The Typhoon still had a long way to go before it could be given a clean bill of health.

At the beginning of January 1943 Squadron Leader Beamont was summoned to a meeting at Bentley Priory: 'I was told to report to Fighter Command HQ to attend a meeting to discuss the role of the Typhoon. No more than that. When I got there I found that the meeting was chaired by the Commander-in-Chief and that the main topic was not how best to use the aeroplane but whether it was to continue in service, or to be replaced by an American heavy fighter, such as the P-47. I hadn't heard about this before and during the course of the meeting the subject became a very hot argument indeed. Towards the end of the meeting – I was a fairly junior office present – I was asked to say my piece. So I just described

the activities of 609 at Manston and how the Typhoon was proving to be an extremely accurate ground-attack aeroplane, and was capable of inflicting a lot of damage with its 20mm cannon on a wide range of targets. It was also capable of accepting punishment and coming back. I was asked how it should be best used in the future and I said it would be an ideal ground-attack fighter provided we developed certain aspects, particularly the vision from the cockpit. This was listened to and then challenged with some derision by members of the meeting, particularly the engineering officers. Eventually 609 Squadron were again asked to report on their activities – we still said it would make a very practical ground-attack aeroplane – and 3 Squadron, who had just joined us at Manston, supported our case.'

So the Typhoon remained in service, but it was to be touch-and-go for some months yet.

The start of 1943 saw 13 squadrons fully equipped with Typhoons, although five of these were still working-up, and were not yet operational; one more was about to receive its first aircraft. The fourteen squadrons were as follows.

10 GROUP (south-west):

Exeter	257 Squadron
Warmwell	266 Squadron
Charmy Down	245 Squadron (non-operational)
Harrowbeer	193 Squadron (awaiting aircraft)

11 GROUP (south-east):

Manston	609 Squadron
Tangmere	486 Squadron

12 GROUP (midlands):

Matlaske	56 Squadron
Snailwell	181 Squadron
Sawbridgeworth	182 Squadron
Church Fenton	183 Squadron (non-operational)
Hutton Cranswick	195 Squadron (non-operational)
Digby	198 Squadron (non-operational)

13 GROUP (north):

Acklington	1 Squadron
Drem	197 Squadron (non-operational)

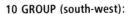

Top left: These 486 Squadron pilots were responsible for the destruction of seven enemy aircraft during the last weeks of 1942. Left to right: Pilot Officer G. G. Thomas, Flight Sergeant Frank Murphy, Sergeant 'Hyphen' Taylor-Cannon, Sergeant 'Arty' Sames, Flying Officer 'Spike' Umbers and Flight Sergeant 'Norm' Gall. (via P. Sortehaug)

Left: Some of the men who bore the brunt of the Typhoon's teething troubles – ground crew of 56 Squadron gathered round one of their charges at Matlaske, early 1943. (BAe)

CHAPTER FOUR

'Anti-Rhubarbs': defensive operations, 1943

THE availability of increased numbers of Typhoons at the beginning of 1943 was opportune, for the Luftwaffe's fighter-bomber activity over southern England was just about to increase. Until the start of the new year these operations had been undertaken almost entirely by two specialist Staffeln in the two main western-based Jagdgeschwadern – JG 2 and 26. During February 1943, however, the Stab (HQ flight), I and II Gruppen of a new Schnellkampfgeschwader 10 were formed for service in western France, equipped with Fw 190A-4/U8 fighter-bombers. These new units would operate both over England and against shipping in the Bay of Biscay. Originally formed to undertake the latter function, the Gruppen were moved to Amiens during the spring of 1943 for the former duty when JG 2 and 26 became too involved in the defensive role to be able to continue such action. At this time the Jabostaffeln from these latter Geschwadern were transferred to SKG 10 to form the basis of a 1V Gruppe [III Gruppe was based in the Mediterranean area throughout 1943].

There were also changes in the British defences. Although the low-looking Chain Home Low radar and Naval surface-watching radar operators were specially briefed to watch for the incoming fighter-bombers, the first warning often came from the Observer Corps posts or the Coastguards. These were now issued with ex-Admiralty 'Snowflake pyrotechnics' (under Operation 'Totter'), which were launched to alert the patrolling fighters to the position of intruders which had eluded them and the radars. A desperate measure perhaps, but it worked quite well. The Typhoons were now maintaining standing patrols (which soon became known as 'anti-Rhubarbs') from dawn until dusk, pairs of aircraft flying parallel to the coast on regular beats – Ramsgate to Dungeness, Dungeness to Beachy Head, Beachy Head to Shoreham, Shoreham to Selsey Bill, Selsey Bill to St. Catherine's Point, and so on, down to Start Point in Devon. Typically, patrols lasted about 75 minutes and, though mostly uneventful, were no sinecure. The usual height was anything between 10 and 200 feet above the sea – any higher and it would have been difficult to spot the Jabos – and this allowed little chance of a successful bale-out in the event of that ever-present danger, engine failure. During the early months of 1943, in order to keep this possibility to a minimum, Sabres were removed for overhaul after just 25 hours' running. The engineering effort to keep sufficient numbers of Typhoons flying was enormous, and to help this Typhoon squadrons had flight lieutenants (rather than the usual flying officers) as Engineering Officers, with twice as many staff as on other fighter squadrons. The complement of aircraft was also 50 per cent higher in order to keep the required number of Typhoons serviceable. Even so, in May 1943, when the supply of Sabre engines could not be maintained because of essential modification work, and despite the time between overhauls being raised to 30 hours, the squadrons found themselves rationed to 300 hours per month (200 in the case of bomber squadrons). Despite these efforts at least 50 Typhoons were lost through engine failure in the first five months of 1943, and many others were sentenced to lengthy periods of repair.

One ray of hope for the pilots was the first successful ditching of a Typhoon in deep water. This had been thought inadvisable, if not impossible, as the huge air intake beneath the nose made a dive to the seabed the most likely outcome. Then, on 20 February, when Flying Officer Furber of 266 Squadron had an engine failure at 300 feet while chasing a bandit, he was unable to gain sufficient height to bale out and was forced to ditch. He did so successfully by keeping the tail well down, but even so he had a narrow escape when dragged under by the IFF aerials (wires stretching from mid-fuselage to the tailplane tips) as the Typhoon sank; however he struggled into his dinghy and was picked up by a minesweeper.

Throughout the first five months of 1943 the Typhoon units in 10 and 11 Groups of Fighter Command saw good return for their efforts against the Jabos and their fighter escorts. By 1 June, 32 Fw 190s, eight Bf 109s and a single Ju 88 had been claimed shot down, while probable claims totalled four more Fw 190s, one Bf 109 and a Do 217; eleven Fw 190s and one Do 217 were claimed damaged. Of the confirmed successes, 19 Fw 190s and three Bf 109s were credited to 609 Squadron, six Fw 190s to 266 Squadron and three Fw 190s, three Bf 109s, and the Ju 88 to 486 Squadron. On only two occasions were the Luftwaffe able to inflict casualties in return, once on 14 February when two of 609 Squadron's Typhoons flown by Flight Sergeant Haddon and Sergeant Wiseman were 'bounced' during a defensive patrol over a disabled MTB in mid-Channel, and were shot down into

Below: Flight Sergeant 'Babe' Haddon (left) was responsible for some of 609 Squadron's early successes, but both he and Sergeant 'Johnny' Wiseman (with the dog) were shot down and killed while escorting an MTB in the Channel on 14 February 1943. (R. Lallemant via R. Decobeck)

the sea. The second occurred on 29 March when Flying Officer Bolster of 1 Squadron – which had moved to Biggin Hill from Acklington in February and thence to Lympne in March – was shot down south of Beachy Head when undertaking a lone interception sortie. The single Ju 88 had been detected at 'zero feet', no less than thirty miles south of St. Catherine's Point, by 'Blackgang' – a low-looking radar at Blackgang Chine on the Isle of Wight. Following the Controller's directions, and despite gathering February gloom, it was sighted and promptly dispatched by Flight Sergeant Frank Murphy,* who was leading a 486 Squadron section.

One of the outstanding interceptions occurred on 20 January when 28 Jabos escorted by fighters of JG 26, made an attack on London, with diversionary raids on the Isle of Wight and off the Kent coast. Little warning was obtained, and the balloon barrage was grounded at the time. Some considerable damage was done in the London docks, and civilian casualties were heavy, but Luftwaffe losses totalled three Jabos and six fighters. Six were credited to 609 Squadron, which claimed three Focke-Wulfs and three Messerschmitts, plus one Fw 190 damaged. The three Bf 109Gs were claimed by one pilot – Flying Officer

*After his tour on Typhoons, Frank Murphy was promoted to Squadron Leader and seconded to Hawker Aircraft as a test-pilot; continuing with Hawker after the war, he was Chief Production Test-Pilot in the Hunter's heyday.

'Johnny' Baldwin – in an unusually high combat at 20,000 feet; not to be outdone Flying Officer Van Lierde had dispatched his 190 at 27,000 feet.

609 Squadron enjoyed other successes of note during this period, particularly on 14 February, the day on which Haddon and Wiseman were lost, for later that same morning two other sections were more fortunate, claiming four Fw 190s shot down and two probables. Two of the confirmed victories and one probable were credited to Flying Officer 'Cheval' Lallemant, a Belgian pilot who would later command the unit.

On 9 April, 10./JG 26 lost Unteroffizier Karl Heck to fighters during an attack on Folkestone, and subsequently Leutnant Otto-August Backhaus of this unit was lost while searching for Heck in mid-Channel; two of II/JG 26's fighters were also lost. During these actions Fw 190s were claimed by 1 and 609 Squadrons, 486 Squadron claimed a probable, and two more were shot down by Spitfires of 611 Squadron.

A landmark during this period was the first successful 'scramble' by Typhoons to intercept one of the raids, rather than interception by the patrols. This took place on 29 April and was achieved by two Typhoons of 486 Squadron based at Tangmere. The event is vividly recalled by Allan Smith, then a flying officer: '. . . with Frank Murphy as my No. 2 we headed straight out to sea keeping low on the water and awaiting instructions from "Blackgang". They had plotted

"bandits" approaching from the south and their first vector was to put us between the "bandits" and the French coast. The "bandits" kept on coming and the trap was set. We were then given further vectors which would position us behind the "bandits" and then were given the code-word "Buster" [full throttle]. Shortly afterwards I saw two aircraft low on the water and called "Tallyho" to "Blackgang". At about the same time the "bandits" either saw us or received a message from their base that they were being intercepted and decided to handle the situation by making a run for France at full throttle. Their turn towards France gave us the chance to close the gap further and I identified them as Me 109s. We tucked in behind them and it must have been very difficult for them to know just where we were because they were not flying far enough apart to cover each other's tails properly.

We were flying about ten feet above the water and as we moved into firing range I told Frank to attack the second aircraft, which was lagging a bit behind, while I kept an eye on the leader. I didn't know it at the time but Frank was having trouble with his reflector sight and had to use the splashes of the cannon shells on the water to direct his guns on to the target aircraft. There were a number of strikes on the wings and the fuselage and the 109 started to move to port and eventually flew between my plane and the 109 I was following. As it came into my

Left: Two 486 Squadron New Zealanders, Frank Murphy and Allan Smith, whose successful interception of two Bf 109s is described below, are seen here sharing a joke at Tangmere, January 1943. (F. Murphy)

Below: Flying Officer 'Norm' Gall (left) of 486 Squadron with factory-fresh JP532 'SA-T' in one of the blast pens along Tangmere's north-eastern perimeter, July 1943. (Harman via Chris Ashworth)

Above: Squadron Leader Charles Green and some of his Rhodesians at Exeter in the summer of 1943. (IWM)

Above: Re-arming R8656 'FM-L' of 257 Squadron at Warmwell in May 1943. (RAF Museum/ C. E. Brown)

Below left: Flying Officer Cedric Henman, an Anglo-Argentinian flying with 257 Squadron, intercepted a pair of Bf 109s while on an 'anti-Rhubarb' patrol near Portland; they split and ran for home but he managed to dispatch one into the sea. His usual aircraft, R8639 'FM-B', was decorated with a portrait of 'Patoruzu' – an Argentinian cartoon character. (IWM)

Bottom left: 257 'Burma' Squadron's four Burmese pilots – left to right: Flying Officers Lao, Yi, Khin and Clift. Yi was reported missing on the last day of 1943 and Lao was killed on his second tour, but Khin and Clift survived to command the post-war Burmese Air Force. (IWM)

Below right: Squadron Leader 'Ronny' Fokes, CO of 257 Squadron, with his two fitters and his 'FM-A', believed to be JP510. (RAF Museum)

Right: Some of 56 Squadron's pilots in front of one of their Typhoons at Matslaske early in 1943, including Flight Lieutenant R. H. Deugo, RCAF (third from the left), who had survived being shot down by Spitfires on 1 June 1942, but was killed on operations with 198 Squadron on 20 July 1943. (BAe)

sights I gave it a couple of short bursts, getting strikes on the fuselage and tail section, and shortly afterwards it crashed into the sea. I then closed in on the leader and gave him several bursts of cannon-fire from dead astern. There were strikes all over the aircraft, pieces started to come off and it burst into flames. I moved off to port to avoid the debris and as the 109 lost airspeed I finished up in close formation about twenty feet to the left of the 109. At this stage the pilot turned and looked at me – it was my first face to face meeting with a German and I will remember that face until the day I die. I suddenly realized that if I were in his position I would have turned hard port and rammed the Typhoon – he took no such action – perhaps his controls were damaged. I pulled away and shortly afterwards he hit the sea.'

Having exchanged bases with 266 Squadron in January, 257 Squadron were now at Warmwell, and carrying out anti-Rhubarbs between Portland and the Isle of Wight. These bore fruit twice in April when Bf 109s were caught running for home. On the second of these occasions Flying Officer Henman, an Argentinian with 257, was attacked by two 109s as he cut them off, but evading them with a stall turn he was able to use the Typhoon's vastly superior speed to overhaul one, firing down to fifty yards' range before it pulled up and crashed into

the sea. Then on the 30th of the following month 'twenty plus' Fw 190s attacked Torquay, bombing the hospital which was used by recuperating aircrew. There had been no warning, but five sections were scrambled from Warmwell in an attempt to intercept the outgoing raiders. One Focke-Wulf was spotted by Yellow Section, some five miles ahead, and they were joined by a third Typhoon in a chase across the Channel. The Tiffies were clocking 350mph against the 190's estimated 300–320, and it was overhauled at 1,000 feet as it approached Guernsey. Flight Sergeant Calnan gave it a 1½-second burst as he closed to 150 yards, and the Focke-Wulf rolled over and dived into the cliffs.

The last big interception of the period occurred on 1 June when a further five Focke-Wulfs were claimed by 609 in the course of two engagements. First, Flight Lieutenant Wells was alerted by a gasometer exploding at Margate while he was patrolling nearby. Giving chase, he caught and flew through the formation of twelve Fw 190s, shooting down two of the leaders and attacking a third until he ran out of ammunition. Flying Officer Davies then attacked four more Focke-Wulfs which were strafing Broadstairs, claiming one shot down before pursuing others out to sea. Here he claimed a second victim in mid-Channel, and then a third, which he pur-

sued almost to the coast of Belgium. At this point the remaining Germans turned on him and, low on ammunition as well as outnumbered, he was obliged to break off and take advantage of the Typhoon's speed to make good his withdrawal.

After this the Jabos were not met again in any numbers until much later in the year, but this did not indicate that they were defeated, despite the losses they had suffered. On 18 June Stab, II and IV/SKG 10 had been posted to Sicily to reinforce Luftflotte 2; only the thirty aircraft of I/SKG 10 remained in France for offensive operations.

Not all the action had been in the south. The irritating Jabos had also made attacks on East Anglian coastal targets, although successes against these were limited to a single claim for a Bf 109. This was one of 26 which attacked Southwold on 15 May and was intercepted and shot down by Sergeant Hough* of 195 Squadron (by then operating from Ludham) on his 21st birthday. Not all interceptions went to plan, and one miscalculation on 6 July had tragic results. Although still based at Matlaske, 56 Squadron maintained two Typhoons on runway readiness at Ludham – nearer the likely coastal targets. In the evening of that day the

*Richard Hough, author of controversial biographies of Lord and Lady Mountbatten, has described his wartime experiences with 195 and 197 Squadrons in 'One Boy's War', Heinemann, 1975.

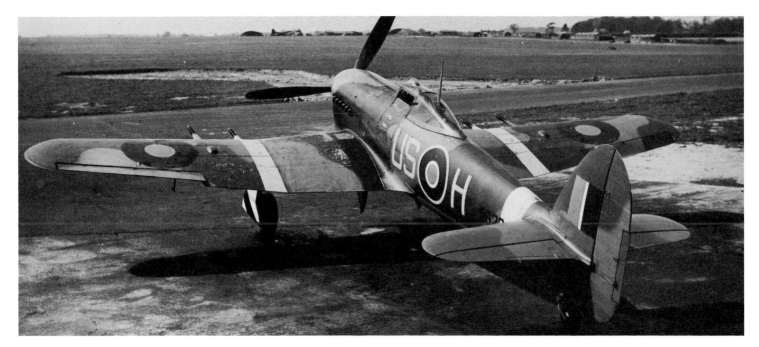

cockpits were occupied by Flight Sergeant Plumb and his No. 2, Flight Sergeant Clusas. 'Vic' Plumb remembers:

'I heard cannon-fire and two Fw 190s pulled up over the airfield to attack another ground target. I signalled to my No. 2 and roared off, hoping not to be caught in the act. As we were off the ground, doing about 200mph, I saw a red flare from airfield control but I had lost sight of the Focke-Wulfs. I called GCI which was nearby at Neatishead and was given vectors to the east, at full speed and staying at low level. When a few miles out to sea we were requested to increase speed if possible as the target was ahead and appeared to be gaining. We increased to maximum boost and revs. More calls informed us that the target was still ahead and increasing the gap. The plot and R/T were fading so we were told to go for ten minutes and if nothing was seen to return to base. After about ten minutes or so with no R/T contact, I called No. 2 and said I was returning. Reducing boost I turned and climbed to about 1,000 feet and called control for a bearing. I had just set this bearing on my compass when I saw a Focke-Wulf behind my No. 2; I shouted "Break!" and turned sharply to make a head-on attack. My No. 2 did not respond and I saw strikes on his aircraft. I had time for a brief squirt and then tracers were flying by me and some struck the wings – the other 190 was behind me. As I turned very steeply to avoid it I saw my No. 2 hit the sea in a shallow dive. The two Focke-Wulfs then tried to line me up but I made very steep turns which they were unable to turn inside; although I tried to get my sights on them I was unable to get enough deflection in the turns. By now we were down to sea level where the 190s did not seem to like steep turns so much, and as they pulled up for an attack I edged a bit nearer home. After a

Above: R8224 was one of only 15 production Typhoons built by Hawker, and was named 'Land Girl' to commemorate subscriptions from the Land Army. It carried the name on the port door, repeated with the Land Army badge on the starboard door. (RAF Museum/C. E. Brown)

while they gave up. I noticed skin damage on my wings and when I had landed and taxied to dispersal the ground crew opened up the starboard gun bay which was on fire. This was soon put out but poor old "Land Girl"* stood there looking rather sorry for herself. Of course, GCI had put us in front of the target and that is why they appeared to be gaining on us; visibility behind us was poor, with the sun low in a cloudless evening sky. So the Focke-Wulfs were in an ideal position to catch us from behind and below as we throttled back and climbed.'

The pressure on the original coastal defence Typhoon squadrons had been steadily reduced during the spring and summer. As radar techniques and alerting systems began to prove more effective, more reliance was placed on pairs of Typhoons held at readiness at the end of the runways

*'Landgirl' was a Hawker-built Typhoon IB, R8224, a presentation aircraft purchased by subscriptions from the Land Army. See photo caption above.

of advanced airfields, with pilots in the cockpits. The burden of the coastal patrols, which were still maintained, were now shared by some of the new Typhoon squadrons which had re-equipped in the north and had now moved south, to the scene of action. After a brief stay at Peterhead 245 Squadron had arrived at Gravesend, while 197 had come down from Drem to join the New Zealanders at Tangmere. At Manston 609 was joined by 198 Squadron. Other units now swelled the ranks of the defenders: 193 Squadron had become operational at Harrowbeer, while at High Ercall 247 Squadron had traded their Hurricane night-fighters for Typhoons before moving to Middle Wallop in March. During April 174 Squadron, a Hurribomber unit at Gravesend, also began conversion, increasing the number of Typhoon squadrons to sixteen.

From April, the Typhoons were joined in their patrols by the new Griffon-engined

Spitfire XIIs of 41 Squadron, based at Hawkinge; in May 91 Squadron also became operational on these aircraft. The Griffon enhanced the Spitfire's low-level performance considerably. In July 1942 the prototype Mk XII, in the hands of Jeffrey Quill, had unexpectedly won a 'race' against a Typhoon flown by Ken Seth-Smith and a captured Fw 190 piloted by Squadron Leader Wilson, which had been laid on as a demonstration for visiting VIPs at Farnborough. However, the production Spitfire XII was found to be substantially slower than the Typhoon at sea level, and marginally slower than the Fw 190. Shortly before handing over command of 609 Squadron, Squadron Leader Beamont flew a Spitfire XII at Hawkinge: 'Afterwards I took off in Typhoon "PR-G" with Squadron Leader Ray Harries (CO of 91 Squadron) to race round the coast to Pegwell Bay. Harries gave up around Deal, saying afterwards on the 'phone, "You were bloody miles ahead by then!" In this and subsequent tests I found that the Typhoon was at least 20mph faster at sea level.'

After an uneventful summer of patrols, two 197 Squadron Typhoons finally intercepted and shot down a Bf 109 off St. Catherine's Point on 14 September. This was credited to Flying Officer 'Wally' Ahrens, a Canadian who would later command 257 Squadron. He was flying JP546, a Typhoon named 'Borough of Sutton and Cheam'; this was a symbolic victory as the original bearer of this name, R8199, had been the first Typhoon shot down [by Spitfires] in June of the previous year.

A month later, on 15 October, two sections from 266 Squadron were scrambled, meeting Jabos in some strength east of Start Point; two were claimed shot down and one damaged. Finally, on 21 October Flying Officer Wiley and Flight Sergeant Fairburn of 1 Squadron claimed a single Fw 190 shot down off Beachy Head – it was the Typhoon's last victory in the battle of the Jabos and, barring a stray Ju 188 in April 1944, and a pair of 109s the following month, its last defensive victory of the war.

Top right: One of 245 Squadron's Typhoons, DN591 'MR-K', at Peterhead where the unit's first operational sorties with their new aircraft were carried out. (E. Brewer)

Centre right: During 1943 the other regular Tangmere resident was 197 Squadron, which had several Belgians among its pilots. One of them, Pilot Officer Jean Parisse, had flown with the 4ème Escadrille, IIème Régiment of the Aéronautique Militaire Belge, and decorated his Typhoon, DN473 'OV-E', with their paper horse badge. On 11 May 1943, soon after this photograph was taken, DN473 suffered an engine failure and crashed in the sea off Selsey, Pilot Officer Patullo baling out safely. (J. Parisse via R. Decobeck)

Right: Flight Lieutenant 'Wally' Ahrens, RCAF, shared in 197 Squadron's first confirmed victory, on 14 September 1943. He is seen here on the wing of JP546 'OV-D' which had been named 'Borough of Sutton and Cheam' after the original (R8199) had been so swiftly lost, tragically shot down by Spitfires on 1 June 1942. (IWM)

CHAPTER FIVE

'Rhubarbs', 'Roadsteads', 'Rangers': offensive operations, 1943

AFTER the initial operations of the Duxford Wing, few offensive sorties were flown during the closing months of 1942, as the existing Typhoon units concentrated on ironing out the problems with the aircraft and undertaking the defensive function, while the new units were busy working-up to operational standard.

Despite the pioneering efforts of 56 and 609 Squadrons on day and night 'Rhubarbs' (as already recorded), early 1943 still saw only a relatively limited number of offensive flights by the Typhoons, partly because of the adverse weather of winter as well as the defence commitment. When flown, these usually took the form of 'Rhubarbs'; they were of little more than nuisance value, and were to bring quite heavy losses – mainly to Flak. During 1943 the number of aircraft on operations lost to technical faults or accidents fell very steeply, reflecting the progress made throughout 1942 both with the airframe, and particularly with the engine. From April 1943 onwards the number of offensive sorties flown rose rapidly, and once the threat of the Jabos had diminished in mid summer, offensive activity became increasingly the Typhoon's main function.

This activity was to take several forms; 'Rhubarb' has already been described, but the other operations were also known by RAF code-names and these may be defined as:

'Circus' – a sweep accompanied by a small force of bombers designed to draw enemy fighters into action.
'Ramrod' – a 'Circus', but with emphasis on the destruction of a ground target by the bombers.
'Roadstead' – a low level attack on shipping and coastal defences or ports.
'Ranger' – freelance fighter sweep.
'Rodeo' – pure fighter sweep.
'Intruder' – a night 'Rhubarb'.
In addition the Typhoon squadrons also undertook shipping reconnaissance (sometimes known as 'Lagoon'), escorts to convoys, air/sea rescue aircraft and launches, and air/sea rescue searches for downed colleagues.

Towards the end of 1942, 181 and 182 Squadrons had been formed specifically as the first Typhoon fighter-bomber units, and during the spring of 1943 these two were joined by three more such specialist squadrons. 183 Squadron formed at Church Fenton in Yorkshire, eventually commencing operations from Colerne in April; 3 Squadron traded its Hurricanes for Typhoons at Hunsdon and began bombing with them from West Malling in May; and 175 Squadron, another ex-Hurricane unit, made their first sorties the following month.

At first a 250lb bomb was carried under each wing, but these were soon replaced by 500-pounders. The 'Bombphoons', as they were initially known, were generally escorted by fighter Typhoons from the other squadrons, although once rid of their bombs, the racks had little adverse effect on their fighting performance. Targets on the early bomber operations were mainly airfields in France – Poix and Abbeville were the favourites – but it was soon realized that with its startling low-level performance and heavy armament, with or without bombs, the Typhoon would be very effective in the anti-shipping role. Consequently Typhoons terrorized coastal shipping along the occupied coast from the Dutch Islands to the southern Brittany ports.

The New Zealanders at Tangmere got a very early lesson in the dangers of 'Rhubarbs' when Flying Officer Allan Smith and Flight Sergeant Bill Mawson set out for 486's first foray over France. Allan Smith was leading:

'Rhubarbs took place when there was 10/10 cloud with a base of 2,000 to 3,000 feet. The idea was that if enemy fighter reaction was too strong, you could take evasive action by simply pulling up into the cloud. On this particular one we had decided to cross the coast at Fécamp and patrol the nearby railway lines. We hammered across the Channel on the deck, to avoid radar detection, and made the correct landfall. As we crossed the coast there was some Flak and I turned slightly to starboard to get an accurate pinpoint and to start the patrol. When I straightened out there was no sign of Bill. One minute he was there and the next he was gone and I had heard nothing on the R/T.'

Although Mawson was reported to be a PoW the following month, it was not until the war was over that Smith discovered what had happened:

'As we approached the French coast I was about fifty yards behind Allan. At this point an explosion occurred at the front of the aircraft and vapour came from around the wing root at the starboard side of the engine, while at the same time I could see tracer flashing past the fuselage. I could not maintain height and barely avoided trees before belly-landing in a field. I couldn't find any means of destroying the aircraft, but seeing people from a farmhouse about 150 yards away I ran to them and asked for matches, which they gave me. I ran back but by this time German soldiers had emerged from the trees and were converging on the Typhoon. I managed to hide until nightfall but was eventually caught by a German patrol the following evening.'*

The Typhoon's best defence against Flak was to fly as low as possible but if the aircraft were hit it gave the pilot little time to react. The instantaneousness of disaster is well recalled by Flying Officer Peter Brett of 183 Squadron: 'We went in over the French coast and just after that – he was flying fifty or sixty feet to my left – flames suddenly issued from his radiator and he jettisoned his hood. I saw him start to get out but he only got about half way before the flames engulfed him and he dived into the ground. He was flying slightly faster than me so he crashed in front and to the left of me. There was a big explosion and I saw something, presumably the engine, shoot along the ground in a ball of fire. And then we were gone.'

Losses to Flak were frequent on all the operations flown, but the Luftwaffe was less in evidence generally. This was not always the case however and 3 Squadron was to prove a particularly unlucky unit in this respect. On 18 May eight of their aircraft took off to bomb Poix airfield; cover over the target was provided by fighter Typhoons of 486 Squadron, while others from 1 Squadron were to provide withdrawal support. Unfortunately there was some confusion and after bombing 3 Squadron's aircraft did not climb to meet 486 as expected but attempted to escape at low level. One fell to Flak, but the rest were badly bounced by Bf 109Gs of I/JG27 which had recently arrived in France after long service in North

*The Typhoon, EJ956 'SA-I', was repaired by the Germans and test-flown at Rechlin, later serving with Versuchsverband/Obdl (the famous 'Zirkus Rosarius'), whic toured German airbases demonstrating captured Allied types. This unit also used JP548 (which had force-landed on the Cherbourg peninsula on 14 February 1944) and a third as yet unidentified Typhoon. EJ956 was written-off for the second time when it turned over in a forced-landing near Meckelfeld on 10 August 1944; the pilot was unhurt. JP548 crashed at Reinsehlen on 29 July 1944, killing the pilot, Feldwebel Gold. A captured Tempest was also evaluated at Rechlin.

Africa. In quick succession four more Typhoons went down and none of their pilots survived. This was not to be 3 Squadron's only adverse encounter with the Luftwaffe, for on 1 July eight more of the unit's aircraft on a 'Roadstead' off the Hook of Holland, were engaged by Fw 190s of JG 2 which shot down three of them; only two damaged could be claimed in return. On this occasion 3 Squadron was up against the strongest of opposition; two of the claiming pilots were great Luftwaffe aces, Kurt Bühligen and 'Sepp' Wurmheller.

The two Norfolk-based squadrons, 56 and 195, with vast areas of the North Sea as their territory, were much involved in anti-shipping sorties. Flight Sergeant 'Vic' Plumb describes the techniques: 'These were usually flown very low over the sea. I remember a pilot coming back with the tips of his prop bent back through touching the water.* The

*Other Typhoon pilots have reported that propeller tips were bent forward on striking the sea.

Typhoon was an excellent low-level aircraft and we assumed that the radar could not detect us on the wave tops because we were never intercepted. We flew in flights of two or four in loose line abreast, about 100 yards apart; this formation enabled us to keep a good lookout at all times. During an attack we all tried to go in at the same time, if possible passing to the side of the target and using heavy rudder movements until we were out of range of the guns. I was never involved in a second attack on ships, but I remember two of our pilots on a weather "recce" coming across two E-boats which they eventually sank with repeated cannon-fire attacks. One of them came back with pieces of whip aerial wrapped round the leading edge of the wing. We did not regard the Sabre as unreliable – well not more than any other aero engine at that time. We were happy about low-level work over land or sea. The enemy was always above or across the sea and we just accepted that it had to be

crossed. It took 29 or 30 minutes to cross from Norfolk to Holland or Belgium and if we were given the choice it was always at low level.'

Low-level flying over the sea did demand enormous concentration, any lapse in which could be fatal. Sergeant Freddie Jones of 195 Squadron had an extremely lucky escape on 24 July, when during low-level formation flying, he caught the slipstream of the preceding aircraft; one wing touched the sea and the Typhoon cartwheeled in at 300mph. When he gathered his senses he was still sitting in the cockpit, on the seabed eighteen miles off Yarmouth. Fortunately he was in shallow water and, releasing the

Below: Flight Lieutenant Walter Dring with a 183 Squadron Typhoon, R8884 'HF-L', at Gatwick in April 1943 (note the old racecourse grandstand in the background). Dring later commanded the Squadron, becoming Wing Leader, 123 Wing in July 1944, but was killed in a landing accident, at snow-bound Chièvres in the following January. (IMW)

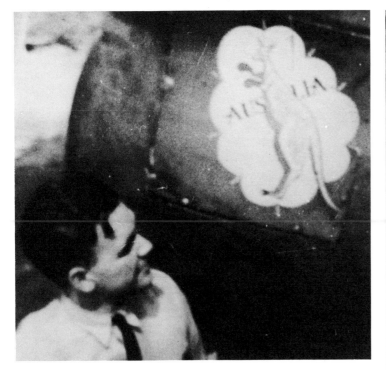

Top Left: Flight Sergeant Tom McGovern, RAAF, with patriotic artwork on the nose of his Typhoon, DN361 'JE-M'. (Justice T. H. McGovern)

Top right: Flying Officer 'Wally' Coombes, RCAF, pauses by 195 Squadron's list of 'services' on offer, outside their dispersal hut at Ludham, summer 1943. 'Butch' was Squadron Leader Don Taylor, the commanding officer. (Group Captain F. W. M. Jensen)

Centre left: Refuelling EK273 'JE-DT' at Ludham in June 1943. 'DT' were the initials of 195 Squadron's commander, Don Taylor. This aircraft was 'borrowed' by Coltishall Wing Leader, Wing Commander Rabagliati, for the sortie on which he went missing, on 6 July 1943. (K. A. J. Trott)

Left: Pilots of 174 Squadron lay on a 'scramble' for the benefit of the Press, at Gravesend in June 1943. Flight Lieutenant Ian Mallet, who describes his part in the Amiens raid in the text, is third from the left. (G. I. Mallet)

harness which had saved his life, he bobbed to the surface to be picked up by a conveniently passing trawler.

Sometimes discretion proved the better part of valour. Flight Sergeant Tom McGovern of 195 Squadron: 'Six of us, with Flight Lieutenant Frank Jensen, OC "A" Flight leading, set off for the Dutch coast to locate some German shipping which had been reported by a Mustang. We were flying at zero feet and were assigned to pinpoint the exact whereabouts of the shipping for the benefit of the torpedo-carrying Beaufighters which were following us out. Sighting no shipping at the expected point we swung north towards Den Helder. As we got close we saw some dozens of specks moving about the sky, just under the cloud cover. These began to converge on us, diving. There were forty plus Me 109s and Fw 190s, obviously guarding the shipping which had got into the harbour. We broke left, out to sea, as this horde was almost on us and, just as we were within range of their fire, gradually drew away from them. I was never so thankful for the immense speed of the Typhoon – I had something like 410mph on the clock from truly straight and level, for we had not risen an inch off the deck during the whole exercise. Jensen advised against the Beaus going in and they were sent home before reaching the scene.'

These operations over the North Sea could be costly, for it was a long way home to nurse a damaged aircraft. 56 Squadron's CO, Squadron Leader Pheloung, survived one bale-out in March, when he was picked up by a Walrus 35 miles off the coast, but the next time, on 20 June, his luck deserted him. Hit by Flak while attacking shipping, he climbed to 1,500 feet to bale out but before he could do so his Typhoon plunged into the sea. The following month Wing Commander Rabagliati – Battle of Britain and Malta pilot and now Wing Leader at Coltishall – forsook his usual Spitfire and borrowed the 195 Squadron CO's Typhoon to join 56 Squadron on a shipping strike. Leaving three ships in a convoy somewhat worse for their attentions, the Typhoons were sixty miles from home when the Wing Leader, his aircraft damaged by Flak, was forced to bale out. Despite a massive air and sea search he was not found.

By the middle of June 1943, as the period of offensive action began to increase to a maximum effort, the disposition of Typhoon units was as follows.

10 GROUP:

Harrowbeer	183 Squadron
	193 Squadron
Warmwell	257 Squadron
Exeter	266 Squadron

11 GROUP:

Lympne	1 Squadron
Manston	3 Squadron
Gravesend	174 Squadron
Appledram	175 Squadron
	181 Squadron
	182 Squadron
Tangmere	197 Squadron
	486 Squadron
Martlesham Heath	198 Squadron
Selsey	245 Squadron
Bradwell Bay	247 Squadron
Manston	609 Squadron

12 GROUP:

Matlaske	56 Squadron
Ludham	195 Squadron

At the beginning of July further moves took place, forming the first Typhoon wings since the disbandment of the ill-fated Duxford Wing. Earlier in the year the first 'Airfields' had been formed; these were, in fact, completely self-contained and fully mobile units capable of supporting fighter or fighter-bomber wings. Initially the squadrons posted to these Airfields were changed at frequent intervals, but when 174, 175, and 245 Squadrons were allocated to 121 Airfield at Lydd, and 181, 182, and 247 Squadrons joined 124 Airfield at New Romney, it was the start of associations which would last for the duration of the war. Both Airfields came under the command of Group Captain 'Paddy' Woodhouse as 16 Wing, with [rather confusingly], Wing Commanders Crowley-Milling and Ingle as 'Wing Leaders' of 121 and 124 Airfields respectively.

Not surprisingly it was the 'Ramrod' operations which provided the Typhoon units with the greatest number of engagements with the Luftwaffe during the second half of 1943, and some hard battles were fought. On other occasions the enemy was encountered in less expected circumstances, as on 15 July when 486 Squadron spotted a downed Wellington crew in a dinghy off Le Havre. Four Typhoons were detached to cover the dinghy while Squadron Leader Scott returned to Tangmere to organize a rescue mission. Eight more of 486's Typhoons were soon airborne, escorting a lifeboat-carrying Hudson back to Le Havre. The boat was successfully dropped, but while covering its withdrawal from the enemy coast 486 were bounced by a dozen Fw 190s. Fortunately the German aircraft were spotted before they had a chance to open fire, and in the furious dogfight that developed the New Zealanders claimed two 190s destroyed and two probables without loss to themselves. The Wellington crew was rescued, one of several which owed their lives to these sharp-eyed pilots.

While engaged in a 'Circus' on 15 August, 266 Squadron lost their commanding officer, Squadron Leader MacIntyre, who had taken over from Charles Green during the previous month, and two other pilots to Fw 190s over Guipavas. The Focke-Wulf which shot down MacIntyre was promptly attacked and claimed destroyed by Flight Sergeant Derek Erasmus, who by the end of the next year would be leading his own Typhoon squadron. Four days later during a 16 Wing 'Ramrod' to Amiens, 182 lost three out of six aircraft, following an encounter with fighters of II/JG 26. The Wing ran into a formation and in the ensuing mêlée Flight Lieutenant Geoff Ball latched on to an enemy fighter: 'He rolled on to his back and tried to escape by diving but I followed him and shot him down. God knows what speed we got up to – the ASI was "off the clock" (i.e., more than 550mph!). The cockpit hood burst open and the propeller overspeed threw oil back all over the windscreen. I took some cine shots of the 109* and started to hedge-hop my way home, when I went straight over the top of a Flak-post and got a belly-full. As well as the engine I lost the rudder and had to go straight ahead . . . into an orchard. The aircraft hit the trees, turned over and exploded – if I had stayed the right way up I would have frizzled but, upside down, the fire was above me.' Despite burns to his face and hands, Ball managed to struggle clear, only to be caught, with four other evaders, within sight of the Pyrenees, as a result of which he spent a harrowing six months as a 'guest' of the Gestapo. One of the other 182 Squadron pilots lost during this combat, Flight Sergeant Ron Dench, was more fortunate, evading successfully and returning to England in November; he subsequently resumed operational flying with 182 Squadron.

Another 16 Wing operation which resulted in losses took place on 11 September when Group Captain Woodhouse and Wing Commander Alex Ingle [recently promoted after leading 609 Squadron] led 175, 182 and 245 Squadrons on a 'Ramrod' to the Poix area. Here II/JG 26 Focke-Wulfs attacked, Ingle and one of the 175 Squadron pilots being shot down – only three claims for damage to the German aircraft being submitted in return.

It was the Flak that was the most serious enemy, however, and of 66 aircraft lost on offensive operations from 1 June to 30 September, more than half are known to have fallen to this cause, while enemy fighters were reckoned responsible for about 25 per cent. From 20 June to 25 October 1943, casualties included two wing leaders and nine squadron commanders (two of them from 198 Squadron), Wing Commander Ingle and Squadron Leader MacIntyre being the only ones known to have fallen to German fighters. Usually this

*It would appear that no claim was ever submitted for this aircraft, which therefore is not listed in the Claims appendix. Owing to the large number of Allied claims on this day, it has not been possible to isolate a likely German victim.

attrition was suffered in ones and twos, unlike the more dramatic [but in the longer term, less costly] battles with the Messer-schmitts and Focke-Wulfs. There were, however, several occasions on which some units were particularly hard hit by ground fire. On 16 September, for instance, 486 Squadron lost three aircraft and pilots while on a 'Roadstead' to Le Havre.

Two special operations also brought heavy casualties. A fast, modern 10,000-ton cargo ship, *Münsterland*, had run the gauntlet of Allied naval and air patrols from Japan, loaded with urgently needed latex rubber and special metals. She eventually reached the heavily defended port of Cher-bourg, where she was spotted by aerial reconnaissance. It was decided that despite the known efficiency of Cherbourg's de-fences, *Münsterland* must be attacked; the task fell to 263 Squadron's Warmwell-based Whirlwinds and 183 Squadron's Typhoons which flew to Warmwell, from their new base at Predannack, to make the attack. The Whirlwinds went in early on the morning of 24 October, six with bombs and six more in the anti-Flak role; they were covered by eight Typhoons of 257 Squadron. Despite the benefit of surprise the Whirlwinds were met with what one of the pilots described as 'a horizontal hailstorm painted red'; two Whirlwinds went down and two more crashed on landing. After a reconnaissance by 257 it was 183's turn in the late after-noon. Eight Typhoons made their attacks below mast height and claimed two direct hits, but the alert defences clawed down three Typhoons, including that of Squadron Leader Gowers who was seen to crash out-side the mole. Flying Officer Munrowd's aircraft was badly hit in the tail but he nursed it back to Warmwell for a wheels-up landing. However, *Münsterland* had been damaged, her progress delayed, and she had not seen the last of Typhoons or Whirl-winds.

Top left: German soldiers inspecting the wreck of JP577 'HH-T', brought down by Flak while returning from escorting Bostons to Albert. Sergeant H. E. R. Merlin managed to evade capture, eventually becoming the driver for a French engineer in charge of 'Noball' site construction! After much information had been passed back to England, Merlin made a spectacular return to 175 Squadron, in a captured Kübelwagen (jeep), at B.50 Vitry-en-Artois, 14 months after his disappearance. (via A. S. Thomas)

Centre left: Wing Commander R. T. P. Davidson, RCAF, in the cockpit of JP596 which had been his aircraft (HH-W) when commanding 175 Squadron, and which he retained on promotion to Wing Commander Flying, 121 Wing in September 1943. A second swastika would be added to his scoreboard on 8 January 1944. (Public Archives of Canada)

Left: Frank Jensen (centre), seen here as a flight commander on 195 Squadron in mid-1943, was promoted to command 181 Squadron in August 1943. (Group Captain F. W. M. Jensen)

The very next day six 181 Squadron pilots were briefed to make what, in light of later developments, would be a historic operation – the first attack by Typhoons with rocket projectiles, their target being Caen power-station. The squadron had begun practising with this new weapon on 22 September and had tried a first operation with them on 21 October – an abortive sweep after shipping between Cherbourg and the Channel Islands. The operation on the 25th was to be on a much grander scale, involving all six squadrons of 16 Wing, although it would be recorded in 181 Squadron's 'diary' as 'Black Monday'.

174 Squadron, escorted by 245, were to dive-bomb Caen marshalling yards from high level, while 175 and 182 Squadrons made 'dummy runs' over Caen to draw the Flak, and 181, having been escorted to the target area by 247 Squadron, were to make their run in across the marshalling yards which would, hopefully, have been reduced to shambles by the bombers. In the event the plans went awry when cloud cover prevented the bombing; the Flak, possibly alerted by signalmen as 181's route to Caen had been at low level along a railway line, refused to be decoyed by the higher squadrons' antics. Squadron Leader Frank Jensen, previously a flight commander in 195 Squadron, was leading 181 Squadron in two 'vics' of three: 'Just before the target was a line of poplars which marked the point where it was necessary to pull up into the rocket-launching position. At that moment all hell let loose as the Flak batteries opened up; Flying Officer Hugh Collins and myself were hit immediately and Flying Officer "Paddy" King a few seconds later. I prepared for a forced landing, jettisoning my rockets and cockpit side panels; with forward vision obscured by oil on the windscreen I had to stick my head out of the side of the cockpit but fortunately spotted a ploughed field on which to put the Typhoon down. I remember trying to keep the Tiffie straight with the rudder, as normal, and the rudder bar nearly broke my ankles! I was able to warn the second formation of the hot reception and pass a message for onward transmission to my wife.' Jensen and Collins were captured but King was killed. The second formation, despite Jensen's warning, carried out their attack and registered hits with all three salvoes of rockets.

The air fighting which often accompanied the 'Ramrod', 'Rodeo' and 'Circus' operations provided Typhoon squadrons with fourteen more victories by the end of October 1943. 'Roadstead' operations in their totality gave the opportunity for only a single aerial success during this period, but pilots on the low-level 'Rhubarbs' frequently encountered German aircraft of many and various types, and these sorties contributed an additional thirteen claims. 609 Squadron

Top: Jensen led 181 Squadron on the first Typhoon rocket attack, on 25 October 1943 in JP513 'EL-F', seen here after overshooting the runway at New Romney on 4 August 1943. (D. J. Coxhead)

Above: Although three Typhoons were shot down during the attack, the only fatality was Flying Officer 'Paddy' King flying JP590 'EL-C' (photographed somewhat earlier, displaying his personal shamrock emblem and still equipped with bomb racks). (Group Captain F. W. M. Jensen)

particularly enjoyed a number of profitable encounters during October. On the 4th of that month three sections undertook 'Rhubarbs' during the day, one pair claiming two Bf 109s shot down and an He 111 damaged over Juvincourt, while a second pair claimed a Bf 110 in the Florennes area; the third pair suffered one loss to Flak east of Dieppe. It was one of the more costly days for the Typhoons generally, however, a section from 245 Squadron on a 'Rhubarb' over northern France failing to return, while single aircraft of 3 and 198 Squadrons on 'Roadsteads' to the Dutch coast were lost to Flak. One of the missing 245 Squadron pilots was the redoubtable Flying Officer James, MM, DFM. As pilot of a Hampden bomber, he had been shot down over Germany and had an injured hand amputated by a harassed German doctor; repatriated, he was inspired by the famous one-armed Hurricane pilot, Squadron Leader Maclachlan, and returned to 'ops' on single-seaters. He had been held in great awe by the younger pilots in 245.

The next day was ideal weather for 'Rhubarbs' and 609 Squadron again had two sections out over France, both fitted with long-range tanks. In the early afternoon Pilot Officer 'Pinkie' Stark and Flying Officer 'Arty' Ross located an airfield about seventy miles east of Paris [believed to be Connantre] and strafed Bf 110s there, including a group refuelling. As the Flak opened up they headed south and almost immediately sighted a Ju 88 at 3,000 feet, some five miles to starboard and heading north. Turning smartly in pursuit the Typhoons soon closed the distance and Stark opened fire at 400 yards, setting the starboard engine on fire. Closing to 100 yards a second burst fired the other engine and strikes were also seen in the cockpit area. The Ju 88 crashed into a wood – 609 Squadron's 200th victory and the excuse for an enormous party at the Hotel Majestic in Folkestone. Later in the day, south of Paris, Flying Officer Van Lierde shot down another Ju 88 and destroyed a second on Soissons airfield.

Losses of highly trained pilots and their aircraft on 'Rhubarbs', in exchange for dubious results, were causing serious concern within Fighter Command, and eventually they were restricted to 'special targets'. One such 'Rhubarb' fell to 609 Squadron on 16 October when Squadron Leader Pat Thornton-Brown led six Typhoons to the south of Paris, where the special target was no less than Field Marshal von Rundstedt. The timetable of his train from the south was known and an interception as it approached Paris was laid on. Fortunately for the Field Marshal the Typhoons ran out of the essential cloud cover and had to turn back, but not before two Ju 88s and a Me 410 had been claimed shot down.

Thornton-Brown participated in both the victories over the Junkers aircraft, sharing one with Flight Lieutenant 'Johnny' Baldwin, whose personal score now stood at six and a half.

The pattern of Typhoon operations was gradually changing as 1943 passed. From August, underwing 45-gallon drop-tanks became available in increasing numbers, giving a range increase from 610 to 980 miles. With the aid of these, 609 Squadron's Flight Lieutenant Smith became the first Typhoon pilot to fly over Germany; hit by Flak on the return trip he was forced to ditch off Deal. The tanks also brought new problems; they were not the cheap, light type of tanks used in quantity later in the war, but were expensive items, and pilots were encouraged to bring them back empty whenever possible. The fuel carried in these tanks was used before that in the main wing tanks, but the tank switching cocks were not reliable in operation. On occasion they could allow fuel in the main tanks to run down into the empty underwing tanks, starving the engine and causing it to fail. At reasonable altitude this was fairly easily remedied, but at low level could lead to disaster before the pilot had a chance to rectify the situation.

By mid-summer all Typhoons coming off the production line were capable of carrying bombs; at first the Typhoon 'fighter' squadrons used this facility infrequently and on a small scale [e.g., pairs on Intruders], but in the autumn they began training in earnest and by November nearly all the Typhoon force had converted to the fighter-bomber role. Only 198 and 609 Squadrons continued their predominantly low-level fighter function.

Earlier in the year, during March, a major exercise had been held in the south of England under the code-name 'Spartan' to prepare the forces for their forthcoming enterprise – the invasion of France. Four Typhoon squadrons had taken part in this: 181 and 183, operating from Cranfield as part of the 'Eastland' (German) forces; 182 and 247 from Middle Wallop, supporting the 'Southland' (Allied) forces. Since July the personnel of the six squadrons of 16 Wing, operating with the two mobile 'Airfields', had been living under canvas, experiencing the difficulties and ironing out the problems of a life-style which was to be the lot of all the Typhoon force during the following year. These changes were all part of the plans for a tactical air force which was gradually being constructed within Fighter Command, and which would eventually take on a separate identity to support the ground forces during the planned invasion. The Typhoons would play a major part in this new air force, not as fighters but as direct ground-support aircraft.

Top left: Flight Lieutenant 'Moose' Mossip, RCAF, seen with his usual aircraft, JP677 'JX-C', built up a reputation for aggressive intruder work with 1 Squadron in the autumn of 1943. He was killed on his second tour, with 245 Squadron. (IWM)

Centre left: 609 Squadron pilots describing the action after the abortive attempt on Field Marshal von Runstedt's train, on 16 October 1943, which turned into a successful 'Rhubarb'. Left to right: Flying Officer 'Manu' Geerts, Flying Officer John Niblett, Flight Lieutenant 'Mony' Van Lierde, the Squadron's Medical Officer, Squadron Leader 'Pat' Thornton-Brown, Flight Lieutenant L. E. 'Smithy' Smith. (F. Ziegler via C. Goss)

Bottom left: Four 609 Squadron pilots who were awarded the DFC in the autumn of 1943 – left to right: Flight Lieutenant 'Mony' Van Lierde, Pilot Officer 'Pinkie' Stark, Flying Officer Charles Demoulin, Flight Lieutenant 'Johnny' Baldwin. (L. W. F. Stark)

Top right: 183 Squadron Typhoons dispersed around Cranfield's perimeter during Exercise 'Spartan' in March 1943. They wear the markings of 'Eastland' forces – white nose stripe, black spinner and port wing undersurfaces. (IWM)

Right: Squadron Leader Denis Crowley-Milling (5th from right) reports the results of a 181 Squadron sortie for the 'Eastland' forces during Exercise 'Spartan', Cranfield, March 1943. In the background R8742 'EL-A'. (IWM)

CHAPTER SIX

Second Tactical Air Force expansion

THE beginning of November 1943 found RAF Fighter Command with eighteen operational Typhoon squadrons on strength, four in 10 Group in south-west England, thirteen in 11 Group in the south-east, and a single unit with 12 Group in the Midlands. The 11 Group units were by now organized into two wings of three squadrons each, three of two squadrons, and a single unit at Fairlop. All but two of the units (198 and 609) were fitted and trained for the carriage of bombs beneath the wings of their Typhoons, while one squadron (181) had some aircraft fitted with the new rocket projectile launching rails.

Major changes were afoot, however, for on 13 November the Second Tactical Air Force (2nd TAF) was formed from within Fighter Command as a component of the Allied Expeditionary Air Force which was to support the forthcoming Allied invasion of Normandy. Already 2 Group of Bomber Command, with its light day bombers, together with the squadrons of Army Co-operation Command, had been amalgamated into Fighter Command, and now that illustrious organization ceased to exist for the time being. Into the new tactical air force went these light bombers and reconnaissance aircraft, numerous Spitfire squadrons and, initially, two Typhoon 'Airfields', 121 and 124, now located at Westhampnett and Merston (and for the moment still

operating under the control of 16 Wing). The wing leaders were now both Canadians who had served with distinction in the Middle East: Wing Commanders Davidson and Walker. The rest of the squadrons were to form a new home defence organization, ponderously named Air Defence of Great Britain (ADGB); initially the other twelve Typhoon squadrons remained part of this command, although most would soon join 2nd TAF.

Second TAF was commanded by Air Marshal Arthur Coningham, and contained, in addition to 2 Group already mentioned, two new groups: 83, which was to provide support for the British Second Army and was commanded by Air Vice-Marshal Harry Broadhurst, and 84, which would support the Canadian First Army and was commanded by Air Vice-Marshal Brown. All three commanders were ex-Mediterranean theatre men. Both the new Typhoon wings were assigned to 83 Group.

At first the change was administrative only, and had no real effect on the operations flown, for these continued to be controlled by 11 Group until the actual invasion took place. Life as a Typhoon pilot remained fairly hazardous, November bringing no less than 25 losses to various causes – at least a dozen of them to Flak – on a range of activities mainly of the 'Ramrod' and 'Rhubarb' varieties. Indeed it was 13 November, the day of 2nd TAF's official

formation, which was to bring the heaviest losses of the month. Four 181 Squadron aircraft undertook a 'Rhubarb' to the south of Paris, an area rich in targets but heavily defended by Flak; one Typhoon was seen to go down to ground fire, a second went missing over France and a third, flown by Flight Lieutenant Peacock, one of the three survivors of 'Black Monday' (25 October 1943), suffered engine trouble while crossing the Channel on the return trip. He attempted to bale out but was killed when the Typhoon dived into the sea south of Shoreham. Flak claimed another victim when one of 56 Squadron's aircraft, also on a 'Rhubarb', was hit over Holland and forced to land just south of The Hague.

November was not without 'profit' however, three German aircraft being brought down on 'Rhubarbs' early in the month, while the 30th brought considerable success for 198 Squadron. Nine of their aircraft, led by Squadron Leader Bryan, undertook a 'Ramrod' to the area south of Gilze-Rijen in Holland, as indirect support to a raid on Germany by Eighth Army Air Force B-17s.

Below: Wing Commander Desmond Scott, RNZAF, Tangmere Wing Leader, with his dog 'Kim' and R8843 'DJS', late in 1943. This is believed to be the first Typhoon to see operational service with the new sliding hood. (Group Captain D. J. Scott)

Below right: One of the first Typhoons in service with the new canopy, JR503 'US-K' of 56 squadron, after an obviously expert wheels-up landing at Martlesham Heath early in 1944. It had previously been coded 'US-B'. (L. Woodhouse)

Here a Ju 88 was seen and dispatched by Flight Lieutenant Smith, following which three sections of Fw 190s were spotted going in to land at Deelen. Catching these at a disadvantage, Bryan and three of his pilots claimed four shot down and a fifth damaged as it taxied clear of the runway.

Many changes to the Typhoon scene took place during the winter of 1943–44. More squadrons received rocket-equipped aircraft, although at first there was no specialization, Typhoons being converted from rocket- to bomb-carriers and vice versa as the tactical situation required. With the Sabre's shortcomings now under control, supplies of new and serviceable Typhoons were relatively plentiful, and by the end of 1943 most units had been re-equipped with JP- and JR-serialled aircraft. Among these were the first of the Typhoons with the long-awaited sliding hood, which afforded such an improved field of view. The new aircraft off the production line were also supplemented by Typhoons which had been held in storage since their initial delivery, because of Sabre supply problems; these were returned to Glosters, re-emerging from the factory rebuilt to the latest standard. In fact it was Typhoons of this category which were the first to introduce the delights of the new canopy to the operational squadrons. One of the earliest recipients was 486 Squadron which received R8843 in mid-September; adopted by Squadron Leader Scott who was then promoted to become the Tangmere Wing Leader; it carried his initials 'DJS'.

The increased flow of Typhoons also allowed the formation of some new Typhoon squadrons. 186 Squadron was the first of these; previously having been equipped with Hurricane IID aircraft, on which it had never become operational, it began receiving Typhoons at Ayr in November 1943, but before training was complete these were exchanged for Spitfire Vs. In the event, this ill-fated unit was disbanded in February 1944 without ever becoming operational as a fighter squadron. In the same month, one of the newer Typhoon units, 195 Squadron, was also disbanded, their aircraft swelling the numbers available for an ambitious re-equipment programme. This included two rocket-firing Hurricane squadrons, 164 and 184, the two Whirlwind squadrons, 137 and 263 (although 137 had by now exchanged its Whirlwinds for Hurricanes) and three squadrons of the Royal Canadian Air Force. The latter had flown Kittyhawks or Hurricanes in Canada and were transferred to the UK at the end of 1943, initially receiving Hurricanes for training. By the end of January 1944 they were based at Ayr and their first Typhoons had arrived; they also changed their RCAF squadron numbers, 111, 118, and 123, to 440, 438, and 439 respectively, in line with the UK-based RCAF numbering system. The three squadrons together formed 143 Air-field, and in March they would move down to Hurn to begin operations.

Within 83 Group, 16 Wing, still commanded by Group Captain 'Paddy' Woodhouse, was now joined by 22 Wing, comprising two RCAF Airfields, the new 143 with Typhoons, and 144 with Spitfires, under Group Captain Davoud. These large wings were found to be unwieldy and eventually disappeared in a further bout of reorganization shortly before D-Day, as will be seen later.

While these preparations continued, operations were intensifying. By the end of November 1943 Intelligence had identified a new target for the attention of Allied bombers. Construction works incorporating distinctive ski-shaped structures, were springing up in many areas of the Pas-de-Calais, and were known to be launching sites for the new Fiesler Fi 103 pilotless flying bombs – later known as the 'V-1'. The French Resistance had provided information on the structure and materials used in these works and they were calculated to be vulnerable to attack with bombs of 500lb weight or greater. Typhoon dive-bombers joined a host of Allied bombers, medium and heavy, in an all-out assault on these priority targets, which were soon code-named 'Noballs'. The attacks, in the face of stiff opposition at some sites, were made throughout December and into the New Year, continuing until July 1944; some

Typhoon squadrons would make as many as three visits to the Pas-de-Calais in a single day. After February, the Typhoon's participation, which by now included rocket-armed aircraft, was somewhat reduced because of the preparations for D-Day. In fact, by mid-February the Germans had realized that they were fighting a losing battle, and while maintaining token work on the original sites, had concentrated their major effort on new, smaller, and highly camouflaged sites; it was these that were eventually used to launch the V-1 campaign. The technique used in attacking the well-defended 'Noball' targets is described by Warrant Officer Bob Betts of 247 Squadron: 'We would approach the target, keeping radio silence, in squadron formation at 8,000 feet. The anti-aircraft guns would keep silent, hoping that we had not seen the site. We would fly over the target and position for the best angle of attack, break radio silence, fuze the 500lb bombs, fall into line astern and be prepared to dive within seconds. The angle of dive was 45 degrees but this felt like 90 degrees in the cockpit. In the dive you had to watch the small hand (thousands of feet) of the altimeter since the big hand (hundreds) was moving too fast, watch the ASI which would go above

550mph, trim out any skid by keeping the needle and ball central, line the target up on the vertical red line on the gunsight, and watch for other Typhoons, especially those underneath. On approaching 4,000 feet you checked for skid once more, pulled gently back on the stick, keeping the target so that it moved down the vertical red line of the gunsight. When it disappeared below the nose you counted up to five slowly, or ten fast, then pressed the bomb release button at the end of the throttle in your left hand. This business of counting five slowly or ten fast always struck me as being rather "Heath-Robinson", however it proved to be an extremely accurate method with an average error of less than fifty yards.'

Although these activities were to provide the main focus of attention for the Typhoon pilots throughout the winter and early spring of 1944, those units still operating as fighters were to enjoy a final 'fling' before their conversion to the more prosaic, but even more dangerous close-support role. December and January were indeed to prove the most successful months of the war in this respect. For many months 609 Squadron had maintained a flight of Belgian pilots on its strength, and numbers of these were now receiving promotions to flight and

Above left: Warrant Officer 'Bob' Betts, 247 Squadron, in a bombed-up Typhoon (500 pounders) during the 'Noball' campaign. (Captain R. W. Betts)

Top: Bombing-up Typhoons of 247 Squadron at Merston in March 1944. The nearest aircraft carries a squadron leader's pennant below the windscreen, identifying it as Squadron Leader Robin McNair's Typhoon, MM951 'ZY-G'. (Captain R. W. Betts)

Above: Sergeant 'Sammy' Samuels of 193 Squadron in the cockpit of R8890 'DP-G', 'Salome', at Harrowbeer, summer 1943. Due to a shortage of muzzle caps, canvas has been doped over the ends of the cannon barrels. (P. G. Murton)

Top right: Pilots of 193 Squadron at Harrowbeer, including Flying Officer John Pressland and Flight Lieutenant 'Johnny' Crabb, in the front row, second and third from the right respectively. (P. G. Murton)

squadron commander level. For these pilots the winter of 1943–4 was to provide several opportunities to harry the Luftwaffe over, or near, the soil of their own homeland – a situation to which they were to respond with vigour and relish.

It was not only the units based in the south east that saw action during this period. On 1 December twelve Typhoons, eight from 266 Squadron and four from 193 Squadron, both based at Harrowbeer, set out to escort a single Mosquito (a second had gone 'u/s' at the last moment) on a

'Roadstead' off the Brittany coast. A 4,000-ton freighter was located near the Ile de Groix, and as the Mosquito began its attack, 193 Squadron, which had been allocated the anti-Flak role, dived on the escort of several armed trawlers. Unfortunately, the Mosquito's bombs fell short of the target and soon afterwards it hit the waves and disappeared immediately. Meanwhile 266 were orbitting the area and keeping a sharp lookout for German fighters. To their delight a Ju 52 lumbered into view at 300 feet. This was one of the Ju 52s fitted with a large dur-alumin hoop which could be energized for exploding magnetic mines (the RAF used similarly equipped Wellingtons); it was quickly dispatched. Rejoining the 193 Squadron Typhoons, the first section of 266 turned for home, but almost at once spotted two Ju 88s. One escaped into cloud but the other was caught by Flying Officer John Pressland of 193 Squadron. After a short burst from 400 yards he quickly closed to 250 yards and continued firing short bursts, despite return fire from the dorsal position, until he was forced to break away to avoid a collision. Two 266 Squadron pilots joined the attack and the Ju 88 went down in flames into the sea. Meanwhile, the remaining section of 266 Squadron had also run into a Ju 88 and this soon joined its comrade in a watery grave. However, both rear gunners had their revenge, for Flying Officer Blackwell, who had made the attack on the second Junkers, was not seen after making his attack, while during the return trip across the Channel Pressland's Typhoon started trailing vapour. He recalls:

'There was not much warning, the engine coughed a couple of times and stopped dead. I was at about a thousand feet, possibly less, so I knew I had to bale out pretty smartly. I undid my straps, jettisoned the doors and roof, pushed the stick forward with my foot, and did just that! [He was thirty miles south of Land's End.] The rest of the Typhoons milled around for a while and got off a long transmission for a fix, but they could not stay too long as fuel was running low. After what seemed an age, but was

probably quite a short time, some ASR Spit-fires arrived. There were some hand-launched rockets in the dinghy and I fired one of these but it slipped from my grasp and sizzled and spluttered in the bottom of the dinghy. I managed to get the next one off OK and the Spits saw me; they dropped a succession of smoke floats to mark my position until the Walrus arrived. It was too choppy for the Walrus to land but he hung around until the ASR launch finally picked me up.' It was one and three-quarter hours since he had baled out.

At about noon on the same day, eight of 198 Squadron's aircraft in company with ten from 609 Squadron, which had just moved to join them at Manston, flew a 'Ramrod' over Belgium and Holland. 198's new commanding officer, Squadron Leader 'Johnnie' Baldwin, claimed one Fw 190 shot down, and another of his pilots a probable in the Arnhem area, while 609 claimed a Bf 109 over Brussels, but this latter unit's Flight Sergeant Aitken-Quack – a pilot who had gone to Finland as a volunteer in 1940 – was shot down by Unteroffizer Gerhard Guttman of II/JG 26, and was made a prisoner of war.

Three days later these two units were again out over Holland on an afternoon 'Ramrod' to support another 8th USAAF raid. Approaching Gilze-Rijen airfield, 609 Squadron's six pilots spotted bombers in the immediate area. A swift check showed that these twin-tailed machines were not friendly Mitchells, but Do 217s of KG2, and in quick order six were claimed as shot down, two by one of their Belgians, Flying Officer Charles Detal, and another by his compatriot, Flying Officer Manu Geerts, while the commanding officer, Squadron Leader Pat Thornton-Brown, claimed one and one shared. 198 Squadron had by now appeared on the scene, and encountered a number of Do 217s in line abreast. These were promptly set upon, one more bomber being claimed by Squadron Leader Baldwin while three others were credited, in shares, to six of his pilots, for a total claim of ten without loss to the Manston squadrons.

In addition to the indirect support operations like these, close escort duties for 8th USAAF bombers became an increasingly familiar duty for many of the Typhoon squadrons at this time; they were not too popular, for reasons detailed below, but there was the consolation that 'targets of opportunity' could be attacked on the way home. Flying Officer Peter Roper of 198 Squadron describes some of the problems on one of these missions:

'. . . we rendezvoused with the bombers just off the coast; they were B-26 Marauders. We liked escorting them because they were faster than any of the other bombers, so we could keep position more easily and maintain our speed. Important considerations if the formations were attacked. There were two things we didn't like, but they always seemed to happen and there was nothing we could do about them. These medium bombers always seemed to fly at about 12,000 feet. So we were up at thirteen or fourteen thousand, just about the worst height for us performance-wise. There was a two-stage supercharger on our engines and at this height it was just between the best change levels. We were always shifting from one stage to another and watching our boost gauges as the engine revs surged around. As if we didn't have enough to do! The other thing wrong was the sun. "Watch for the Hun in the Sun" was something that had been drilled into all fighter pilots from their early training days on. Looking up sun, it was almost impossible to see other aircraft, even with smoke-tinted goggles. At best they would be shadowy silhouettes, close at hand and diving fast. The Luftwaffe always had this advantage in the mornings when the sun was in the east. Why most operations, especially bomber escorts, were always in the mornings we never found out.

As we got near the enemy coast it was time to do other checks. Gun sight on, gun button to "Fire". Seat right down and feet on the anti-G rudder pedals. We might have only a split second's warning, if at all, and might have to pull maximum G to turn inside an attack. To black-out usually spelt disaster. There were 48 Marauders in two equal groups; we were looking after the first group and 609 the other. There was the usual Flak as we crossed the coast, black puffs of smoke, mainly at the bombers' height. By this time we were above and between them and the sun, weaving around, watching them, watching the rest of our sections, and searching up sun, trying to catch a glimpse of something against the glare. We were close escort and there would be no top cover until the Spits met us on our return. The only clouds around were in a nice white layer at 10,000 feet just below the bombers – ideal to silhouette them for an attack from above – but for us it just made the glare worse. We knew the enemy fighters

were up there. While we were still in radar range the voice of our Controller was spelling out their height and direction in his calm distant voice, "20 plus Bandits at 1 o'clock. Angels 20." As close escorts we couldn't leave the bombers and go after them, even when we saw a 109 diving down to one side as a decoy. We just had to weave around, wait and watch. Watch our position all the time, watch behind our tails, watch behind the other sections, and especially, watch up sun. No wonder we all wore neck scarves, even the softest collar rubbed the skin off our necks on a show like this. We could see Eindhoven coming into view and the clouds cleared away. We had been there a few times before; it always seemed such a splendid target. The large sprawling Phillips factory stood out from the flat countryside. It never seemed to be camouflaged in any way and we always saw it in cloudless skies.

The Flak, which had been intermittent and inaccurate up to now, became heavier as the first group of Marauders closed for-

Top: Pilots of 56 Squadron in mid-1943, including Flight Sergeant 'Vic' Plumb (second from the left), and Flying Officer Peter Roper (second from the right), who transferred to 198 Squadron shortly after the photograph was taken. (BAe)

Left: Squadron Leader 'Johnny' Baldwin of 198 Squadron in the cockpit of his 'TP-X' at Manston, January 1944. Behind is JR361 'TP-Y', shot down by Flak, with the loss of Flight Lieutenant Curtis, on 20 January 1944, after only 10 hours' flying time. (R. A. Lallemant)

mation and got set on their bombing run. It was like a black carpet below and amongst the planes. This was the most dangerous time for any bomber – on the run in to the target they had to fly straight and level without change in height. The Americans also used pattern bombing, all dropping their bombs at once on orders from the lead bomb aimer. This made them more vulnerable still. This was the time the enemy fighters should attack if they were going to do so. We were weaving around waiting for them and keeping up sun as the bombers turned together. We caught a glimpse of some of the explosions on the ground, but we couldn't look for long enough to see how accurate the attack had been. Now we were on our way back, above and behind the bombers, with our necks craning more and more over our shoulders and weaving more and more to get a good view behind us. 609 was now coming in with the second group and we could hear some excited chatter on the R/T. One of the Belgians had started after a decoy and was being called back with very rude words!

The 109s and 190s stayed above and did not venture down. They seemed to be more scared of Typhoons than they were of Spits. The Marauder formation seemed to be intact with no stragglers so we were relieved when the Hornchurch Spits came into sight right on schedule. Relieved because we could now get down and do some attacking and not hang around in the sky waiting, waiting and nothing turning up. The new close escort got into position and the top cover seemed to dispel the enemy fighters even further away. We dropped our overload tanks, closed up to formate down through the cloud layer, and descended rapidly; I blew my ears as we went down. We got down below 1,000 feet where we felt comfortable. It was quite a change from the glare above cloud and although the air was a bit bumpy we were more at home at low level. It was usually more exciting too.'

The good spell faltered in mid-December when 198 Squadron lost one of its veteran flight commanders, Flight Lieutenant V. Smith, during a 'Ramrod' over Leeuwarden, victim of the perennial engine failures of the Typhoon's Sabre. Next day six of 609 Squadron's aircraft escorted US B-26 Marauders over the Somme estuary, but here 8th USAAF P-47 pilots engaged on another mission, mistook the Typhoons for Fw 190s and attacked them, near Doullens, shooting down Squadron Leader Thornton-Brown and Flying Officer Miller, both of whom lost their lives. According to eyewitnesses on the ground, Thornton-Brown had baled out safely, only to be shot by German troops as he descended under his parachute.

While 183 and 266 Squadrons were to further raise the victory tally late in the month, casualties for December were again rather heavy – 28 aircraft and 22 of their pilots, although one of the latter evaded capture and eventually returned home. Five losses were the result of mid-air collisions and at least seven had fallen to fire from bombers and fighters – both 'friendly' and hostile. The last of these, an aircraft of 257 Squadron on withdrawal support for 'Ramrod 118', came down off St-Brieuc on the last day of the year, after a fight with Fw 190s. It was flown by Flying Officer Yi, one of four Burmese pilots who had joined 257 (Burma) Squadron earlier in the year; he had gone after two Fw 190s with Flight Lieutenant Scarlett, and, latching on to one of them, was heard on the R/T to say that he had 'got it'. With the rest of the squadron absorbed in the drama surrounding the ditching in the Channel of a B-17, the outcome of his action was unobserved, but when he was eventually missed, only a patch of oil and two bobbing long-range tanks could be found to bear mute testimony to his fate.

The New Year of 1944 brought a resumption of success – indeed January was to net some 46 aerial victories but it began with a tough mission for 198 Squadron; reconnaissance had shown that *Münsterland* was now in Boulogne harbour, ringed by defences, and it remained a priority target. Two of 198's Typhoons had now been fitted with rocket rails (Squadron Leader Baldwin had resisted the modification of any more, and these two were their oldest aircraft); these, accompanied by seven more armed with cannon only, carried out the attack. Squadron Leader Baldwin was first in and silenced *Münsterland*'s own Flak, but even so the shore defences and three armed trawlers moored in a protective crescent poured intense fire at the attacking aircraft. The two RP Tiffies, flown by Flight Lieutenant R. Curtis and Flying Officer Roper, both managed to release their rockets and although Roper's salvo fell short due to a malfunction, Curtis's rockets caused a large explosion amidships. Five of the Typhoons were hit but all made it back to Manston, where two made crash-landings. Although the ship had been damaged again, the *Münsterland* episode would not be finally resolved until the 20th of the month when, in the early hours of the morning, the freighter was reported to have left Boulogne. Again 198, this time accompanied by 609 Squadron, was scrambled, and they located *Münsterland* one mile off the enemy coast. They had, however, been cheated by the Dover long-range guns, which had already done fatal damage to the German ship, the decks of which were now awash. The Typhoon pilots, in spite of desultory Flak from the shore, relieved their frustrations by using the superstructure of the doomed vessel for target practice.

On the 2nd, four 198 Squadron aircraft on a sortie west of Paris, found an airfield occupied by at least five German twin-engined fighters, identified as Bf 110s and Me 210s, all of which were strafed. A number of Bucker Bu 131 biplane training aircraft were then seen flying around the Eiffel Tower; one of these was shot down and a second claimed as damaged. As the formation headed for home, a lone Fw 190 was encountered and dispatched by Squadron Leader Baldwin. Two more of the unit's pilots on a separate operation claimed an Me 210 over St-Quentin, while 609's veteran Belgian, Manu Geerts, claimed another Fw 190. The incident with the Bu 131s was widely reported in the British Press at the time, and, perhaps surprisingly after four years of ruthless war, generated some correspondence as to the ethics of such attacks. It was not, however, the first time that Luftwaffe trainers had fallen victim to intruding Typhoons, Pilot Officer Jaspis of 609 Squadron having claimed a Bu 133 (the single-seat version of the Bu 131) the previous November; two more Bu 131s were to fall to 257 Squadron Typhoons at the end of January.

Next day 198 Squadron's Flight Lieutenant Curtis claimed a Bf 109, while 609's Charles Detal claimed an Fw 190, but each unit lost one aircraft, that from 609 Squadron being shot down north of Cambrai by Fw 190s of II/JG 26 – again Unteroffizier Guttmann was the successful pilot. Three other Typhoons were lost on this date, one of 197 Squadron being reported missing near Ligecourt, while two from 198 and 609 Squadrons were lost over Belgium; all fell victim to Flak. On 4 January 198 and 609 Squadrons returned to Holland where again they were able to catch KG 2's Do 217s in the circuit, this time at Eindhoven. Five were claimed on this occasion, four by 609 where Charles Detal was again successful, as was Manu Geerts who shared one with Pilot Officer 'Pinkie' Stark, another being credited to Flight Lieutenant Davies. Two more Dorniers were attacked on the ground and a Ju 88C coastal fighter which was taxiing was set on fire. The cost was a single 609 Squadron Typhoon which dived into the sea during the return flight due to an engine failure, with the loss of another Belgian pilot, Flying Officer Daix.

Crossing the Channel for 'Ramrod 122' on 7 January, three Typhoons of 193 Squadron were 'bounced' by Fw 190s of JG2 just north of Guernsey as they began their climb to cross the French coast. The first burst of fire hit the 'B' Flight commander's rudder; the other two Typhoons managed to evade their attackers, but Flight Lieutenant 'Johnny' Crabb was not seen again. On the next day Wing Commander Davidson led his 121 Airfield Typhoons on a 'Ramrod' north of Paris. Here he and his wingman saw and shot down a transport aircraft, and Flight Sergeant Bill Waudby gave chase to a Ju 88. He was hit by return fire, and although he was not seen again by his comrades, he managed to force-land and evade capture. He eventually returned to his unit, 245 Squadron, at the end of May to continue his tour of operations. On the 13th, 198 Squadron was in action again, six Tiffies on a 'Ranger' sweeping over airfields west of Paris. Squadron Leader Bryan, who was visiting his old unit, and Squadron Leader Baldwin spotted two Caudron Goelands, and shot down one each. Two Bf 109Es were then seen near Rosières, and while Flight Lieutenant Niblett claimed one of these, Bryan was able to share the other with Flying Officer Freeman; Flying Officer Max Laman, an Australian, was shot down by light Flak. Meanwhile, another four of the unit's aircraft on a similar 'Ranger', caught a number of Ju 88s and an Arado Ar 96B trainer, claiming three of the former and the latter shot down; they then fought briefly with five Bf 109s before making good their escape.

While the Manston Typhoons were gaining much of the success at this time, those in 10 Group were also able to achieve a share – notably 266 Squadron. On 21 January this unit's outstanding commander, Squadron Leader 'Pip' Lefevre, a veteran of the Norwegian Campaign and service in Malta, claimed a Bf 109, and two days later he and three of his pilots claimed an Fw 190 between them. However, the majority of the action still came the Manston squadrons' way; on 24 January 22 Typhoons of 3, 198 and 609 Squadrons, detached to Norfolk for the day, to operate from Coltishall, set out to escort Coastal Command Beaufighters on a shipping strike off the Frisian Islands. The Beaus arrived over Coltishall two minutes early and failed to orbit. Most of 3 Squadron and four aircraft of 198 Squadron managed to make contact with the Beaus but the rest of the Typhoons were forced to return after twenty minutes' fruitless searching. Flying Officer Geoff Eagle of 198, who had been with the latter group, chose to continue on course, on his own, in the hope of catching the main formation. In this he was unsuccessful, but about thirty miles north of Ameland, flying at zero feet, he ran into twelve Bf 109Gs! They were flying in three sections of four, in a shallow vic, at 300 feet, approaching from port on a course at right angles to his own. His combat report read:

'I broke port and attacked the squadron leader with a short burst from 300 yards and 90 degrees allowing some three and a half rings deflection for a target speed of 260–280mph. This produced cannon strikes on his belly jettison tank, and caused it to explode and envelope the entire aircraft with blazing fuel, sending it plunging into the sea. Maintaining same line of flight and

deflection I transferred my aim to No. 3 of the same section, firing a longer burst while closing from 200 to 80 yards. For a while I saw nothing, then a strike caused an issue of greyish-white smoke from the cockpit. Hun immediately lurched to port, collided with his No. 4 and took both of them down to join their late leader.'

One of the other two sections made a half-hearted attempt at a head-on attack as Eagle broke to port, before joining the other section in running for home with 'black throttle smoke' streaming from their exhausts! This left the sole survivor of the first

Top: Typical of 198 Squadron's long-range Typhoons, JR371 'TP-R' taxies out at Manston, January 1944. JR371 was one of the last Typhoons to leave Gloster's production line with the old framed canopy. (via G. Seager)

Above: Some of the successful 198 Squadron pilots, early in 1944. Top row, left to right: Flying Officer H. Freeman, Flying Officer J. F. H. Williams, Flying Officer C. Rainsforth, Flight Sergeant J. S. Fraser-Petherbridge, Warrant Officer J. Allan, Flight Lieutenant J. W. Scambler, Flight Lieutenant D. Sweeting, Warrant Officer H. A. Hallett. On the wing: 'Spy', Flight Lieutenant P. D. Roper, Flight Lieutenant R. J. Dall, Flying Officer W. Parkes, 'Sarah', Warrant Officer G. J. Stokes. On the ground: Flight Lieutenant J. Niblett, Flying Officer W. G. Eagle, Flight Sergeant R. C. A. Crouch, Sergeant J. S. Madgett, Flight Lieutenant J. M. Plamondon, Flight Lieutenant R. A. Lallemant. (IWM)

Top: A German sentry with a makeshift shelter stands guard over Flight Lieutenant Wardsinski's 3 Squadron Typhoon, JP921 'QO-P', force-landed in Holland on 29 February 1944. With the help of the Dutch Resistance Wardsinski was able to avoid capture. (via P. Truren)

Above: Typhoons were always prone to tyre-bursts. JR365 'HE-P' of 263 Squadron suffered such a mishap at Beaulieu in February 1944, and after repair it suffered a similar accident at Predannack a month later. Note that the underwing identity stripes have been removed in accordance with an order dated 7 February 1944. (263 Squadron via A. S. Thomas)

and a Bf 109 shot down over Brussels for his fifth and sixth individual victories, while 'Pinkie' Stark claimed a Goeland; but it was 30 January which was to prove the outstanding day of this outstanding month. While Charles Detal, Squadron Leader Wells and another pilot claimed two Ju 88s destroyed on the ground, 'Pinky' Stark was able to claim an Fw 190 shot down and Flying Officer Demoulin (Belgian) two more.* Honours went to 198 Squadron, which engaged in a big fight with JG 2 Fw 190s, no less than nine destroyed, one probable and two damaged being claimed, including two each for Squadron Leader Baldwin, Flight Lieutenant Niblett, Flying Officer Williams and Warrant Officer Stanley. It is believed that in this combat at least four of III/JG 2's aircraft were lost, together with that flown by Hauptman Fritz Edelmann of Stab/JG 2 and Hauptman Bernhard Schenkbier of 10/JG 2.

Despite this excellent month, which had cost only two Typhoons to German fighters and one to a bomber, losses to other causes had been very severe. Of the other 31 suffered most were to Flak, but still at least seven to engine failures, mid-air collisions, and other accidents. February would prove to be even worse, with nearly forty operational losses. These included three squadron and five flight commanders, while the recently successful Flying Officer Eagle was wounded by Flak over Calais during a 'Ranger' on 13 February, and was off operations as a result. One of the hardest losses occurred on the 6th, when Squadron Leader Lefevre of 266 Squadron was seen to bale out during an attack on shipping in the Abervrach estuary; he was not found.

During the month the ex-Whirlwind unit, 263 Squadron, had resumed operations, led by their outstanding commander, Squadron Leader 'Geoff' Warnes, unusual in that he was short-sighted, and wore corrective lenses in the air. In the course of an early 'Rodeo' on the 12th, Warnes personally shot down a Do 217 south-west of Rennes, and next day he claimed a Bf 109 in the Chartres area, Flight Lieutenant Gerry Racine claiming the destruction of three more of these fighters on an airfield, although two of the unit's aircraft were brought down by Flak. Nine days later, on the 22nd, Warnes led eight Typhoons of 263 on a sweep, intending to search the area between Kerlin Bastard airfield and Vannes in Brittany. Crossing the French coast the formation ran into 10/10 snow clouds and abandoned the primary mission for a shipping reconnaissance. At low level, approximately eight miles north-west of Guernsey, Warnes announced that he was going to ditch; the reason for this has never been established, but it was probably due to an engine failure,

section who, after an unsuccessful attempt to turn on to Eagle's tail, also ran for home, leaving Eagle to set course for Coltishall. Eagle's three victories brought him a DFC, and, added to those he had already gained flying Hurricanes in the Libyan Desert, made him an 'ace'. Sadly, Eagle was to perish in the last Typhoon structural failure when, while undertaking propeller trials for De Havilland, his aircraft broke up near Brockenhurst in the New Forest, just a few days after VE-Day.

Three days later it was the turn of 609 Squadron, Charles Detal claiming a Bf 110

*Charles Demoulin has described his wartime experiences in *Firebirds*, Airlife, 1987.

possibly caused by fuel-flow problems on switching from drop-tanks to main tanks. The squadron orbitted and Warnes was next sighted in the sea, apparently having difficulty in reaching his uninflated dinghy. One of the two pilots that could see their popular commanding officer was Flying Officer Tuff, an Australian, and he announced that he was going to bale out to help Warnes. Despite an order to the contrary, and in what must be one of the most calculated acts of bravery recorded in the air war, he did so, leaving the warmth and relative security of the cockpit of his Typhoon for the near-freezing, snow-swept Channel and the faint hope of bringing aid to his struggling squadron commander; the hope of eventual rescue was even fainter. Meanwhile the other Typhoons were orbitting and transmitting, allowing Middle Wallop and Exeter to get a good fix, but a third aircraft, flown by Flying Officer Hunter went missing, possibly having stalled in a tight turn during the low-level search. Despite extensive ASR operations no trace of any of the three pilots was ever found. Tuff's cool act of gallantry was recognized by a mention in dispatches, the only possible posthumous award other than the Victoria Cross.

February brought twenty aerial victories, plus the destruction of eight more aircraft on the ground, but the Typhoon's time as a pure fighter was fast running out, concentration upon bombing, rocketing and strafing steadily becoming of greater importance. Undoubtedly the most successful day of a busy and costly month was the 10th when Wing Commander Reg Baker led three 266 Squadron aircraft on a 'Rodeo' over the Bretigny-Paris area. Here Baker claimed an Fw 190 and a Do 217 shot down to bring his total for the month to three, Flight Lieutenant Deall claiming a Ju 88 and Flying Officer McGibbon three trainers identified as North American Yales – obviously ex-Armée de l'Air machines taken over by the Luftwaffe. Deall, McGibbon and the third 266 Squadron pilot joined to strafe aircraft on the ground, claiming a Ju 88, He 111 and Bf 110 destroyed and two others damaged. 266 Squadron was less fortunate on the 15th when a Sunderland in the Bay of Biscay signalled that it was under attack by Ju 88 fighters. Six of the unit's Typhoons were scrambled from Harrowbeer and made for Brittany where it was hoped they would intercept the coastal fighters as they returned to Poulmic or Kerlin Bastard. Unfortunately, in poor visibility, a small error in navigation took the formation straight over Morlaix airfield. The airfield defences were apparently forewarned and opened up with a devastating barrage; three of the Typhoons went down immediately and just to emphasize the changing fortunes of war, the three remaining aircraft failed to find the returning Junkers. Engine failure claimed another victim on this day, when Flight Sergeant Cecil Eckel, a West Indian pilot of 247 Squadron, was forced to abandon his Typhoon near Mortain. Thanks to a hair-raising last-second bale-out he managed to elude the searching Germans and eventually was hidden by the Resistance in Paris until the city was liberated.

A more unusual operation was undertaken on 18 February under the code-name 'Jericho' – the now-famous low-level attack on the German prison at Amiens, by Mosquito fighter-bombers of 2 Group. The plan involved eighteen Mosquitoes from 21, 464, and 487 Squadrons, in three waves; the first two waves would attack specific targets while the third wave would be held in reserve against failure of either of the first two. The attacking formations were to be accompanied by a Mosquito of the Film Production Unit. Each wave was to have an escort of eight Typhoons and the operation was timed for midday in order to catch many of the guards at lunch. The Typhoon escort was to be provided by 174 and 245 Squadrons from Westhampnett and a third unit from Manston, but there seems to have been some failure in communications, for briefing at Westhampnett was carried out in great haste at 1055 hours, and the first Typhoons were airborne at 1110! There had been no time to fit the long-range tanks which were desirable for an operation of this duration. At Manston, where the weather was appalling, with very low cloud and snow storms, there was also confusion. Flight Lieutenant Peter Roper of 198 Squadron recalls:

'It was another squadron at Manston that was supposed to fly the escort, but the CO refused to take off at the last moment because of the bad weather. Flight Lieutenant 'Bluey' Dall was passing by the Ops room at the time and the Intelligence Officer was in a desperate state, so Bluey said he would get an escort together. Anyway Bluey came into our "B" Flight dispersal hut and shouted out "No time for a briefing, there is a show on, follow me!" We had no idea where we were going and I don't know whether Dall had either. I remember Jack Armstrong and Bud Scambler coming with us. Scambler was Dall's number two and Armstrong was mine. We got off alright, but Armstrong lost us in the snow and returned to base. [Two more 198 Squadron Typhoons also took off but were forced to return.] Dall, Scambler and myself got out to about mid-Channel flying right down on the wave tops before the weather cleared. Typically of Bluey, he didn't seem to know where we were going. The only Mosquito we saw was the FPU one . . .'

Meanwhile, at Westhampnett where the weather was slightly better, eight Typhoons of 174 Squadron led by Flight Lieutenant 'Granny' Grantham were followed into the air by eight more from 245 Squadron, led by Squadron Leader Collins. Both these units had been briefed to rendezvous with their respective Mossie formations at Little-hampton. The bad weather had its influence here too, but 174 managed to meet up with four Mosquitoes of the second wave [and were joined by another three in mid-Channel] and 245 located the three Mosquitoes which were all that remained of the third wave. Flying Officer 'Junior' Markby, an Australian flying one of the 174 Squadron Tiffies, takes up the story:

'After crossing the French coast we descended to ground level and escorted the Mosquitoes to the target, then formed a defensive circle while the bombing runs were made. There was a thin veil of cloud over the area, at about 1,000 feet, and this provided some excellent cover for some Fw 190s who made attacks from above this cloud, breaking back above where they could still observe our aircraft. Another Typhoon and myself had been delegated to

Left: Flying Officer R. B. Tuff, RAAF (right), who lost his life while trying to save his CO from the Channel on 22 February 1944, photographed at OTU, prior to posting to 263 Squadron. On the left is Flying Officer George Chapman who later flew Typhoons with 174 Squadron and was one of several 2nd TAF pilots shot down by USAAF fighters in 1945; he survived as a PoW. (G. B. Chapman)

Above: Pilots of 247 Squadron outside their mess tent at Merston in August 1943. Only two of the ten in the picture would complete their operational tours – indicative of the odds facing Typhoon pilots at this time. Left to right: Flight Sergeant R. W. Betts (wounded), Flying Officer G. W. Waugh (killed), Sergeant C. E. B. Eckel (shot down over enemy territory, evaded), Flying Officer J. B. Watchorn (killed), Flying Officer B. T. Tatham (completed tour January 1945), Flying Officer P. A. Chappell (killed), Flying Officer H. L. Van Zuilecom (killed), Flying Officer K. F. Gear (completed tour August 1945), Flight Lieutenant C. E. Brayshaw (killed), Flight Sergeant W. J. L. S. Lowes (killed). (C. E. B. Eckel)

Below: Pilots of 245 squadron on the peritrack at Westhampnett (now Goodwood) in February 1944. Second from the left is Flight Lieutenant Bob Lee who would later survive five days trapped in his crashed Typhoon in Normandy. Behind them is JR311 'MR-G' which was transferred to 175 Squadron and became another victim of structural failure on 24 May 1944. The quilted engine covers with canvas 'chimneys' for oil heaters are also worthy of note. (IWM)

stay with the FPU Mosquito, and when the other aircraft turned for home, we remained, while several photographic runs were made, and kept the enemy from interfering. We were pleased to formate on him on the way home as the weather deteriorated again and we figured he was better equipped to guide us in the blind flying conditions, and we were running out of fuel.'

Flying Officer Renaud was forced to land four miles north of Amiens and was taken prisoner. At the time his loss was put down to Flak, but post-war examination of German records has revealed that his Typhoon was brought down by Leutnant Waldemar Radener of II/JG 26. Two Mosquitoes also failed to return, including the strike leader, Group Captain Pickard, DSO, DFC, who was shot down by Leutnant Wilhelm Mayer (also of II/JG 26) for his 15th victory.

Flight Lieutenant Ian Mallet was among the remaining Typhoons:

'Flight Lieutenant Grantham set course on 030 degrees but being low on fuel I led the remainder of my section back on a course of 330 degrees, dropping to sea level as the weather further deteriorated with flurries of snow. Boucher and Brown lost contact and climbed into cloud; Boucher managed to land at Lydd to refuel before returning to Westhampnett but Brown, regrettably did not return to base. Either he ran out of fuel before reaching land or iced-up in the cloud. I continued at sea level on a revised course given to me by "Redhead" Control and later caught a glimpse of cliffs right in front of my nose. After pulling up into the cloud I saw ice on the wings, so I turned south and let down over the sea and thence back to Westhampnett which was relatively clear. Flight time was 1 hour 55 minutes and there was very little fuel left.'

The third wave, still escorted by 245 Squadron, cruised around northern France for 45 minutes, but the bombing of the first two waves had been so accurate and effective that they were not required. The trio from 198 Squadron also returned safely, but they were forced to land at Tangmere.

Two days later four Typhoons of 247 Squadron escorted a pair of Mosquitoes on a PR sortie to photograph the results of the raid. The escort was led by 247's 'press-on' 'A' Flight commander, Flight Lieutenant Brayshaw, who had, the previous September, survived a ditching off the coast between Dymchurch and Hythe, remaining in his Typhoon [recorded in the Squadron diary as the 'Subphoon'] until it came to rest on the seabed and then swimming to the surface. Crossing the French coast on the return trip the formation came under intense fire and this time Brayshaw's luck ran out; his aircraft, badly hit, shed both elevators and plunged into the sea north of Cabourg.

Top: A still from a historic film – JP535 'XP-A' of 174 Squadron, flown by Flying Officer 'Junior' Markby, RAAF, formates on the starboard wingtip of the FPU Mosquito in appalling weather over the Channel, on the return from Operation 'Jericho'. (IWM)

Centre: 'Junior' Markby pictured in weather more suited to photography! (H. V. Markby)

Bottom: Salvaging Flight Lieutenant Brayshaw's 'Subphoon' – JP653 'ZY-E', beached at Dymchurch following his spectacular escape on 24 September 1943. (via A. J. Cranston)

CHAPTER SEVEN

Preparations for Invasion

MORE changes now took place as units prepared for their new role in the tactical air force. During January, 174 Squadron had been the first of the Typhoon squadrons to attend the Armament Practice Camp at Eastchurch to learn how best to use its new rocket-firing equipment. During March and April nearly all remaining units were to attend APCs at Eastchurch, Llanbedr, or Hutton Cranswick, in rotation, training in either the rocket-launching role, or as dive/fighter-bombers. Experience had shown that constant practice was necessary to maintain efficiency in either of these arts, and in addition, the manpower required to change Typhoons from bomber to rocket-firing configuration and vice versa, was prohibitive, therefore each squadron was to specialize. Initial plans were to equip the following squadrons with RP Typhoons: 174, 175, 181, 182, 184, 245, and 247 in 83 Group, 164, 183, 198, and 609 in 84 Group, and 137 still in 11 Group – the remainder were to specialize as bombers. At first RP Typhoons were in short supply, but an accelerated modification programme by Hawkers and RAF Maintenance Units ensured that all the designated units were equipped by the end of April.

In a series of bewildering moves, 84 Group's Typhoon squadrons were now reorganized. After their final burst of successful fighter operations, 198 and 609 Squadrons were transferred to 2nd TAF on 1 March, becoming the nucleus of 123 Airfield at Manston, and moving to Tangmere a fortnight later. Their place at Manston was

Below: A formation of 181 squadron Typhoons, operating from Hurn and photographed by a 430 Squadron Mustang over nearby Sandbanks, on 11 April 1944. The formation includes RP and bomber Typhoons; only one with the new canopy is visible in this photograph (EL-A MN208, the others are EL-B JR297, EL-Q JR244, EL-C JR294, EL-P JR292, EL-S JP551). (W. Grey)

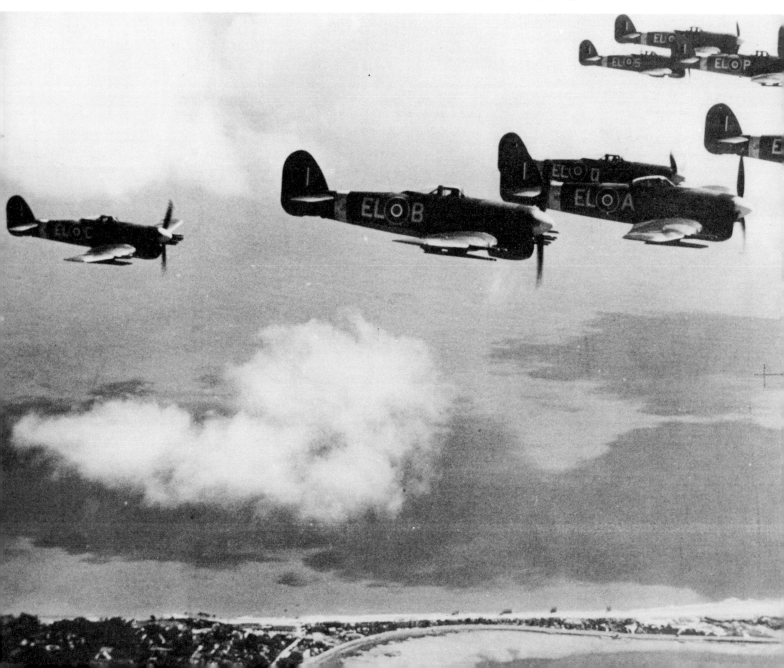

briefly taken by two Tangmere squadrons, the long-term resident 197, and 183 which had recently moved up from the south-west. Two weeks later 197 Squadron returned to Tangmere, where 257 and 266 Squadrons were now also based; 183 moved to Thorney Island to join 164 Squadron (now fully operational), becoming 136 Airfield. 193 Squadron had also forsaken its home in the south-west for Thorney Island, but this unit, after a spell at APC, moved along the coast to a new ALG at Needs Oar Point, near Beaulieu, on 11 April. Three of the Tangmere squadrons, 197, 257, and 266, had arrived there the previous day, and 193 Squadron completed the final line-up for 146 Airfield. These three 84 Group Airfields came under the control of 20 Wing.

At this time, the squadrons were also split up for service on the continent. While the air parties, with small administration sections, retained the unit number, the ground staff were organized as separately numbered Servicing Echelons, and were supplied with sufficient transport vehicles to become fully mobile. Initially all such echelons remained with their squadrons, but the intention was that during the Invasion and any advances which followed, the echelons could move from landing-ground to landing-ground at short notice, servicing any air party which happened to arrive. While a convenient and sensible arrangement in many respects, it had the less fortunate aspect of seeking to separate the faithful ground crews from 'their' squadron, with consequent deleterious effect on morale and sense of belonging. In the event most servicing echelons were to remain closely linked with their original squadrons throughout the rest of the war.

March had seen some reduction in overall activity as the moves and training took their toll, although attacks on V-1 sites were maintained, both directly and as escorts to formations of US B-26 Marauder and 2 Group Mitchell bombers attacking these targets. The month brought 31 losses to all causes in the operational squadrons, including three flight commanders, but no squadron or wing leaders, and in fact only seven or possibly eight of these were directly due to enemy action. German aircraft were met on only three occasions, the first on the 6th when six 3 Squadron Typhoons were escorting B-26s to Poix. Here Bf 109s attacked, shooting down one Typhoon and damaging a second. The balance was more than re-

Right and opposite page top: New Typhoons for old . . . P504 had a lengthy career, first as 'OV-Z' of 197 Squadron, Squadron Leader 'Jacko' Holmes' aircraft (IWM). After canopy and RP mods at Hawker's in March 1944, its next operational unit was 137 Squadron, becoming 'SF-R', Flying Officer Ken Brain's regular mount, at the end of August 1944. Re-coded 'SF-E' after repairs in November 1944, it was shot down by Flak on 27 December 1944. (K. G. Brain)

established ten days later when a dozen aircraft from 174 and 175 Squadrons, joined by two from 245 Squadron, undertook a 'Ramrod' to Villaroche, where a Ju 88, a Bf 108 communications aircraft, and two Ar 196 floatplanes were shot down, with a third of the latter damaged and two more aircraft destroyed on the ground. The cost was two Typhoons to Flak and a third crash-landing with a wounded pilot at the controls on return to base.

On the last day of the month, four 263 Squadron aircraft flew a late evening 'Rodeo' down to Kerlin Bastard on the Brittany coast, in another attempt to surprise the Luftwaffe's long-range Ju 88C coastal fighters, returning from patrol over the Bay of Biscay. Hindered by heavy cloud in the target area, the flight crossed the coastline into an area of substantial anti-aircraft defences. Turning for base, the formation leader, Flight Lieutenant Gerry Racine, lost contact with the rest of flight when his R/T set burnt out and evasive action was taken to avoid the Concarneau Flak. Climbing through cloud and on up to 18,000 feet, he headed north. It was now night, and while passing the Morlaix area he was surprised by tracer flashing past him, and then strikes on both wings. Breaking hard into a starboard diving turn, he straightened out after 270°, some 4,000 feet lower, and almost collided with the enemy aircraft which he took to be an Me 410. He was behind it and he opened fire, seeing strikes and then a burst of flame, which continued as it dived into the clouds below. Racine now had his own problems; the Typhoon was uncontrollable, and would only fly in a shallow spiral glide. He struggled to regain control for twenty minutes before the Typhoon stalled at about 10,000 feet and flicked over on its back. After a brief struggle, he managed to bale out and on the way down saw his Typhoon explode with an enormous streak of flame. It fell on Penguen Point, north-west of Morlaix, setting fire to brushwood; two Germans were killed in their own minefield while trying to reach the wreckage. Despite damage to his ankles, Racine managed to evade capture, eventually returning to the UK via Spain and Gibraltar. His victim was confirmed as an Me 410 which had crashed in the shallows between Ile de Batz and the mainland.

Centre left: JP736 also began its service life as a squadron commander's aircraft – 'HH-L', 'Lulu', personal mount of 175 Squadron's Mike Ingle-Finch. After a trip to Langley for mods, in January 1944, it was (unusually) returned to the squadron in March. By then Squadron Leader Ingle-Finch had a new 'Lulu' – MN194 – so JP736 became 'HH-B' (which accounts for the square bottom to the 'B') and its new 'owner', Flight Lieutenant 'Jack' Frost.

Left: Flight Lieutenant 'Gerry' Racine, RCAF, seated in the cockpit of his 263 Squadron Typhoon, 'Lil Jig III' at Harrowbeer in the spring of 1944. (L. W. F. Stark)

Top: Among the new 2nd TAF Typhoon units was 184 Squadron, one of whose first Typhoons, JP440 'BR-R', is seen here flying from Odiham in April 1944. (J. Rose)

Above: Typhoons of 137 Squadron at readiness at Lympne in February 1944. Nearest the camera is JR504 'SF-Z', with MM974 'SF-R' behind. (L. P. Boucher)

With the attendance of so many squadrons at APCs during April, activity was even further reduced. By this time too, the US 8th AAF escort fighters had been strengthened and were engaged in the great battles of the spring which came near to breaking the Luftwaffe fighter defences. It proved to be a very much quieter month for the Typhoons, therefore, losses to all causes falling away to just fifteen aircraft in the operational units; only six of these were due to enemy action and did not include any formation leaders. Four and a half aerial victories were claimed against a variety of types although no single-engined fighters were engaged. The 'half' was a Ju 188 which 266 Squadron shared with AA Command on the 18th of the month. Four of their aircraft were returning from an early morning exercise and while passing over their new base (Needs Oar Point) in line astern, prior to landing, the leader's attention was drawn by a series of AA bursts about a mile ahead. Their target was quickly identified as a Ju 188 and closing rapidly the leader, Flight Lieutenant Sanders, and Flight Sergeant Dodd each made a single pass firing 100 rounds apiece.

The 188 went down immediately, and when the wreckage was investigated it was found to have seven crew (more than usual) on board; their presence has never been adequately explained.*

The all-Canadian 143 Airfield became fully operational during April and Wing Commander Davidson moved across from 121 Airfield to lead his compatriots in the air. His place with the latter unit was taken by Wing Commander Green, the tough Rhodesian, who had been promoted after his tour commanding 266 Squadron. On 24 April one of Davidson's units, 438 Squadron, dropped pairs of 1,000lb bombs on a bridge at St-Sauveur – the first time that such missiles had been released operationally by Typhoons – although because of a shortage of aircraft in the Wing the unit had to use 439 Squadron Typhoons to do it! These weapons were particularly useful against bridges and the Canadians made many such attacks in the coming weeks, as part of the campaign to disrupt communications in northern France.

Even as the re-equipment of 137, 164, 184, and 263 Squadrons and the Canadian Wing had been taking place, other units had been giving up their Typhoons. During January, 486 Squadron had received a few of

*This incident was observed by Nevil Shute Norway who later used it as the basis of a scene in his novel, *Requiem for a Wren*.

the new and potent Tempests to try out, although in the event, these were passed on to 3 Squadron during February. This latter unit became the first to be fully operational on the new type, flying its last Typhoon operation, an ASR patrol, on 24 March. 486 Squadron soon followed suit, undertaking its final Typhoon sorties on 14 April, while early in May, 56 Squadron, which had already swapped its newly received rocket-Typhoons for 137 Squadron's unmodified aircraft, converted temporarily to Spitfire IXs until sufficient Tempests were available. Meanwhile, at the start of April, 1 Squadron had also ceased to fly Typhoons, moving to North Weald where it also re-equipped with Spitfire IXs, but on a more permanent basis. These proved to be the last major changes before the Invasion, leaving twenty fully operational Typhoon squadrons available for the final month of operations before the great day. All but two of these squadrons had now been allocated to 83 and 84 Groups in the 2nd TAF, 137 and 263 Squadrons remaining with the ADGB. They were based at Manston and Harrowbeer respectively; 137 was equipped with rocket-Typhoons and 263 at this stage still operated as a bomber squadron. They were committed in the main to anti-shipping operations at their respective ends of the Channel. In April and May further organizational changes took place; the Canadian Spitfire units left 22 Wing, their place being taken by the Typhoon Airfields from 16 Wing which was then disbanded. By mid-May the names were all changed – Wings became Sectors and the Airfields were then known as Wings, retaining their original numbers.

May was to see a great resurgence of activity, directed against a variety of priority targets. While the 'Noball' sites continued to be candidates for regular assault, much effort was also directed against the railway system of north-west France, but from 10 May the coastal radar network from the Pas-de-Calais to Brittany became the prime target. These radar sites were particularly difficult objectives to hit accurately and effectively; the aerials in most cases were relatively small, dispersed, protected by blast walls, and very heavily defended by Flak batteries of all calibres. The nature of the targets, whose destruction or severe reduction would be vital to the success of D-Day, meant that the task fell largely on the Typhoon squadrons. Back on 16 March, 198 Squadron had established the credibility of rockets against radar sites, with two attacks on the De Haan 'radar chimney', which had been so badly damaged that it had to be totally dismantled for repair. However, some radar sites had to be attacked several times, with defences therefore fully alerted; losses rose alarmingly and were to include a high proportion of formation leaders – against the concentrated fire of the ground defences, experience was little defence, the second and third tour fighter 'aces' from Fighter Command and Desert Air Force, who were now leading the Typhoons, proving as likely to fall victim to this impersonal scourge as were the young novices straight from OTUs. The first attacks were on the long-range aircraft-reporting stations and a week later the assault on night-fighter and coastal battery stations began. To conceal the intended invasion beaches, it was necessary to attack two sites outside that area for every one within it. During the last week before D-Day an intensive series of attacks were made on 42 sites, and finally on the last three days, twelve sites selected as especially worthy of attention received last visits. Rocket Typhoons made 694 sorties, firing 4,517 RP, and a further 759 sorties were shared between Typhoon and Spitfire bombers, dropping 1,258 bombs. Countless rounds of cannon shells were expended, which post-Invasion examination of the sites and interrogation of the German operators revealed to have been particularly effective against unarmoured control cabins, with consequent lowering of the operators' morale. By weight RP were roughly four times as effective as bombs, but numerically bombs were twice as effective as RP; the rockets had proved most efficient against the larger aerial displays ('chimneys' and 'hoardings') whereas the bombs had been most damaging in the disruption of the multitude of power and telephone lines associated with these sites.

Just before the anti-radar campaign began, the Canadian Wing lost its leader when Wing Commander Davidson suffered an engine failure while leading an attack on Douai marshalling yards on 8 May. He was forced to land in France, joining the growing list of evaders, but instead of passing along one of the escape routes, he remained in France and fought with the Maquis, eventually linking with Allied forces after the Invasion. His place at the head of the Canadians was taken by another Desert Air Force veteran, ex-Kittyhawk 'ace', Wing Commander Judd. The very next day, 124 Airfield's popular Norwegian leader, Erik Haabjoern, had the first of two narrow escapes during May. Squadron Leader Robin McNair, commanding 247 Squadron at that time, witnessed both:

'The Wing was based at Hurn, but all three squadrons had flown east in worsening weather, arriving at Manston on a gloomy afternoon. We took off on a fighter sweep, to enter enemy territory at Knocke, go on to Reims, and come out at Dieppe. The area contained a substantial number of Luftwaffe fighter stations, so everyone was pretty alert. We crossed the Kent coast at ten or fifteen feet and passed over the wrecked ships on the Goodwins with their hazardous

Top: One of the last Typhoons operated by 1 Squadron, MN207 'JX-I', here carrying 45-gallon long-range tanks at Martlesham Heath in March 1944. (Harkness via P. Sortehaug)

Above: Robin McNair, who commanded 247 Squadron from February to August 1944, seen here during his earlier service as a flight commander with 245 Squadron. 'MR-G' was DN492 at this time. (R. J. McNair)

Right: Wing Commander Erik Haabjoern, the popular Norwegian who commanded 124 Wing during the Invasion period, and who survived three immersions in the Channel while flying Typhoons. He flew with 56 and 609 Squadrons before commanding 247 Squadron and 124 Wing; he was killed on a ferry flight after the war. (Group Captain F. W. M. Jensen)

masts poking out of the sea. These came at you very swiftly in the mediocre visibility and required a quick jerk on the stick to skim over. The squadrons flew abreast in a wide formation, 247 to the starboard. About forty miles from the Kent coast Erik gave his callsign and said "My engine's stopping." The next thing I saw was Typhoon "EH" zooming up from sea level with a dead propeller. At 500 feet or so, when the aircraft was nearly stalling, Erik jumped out, very quickly and cleanly, and almost at once his parachute began to stream and open. The whole thing was an amazingly deft performance. As his deputy, I detached two aircraft to remain over him, and radioed Ops Control. By that time we were well on our way, but it was an ill-fated sweep; my engine began to vibrate badly fifteen miles into Belgium and my radio ceased to function. I turned back with my number two, nursing the engine. A third leader took over and the sweep was completed without further drama.'

Haabjoern was picked up safely, but just thirteen days later it was a somewhat closer call: 'We attacked a radar station just north of Dieppe with cannons and rockets and Erik went in first, from landward, leading 181 and 182, and I came in second with 247. He flew very low to be sure of hitting the target and I feared that he might be hit by debris from the buildings, but he was hit by Flak as we headed out over the coast, just north of the harbour. His engine was trailing smoke and he was flying very low still. Just after he had passed the outer harbour wall his engine stopped. He pulled hard on the stick, came up to about 700 feet, and leapt out in his practised manner! Soon he was in his dinghy, but in easy sight of the harbour wall; he told me afterwards that he could see a German sentry pacing up and down. Since he was so close to the shore and in danger of being picked up by an enemy vessel, or shot up by an aircraft, a protective beehive of Typhoons gathered over Erik.

Eventually Spitfires turned up to mount guard and we went home to Hurn. Then came the 190s and 109s, more Spitfires, and the inevitable dogfights, as Erik sat in his dinghy. In due course, a stout-hearted Walrus pilot landed three miles off Dieppe and picked him up. He was soon around again at Hurn; to one who had escaped from Norway, across the North Sea in an open boat, a few hours in a rubber dinghy was small trouble. He was a brave and fine leader, and all this was good for morale.'

Meanwhile, the campaign against communications continued; bridges of all descriptions, river and rail traffic, junctions and marshalling yards, were the most common targets, but anything of military value was fair game. On 23 May 193 and 257 Squadrons jointly attacked a rail tunnel into which a train had just disappeared, bombing each end simultaneously, blocking them and sealing in their intended target. On this particular day 257 Squadron noted a record delivery of ordnance, firing 9,615 20mm shells and dropping 62 500lb bombs. 184 Squadron paid several visits to the marshalling yards at Gamaches [which soon became known as 'Gamages'], which was also attacked by 245 Squadron on 28 May. On this occasion they came up against a new hazard – rocket-launched cables which then descended slowly by parachute. Flight Sergeant Lush brought back fifteen yards of cable trailing from his wing; it had cut eighteen inches into the leading edge. 184 had joined 121 Airfield at Holmsley South for a week commencing 13 May; after the Invasion the unit would become a permanent member of that Wing. Also resident at

Holmsley at this time was 1320 Flight, the unit specially formed to conduct the operational trials of 'Abdullah', a radar-homing device, which was fitted in the Flight's three Typhoons, MN236, MN263 and MN296. These trials were flown from 14 to 21 May, each sortie involving a single 'Abdullah' Typhoon flown by Squadron Leader Daniels or Flight Lieutenant Jones (who were on detachment from the FIU), escorted by two or three aircraft from one of Holmsley's other Typhoon squadrons. Briefed only to act as escort, the regular Typhoon pilots were intrigued. Flight Sergeant Peter Baden of 175 Squadron was one of them:

'We didn't speak to the pilots, and were told nothing about the aircraft, which were unarmed, except that they were very "hush-hush". We weren't supposed even to look in them. With another pilot I was merely told to formate on one of the aircraft as close escort over the Channel, wherever it went; no information on the purpose of the mission or where we were going. We learnt nothing more on the sortie as the weather was so hazy that there was no horizon and we saw nothing, although from the flight time I assumed that we must have been close to the French coast at about 500 or 1,000 feet. After landing we sneaked a look in the cockpit while the plane was unattended but saw no CRT or other indicator, just a few small black boxes with switches.'

In a dozen such sorties, 1320 Flight established that technically the equipment worked as intended, but tactically it was of little use, mainly because the radar operators lost no time in shutting down their transmissions on the approach of aircraft. Besides which, in the present campaign at least, the location of all the German radar stations were well known and photographed.

The radar war continued to exact its toll, particularly among the squadron commanders. On 23 May Squadron Leader Keep was hit while leading 181 Squadron in the anti-Flak role at Cherbourg; he managed to ditch successfully ten miles off the French coast and was picked up by a Walrus. He had however sustained facial injuries, including a broken jaw, which would keep him off operations for some time. 164's Squadron Leader Russell was forced to bale out attacking a 'Freya' at Fruges on the 28th and was posted missing. Squadron Leader Ross of 193 Squadron was also missing after baling out nearer home, just fifteen miles off the Isle of Wight, on the eve of D-Day. On 2 June 198 Squadron had lost its commander, Squadron Leader Niblett, during a joint attack with 609 Squadron, on the night-fighter and coastal battery control radars at Caude Côte, just west of Dieppe. While four of 198 led by Niblett ran in from the sea, twelve others from both squadrons dived

out of the sun. Flight Lieutenant Denis Sweeting was Niblett's number two and his account gives some idea of the ferocity of the defences:

'Before we were a mile distant I had checked that my electric sight was on and that the firing buttons for the rockets and cannon were on "Fire". The top of the radar arrays were now clearly visible, being set on concrete emplacements only some forty yards back from the cliff edge. I was looking to "Nibby's" aircraft for the lead in, when it seemed to flash. It looked as if he had fired his rockets, which I thought was too early, as we had decided before take-off to fire as we crossed the cliff-top. Then, petrified with horror, I realized that his aircraft had been hit and had burst into flames. In a second all that became visible of the aircraft was its wingtips sticking out of a ball of fire. The tips turned slowly over and the aircraft must have been on its back when it exploded into the base of the cliff.

As if released from a spell, I realized it could well be me next. I shoved the throttle wide open and started jinking the Typhoon like mad. Crossing the cliffs at speed, I straightened to line up the sights with the base of the array and fired a salvo of eight rockets simultaneously with cannon-fire. Breaking steeply away from just about ground level, I was turning and jinking the aircraft in a way which I had not thought possible, for there seemed to be fire coming from every quarter. Wondering how I was going to get out of this predicament, I decided that rather than continue inland and risk more defences, I would take a chance and break back over the coast. Twisting and weaving and firing my cannons I reached the cliff edge again on my way out. There were flashes all around of guns firing at me – and then I was once more over the sea chucking the aircraft about like mad with the engine flat out. The sea beneath me seemed to be boiling with exploding Flak shells.'

This attack was not successful and had to be repeated the following day. 198 Squadron had also suffered losses earlier, on 24 May, when Squadron Leader Niblett had led four Typhoons against the Jobourg site, on the north-west tip of the Cherbourg peninsula. A German PoW later described it: 'Three [sic] Typhoons came in from the valley flying very low in line astern. The second aircraft got a direct hit from 37mm Flak which practically shot off the aircraft's tail; the pilot, however, managed to keep some sort of control and continued straight at the target. He dived below the level of the Mammut's rim, released rockets into the structure, and then tried to climb at the last moment to clear. The third aircraft in trying to avoid the damaged Typhoon touched the latter's fuselage with a wing tip. Both aircraft locked together and crashed some 100

Top: One of the German radar sites on the French coast, under attack by rocket Typhoons. (IWM)

Above: Flying Officer 'Neufy' Taylor, a Canadian with 183 Squadron, who shot down two Bf 109s on 29 May 1944, using only 20 rounds per gun! He was subsequently shot down and killed on D-Day. Note that his Typhoon, like many at this time, has a stone-guard to protect the radiator when operating from rough strips. (IWM)

yards beyond. The Mammut was never again serviceable.'

The two crashed Typhoons had been flown by Flying Officer Freeman and Flight Sergeant Vallely and it is thought that the aircraft which hit the 'Mammut' was Freeman's. It was also impossible to establish whether or not the Typhoon had been flown into the aerial deliberately, as some thought, including German witnesses. Had it been so, one would like to think that the citation for a Victoria Cross, mooted by Professor R. V. Jones, would have been successful.*

One of the radar sites was unique in being on UK territory! This was the complex at Fort St. George, St. Peter Port, Guernsey, and it proved a tough nut to crack. An attack by 181 and 182 Squadrons on 27 May was followed by a visit from all three squadrons of their Wing on 2 June. Some equipment remained serviceable so the next day 439 Squadron plastered the site with bombs; still one stubborn 'Freya' appeared to be operational. The installation received its *coup de grâce* on the eve of D-Day when 439 paid another visit, but it cost this unit its first casualty to enemy action. The formation leader, Flight Lieutenant Saville, had led eight Typhoons in a dive from 12,000 to 4,000 feet before releasing their bombs, but when the squadron reformed Saville was not to be seen, although an ominous disturbance in the sea, just off shore, was noted. Apparently Saville had been hit in the dive and had been unable to pull out.

Few German aircraft were seen at this time, but during an armed reconnaissance over the Gisern-Pontoise area on 18 May by 164 and 183 Squadrons, two Bf 109s were claimed shot down in a two-minute dogfight, Wing Commander Bryan sharing one of these with a pilot of 183 Squadron. In rather different circumstances on the 29th, Flying Officer 'Neufy' Taylor and another pilot of 183 Squadron were scrambled from Thorney Island after a pair of raiders. Taylor

*See Chapter 43 of *Most Secret War* by Professor R. V. Jones, published by Hamish Hamilton Ltd., 1978.

caught the Bf 109 fighter-bombers and rapidly dispatched both with an expenditure of only twenty rounds per gun. Sadly this gifted pilot would be lost in combat with Bf 109s on the first day of the Invasion, barely a week later.

Losses were also suffered on other operations in May, one of which is recalled by Squadron Leader Jack Brandt, a Burma campaign veteran who was flying with 137 Squadron as a supernumerary: 'Four of us went on a "Ranger", egging the Jerries to get airborne with little success. On our way home we spied an ammo train, shot it up, and in return I was shot down. It was a classic bit of ground to air shooting, mostly in the engine and cockpit. I was too low to bale out, the engine was on fire so I did the next best thing – guessed where the ground was and pulled the stick back. I think I was doing about 300 knots. Fortunately, traversing several farms, two roads and knocking down two posts, the fire was put out and I managed to crawl out. This happened somewhere south of Amiens. Thank God it was a Typhoon, because if it had been a Spitfire or a Hurricane I am sure the engine would have ended up in my lap. After a few traumas I managed to escape capture and ended up in Paris, aiding, in a small way, the French Resistance.'

The three RCAF squadrons of 143 Wing attended 16 APC at Hutton Cranswick during mid-May for their week of instruction; they were the last before the great day. By the beginning of June they were also practising the art of smoke-laying. Two other bomber squadrons, 197 and 266, had also undergone training in this role, 197 giving a demonstration of its efficiency before General Eisenhower at Thorney Island on 21 April, while 266 spent ten days at Snaith in Yorkshire exercising with Army units. In fact these skills were never put to the test, as it was decided that the Typhoons could not be spared from their primary roles; on D-Day smoke-screens were laid by Bostons of 88 and 342 Squadrons, as already recorded.

By the eve of D-Day the costly operations of May and early June had raised Typhoon casualties among the operational squadrons by another 53 aircraft. Most squadrons had suffered at least one loss, but the prime sufferers had been 609 Squadron, which lost a flight commander and four other pilots, and 137 Squadron, which had also lost five, mainly on anti-shipping operations. However, most of the losses had come in the battle to blind the German radar; it had been expensive but extremely effective. All six long-range aircraft reporting-stations south of Boulogne were destroyed and at least 15 other installations in the area were rendered unserviceable. Large stretches of the French Channel coast were therefore bereft of their normal radar coverage; also the personnel manning the radar stations were suffering from a severe loss of morale from the frequent and sudden, shattering attacks. It was calculated that on the night of the Assault there was never more than 18 per cent of the radar in north-west France in operation, and at times it was as little as 5 per cent. The Germans did not receive the early warning that the radar should have given; no fighters interfered with the airborne operations; the coastal batteries were impotent; the enemy was confused and hesitant; vital decisions were delayed. Thousands of Allied lives were saved.

On 3 June orders were received to paint the famous 'Invasion stripes' on the Typhoons (and on all Allied aircraft operating in the area); this was accomplished by the next day. All was now ready, bar the weather, and on 5 June 1944 the RAF's Typhoon units were disposed as follows:

Second Tactical Air Force

83 GROUP:

121 Wing Holmsley South;
Wing Commander C. L. Green, DFC
174 Squadron

175 Squadron
245 Squadron

124 Wing Hurn;
Wing Commander E. Haabjoern, DFC
181 Squadron
182 Squadron
247 Squadron

129 Wing Westhampnett
184 Squadron

143 Wing Hurn;
Wing Commander M. T. Judd, DFC, AFC
438 Squadron
439 Squadron
440 Squadron

84 GROUP

123 Wing Thorney Island;
Wing Commander R. E. P. Brooker, DFC ☆
198 Squadron
609 Squadron

136 Wing Thorney Island;
Wing Commander J. M. Bryan, DFC ☆
164 Squadron
183 Squadron

146 Wing Needs Oar Point;
Wing Commander E. R. Baker, DFC ☆
193 Squadron
197 Squadron
257 Squadron
266 Squadron

Air Defence of Great Britain

10 GROUP
263 Squadron Harrowbeer

11 GROUP
137 Squadron Manston

Among the Wing Leaders, Green, Haabjoern, and Bryan were all experienced Typhoon pilots; Judd, as already mentioned, was an ex-Desert Kittyhawk pilot, and Baker had flown Typhoons with 182 Squadron before commanding a Whirlwind fighter-bomber squadron. Brooker was very experienced on Hurricanes, having flown both in the UK and Singapore, claiming a total of seven victories and two probables by early 1944, and had just completed a spell as CO of the Fighter Leaders' School.

Left: Wing Commander E. R. Baker of 146 Wing at Needs Oar Point, shortly before D-Day, and minus his familiar red moustache, half of which had been shaved off at a mess party a few days earlier. 'An extraordinary character – he held his morning briefings on "the throne" – a canvas convenience in the centre of the airfield. His personal callsign was "Lochinvar", which he was forced to replace, after much resistance from him, just before D-Day. He was killed just 10 days after D-Day.' – Flight Sergeant 'Jock' Ellis, 197 Squadron. (J. C. Rook)

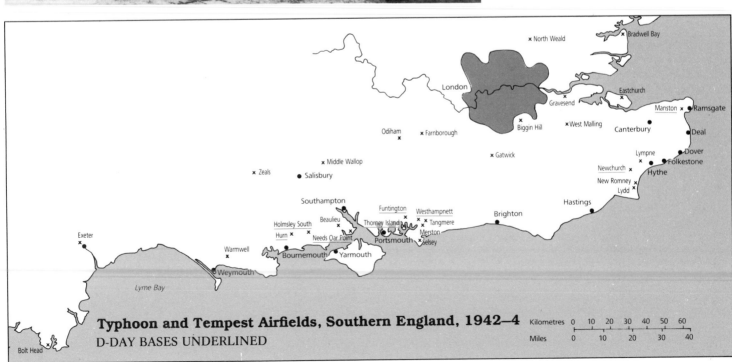

Typhoon and Tempest Airfields, Southern England, 1942–4
D-DAY BASES UNDERLINED

CHAPTER EIGHT
D-Day to Breakout

OF the eighteen Typhoon squadrons available to the 2nd TAF
on D-Day, nine were allotted to
the 'Air Alert' role. These nine
were to be employed three at a time, with
one squadron allocated to each of the three
British and Canadian Assault Forces. The
honour of being first in over the invasion
beaches fell to the three Canadian squadrons of 143 Wing; their arrival was timed to
coincide with the approach of the first
landing-craft at H-hour – 0725 hours. They
were briefed to call the HQ ships on arrival
in case the Assault Force Commanders
required them to take on more urgent
targets, but in the absence of new instructions they dive-bombed the pre-arranged
targets which were strong points at Le
Hamel and La Rivière (Gold beach), Cour-
seulles (Juno beach), and Hermanville
(Sword beach). Flying Officer James H.
Beatty was flying with 440 Squadron:

'Twelve aircraft were used and the pilots
were briefed the night before, everyone was
confined to the airfield. I believe that we
were the only aircraft, during the initial
assault, allowed below the cloud base – the
only other aircraft we saw at our elevation
were two Focke-Wulfs and they climbed
into the clouds. At the briefing we had been
given our targets and told, that if we were
hit, to bale out over the Channel and the
odds were that we would land on a ship.
They also suggested that we land on an
empty one headed for England!

The flight across the Channel was something to see. There was every kind of ship,
barge and landing-craft that you could
imagine. Battleships – six of them, firing big
guns. Landing-craft would run in towards
the beaches, fire a volley of rockets, and
then back off. We went into the initial target
in line astern and bombed at low level with
delayed-action bombs; we then went behind
the beaches, after gun positions. The visibility was very poor due to weather, smoke
and dust, so it was difficult to assess results.
As we left we watched the landing-craft go
in on the assault . . . the German defenders
were more concerned with what was in
front of them at the start, but later in the day
and in the following days things changed
and casualties rose.'

Targets were also pre-arranged for the
other nine Typhoon squadrons not on Air
Alert and these included four more gun-sites
and two German Army HQs, Château-le-

Above: Flight Lieutenant K. J. Harding of 198 Squadron climbing away from Thorney Island on the evening of D-Day, in MN409 'TP-G', for an armed reconnaissance in the Caen–Falaise area. Note that the hastily applied 'Invasion stripes' have obscured the aircraft's code-letter, which has therefore been repositioned on the nose. (IWM)

Parc, south-east of Bayeux, and Château-la-
Meauffe near St-Lô. During the day calls for
assistance resulted in attacks on a radar
station near Le Havre, which had been
directing coastal guns, and strong points
met by the advancing Allies. By late morning it was apparent that there were not
enough targets in the assault area to keep

the Typhoon force fully occupied and some
squadrons were then redirected on to
'armed recces' of the area south of Bayeux,
Caen and Lisieux, their prime purpose being
the disruption of reinforcements. First in
this area was 164 Squadron which became
the first Typhoon unit to bring the Luftwaffe
to combat, forcing an Fw 190 to land and

Below: Wing Commander R. E. P. Brooker, Wing Leader 123 Wing, just airborne from Thorney Island on D-Day. His Typhoon, MN570, was simply marked 'B' (for Brooker), as was his Tempest when he later led 122 Wing. (IWM)

then destroying it on the ground. 183 Squadron was not so fortunate; absorbed with its ground targets, this unit was bounced by Bf 109s and three Typhoons went down, including one flown by the recently victorious Flying Officer Taylor.

Throughout the afternoon the Typhoons continued with the 'armed recces', scarcely hindered by the Luftwaffe, although 164 again met Fw 190s. This time honours were even, each side losing one aircraft.

At the end of the day Typhoons had flown 400 sorties for the cost of eight aircraft and pilots (although one of these successfully evaded). Four had gone down to enemy fighters and four to ground fire or debris damage. Resistance had been much lighter than expected, but the next day would be a rather different story.

Dawn on the 7th revealed a solid cloud base between 1,500 and 3,000 feet but the Typhoons were airborne at first light. The 83 Group squadrons were assigned to the area Caen-Mézidon-Falaise to a point south of Villers-Bocage, while 84 Group patrolled the area east of this, as far as Evreux. 2nd TAF Mustang IIIs with their superior range, policed the routes to the south of the Typhoons' areas. To allow sufficient time on patrol the rocket squadrons carried long-range tanks and a reduced load of four RP, the bombers a tank under one wing and a bomb under the other. Much execution was done, particularly of unarmoured vehicles, but this work was hampered by the low cloud which also forced the Typhoons to fly within easy range of light Flak – this was reflected in increased losses. From a total of 493 sorties flown during the day, some of which were diverted to give direct support, fifteen Typhoons were lost. Hardest hit were 184 and 245 Squadrons, both of which lost three aircraft. 184's were all shot down in one action; Flight Lieutenant 'Dutch' Holland was leading a formation of eight:

'We flew over Mezidon marshalling yard at approximately 1,000 feet and attacked on a reciprocal course. The marshalling yard was full of tanks, anti-aircraft guns, military vehicles and troops. Everything in the world seemed to open up at us and I was hit before we started the attack. I led the Squadron down to 300 feet, close enough to see the eyes of the gunners, and fired rockets into the vehicles. With the satisfaction of seeing the rockets explode among them, I pulled up – 200 feet my clock showed – and waited for things to happen. I gave instructions for the squadron to carry on, as I was baling out, and pulled up to 1,200 feet. I had never baled out before and I felt no fear until trying to get out of the plane. Being very low I decided that the best thing was to roll the plane and get out on its side. I had carried out all the preliminaries of releasing the harness, pulling the R/T plug out, but alas the hood would not jettison. Fire was com-

Top: Among the heavy losses of 'D+1' was MN377, 'MR-B' of 245 Squadron, hit by Flak and force-landed near Falaise by Flying Officer K. J. A. Dickie, who managed to evade capture. After Dickie had scrambled clear, the aircraft was strafed by accompanying Typhoons. (Jean-Pierre Benamou)

Above: Squadron Leader 'Jack' Collins of 245 Squadron, like Squadron Leader Horden before him, usually flew 'MR-?'. In June 1944 this was MN819, seen here on the runway at Holmsley South, in the New Forest. (N. B. Wilson)

Below: Sommerfeld tracking being laid on one of the strips in Normandy which would be the home of the Typhoon squadrons for two months. (IWM)

Right: Council of war on one of the strips used before the Typhoons were based in Normandy, probably B.2. The pilots are from 121 and 124 Wings and include Flying Officer 'Tommy' Hall (far left), Squadron Leader Mike Ingle-Finch (fourth from left, standing), Flight Lieutenant 'Jimmy' Bryant (centre, wearing beret), Flying Officer Pete Tickner (far right, standing) and Wing Commander Erik Haabjoern (left foreground, seated on a box). (IWM)

ing from the starboard side. Things were getting very hot. I got my feet on the dashboard and undercarriage lever and pushed at the hood with all the force I knew. The next thing I knew I had hit the tail with my parachute and done a somersault – my first instinct was to pull the ripcord – I must have done although I do not remember. But I do remember my seeing my plane hit the ground before the chute opened.'

That was just the start of his ordeal; after seventy days on the run 'Dutch' Holland found a way through to the Allied lines. Later he returned to action flying Tempests with 33 Squadron.

With the beachhead firmly established, Typhoon operations continued in the pattern set on the 7th. On that date work had commenced on the construction of the first landing-grounds in France. Runways were bulldozed from the Normandy farmland, ditches and hedges levelled, and surfaced with 'Sommerfeld tracking' (wire mesh). The first of these were given B (British) or A (American) numbers, dependent upon which nation's area of operations they were located within; a full list of those mentioned in this book appears in Appendix 2) were ready for use on 10 June. Early that morning the first aircraft to make a wheels-down landing was flown in by Flying Officer Smith of 245 Squadron, after being hit by Flak which caused the engine to vibrate badly. When he came to a halt on B.3 he was met by a swarm of photographers and 'brass' who were expecting to greet A. V.-M. Broadhurst in his Spitfire!

The operation on which Smith had been hit was one of three laid on that day against two German Army HQs, in an attempt to thwart counter-attacks which were about to be launched. Two of the attacks against what was thought to be the HQ of 1st SS Panzer Corps, were without success, but in the evening forty Typhoons from the three squadrons of 124 Wing, plus 245 Squadron, swept in to rocket the Panzer Gruppe West's HQ at Château-la-Caine, about twelve miles south-west of Caen. They were immediately followed by 71 Mitchells bombing from 12,000 feet. The château itself was not badly damaged, but the orchard which sheltered the HQ's vehicles was saturated with direct hits. The Chief of Staff, General Von Dawans, and several of his officers died, and the HQ was out of action until 28 June. Later in the month, on 27 June, 146 Wing joined the Mitchells for a similar attack on the Headquarters of Lieutenant-General Dohlman's infantry division in the St-Lô area; here again the target was destroyed and the General killed. No General was safe in his HQ in this campaign.

From 13 June the Typhoons began using the new strips to refuel and re-arm during the day, returning to their south coast airfields at night. B.2 was used by 181 Squadron on this day, B.3 came into use [by 174 Squadron] the following day, and B.6 received its first visitors, 247 Squadron, on the 18th. Meanwhile, on 17 June, Dakotas had

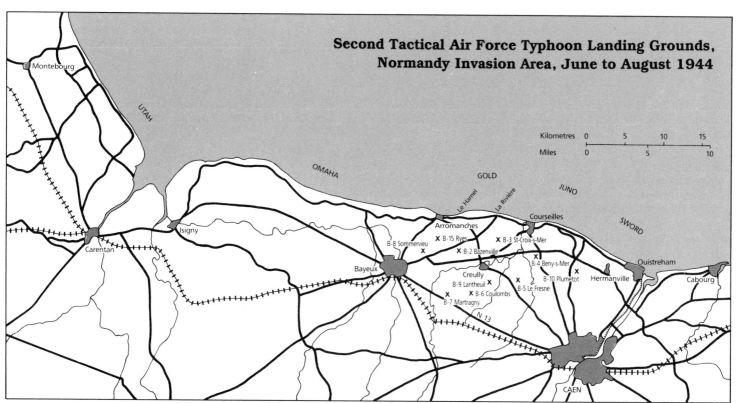

Second Tactical Air Force Typhoon Landing Grounds, Normandy Invasion Area, June to August 1944

Top left: The problem – MN371 'XP-A' of 174 Squadron taxiing through clouds of fine, abrasive dust at B.5 . . . (IWM)

Left: . . . and the solution –the original domed 'filter', designed by Napier and fitted in haste to all 2nd TAF's Typhoons, can be seen in the centre of the air intake. (Australian War Memorial)

Above: Has the shelling stopped? Flying Officer 'Tommy' Hall, RAAF, 175 Squadron, demonstrates two essentials for occupants of B.5, Le Fresne-Camilly in July 1944, a dugout and a 'tin hat'. (T. Hall)

Right: Four Canadian pilots of 245 Squadron: Pilot Officer Sam Bennet, Flying Officer George Wharry, Warrant Officer Chester West and Flying Officer John Thompson, study their maps among the harvested corn at B.5, Le Fresne-Camilly in late July 1944. (Public Archives of Canada)

delivered the ground echelon of 174 Squadron, 121 Wing, to B.5, scheduled as that Wing's new base, but heavy shelling had forced a temporary move to B.2. Three days later 175 Squadron moved into B.3 while the whole of 124 Wing plus 245 Squadron settled in on B.6; on this latter strip there were now 65 Typhoons just over three miles from the front-line. In the evening of the next day a Bf 109 flew over the strip at fifty feet, obviously on a 'recce'. 245 Squadron's diarist remarked, 'We shall be shelled or bombed soon and this will be expensive with no blast shelters for the aircraft.' He was right. Salvoes started arriving on the morning of the 22nd and by 1030 the Typhoons had been ordered back across the Channel. By this time all the squadrons had suffered severely, 247 Squadron for example flying back fourteen aircraft, of which only four were unscathed, and leaving four unflyables at B.6 (these were all repaired; only 181 Squadron had a single write off).

With all the Typhoon squadrons back on British soil the next major problem became apparent. Already the squadrons had been experiencing more engine trouble than normal, though this was thought to be due to the Servicing Commandos in Normandy being more familiar with Merlins than

Sabres. However when the aircraft of the four squadrons now at Holmsley South were examined, no less than 37 engines showed sleeve wear sufficient to require replacement. Construction of the strips in Normandy had robbed the soil of its natural covering and the resulting clouds of fine dust which had billowed over the landing-grounds, fed by every aircraft movement, had not only turned the surrounding countryside white, but had relentlessly scoured the Sabres' moving parts. Napiers responded magnificently to the crisis, designing, manufacturing and flying the prototype of a dust deflector in one day. Half the company's sheet metal workers were at work by midnight of the same day, turning out the finished product, which was fitted to the whole of the Typhoon force within a week! The device consisted of a mushroom-shaped dome which sat over the carburettor air intake, deflecting the heavier dust and sand while allowing the air to be sucked in behind it. Unfortunately it was not the complete answer as the Sabre had a habit of backfiring, on which occasions a red-hot dome would be projected across the airfield, to the consternation of those in line! Eventually the domes were replaced by drum-shaped filters which had 'cuckoo-doors' to cope with backfires.

Thus fitted, and with the shelling much reduced, the Typhoons returned to France, where the ground-crews had had to sit it out. By the end of June 121 Wing were established at B.5, 124 Wing at B.6, and 143 Wing became the first Typhoon bombers based in France, arriving at B.9 on the 27th.

Much had been achieved, for while there had still been no breakout from the beachhead, the Allied positions had been expanded and secured. German reinforcements had been critically delayed by the cumulative effects of constant air attack on the rail and road systems of the area, while a very close and effective system of support to the ground forces was rapidly developing. By now all the 83 Group Typhoon units were based in France, where they were joined on the last day of the month by the first of the 84 Group Wings, 123, which arrived at B.10. The period since 6 June had, however, cost 2nd TAF nearly seventy Typhoons in action, well over half of them to ground fire of one sort or another; little more than half a dozen had fallen victim to German fighters, however, while claims against the latter totalled nine. Of these nine no less than five were claimed in one engagement which took place on 29 June. Wing Commander Baldwin was leading ten aircraft of 193 Squadron, covering RP Typhoons, when several Bf 109s were sighted near Conches airfield. Giving orders to jettison long-range tanks he led the Typhoons into the attack, but then a further formation of 109s appeared through the clouds, behind the Typhoons; a dogfight immediately developed, in and out of cloud. After downing two himself, and damaging a third, Baldwin found there were now large 'numbers of enemy aircraft milling around, so he called on his pilots to make use of cloud cover and return individually. This they did successfully, although two damaged Tiffies were forced to land at A.3 and B.2. In addition to Baldwin's claims (which brought his confirmed total to 14½) three more 109s were claimed destroyed and three damaged.

Heaviest losses among the Typhoons had been suffered by 84 Group units, 198 Squadron losing eleven aircraft and 193 Squadron seven; 84 Group also lost two very experienced Typhoon Wing Leaders, Mike Bryan and Reg Baker, to the old enemy, Flak. Wing Commander Baker was last heard transmitting instructions to his Wing as his crippled Typhoon plunged almost vertically to the ground west of Caen.

These were not the only operational Typhoon losses for the RAF during June, for it will be recalled that both 137 and 263 Squadrons had remained under the command of Air Defence of Great Britain (as Fighter Command had temporarily been renamed) and had continued to operate against shipping in the Channel from their bases at Manston and Bolt Head respectively. In the area over which it was operating (the Brittany coast and the Channel Islands) 263 Squadron suffered heavy casualties to defending Flak ships during the month, six of the unit's Typhoons failing to return. Included among these was the squadron's commander, Squadron Leader Gonay, a Belgian who had flown with the RAF since the Battle of Britain. He was hit by fire from an armed trawler attacked off Corbière Point and, attempting to force-land on Jersey, was killed when his Typhoon hit a farmhouse. The unit was unique at this time, being established as a 'double squadron' – one flight operating with rocket-Typhoons and the other with bombers; an increased complement of aircraft ensured that eight of either type could be provided for operations at all times. One of the flight commanders was 'Pinkie' Stark, who had transferred from 609 Squadron. His tour finished abruptly when he was shot down by Flak attacking a power-station in Brittany but, thanks in part to some tips from 263's earlier evader, Gerry Racine, he was back in the UK in ten days!

From the opposite end of the south coast 137 Squadron attacked E-Boats and other coastal vessels on the northern flank of the invasion area without loss. From the early hours of 13 June southern England was under steadily mounting attack by the new 'V-1' pilotless 'Flying Bombs', launched from the many sites in the Pas-de-Calais. While squadrons of high-performance Tempests and Mustangs were withdrawn from 2nd TAF to join the new Spitfire XIVs and Mosquitoes in facing this new threat, 137 Squadron was well-placed at Manston to intercept the 'Divers', as they were code-named. For a week 137 continued with their normal operations but on 22 June they were given permission to join in with the 'anti-Diver' patrols when their other duties permitted. The Typhoon was still a formidable interceptor at low altitude, and during the next few weeks the unit would shoot down thirty V-1s, Flying Officer 'Arty' Sames, a New Zealander, claiming five and Flight Lieutenant Brandreth, Flying Officer Holder and Pilot Officer Brain each claiming four individually.

One of 137's Australians, Warrant Officer 'Jack' Horne, having opened his score some days earlier with a 'Diver' destroyed over the Channel, was returning from an early morning shipping reconnaissance: 'I saw a flying bomb coming out from France and I turned to chase it. The "doodlebug" was doing about 380mph, but I had a slight advantage in height so I put the nose down, opened the throttle, put the pitch in fully fine and got after it. I opened fire at long range but I could see that the cannon-shells were not hitting it and the range was getting greater. In desperation I raised the nose of the Typhoon and fired four pairs of rockets at it (I'd seen no shipping on the reconnaissance). At least one of the rockets hit the bomb, because it started to break up and spun down into a field (I'd gone too far in the chase – we were supposed to break off five miles from the coast to give the Flak a chance). The following day, a Group Captain from an experimental station arrived at Manston in a Mustang, which was equipped with rockets unlike any we'd seen before. They had Bakelite heads with a photoelectric cell which would trigger the 25lb warhead if the rocket passed close to the 'doodlebug'. The Group Captain told me that the rockets had originally been intended as a make-shift anti-aircraft defence earlier in the war. They loaded my aircraft up with similar rockets which had been sent down by transport and we both stooged up and down the Channel, but no flying bombs appeared that day.'

The trials continued, however, and on 27 July Flying Officer Sames was the first to fire the special rockets in earnest. On this first attack the rockets exploded about forty feet above the 'Diver' which continued on its way, apparently unharmed. The following night Flight Lieutenant Doug Brandreth took off in a similarly armed Typhoon; after several unsuccessful attempts he managed to make an interception south-east of Folkestone, of a 'Diver' flying at 3,000 feet and 320mph IAS. Launching one pair of rockets from 5–600 yards astern, he too saw them explode above the 'Diver', but this time the light from the jet exhaust went out and the V-1 crashed into the sea. This was the only effective use of this imaginative weapon. Because of the involvement of most other squadrons in Normandy, 137 would remain the only Typhoon unit committed against the flying bombs throughout the summer.

The arrival of the V-1s did however lead to some diversion of effort from targets in Normandy during July, the 2nd TAF fighter-bombers frequently flying north to attack the launching sites during the month, while remaining coastal radar stations were also put back on the target list. When coupled with the primary ground-support duties, as the armies in the beachhead struggled to break out with a succession of offensives around the Caen area, the month proved busy for the Typhoons once again, though not as costly as had June; less than sixty aircraft were lost on operations this month.

The sojourn in Normandy of the first 84 Group squadrons had been brief; within days 123 Wing was forced to return to Hurn due to B.10 having become waterlogged following heavy rain, and also having come under regular shellfire. 136 and 146 Wings both also moved to Hurn, consolidating all the Group's close-support aircraft at this single airfield for a week or so. B.15 was now used as a forward refuelling base until the units once again began moving over to the Normandy airfields on a more permanent basis.

More changes came about as the move to France was continued. It was by now clear that seven wings of Typhoons of varying sizes were not administratively effective. On 10 July, 263 Squadron was posted to 2nd TAF from England, to join 136 Wing; within days it was dispatched to 18 Armament Practice Camp at Eastchurch, but on completion of this course, returned to find that its new Wing was about to be disbanded! Instead, 263 went to 146 Wing at the start of August, while 164 and 183 Squadrons were posted to bring 123 Wing up to four-squadron strength. At the same time Wing Commander Dring moved over from 136 to take over from 123 Wing's leader, Wing Commander Brooker, who was rested from operations. In 83 Group, meanwhile, 129 Wing was also disbanded, the lone Typhoon squadron, 184, then being posted to 121 Wing.

All five remaining Typhoon Wings were now operating from a very small area indeed; the crowded strips and airspace were still harrassed by occasional shelling and strafing German fighters, while despite spraying with old oil, dust made aircraft movements hazardous.

There were a number of accidents, one of the more serious occurring on 7 July at B.6, where only prompt action by ground staff prevented a disaster. Flight Lieutenant Allison of 181 Squadron was hit by Flak but

made it back to base; unfortunately a leg wound left him unable to control his damaged Typhoon adequately during his landing and he ran into a group of eight fully armed 247 Squadron Typhoons, parked ready for the next sortie. Immediately the aircraft began to burn. While ground crew and pilots hurriedly arranged the doomed Typhoons so that their rockets pointed in relatively harmless directions and taxied others to safety, Flight Lieutenant Harboard of Flying Control, aided by Leading Air-craftsman Eason, braved the flames to drag clear the unfortunate Allison, who survived his burns; Flight Lieutenant Harboard received the MBE. Despite exploding rockets, cannon-shells, flares and petrol, the prompt action had kept 247's losses down to three aircraft.

Throughout July and into August the round of 'armed recces' and pre-assigned target strikes continued, targets varying from the keenly sought tanks and transport, to troop concentrations or ammunition dumps merely identified as map references to be attacked. Sometimes the results were spectacular, as on 1 August when several formations were instructed to attack tank concentrations in the Bois du Hommet. The attacking pilots could only claim three damaged but the next day the Army found thirty tanks had been destroyed, of which twenty were credited to the Typhoons.

While close support was the primary consideration, interdiction also became of increasing importance. Now, while Spitfires patrolled overhead to keep the Luftwaffe off the backs of the ground-attack aircraft, and Mustangs flew far into the interior to hit convoys on their way to the area, the Typhoons concentrated much of their efforts against the zone immediately behind the battle area to prevent build-up and resupply of the defenders.

The squadrons equipped with rockets sought to use these against the many targets

available, whilst those units still carrying bombs, made diving attacks with pairs of either 500lb missiles, or – on increasingly frequent occasions – big 1,000-pounders. The Canadian Wing in particular used these against vital bridges over the River Orne. As in the costly weeks before D-Day, it was the concentrated and deadly automatic Flak which was still the Typhoon's most danger-ous enemy; it was the presence and strength of Flak and other ground fire which was to determine the form of attack made by Typhoons, particularly the rocket-armed aircraft. One new tactic, first employed in 2nd TAF on 17 July, was destined to be widely used and made famous by Typhoons – 'VCP' or Visual Control Post – better known as 'cab-rank'. The VCP was usually an armoured car in the front-line, manned by a Forward Air Controller and an Army Liaison Officer, in radio contact with the 'cab-rank' of patrolling fighter-bombers and local army units respectively. Flight Lieu-tenant Tom Hall, who used this system many times during his tour with 175 Squad-ron, describes the way it worked:

'Direct support for the Army was con-trolled by a VCP with the advancing troops. In our aircraft we carried gridded maps and initial indication of the target was given by reference to these. When we arrived at the scene the Controller would indicate where the rockets were to be placed by firing mortar-shells, which gave off coloured smoke, on the target. In organizing the attack you had to take into account the position of the sun, the surface wind, and the respective positions of the troops ac-cording to the 'bomb-line' (i.e., the line between the two armies – quite theoretical at times). And you had to be wary of the Germans firing similarly coloured smoke-shells on our boys as soon as our own smoke-shells had indicated their target.' The system worked well and allowed very close support to be given with relative safety.

Top left: Some of 137 squadron's successful anti-'Diver' pilots at Manston in July 1944. In the centre is Flying Officer 'Arty' Sames, a New Zealander who has perviously flown with 486 squadron, the sole Typhoon V-1 'ace' (5 kills). (IWM)

Centre left: Having successfully evaded capture and returned to the UK after being shot down over France in August 1943, Flying Officer Ron Dench (left) returned to France with 182 Squadron. JR513 had originally served with 182 Squadron as 'XM-K', Flight Lieutenant C. D. North-Lewis's aircraft; it went with him to 181 Squadron on his promotion to squadron leader, but was later returned to 182 Squadron as 'XM-N'. (D. J. Coxhead)

Left: Usually captioned as '609 Squadron and Rommel's HQ', this photograph in fact shows Squadron Leader Mike Ingle-Finch (pointing) and pilots of 175 Squadron examining the results of their extremely effective attack on a château north of Caen, on 8 July 1944. (IWM)

Right: A 438 Squadron Typhoon, MN426 'F3-H', being serviced at B.9, Lantheuil. This aircraft was lost on 15 August 1944 when it hit a tree while ground strafing and spun in, killing the pilot. In the foreground, 1,000lb bombs, the normal offensive load for the bombers by this time. (IWM)

July saw two rather more sustained engagements with the Luftwaffe – both with the same German unit. On the 13th Wing Commander Baldwin led a trio of 197 Squadron aircraft on an armed reconnaissance towards the Seine, 257 Squadron following close behind to attack rail yards at Verneuil. One of the 197 Squadron pilots, Pilot Officer Ken Trott, spotted a half-track and requested permission to attack. 'I went down with Johnny Rook and we both attacked the half-track with cannon-fire. I then heard Wing Commander Baldwin call on the R/T to the effect that they were in the middle of about thirty 109s. We climbed to about 4,000 feet and met the 109s, in and out of cloud. I made one attack and then turned to make a head-on attack against another 109. This proved fatal as we collided and I was thrown out of my aircraft at about 2,500 feet; I pulled my ripcord and passed out. I came to hanging from a tree with several Germans standing round.'

While Ken Trott was attacking his Bf 109, Flying Officer Johnny Rook had latched onto the one on Trott's tail. As he was about to enter cloud: 'I was hit in the rear fuselage by 20mm ground fire. I broke away

to avoid this and not seeing any further aircraft decided to return to base. I came down out of cloud and was suddenly bounced by a 109. The first I knew of the attack was seeing 20mm fire passing my cockpit and hitting the wings. I threw all the controls in one corner and opened the throttle wide with full fine pitch. The engine responded perfectly, I screamed round after the 109 and saw him suddenly stall and spin off. By this time I was so close to the ground I am sure he went straight into the deck.'

When he landed he found seventeen 20mm cannon-shells had hit the wings – one in the main spar – and there were holes in the propeller and gouges out of both sides of the engine cowling. The Bf 109s of I/JG 5, had been led by a great 'Experte' from the Eastern front, Hauptman Theodore Weissenberger, who personally claimed two shot down, while Obergefreiter August Mors claimed a third. Although outnumbered, the Typhoon pilots had fought back, Wing Commander Baldwin and Flight Sergeant Shannon of 257 Squadron each claiming a Bf 109 shot down, while the latter unit claimed one more probable and four damaged. At least one Messerschmitt is known

to have gone down, Leutnant Dieter Sachse baling out. 257 Squadron also lost one Typhoon, Flight Sergeant Marriot baling out into captivity, but he was liberated when Bayeux fell to the Allies.

Six days later I/JG 5, this time accompanied by elements of Stab and III/JG1, were again out in the evening, over the St-Quentin–Le Havre–Bernay area, when Typhoons were once more seen below. This time it was another of 146 Wing's units, 266 Squadron, on an armed reconnaissance to the Lisieux area, and the fighter-bombers were taken badly by surprise, three Typhoons and their pilots being lost, while Pilot Officer Forrester managed to claim a single victory in return. The JG 5 pilots overestimated somewhat on this occasion, Weissenberger claiming three personally to bring his own tally to 197 victories, while Mors, newly promoted Leutnant, claimed two more to reach a personal score of 57, and Leutnant A. Lehner added another as his 37th victory. Not all the unit's pilots were apparently as aggressive as these three, the British listening service reporting that Weissenberger was heard to become quite hysterical, screaming at two reluctant pilots

Left: Pilots of 197 Squadron at Needs Oar Point in June 1944. Left to right: Pilot Officer Johnny Rook, Pilot Officer 'Dumbo' Taylor, Pilot Officer Bob Jones, RCAF, and Flying Officer Bruce Gilbert. (B. L. Gilbert)

Below: Flight Sergeant N. L. Gordon of 440 Squadron was forced to make a wheels-up landing due to an undercarriage malfunction. His aircraft, MN413 'I8-T' is seen here being recovered by a Repair and Salvage Unit; it was later returned to service with 184 Squadron. (IWM)

Top right: Wing Commander Charles Green of 121 Wing setttles into the cockpit of his 'CG' (possibly MN666) at Holmsley South, June 1944. (N. B. Wilson)

Centre and bottom right: Hit by Flak near Vire on 7 August 1944, Flying Officer A. W. Kilpatrick was forced to land MN535 'DP-A' half a mile inside enemy lines. He was eventually captured and taken deeper into occupied territory, but on the sixth night managed to escape during an Allied dive-bombing attack. While taking shelter in a ditch he encountered five German soldiers, who were persuaded to act as his escort back to Allied lines, in exchange for safe conduct on the other side! After nine days behind the lines he (together with his 'guards' who now numbered 27!) managed to make contact with advancing Allied columns. (Centre Jean-Pierre Benamou, Bottom D. H. G. Ince)

in his Gruppe to come down and join in the fight, threatening to shoot them down if they refused! It seems that again one of the unit's Messerschmitts was lost, the pilot baling out unhurt.

Between these two combats, on 17 July the German Supreme Commander in the West, General Feldmarschall Erwin Rommel was severely injured, suffering a fractured skull when his staff car was strafed and driven off the road by British fighters. Responsibility for this attack remains disputed, claimed both for Typhoons of 193 Squadron led by Wing Commander Baldwin and by Spitfires of 602 Squadron led by the South African 'ace' Squadron Leader Chris Lerroux. The latter claim is believed to be the more likely.

On 7 August early morning mists obscured the first movements of a fullscale German counter-attack in the countryside around Mortain. Spearheaded by five Panzer divisions, the attack was opposed by only two US Infantry divisions. By midday the mists had cleared, but the 2nd SS Panzer Division had taken Mortain, while the Wehrmacht's 2nd Panzer Division had captured three key villages, threatening to cut off General George Patton's US Third Army as it began moving into Brittany. It is now known that this German thrust did not present the menacing situation apparent at the time; it did however hold the key to the Allied breakout from Normandy. Forewarned by the highly secret 'Ultra' Intelligence (from decoded German signal traffic), the Allied commanders were content to draw the German forces, and particularly their armour, into a trap of their own making. In a superb example of Allied co-operation it was agreed, in advance, that as USAAF tactical support aircraft (P-38s and P-47s) were equipped only to carry bombs, and were thus not so well-placed to counter armoured vehicles, 2nd TAF's rocket-firing Typhoons would attack the armour while the US Ninth AF would restrict their own fighter-bombers to the enemy transport moving to and from the battle zone. In addition, the Americans would provide a defensive screen of fighters, to keep the Luftwaffe at bay.

Wing Commander Green returned from a reconnaissance of the battle area, reporting the presence of 300 tanks, and lost no time in organizing his 121 Wing. 174 Squadron was the first airborne, departing B.5 at 1215 hours, with 181 Squadron from B.6 following just ten minutes later. The pilots spotted fifty or sixty tanks and 200 vehicles lining the road from St-Barthélemy to Chérencé; using classic fighter-bomber tactics they halted the column by attacking the lead and rear vehicles, and then set about those between. Meanwhile another two squadrons were getting airborne, and by 1400 hours a 'shuttle-service' had developed,

△1

△5

△2

△6

△3 ▽4

△7 ▽8

Left: Normandy 'Op'
1. The 'Wingco' briefs 193 Squadron . . .
2. 1530 hours, Squadron Leader Button is first away from B.3, St Croix.
3. 1530 hours, and an already anxious 'Chiefy' awaits the Squadron's return.
4. 1600 hours, they're back – MN602 'DP-H' is first to touch down.
5. Phew! The 'Boss' indicates the Squadron had a hot reception.
6. The pilots discuss who had hit the target . . .
7. . . . and then pass the 'gen' on to the 'Spy'.
8. The 'Groupie' hears how the 'show' went. (D. H. G. Ince)

with another squadron of Typhoons in the air every twenty minutes, seeking their targets, making their attack, and returning to refuel and rearm. The brunt of the sorties were made by 83 Group squadrons, especially those of 121 and 124 Wings. Although 84 Group Tiffies made some sorties at Mortain, their main task remained the rest of the front. Here, aided by some 124 Wing squadrons diverted from Mortain, they dealt with another Panzer attack which developed at Vire. The USAAF had been true to its word and the Luftwaffe fighters got no nearer than 25 miles from Mortain.

Flak was not as bad as that frequently experienced from prepared positions, and losses in the Mortain area amounted to just three aircraft, with one pilot killed. One of the others, however, had a miraculous escape; Flight Lieutenant Bob Lee of 245 Squadron was hit by Flak, lost consciousness, and when he came round found that his Typhoon had ploughed into the ground upside down, in no-man's land. He managed to release his harness but was trapped in his aircraft, where he was to spend the next five days. During that time the Germans used the wreck for target practice; he was hit in the hand and leg and on one occasion a fire started, but fortunately it soon went out. Just in time, he was found by an American unit clearing the battlefield, when they pulled the Typhoon from the grave it had dug for itself and almost for its pilot.

By dusk on the 7th, nearly 300 sorties had been flown in the Mortain area and claims against tanks totalled 84 'flamers', 35 'smokers' and 21 damaged. Claims made against enemy transport amounted to 54-19-39. There has been much controversy about the accuracy of these and other similar claims in recent years, particularly in relation to the efficacy of the Typhoon/rocket combination as a 'tank-buster'. If examination of battlefield debris showed less than the expected number of rocket victims, several factors should be borne in mind:

(i) The difficulty of pilot assessment of RP attacks; camera-gun film rarely showed rocket strikes since by the time they hit the target the Typhoon was already taking evasive action.

(ii) Visual assessment was constantly hampered by smoke, dust and the general confusion of battle.

(iii) The likelihood of repeated attacks being made on tanks already destroyed and claimed previously.

(iv) The efficiency of the German battlefield recovery service.

A factor difficult to assess accurately but very significant, was that of the effect of repeated rocket attacks on enemy morale. During the battle pilots reported crews abandoning their tanks and running for cover and this was also observed, with glee, by US ground forces. Interrogation of prisoners showed that they were extremely nervous of RP attacks.

Perhaps the only fair conclusion is that in the hands of an average pilot, in the turmoil of battle, the rocket-Typhoon was not a precision anti-tank weapon. Nevertheless on numerous occasions it proved to be extremely effective in dealing with troublesome armour and the Typhoon squadrons were recipients of frequent 'strawberries' (the opposite of 'raspberries') from the Army in gratitude for their close support, which was the aircraft's true forte. It should also be remembered by those intent on impugning the Typhoons' efficiency in Normandy, that if the battlefield research teams were correct and the 20mm cannon caused the greatest measurable damage (by crippling enemy transport and supplies), the Typhoon carried twice as many of these as the other main 2nd TAF fighter-bomber, the Spitfire, and was a far more accurate gun platform. As to the situation at Mortain, the Typhoons had certainly been the weapon which crushed the enemy armour and destroyed all German hopes of a successful counter-attack. At 1940 hours on that day a signal from the Chief of Staff of the 7th German Army was intercepted, in which he was forced to admit that the attack had been at a standstill since 1300 hours due to 'employment of fighter-bombers by the enemy and the absence of our own air support'. No greater accolade than this is necessary, and must surely be accepted as incontrovertible proof of the effectiveness of the Typhoon Wings on this occasion.

Coupled with the long, slogging battle to which the British and Canadian Armies had held the main German forces further north, the defeat at Mortain put a virtual end to the defence of Normandy. Following up Von Kluge's retreating forces, the US First Army moved forward, making contact with British Second Army on its left. Heavy attacks on the German defences were made that night by a strong force of Bomber Command Lancasters and Halifaxes, the Canadians then attacking towards Falaise. To the south the US Third Army now gathered momentum, taking Le Mans on the 9th and then Argentan on the 13th, only fifteen miles south-east of Falaise. There was now a strong possibility of surrounding the German 7th Army, and Field Marshal Bernard Montgomery ordered the Canadians to attack again on the 14th in an effort to meet Patton's spearheads at Argentan. 2nd TAF close-support aircraft headed the Canadian attack, while Bomber Command raided Falaise, almost reducing the town to a heap of impassable rubble. By 18 August only a small gap remained at Chambois, where the Germans fought desperately to prevent the 'pocket' being closed. Now the fighter-bombers came into their own again, and throughout mid-August the 7th Army's columns, trapped in the narrow lanes of Normandy, were repeatedly attacked and suffered the most fearful carnage. The density of ground fire above the packed targets was very heavy, however, and Typhoon

Below: Flight Lieutenant Bob Lee survived five days trapped inside the cockpit of MN 459 'MR-R', seen here after it had been dragged clear of its crater by a battlefield clearance team. (Jean-Pierre Benamou)

losses during August were to reach an all-time high for the war, with more than ninety total losses on operations, and many others damaged. Peak losses occurred on 18 August when seventeen Typhoons failed to return and a dozen pilots lost their lives. The majority of these were caused by Flak or small-arms fire, for while the Luftwaffe was thrown in over the Falaise area in a desperate attempt to aid their hard-pressed comrades on the ground, they were cut to pieces by the Allied fighters above, and on only two occasions were they able to break through to the fighter-bombers; total losses inflicted by them on the Typhoon units did not even reach double figures. Nearly all these engagements occurred on 17 August, the first in the early afternoon when eight 183 Squadron aircraft set off on an armed reconnaissance between Le Neubourg and the Evreux area. North-west of Bernay, Bf 109s of III/JG 27 attacked, shooting down four and damaging a fifth Typhoon; one of the successful German pilots was Oberfeldwebel Fritz Gromotka, who made his 28th claim during this combat. On the receiving end was Flight Sergeant John Davidson:

'We were looking for transport escaping from the Falaise area and we split up in pairs. I spotted some trucks pulled up under trees; I pointed them out to Geoff (Flight Lieutenant Campbell-Brown) but he couldn't see them, so he said, "You go down, I'll follow you." I started to make my attack when I saw some aircraft milling about to our right, high up. I warned Geoff and as I dived I glanced up and saw them all coming down at us and recognized them – I instinctively called out, "Oh Christ they're 109s!" Geoff said, "Turn for cloud," which was on our port side, away from them, but I said, "No, turn into them," which I did as they were coming down. I went straight up through about a dozen, without firing and without them firing at me. Then Geoff called up to say he had four on his tail, so I pulled hard round to find him but I couldn't see him, and I had four coming down after me! I out-turned them and went through them, firing head-on at one, and then pulled up, hoping to God that they didn't do the same. Then I was in cloud, but I never heard from Geoff again.'

Flight Sergeant Ron Brown survived a last-second bale-out and burns, to be hidden by the French until liberated a week later. In subsequent engagements one Typhoon of 184 Squadron was shot down by Fw 190s over Vimoutiers, in which area an aircraft of 197 Squadron was also lost to Bf 109s – probably that claimed by Major Ernst Düllberg of III/JG 27 for his 38th victory. 266 Squadron was also attacked by Fw 190s which shot down one Typhoon and badly damaged a second; two of the Focke-Wulfs were claimed damaged. One of the aircraft shot down by Fw 190s was claimed

Left: Squadron Leader Paul Ezanno (Free French), commanding officer of 198 Squadron in Normandy, a very experienced pilot who had taken a step down from Wing Commander to have the honour of leading a 2nd TAF Squadron in the liberation of his homeland. (via H. Linter)

Below: Squadron Leader Ezanno usually flew 'TP-E', which from July to September 1944 was MN882. Note the code-letters repeated on the fin and under the spinner; the 'Invasion stripes' appear to have been 'toned down'. (M. Robinson)

Bottom: One of the many Flak victims during 'Falaise gap' operations, was Flight Lieutenant 'Eddie' Edwards, 245 Squadron's new 'A' Flight commander, who managed to put JR429 'MR-A' down in a cornfield near Trun, just inside Allied territory. (Jean-Pierre Benamou)

Right: It wasn't all action – 175 Squadron pilots pass the time with a game of cards at their dispersal on B.5. (P. H. Baden)

Centre right: Soon after the Typhoons began operating in Normandy it was realized that 'Invasion stipes' rendered the aircraft too visible on the ALGs. Accordingly the stripes were painted out on the upper surfaces of wings and fuselages. Most units, with apparent exception of 124 and 143 Wings, favoured black spinners. MN582, 'HH-A' of 175 Squadron, which was usually flown by Flying Officer Peter Baden, shows the typical markings. (P. H. Baden)

Below: During the German retreat several of the Typhoon bomber squadrons dropped 'nickels' (also known as 'bumph bombs'), one of which is here being loaded with leaflets urging surrender. (IWM)

Flight Lieutenant 'Poppa' Ambrose kept the heads of the Flak gunners down until he landed safely. Then while hiding in woods the undergrowth was sprayed with machine-gun fire by the searching Germans. Eventually captured, he was tied to a tree and twice faced summary execution only to be rescued in the nick of time by passing officers. Then during evacuation in a convoy he found himself under attack by his own squadron! In front of his lorry was a Tiger tank, and when the first rockets were launched, it surged forward in a frantic attempt to evade the attack, flattening the staff car, and its occupants, which was blocking its way.

In their desperation to escape, growing numbers of vehicles posed as ambulances, laying Red Cross flags across their roofs. This had been noted as early as 12 August, and on the 14th the Supreme Allied Commander directed that such vehicles, despite clear evidence of misuse, were not to be attacked. There was a 'let-out' however, for this did not preclude self-defence if fired on and frequently 'ambulances', impostors or not, were attacked without mercy. On the 18th, Flying Officer Bill Grey of 181 Squadron was leading a section near Livarot:

'I received a direct hit under the cockpit from what I think must have been an 88mm shell. The cockpit filled with scorching fumes and I baled out the best I could – a leg hit the tailplane – and I landed in a cornfield surrounded by trees. In some pain from burns on the face and arms, I limped over to figures beckoning, who I took to be French 'underground', but to my despair I was surrounded by German soldiers. In the evening I was placed in an ambulance with four German stretcher cases. A French youth gestured for me to lie on the floor; I was puzzled by this but an hour later understood. The convoy was attacked by a Spitfire and our ambulance received a 5-second burst of 20mm cannon-fire. Inside was carnage. I was hit in both legs and the left shoulder; I don't know if the Germans survived.' After treatment Bill Grey was left in Bernay by the retreating Germans.

On the 19th most of the action was around Vimoutiers and of the eleven Typhoons lost this day, seven were missing in that area. It was here that Flight Sergeant Cliff Pole, was flying No. 2 to Flight Sergeant Ted Jarvis of 181 Squadron: 'During the Falaise campaign it was the custom for squadrons to dispatch their aircraft in pairs as opposed to the usual eight-aircraft sections. Each pair would scour the battle area looking for targets. Cliff and myself arrived in the battle area and eventually spotted a small column of enemy vehicles, including tanks, near the town. We made several passes firing rockets in pairs, and cannon. I fired my final pair and did the usual climbing turn to look back and down, and saw a

by Feldwebel Soldner of I/JG 2 for his seventh victory.

All day on the 18th, the Allied fighter-bombers poured a murderous hail of bombs, rockets, cannon- and machine-gun fire on the German forces massed in the jaws of the gap, between Trun and Chambois. By late afternoon hundreds of military vehicles of all kinds were forming huge jams outside Vimoutiers, and the 83 Group Typhoons zeroed in on this area. Soon the roads were blocked by blazing trucks, while drivers of those still serviceable sought to escape by driving cross-country. The desperation of those trapped in the long columns as they came under air attack was experienced at first hand by more than one Typhoon pilot. Flight Lieutenant Cedric Henman of 175 Squadron had been forced to bale out of his crippled Typhoon near Falaise on the 14th; he bore a charmed life. As he descended

tank on fire. Almost immediately Cliff's Typhoon hit the deck and exploded. He had been close behind me and had obviously been hit by Flak. Just then I saw his parachute floating to earth – he must have made a very rapid exit from his cockpit! My own aircraft had also been hit and the cockpit filled with an oily mist which settled on the interior of the canopy, instruments, clothes, etc. I had to wind my canopy back and fly as slowly as possible back to B.6 with my head outside the cockpit.' Despite the chaotic retreat, the Flak gunners were still on the mark.

As Polish and Canadian forces sought to complete the closure on the 20th, the Germans attacked them with local armour superiority in the Vimoutiers area. Wing Commander Dring led 32 Typhoons from 123 Wing to attack, breaking up the concentrations with precision attacks under VCP control. Thirteen tanks were claimed and Dring was awarded an immediate DSO. Attacks on the many targets in the pocket continued until the 25th, by which time there was little left worthy of further effort. Once clear of the gap itself there was still no respite for the retreating hordes as they were pounded again in bottlenecks at Orbec, Bernay and Broglie. Subsequent Army investigations showed again that the greatest damage had been done by cannon-fire which had destroyed or disabled large numbers of vehicles, including the more lightly armoured halftracks and armoured personnel carriers, and inflicted damage on self-propelled artillery. The number of tanks actually destroyed by the rockets and bombs was not as high as had at first been thought, although whenever a rocket had struck home on a tank, destruction had been complete. Of the estimated total of 12,000 vehicles abandoned in France, about one-third were reckoned to have been destroyed by direct air attack, but many others had been abandoned in panic or had run out of fuel.

In air support, identification of friendly and enemy forces is always a problem and in the fluid situation around Falaise this was especially so. There were unfortunate instances of Typhoons attacking Polish armoured forces, who retaliated by shooting one down. American fighter-bombers also attacked Canadian troops in error. However, the most tragic incident did not occur on the battlefield. On 27 August, fifteen Typhoons of 263 and 266 Squadrons, led by Wing Commander Baldwin, located six ships heading south-west off Etretat. Suspecting that they were Allied, Baldwin queried their identity with Operations, but was told that there was no Allied shipping in the area, and to attack. Despite querying the instruction a further three times and describing the coloured signals fired, the order was still to attack. The Typhoons swept in

and opened fire with cannon and rockets; the four minesweepers and two trawlers were indeed British and the onslaught was devastating. None of the ships escaped without damage or casualties, but the brunt of the attack was borne by three of the minesweepers, two of which were sunk and the third so badly damaged that it was eventually scrapped. Of the Royal Navy crews, 78 were killed and 149 wounded, although these figures include casualties caused by German shelling of the survivors. This horrendous incident had been caused by a failure to communicate a change of course by the minesweeping flotilla to Naval HQ, who therefore did not expect any shipping in the area and authorized the attack. No attempt was made to lay blame at the RAF's door. Those who doubt the effectiveness of rockets should heed the words of the Commander of the surviving minesweeper in his official report: 'It is felt that the fury and ferocity of concerted attacks by a number of Typhoon aircraft armed with rockets and cannon is an ordeal that has to be endured to be truly appreciated.'

Now as the remnants of 7th Army sought to flee across the Seine, all efforts by the Air Force were turned on the river crossings and the last remaining bridges; indeed the last permanent bridge still standing over this river was destroyed by 146 Wing Typhoons at this time. This was virtually the end of German resistance in France. On 15 August, US and French forces had landed in the south on the Mediterranean coast, and on the 25th, Paris was liberated by its own citizens as the Germans began withdrawing and as the French Armoured Division sped to the city. Next day British Second Army crossed the Seine at Vernon and began a dash into Belgium, towards the vital port of Antwerp. The chase was on and over the next few weeks movement would be rapid, as the front continually moved beyond the range of the fighter-bombers.

While the operations of July and August had been at their height, two of 146 Wing's bomb-carrying units, 257 and 266 Squadrons, had been sent to England to Armament Practice Camp to learn the use of rockets. At the same time the last of the ADGB Typhoon units, 137 Squadron, arrived in France to join 124 Wing. With the increase in size of the Wings, the command position was upgraded to group captain rank (the large 146 Wing was already commanded by Group Captain Denys Gillam), and Wing Commander Charles Green, Wing Leader of 121 Wing, was promoted to command 124 Wing, his place being taken by Wing Commander Pitt-Brown who had been 174 Squadron's commander, and who had previously led a Mohawk Wing in Burma.

Late in August, 121 and 143 Wings had moved to B.24 at St-André de l'Eure, while

124 Wing went to B.30 at Creton. By the third day of September they had moved to Beauvais and Glissy, then to Tille and Vitry, before moving to Moirainville and Merville. For 146 Wing there was no forward airfield available, so the Wing returned to England, operating from Manston over the French and Belgian coastal areas, attacking bypassed German garrisons in the ports, and continuing to support Canadian First Army as it held the far left of the advance, moving up the coastal belt into Belgium. Soon however a base in Belgium was available, and during 11 and 12 September, 146 Wing moved to B.51 at Lille/Vendeville. By the 17th Antwerp was in British hands and 121 Wing moved to B.70 at Antwerp/Deurne. During this period the retreating Germans were continuously harried; on 10 September Wing Commander Bill Pitt-Brown led his old squadron, 174, in a most effective attack on a pair of large barges which were attempting to cross the Westerschelde: 'We saw two large self-propelled barges leaving Terneuzen, absolutely crammed to the gunnels with Huns. We waited until they were in the middle of the estuary, so as we would be at maximum distance from the Flak on both banks, and then ran in towards them, parallel to the banks. We hit them with everything we had. It was a gin-clear day and you could see every shade of blue and brown in the estuary, but as they sank the water round the barges turned pink. The carnage was terrible.'

In mid-September British forces were into Holland, while the US armies had pressed right across France to the German frontier, coming up against the Siegfried Line fortifications. The long German retreat was over and soon the Typhoons would be fighting a rather different war.

Right: A Canadian Typhoon dive-bomber of 439 Squadron, PD603 '5V-H', photographed at B.24, St-André, where 143 Wing spent just four days during the rapid advance following the breakout from Normandy. (E. McKay)

Right: 198 Squadron pilots gathered round Flight Lieutenant Denis Sweeting's Typhoon at B.70, Deurne – the pre-war Antwerp civil airfield. MN951 'TP-A' (which previously had been coded 'TP-K') carried the apt name 'The Uninvited', inspired by the Hollywood film of that title. (via R. Decobeck)

Right: Wing Commander Bill Pitt-Brown, Wing Leader 121 Wing, in the cockpit of 'WP-B' (believed to be MN255) at B.80, Volkel in October 1944. (E. Little)

Left: Flight Sergeants 'Ted' Jarvis and Cliff Pole of 181 Squadron, in front of MN640 'EL-C' in August 1944 (E. C. Jarvis)

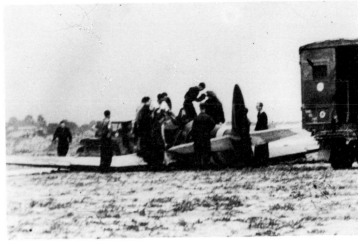

Above: On 10 August 1944, Flying Officer Geoff Murphy of 245 Squadron made an emergency landing at B.5 with one undercarriage leg hanging down. . . .

'I was flying as No. 2 to the CO, Jack Collins, and we commenced to dive on the target – a château being used as 21st Panzer Division HQ – at an angle of 55 or 60 degrees. Heavy Flak was streaming up at us. In a way it semi-hypnotises you, but as you are concentrating on what you are doing, and it's all flashing past, you are unaware of the danger until you are hit. On this occasion, I heard and felt a tremendous thump under the port wing. The aircraft immediately started to yaw to port, taking me straight through the CO's slipstream and my aircraft was being peppered by what I thought was shrapnel; I quickly realized that this was cannon-shell cases and ammunition links from Jack's cannon. I now began to panic as my airspeed was in excess of 500mph and even with the control column fully back, I could not pull out of the dive. I jettisoned my rockets and in desperation kicked on full left rudder to try to yaw the nose up towards the horizon.

The nose at last started to come up and I then noticed a red light, indicating that the port undercarriage leg was hanging down. As the airspeed reduced with the nose rising, the controls became more normal and I was able to roll out to level flight at just under 1,500ft. On the way back to B.5 the CO flew close alongside and confirmed that the port undercarriage

radius arm was shattered, advising me to make a wheels-up landing.

After the rest of the Squadron had landed, I joined the circuit and commenced my pre-landing drills. I had just turned downwind when the Wing Commander Flying, Charles Green, called on the R/T and started double checking the drills I was carrying out. He was obviously trying to assist, but only served to confuse, as we both missed the essential drill of jettisoning the cockpit canopy on approach! This was presumably because, as a result of the dense dust clouds on the strip, we had formed the habit of taking-off and landing with the canopies closed. As it was, because I feared I might hit my head on the canopy during the landing, I lowered my seat and thought nothing more about it! Turning on to finals, I lined up clear of the runway tracking so as not to rip it up, turned off the fuel and switches and as I touched down, up came the port wheel. The aircraft came to a grinding halt in a great cloud of dust which shut out the light – I thought it was smoke – and went to wind back the canopy, but of course the rails had twisted and it wouldn't budge as the rails had twisted. Then panic set in again – I'm trapped in this thing and it is going to catch fire! Fortunately Mike Parkes, our engineering officer, came shooting out in a jeep with the best-looking crowbar I've ever seen and managed to lever it off . . .'

(1–5 IWM, 6 G. Murphy)

CHAPTER NINE
Holland and Germany

IN a desperate effort to keep the momentum of the advance going, a major airborne operation, 'Market Garden', was launched from England on 17 September. US paratroopers were dropped at Grave and Nijmegen, and the British 1st Airborne Division at Arnhem, to capture bridges across the Maas, Waal and Rhine. Prior to the drop 107 Typhoon sorties were flown to neutralize gun positions, but 2nd TAF fighter-bombers were not allowed over the dropping-zone when the actual landings were taking place. Simultaneously XXX Corps, spearheaded by the Guards Armoured Division, were to thrust northwards to link up with the airborne forces. Their advance was preceded by a rolling barrage, and 'cab-rank' Typhoons were on hand to lend aid as required. In fact they began by contributing a rolling barrage of their own – for the first hour new formations of Typhoons arrived every five minutes to make successive strikes. After that more normal 'cab-rank' operations were resumed, sometimes operating within 200 yards of the advancing Guards. Unfortunately, on the 18th, the weather over their bases in Belgium much reduced the support given by the Typhoons, and on the 19th it was even worse. The Allied advance was slowed by determined opposition, and in Arnhem the 1st Airborne hung on to their positions against unexpectedly strong enemy forces. Grave and Nijmegen were taken, but after a hard, costly fight, Arnhem was retained by the Germans. Because the operation had been controlled from England, and because weather was frequently poor, there was little the Typhoons or other 2nd TAF aircraft could do to help.

The advance had, however, made new bases available in Holland, and on 22 September 124 Wing landed at Eindhoven (B.78). The arrival in Holland was particularly significant for two of the pilots, Flying Officers van Zinnicq Bergmann and Wiersum, for it was their homeland. 'Fricky' Wiersum recalls: 'All the squadrons of the Wing had been on ops in the Arnhem area and when we returned to Eindhoven one of the first aircraft to land pranged. We circled with three squadrons waiting for the strip to be cleared and in the meantime it was getting dark and a lot of us didn't feel too happy. Wing Commander Flying, North-Lewis, gave instructions for us to put on navigation lights. Very few were switched on, whereupon there was a curt transmission from the Wing Commander as to where the switch was located! All went on and there we were circling like a Christmas tree. That night aircraft were left all over the airfield!'

Three days later 143 Wing joined 124 at Eindhoven and by the end of the month 121 Wing were settling in at Volkel (B.80), further to the north-east.

Now, with the advance spreading across north-west Europe, the units of 83 and 84 Groups had at last parted company. While 121, 124, and 143 Wings continued to give close support to British Second Army into Holland and along the German frontier, 123 and 146 Wings, flying from bases in northern France and Belgium, were much involved attacking the by-passed garrisons, and targets around the Scheldt estuary and on Walcheren Island, German possession of which was still preventing the use of Antwerp's port facilities by the Allies. Coastal shipping was also attacked. On 29 September the Canadians besieging Calais arranged a 24-hour truce with the German garrison, to allow evacuation of civilians and casualties, and following success at Boulogne a week earlier, it was decided to use Typhoons to intimidate the defenders into a possible surrender. Half an hour before the truce was due to expire, 183 Squadron arrived to orbit the town in menacing fashion. One of the flights was led by Flight Lieutenant Alan Cocks, RAAF:

'The German gunners' watches must have been fast, or they couldn't resist opening up on the planes they disliked so intensely. I received a direct hit from 40mm Flak on the right tailplane, shattering the elevator and bending up some of the metal skin which, acting like an elevator, forced the aircraft to climb. Had the shot been about twelve inches to the left it would have destroyed the complete tail assembly, but as it happened, the left elevator was still functioning and by pushing on the control column with both hands I was able to keep the plane flying more or less straight and level. As I had no trim control, the cable having been cut, I did not attempt to use flaps or undercarriage, but made a belly-landing back at Merville.'

The 83 Group units were now able to operate over German soil, where the newly arrived 137 Squadron was soon undertaking armed reconnaissances. On 24 September this unit was attacked near Goch by 30 Fw 190s of I/JG 26, and the Norwegian CO,

Below: Flight Lieutenant Alan Cocks, an Australian with 183 Squadron, ruefully examines the damage to his Typhoon, MN871 'HF-N', at B.53, Merville, after being hit by Flak (as described in the text) on 29 September 1944. (P. G. Murton)

Squadron Leader Piltingsrud, was shot down in flames by Leutnant Ellenrieder for his twelfth victory. Two days later 175 Squadron went out after barges near Tilberg, but in the Apeldoorn area the unit was attacked by '50 plus' Bf 109s, one Typhoon being shot down by Leutnant Klaffenbach of III/JG 4. In return Warrant Officer Speedie and Captain Hopkins fired off their rockets at the Messerschmitts – without effect! Lieutenant Capstick-Dale, like Hopkins a member of the SAAF, was attacked by three or four fighters and his aircraft suffered damage. He managed to make a wheels-down landing on a forward landing-strip which was being used by Auster artillery-spotters, and from there he was picked up by one of these. As they took off, German troops opened fire, Capstick-Dale shooting back with his revolver.

In an effort to strengthen the fighter-bomber force, one of 83 Group's tactical reconnaissance units, 168 Squadron, had its Mustangs replaced by Typhoons late in September. After re-training, the unit joined the Canadian 143 Wing at Eindhoven, early in October, where it would mainly be employed flying fighter escort to the 'screamers', as the dive-bombers were sometimes known.

With the advance at an end for the time being, the Typhoon ground-attack units became more involved in interdiction work behind the German lines, attacking everything that moved by day – particularly trains and motor vehicles on the rail and road networks. This was intended not only to disrupt normal military movement, but in particular to starve the V-1 and V-2 launching sites of their supplies of bombs and fuel. The V-2 launchers were mobile and easily camouflaged, and interdiction was the only effective counter to this weapon, whose main target was now Antwerp. Among the sufferers there was 146 Wing which moved to Deurne airfield on 2 October; the worst incident occurred on the 25th when a V-2 killed five airmen and wounded six others. One of Wing Commander Baldwin's personal Typhoons (he used two – one fitted for RP, the other for bombs) was also severely damaged.

From time to time more spectacular operations came the way of the Typhoon Wings. Information from Intelligence sources led to a series of 'set piece' attacks on German HQs. These were known as 'cloak and dagger jobs' or, from the precise timing involved, 'tit shows'. On 24 October all five squadrons of 146 Wing undertook such an attack on Dordrecht, where the Dutch Resistance had pinpointed the HQ of the German 15th Army in a park in the centre of the city. The attack was planned for 1200 hours, when it was hoped that the German staff officers would be together at lunch. The attack was led by Group Captain Gillam, who marked the target by placing two smoke-bombs right in the middle of the park. A hail of rockets from 266 Squadron was followed by eight 1,000-pounders, all delivered in the target area by 193 Squadron. Then the three remaining squadrons swept in, adding 70 500-pounders to the chaos. The attack proved to have been an outstanding success, two Generals, seventeen general staff officers and 36 other officers, plus many other ranks being killed. An attack on the funeral was subsequently planned, but called off because of bad weather.

Operations since August had been over a wider area and against less concentrated defences; losses had reduced considerably, falling to 36 on operations in September and 42 in October; they would fall further to only thirty in November, very few of the casualties during these three months being due to German fighters. The exception in

Below left: Group Captain Denys Gillam briefing 146 Wing pilots before one of their operations. (197 Squadron)

Below right: Flying Officer 'Bergy' Bergmann, RNethAF, of 181 Squadron, who took part in the attack on the Dutch Royal Summer Palace. (Air Commodore R. J. E. M. Van Zinnicq Bergmann)

Bottom: Typhoons of 168 Squadron dispersed in a sea of mud at B.78, Eindhoven in December 1944; 'QC-L' was MN267. The van on the left carries the hot-air equipment used to pre-heat the Typhoon engines. (RAFM/C. E. Brown)

October occurred on the 28th when Fw 190s of II/JG 26 'bounced' aircraft of 182 Squadron near Venlo, one Typhoon being shot down in flames, although two claims were made by the Germans on this occasion, one by Major Anton Hackl for his 166th victory, and one by Leutnant Gerhard Vogt for his 45th.

At the beginning of November the Canadians assaulted Walcheren Island, strongly supported by the 84 Group Typhoons, in their now familiar 'cab-rank' role. The Typhoons flew many sorties against guns in pillboxes and larger fortifications; it was for spectacular success during one of these that Squadron Leader Rex Mulliner of 183 Squadron was awarded an immediate DFC, rockets from the attack he led having been slotted through the embrasures of the fortification. In two days Walcheren and the Breskens 'pocket', on the other side of the Scheldt estuary, were taken. This allowed the port of Antwerp to be opened, and the Allied build-up for the advance into Germany to be resumed.

Following these operations, 123 and 146 Wings concentrated their attacks on strong points in the Arnhem and Nijmegen areas, but a more unusual target on 4 November was a 'human torpedo' factory at Utrecht; this was plastered with 38 500lb bombs by 193 and 197 Squadrons led by Group Captain Gillam. Another 'cloak and dagger' job, or 'CD target' as they were now officially known, came 146 Wing's way on 19 November when Group Captain Gillam led the Wing to the Gestapo HQ in Amsterdam, but this was aborted when 10/10 cloud was encountered at 3,000 feet. The operation was laid on again one week later and this time the weather co-operated. Once more the attack was timed for the lunch-hour, with the dual purpose of safeguarding children in a nearby school and catching the Gestapo gathered together in their mess behind the HQ building. Gillam marked the target with phosphorus rockets, and there followed a co-ordinated attack by 193, 257, 263 and 266 Squadrons with rockets, 500-pounders, 1,000-pounders, and incendiary bombs. Four aircraft from 263 Squadron led by Squadron Leader Rutter made a low-level attack. His No. 2 was Flight Lieutenant 'Ronnie' Sheward, a British Argentinian, sometimes known as 'Bentos'!:

'Squadron Leader Rutter was the sort of chap you had confidence in and would follow anywhere. He was spot-on in finding the target (models of this and the surrounding area had been studied) and we went straight in at "zero" feet, crashing the bombs [fuzed for eleven seconds' delay] through the front door and the front of the house; we pulled up into the sun and were away. Wing Commander Wells visited Amsterdam some months later and was hailed with delight by the Dutchmen who vividly described just

what we had done to the hated Gestapo.' Three days later Wells led the Wing in a similar attack on another Gestapo building in Rotterdam.

Pin-point attacks were not, however, the monopoly of 146 Wing. On 4 November 124 Wing took a break from army support and their regular interdiction route – 'the Münster milk run' – to make attacks on two special targets. Wing Commander North-Lewis led 247 Squadron to Apeldoorn where the target was Dutch collaborator, Seyss-Inquart's HQ. The other target was attacked by 181 Squadron and demanded particular care and very accurate shooting. This was a tower on the north wing of the Dutch Royal Family's summer palace which was in use by the SS as an HQ; the rest of the building was believed still to be occupied by members of the Royal Family. The attack was made parallel to the main building so that any overshoots would go into the open area beyond the wing. Included in the attacking force was 181 Squadron's Dutchman, Flying Officer van Zinnicq Bergmann: 'The whole north tower was flattened and hardly anything else damaged. Queen Wilhelmina, who appointed me ADC at the end of the war, always told her grandchildren that this was my work and the young Princesses were very astonished that I was not punished for doing so much damage to their grandmother's property. The Queen

loathed her palace in The Hague and said that would also have been a marvellous target, and it was a pity I never did attack the place!'

On 18 November the Canadians of 143 Wing were given yet another bridge to deal with, but this one would be remembered by the pilots for its stubborness. The bridge was at Hilfarth and was vital for the Germans bringing up supplies for their forward troops; it was attacked by all three squadrons, several times, but despite this rain of 1,000-pounders it remained standing. As the third attack commenced, a horse-drawn transport was seen, its driver flailing his whip in an effort to get off the bridge before the bombs fell. An anonymous voice came over the R/T, 'Stay on the bridge you silly bugger, its the safest place to be!' Not conducive to good bombing!

As weather worsened, and the Wings settled down to see the winter through on the more permanent airfields at which they were now based, one squadron at a time, from each Group, was sent to Armament Practice Camps at Warmwell and Fairwood Common. This not only allowed the pilots

Below: Bergmann's usual aircraft was MN875 'EL-B', seen here taxiing at B.86, Helmond on 23 February 1945. (IWM)

Bottom: 439 Squadron's dispersal at B.7, Eindhoven in October 1944, seen through the remains of a wrecked German hangar. Note the crushed Bf109G in the foreground. (Public Archives of Canada)

to hone their bombing and rocket-firing skills without the distraction of Flak and fighters, but also provided a welcome break from the ceaseless round of operations.

The winter of 1944/5 proved to be a hard one, flying being considerably reduced by fog, snow and generally inclement weather; ground crews had to work in almost intolerable conditions in the open, as few airfields boasted hangars after German demolitions and earlier Allied attacks. Interdiction and attacks on strong points continued to be the main duties of the Typhoons during early December, but at this time several squadrons were attacked on a number of occasions by American fighters, which frequently mistook the aircraft for Fw 190s; at least four Typhoons would be shot down in error by their allies in this way before the winter was over.

On 17 December, taking advantage of the appalling weather which grounded the Allied fighter-bombers, the Germans launched their Ardennes offensive. It was not until the 24th that the skies cleared sufficiently for the air forces to play a major part in slowing down the German advance. However, during that day the German effort on the ground was matched by the endeavours of the Luftwaffe to provide support, more encounters with their fighters occurring than for many weeks. 440 Squadron had lost one aircraft to Flak during the morning of the 24th, but on return from a second strike over the Malmédy area a lone Fw 190 dived on Flying Officers Dunkeld and Cumming as they provided top cover for six other Typhoons, and shot both of the Canadians down. At once a Tempest of 274 Squadron, flown above the combat by Squadron Leader Mackie, dived on the Focke-Wulf and sent it crashing down; the identity of his obviously expert Luftwaffe pilot has not been definitely ascertained. Elsewhere on this day 146 Wing was also hit by German fighters; during a sweep 193 Squadron was attacked by many Bf 109s and Fw 190s which shot down one Typhoon and damaged a second. 197 Squadron attempted to come to the rescue, but was also attacked by the fighters and fired on by Flak; two Typhoons were shot down and a third damaged. Further losses over the Ardennes suffered by the other 143 Wing squadrons and 124 Wing, plus casualties among the squadrons still operating over Holland and Germany, made this the most costly day since Falaise.

Next day – Christmas Day – 266 Squadron dispatched 'B' Flight on a train reconnaissance in the Duigen-Dortmund area, covered by other Typhoons from 193 Squadron. A train had just been destroyed, when a large force of Messerschmitts and Focke-Wulfs, estimated variously between 60 and 150 strong, attacked the lower formation, shooting down two of 266's aircraft. 193 came to the rescue, Flying Officer Bulleid claiming one Fw 190 in flames, while Flight Lieutenant Smith claimed a probable, his own aircraft being damaged in return.

Although the Typhoons did their best to bring support where it was needed, the situation was confused and the lines fluid. In an attempt to overcome these difficulties, Wing Commander 'Kit' North-Lewis dispatched 181 Squadron's Flight Lieutenant Boucher to Dinant, with a radio car and orders to guide the Wing in on the German armour. On Boxing Day, when the weather had improved, the Wing was summoned to deal with a German thrust towards the nearby bridge over the Meuse. Lew Boucher was in the radio car alongside the Brigadier's Divisional HQ:

'Once the Wing was airborne I was in direct contact with Kit and directed him by map-reading over the Div HQ. From there I was able to guide him via a bend in the river on to the German tanks. We had a pretty accurate description of their position from a detailed map and reports sent back from the front line, although I couldn't see it from the ground. At what I judged to be the crucial moment, I called for the smoke-markers and I was very relieved when Kit reported that he could see the enemy tanks and was going in to attack.' With him North-Lewis had another seven Typhoons of 181 Squadron and they made repeated low-level attacks with RP and cannon, despite fierce Flak

Below: Squadron Leader J. R. Beirnes of 438 Squadron taxiing out for a sortie in 'F3-B', armed with 2 × 500lb bombs, instead of the more usual 1,000-pounders. (J. A. Lord)

Bottom: Some idea of the targets awaiting the Luftwaffe on New Year's Day can be gained from this view of MP149 'I8-P' of 440 Squadron taxiing out at B.78, Eindhoven in October 1944. It has a row of operational sortie symbols and the name 'Pulverizer II' on the nose. (Public Archives of Canada)

which riddled the Wing Leader's aircraft. As the formation reformed, Flight Lieutenant Dennis Luke sought and was given permission to make a final cannon attack to use the last of his ammunition. As the lone Tiffie swept in, the German commander emerged from the turret of his tank, perhaps believing that the storm had passed . . . Lew Boucher continues:

'We got a running commentary from the forward troops and the Brigadier was jumping up and down with excitement as it became apparent that the attack was a success. Before returning to Eindhoven I had a look at the site of the attack. There were several burned-out tanks [four and two halftracks were claimed] and one, which appeared to be the lead tank, was standing seemingly undamaged in the middle of the field. I was puzzled by this, the hatch was open so I climbed up to look inside. The tank commander's body was still in it and his head had obviously been smashed by a cannon-shell which had ricocheted off the edge of the hatch opening.'

Luftwaffe fighters were again encountered three days later, on the 29th. The first were seen by 168 Squadron which went out at full unit strength on an armed reconnaissance over the Münster-Rheine area. Here a mixed force of twelve Messerschmitts and Focke-Wulfs were encountered, which managed to shoot down both of the unit's flight commanders, Flight Lieutenants Gibbons and Plant. In return seven pilots poured fire into a single unfortunate Focke-Wulf which spun down, the pilot baling out; two more German fighters were claimed damaged. During the day Fw 190s also shot down one of 439 Squadron's Typhoons near Coesfeld, while on the 31st they similarly dealt with a 247 Squadron aircraft near Steinhuder Lake. Never had 2nd TAF lost so many Typhoons [at least ten] in aerial combat in a single month, and when added to 37 other operational losses in the same nine-day period, one to a USAAF P-47, but mostly to Flak, the Ardennes fighting had proved very expensive to the close-support force. 124 Wing was particularly hard hit. On the 23rd they lost the 247 Squadron commander, Battle of Britain veteran, Squadron Leader 'Stapme' Stapleton, who was apparently hit by debris in a low-level attack on a train and was last seen going down in poor visibility; it was some time before he was known to be a PoW. On the 26th Group Captain Charles Green failed to return from a 'weather recce' with Flight Lieutenant Derry.* This was a convenient way of by-passing the order that Group Captains were not to fly on 'ops' but the old enemy, Flak, claimed this highly experienced and aggressive Rhodesian,

Top: Some of 181 Squadron's pilots at B.78, Eindhoven just before the Ardennes offensive. Third from the left is Flight Lieutenant 'Lew' Boucher, and in the centre Norwegian Flight Lieutenant 'Pete' Isachsen who had shot down a Fw 190 a few days earlier. (L. P. Boucher)

Centre: Flying Officer Mike Cole of 137 Squadron had a lucky escape on 29 December 1944 when Flak shattered one of his rockets without serious damage to his aircraft, MN822 'SF-B'. (Captain P. E. Tickner)

Bottom: Battle of Britain veteran, Squadron Leader B. G. 'Stapme' Stapleton had flown Typhoons with 257 Squadron before taking command of 247 Squadron in August 1944. His Typhoon, MP126 'ZY-Y', was hit by Flak and force-landed in enemy territory while flown by Flying Officer 'Frickie' Wiersum, RNethAF. Inspecting German troops were most interested in the artwork on the aircraft – the handiwork of 247's Intelligence Officer. (F. K. Wiersum)

*John Derry of 181 Squadron later commanded 182 Squadron, and after the war became famous as a De Havilland test-pilot in the forefront of research into high-speed flight. He was killed in the tragic DH 110 crash at Farnborough on 6 September 1952.

although he survived as a PoW after some rough treatment from his SS captors. His place was taken by Group Captain Bitmead. A third bitter blow was the loss of Squadron Leader Short, who had risen from Flight Sergeant to the command of 181 Squadron, when he collided with an unidentified Typhoon near St-Vith. In 146 Wing, 197 Squadron lost their popular commander, New Zealander Allan Smith, who after his tour with 486 Squadron and a rest tour production testing at Glosters, had returned to operations to lead this bomber unit. Hit by Flak while dive-bombing a bridge at Culemborg, he managed to force-land on a frozen lake but was quickly taken prisoner.

The Luftwaffe's last major input in the Ardennes fighting occurred on 1 January 1945, early in the morning, when the surprise attack on Allied airfields in the area was launched under the code-name Operation 'Bödenplatte'. Generally this proved a costly exercise for the Germans, who lost more manned fighters during the attack than the mostly unmanned aircraft they managed to destroy on the ground. The most successful of all the German attacks was that made on Eindhoven airfield by Jagdgeschwader 3. This was the home of eight Typhoon squadrons of 124 and 143 Wings and three reconnaissance Spitfire squadrons, as well as 83 Group Communications Squadron and 403 Repair and Salvage Unit. 143 Wing had been first to operate on this date, with four Typhoons of 439 Squadron and six of 168 Squadron already in the air on a weather reconnaissance to St-Vith and an armed reconnaissance over the Frith-Prum area respectively, when six incoming Bf 109s passed the latter formation. One of these attempted to attack the British aircraft but was shot at and claimed damaged for its trouble. A 137 Squadron formation was also airborne and missed the holocaust that was about to come. As the Messerschmitts and Focke-Wulfs reached Eindhoven, at 0920 hours, they found another 168 Squadron aircraft just getting airborne for an air test, piloted by Flight Lieutenant Gibbons; he managed

to swing his Typhoon round to meet the attackers and was seen to blow the tail off one Fw 190 before succumbing to the fire of three Bf 109s.

Next on the runway after Gibbons were eight bombed-up Typhoons of 438 Squadron, lined up in pairs, and led by their new CO, Flight Lieutenant Pete Wilson; behind them eight more bombers from 440 Squadron awaited their turn for take-off. The first pair from the former unit were actually on their take-off run as the JG3 aircraft swept in, the Typhoon leader being hit and mortally wounded, while the second aircraft was shot down in flames; Wilson pulled off the runway and climbed out, but died within minutes from a stomach wound. Strapped into one of the other 438 Squadron aircraft was Pilot Officer Andy Lord:

'The Boss gave the "Go" signal to his No. 2 and both started to roll. Midway in their take-off run All Hell Broke Loose, And Then Some . . . The first wave of Me 109s and Fw 190s surged on the deck from the opposite end of the runway, all guns firing. Our first two guys never had a chance. Then a second wave, a third, eventually well over fifty enemy fighters bombed and strafed the

airfield. There were so many that two of them collided. I saw the right wing of Red 3 fold straight up. I looked to the left, my wing was on fire – same on the right. Yanked the helmet off, undid all my straps and jumped to the ground. In normal times one should at least break a leg. I ran about fifty feet and fell flat behind a two-foot high pile of scraps. Then I got mad. I pulled out my .38 Webley and started shooting at the unwelcome visitors. They were all over the place, right on the deck, shooting us up real good. Our AckAck, the Bofors, were blasting away with some success; smoke from burning aircraft, ours and theirs, bombs exploding, enemy planes crashing on the field, parachutes coming down, ammo from our kites exploding. A real madhouse.' Other pilots leapt from their cockpits to cover as their Typhoons burst into flames, two more of them suffering wounds. Pilot Officer Watson of 440 Squadron managed to open fire from the ground, claiming hits on one Focke-Wulf before his own fighter was set on fire.

124 Wing was also hit, one of 137 Squadron's pilots being killed as he was taxiing to dispersal, but their losses were much lighter

than those of the Canadian Wing. The Reconnaissance Wing lost a dozen more aircraft including three Mustangs (which were about to be replaced by Spitfires) and many others were damaged. Losses of Typhoons at Eindhoven were:

124 Wing	Destroyed	Damaged
137 Squadron		2
181 Squadron	1	
182 Squadron	3	2
247 Squadron		2
143 Wing		
168 Squadron	1 (shot down)	1
438 Squadron	5	2
439 Squadron	1	1
440 Squadron	8	4

In addition, the 143 Wing Leader's aircraft, which was under repair at 403 R&SU was also destroyed. In the above table 'damaged' refers to aircraft effectively out of action, i.e., which had to be repaired off unit; aircraft with minor damage, reparable locally, have not been included. Totals for the latter are not available, but few Typhoons escaped some damage. 182

Top left: The aftermath of 'Bodenplatte' at B.78, Eindhoven on New Year's Day 1945 – the Typhoon on the left has been totally destroyed but the one on the right, believed to be RB257 '5V-S', has apparently just lost most of its fin to a cannon-shell. (via D. Howley/R. L. Ward)

Left: 438 Squadron pilots examining leaflets about to be dropped on German forces surrounded in the Ruhr area. Left to right, back row: Flying Officer 'Johnny' Brown, Flying Officer 'Andy' Lord; front row: Flying Officer 'Pete' Hay, Flight Lieutenant A. MacDonald, Flying Officer 'Buck' Kirlin, Flight Lieutenant 'Bob' Spooner, Flying Officer Ray Oldfin, Flight Lieutenant Roy Burden. (J. A. Lord)

Below: 143 Wing's Leader, Wing Commander F. G. Grant, taxiing at B.78, Eindhoven in his personally marked RB205 'FGG', December 1944. It was the usual practice to position airman on one or both wings to help the pilot avoid bad ground on temporary or damaged airfields. (RAFM/C. E. Brown)

Squadron for example, had no aircraft serviceable and 247 had only five! Furthermore, five of the aircraft listed as 'damaged' were eventually scrapped in the UK before repair was completed (see Appendix 4).

The attack had been led by JG 3's Kommodore, Oberstleutnant Heinz Bär, who claimed two of the Typhoons destroyed to raise his personal score to 204. However, his unit lost sixteen pilots, ten of whom were killed and six taken prisoner, while two more returned wounded.

The Typhoons had the last word when the four 439 Squadron pilots returning from their weather reconnaissance, spotted fifteen Fw 190s east of Helmond, running for home. Attacking these, in company with two Spitfires, the Canadian pilots claimed four shot down, two each by Flying Officers Lawrence and Fraser, although one Typhoon was lost in return. This was the second time that Lawrence had claimed two victories in a single combat, and he was awarded an immediate DFC.

In the aftermath of the destruction at Eindhoven it was considered of paramount importance to let the Luftwaffe know that the Typhoons were still in business, so on missions flown later in the day the pilots were for once encouraged to chatter on the R/T and to use all the callsigns of the Wing for the benefit of the German listening service.

Other Luftwaffe fighters attacked a USAAF airstrip, A.84 at Asche, where 164 and 183 Squadrons had just arrived on detachment from 123 Wing. Already scrambled to meet the incoming Germans, US P-51s mistook the Typhoons for the enemy, shooting down one 183 Squadron machine as it approached with its wheels down. The rest landed safely, but were then subjected to the Germans' strafe, which damaged two 164 Squadron Typhoons. 146 Wing's airfield at Antwerp/Deurne was also

attacked, but ineffectually, a single 266 Squadron Typhoon and two of 257 Squadron's aircraft suffering damage. Few of the German fighters which had been assigned Volkel as a target managed to make attacks and the Typhoon squadrons there escaped without loss or damage.

Within a few days the units which had suffered most were back at full strength, their pilots having been ferried back to the UK to pick up new Tiffies from 83 GSU, but with the end of the German offensive, and a resumption of poor weather, January was not thereafter a month marked by much action. In the middle of the month 124 Wing moved into a newly built airfield at Helmond, closer to the scene of operations. Another specially constructed base was nearing completion further north at Mill, but would not be occupied by 146 Wing until the following month.

The start of February saw some improvement in the weather, and on the 8th the British and Canadian armies launched an offensive – Operation 'Veritable' – to move up to the Rhine prior to the crossing of this major obstacle to deployment into Germany proper. 'Cab-rank' operations to provide direct support became once more the order of the day, the next week bringing the biggest killing of tanks, armoured vehicles and other motor transport since the Falaise operations of the previous August. Generally now very experienced, the Typhoon units sought also the deadly '88s', the six-barrelled mortars (Nebelwerfer), machine-gun nests, observation posts and other such 'pin-point' targets. Casualties among pilots since the Invasion had been such that by this time a constant flow of suitably experienced replacements was becoming difficult to maintain. Volunteers from the Spitfire squadrons had been called for, but the reputation of the Typhoon units as virtual suicide squads brought a very disappointing

response – almost nil! There is no doubt that casualties had been very heavy, and by mid-February had included twenty squadron commanders and Wing leaders since D-Day, as well as large numbers of experienced flight commanders. Experience and flying skill were of some advantage when the deadly Flak was the main enemy, but chance and luck seemed to count for more! To keep the other squadrons at full strength and to allow the posting of tour-expired pilots to instructor jobs at the new Typhoon OTUs, each of three Wings now shed a squadron. At the end of February 168 Squadron was the first to be disbanded, followed by 257 Squadron the next month and 174 Squadron at the beginning of April.

Despite the odds against such happenings, the Typhoons were to enjoy some unexpected successes against the new Luftwaffe jets before Operation 'Veritable' was over. On 14 February, 55 Messerschmitt Me 262 fighter-bombers were sent to attack British forces advancing near Kleve, and some of these were to fall foul of 83 Group Typhoons as they did so. Two flashed past aircraft of 184 Squadron near Arnhem, Captain Green, a SAAF pilot, getting in a quick burst which allowed him to claim damage to one. That same morning four 439 Squadron pilots saw below them two jets from 5/KG(J) 51 heading west. Diving to attack, Flight Lieutenant Lyal Shaver hit one which blew up at once, and Flying Officer Fraser obtained hits on the second, which was later confirmed as destroyed; they had shot down Oberleutnant Hans-Georg Richter in 9K+BN and Feldwebel Werner Witzmann in 9K+HN.

Late February also saw an almost complete change in the command of the Typhoon Wings. The veteran (at 25!) New Zealand pilot, Group Captain Scott, handed over command of 123 Wing to 'Johnny' Baldwin, who had been Wing Leader of 146 Wing until October of the previous year, and within a week he was followed to England by Denys Gillam, now recipient of two Bars to his DSO; Wing Commander 'Johnny' Wells was promoted from Wing Leader to command 146 Wing in his stead. 146's new Wing Leader was Wing Commander Deall, Rhodesian ex-commanding officer of 266 Squadron. 123 Wing had lost their Wing Leader, Wing Commander Dring, in a tragic landing accident in January, when his Typhoon hit a snow bank on landing and turned over; his place had been taken by Wing Commander Button, who had previously commanded 193 Squadron. In 83 Group, command of 143 Wing passed from the long-serving Group Captain Paul Davoud to Group Captain Nesbitt.

During early March the Germans were in full retreat to the Rhine, but once the river was reached, the line once more became static, and attacks on interdiction targets

were resumed. These were normally flown in formations of six or eight, although one or two 'spares' would be taken along in case of technical failure, turning back at the 'bomb line' if not required. The remainder then pressed on in 'loose pairs', the leader searching for targets while under the cover of the rest of his formation. Railway targets in particular were avidly sought but trains could be a deadly trap, even for the wary – Flight Lieutenant Lew Boucher, 181 Squadron:

'We spotted a goods train which had just cleared a cutting and was puffing along on an open plain. It was a perfect target but for some reason I felt uneasy. We circled a couple of times and I could see nothing special about it, but I still had that feeling although there seemed to be no logical reason for it. John Derry was flying with me on that occasion; he was very much the 'press-on type' and called up to ask what we were hanging about for. I wasn't at all sure myself, so decided to go in. As I turned into the dive intensive AA fire opened up from the train itself – a Flak train. I broke off the attack immediately, toyed with the idea of splitting the flight to attack from different directions, but decided it wasn't worth the risk.'

Two pilots of 182 Squadron had fallen foul of a more elaborate trap, as Flying Officer Ian Ladely recalls: 'Just two went

down on this train, Bill Cutherbertson and Jack Taylor, while the rest of us gave top cover. There was a call from Jack, "I've been hit," and as Bill circled to watch him force-land he was hit too. Both of them belly-landed OK and were seen to climb out of their cockpits. We then saw that the train had been parked alongside the main line, with several Flak-cars, and with Flak positions hidden in the woods all around.' The unfortunate Cuthbertson and Taylor were captured by the Volkssturm and were shot, in accordance with orders that the part-time soldiers had, namely to execute all 'terror-flieger' captured deep in German territory. The perpetrators of this crime were hunted down immediately after the war, one being shot while trying to escape and the rest were hanged. 2nd TAF pilots were well aware of the dangers that they faced if they found themselves behind enemy lines. Several were known to have been murdered in cold blood in Normandy and more would meet this fate on German soil. Pilots were armed with revolvers, but some carried additional weapons such as knives; Bob Merlin, who returned to 'ops' with 175 Squadron after his long sojourn in enemy territory, carried a Sten gun in his cockpit!

At this time 146 Wing carried out a new form of attack as recalled by Flight Lieutenant David Ince of 257 Squadron: 'Most uncertain in its results and most uninspiring to the pilots was the technique of blind bombing carried out from above cloud under the direction of a Mobile Radar Control Post. MRCP squadrons would join up in close formation and the leader would be directed to a pre-determined bomb-release point, in level flight, on radio instructions from the ground. I took part in trials off the Belgian/Dutch coast flying an FR Typhoon as No. 2 to Wing Commander 'Johnny' Wells, and taking a vertical line overlap series of photographs from which to assess the bombing accuracy under MRCP control. Following this trial a limited number of MRCP operations were flown in February and March 1945. Usually the results were unknown but on one occasion the Army did report all bombs in the target area.'

The technique was tried out, with rather less success, by some of the RP squadrons, although in their case the aircraft were positioned above the cloud but dived through it to release their rockets.

As preparations were made for a massive crossing of the Rhine by both ground and airborne forces, a number of 'CD' targets were dealt with by the Typhoons. On the 18th 146 Wing attacked the HQ of General Blaskowitz, who had taken over from General Student; the target was hit hard and 62 of his staff died. Three days later five squadrons of 84 Group Typhoons supported by three of Spitfires, attacked the camouflaged village of Zwolle, which was being used as a paratroop depot, and also attacked the HQ of the German 25th Army, a hotel at Bussum in Holland. The General

had left the previous day, but vital staff were killed and documents destroyed.

While this Group's Wings continued to hammer at strong points, rail and road transport and barges on the rivers, all units now prepared to provide strong support for the Rhine crossings. On 20 and 21 March, 121 Wing moved forward to B.100 at Goch, the first British airfield on German soil, while 123 Wing moved to B.91 at Kluis in Holland; 143 Wing would follow to B.100 within a few days. On the 23rd Wing Commander Keep, who had replaced Wing commander Pitt-Brown the previous month, led 121 Wing on a sustained attack on Flak positions in the area selected for the airborne operations across the Rhine.

Next day as the crossings took place, spearheaded by a massive airborne force of paratroops and glider-borne infantry, it was maximum effort for all the Typhoon Wings, with the first sorties taking place shortly after dawn. Some operated on cab-rank patrols, while others were allocated a Flak-

suppression role. The latter was not too popular with the pilots for it involved a pair of Typhoons acting as bait while the following pair watched for gun flashes to reveal the Flak positions and carried out the attack. Most of the Wings launched sections of four aircraft every fifteen minutes from 1000 and 1600 hours, 245 Squadron, to quote just one example, flying 52 sorties during the day. The landings proved a total success, and the Typhoons had certainly played their part once again; out of the 440 para-dropping and glider-towing aircraft employed by the RAF, only six were shot down by Flak. Despite the dangerous task they had undertaken, losses among the Typhoons had been relatively low and those pilots who were hit managed, in the main, to bale out or force-land in Allied territory. Two exceptions were 124 Wing Leader, 'Kit' North-Lewis and 247 Squadron's Flying Officer Cliff Monk. The latter crash-landed in enemy territory and jumped into a trench occupied by two German soldiers, who promptly sur-

Left: Flying Officer A. H. Fraser of 439 Squadron in his Typhoon 'Nicky' a few days after his third victory – an Me 262 claimed on 14 February 1945. (Public Archives of Canada)

Right: Wing Commander 'Kit' North-Lewis of 124 Wing with his RB208 'KN-L' which he force-landed on Gravel Island near Wesel during the Rhine crossings. (Air Commodore C. D. North-Lewis)

Below: You can almost hear the roar of the Sabre as this 183 Squadron Typhoon struggles to get airborne from B.91, Kluis in April 1945. (RAF Museum/C. E. Brown)

rendered when he brandished his pistol. They were followed by 28 more, eager to find a British officer to take them into captivity, which he did! North-Lewis was hit on the first sortie of the morning and, too low to cross the Rhine, was forced to make a wheels-up landing on Gravel Island, near Wesel. He was immediately captured by the German paratroops there, but the roles were reversed when they learnt they had been cut off by the British advance. The next day he was allowed to take a convenient canoe, paddle to Allied territory, and direct British troops to the island, where they rounded up 120 Germans. He was awarded an immediate DSO and taken off operations; his tour had started in February 1944 and he had logged 175 operational sorties.

Back in January, 2nd TAF aircraft markings had been revised in an attempt to make them more recognizable, in particular to the USAAF pilots who were inclined to shoot first and identify later. Spinners were uniformly painted black, the red/blue roundels on the wing upper surfaces had a white ring inserted and all roundels were outlined in yellow. In addition, all remnants of the D-Day stripes, which were still carried below the fuselage, and the rear fuselage 'sky' bands were painted out in order to avoid confusion with the similar 'home defence' bands which were appearing on Luftwaffe fighters in increasing numbers. Despite these precautions the Typhoons were still regularly molested by P-47s and P-51s, and occasionally by Spitfires; one of the losses on the 24 March was a 174 Squadron aircraft which had been forced into a dogfight

with friendly fighters and was left with insufficient fuel to reach base. Three days earlier Flying Officer George Hill, an Australian pre-war racing driver flying with 247 Squadron, had a narrow escape, details of which indicate the hazards facing Typhoon pilots at this time. When his Typhoon was hit in the nose tank by Flak, he had turned for home but the aircraft was hit again, losing all its glycol and four feet off one wing tip. Just then he was bounced by a squadron of P-47s, and his aplomb was much admired when 'Kenway' control inquired if he was getting on all right and he replied in his Aussie drawl, 'Yes, just sorting these Thunderbolts out.' As he roared across the lines the Germans 'threw everything up but themselves,' but he still managed to skim the Rhine and force-land in the American lines!

In March losses on operations totalled more than forty, similar to February's figure, despite the increased tempo of sorties. Two more unit commanders had gone down – 193's Squadron Leader Erasmus and 609's Squadron Leader Roberts. The latter was replaced by Squadron Leader 'Pinkie' Stark, scorer of that unit's 200th victory, who would remain in command for the rest of their time as a Typhoon squadron. Another squadron leader lost during the month was Mike Savage who joined 175 Squadron as a supernumerary and went missing on his first sortie. Hardest hit had been 247 Squadron, which had lost eight aircraft during the month, a rate of casualty considerably heavier than that suffered by any other squadron in either of these two months. As a further reminder that Flak was no re-

specter of experience, one of the losses was Flight Lieutenant Tom McGovern who became a PoW on the third trip of his second tour. Not surprisingly, the CO at the time, Squadron Leader Jim Bryant, who had been one of the original members of 181 Squadron and had returned to 'ops' after a four-month spell instructing at 83 GSU, remembers this period, and particularly 24 and 25 March, when support for the bridgehead across the Rhine continued, as the most dangerous for Typhoon pilots:

'I can think of no other period when so many Typhoons were written-off by anti-aircraft fire in such a short period. Those gunners were really making a last-ditch stand for the Third Reich, and we were equally determined that our airborne troops should encounter as little opposition as possible. On one of these sorties, in which we operated as pairs, my No. 2 was "Pop" Arnold, some 400 yards to starboard, and we were flying at 1,500 feet, looking for guns near Dingden. Three were spotted, each in the corners of a field. My first pair of rockets knocked one out and as I started to climb away a shell from another hit my port wing and removed a large chunk, from the tip to the roundel. This immediately threw the aircraft on its back and at 200 feet heading straight into a forest. It took all my strength, using both hands on the stick to right the aircraft. I was travelling south at the time with an airspeed of about 350mph. Unable at this speed to make a right-hand turn on to a westerly course, I throttled back and was obliged to make a 270 degree climbing turn to port to head back towards the Rhine. All

Left: Complete hydraulic failure following an anti-Flak patrol forced Flight Lieutenant Pattison of 182 Squadron to make a wheels-up landing at B.78, Eindhoven on 25 March 1945. (Public Archives of Canada)

Above: To supplement the supply of new production Typhoons, many older airframes were taken out of storage and modified to the latest standard, seeing active service, often for the first time, in the last months of the war. Here R8824 'PR-M', which had first seen service with 182 Squadron in September 1942, is seen alongside another 609 Squadron Typhoon, SW392 from the last production batch. (L. W. F. Stark)

Below left: Sergeant John Dick took this photograph of 247 Squadron colleague, Warrant Officer 'Bert' Collins, over the Ratzenburger Lakes, on the return from attacking Altenwallingan, 13 April 1945. 'ZY-S' was JR247 which had seen previous operational service with 197 Squadron as 'OV-V' and had survived a 200mph landing at Manston on 18 March 1944. (Flight Lieutenant 'Zipp' Button had lost three feet off JR247's starboard wing when he hit a tree on a 'Ranger' over France, and was forced to retract the undercarriage to avoid overshooting the runway.) (J. Dick)

Below: Squadron Leader 'Jimmy' Bryant with his groundcrew and SW422 'ZY-V', the replacement for RB225 'ZY-V' which he had been forced to abandon near Helmond on 25 March 1945. (J. H. Bryant)

Above: On 7 April 1945 a 175 Squadron Typhoon ran into the back of JR194 'BR-N' on the runway at B.100. After shredding the rear fuselage of 'BR-N', the 175 squadron aircraft somersaulted over its victim and never flew again, but amazingly, JR194 received a new rear fuselage and tail unit at 419 RSU, and was back in service with 184 Squadron in just five days! (Public Archives of Canada)

Below: Flying Officer 'Johnny' Rook of 197 Squadron taxiing RB251 'OV-G', 'Brenda IX', for take-off at B.89, Mill in March 1945. It was from this aircraft that Flight Lieutenant G. R. Gibbings made his involuntary departure on 12 April 1945. (J. C. Rook)

the guns in the area were now firing at me and I could feel the odd dull thud as bullets hit the fuselage behind me. Climbing slowly I crossed the Rhine at about 2,000 feet and found that at 210mph the port wing stalled in an incipient flick roll. At 220mph a jagged piece of metal skin, on the edge of the missing part of the wing, curled back and threatened to foul the aileron, the far end of which was sticking out on its own, with only the rear spar in front of it. Flying in this restricted speed range still required both hands to prevent the aircraft from rolling; landing was clearly out of the question. On approaching base [Helmond], and then at 5,000 feet, I advised Ground Control of my intention to bale out south of the airfield. Heading for open country, I pulled out the R/T plug, undid safety straps, jettisoned the hood and held back pressure on the stick as I set elevator trim fully forward. On releasing the stick I flew out of the cockpit as the aircraft plunged down and to port, to bury itself in a swamp.' Another 247 Squadron pilot, Flight Lieutenant 'Dizzy' Compton, was forced to bale out over the airfield later in the day.

After crossing the Rhine, the British and Canadian forces were once more in hot pursuit, as their armoured columns cut deep into north and north-west Germany. During the first week of April, 123 Wing aided in the final, and long-delayed liberation of the shattered remains of Arnhem. A mixture of

close support and interdiction sorties were flown during the first part of the month, the last losses to the Luftwaffe being suffered during one such operation. These occurred on 4 April, when twelve Bf 109s 'jumped' Typhoons of 438 Squadron and shot down two which were providing top cover for the rest of the unit. Attacks were also made against remaining Luftwaffe airfields, where a considerable number of aircraft – mainly twin-engined types – were claimed destroyed. Harbours and waterways were attacked as some German elements strove to escape across the Baltic to Norway. Further moves were made to airfields deeper in Germany, but on 20 April six Bf 109s and three Fw 190s strafed B.150 at Fassberg where one or two Typhoons of 121 and 143 Wing, which was newly arrived, were damaged.

Although German airfields were a profitable target for the Typhoons, they were ferociously defended by automatic Flak, and other dangers lurked as Flight Lieutenant Bob Gibbings found out during a 197 Squadron attack on Broeksketel. As he swept across a hangar complex on a strafing run, his cannon-shells struck an ammunition dump, which blew up in a massive ball of flame right in his path. It was a battered and burnt Tiffie with a very shaken pilot that emerged from the other side of the fireball! As he set course for Allied lines, with engine temperatures creeping inexorably into the

red, he jettisoned his canopy, undid straps and other connections and gave some thought to the method of baling out, which was looking increasingly necessary. Having elected to try the 'stick forward' method, he unthinkingly gave the control column a gentle push – and found himself in space – just the wrong side of the lines! He spent the rest of the war as a PoW, as did Flight Lieutenant Tommy Clift, one of the two surviving Burmese pilots, who had gone down on the same operation.

On 26 April as a section of four 263 Squadron Typhoons were breaking away from an RP attack on a train in Niebull station, two Me 262s 'jumped' them. One of the 262s attacked Pilot Officer Morgan, the formation leader, who had been hit by Flak and was attempting a forced-landing, but it overshot. Immediately Morgan's No. 2, Warrant Officer Barrie, gave it a long burst, which was followed by attacks from the other two Typhoons. The jet turned on its back, flames pouring from the centre section, and dived into the ground from 3,000 feet. It was the last German fighter to fall to the Typhoons' guns.

Operations continued into early May with sustained attacks on communications and airfields as well as on the Baltic ports and coastal shipping. Among a number of float-planes and flying-boats destroyed at this time were two six-engined Blohm & Voss Bv 222s. One of the latter was claimed by

Right: Typical of Typhoons in 1945, this trio from 263 Squadron carry long-range tanks with rocket load reduced to two pairs. 'HE-A' was a PD-serialled aircraft, the rest of the number having been obscured when the rear fuselage band was painted out. (IWM).

175 Squadron when a flying-boat base was spotted while on a shipping reconnaissance on 2 May. The formation was led by Flight Lieutenant Harry Pears whose combat report read: '. . . when approaching Trave-munde/Potenitz I saw an Ha 139 taking off on the water. I attacked this with two bursts of half and two seconds, 1,000 yards to 500 yards head on. I also released a pair of rockets and got a direct hit. I claim this E/A as destroyed* I then saw a Bv 138 about to take-off. I attacked from 1,600 yards to 800 yards with two bursts of half and three seconds. I saw strikes round the cockpit and port engine which started smoking. I claim this E/A as damaged. I noticed that the Bv 222 attacked by Warrant Officer Wyper was on fire and sinking. I saw Flight Sergeant Slay attack another Bv 138. This was seen to be smoking from the fuselage after his attack.'

Great masses of motor transport – more even than at Falaise – packed the roads of north-west Germany, and great execution was done to these and to rail locomotives. In the first days of May shipping in the Baltic became a priority target; fleeing from the northern German ports and heading for Denmark or Norway were vessels of all shapes and sizes, even sailing-ships, thought to be carrying German leaders and SS troops intent on carrying on the war. Two of

*It is thought that the aircraft claimed as an 'Ha 139' was more likely a He 115, or another Bv 138, as the Blohm & Voss Ha 139 was an experimental type of the late thirties, unlikely to have survived to 1945.

the largest vessels sunk were the 21,000-ton *Deutschland* and the 27,500-ton *Cap Arcona*, both passenger liners, but unfortunately the latter was not carrying fleeing SS. *Cap Arcona* and *Thielbek*, a much smaller freighter moored nearby, were floating prison-ships in which 4,500 and 2,800 concentration-camp inmates, respectively, had been incarcerated for some days. This fact was not known to RAF Intelligence, so 83 and 84 Groups laid on shipping attacks. Both ships were hit by an extremely accurate RP attack pressed home by an unsuspecting 198 Squadron and approximately 6,900 of their wretched cargo perished, along with 100 of their SS guards. *Deutschland* had been earmarked as a hospital-ship and had a small medical team on board, but the necessary Red Crosses were limited to a single example on one of the funnels; she was sunk following rocket attacks by 184 and 263 Squadrons and dive-bombing by 197 Squadron. The crew managed to escape in lifeboats.

The volume of Flak encountered in the last weeks sent casualties soaring again; at least 38 aircraft were lost to this cause alone during April, with seven more during the first four days of May. The latter included Wing Commander Webb, 124 Wing's new Wing Leader, shot down in flames on 2 May while attacking a train north of Lübeck. Eight more Luftwaffe aircraft destroyed on airfields or on the water during these days brought such claims to over thirty in a four-week period.

Above: The only known 'sharkmouth' Typhoon. It was flown in the last months of hostilities by Squadron Leader Tony 'Zweigbergk, CO of 245 Squadron, seen here (on the right) with Flight Lieutenant Geoff Murphy, admiring the fiercesome design. (G. Murphy)

Below: 'Pulverizer IV' (RB389 'I8-P' of 440 Squadron) being armed with segmented anti-personnel bombs at B.100, Goch in April 1945. (Public Archives of Canada)

Then suddenly it was over: On the evening of 4 May 1945, all German armies in Holland, Denmark and north-west Germany surrendered, prior to the complete cessation of hostilities in Europe three days later. The final Order of Battle of the Typhoon units as the war ended was:

83 GROUP:

121 Wing B.150, Hustedt;
Wing Commander J. G. Keep, DSO
175 Squadron
184 Squadron (at Warmwell APC)
245 Squadron

124 Wing B.158, Lübeck;
Wing Commander M. R. Ingle-Finch, DFC, AFC *
137 Squadron (detached to 125 Wing, B.118)
181 Squadron
182 Squadron
247 Squadron

143 Wing B.150, Hustedt;
Wing Commander F. G. Grant, DSO, DFC
438 Squadron
439 Squadron
440 Squadron

84 GROUP:

123 Wing B.103, Plantlunne;
Wing Commander J. C. Button, DFC
164 Squadron
183 Squadron
198 Squadron
609 Squadron

146 Wing B.111, Ahlhorn;
Wing Commander J. H. Deall, DFC
193 Squadron
197 Squadron
263 Squadron
266 Squadron (at Fairwood Common APC)

In both 83 and 84 Groups the Typhoons had provided the backbone of the close-support force, backed by larger numbers of Spitfire fighter-bombers, which carried a smaller bomb-load and doubled as fighters. Vast numbers of vehicles of all kinds had been destroyed since 6 June by the two Groups, together with many locomotives and rolling-stock, armoured vehicles, guns, head-quarters, barges and other shipping. Of more than 220,000 rocket projectiles launched, virtually all had been delivered by Typhoons, as had a substantial proportion of the bomb tonnage dropped. Although operating specifically in the close-support role, the Typhoons had been able to claim the destruction of fifty German aircraft in the air during this period, and nearly as

Top: Sergeant John Lincoln of 175 Squadron returning from a sortie over the Baltic in SW464 'HH-D', in the first days of May 1945. (W. J. Lincoln)

Centre: Wing Commander J. C. 'Zipp' Button of 123 Wing flew this personally marked ('JCB' aft of the fuselage roundel and on the undercarriage fairings) Typhoon, RB431, from February to November 1945, when it was probably the last Typhoon in service in BAFO. The cannon, propeller and undercarriage markings were black and white. (via R. M. Rayner)

Above: The pilot of this 137 Squadron Typhoon is carefully watching the guiding airman's instructions. The aircraft is armed with anti-personnel rockets under the port wing and the more usual 60lb HE rockets under the starboard wing. (via J. Rendall)

* Wing Commander M. R. Ingle-Finch replaced Wing Commander G. F. H. Webb, who was killed in action on 2 May 1945, although he did not take command until 19 May 1945.

Left: Flying Officer 'Paddy' Byrne with MP188 'OV-Q'; both survived well over 100 operational sorties with 197 Squadron. (J. K. Byrne)

Right: The efficiency of 146 Wing's forward-facing camera modification on their Typhoon FR.1Bs can be judged from this enlargement of a small section of a photograph taken from a Typhoon 'beating up' the apron at Hildesheim. The nearest of the two red-spinnered 266 Squadron Typhoons, 'ZH-B', can be identified on the original print as RB248. (R. E. G. Sheward)

Left: Symbolic of victory, a 247 Squadron Typhoon, RB458 'ZY-B', parked among the remains of its foes on a shattered Lübeck airfield, in the first days of peace, May 1945. (RAF Museum/C. E. Brown)

Centre and bottom right: Typhoons were always prone to fires on start-up. Despite the best efforts of the fire crew, MN739 'ZH-U' was a 'write-off' after this conflagration at R.16, Hildesheim on 26 June 1945. (I. J. W. Pugh)

Left: 146 Wing lined up at R.16, Hildesheim prior to a Wing formation flight in June 1945. Among the 'ZH'-coded 266 Squadron Typhoons in the front row can be seen Wing Commander 'Johnny' Deall's 'JH-D'. (R. E. G. Sheward)

many again on the ground. More than 500 Typhoons had been lost on operations since the Invasion – less than fifty of them to hostile aircraft – while many more had been damaged.

The Typhoon had been the very epitome of close support during its ten months of operations with the British Second and Canadian First Armies in Europe. Accurate, swift-responding, hard-hitting, it had been the scourge of the Wermacht's mobile forces whenever weather allowed uninterrupted operations. Yet the aircraft saw no service in any other theatre, nor with any air force other than the RAF.* Too specialized for a peacetime air force, and with increasing numbers of its successor, the Tempest, becoming available, its days were numbered the day the war with Germany ended.

After some hectic celebrations, the Typhoon squadrons settled down to a routine of flying training, interspersed with flag-waving formation flights. Some of the luckier 83 Group squadrons rotated on detachments to Copenhagen, where almost forgotten food was plentiful and the populace most welcoming. However, by the end of May, 164 Squadron had gone, re-equipping with Spitfires in the UK, and the following month 183 Squadron followed suit (although the new Spitfires would soon be exchanged for Tempest IIs). At the end of July, 266 Squadron disbanded and August brought a whole rash of departures including the whole of the Canadian Wing. The Typhoons were flown back to Dunsfold or Lasham, where the GSUs had become 83 and 84 Group Disbandment Centres respectively. War-weary Typhoons were scrapped on the spot, but more serviceable examples were flown to 5, 20 or 51 MUs where they were put into storage.† 247 Squadron joined 183 at Chilbolton, to begin conversion to the Tempest II, but still had enough Typhoons to be the sole representative of the rapidly disappearing genre to take part in the massive Battle of Britain flypast over London on 15 September 1945. Most appropriately the Chilbolton Wing formation was led by Wing Commander 'Bee' Beamont, at the head of 183 Squadron's Tempest IIs, with 247 led by Squadron Leader Jim Bryant, both of whom had flown Typhoon operations since the early days. For the occasion they were joined by 222 Squadron's Tempest Vs – probably the only time all three types were seen together in the air in any significant numbers.

By the end of September, the last of the Typhoon squadrons in Germany had also disbanded; the Typhoon had served its purpose most admirably – and gone!

*Although RCAF and RNZAF units flew Typhoons/Tempests, these were RAF aircraft and the units came under RAF control.
†By the end of 1945 674 Typhoons were held in storage; they were eventually scrapped in batches during late 1946/early 1947.

△1

△4

△2   ▽3

△5   ▽6

After the surrender the Typhoon squadrons lost no time in embellishing their camouflaged aircraft with brighter colours and 121 Wing's were perhaps the most colourful.

1. 175 Squadron favoured scarlet spinners with chrome-yellow backplates, the colours being repeated on the inner surfaces of the undercarriage leg fairings; two yellow horizontal bands flanking one red for 'A' Flight, with the colours reversed for 'B' Flight. Intake filters were red with a yellow code-letter. 'Babs VIII' (in white) shown here was SW399 'HH-K', (W. J. Lincoln)

2. 184 Squadron's aircraft featured white spinners, rear fuselage bands and inner surfaces of the undercarriage leg fairings, with red stripes and edging, as seen on RB382 'BR-M'. (I. G. Handyside)

3. Mid-blue and white chequers with a blue spinner and white backplate identified 245 Squadron as shown on SW417 'MR-X'. (G. Murphy)

4. 609 Squadron's Typhoons sported gloss-black spinners with yellow backplates and trim on the undercarriage leg fairings, as on Squadron Leader 'Pinkie' Stark's SW411 'PR-J', which also had a Squadron Leader's pennant and 609's crest below the windscreen. (L. W. F. Stark)

5. 124 Wing Typhoons featured two-tone spinners, although the colours are not known; an example is 182 Squadron's RB195 'XM-K' photographed at Lübeck in July 1945. (P. Riley)

6. 440 Squadron painted their Typhoons' spinners white with red tips and backplates; some aircraft, like JR336 'F3-X', had their 'Mod 286' plates in white edged with red. (J. A. Lord)

CHAPTER TEN

Tempest Development

EARLY in the Typhoon development programme the major limitation on the aircraft's performance had been identified as the wing section. The Typhoon employed an NACA 22 section which had its maximum depth at 30% chord; the thickness/chord ratio was 19.5% at the root, tapering to 12% at the tip. This allowed great structural strength with plenty of room for fuel and armament, and although ideal at speeds up to 400mph, when diving trials were carried out on the Typhoon prototype, a sharp increase in drag was evident as 500mph was approached, followed by buffeting and trim changes. Accordingly, in March 1940, investigations into the advantages of a thinner wing section were undertaken. However, because of changing priorities occasioned by the Battle of Britain, the actual design of the wing was not commenced until September of the following year. The maximum depth of the new section occurred farther back, at 37.5% chord, while the thickness/chord ratio was reduced to 14.5% at the root tapering to 10% at the tip. This meant that the new wing was five inches thinner at the root than the original Typhoon wing. The profile of the new wing was also radically changed, to a semi-elliptical planform, not unlike the Spitfire's. There were, apparently, no aerodynamic reasons for this decision – it is said that it was made at the insistence of Spitfire enthusiasts at the Ministry of Aircraft Production!

The new thin wing meant that alternative space for fuel had to be found and this was achieved by moving the engine forward 21 inches and inserting a 76-gallon tank between the firewall and the oil tank. The redesign also included a new undercarriage unit and the latest version of the Sabre engine, the Mark IV. A contract for two prototypes to specification F.10/41 was placed in November 1941; the new type was to be known as the Typhoon II. There followed much discussion between the Ministry of Aircraft Production and Sydney Camm as to the most suitable cooling arrangements for the Sabre IV. Camm had designed radiators to be fitted in the inner wing sections with intakes along the leading edge (similar to the Mosquito), allowing a beautifully slim nose cowling which belied the bulk of the Sabre. Hawker wind tunnel tests showed that the wing radiators gave little advantage over the existing Typhoon positioning, under the nose, but calculations made by RAE Farnborough suggested that they would reduce drag from this item by nearly two-thirds, so work on the wing radiators continued.

By the spring of 1942 the Sabre engine problems were casting severe doubts on the viability of future projects with this power plant. With the Rolls-Royce Vulture now out of the running, the same company's Griffon came under scrutiny. A Griffon-engined variant of the Typhoon I was hurriedly designed and a Typhoon airframe was dispatched to Derby for a trial installation, while one of the Typhoon II prototypes was now planned to have a Griffon 61. The only other alternative was the Bristol Centaurus, but this was only in the very early stages of development and could not meet the time-scale required for Typhoon II production. By June 1942 it had been decided to double the existing prototype order. Two were now to have Sabres; one would have the Mk IV, but as this was also behind schedule, the other would have the Mk II – the standard production Typhoon engine. Two more would have Griffon engines and the intention to order a further two Centaurus-powered variants, when this engine became available, was declared. Two months later the position was clarified when the Typhoon II was renamed and Mark numbers were allocated to the different variants. The name change was justified because the projected developments were significantly different in appearance from the Typhoon I, but one also suspects that it was politically expedient as the Typhoon's reputation was at its nadir. The name chosen, 'Tempest', followed Hawker's established 'winds' theme, and the Mark numbers were:

Mk I	Sabre IV	(serial no. HM599)
Mk II	Centaurus IV	(LA602 and LA607)
Mk III	Griffon IIB	(LA610)
Mk IV	Griffon 61	(LA614)
Mk V	Sabre II	(HM595)

Perversely, owing to the delays with the Sabre IV and Centaurus engines, and the redesign necessary for the Griffon installation, the Mk V was ready to fly long before

Below: This view clearly shows the extra bay inserted in the fuselage (between the oil tank and the fire-wall) in order to accommodate a fuel tank (cf., Typhoon on page 17). (BAe)

the others. This event took place on 2 September 1942 with Phillip Lucas at the controls. At the time the aircraft featured the early Typhoon-style heavily framed canopy, although a mock-up of a proposed one-piece 'bubble' sliding hood was already under construction. Inevitably the extra length of the nose needed compensation, and both vertical and horizontal tail surfaces were increased in area, the former by the addition of a fin fillet and the latter by replacement with a unit of greater span and chord. It was soon evident that the new wing was giving its expected benefits, handling at speed proving smoother and crisper, and there was no evidence of the vibration experienced by Typhoons.

Arguments as to the fixed armament to be carried in the wing had raged for more than a year, three 20mm cannons per wing losing favour to the 'universal wing' which would allow two 20mm cannon, or a single cannon with either a 0.5in machine-gun or two 0.303in machine-guns. It proved impossible to incorporate all these alternatives in the new slim wing and two 20mm Hispano Mk II cannon with 200 rounds per gun, was the eventual decision.

In February 1943 RAF pilots got their first chance to fly the Tempest when three test pilots from A&AEE made a brief assessment. They were impressed, reporting HM595 to be 'a manoeuvrable and pleasant aircraft to fly, with no major handling faults'. It was thought that the elevator was a little on the heavy side but by no means excessively so. Although HM595 still had the old canopy at this time, they were able to examine the new sliding hood which had been installed on Typhoon R8809, and this was considered excellent.

Meanwhile work on the Tempest I had been further delayed by problems with manufacture of the wing radiator, but it eventually flew on 24 February 1943. It performed well and only minor problems such as poor elevator control at low speed and slow throttle reaction were noted. It was an exceptionally clean design and its maximum speed was soon established as a promising 466mph at 24,500 feet.

Below: The Tempest V prototype, HM595, at Langley in September 1942, in its original form, with Typhoon canopy and tail unit. (BAe)

Bottom: The Tempest V prototype after the addition of an interim fin fillet and a larger tailplane. It is seen during altitude measurement at A&AEE Boscombe Down, hence the datum line on the fuselage. (Mod)

Top right: The Tempest I prototype, HM599, at Langley in February 1943. (BAe)

Centre right: This view of the Tempest I, HM599, clearly shows the controversial leading-edge radiators. (BAe)

Bottom right: The first production Tempest V, JN729, spent all its life with Hawker, engaged on various trials. (BAe)

Unfortunately, there still remained much development work to be done on the Sabre IV and this, plus Air Staff distrust of the wing radiators, which were thought to be prone to battle damage (the Mosquito managed!), led to abandonment of the Tempest I in favour of the less spectacular but more certain progress of the Tempest V. Production orders for the latter had now been placed and development of the Tempest II (whose Centaurus engine was now proceeding well, thanks in part to the Centaurus-powered Tornado programme) would continue as a more long-term prospect. The Griffon-powered Tempest III and IV were also axed, Griffon production being largely earmarked for Spitfires. In the event, the Tempest III airframe, LA610, was eventually completed as a Hawker Fury with a Griffon 85; later still it was re-engined with the final version of the Sabre, the Mk VIII, which developed over 3,000hp, and in this form it achieved 483mph making it the fastest of the Hawker piston-engined fighters.

The first production Tempest V, JN729, took to the air on 21 June 1943, piloted by Bill Humble, and was part of an order for 100. These aircraft were known as the Mk V Series I and were distinguished from later Mk Vs by having long-barrelled Hispano Mk II cannon which protruded some eight inches beyond the leading edge.

In October of the same year, the third production Tempest V, JN731, was delivered to A&AEE Boscombe Down for a series of tests including performance and handling trials. The resultant report was generally satisfactory, main areas of criticism being heavy ailerons (although they could still be moved at 535mph IAS in a dive) and poor roll rate. These aspects would soon be greatly improved with the fitting of spring-tab ailerons. The view from the cockpit (JN731 had the new canopy) was considered excellent. Maximum speed was found to vary between 376mph at sea level and 432mph at 18,400 feet, a very useful 411mph being recorded at 6,600 feet. Service ceiling was 34,800 feet.

It was apparent that with a little more refinement the RAF was about to receive its most potent medium- and low-level fighter yet. To find out just how good it was going to be, an early production aircraft, JN737, was dispatched to the Air Fighting Development Unit at Wittering on 8 January 1944, for comparative trials with current Allied and German fighters. By now production Tempests were fitted with spring-tab ailerons, which dramatically improved the roll rate, especially at speeds above 250mph IAS.

First it was flown against a Typhoon (with the old canopy, although the new canopy was already in service on Typhoons). The advantages of the Tempest's new canopy

were immediately apparent in take-off, landing, formation flying, and dogfighting, the all-round view being superior to any Allied or enemy aircraft in service at that time. The engine was smoother, and rudder, ailerons and elevators were all found to be more effective than its predecessor's. Maximum speeds at various altitudes and settings were all found to be 15–20mph higher than the Typhoon's. The extra speed compensated the reduced internal fuel capacity (132 gallons as opposed to the Typhoon's 154 gallons) to give the Tempest a similar range. Climb rate was about 300ft/min better at maximum rate of climb but 'zoom' climb was greatly improved due to the aircraft's clean airframe, and dive performance similarly benefited. In fact the Tempest's acceleration in the dive was remarkable; this and its steadiness as a gun platform would be the keys to its success in combat over north-west Europe.

Comparisons with the Mustang III, Spitfire XIV, Bf 109G and Fw 190A, revealed that the Tempest was faster than all of them below 20,000 feet – 15 or 20mph in the case of the Allied types, 40 or 50mph for the German aircraft. At higher levels the Mustang and Spitfire soon reversed this, but while the Bf 109G could match the Tempest, the Fw 190A remained slower.

The Tempest could just be out-turned by the Mustang, and more easily by the Spitfire, but it could hold its own with the 190 and out-turn the 109, which was embarrassed by

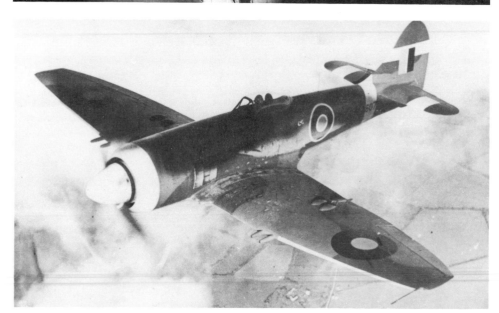

Top left: The Sabre II on a production Tempest V. (BAe)

Left: The second prototype Tempest II, LA607 under test. This aircraft was for many years the sole surviving Mk II in the UK, but has since been sold to American collector, Kermit Weeks.

Below: The second production Tempest V, JN730, was used for the development of the Tempest's specially designed 45-gallon underwing tanks. (BAe)

Below right: The first prototype Tempest II, LA602, at Langley June 1943. Like the other Tempest prototypes it started life with a Typhoon fin and rudder. (BAe)

its leading-edge slots opening near the stall. In roll rate the Tempest could not compare with the Fw 190 and was also inferior to the Mustang and the Spitfire, although the situation was reversed with the Spitfire at speeds above 350mph. Below this speed it was roughly equal to the Bf 109 but above it the 109 could be lost by making a quick change of bank and direction.

It was concluded that the Tempest V was superior to the Typhoon in all respects and faster than any other fighter up to medium altitude, having the best zoom-climb and dive characteristics yet seen by the AFDU.

In comparing the Tempest with the Spitfire XIV the AFDU had noted that the tactical attributes of the two aircraft were completely different, and for this reason Typhoon squadrons should convert to Tempests and squadrons equipped with earlier Spitfires should convert to the Mk XIV. Initially this was the policy, but after the first three units no further Typhoon squadrons received Tempests during the war, as neither the aircraft nor their pilots could be spared from 2nd TAF. The first Tempests arrived at Tangmere in January 1944 and were used by 486 Squadron, RNZAF, for familiarization; they were soon passed on to 3 Squadron which became the first unit to equip with the type.

Meanwhile, the Hispano Mk V short-barrelled 20mm cannon had become available, and follow-up orders for the Tempest were for the Mk V Series 2 aircraft which featured this gun, completely contained within the wing, and the facility for a 45-gallon drop-tank under each wing. The drop-tank had been specially designed for the Tempest by Hawker, much to the annoyance of the Ministry of Aircraft Production which was committed to the manufacture of the cylindrical tanks, as used on Hurricanes and Typhoons. However Camm made a good case for the new streamlined tanks,

which had less than half the drag of the original model, and the argument was won when it was discovered that the standard tanks would require internal modifications before they could be fitted to the Tempest. The Mk V Series 2 Tempests began reaching the squadrons towards the end of June 1944 and deliveries of this sub-type continued until September 1945 when SN355, the last of 801 Mk Vs was delivered.

While much effort was made to get the Tempest V into service, it was still regarded as an interim measure, with the Mk II being considered the ultimate Tempest. The first prototype of this version, LA602, eventually flew on 28 June 1943. Like the Mk I and Mk V prototypes, it began life with a Typhoon-style fin and rudder; it was powered by a Bristol Centaurus Mk IV air-cooled radial engine, rated at 2,520hp, rigidly mounted and driving a 4-bladed propeller. Carburettor air intakes were sited in the leading edges of both wings adjacent to the fuselage, and an oil cooler with a leading edge intake was mounted in the inner section of the starboard wing.

Serious engine vibration was soon apparent and this was to be the Mk II's main problem during the early days of the programme. The second Mk II, LA607, flew on 18 September 1943 and was assigned to engine development.

The engine originally projected for the production Mk II was the Centaurus XII, but protracted delays with this version placed it beyond the time-scale required for Mk II production. In addition, the answer to the engine vibration was found to lie in replacing the original eight-point rigid mounting by a six-point rubber-packed mounting and this was unsuitable for the Centaurus XII, so production plans settled on the Centaurus V which had a similar output to the Mk IV. Another measure taken to control the vibration was the intro-

duction of a 5-bladed propeller; this was flown on LA607 but abandoned in favour of a finely balanced 4-blader. Further engine problems, including overheating, exhaust malfunction, crankshaft lubrication and reduction gear seizure, combined to delay the flight of the first production aircraft, but in May 1944 LA602 was delivered to A&AEE Boscombe Down for assessment. It was not up to production standard, particularly in respect of engine mountings and exhaust system, both of which were still under development, and it was armed with Hispano Mk II cannon with protruding barrels (as for the Tempest V Series I) whereas the production version would have the shorter barrelled Mk V cannon. It was generally satisfactory but many small faults were found. Noise level was considerably lower than the Mk V, making the aircraft more pleasant and less tiring to fly, but below 2,000 and above 2,400rpm the engine vibration was still higher than normally permissible. All control characteristics were similar to the Mk V, but the ailerons were even heavier (this was before introduction of spring-tabs). The rudder was moderately light for small deflections but heavier for larger ones. Power changes necessitated adjustment of the directional trim only at high speeds. The elevator was moderately light and changes in longitudinal trim at speed were very small. Approach and landing were very easy although with engine off there was insufficient elevator control to get the tail down for a three-point landing.

Dimensionally the Mk II was, of course, very similar to the Mk V; span was identical, but it was slightly longer (34ft 5in) and lower (15ft 10in). Fully loaded the weight was up by only 20lb, to 14,500lb. There were all round increases in performance – maximum speed was measured at 442mph at 15,200 feet and climb to this level took four and a half minutes as opposed to the Mk V's

joined the two prototypes and JN750 (a Mk V converted to Mk II) to expedite service clearance of the type.

By now the Tempest II had been selected for use in south-east Asia – to replace the RAF's ageing Hurricanes and lease-lend Thunderbolts. Original plans for tropical trials in this area were abandoned in favour of the Middle East and six aircraft (MW801 to MW806) were flown to Khartoum in April 1945 for intensive flying trials. Despite the loss of one Tempest in a landing accident during the trials (a further aircraft was lost on the ferry flight back to the UK), 740 hours had been flown by completion of the trials in August 1945. The Tempest Mk II was considered 'very satisfactory by all attached pilots, particularly in the role of low attack', but for the hurly-burly of squadron use some 29 minor modifications were considered necessary.

While these tropical trials were still in progress, the first Mk IIs, which had been steadily stock-piled at Maintenance Units, were released for service, the first examples going to 13 OTU at Harwell in June 1945, quickly followed by deliveries to front-line squadrons. The ending of the war against Japan was to cut back re-equipment plans, however, and the Mk IIs which were now pouring off the production lines were delivered to MUs for storage. Bristol's production order was cut back to fifty aircraft, and twenty of these were actually assembled by Hawker from Bristol-built components, while Hawker's orders were also reduced, final production of this version totalled 452.

Returning to 1944, it had been calculated that Tempest II production would be limited by the availability of Centaurus engines and therefore Sabre-powered Tempest development and production would continue to make up the deficit. A new version of the Sabre – the Mk V – with nearly 10 per cent more power output over the Tempest V's Sabre II, was fitted in HM595 which now became the prototype Tempest VI, first flying in this guise on 9 May 1944. The new

five minutes. Service ceiling was also improved – 37,500 feet.

The main improvements required were lighter ailerons and complete eradication of engine vibration. These were eventually achieved with the fitting of spring-tab ailerons and improved engine mountings.

Originally the Tempest Mk II was to have been built by the Gloster Aircraft Company, as the parent company was committed to Mk V production and could not build Mk IIs at the required rate. However, continuing demand for the Gloster-built Typhoon, then suffering its highest loss rate in 2nd

TAF, coupled with the prospect of Meteor production, meant that the contract for 300 aircraft had to be transferred to a new sub-contractor. The Bristol Aeroplane Company, whose engine division was responsible for the Centaurus, was chosen, but it would be February 1945 before the first Tempests produced at their new plant at Banwell, near Bristol, came off the line.

Meanwhile Hawker's own production line at Langley had been turning out Mk IIs alongside Mk Vs, the first aircraft having been completed in October 1944, much later than planned. The first six aircraft

reverse took place, although there was a manual switch in the cockpit which could override this system, in the event of, for example, a dust-laden atmosphere. The aircraft was also equipped with desert survival gear which included two cylinders of water strapped to the fuselage behind the pilot's head armour. The first seven production aircraft, NV997-999 and NX113-116, which became available in July and August 1945, were retained by Hawker and Napier for their own trials.

With the war in Europe over and that in the Pacific coming to its dramatic close, the Tempest VI looked ripe for cancellation, especially as the RAF would now have many Tempest IIs surplus to requirements. But, if the Tempest VI project had been allowed to founder, Napier would have been in severe trouble, needing continued Sabre V production to survive until more advanced projects came to fruition. In the event, Tempest VI production was allowed to proceed, although orders were cut from 250 to 142. Full performance and cooling trials were carried out on NX119 at Khartoum between December 1945 and February 1946. The more powerful Sabre gave the Mk VI a top speed of 438mph at 17,800 feet and a service ceiling of 38,000 feet. Deliveries took place throughout 1946 and at the end of that year the first of five squadrons in the Middle East began re-equipping.

Development of underwing stores for the Tempest followed much the same lines as the Typhoon. During the summer of 1944 trials with rockets, bombs and other stores were undertaken by Hawkers and A&AEE. A pair of bomb racks reduced the maximum speed by up to 10mph and the addition of two 500lb bombs caused a further reduction of approximately 30mph (it varied with height). Mk III lightweight rocket rails gave a drop of 16mph and a further 21mph when eight 60lb RP were added. Neither affected handling to any significant extent, but service use of underwing stores was limited to the 45-gallon drop-tanks mentioned earlier, until the last few days of the war when 33 Squadron carried 500lb bombs into action. Post-war, Mk II, V, and VI squadrons were equipped to carry up to 1,000lb bombs or four rocket rails under each wing; the rails were eventually replaced by 'zero-length' launchers.

Trials were also undertaken with a 47mm Vicker's 'P' gun (a development of the Vickers 'S' gun carried by Hurricanes in the Western Desert in 1943) under each wing, but these came to nought and the RAF continued, despite some post-war doubts, in its reliance on rockets.

As with the Typhoon, Napier investigated the efficiency of annular radiators, converting two Mk Vs, EJ518 and NV768, the latter employing a Sabre V and a huge ducted spinner with the air intake ahead of the pro-

engine's 2,340hp required greater cooling capacity and this was provided by removing the oil cooler and carburettor air intake from the centre of the radiator, the resulting space being filled with additional radiator area. The carburettor air intakes were repositioned in the leading edges of the inner wings and the oil cooler was now fitted behind the radiator.

It was decided early in the Mk VI's career that it would be developed for use in the Middle East; to help the project, a Tempest V, EJ841, was modified to Mk VI standard, and a standard Mk V, EJ759, was sent to Khartoum for engine cooling and air cleaner trials. Cooling was not satisfactory and a subsidiary oil cooler was fitted in the leading edge of the starboard wing as in the Tempest II. The air cleaner was similar to that fitted on the tropical version of the Typhoon, and was installed beneath the fuselage, between the wings. During ground running and taxiing, when sand and dust were a problem, air for the carburettor was drawn in via the filter system, but after take-off, retraction of the undercarriage automatically initiated transfer to air from the leading edge intakes. When the undercarriage was lowered, the

peller blades. Although these installations were successful they did not result in any changes to the Tempest production models.

One version of the Tempest which never left the drawing-board was the Hawker P.1027, powered by the Rolls-Royce 46 Eagle. This 2,690hp engine was to drive contra-rotating propellers and the radiator was moved back to a ventral position similar to the P.51 Mustang. The only further development of the Tempest to fly was the 'Tempest Light Fighter' produced to specification F.2/43. With span reduced by the simple expedient of removing the centre section and bolting the wings together, and a new all-monocoque fuselage, the new fighter was produced in Sabre-, Griffon- and Centaurus-powered versions. The latter saw production as the Hawker Fury and Sea Fury – Hawker's last piston-engined fighter.

By mid-1947 many Tempest Vs had been removed from front-line service and large stocks were held in storage at 5 MU Kemble and 20 MU Aston Down. The RAF had a requirement for a high-speed target-tug to replace its Martinets, and provide realistic targets for its new jet fighters. The availability of the Tempest, with its high cruising speed, made it an ideal choice for the role. Consequently in May 1947, SN329, fresh from refurbishment by Hawker, was allocated for conversion to prototype Tempest TT.Mk 5 (Roman numerals for Mark numbers were replaced by Arabic numerals about this time). Trials with the towing equipment were carried out by the Airborne Forces Experimental Establishment at Beaulieu (which undertook all glider-towing and similar trials) during 1948 and 1949 and with modified equipment by A&AEE Boscombe Down, following closure of the AFEE in 1950. Meanwhile, in December 1948, the first of eighty Tempests were withdrawn from storage and delivered to Langley for the conversion to TT.Mk 5 standard; the programme was not completed until May 1952. These Tempests were the last of the breed to see RAF service and the final examples were retired from 233 OCU Pembrey in July 1955.

Top left: The prototype Tempest TT.5, SN329. Here it is carrying a wind-driven winch which was not fitted to production TT.5s. The standard fixed towing point is visible beneath the fuselage just forward of the IFF aerial. The tail surfaces are protected from cable damage by wire guards. (MoD)

Centre left: Tempest V NV768 was fitted with an annular radiator by Napier and is seen here in company with a standard Mk VI, NX121, July 1945. At this time it was fitted with a conventional spinner, but it also flew with a huge ducted spinner, of the same diameter as the engine cowling. (RAFM/C. E. Brown)

Left: The 'Tempest Light Fighter' project resulted in the Hawker Fury, which was successfully developed as the Sea Fury. One of the Centaurus-engined prototypes, NX802, in demonstrator colours, is seen here on the apron at Langley in 1947. In the background are two Tempest Vs, JN876 'RH', Air Marshal Sir Roderick Hill's aircraft (probably visiting), and SN213 '5R-S', ex-33 Squadron, awaiting repair. (BAe)

CHAPTER ELEVEN

The Tempest in Service, April 1944 to May 1945

AS the first production Tempest Vs became available, strenuous efforts were put in hand to make a Wing of these formidable aircraft ready for air superiority duties during the impending invasion of western Europe. These efforts were almost, though not entirely successful, although in the event the very limited initial reaction of the Luftwaffe, and the manifest ability of the Spitfire IX and Mustang units to deal with any threat posed by such Messerschmitts and Focke-Wulfs as did appear, prevented this proving to be anything of a problem.

In line with the AFDU's recommendations, three of the existing Typhoon units were chosen to be the first to re-equip. The first of these, 486 Squadron, received five Tempests for 'experience', these arriving at Tangmere in mid-January 1944. At the end of February these aircraft were transferred to 3 Squadron at Manston, this unit moving to Bradwell Bay a week later where full conversion to the new fighter began. Early in April a week was spent at Ayr's APC for some air-firing experience, before a return to Bradwell Bay allowed the first operational sorties to be flown on 23 April – an ASR patrol. Meanwhile 486 Squadron had also undertaken full re-equipment at Castle Camps in Cambridgeshire, also spending a week at Ayr before joining 3 Squadron at a new advanced landing-ground (ALG) at Newchurch in Kent, near the south coast, to be known as 150 Airfield.

A third unit, 56 Squadron, had been spending its time in relative inactivity in the north-east at Scorton and Acklington, in anticipation of early re-equipment. At the end of March a dozen of the unit's recently received rocket-Typhoons were exchanged with 137 Squadron for that unit's older, unmodified aircraft. But when new mounts became available in April, they were Spitfire IXs! The flow of Tempests from Langley had been stemmed by industrial troubles arising from a dispute over pay rates for work on the new type. After a session at Ayr, 56 Squadron arrived at Newchurch on 28 April, still with a few Typhoons among its Spitfires, to complete the formation of 150 Wing, 85 Group. The Wing was to be led by Wing Commander Roland Beamont, DSO, DFC✭, who was returning for a further tour of operations after a period as a test-pilot with Hawker, where he had played an important part in the development of the Tempest.

The Tempests of 3 and 486 Squadrons were soon in action, shipping reconnaissance and strafing sorties being flown by pairs of aircraft throughout most of May. The old problems with the Sabre had still not entirely cleared themselves, however, and by mid-month each unit had suffered two forced-landings because of engine failure. On the 27th two 3 Squadron aircraft failed to return from a shipping reconnaissance off the Ostend–Dunkirk stretch of the

Top left: Goodbye Typhoon, Hello Tempest! One of 486 Squadron's last Typhoons, 'SA-R' MN282, in formation with one of its replacements, Tempest V 'SA-N' JN766. In addition to the more obvious differences in the fin and wing shapes, note the longer nose of the Tempest. (IWM)

Left: The same Tempest photographed during 486's re-equipment period at Castle Camps in April 1944. Note that at this time the Tempests still wore Typhoon-style identity stripes beneath the wings. These had been removed from Typhoons two moths earlier. (IWM)

Belgian coastline, no indication of their fate being forthcoming. That both were lost would seem to presuppose interception by German fighters, but no claims have been found.

After all the effort expended to have at least two squadrons of Tempests ready for D-Day, in the event they were not called upon to operate over the beaches until late on 6 June, the day of the Invasion, being held in reserve against any serious attempt at intervention by the Germans. To Beamont's chagrin the Spitfires of 56 Squadron *were* called upon, joining units of the Detling Wing to escort formations of gliders and their tugs during the initial assault. Two of the units with which they flew on that memorable day, 80 and 274 Squadrons, were soon to become familiar companions when they too converted to Tempests.

At last, on 8 June, with the Invasion already two days old, came the call. Beamont led a formation of nine 3 Squadron Tempests in a sweep over the beachhead, where five Messerschmitt Bf 109Gs were seen to the east of Rouen. The British pilots attacked at once, Beamont personally claiming one of the opposing

fighters shot down, while Flight Lieutenant Moore accounted for another. Two more Messerschmitts appeared and attempted to 'bounce' the formation, but a vigilant Pilot Officer Whitman turned into these and reported that he had sent one down. Three for no loss! The Tempest had demonstrated its capabilities in unmistakable fashion.

Despite further patrols and sweeps, nothing more was seen of the Luftwaffe during the rest of the week. Even as the Allied forces struggled to secure their beachhead in Normandy, however, southern England came under a new threat as the long-anticipated V-weapon campaign was launched by the Germans from the Pas-de-Calais. As recounted earlier, Typhoon squadrons along with many others had played their part throughout early 1944 against the 'Noball' targets – the launching sites for the V-1 flying bombs. These robot mini-aircraft, Fieseler Fi 103, to give them their formal title, were little more than bombs fitted with rudimentary wings and control surfaces, and powered by a single pulse-jet engine. The amount of fuel carried dictated the range of the missile, which was launched in the general direction of

Above: Wing Commander R. P. Beamont, Wing Leader of 150 Wing, the first Tempest Wing. (IWM)

Left: Armourers at work on Wing Commander R. P. Beamont's 'R-B' JN751, at Castle Camps in April 1944. This was his personal aircraft from the formation of 150 Wing until replacement by a Tempest V Series 2 aircraft at the beginning of September 1944. To aid swift identification in the air its spinner was painted yellow. (IWM)

Left: Pilots of 3 Squadron discuss tactics at the height of the V-1 campaign, using the tailplane of 'JF-M' as a map table. (IWM)

Right: Flight Sergeant R. W. Cole of 3 Squadron examines his damaged Tempest after having flown through an exploding V-1. His score would eventually reach 21 plus two ⅓ shares. (IWM)

London, and which dived to explode on any target in its path when the fuel was exhausted.

The first of these missiles – 'Divers' as they had already been code-named – to be seen by the Wing was spotted by pilots of 3 Squadron on 13 June; they were about to become extremely familiar. Three days later the Newchurch Wing was detached from 2nd TAF to ADGB, together with a number of other units of high-performance fighters, to form part of the defences being prepared to counter this new menace. Indeed the Tempests had been positioned at Newchurch ready to meet this threat, which British Intelligence had been well aware was about to manifest itself.

Patrols against the 'Divers' commenced on the 16th, the first being shot down south of Maidstone at 0750 hours by Flight Sergeant Rose of 3 Squadron, and later in the day Flight Sergeant O'Connor claimed the first for 486 Squadron between Hythe and Dungeness. By nightfall thirteen had been dealt with by the Wing, eleven of which were credited to 3 Squadron. Thereafter patrols were maintained throughout the hours of daylight, and there was not to

be a day when claims were not submitted by the Wing's squadrons until mid-July.

Roland Beamont has provided a graphic description of the problems encountered initially in intercepting the bombs, and the measures developed to overcome these: 'The interception and destruction of V-1s presented some interesting problems for 150 Wing. I knew we had been positioned to counter the V-weapons, but beyond the general brief that the flying bombs when they came would be small and very fast, and that the V-2s would be supersonic rockets against which there would be no defence except attacks on the launching sites, there was no detailed Intelligence to go on. These pulse-jet auto-piloted aircraft measured 16 feet span by 20 feet length and flew at 1,500–2,000 feet at speeds approaching 400mph. At that height the Tempest proved to have a greater speed margin than all other fighters, and with its excellent gun-aiming stability was immediately successful in destroying ten V-1s over the Channel, Kent and Sussex by midday on the first day, 150 by the end of the first week, and in all 632 by mid-August. Then the AA guns were able to take over with radar and proximity-fuzed shells and so allowed the Tempests to return to the Battle for Europe.

. . . on the first day, speed, height, size and best methods of attack were all unknown. In the event, the attack came generally at below 2,000 feet and at speeds between 340 and 370mph IAS; and with a three-foot cross-section fuselage and eight-inch thick wing they proved extremely small targets to hit from the stern quarter which, by virtue of their high speed, was the segment in which the vast majority of fighter attacks ended up. Then there was the question of firing range and how close to go in, relative to the chances of blowing yourself up when the warhead exploded. Starting at 400 yards we experienced much wastage and frequent missing altogether until, when closing to 200 yards before firing, a higher success rate was achieved but losses were sustained due to debris and fire damage. I was convinced that the standard Fighter Command 'spread harmonization' pattern for the guns was unsuitable for this operation and, after failing to obtain official approval, had my own guns point-harmonized at 300 yards. This had an immediate effect for the better on my shooting and I was able to hit the next lot of V-1s with my first burst and with good effect. Accordingly I ordered all 150 Wing guns point-harmonized in disregard of Command policy with two results: the first an immediate and sustained improvement on the Wing's scoring rate, and the second, not unexpectedly, was a different sort of rocket from Headquarters!

Interception of these small, fast targets was also a problem; although the radars could see them they could rarely put my

fighter into the 500 yards or nearer position which was generally necessary for them to be picked up visually in all but perfect light conditions. The situation became even more difficult by the end of the first week when it became fashionable to do 'training sorties' in the south-east, and the skies of Kent became a sort of free-for-all with fighters of all types and from many Commands joining in. This showed commendable zeal for the fray but it often resulted in confused intercepts, and many V-1s got through when the Tempests were baulked by slower fighters. I reported to 11 Group Headquarters and asked for a special defence zone to be created in which all aircraft would be banned except those few squadrons most suitable for this activity, namely Tempests, Spitfires XII and XIV, and later Mustangs with uprated engines. I also asked for a deployment of the Royal Observer Corps round the coast with signal rockets which they would fire towards any V-1 seen, to give visual clues to the radar-vectored fighters. Within a very few days, thanks to the immediate reaction of Air Vice-Marshal Bouchier of 11 Group, these measures were in operation, and significant improvement in the kill rate was achieved.

In parallel with all this activity was the fact that daylight did not see an end of the V-1 attack, and they were launched throughout the 24 hours on an 'as available' basis, so that in the short summer nights there were on average as many V-1s coming across per hour as in daylight. The interception of these vehicles at night was in itself a unique operation as there had been no previous experience anywhere in the world of intercept and attack on a brilliant light, which was all that could be seen of the V-1. The Mosquito night-fighters had had some success and on the night of 22 June I took off for an experimental sortie from Newchurch and succeeded in intercepting and shooting down a V-1 north of Hastings, but it was an imprecise and hazardous occupation at first. The radar interception was made far easier than in daytime of course, by virtue of the fact that the brilliant flame of the pulse-jet could be seen at night for ten or fifteen miles in good weather, and all one had to do was to close at full throttle until at firing range. But here was the problem. With nothing to judge distance by except the light, which got progressively bigger and more dazzling, it was not easy to get into an effective firing range without suddenly overshooting and possibly even running into the target. I found that the best method was to approach the target from astern until we appeared to be within about 1,000 yards and then to descend below it until in a relative position of approximately 100 feet below and 300 yards behind. This could be judged reasonably well by looking up through the transparent canopy and over the top of the windscreen arch. From this situation a gentle climb was made into the dead astern position until preferably the wake of the V-1 was felt in the Tempest and then with the gun-sight centred directly on the exhaust flame, a long burst was generally enough to deal with it.'

Help in dealing with the night threat was soon to arrive, for on 22 June the FIU at Wittering, a test unit which experimented with night-fighting techniques on actual operations, was issued with a small number of Tempests and immediately commenced night-flying and air-firing tests with them. These proved successful, and on the 25th, Squadron Leader 'Tubby' Daniel, earlier in the war a successful night-fighter 'ace' over Malta, and Flight Lieutenant 'Joe' Berry, arrived at Newchurch on detachment. Weather prevented night sorties being made until the evening of 28 June, but by dawn of the next day the two pilots had each des-

troyed two V-1s – the start of a remarkable run of success that was to be achieved as this small detachment was steadily reinforced until it had reached the strength of a full Flight.

Meanwhile the effectiveness of the defence was indeed increasing as Roland Beamont indicates. On 23 June, a day on which the Newchurch Tempests claimed the destruction of more than two dozen V-1s, no less than five were credited to 3 Squadron's Flight Lieutenant Remy Van Lierde alone. On the 28th Flying Officer Clapperton of the same unit claimed three in a single sortie, 3 Squadron's tally reaching 100 on this date. 486 Squadron was close behind, having claimed 92½ by the end of June, but it was this unit which was to suffer the first casualties on these operations when on the 28th one Tempest was hit by British AA fire and two more were struck by debris from exploding V-1s. Flying Officer

Williams managed to land his damaged aircraft at base, Pilot Officer Lawless force-landed, but Flight Sergeant Wright crashed near Beachy Head and was killed. Three days later it was 3 Squadron's turn; Flying Officer Kosh crashing to his death southwest of Rye after chasing a V-1 into cloud, and on 3 July Flight Sergeant Domanski (Polish) was also killed when hit by AA firing at a bomb which he was chasing; between them the two pilots had accounted for seven 'Divers'.

After gaining a single success against the new enemy with their Spitfires, 56 Squadron had at last received their Tempests on 24 June, commencing operations with these aircraft on 2 July. Next day this squadron's Tempest 'bag' was begun by Flight Lieutenant 'Digger' Cotes-Preedy, who brought down a 'Diver' near Dungeness. One of the unit's Canadians, Flying Officer Ness, having used up all his ammunition without

Left: Refuelling and re-arming Tempest 'JF-G' of 3 Squadron at Newchurch in June 1944. (IWM)

Left: JN765 'JF-K' of 3 Squadron taxiing out at Newchurch in June 1944. This aircraft was one of the casualties of the V-1 campaign, when Flying Officer Kosh chased a flying bomb into cloud, lost control and crashed. (IWM)

success, attempted three times to turn one of the bombs over with his wingtip, but again he was unsuccessful. On the 4th, however, Flying Officer MacLaren managed this feat, flying alongside one V-1 and placing the wingtip of the Tempest a few inches below that of his quarry. A quick flick and the bomb turned over, its gyros tumbled and it crashed to the ground. This third day of interceptions was to bring 56 Squadron five successes, and thereafter the unit's score rose steadily if unspectacularly – but the squadron was never to achieve the rate of scoring enjoyed by its two companions.

July had brought the first decorations for the 'Diver' operations, Flight Lieutenant Moore and Pilot Officer Feldman (American), both members of 3 Squadron, receiving DFCs, and two days later the same unit's Flight Lieutenant Umbers, received a Bar to his DFC, and Wing Commander Beamont a Bar to his DSO. As the sorties continued, highlights succeeded each other in rapid succession. On 4 July, 3 Squadron achieved its best day to date with claims for 14½; Flight Lieutenant Van Lierde's four in one sortie also recording a new best performance. Next day the squadron score passed 150. The increasing success of the FIU detachment at night was underlined on the 6th, when Flight Lieutenant Berry claimed four in one night, and on the 8th 486 Squadron's Flight Lieutenant McCaw matched Van Lierde's four in one sortie, as would Warrant Officer Kalka, another of the New Zealanders on the 12th.

On the 5th, Warrant Officer C. J. Sheddan of 486 Squadron attacked three V-1s, two of which were destroyed, one being credited to his efforts, but a 20mm shell-case from another aircraft entered his Tempest's oil cooler intake, and he was obliged to crash-land. The 12th proved to be the best day of the whole campaign for the Tempests, and particularly for 3 Squadron which claimed seventeen of the 28½ V-1s credited to the Wing on that date. The cost was 56 Squadron's first loss, when Flight Lieutenant Mansfield was badly injured in a forced-landing after his aircraft had been hit by the ever-dangerous 'friendly' AA.

Although proving very successful, FIU's night operations were also, by their very nature, more hazardous, and a number of notably successful pilots were to be put out of action while so engaged. During the night of 5 July, Squadron Leader Daniel's engine cut after a V-1 exploded close by; although he baled out, he was not found. Having previously commanded the Typhoon 'Abdullah' Flight at Holmesly South, he had claimed six victories at night and then three V-1s. Five nights later, Flight Lieutenant Wagner, who had recently joined the detachment at Newchurch, flew into the ground at high speed in foggy conditions and was killed. This eight-victory 'ace' had

also shot down two V-1s. Wing Commander Hartley, FIU's commanding officer, had joined the detachment on 10 July, but on the 17th he collided with a Mosquito and baled out with a broken leg; the Mosquito crew were killed.

Despite these setbacks the record of the detachment was unsurpassed, and it was Flight Lieutenant Berry who was to set the record for 'Divers' shot down in a single night (or day!), accounting for seven during the hours of darkness of 23/24 July. He was to add four more on the 25th, and on the 27th he closed to within 100 feet of a bomb over West Malling airfield in order to destroy it before it fell on the base below. The explosion damaged his Tempest, but despite this gallant effort, he was obliged by the authorities to share his success with a Mosquito crew who had fired from 1,000 yards' range, and according to FIU 'missed hopelessly!' Next day it was announced that FIU's score had reached fifty, of which 36½ were the work of one man – Joe Berry! When July came to a close, 150 Wing announced that to date Berry was top-scorer, followed by Wing Commander Beamont (23), Flight Lieutenant Van Lierde (22), Flight Lieutenant McCaw (19), Flight Lieutenant Moore (17) and Flying Officer Cammock (15).

As the month drew to a close, a fourth Tempest squadron was approaching readiness for action. On 29 July 501 Squadron at Westhampnett, which had been operating elderly Spitfire VBs during the Invasion, received a full complement of the big Hawker aircraft in a one-day changeover, and at once went non-operational for training. A move was made to Manston on 2 August, and from here the first anti-'Diver' patrols were flown on the 5th, Flight Sergeant Ryman and Flying Officer Polley each claiming one shot down. Two days later a third was claimed by a Free French pilot, Flying Officer Deleuze. A rather complicated series of changes then followed. In the meantime the FIU Tempests at Newchurch had continued their successes apace, Flight Lieutenant Berry in particular achieving great things. On 3 August he had claimed five, as he had again on the 5th, while the 7th brought a further four to raise his total to 52½, and a Bar to his DFC. On the 10th, however, the whole detachment moved to Manston to be amalgamated with 501 Squadron, which was to convert at once to the night role. Berry took over the squadron from Squadron Leader Barnett, and the five remaining FIU pilots were posted in to replace sixteen who left with Barnett next day to join 274 Squadron. This latter unit was another Spitfire squadron which had been flying Mark IXs from West Malling, led by a great Canadian 'ace', Squadron Leader 'Stocky' Edwards. Now, as Tempests replaced the Spitfires on 11

August, Edwards and two other Canadian pilots, together with the two flight commanders, all departed, tour expired. Indeed only eleven of the original 29 pilots were to remain as Barnett with his two flight commanders and fourteen other pilots arrived from 501 Squadron. Daylight anti-'Diver' operations commenced on 12 August, although Flight Sergeant Ryman, who had claimed the first such for 501 Squadron while with that unit, was killed in a crash near Canterbury next day while on such a sortie. The first claim for the squadron was made on the 15th by Flight Lieutenant Willis. Meanwhile 501 Squadron had at once started to emulate FIU's earlier success at night with claims for eight 'Divers' during the night of 11/12 August, and by the end of the month would add at least 22 more. Not all these would be achieved at night, however, for at dawn on the 27th six were to be destroyed, four of them by Flight Lieutenant Bonham, three by tipping their wings after he had used all his ammunition on the first.

The 150 Wing squadrons continued their patrols during August, but now the rate of interception began to fall away. Partly this was due to the re-arranged defences, the coastal 'belt' of AA guns now putting up a great density of fire, aided by radar prediction and proximity-fuzed shells, which greatly reduced the number of 'Divers' breaking through to the area patrolled by the fighters. Coupled with this, the Allied breakout from Normandy during the month, and the destruction of the German 7th Army at Falaise, caused a rapid roll-up of the Wehrmacht in France and a withdrawal from the launching areas in the Pas-de-Calais before the month was out. By mid-August whole days were passing during which not a single claim was being submitted, and it was clear that the battle had been won by a combination of arms and circumstances.

On 11 August the ex-Malta veteran, Squadron Leader Dredge, ended his tour with 3 Squadron, having personally destroyed six of the V-1s. His place was taken by Squadron Leader Wigglesworth, who moved over from 56 Squadron, the very successful 'Diver'-hunter, Flight Lieutenant Moore, leaving 3 Squadron to take over Wigglesworth's old flight. By the 25th, 56 Squadron could be spared to fly an offensive reconnaissance across the North Sea to the Cassel area, led by Wing Commander Beamont. This was a sign of things to come, for next day 486 Squadron aircraft swept across the Channel to Calais, Béthune and Dunkirk, strafing ground targets in the area, and on the 28th, nine Tempests of 3 Squadron flew a sweep as far as Brussels.

Patrols continued unabated, but with steadily diminishing returns, and on 29 August Flight Sergeant Foster and Flying Officer Barckley made the last two claims

Above: Flight Sergeant O. D. Eagleson of 486 Squadron indicates success as he climbs out of the cockpit of 'SA-G'. With a total of 21 he would be the New Zealand Squadron's top scorer against V-1s. (IWM)

Below: Armourers feeding belts of 20mm ammunition into the gunbays of a 501 Squadron Tempest, at Bradwell Bay, October 1945. (RAFM/C. E. Brown)

Opposite page: Pilots of 501 Squadron pose in front of one of their Tempests which has been stripped of its camouflage paint and polished – a rare sight in the autumn of 1944. (J. Grottick via D. Watkins)

for 3 Squadron against the 'Divers', bringing that unit's total to a record 305½. Two days later both the other Newchurch units recorded their last 'Diver' claims, Flight Sergeant Shaw claiming one for 56 Squadron, and Flight Sergeant O'Connor, who had gained 486 Squadron's first such success, also claiming its last – his own score reaching 8½. On 1 September, 274 Squadron's Flight Sergeant 'Ben' Gunn (later Boulton-Paul's Chief Test-Pilot) made the last claims for the Tempests for a 'Diver' by day over England, to raise his unit's 'bag' to nineteen (later reduced to fifteen to allow for shares with other units).

In the meantime, on 29 August another Spitfire IX unit, 80 Squadron, which had served alongside 274 Squadron in North Africa and Italy, and had returned to the United Kingdom at the same time, in spring 1944, converted to Tempests and moved to Manston to rejoin its old companion. Anti-'Diver' patrols were at once instituted, but it was already too late, and none were seen. All was therefore ready for a return to full offensive operations by the Tempests, and on 6 September all three Newchurch squadrons flew their first Wing 'show' to Emden. Four days later, Wing Commander Wray, the Manston Wing Leader, led nine 274 Squadron aircraft on an offensive patrol to Holland's Leeuwarden airfield where six Bf 109s were seen on the ground, two of these being strafed.

What then had the Tempests achieved against the V-1s? Most certainly they had emerged as the most successful of the fighters against this robot menace, but every record that has been consulted differs as to the final sum of their claims. Roland Beamont has recorded that the Newchurch Wing destroyed 632 'Divers', of which his own score was 32, but totals recorded for the individual units and, indeed, many of the pilots therein, differ. Certainly Beamont's total appears not to include those claimed by the FIU detachment, which was credited with 86½ (all but two of them at night) in its own right. The varying totals quoted for other units are:

3 Squadron	288–305½
486 Squadron	239½–241
56 Squadron	70½–77 (one by a Spitfire)

Additional to these totals are those gained by the Manston units – nineteen, later reduced to fifteen, for 274 Squadron, and at least 88 by the end of the war by 501 Squadron, for a grand total well in excess of 800. The cost had not been light; during the three months of patrols eight Tempests had been lost while attacking bombs, either by the explosion of their targets, by 'friendly' AA fire, or by collision with other attacking aircraft. No less than 23 more had been written-off as a result of accidents or engine failure while engaged in these operations. A list of successful V-1 hunters is given in Appendix 3.

501 Squadron continued to operate against 'Divers' by night, as these were now being air-launched over the North Sea by Heinkel He 111 'mother' aircraft. Late in September this unit moved to Bradwell Bay to be better positioned for the new area of approach of the missiles, and continued to take a regular toll of them during the longer nights of the autumn and early winter. As a result of this continued defensive activity, 501 Squadron was to undertake few missions of an offensive nature. During the night of 27/28 September, however, Squadron Leader Berry led a 'Ranger' sortie by two Tempests over Holland to strafe trains, but on the next such operation, flown before dawn on 1 October, when three Tempests flew to Zwischenwalter, and over airfields between there and Rheine, Berry, who was again leading, flew into a barrage of light Flak, his blazing aircraft being seen to crash into the ground. With 60⅓ 'Divers' shot down, 52½ of them with the FIU, he had been top-scorer by a wide margin.

No more offensive sorties were undertaken by the squadron after this experience. The final major success against the bombs came during the night of 17/18 December 1944 when four were brought down, few being seen after that date. On 3 March another move was made to Hunsdon where the final two claims were made, Flight Lieutenant Grottick claiming the last to be shot down, near North Weald on the 27th of that month. On 1 April, with no defensive duties remaining, the squadron resumed daylight duties, but at this late stage of the war there was no employment for it, and disbandment followed on 20 April 1945.

The role of the Tempest against the V-1s is well summed-up by Flying Officer Ronald Dennis, a New Zealander, who served with 56 Squadron throughout this period:
'The Tempest was the best all-round machine for the job. All our aircraft were fitted with Rotol airscrews when the maximum rpm were increased to 3,850 from 3,700 and boost to +13 from +11, as the De Havilland airscrew could not absorb the added power and more than once shed a blade, with somewhat detrimental effects on the engine! The aircraft were highly polished, and I can recall overhauling a V-1 which was heading for London at the unusually high speed of 400mph. I shot it down just as the Royal Observer Corps fired red rockets to warn me I was about to enter the London Balloon Barrage. I haven't forgotten another one I shot down, only to find it had been claimed by a pilot of a Mustang flying in the vicinity. We operated against the V-1s from Newchurch, Dungeness – from Somerfeld tracking – no problems for the aircraft. At night each pilot was allocated a sector bounded by single searchlights flashing a single letter code.'

CHAPTER TWELVE

The Tempest with Second Tactical Air Force

WHILE 501 Squadron had continued operating over the United Kingdom, the other Tempest squadrons had been most active during the autumn period, and it is now appropriate to resume their story from early September 1944. After the attack on Leeuwarden airfield by aircraft of 274 Squadron on 10 September (as recorded earlier), this target was again visited next day when 80 Squadron escorted a dozen of the new Douglas A-26 Invader light bombers of the US Ninth Air Force to attack; both Manston squadrons then provided escort to medium bombers on the 12th. Groundstrafing sorties against targets in Holland remained the main activity of all units, with occasional losses to Flak, but on 17 September one of the reasons for the continued retention of the Tempests in England became clear with the launching of Operation 'Market Garden' – the airborne landings at Arnhem, Nijmegen and Grave to capture vital bridges. The Manston units operated in the Flak-suppression role as the troop carriers approached the drop-zone, attacking gun positions on Wallensee and Schowen islands in the Scheldt Estuary. Barges were also strafed, 80 Squadron claiming to have sunk five of these, but losing one Tempest which crashed into the sea after being hit by a burst of Flak. Next day the latter unit was again attacking Flak positions around Vlissingen, two Tempests being lost, one definitely to Flak.

Thereafter all the Tempest units were to change airfields, 80 and 274 Squadrons moving to Coltishall on 19 and 20 September, while next day 3 Squadron moved to Matlaske, where it would be followed by 56 Squadron on the 22nd. From its new base at Coltishall, 80 Squadron was soon active over Holland again, and on the 25th a squadron-strength strafing attack south of The Hague was ordered. While the rest of the unit's aircraft carried out this duty, one pair of Tempests remained above as cover, but both failed to return. One of the pilots was heard to report over his R/T that he was baling out, but no one saw what happened to them and it was surmised that they had been 'bounced' by German fighters and shot down. This was not so; they had been hit by Flak from an emplacement at Steenbergen, Rotterdam.

At last came the return to direct 2nd TAF command, when on 28 September 3 and 56

Squadrons flew over to B.60 airfield at Grimbergen, near Brussels. Here they came under the control of 122 Wing, a unit which had previously comprised a trio of Mustang III units. These had been ordered back to England to provide long-distance escort to Bomber Command heavy bombers on recently reinstated daylight raids into Germany, under the control of 150 Wing – in effect, a direct exchange. As 3 and 56 departed, the third element of the original Newchurch Wing, 486 Squadron, took their place at Matlaske; the New Zealand unit would follow them to Grimbergen on the last day of the month. On 29 September, 80 and 274 Squadrons moved to Antwerp, also in Belgium. 3 and 56 Squadrons were already in action, endeavouring to provide fighter cover over Arnhem, Nijmegen and Eindhoven, where Operation 'Market Garden' was reaching its climax. In this area 3 Squadron suffered its third loss of the month to Flak, but 56 Squadron re-opened the scoring when a large formation of more than thirty Fw 190s was reported over the battle zone, Squadron Leader Cotes-Preedy claiming one shot down, as did Flight Lieutenant Moore, two more being credited to Flying Officer Ness, and a probable to Flying Officer Payton. The Antwerp-based units were also at once active over the same

area, 274 Squadron losing an aircraft during a sweep near Eindhoven on the last day of the month to bring September's cost to a rather high fourteen Tempests, six of which had been suffered by 80 Squadron alone, while 3 and 274 had each lost three.

The month's end also brought 486 Squadron over to join its companions at Grimbergen, bringing to five the number of Tempest squadrons on Belgian soil. Their stay here was to be brief, however, for on 1 October 122 Wing and its three new units moved to a new base, B.80, on Dutch soil at Volkel – a permanent airfield which was to remain their home for several months.

Below: Groundcrew manhandling a 45-gallon drop-tank from EJ719 'JF-R' of 3 Squadron, Volkel, December 1944. On 1 January 1945 this aircraft was shot down by Flak and Pilot Officer Ron Pottinger baled out into captivity. (RAFM/C. E. Brown)

Top right: EJ713 'W2-K' of 80 Squadron about to lift off from Volkel early in October 1944. Flight Lieutenant J. M. Weston scored 80 Squadron's second Tempest victory, a Bf 109, in this aircraft on 8 December 1944. (IWM)

Right: The pilot of EJ714 'JJ-W' of 274 Squadron strains for a better view as his Tempest picks up speed on Volkel's runway, October 1944. (IWM)

Far right: When Wing Commander Beamont was shot down behind the lines, his place as Wing Leader 122 Wing was taken by Wing Commander J. B. Wray, seen here with his Tempest EJ750 'JBW' (Group Captain J. B. Wray via N. L. R. Franks)

At the same time 80 Squadron moved to another Dutch airfield, B.82 at Grave, to join 125 Wing, all other units of which were Spitfire-equipped. 274 Squadron followed next day, their arrival coinciding with the appearance of one of the Tempest's arch-enemies – the Messerschmitt Me 262 jet fighter-bomber. One of these swept over Grave, releasing a single bomb which killed 125 Wing's adjutant and a cook, and wounded a number of personnel. During that same day a trio of these formidable aircraft were also seen by 3 Squadron pilots from Volkel – a sign of things to come.

More reorganization was under way, for on 7 October 80 and 274 Squadrons moved to join 122 Wing at Volkel, raising this unit to five-squadron strength under the command of Group Captain Jameson, DSO, DFC✶, a notable fighter 'ace' who had served in Norway in 1940 and been one of only two pilots to survive the sinking of the carrier HMS *Glorious* during the withdrawal from that campaign. At the same time their Wing Leader from Coltishall,

Wing Commander Wray, DFC, was posted in to relieve 'Bee' Beamont, who was now virtually tour-expired. Beamont was not to go home for a well-earned rest, however, for on the 12th he took-off at the head of 3 and 80 Squadrons on a 'last sortie', strafing ground targets. Over German-held territory Flak hit JF-L (EJ710), a 3 Squadron aircraft which he was flying in place of his own Series 2 'RPB' (which had replaced the earlier 'RB'); he was obliged to crash-land, and spent the rest of the war as a prisoner.

The role of the Tempest in north-west Europe was now to be that of a medium- and low-altitude air-superiority fighter, seeking the Luftwaffe wherever it could be found, and clearing the air for the ground-support Typhoons, dive-bomber Spitfire IXs and XVIs, and the medium bombers of 2nd TAF. While frequently the absence of opposition by German fighters led the pilots down to strafe targets of opportunity on the ground – a task for which the stable Tempest, with its heavy armament, was as well-suited as the Typhoon – they were not

to carry bombs or rocket projectiles operationally until the last few days of the war, although they were fully capable of doing so. Their story during the final seven months of the war was therefore very much one of aerial combat, a role in which the fighter was soon to achieve a formidable reputation and an enviable kill/loss ratio.

After the success achieved by 56 Squadron on 29 September, a couple more victories had been claimed during the following three days, the second of these by Wing Commander Beamont to raise his personal score to seven. 6 October proved to be a day of mixed fortunes; during an early reconnaissance, Pilot Officer Cammock, one of 486 Squadron's leading scorers against the 'Divers', was shot down and killed by Flak while attacking a train near Arnhem, and in similar circumstances another of this unit's aircraft was to be lost that same afternoon, although the pilot managed to bale out. Four of 56 Squadron's Tempests were scrambled to intercept an attack on Nijmegen bridge, and were successful in shooting down two Fw 190s. 486 Squadron suffered a further loss to Flak next day, while on the first operation mounted from Volkel by 274 Squadron during the afternoon of the 7th, Flying Officer Mears failed to return from the Zwolle area. There seems little doubt that his was the first Tempest to fall victim to a German fighter, a claim for a Tempest being submitted by Oberleutnant Heilmann of III/JG 54.

The elusive Me 262 jets were frequently seen during October and November of 1944, but catching them was a matter of great difficulty. At last the opportunity arose on 13 October, when two of 3 Squadron's aircraft were patrolling over Grave. Here a single aircraft from I/KG(J) 51 was seen, and the Tempests gave chase. Pilot Officer Cole was well-positioned, gaining speed in a dive and closing from 400 to 100 yards. A quick burst of fire and 9K+FL, flown by Unteroffizier Edmund Delatowski, blew up violently. Further interceptions by the end of the month would bring claims for four more Me 262s damaged, but no further confirmed successes. Damage to yet another was claimed on 2 November, but on this occasion the jet pilots fought back, one Tempest of 274 Squadron being damaged Category 'B'. That same day eight Tempests were scrambled by 3 Squadron during the afternoon, four to patrol over Achmer and four over Rheine. Those over the former airfield were 'bounced' by Fw 190s and one Tempest was hard hit. The pilot managed to get back to Volkel, but his aircraft was too badly damaged for repair and was written-off.

It was the turn of the Wing Leader, Wing Commander Wray, to intercept a Me 262 on 3 November, claiming this probably destroyed. It seems that 2nd TAF Headquarters down-graded his success to a 'Damaged', but in fact he appears to have actually shot down a fighter version of the jet, flown by

Unteroffizier Willi Banzhoff of 3/Kommando Nowotny.

At this time confusion must have been caused by the number of pilots in the Wing named R. Cole. On 7 November Flight Lieutenant R. B. Cole led eight 274 Squadron Tempests on a patrol over Duerne–Nijmegen–Volkel, during which Flight Lieutenant Malloy and his wingman, Flight Sergeant R. C. Cole (neither of them to be confused with 3 Squadron's successful Pilot Officer R. W. Cole!) dived to attack a train. As they did so, they were in turn attacked by Fw 190s, and Flight Sergeant Cole was shot down. Malloy escaped one, but was pursued for ten minutes by another, finally crash-landing his damaged Tempest on return to Volkel. The Luftwaffe was beginning to claw back the advantage!

Pursuit of the Me 262s continued; on the 19th pilots of 486 Squadron claimed one probably destroyed as it attempted to take-off from Rheine, and on the 26th 3 Squadron also attacked this airfield where two jets were seen on the ground, one being claimed destroyed and one damaged. Pilot Officer R. W. Cole, who had shared in the destruction of the former, was hit by Flak as the formation turned for home, and he baled-out into captivity. The month ended on a successful note, however, for that same morning ten 486 Squadron Tempests on a sweep, encountered a Ju 188 near Münster which blew up after an attack by Flight Lieutenant Taylor-Cannon. Another such aircraft was seen going into land at Rheine and was claimed probably destroyed by Pilot Officer Stedman. Two days later, on the 28th, Flight Lieutenant Moore of 56 Squadron was leading an armed reconnaissance when again a twin-engined aircraft was spotted near Münster – this time a Heinkel He 219 night-fighter of I/NJG 1, flown by Leutnant Kurt Fischer. Moore at once shot this down, but again a second

aircraft was seen; four others joined with him in attacking this, but only a probable could be claimed, and this was subsequently down-graded to 'Damaged'.

The first two months of operations on the Continent had cost the Wing 21 aircraft and ten pilots, five of whom were prisoners. Of these at least seven had fallen to Flak and three to enemy aircraft, but the largest number, eight, were still victims of engine failure – the old Sabre 'disease'. On 21 November 274 Squadron's commanding officer, Squadron Leader Heap, had been killed when his Tempest crashed and burst into flames following such a failure; his place was taken by Squadron Leader Baird.

A cold, grey autumn deteriorated into the start of a bad winter as December arrived, and activity in the air was much curtailed during the first half of the month by fog, low cloud, rain and snow. None the less, the month opened well with another victory over the Me 262s. This one fell to 80 Squadron, and occurred during an offensive reconnaissance to the Quackenbrück area. Flying Officer 'Judy' Garland, a veteran of the squadron's service in North Africa and Italy, was strafing when he saw a jet (9K+ BH of I/KG(J) 51) pass by. Unobserved, he attacked and sent it crashing down by a railway line to the south of Rheine; Oberleutnant Joachim Valet did not survive. Five days later both 56 and 80 Squadrons recorded successes against piston-engined

Below: Groundcrew and pilots struggle to free 'W2-U', an 80 Squadron Tempest, from the mud at Volkel. (Australian War Memorial)

Below right: Flight Lieutenant D. C. Fairbanks of 274 Squadron with Tempest EJ762 ('JJ-E' or 'F') which survived a hit by Flak on 19 November 1944. Note the damage to the leading edge of the wing which contained a fuel tank – the subsequent fire having stripped the tail surfaces of paint and fabric. Fairbanks went on to become the most successful Tempest pilot in air combat, with at least 11 confirmed victories. (A. E. Gunn)

fighters, and on 11 December the former unit, on an afternoon sortie, spotted a train over which three Bf 109s were circling near Rheine. In a matter of minutes the train had been destroyed and two of the Messerschmitts shot down, one by Squadron Leader Perry St. Quintin, who was flying with the unit as a supernumerary to gain up-to-date experience. One day earlier another of 56 Squadron's pilots, Flight Sergeant Jackson, had attacked a Me 262 near Volkel, claiming damage; as had happened during the previous month, the attack seems to have been more effective than was realized and 9K+FL of I/KG(J) 51 flown by Leutnant Walter Roth failed to return.

At this stage 56 Squadron was certainly proving to be the premier unit of the Wing, and was obtaining the lion's share of combat successes. On the 14th the unit was again in the right place at the right time, encountering eighteen Bf 109s south of Rheine, three of which were claimed without loss, to raise the squadron's total for the war to over 100. One Messerschmitt was shot down by Flying Officer David Ness, who was fast becoming the Wing's most successful pilot. The young Canadian expended all his ammunition on his victim, overshot a second German fighter, and was pursued in his defenceless state for twenty minutes before escaping unscathed.

By now the German offensive in the Ardennes – the famous 'Battle of the Bulge' – had been launched and was making headway in the northern sector of the American front. In this it was protected from the full depredations of Allied airpower by particularly inclement weather, and by an effort by the Luftwaffe unprecedented since the previous summer. The skies cleared briefly on 17 December and 2nd TAF put up a maximum effort in support of their allies, resulting in the most active day yet for 122 Wing. At 1010 hours

eight 274 Squadron aircraft scrambled over the Münster area, engaging Bf 109s believed to be from III/JG 3 over the Burghstein Forest-Emmerich area, where in a period of about twenty minutes three were claimed shot down and one damaged. All but one were credited to Flight Lieutenant Fairbanks, who caused one to crash without firing a shot. At much the same time eight 3 Squadron Tempests headed for the Rheine area where Flight Sergeant Rose spotted six Bf 109s and claimed one shot down. Eight more were later seen over Nijmegen and one claimed damaged, but while strafing ground targets after these actions, Rose flew into a tree and returned alone with his damaged aircraft.

56 Squadron was again in the thick of things, recording two successful engagements. In the morning four pilots, scrambled towards Rheine, were recalled to Helmond, where many aircraft were seen. Most of these proved to be US P-47s, amid a forest of Flak bursts, so the quartet turned and swept up the road towards Grave when four Bf 109s appeared out of cloud, one of these attacking Flight Sergeant Kennaugh's Tempest. It was at once engaged and shot down by Flight Lieutenant Ross and Pilot Officer Shaw. Four more Messerschmitts then appeared, one being shot down in flames by Flight Lieutenants Moore and Ross, the pilot baling out to become a prisoner. Meanwhile more Tempests had been scrambled from Volkel and appeared on the scene, the pilots of two of these accounting for a third Bf 109 in flames. During the afternoon eight of the unit's aircraft were again airborne, this time over Münster and Paderborn, two He 219s of I/NJG 1 being seen flying low above the ground in the former location. One of these made good its escape, but the other was attacked by Pilot Officer Shaw, who set one engine on fire. The big night-fighter made

two circuits of an airfield and put down its undercarriage at which point the fire went out. Flight Lieutenant Ross now attacked and the aircraft landed and ran straight into a ruined building; he and Shaw jointly claimed its destruction.

Flight Lieutenant Moore then led one section down to strafe a train, but at this point 25 Bf 109s were seen above, and these were attacked, two being claimed, one each by Moore and another pilot. Warrant Officer Alexander was set upon by nine, but managed to escape after damaging one, with only slight damage to his own aircraft. The opponents of both morning and afternoon are believed to have been from JG 27.

Elsewhere during the day, Wing Commander Wray had achieved further personal success, shooting down another of KG(J) 51's Me 262s, this time 9K+BP from II Gruppe, flown by Leutnant Wolfgang Lübke. The Wing's ten for no loss was marred, however, when two of 80 Squadron's Tempests were shot down by intense Flak while on a reconnaissance over the Bielefeld area; one of the missing pilots was a Norwegian, Lieutenant Gilhaus. The weather then closed in again, as the Panzers ground on through the thin defences facing them. While forces on the ground were rushed to the area and the US airborne troops began their famous stand at Bastogne, there was little more that could be done in the air until Christmas Eve. Then the clouds and fog cleared and in the sunlit blue sky above the snowclad landscape, the Allied air forces were continuously in action. For 122 Wing the final week of December 1944 was both busy and eventful.

Efforts were being made at this time to introduce experienced Spitfire pilots into the Tempest Wing as potential squadron commanders, since suitably qualified flight commanders within the units were in short supply. 486 Squadron's long-serving commander, Johnny Iremonger, was rested on the 13th, 'Spike' Umbers being posted in from 3 Squadron in his stead. On the same day a most notable Spitfire pilot, who had seen considerable service in the Mediterranean theatre, New Zealander Squadron Leader Evan Mackie, joined 274 Squadron as a supernumerary; he was soon to be in action.

With the improved weather on 24 December, patrols were instituted over the battle zone in the area Aachen–Jülich–Malmédy. A formation of 274 Squadron aircraft off at 1105 hours, were soon followed by others from 3 Squadron. At 1240 hours the latter flight spotted ten Bf 109s to the north-west of Malmédy, Flight Lieutenant Thiele getting a burst into one of these which caused the starboard wing to crumple. P-47s were then seen and investigated, but Flying Officer Dryland was found to be missing. Meanwhile at 1245 hours,

near Eindhoven, the 274 Squadron formation saw below them a Fw 190 – almost certainly from IV/JG 54 – in the process of shooting down two Canadian Typhoons of 143 Wing (see page 90). Squadron Leader Mackie at once broke away and engaged, his opponent being seen to spin into the ground and blow up after his attack. Next day Dryland returned; he too had engaged a Fw 190 (also believed to be from IV/JG 54) and had shot this down, but his Tempest had then been hit by Flak. Forced to come down behind German lines, he had evaded capture and got through to the US troops.

Christmas Day brought a present in the form of further engagements with the German jets. Wing Commander Wray led 80 Squadron on a patrol during which Pilot Officer Reg Verran gave chase to a new opponent – an Arado Ar 234 reconnaissance-bomber of III/KG 76 – to which he

claimed damage. Again the attack had exceeded estimation, and while the jet escaped initially, Leutnant Alfred Frank was obliged to crash-land the damaged aircraft in Holland, leaving it in a written-off condition. During the afternoon Flying Officers Bremner and Stafford of 486 Squadron intercepted a Me 262 over Aachen, the pilot being seen to bale out, although his parachute failed to open.

Considerable further success was achieved on the 27th. During the morning 274 Squadron claimed two Bf 109s (II/JG 27) shot down, and immediately after midday 80 Squadron shot down all of four Fw 190s of 14/JG 54 encountered near Rheine. A few minutes later four more such aircraft from 10/JG 54 also went down near Münster when 486 Squadron attacked 40-plus Fw 190s and Bf 109s, claiming four destroyed, one probable and one damaged.

On this occasion JG 54's Leutnant Peter Crump managed to retaliate, shooting down Flying Officer Hall's EJ627.

29 December proved to be a more costly day for the Wing, when small formations on armed reconnaissances were twice greatly outnumbered. On the first occasion, during the morning, four 3 Squadron aircraft were attacked from above by 20-plus Messerschmitts and Focke-Wulfs, a similar-sized second formation then appearing. Flight Lieutenant Thiele escaped his attackers and engaged a lone Bf 109, which he claimed shot down, but Flying Officer Slade-Betts, one of the V-1 'aces', and Flight Lieutenant Edwards both failed to return. During the afternoon eight 56 Squadron pilots flew a similar sortie, but became engaged in a hectic and confused dogfight when 50-plus Fw 190s and Bf 109s appeared. Initially 1:1:4 were claimed, but 2nd TAF HQ subsequently up-graded these claims to 4:0:2. (Two of these late confirmations were subsequently to make Flying Officer James Payton the squadron's Tempest top-scorer.) However, Flying Officer Kenny Watts and

Flight Sergeant Jackson were both lost. Their main opponents were believed to be from 12/JG 54, at the end of a day of great slaughter suffered by III/JG 54 to 2nd TAF Spitfires and Tempests. Twelve Fw 190Ds had taken off from Münster, losing two aircraft, while 7/JG 6 had lost at least one Fw 190A-8 in the same area. During one of these combats Feldwebel Steinkamp of 13/JG 27 had claimed two Tempests shot down and a third was credited to pilots of that Geschwader's 11 Staffel. However, the combats of the 29th had raised 122 Wing's total since the Tempests had arrived to 48:4:12, of which 21:2:6 had been credited to 56 Squadron.

The year 1945 opened with the Luftwaffe's surprise attack on Allied airfields at dawn on 1 January – Operation 'Bodenplatte'. Volkel, the Tempests' base, escaped attack, however, and aircraft of 486 Squadron, which were in the air on an early reconnaissance to the Hanover area, were recalled to Arnhem, intercepting German fighters near Venlo and Helmond; here five Focke-Wulfs were claimed shot down, and two Messerschmitts damaged. The Luftwaffe remained in evidence during the rest of the day, five more victories being claimed by 3, 56 and 80 Squadrons, Flying Officer 'Judy' Garland of the latter unit diving on two Fw 190s near Münster during a midmorning armed reconnaissance to Paderborn and Bielefeld; his fire hit both aircraft, and both blew up. A single loss was suffered when Pilot Officer Pottinger, one of 3 Squadron's V-1 'aces', baled out over Dulmen after his Tempest had been hit by Flak; he became a prisoner.

Four days later, five more claims were made, three of them in the early afternoon against Fw 190s which may have been from II/JG 26, this unit losing 27-victory Ritterkreuzträger Leutnant Wilhelm Mayer among others during the day. Thereafter the Luftwaffe was rarely to be seen during the next ten days, as the weather closed in and German units sought to make good their recent losses. Despite the lack of opposition in the air, 122 Wing was to take a hard knock on 13 January, though mainly from a most unexpected source. On this date both 80 and 274 Squadrons lost pilots on operations, the former to Flak, the latter when Flight Lieutenant Malloy failed to pull out of a dive near Euskirchen, and crashed. It was 486 Squadron which took the brunt of the losses, however, while on a reconnaissance over the St-Vith area. Here US Army anti-aircraft gunners opened fire on the unsuspecting formation, shooting down Squadron Leader Umbers, Pilot Officer Kalka and Fight Lieutenant Appleton, and seriously damaging two other Tempests; fortunately there were no fatalities, Kalka baling out (to be fired on while parachuting down, it must be added), while Umbers and Appleton both force-landed near Euskirchen! Next day the Luftwaffe was to be found again, six single-engined fighters being claimed by 3, 56 and 486 Squadrons, Flight Lieutenant Fairbanks, who had been posted from 274 to 3 Squadron, during December, being credited with a Focke-Wulf and a Messerschmitt to make him the first pilot to claim five victories flying Tempests. Flight Lieutenant Crafts of 274 Squadron claimed a He 219 night-fighter shot down near Hamm.

On 23 January, 122 Wing and the Tempest squadrons were to enjoy their single most successful day of the war. Early in the morning 80 and 274 Squadrons engaged Messerschmitts and Focke-Wulfs in the Gütersloh area, each unit claiming two of each type, to which 80 Squadron added a Fw 190 probable (indeed one of 274 Squadron's Messerschmitts was initially claimed as a probable, but was subsequently upgraded). About two hours later 3 Squadron engaged ten Fw 190s which were fitted with rocket-launchers beneath the wings, catching these at low level to the west of Bielefeld and claiming four shot down and two damaged. Two confirmed and one damaged were credited to Flying Officer Basilios Vassiliades, a pilot of Greek extraction who had recently joined the squadron; he had earlier served with 122 Wing as a Mustang pilot in 19 Squadron, having already been credited with five and two shared victories with this unit.

56 Squadron was involved in a sweep over the Paderborn area at about the same time, as Flying Officer Ronald Dennis recalls:

'. . . we were flying at 7,000 feet in the vicinity of Achmer airfield. Me 262s were seen taking off, one of them flying low along the railway in the direction of Hanover. I was flying No 2 to "Casanova" McLeod [Flight Lieutenant McLeod] and we were detached in pursuit. The sky was overcast with a light powdering of snow on the ground. At 3,600rpm and maximum boost in a shallow dive we slowly overhauled the Me 262, whose pilot did not appear to be aware of our presence and continued to follow the railway line. As the pursuit continued I could hear a disembodied voice screaming with rage and hatred and suddenly, and rather shamefacedly, realized it was my own reactions! Suddenly the Me 262 went into a gentle left-hand turn over Hanover airfield. "Casanova" and I turned inside the e/a and opened fire. I found myself dead astern at about 300 yards. Following a burst of fire, flames poured from the e/a which went into what appeared to be a controlled descent with the intention of a forced-landing. We slowed our speed and followed down. The e/a hit the ground at the far end of the field, lifted over a hedge and nosed into the ground beyond where it exploded in a ball of flames. The pilot never left the aircraft – I felt quite sad.'

Early in the afternoon, 80 Squadron, led by Squadron Leader Evan Mackie, who had taken over command of the unit from Squadron Leader Spurdle on the 16th, claimed two Bf 109s and one probable over Bramsche; the probable, claimed by Flight Lieutenant Holland and Flying Officer Anders, was to be confirmed on 14 February. Finally, between 1600 and 1700 hours, 486 and 56 Squadrons claimed a further six fighters during two engagements over Rheine to bring the day's total to 21:2:8 without loss! Additionally, Flight Lieutenant Fairbanks and Pilot Officer Torpey of 3 Squadron had destroyed two Ju 52/3m transports on the ground at Gütersloh while on a 'cannon test', and claimed two more damaged.

Next day 80 Squadron rounded out an excellent month with two more Bf 109s south of Rheine to bring claims for the month to 44 confirmed and two probables. Losses during a period of very heavy operations had been relatively moderate, totalling fourteen in December, but only nine in January. At least nine of these losses had been to Flak, but three aircraft fell to 'friendly' forces! Five aircraft had fallen to German fighters during December, and two as a result of engine failure. Of fourteen pilots lost with these aircraft, six had become PoWs.

Worse was to follow, however, as with better weather in February, sorties over enemy territory increased and, in particular, the number of attacks on ground targets – mainly of an interdiction nature – rose considerably. By now German light Flak defences were highly concentrated, and with the eclipse of the Luftwaffe, had become the main defence against Allied air attack. During this one brief month – the shortest of the year – operational losses rose to 31 aircraft. What was worse was the proportionate increase in the percentage of pilots lost – thirty, of whom only two could be confirmed as prisoners at the time. In fact sixteen had become PoWs and five evaded capture, the remaining nine having lost their lives. At least seventeen of these casualties were caused by Flak – possibly more – engine failures and other operational accidents accounting for a relatively modest seven aircraft.

Aerial actions were to bring a further thirty confirmed victories during February, though not all for 122 Wing, as will be recounted later. The first two days of the month both brought single victories over German fighters, while during an afternoon sweep south of Paderborn on the 2nd, a Dornier Do 217 bomber was seen flying low near an airfield, and was dispatched by a trio

of pilots from 486 Squadron. Next day six Tempests from 274 Squadron strafed Vechta airfield, where Flying Officer Mooney claimed a Me 210 destroyed on the ground, damage to several other twin-engined aircraft also being inflicted. On the 8th this unit became engaged with Bf 109s from II/JG 27 near Rheine soon after 0900 hours, three being claimed shot down and one damaged for the loss of the commanding officer, Squadron Leader Baird; the German unit lost at least two aircraft in this engagement, but submitted claims for three Tempests shot down. Shortly afterwards Pilot Officer Verran of 80 Squadron shot down a Fw 190 near Bremen, watching it crash-land and collide with a house.

To replace Baird, David Fairbanks was posted back to the unit from 3 Squadron next day, to the delight of 274; '"Foob" Fairbanks, the "terror of Rheine" is to return to us' exulted the squadron diary. His return was celebrated in suitable style on the 11th when he led eight of the unit's Tempests on a reconnaissance over the Hanover and Paderborn area. Following some strafing, a jet was seen and Fairbanks gave chase, following it for twenty miles through cloud before finally catching it as it went in to land at Rheine. One burst and it disintegrated. Identified at the time as a Me 262, it seems that it was in fact a reconnaissance Ar 234B of 1(F)/123, flown by Hauptman Hans Felden, returning from a photographic sortie over Hull on the English coast.*

274 Squadron had not been the only unit in the Wing to lose their commander during February. On the 10th Squadron Leader Thiele of 3 Squadron was brought down by Flak near Dorsten, baling out to become a prisoner, and on the 14th, Squadron Leader Umbers of 486 Squadron was shot down and killed near Meppen. Earlier in the day, Flying Officer Trott from this unit had been hit while leading a reconnaissance over the Dummer Lake, and was seriously wounded. He managed to get back to Volkel from where he was CasEvaced to England at once with a severe stomach wound; he was subsequently awarded a DFC for this action. Flight Lieutenant Cole was promoted from 274 Squadron to replace Thiele, while in 486 Squadron one of the flight commanders, K. G. Taylor-Cannon, who had first joined

the unit as a sergeant in 1942, took Umber's place.

Activity continued at an increasing rate. On the 14th 80 Squadron also lost two Tempests, one to Flak and the other in combat; on an afternoon sweep to Celle the squadron encountered a Bf 109 which was shot down by Pilot Officer Rankin and Flying Officer Royds, but the latter was seen to fly into a severed wing from the Messerschmitt, and failed to return. In the event the victory was credited to Rankin alone. Squadron Leader Fairbanks of 274 Squadron again encountered a jet during the day, claiming a Me 262 damaged over Rheine, while next day was to prove one of his best. Again he led off eight Tempests, this time to Hildesheim where a locomotive was strafed. At 1730 hours at least an equal number of Bf 109s were seen and attacked near Hildesheim, Fairbanks being credited with two shot down and Flying Officer Mossing with one and one damaged.

It was to be five days before the Luftwaffe was again encountered, and during that period the Tempest force with 2nd TAF was to be substantially reinforced. During mid-December 1944 two of 2nd TAF's Spitfire IX units, 33 and 222 Squadrons, had returned to England where they were posted to Predannack in Cornwall where conversion to Tempests followed. Training began at the beginning of January, proving fairly straight-forward, although 222 Squadron lost two aircraft in training accidents, both crashing into the sea. Now, on 20 and 21 February these units arrived at B.77 airfield, Gilze-Rijen, Holland, to join 84 Group's 135 Wing – of which 222 Squadron had previously been a part. On their arrival the Wing's other two Spitfire units, 349 (Belgian) and 485 (New Zealand) Squadrons departed for the United Kingdom for similar conversion. A new Wing Leader, Wing Commander Mason (previously a Typhoon pilot and commander of 183 Squadron) arrived at the same time. 122 Wing had also received a new Wing Leader at this time, Wing Commander Brooker, DSO, DFC (✭), taking over from Wing Commander Wray, who was rested. Richard Brooker had flown in the Battle of Britain and in the defence of Singapore before leading 123 Typhoon Wing during the Invasion; he already had some seven aerial victories to his credit. 122 Wing was also reinforced during February by the arrival of 41 Squadron, equipped with Griffon-engined Spitfire XIVs, to support the Tempests by providing high cover; the unit would remain until early March.

The arrival of the new units coincided with a marked increase in activity as 2nd TAF launched Operation 'Clarion' in an effort to wipe out all remaining German transport prior to the completion of 21st Army Group's move up to the Rhine. 274 Squadron undertook two strafing attacks on

21 February, during the second of which a lone Ju 88 was seen and shot down in flames by Flight Lieutenant Hibbert. The unit also received some new pilots, one of whom was the American, Flying Officer 'Buck' Feldman, who had flown against the V-1s with 3 Squadron during the previous summer. Next day as 'Clarion' opened, there were several engagements from midday onwards. At 1320 hours Wing Commander Brooker led seven 3 Squadron Tempests on a reconnaissance over the Nienburg-Plene area, where considerable unwelcome attention was received from US Ninth Air Force P-51s. Shaking these off, the formation encountered a lone B-24 near Steinhuder Lake, four pilots breaking away to escort this, while Brooker led the remainder in a strafing attack. Over Rheine a pair of Bf 109s were then seen below, and were attacked, Brooker claiming one destroyed and a second being damaged; as the British pilots were reforming, ten Fw 190s from I/JG 26 attacked and Pilot Officer Bailey's aircraft was shot down by Leutnant Waldemar Söffing. It seems that Brooker's claim may subsequently have been reduced to a 'damaged' by Headquarters.

Immediately behind the 3 Squadron aircraft came others of 56 Squadron, Squadron Leader Perry St. Quintin – still a supernumerary with the unit – claiming a Fw 190 shot down over Cloppenburg at 1425 hours. P-51s again made a thorough nuisance of themselves and on this occasion succeeded in shooting down Flight Lieutenant Green's Tempest after it had been hit by Flak; he failed to return. The New Zealanders of 486 Squadron also had trouble with their American allies during this afternoon when at 1510 hours the unit spotted seven JG 27 Bf 109s over a formation of P-47s south of Münster. At first the Thunderbolts prevented the Tempests becoming engaged, but two Messerschmitts were seen heading away north, and these were both shot down. A pair of Focke-Wulfs were then spotted, but some 20 P-47s attacked the Tempests as the squadron attempted to intercept, one of the New Zealand aircraft being damaged as the German pilots watched with obvious interest from above! The balance was restored during the last operation of the day, Squadron Leader Fairbanks leading elements of 274 Squadron to Rheine where at 1700 hours, he engaged and shot down two of ten 'long-nosed' Fw 190Ds of III/JG 54, one of the pilots baling out.

Fairbanks gained one more success two days later on the 24th while on a morning reconnaissance. A lone Fw 190 was seen near Rheine and was at once shot down in flames. At much the same time 486 Squadron had been scrambled after a 'plot' over Münster. A trio of Bf 109s were seen, and two were claimed shot down at low level near Bramsche. At 1715 hours three 274

*The Germans had been anticipating an invasion of the Low Countries at this time, which accounts for this particular flight.

△1

△2   ▽3

△4   ▽5

△6   ▽7

Squadron Tempests were back over Rheine where Flight Lieutenant Kennedy gave chase to a Me 262, claiming damage before being driven off by intense AA fire. A Ju 88 was then seen near Plantlunne and Flying Officer Mossing attacked, hitting one engine whereupon three members of the crew baled out. The pilot remained at the controls, weaving desperately, but Kennedy then closed in and shot out the second engine at which the aircraft turned on its back and crashed. Elsewhere during the day Flight Lieutenant Vassiliades of 3 Squadron destroyed a Ju 188 on the ground.

Early next morning a formation of Tempests from 56 Squadron were out west of Münster, when, as Ronald Dennis recalls: 'Flying as No 4 in a "Finger Four" formation, I saw the flash of sunlight on wings high at 4 o'clock, closing rapidly. Called "breaking port" and went into a steep left turn, losing contact with the rest of the formation. Gained height to about 7–8,000 feet and found myself at max boost and rpm in a left turn on the point of a stall. Two Me 109s were turning with me, all three at 120° to one another. I found the Tempest could hold the 109s in the turn, in fact gain slightly on the one ahead. After two or three minutes of stalemate the 56 Squadron Tempests appeared and one 109 rolled on to its back and dived away with Tempests in hot pursuit, leaving the second to me. [The other Messerschmitt was claimed shot down by Flight Lieutenant McLeod.] At one stage he began to close with me but then for a reason I am unable to explain he rolled out

and went into a gentle climb which gave me the opportunity to open fire from astern. Upon reflection I think the pilot's idea was that – knowing I was on the point of stalling – he could, by climbing, induce the stall. However, my cannon-fire blew the tail empennage away from the fuselage. The e/a flicked upside down and went into a flat spin. The pilot ejected, his parachute opened, but a large segment of the canopy appeared to be missing and I fear his descent was rather faster than conducive to a safe arrival. Again a feeling of inexpressible sadness. PS. During the actual combat my thoughts at one stage in the steep turn became detached and I found myself thinking of England and home – stupid really!' It is believed that Dennis's opponents were from 1/JG 27, and that the aircraft shot down by him may have been that of the Staffelkapitän, 21-victory 'Experte', Oberleutnant Max Winkler.

During the previous day 33 and 222 Squadrons had flown their first sorties from Gilze-Rijen, and during this same morning, a few minutes prior to the 56 Squadron engagement, a composite formation of eight Tempests from these units had arrived over Rheine on a sweep led by Squadron Leader Matthew, 33 Squadron's commanding officer. Here fifteen Bf 109s – all from I/JG 27 it is believed – were seen below and the Tempests dived to attack. In a near-perfect 'bounce' four were claimed shot down and four damaged, Flight Lieutenant Luckhoff being credited with the destruction of two. In return Flying Officer Harmon was shot

down by the Messerschmitts and one other Tempest was damaged; I/JG 27 did indeed lose four aircraft.

At the end of a month of such success, further achievements must have been in the mind of Squadron Leader Fairbanks as he led off six of his Tempests to Hamm, Münster and Osnabrück early in the morning of the last day of the month. A strafe was carried out, but then at 0800 hours more than forty Fw 190s were seen north of Osnabrück. In typical fashion, Fairbanks led his flight into the attack and a hard fight began, with little chance for the RAF pilots to do more than get the odd shot at their multitude of opponents. Four returned, claiming damage to five Focke-Wulfs (three by Flight Sergeant 'Ben' Gunn alone), but two Tempests were missing, one of them that flown by Fairbanks who had been heard calling that he had five on his tail. The 'terror of Rheine' in fact survived to become a prisoner, and on his return after the war claimed that he had first shot down one of his opponents, but this does not seem to have obtained any late official confirmation; Flying Officer Spence, pilot of the other Tempest, also survived as a PoW. Already awarded a DFC and Bar during early 1945, a second Bar would be gazetted for Fairbanks in July of that year, the citation for which credited him with fifteen victories – one with 501 Squadron while flying Spitfires, eleven in the air, two and one shared on the ground while flying Tempests, but apparently not one on 28 February; he had also shot down one V-1. Flight Lieutenant Hibbert was promoted to take his place.

The day was also marked by a couple of rather unusual victories. Over Hildesheim later in the morning 3 Squadron pilots shot down a Siebel Si 204 liaison aircraft, losing one to Flak themselves, while at Gilze-Rijen Flight Lieutenant Jongbloed of 222 Squadron destroyed a V-1 over the airfield – not to the entire delight of those below! Jongbloed was a Dutch pilot who had claimed 9½ 'Divers' while flying Spitfire XIVs with 322 (Dutch) Squadron during the previous summer.

The losses of February and the absence of Fairbanks brought some considerable change in tactics during March, a month that began with the official stricture 'No, repeat no ground attacks', together with an instruction that formations should not penetrate hostile airspace unless at least 16-strong due to the increasing size of Luftwaffe fighter formations recently met. These new rules would be adhered to for a few days with a resultant marked drop in losses, but before the month was out attacks on ground targets had been resumed, and smaller formations were again straying into German skies. March would bring 23 losses, again at least half of them caused by Flak; seventeen pilots would fail to return.

Top left: Flying Officers 'Ron' Dennis (right) and 'Val' Turner relaxing in 56 Squadron's dispersal hut at Volkel. (R. V. Dennis)

Some of 56 Squadron's successful pilots in the spring of 1945. (R. V. Dennis)
1. Squadron Leader R. W. A. MacKichan
2. Squadron Leader P. R. St. Quintin (supernumerary)
3. Flight Lieutenant F. L. 'Casanova' MacLeod
4. Flight Lieutenant P. H. Clostermann
5. Flying Officer D. E. Ness
6. Flying Officer V. L. Turner
7. Flying Officer J. J. Payton

Below: Sergeant A. E. 'Ben' Gunn in the cockpit of Tempest 'GF-R' while instructing at 56 OTU after completing a tour with 501 and 274 Squadrons (A. E. Gunn)

The month started well for the Tempests of 135 Wing, when on the 2nd an early sweep was made by 222 Squadron to the Rheine–Lingen area. Here at about 0800 hours two Arado Ar 234B jet bombers of 9/KG(J) 76 were seen; Flight Lieutenant Varley attacked Leutnant Eberhard Rögele's Fl+QT, which blew up, while the second was claimed damaged. More than a dozen Bf 109s from IV/JG 27 were then seen, attempting a 'bounce' of the Tempests, but the tables were swiftly turned, and four were shot down, one pilot being seen to bale out, and one Messerschmitt to crash-land.

Varley's combat report read: 'I was flying Yellow 3 on an offensive sweep, Lingen area. While on outward leg at 3,000 feet, we were warned of aircraft 12 o'clock below. I immediately saw crossing our formation from starboard to port what appeared to be a Horsa glider, and I realized this was the Arado jet plane. I dived and turned port and closed to 1,000 yards and fired a one-second burst 10° deflection, and looking down and around saw another jet plane flying below in the other direction. I closed to 200 yards and fired a two-second burst dead astern, and a huge explosion with red flame occurred. When the e/a blew up Yellow 1 yelled "break port" and I broke (now at 2,000 feet) into 12 Me 109s trying to bounce me. One fired head-on at me and I returned fire, turned hard port, and he turned starboard. After about six turns following him with difficulty, he broke away. I chased him and with 20° deflection above, saw hits. He began weaving on deck and with another 30° deflection burst, saw his propeller stop. He turned several times and disintegrated on hitting rough ground. I climbed and saw dogfights above and two or three parachutes, but I returned to base seeing nothing further. I saw object hanging from jet a/c, between fuselage and nascelle, suggesting bomb. This might have been the cause of first explosion, aircraft exploding again on hitting ground. Claim: one Arado destroyed; one Me 109 destroyed.'

During a second sweep to the same area in the afternoon, another Ar 234B was seen and damaged by Flight Lieutenant Varley and Flying Officer Carson; one of the two jets damaged by the squadron during the day was harder hit than realized, Oberleutnant Arthur Stark, also of 9/KG(J) 76 crash-landing Fl+ET at Lippstadt after combat with fighters, the aircraft being damaged beyond repair. The day had not been so favourable for 122 Wing, however, for while Squadron Leader Cole of 3 Squadron had shot down one Fw 190 near Rheine, 80 Squadron had come off worst in a fight with twenty Bf 109s and Fw 190s in the same area, Captain Olof Ullestad (Norwegian) becoming a prisoner when his Tempest was shot down by one of the Messerschmitts; only claims for a couple damaged could be made in return.

Early in March Flight Lieutenant Pierre Clostermann, a successful Free French fighter pilot who had previously flown two tours on Spitfires, joined 274 Squadron. On 5 March he set out on a late afternoon cannon test, but became 'lost', finding himself over the Hengelo area, where he spotted

Left: Damaged aircraft beyond the repair capacity of the local Servicing Echelons or Repair and Salvage Units, were transported to 151 Repair Unit at B.55, Coutrai in Belgium. Here 'SA-N' NV763, ex-486 Squadron, and 'W2-M' EJ722, ex-80 Squadron have been receiving attention. (A. R. Gearing via W. Smith)

Right: Tempests of 486 Squadron at B.80, Volkel; 'SA-C' NV937 served with 486 Squadron from 13 to 28 March 1945, when it suffered minor battle damage. After repair it became 'JF-J' of 3 Squadron. (RNZAF)

four Bf 109s. He reported that he had shot down one of these, before making good his escape into clouds.

Two days later 122 Wing gained further successes near Rheine. Elements of all squadrons from the Wing were in the area, four German fighters being shot down without loss, two by 56 Squadron, one by Flight Lieutenant Vassiliades of 3 Squadron, and one by Squadron Leader Mackie who was leading a big formation from his own unit, plus 274 and 486 Squadrons. The Fw 190D which he engaged proved to be expertly flown, and a hard dogfight commenced at low altitude, both aircraft pulling maximum 'G'. At last the German pilot's attention seemed to be momentarily distracted by the approach of two other Tempests, and Mackie was able to get in a good shot which caused the 'long-nose' to crash in flames and blow up. 'The burst which finished him off was at such a deflection that the target was obscured by the engine bonnet, but it started to blaze right in the cockpit. I could almost have wrung the sweat out of my

battledress on return to base. So tight were our turns that we were both making wingtip trails at 3,000 feet!' recorded Mackie.

A week later on the 14th 222 Squadron again intercepted an Ar 234B, north of Quackenbrück, and this was claimed shot down, although it was also seen to be hit by Flak. Next day another of these jets was claimed damaged by 80 Squadron. To the surprise of 274 Squadron's personnel, the unit was ordered to move to B.91 at Gilze-Rijen on the 17th, to join 135 Wing, bringing each Wing to a more even strength. Operations proved similar – armed reconnaissances, patrols, sweeps and escorts to medium bombers over northern Germany – and of course much strafing, but the unit recorded that the methods of operation in the new Group seemed very different initially.

Activity again increased late in the month as 21st Army Group's proposed crossing of the Rhine, scheduled for 24 March, approached. On the 22nd 56 and 80 Squadrons on an afternoon sweep over Hesepe,

became engaged with Fw 190s of II/JG 26, claiming six shot down and two damaged without loss. The German unit had three pilots killed in this engagement, and claimed one Tempest shot down in return; total losses of aircraft are not known.

Three days later, the Rhine crossing successfully achieved under an umbrella of 2nd TAF fighters, it was again the turn of 135 Wing to achieve a notable success. 222 Squadron was undertaking an early sweep over the Lippstadt–Paderborn area when Flight Lieutenant Turney saw three Bf 109s. Diving on these he found not three, but seven, claiming one shot down; within moments three more had followed as other Tempests joined the fight. At almost exactly the same time, pilots of 80 Squadron had encountered a trio of Bf 109s near Wesel, Flying Officer Sheaf shooting down the leader. Seven hours later, during an afternoon sweep, 222 Squadron was again in luck, spotting eleven Fw 190s of III/JG 54 near Quackenbrück, three of which were rapidly claimed shot down; the three

engagements had netted eight victories without loss. However this good day had been sadly marred by losses suffered to the omnipresent Flak which brought down four Tempests with the loss of two pilots. Flight Lieutenant Vassiliades, who had just become a flight commander in 3 Squadron, was killed when his aircraft blew up, and 486 Squadron's long-serving Flying Officer Kalka baled out when his ailerons were jammed by a Flak hit as the squadron was strafing eight Fi 156s seen disposed in a wood, having previously shot down a German balloon. Unfortunately Kalka fell into the River Maas three miles from Grave, and was drowned despite the heroic efforts of a young Dutch girl to save him. The damaging of four unoccupied Storch aircraft seemed poor compensation for his loss. Another such aircraft would be destroyed on the ground three days later by Flight Lieutenant Clostermann, who meanwhile had moved from 274 to 56 Squadron.

On 26 March Squadron Leader Bower, recently posted from 222 Squadron to command 33 Squadron when Squadron Leader Matthew ended his tour, led nine of his new unit's Tempests to escort US B-26 Marauders over Vlotho during the afternoon. While so engaged four Fw 190Ds of III/JG 54 bounced one section, Oberleutnant Hans Dortenmann shooting down Warrant Officer Ligtenstein for his 31st victory, the Tempest pilot being seen to bale out. The rest of the formation were able to shoot down two of the Focke-Wulfs, flown by Obergefreiter Hansen and Unteroffizier Flakowski, before they could escape.

The month was rounded out by 80 Squadron, four of whose pilots shot down a lone Ju 188 west of Dummer Lake during the evening of the 31st, after other members of the unit had claimed a couple of Bf 109s as probables three days earlier. And so the Tempests approached April 1945 – the last

Left: The first section of 80 Squadron to return from an operation on 24 March 1945 – covering the Rhine crossings. Back to the camera is Major 'Dutchy' Henwick (SAAF), and facing it, left to right: Flight Lieutenant Tony Seager, Flying Officer 'Bill' Long (killed the next day), 'Doc' Gallagher, Flying Officer N. J. Rankin (killed six days later) and Squadron Leader Mackie. (F. L. Withers)

Below left: Squadron Leader 'Smokey' Schrader, commanding officer of 486 Squadron in April 1945; he was the second most successful Tempest pilot in air combat, with 9 confirmed claims plus one shared. (K. Smith via P. Sortehaug)

Below right: Squadron Leader 'Jimmy' Sheddan, 486 Squadron's last wartime commanding officer. (W. J. Sheddan)

Bottom: Raw power! Two of 274 Squadron's Tempests scream down the runway on a 'scramble' from B.91, Kluis April 1945. (RAFM/C. E. Brown)

Opposite page: A 486 Squadron Tempest, NV988 'SA-Y', taxies out for another sortie from B.80, Volkel in March 1945. This aircraft was lost on 15 April when it suffered an engine failure, but Flying Officer A. R. Evans baled out safely. (RNZAF)

full month of the war, but a month which was to bring the greatest number of victories and heaviest losses of any in their year of service, as the British and Canadian troops of 21st Army Group advanced from the Rhine through north-west Germany and Holland, to and over the River Elbe in the twilight hours of the Third Reich's existence.

The month began with the departure of 3 Squadron to the United Kingdom to attend Armament Practice Camp at Warmwell – the first of the Tempest units to be dispatched on such a refresher course. The first claim of the month was made by Flight Lieutenant Clostermann when he shot down one of two Fw 190s which he spotted taking off from Ahlhorn airfield on 2 April. Two days later four Tempests were lost, each by a different squadron, and all apparently to Flak. Some may have fallen foul of Luftwaffe fighters on this occasion, however, for the Focke-Wulf pilots of I/JG 26 were to claim three Tempests shot down south of Diepholz on this date. The balance was righted on the 6th, five Fw 190s being claimed, three by 56 Squadron, while at dusk a patrol from 486 Squadron spotted four Ju 87 Stuka dive-bombers low over a bridge in the Steinhuder Lake area, Flying Officer Sheddan dispatching two of these before they could escape in the gloom. Three days later a section from 80 Squadron caught a number of trainers over Fassberg, identifying them as 'Me 108s', although combat film shows them to have been Arado Ar 96s. In short order three were shot down, two of them by Squadron Leader Mackie to raise his tally with the Tempest to five.

At last, after several months at the same airfield, the units were on the move in the wake of the victorious armies. 135 Wing was first to begin this process, 33, 222 and 274 Squadrons moving to B.91 at Kluis, near Nijmegen, on 7 April, but during the next

four days 122 Wing became the first to operate from German soil, the squadrons going to B.112 and B.118 at Hopsten, where 3 Squadron rejoined the Wing on its return from Warmwell on the 17th. There were also some changes in command at this point; early in the month Pierre Clostermann moved again, this time to take over 'A' Flight of 3 Squadron, while 486 Squadron welcomed Flight Lieutenant 'Smokey' Schrader, a veteran Spitfire pilot from the Mediterranean theatre. Schrader claimed a Fw 190 shot down on 10 April to begin a month's meteoric scoring which would leave him second only to David Fairbanks as a protagonist of the Tempest. No sooner had he arrived than, on the 13th, Squadron Leader Taylor-Cannon was shot down by Flak over Domitz and baled out; he was not among those released at the close of hostilities, and was presumed to have been shot by German home guards (Volkssturm) or police. Schrader at once took over the leadership of the squadron, his promotion to Squadron Leader following on 21 April. The successful Jim Sheddan took over Schrader's flight.

Over the front on the 11th, 222 Squadron had strafed a number of jet aircraft at Fassberg airfield, one of which was taxiing. As this latter aircraft (reported initially as possibly a Me 163, but believed by 2nd TAF Headquarters to be a Me 262) took off, it was seen to burst into flames and crash, the pilot baling out; the squadron was credited with its destruction. The following day proved to be very busy, 274 Squadron shooting down a lone Ju 188 near Fassberg during the morning, while on an early afternoon sweep one section of 33 Squadron had just gone down to strafe when seventeen Bf 109s and Fw 190s bounced them, shooting down two of the Tempests and badly damaging a third. The pilot of the latter, Captain Thompson, SAAF, claimed one

Messerschmitt shot down, Flying Officer Ter Beek adding one and two damaged. When one of the missing pilots, Flight Sergeant Watton, was subsequently found safe in hospital, he added claims for one more shot down and one damaged. All claims were later confirmed by HQ to have been against Fw 190s – clearly aircraft of I/JG 26 which lost at least one such aircraft, while claiming six Tempests shot down, two of them by Oberleutnant Dortenmann (previously with III/JG 54) and one by Leutnant Söffing. Later in the evening further Focke-Wulfs were claimed by 56 and 486 Squadrons.

At 0830 hours on the 15th nine 486 Squadron Tempests set out on an armed reconnaissance to the Murite Lake–Pritzwalk area. A flight from 80 Squadron had been in the air over the same general area for an hour longer, and at 0900 hours Squadron Leader Mackie and Sergeant Turner claimed a Fw 190 shot down over Melzer – a claim which HQ, 2nd TAF subsequently confirmed, but credited a one-third share to Flying Officer O'Connor of 486 Squadron. Half an hour later the New Zealanders spotted nine Fw 190s over Uelzen and attacked at once, claiming eight shot down (two of them by Flight Lieutenant Schrader) and one damaged. Flying Officer Evans, after shooting down one of the Focke-Wulfs, discovered that he could not drop his underwing tanks, so he rolled clear of the combat and climbed away. However his engine then seized-up, and he baled out into British-held territory. Meanwhile, at 0930 hours, Flight Lieutenant Seager of 80 Squadron had claimed yet another Fw 190 near Celle, the pilot of which baled out. Warrant Officer Rollo of this unit was obliged to force-land after being hit by Flak, and Squadron Leader Mackie also made a similar landing due to engine failure. Shortly afterwards, at 1015 hours, Flight Lieutenants McCairns and

Cox of 56 Squadron caught a jet over Kaltenkirchen airfield, which they identified as a Me 262. Their claim for its destruction was confirmed – but as an Ar 234.

Activity continued unabated over the next two days, but not without loss. The main action on 16 April occurred during the evening when two Fw 190s were claimed over Ludwigslust by 486 Squadron, while two more were claimed by 80 Squadron, one of them by Flight Lieutenant Kilburn, a 1942 Spitfire 'ace' just beginning his second tour. This latter combat over Neuruppin proved costly, however. Wing Commander Brooker, the 122 Wing Leader, and Sergeant Turner both failed to return, Brooker last being heard to report over the radio that his engine was cutting; both were believed to have been shot down by the Focke-Wulfs.

80 Squadron was again in action against these aircraft next day, when at midday Fw 190Ds of I/JG 26 were engaged over Greves-mühlen and Lübeck, Captain Henwick and Pilot Officer Verran each claiming one shot down and one damaged. In return Ober-leutnant Dortenmann, Leutnant Söffing and Obergefreiter Böcker each claimed one Tempest, although the only loss actually suffered was Flying Officer L. Smith, DFM, who was shot down and killed; two of I/JG 26's pilots were lost in combat on this date.

The squadrons of 135 Wing were also active; after shooting down a Ju 88 early on the 17th, 274 Squadron dispatched five Tempests to strafe Stade airfield next day, a Fw 190 and two Do 217s being claimed destroyed on the ground here, and several other aircraft damaged. On the 19th aircraft from 222 Squadron were strafing Husum airfield when Flying Officer Walkington saw an aircraft flying north at 500 feet. This defied identification at the time, having twin tails, a single engine, wing planform similar

to a Bf 109, and a nose with a 'drooping appearance'. The upper surface was painted mottled green, while beneath it appeared to be yellow – possibly primer. Walkington turned after it, but it proved to be very fast and he was unable to close at 360mph IAS. However, the enemy pilot, although having a lead of 1,500 yards, undertook a 360° turn to starboard, allowing the Tempest to turn inside it and close to 1,000 yards. Although his aircraft was not yet equipped with one of the new gyro gunsights, Walkington trim-med carefully, allowed deflection of three-quarters of his sight ring and fired several short bursts. The little jet climbed through cloud at 3,000 feet, the Tempest in hot pursuit, and before he could fire again it came spinning past him and crashed, the result of some very good shooting. There is little doubt that his victim was one of the first Heinkel He 162s to be seen.

On 19 April Squadron Leader Mackie was posted from 80 Squadron, promoted to take over the leadership of 122 Wing. His place was taken by 'Dutchy' Henwick, SAAF, but he at once led the squadron over the North Sea to attend the APC at Warm-well; the unit would not be back before the war ended. On the 20th the squadrons of 135 Wing moved to B.109 at Quackenbrück, on German soil, from where they were to launch a series of attacks on airfields east of Hamburg. 274 Squadron's commander, Squadron Leader Hibbert, was rested, his place being taken by Squadron Leader Usher.

With the Germans forced into an ever-shrinking area of remaining territory, the Luftwaffe was to be seen more frequently than for many months, and was constantly harried and hunted on and around its own airfields. On the 20th Pierre Clostermann was to claim two Fw 190s within the space

Above: Flight Lieutenant Pierre Clostermann flew no less than four 'JF-E's during his service with 3 Squadron; the one seen here, in April 1945, was NV994. (RAFM/C. E. Brown)

Below: Two 222 Squadron Tempest pilots – Flying Officers Douglas Coxhead and Geoff Walkington – the latter claimed an unidentified aircraft on 19 April 1945 which was almost certainly a Heinkel He 162 of JG1. (D. J. Coxhead)

of forty minutes near Hamburg, and next day 486 Squadron also made two claims, Squadron Leader Schrader shooting down a Bf 109 as it went in to land at Schwerin, for his fifth Tempest victory, and Flying Officer Evans claimed a Fw 190 east of Wismar. One Tempest failed to return, apparently due to engine failure, but possibly shot down by Leutnant Schramm of II/JG 26, who claimed a Tempest near Perleberg, his Gruppe recording the loss of one Fw 190 and its pilot.

At 1135 hours on 23 April Flight Sergeant Inglis of 274 Squadron took off on a routine test flight, but failed to return. He had baled out after being hit by Flak, and evaded capture to walk to Allied lines. Not until after the close of hostilities was he able to complete a combat report, but then he had a remarkable story to tell:

'While on a weather recce and cannon test I found a break in cloud just south of Schleswig town and went through it to a cloud base of approx 1,500 feet. Flying NW I sighted an uncamouflaged a/c ahead and slightly to port flying very low. I closed in line astern and slightly above and identified it as a Ju 188 and opened fire at 400 yards with a two-second burst which set the port engine alight and knocked pieces off the wing. The e/a started a slight turn port and I got in a one-second burst at the cockpit before I pulled over him. I started a climb port and looked back to see the a/c crash into the edge of what appeared to be a planted forest. I was about 800 feet and had turned 90° when I saw a Fw 190 pull up to port in the vicinity of the burning a/c. This Fw 190 was, as I soon saw, accompanied by two on his port side and three on his starboard side. I straightened out and dived behind the starboard a/c and noticed as I did so that those on the port had all followed in the leader's port turn. I gave this last 190 a two-second burst and got good strikes on his engine and cockpit. E/a poured smoke and then flame as it dived steeply into the ground to port. This Fw was carrying what appeared to be a bomb under the fuselage. I pulled hard up to port in a steep climb as by this time the first Fw 190 was almost on my tail. I got a short burst from 30° at the tail end e/a and saw strikes on the port wing root. He straightened out as he entered a cloud and I was about to fire from about 50 yards line astern when it rolled slightly and the pilot baled out. I remained in the cloud at approx 2,500 feet for about three minutes then started to fly north in and out of the low cumulus cloud but couldn't see the other a/c again. After remaining about ten minutes in the Flensberg area and west, I headed south along the railway to Eggebeck airfield where I made three attacks at e/a on the ground at the north-west corner of the 'drome, resulting in one Ju 88 burning and one Ju 52 damaged.

As I crossed the a/f on the third attack, glycol poured out of the exhaust tubes and I pulled up to about 2,500 feet where the engine 'packed up' and a few minutes later seized. I switched on the distress switch and called Longbow on A, B and C but received no reply. At about 1,500 feet spurts of flame came from the engine and I decided to bale out. I claim one Ju 188 and two Fw 190s destroyed in the air, one Ju 88 destroyed and one Ju 52 damaged on the ground.'

Other units of 135 Wing had also been over airfields at this time; 33 Squadron attacked several in the Kiel area on the 23rd, claiming six aircraft destroyed and others damaged, all three units making similar attacks next day. 33 Squadron strafed Ar 196 floatplanes alongside a lake at Ratzenburg, while 222 Squadron attacked Skydstrup airfield in Denmark, claiming two destroyed and thirteen damaged. 274 Squadron, which had claimed five destroyed and nine damaged on Flensberg airfield on the 20th, now struck at several Baltic fields, adding four more destroyed and eleven damaged to the Wing's 'bag'. The cost was not always light, 33 Squadron losing three Tempests to Flak over Tunnewitz airfield on the 24th, one pilot managing to bale out, while another force-landed in Allied territory.

Meanwhile 122 Wing was far from idle. While eight Tempests from 486 Squadron were on an early armed reconnaissance on the 25th, a Me 262 was seen going in to land at Lübeck-Blankensee, and was shot down by Flying Officer K. A. Smith. Unfortunately this pilot was himself shot down next day by Flak, although he was seen to crash-land and get out of his aircraft. 3 and 56 Squadrons moved deeper into Germany on 26 April, going to B.152 at Fassberg – so recently the area of operations. It was still the New Zealanders of 486 Squadron who seemed to find the lion's share of the action at this time however; on the 28th Flight Lieutenant Reid and Flying Officer Eagleson found and shot down a transport aircraft identified as a Ju 352, but credited as a Ju 52. The next day was to be the squadron's best ever. At 1245 hours eight Tempests took off to sweep over the Lauenburg area, home of Schlachtgeschwader 151, a training and replacement unit rendered operational late in the war to fight the Russians approaching from the east. Here many fighters were seen in the air and in quick succession three Bf 109s and three Fw 190s were claimed shot down, with one more of the latter as a probable. Above all, this was Squadron Leader Schrader's day:

'I was leading the squadron on an armed recce of the Lübeck–Wismar area when, just after take-off, Kenway advised that Bandits were in the Bridgehead area. When in the vicinity of Lauenburg and while at 3,000 feet two Fw 190s came down out of the clouds

crossing ahead of us. I took my section of four a/c into the attack – one of the e/a returned to cloud and I attacked the other. After manoeuvring I fired a short burst from 300 yards with 30° angle off. I saw strikes on the port side of the engine and the lower part of the cockpit. The Fw 190 went into a slow steep spiral and I saw it crash and explode on the ground in the vicinity of Zahrensdorf. My No. 2, Warrant Officer Howard, confirmed this. Shortly after this engagement I saw a Me 109 with one bomb centre-slung flying 12 o'clock towards us. The e/a broke port and within 300 yards I fired a burst with 60° angle off. I saw strikes on the port wing root followed by a vivid flash. The e/a rolled on its back and went straight into the deck. I went down and photographed the burning wreckage and noticed that the bomb had been flung clear. This bomb exploded approx ten seconds after the crash.

By this time myself and No. 2 had become separated from the rest of the squadron so we patrolled just north of the Bridgehead for approx ten minutes. At the end of this time I spotted a single a/c flying ahead of us at our height of 4,000 feet. Pulling out alongside of the a/c I recognized it to be a Me 109. My No. 2, Warrant Officer Howard, attacked first and I then closed to 150 yards in dead line astern and fired a burst and saw large pieces of the e/a fall away. It went over on its back and streamed white smoke. I saw it hit the ground and explode just south of Ratzenburg. After this, my No. 2 and myself turned west and went over the outskirts of Hamburg; saw two a/c which we recognized to be Me 109s heading west at about 4,000 feet. We chased them to the area of Hamburg airport. I attacked the leader, instructing my No. 2 to attack the other. After a short dogfight I fired a two-second burst from 300 yards with 20° angle off and saw strikes on the port side of the engine. The 109 caught fire immediately and dived in flames steeply to the deck where it crashed on the secondary railway line just east of the Hamburg a/f. I claim the following a/c destroyed: one Fw 190, two Me 109s and half of a Me 109 shared with Warrant Officer Howard.' During this first engagement 12/SG 151 reported the loss of four Fw 190s.

At 1545 eight more of the unit's aircraft set off for the same destination, and once more ten Fw 190s – again aircraft from 12/SG 151 – were seen, three being shot down by Flight Lieutenant Reid, Flying Officer McDonald and Warrant Officer Duncan. Leutnant Ernst Orzegowski, a notable Ritterkreuzträger of the Stuka and Schlacht force, baled out, as did Feldwebel Erhardt, while Obergefreiter Fricke was killed. At 1957 a third eight-aircraft sweep was flown, two Me 262s being seen south of Bergedorf, and then a Fw 190 which was shot down by Flying Officer Evans. During the day I and II/JG 26 also reported losing three pilots, at least one of them in the Lauenburg area, where Leutnant Söffing claimed one Tempest and one Spitfire XIV shot down. The only Tempest loss of the day was suffered by 3 Squadron when Warrant Officer Crowe force-landed near Lübeck – possibly Söffing's victim. This was the last claim for a Tempest to be made by JG 26, which had claimed fourteen of these aircraft since 22 February. Of these, five had been credited to Waldemar Söffing, a 35-victory 'Experte', and four to Hans Dortenmann (one while with III/JG 54), a 38-victory veteran of the Eastern Front.

During the last day of the month, while the squadrons continued patrolling over the bridgehead thrown across the Elbe by 21st Army Group, the final claims for April were submitted by 3 and 56 Squadrons to raise the total for the month to 61 in the air, 29⅓ of them by 486 Squadron.

The first days of May found 122 Wing patrolling over the northern coastal airfields of Germany to prevent Luftwaffe aircraft flying out to Scandinavia. On the 1st three aircraft were shot down in the Schwerin area, and on the 2nd the tally rose to at least a dozen, seven of them by 56 Squadron. In 486 Squadron, Flying Officer Eagleson, one of the 'Diver' aces of summer 1944, encountered a lone Fw 44 Weihe communications aircraft in the early morning and shot this down in flames. Later in the day he spotted a Fi 156 Storch on the ground and destroyed this, but in the evening on a third sortie, his Tempest was hit by Flak and he was obliged to force-land. Flying Officer Howard and Pilot Officer Shaw of this unit jointly shot down a Fw 190 and a Fi 156 during the early afternoon, but the squadron's new commander, 'Smokey' Schrader, who had raised his score on the Tempest to 9½ during the previous day, was promoted again and posted to command 616 Squadron, the first unit equipped with Gloster Meteor jet fighters, which had just been cleared for operations over the front. He was replaced by Jim Sheddan, who celebrated that evening by shooting down a four-engined, twin-boom flying-boat over Heiligenhafen, shared with Flying Officer Thompson, to bring his own score to 5½ (four and three shared) plus 7½ V-1s.

Early next morning 3 Squadron swept over the Plon area of Schleswig, catching two Fi 156s and a Fw 44 in the air and dispatching these. Three more such sorties were flown during the day, at the conclusion of which eleven more aircraft had been claimed destroyed on the ground and fourteen damaged, for the loss of one Tempest to Flak. Soon after midday a New Zealand Spitfire 'ace', Flying Officer Johnnie Houlton, starting a new tour on Tempests with 274 Squadron, shot down a lone Do

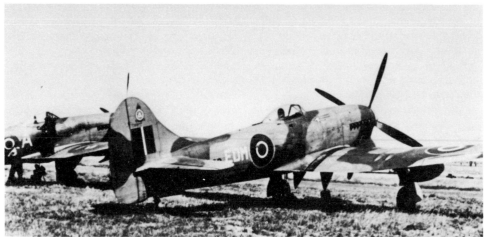

217 bomber over Kiel for 135 Wing's last aerial victory of the war. Two hours later 56 Squadron 'bagged' a Fw 190, and at 1700 hours two of 486 Squadron's pilots caught a pair of Ju 88s near Tegel at low level and shot down both, although two other Tempests were hit by Flak and force-landed. These were to be the last aerial victories claimed by either Wing.

Operations were not yet over, however, for on 4 May during an early sortie 486 Squadron was to claim a Fi 156 destroyed on the ground, and later in the morning in the Kiel-Haderslev area, eight of this unit's aircraft, led by Wing Commander Mackie, claimed three more of these aircraft in similar circumstances. At 1430 hours Flight Lieutenant Clostermann led eight 3 Squadron Tempests to the Danish border, many seaplanes and flying-boats being spotted on the water near Schleswig Holsten. Clostermann personally destroyed two Dornier Do 18s, and when claims for the day were totalled, four Do 24s, a Ju 52, a Bf 110 and a Bv 138 had been added, with five other aircraft damaged. During some of these last operations, 33 Squadron became the first and only Tempest unit to carry a pair of 500lb bombs in action, but it was already too late for this to become standard practice. 222 Squadron attacked an airfield east of Heiligenhafen on the Kiel Peninsula, claiming four destroyed and twelve dam-

Top: A Messerschmitt Me 262, the Tempest's deadly rival. This example, believed to have been from JG 7, elected to land at B.109, Quackenbrück in the last hours before the ceasefire, having encountered a formation of 222 Squadron Tempests near their base. (D. J. Coxhead)

Above: At the end of April 1945, Squadron Leader E. D. Mackie was promoted and took the place of Wing Commander Brooker as Wing Commander Flying, 122 Wing. His Tempest, SN228, probably photographed shortly after the end of the war in Europe, carried his initials, 'EDM', plus his Wing Commander's pennant and scoreboard beneath the windscreen. (Wing Commander E. D. Mackie)

aged during the day, and it was this unit that would have the honour of flying 84 Group's last operational sorties prior to the German surrender.

Even on this last day of real action, a loss was suffered by 486 Squadron – the last of the war – when Flying Officer Austin was brought down to force-land and become a prisoner. Although reportedly to Flak, it now seems that his aircraft was the sole victory to be claimed for the new He 162 jet, Leutnant Schmidt of I/JG 1, just operational on this type, making a claim for a 'Typhoon' on this date.

By 5 May there were no longer any targets left, and most units were not called upon to operate, although 3 Squadron escorted Dakota transports carrying troops and supplies to liberate Denmark. Two days later the war in Europe ended, and with it the period of triumph for the Tempest squadrons of 2nd TAF.

CHAPTER THIRTEEN

The Tempest Post-War

THE end of the war in Europe did not herald the finale of the Tempest's service with the RAF in the way that it did with the Typhoon. Re-equipment with Tempest Vs had ceased, however; it may be recalled that when 33 and 222 Squadrons returned to 135 Wing in Holland with their new aircraft, 349 and 485 Squadrons had been sent to Predannack, in February 1945, similarly to convert. Owing to the intense activity taking place in northwest Europe, few Tempests could be spared for these new units and these were so slow in arriving that a handful of redundant Typhoon FR.IBs were borrowed from the GSUs to give the Spitfire pilots an introduction to the Hawker 'stable'. Early in April it became apparent that sufficient Tempests would not be forthcoming and the conversion course was cancelled. Both squadrons were re-issued with Spitfires and returned to 2nd TAF service during the final weeks of the war. The Tempest V had reached its maximum strength in RAF service of eight squadrons, seven of which were with 2nd TAF and one with ADGB.

Meanwhile the first Tempest IIs had started to roll off the production line in October 1944, although it was March 1945 before examples began reaching RAF Maintenance Units. These aircraft were designated for service in the Far East against the Japanese and first priority was to equip the fighter elements of a new air component which was to be sent out to this area as 'Tiger Force'; Avro Lincolns were to be employed by the 'Tiger Force' bomber units. A Wing of the new fighters began forming at Chilbolton in August 1945, under the command of Wing Commander Beamont, newly returned from his spell in captivity. The first squadron to receive the Mk IIs was 183, previously a Typhoon unit, which had been temporarily equipped with Spitfire IXs. Later in the month 247 Squadron, still Typhoon-equipped, arrived from Germany to join the Wing; this unit took delivery of its first Tempest II at the end of August and had completed conversion by mid-September.

However, the atomic bombs dropped on Hiroshima and Nagasaki brought the war with Japan to an unexpectedly swift conclusion, and the new Wing was no longer required. No further Tempest II squadrons were formed in the UK, although 183 and 247 Squadrons did operate with the type for some time. 183 Squadron, now commanded by Squadron Leader Frank Jensen, another returned PoW and ex-Typhoon pilot, was renumbered 54 Squadron in November 1945. During the following month 247 Squadron lost its highly experienced commander, Squadron Leader Jim Bryant, to

Below: One of 349 Squadron's stop-gap Typhoon FR.IBs gets a full service (for the benefit of the photographer!) at Predannack. Their conversion from Spitfires to Tempests was eventually abandoned, owing to the continuing shortage of Tempests. (349 Squadron via R. Decobeck)

Left: Flying Officer Howard Morley of 54 Squadron in MW798 'HF-M', still resplendent in SEAC identity markings, July 1946. (via P. G. Murton)

Right: A trio of Tempest Vs led by Squadron Leader 'Poppa' Ambrose in SN228 'XC-D', photographed from a fourth Tempest, en route from Fassberg to Gatow. SN228 had previously been Wing Commander Mackie's 'EDM'. (Air Commodore J. W. Frost)

Left: Squadron Leader Frank Jensen in MW800 'HF-V' prepares to lead 54 Squadron on a Victory Day flypast, from Chilbolton, 8 June 1946. (Group Captain F. W. M. Jensen)

Right: First to receive Tempest IIs in BAFO was 26 Squadron, first examples arriving in June 1946. The aircraft pictured here carry RP with concrete practice heads; 'XC-R' was MW417. (Air Commodore J. W. Frost)

Left: A 41 Squadron Tempest V being refuelled at Wunstorf early in 1946. (Air Commodore J. W. Frost)

Right: Outside their hangar at Gatow in May 1946, 26 Squadron's Tempests share the apron with an unserviceable aircraft, 'J5-W', left by previous residents, 3 Squadron. (Air Commodore J. W. Frost)

demobilization. In March 1946 247 Squadron began receiving De Havilland Vampires, the first squadron to be so equipped, and in June moved to Odiham, a more suitable airfield for these jet fighters. 54 Squadron followed suit later in the year, but before surrendering its Tempests it spent several weeks at Molesworth undertaking a conversion unit role. Some 19 pilots were converted to the Centaurus Tempest, prior to posting to the Middle East where they would be flying the Sabre-engined Mk VI. No more operational Tempest squadrons would be permanently based in the UK.

Tempests with the British Air Force of Occupation

With BAFO, as the 2nd TAF had been temporarily renamed, the Tempest was to soldier on for some years yet. The close of hostilities in May had found the greater part of 122 Wing at Fassberg, where 80 Squadron rejoined the Wing on its return from Warmwell APC on VE-Day. 486 Squadron was detached at Celle, but soon moved to Kastrup in Denmark, where the other three squadrons followed in June.

135 Wing was at Quackenbrück, from where in June 222 Squadron departed for England to convert to Gloster Meteors and become part of Fighter Command. The other two units of the Wing, 33 and 274 Squadrons, moved to Dedelstorf, from where 274 proceeded to Warmwell APC in July. While there it was renumbered 174 Squadron (previously a Typhoon unit, which had disbanded in April). Meanwhile, after their spell in Denmark, the 122 Wing squadrons returned individually to various German bases, the Wing being disbanded; there was to be much reorganization of the BAFO Wings in the last quarter of 1945 and the first of 1946.

In September 1945 486 Squadron was disbanded at Flensburg, to allow its New Zealand personnel to return home; its aircraft were then passed on to 41 Squadron at Lübeck; the pilots were not too pleased to receive twelve 'well-worn' Tempests in place of their Spitfire XIVs! This unit remained with 124 Wing at Lübeck for the time being, joined by 80 Squadron. In September, 3 and 56 Squadrons came together again, joining 135 Wing at Dedelstorf, with 174 Squadron and the resident 33 Squadron; this Wing moved to Fassberg in October. This was a short-lived partnership, however, for in January 1946 3 Squadron was posted to 123 Wing at Wunstorf, joining 41 and 80 Squadrons. These Wings, 123 and 135, would remain as the two BAFO Tempest Wings for the remainder of the aircraft's service in Germany. There were to be yet more changes to their constituent squadrons, which occurred on the night of 31 March/1 April 1946. Fighter Command wanted its traditional 'numberplates' back, so over-

night 41 Squadron was renumbered 26 and 56 Squadron became 16; 174 Squadron was disbanded. The final Tempest V line-up was thus:

123 Wing Wunstorf
3 Squadron
80 Squadron

135 Wing Fassberg
16 Squadron
26 Squadron
33 Squadron

From these permanent bases individual squadrons rotated detachments to Gatow (Berlin) and the APC at Sylt. During the summer of 1946 the Fassberg squadrons began receiving Tempest IIs; 26 Squadron was re-equipped in June, followed by 16 Squadron in August and 33 Squadron in October. The two Wunstorf units would carry on with their Mk Vs until 80 Squadron converted to Spitfire F.24s in January 1948, 3 Squadron receiving jet equipment – Vampires – some six months later.

With the disappearance of the rocket-Typhoons from Germany the Tempests had taken over the role, and frequent practise with this weapon was made more realistic thanks to an adequate supply of redundant German tanks. Exchange visits were arranged with their USAAF counterparts, still equipped with P-47s, the Americans expressing great admiration for the Tempest II. In addition to the routine detachments already mentioned, occasional trips to the UK were made to give demonstrations, or in the case of 26 Squadron, to take part in a Combined Operations film in September 1946, RP attacks being staged on Braunton Sands near Chivenor. One of the 'Cold War' confrontations led to a change in routine for 16 and 26 Squadrons, when in July 1947 they flew down to Zeltweg, Austria, the nearest base to the Yugoslav frontier. They returned to Fassberg in August, but shortly after this the Wing moved to a new base at Gütersloh.

As indicated earlier, the Wunstorf squadrons re-equipped in 1948, but the 135 Wing squadrons kept their Tempest IIs into 1949. 16 Squadron was the first to receive jet equipment, Vampires arriving in January; more soon followed in April for 26 Squadron. For 33 Squadron it would be a rather different story; this unit retained its Tempest IIs and in July 1949 flew them to Renfrew, Glasgow, for embarkation on the carrier HMS *Ocean* and passage to the Far East. Their service there is covered later.

Tempests in the Middle East

As recorded earlier, a decision had been made to keep the Sabre-engined Tempest in production as the Mk VI, with modifications to render it suitable for use in the

Left: Tempest V EJ865 'W2-Y' of 80 Squadron, at Wunstorf, 1947, carried a red and yellow lightning flash from its previous service with 274 Squadron, but the significance of a similarly coloured '?' on the nose is not known. Spinner and drop-tanks were blue, denoting 'B' Flight. (P. Berry)

Right: Flown by three successive COs (Squadron Leaders Ambrose, Brandt and Frost) of 26 Squadron, MW416 'XC-D' is seen on the ex-Luftwaffe compass swing base at Zeltweg in July 1947. (Air Commodore J. W. Frost)

Left: Wing Commander Flying, 123 Wing, J. C. 'Zipp' Button, replaced his Typhoon (see page 101) with a Tempest V, NV708 'JCB', which became 'Zipp XII' (just visible above the exhaust stubs on the original print). Markings were in black and white. (via R. C. Sturtivant)

Right: The CO of 33 Squadron flew PR788 '5R-A' which, in addition to his pennant below the windscreen, boasted shadow-shaded code-letters and a small squadron badge on the fin. It was photographed at Thorney Island on a rare visit to the UK. (A. Fraser)

Left: Tempest IIs of 16 and 26 squadrons preparing for a Wing take-off at Gütersloh in 1948. (Wing Commander E. J. Shaw)

Right: A frequent visitor to Tangmere in 1947/48 was Wing Commander Frank Carey of 135 Wing. His 'silver' Tempest II, PR674 'FR-C', had black codes and a red spinner. (A. Fraser)

△1

△2

△3

△4

△5　▽7

△6　▽8

Middle East. Shortly after the end of the war the RAF's fighter-bomber squadrons in this area were equipped with a heterogeneous collection of types – Spitfires due for replacement, lend-lease Mustangs due for return, and Mosquitoes whose wooden structure was suspect in desert conditions – but it was not until the end of 1946 that sufficient numbers of Tempest VIs became available to allow the re-equipment programme to start.

The Tempests were flown out to Fayid in Egypt, usually in formations of four escorted by a Ferry Unit Mosquito, responsible for navigation. 249 Squadron at Habbaniya in Iraq, was the first recipient on 23 December 1946, followed eight days later by 6 Squadron at Nicosia, Cyprus; 213 Squadron which was also at this base took delivery during the following month. A fourth unit, 8 Squadron in Aden, received Tempests in March 1947 and these were soon in action, making a punitive raid on the village of Al Husein, where a Government Agent had been shot. Policing operations by 8 Squadron and the other Tempest units followed a pattern set by the pre-war colonial squadrons. When strikes against dissident tribes were to be carried out, leaflets were dropped – usually 48 hours in advance – warning of the intention. Thus it was empty villages that were on the receiving end of the Tempests' firepower.

In June 1947 324 Wing was reformed, encompassing 6 and 213 Squadrons; it had previously been a Mediterranean-based Spitfire Wing. 8 and 249 Squadrons would, however, continue to operate independently. By the end of 1947, all four squadrons were commanded by wartime Typhoon pilots, 6 and 8 Squadrons by Squadron Leaders Dennis Crowley-Milling and Frank Jensen, who had been successive commanders of 181 Squadron in 1943 and who had led the first Typhoon bomber and rocket operations respectively; Jensen, it will be recalled, had already commanded 54 Squadron on Tempest IIs in the UK. 213's Squadron Leader Colebrook was also experienced on Typhoons and Tempests, and Squadron Leader Peter Steib of 249 Squad-

ron had completed a wartime tour in 257 Squadron.

249 Squadron at Habbaniya, having spent a year training, first with the new aircraft and then with RPs, was kept on alert throughout the first half of 1948 due to unrest in Iraq caused by the unstable situation in Palestine. Four of the unit's Tempests were detached to Ramat David, and 6 Squadron moved from Khartoum to Fayid, to help cover the British withdrawal from Palestine; this was accomplished by the middle of May 1948. Three months later it was 213 Squadron's turn to leave Khartoum, Mogadishu in Italian Somaliland being the destination, to cover another British withdrawal, this time from the Ogaden. Ninety-gallon drop-tanks were now available, however, and with the aid of these four-and-a-half-hour patrols could be carried out; thus when 213 Squadron departed for Deversoir in October 1948, 8 Squadron was able to cover Somaliland from Aden. During October 8 Squadron was particularly busy; in one three-day period seven pilots flew 107 hours against the Mansuri tribe in Wadi Mirria, attacking sixteen forts and rendering fifteen of them uninhabitable. A total of 468 rockets were fired with an average error later calculated as six yards!

In the meantime 213 Squadron's place at Khartoum had been taken by a new Tempest unit, 39 Squadron, which promptly detached three aircraft to Asmara, Eritrea, to support British and native troops against armed Shifta bands which were terrorizing small villages. This short-lived unit disbanded at the end of February 1949.

Early 1949 found 6 and 213 Squadrons at Deversoir in Egypt, as the war which had been raging between the new state of Israel – formerly the British mandate of Palestine – and its Arab neighbours, approached a United Nations-negotiated ceasefire. At the commencement of hostilities Egyptian Spitfires had made attacks on RAF airfields in Palestine in error, and had paid for their mistake with several losses. There had, however, been no further British involvement over the next nine months. Now

Israeli forces were infiltrating into Egypt and also threatening the security of Jordan, considered to be an ally of Britain. Consequently flights of reconnaissance Spitfires were sent out from Fayid by 208 Squadron to check the position. One such flight of four aircraft, dispatched early on 7 January 1949, failed to return in its entirety, and no news of the fate of the pilots was forthcoming. Under the impression that they might have force-landed in the desert, several searches were initiated at once. In fact the Spitfires had met intense ground fire, which had shot down one of them; while the remaining three circled they were bounced by Spitfire IXs of the Israeli 101 Squadron, and all were shot down. The claiming pilots were an ex-RCAF Spitfire 'ace' of 249 Squadron in Malta, J. F. McElroy (who shot down two), and an ex-USAAF test-pilot!

Four of 213 Squadron's Tempests had been sent off to escort a photo-reconnaissance Mosquito over the frontier, while four 6 Squadron aircraft patrolled within easy reach of them over the Ismailia–El Auga road, but nothing was seen. At 1500 hours the Tempest squadrons were called to cover six 208 Squadron Spitfires searching for their missing colleagues. 213 Squadron was led by Group Captain Anderson, to provide medium cover, while eight 6 Squadron aircraft led by Squadron Leader Crowley-Milling gave top cover. The Tempests rendezvoused with the Spitfires over Fayid, but on approaching the frontier 213 Squadron was attacked by five Israeli Spitfires – again from 101 Squadron. Pilot Officer Tattersfield was shot down immediately by another ex-USAAF pilot, William Schroeder, two other Tempests being claimed damaged, one of them by Ezer Weizmann, later Chief of the Israeli Air Force. In fact three Tempests were damaged; P2s Heald and Waddington of 213 Squadron had several bullet holes in their aircraft, while that flown by P3 Liquorish had received a bullet through the mainspar, which necessitated a wing change. The Tempests had taken off in some haste and although fully armed, their guns had not been cocked – rendering them useless – so the pilots were forced to employ

Left: 5 Squadron's Tempest IIs lined up at Poona in 1946. The nearest aircraft is PR530 'OQ-D', and in common with most of the others it wears 5 Squadron's maple leaf badge on the nose. (RAFM)

Left: Tempest IIs of 5 Squadron within the fort walls at Miramshah. The hangars had been built before the war, to house Westland Wapitis, but could just accommodate a Tempest, except for its propeller. (H. Pears)

Left: 'UM'-coded Tempest IIs of 152 squadron at Risalpur late in 1946. 152's badge (the Dastar of the Nizam of Hyderabad) was displayed on the engine cowling, just below the centre-line. Nearest the camera, PR666, was coded 'UM-E' or 'F'. (D. J. Coxhead)

Right: Frank Murphy in the cockpit of his Typhoon, when a flight commander in 486 Squadron, November 1943. (IWM)

the superior speed of the Tempest to break off the action. Several exceeded the maximum speed laid down in the 'Pilot's Notes' and some were also spun with long-range tanks still in place, which was also a forbidden practice. The confusion of the situation had been heightened by the red spinners of the Israeli fighters which made them difficult to distinguish from 208 Squadron's similarly-marked Spitfires.

In March 1949, 249 Squadron left Habbaniya and joined 6 Squadron at Deversoir, 213 Squadron having departed for one of the regular APC courses at Nicosia. Time was now running out for the Tempest in the Middle East, however, for in September 1949 the first of the 324 Wing squadrons began receiving Vampires, all three units completing conversion to this type by March 1950. Khormaksar-based 8 Squadron had begun a slow transition to the light bomber role in May 1949, when Bristol Brigands began to arrive; the last Tempests departed from here too in March 1950.

Tempests in the Far East

Although plans to send Tempest IIs with 'Tiger Force' had been shelved, several fighter and fighter-bomber squadrons in India were due for more modern equipment. Two Mk IIs had been dispatched to India in June 1945, but it would be December 1945 before Tempests were shipped out to Karachi in large numbers, deliveries totalling 180 aircraft over the next eighteen

months. These were assembled by 320 MU at Drigh Road, test-flown, and then delivered; in March 1946 the first went to 5 and 30 Squadrons at Bhopal, others then reaching 20 Squadron at Agra and 152 Squadron at Risalpur.

Representing Hawker in India was Squadron Leader Frank Murphy, who after his successful tour with 486 Squadron had gone to the company 'on rest', and stayed on as a test-pilot: 'I went out to Drigh Road to brief the MU test-pilots on the Tempest, and as the squadrons equipped I spent a short time with each of them giving demonstrations, lectures and so on. They were quite experienced squadrons but they had some trouble with the Tempest at first, because it was a difficult aeroplane when landing, especially if you had a bit of a cross-wind. The reason why it varied from the Tempest V was that with the wider nose, for the radial engine, the airflow over the rear fuselage was quite different when the tail dropped after landing, or when you made a three-point landing. The airflow over the fin was not enough to keep the aircraft straight, you had to use full rudder or sometimes brake. A cross-wind made the problem worse, and a ground loop could result. Indian airfields were not very forgiving as they had monsoon ditches down each side, not far from the runway. So, they had a lot of prangs, often wiping off undercarriage legs. The answer was to do a 'wheeler' landing, which gave you time to line things

up before the tail dropped, or even, on occasions when a long runway was available, to land with less flap, when you'd get more airflow over the tail surfaces and the rudder was more effective.'

5 Squadron was given one of Frank's demonstrations just three days after the first aircraft had arrived; the unit diarist recorded: '. . . a mere ten minutes but that was enough to impress on us all the versatility of this aircraft. To see the initial climb, loop and roll off the "deck", and the turning circle at 450mph, shook us all and if any doubts were held, they have now been dispelled.' Among the 5 Squadron pilots was Flight Lieutenant Harry Pears, whom we last encountered rocketting a German seaplane base:

'Every pilot I met took to the Mk II immediately and appreciated its ability in the ground-attack role. Following a move to Poona, in real 'Brown job' territory, the use of Army ranges soon brought the squadron up to a high standard of live firing. Many live demonstrations were given to local Army formations, and others elsewhere in southern India. Tribal disturbances on the North-West Frontier took the squadron to Risalpur and Peshawar, where again the use of firing ranges kept the shooting standard at a high level. Some dummy operations were flown in very mountainous terrain to "scare" the tribesmen, and the odd sortie with solid RP heads and ball ammunition was undertaken. "A" Flight, detached to the fort at Miramshah, was called on for sorties similar to those flown by Westland Wapitis between the wars. ROD (Road Open Day) patrols in support of convoys supplying outposts, along with R/T and visual checks of the outposts, were interspersed with weapons training on the airstrip's own range. Armed aircraft were at stand-by during daylight hours every day; at the end of each day's flying the Tempests were moved into the fort and placed in individual hangars, originally built for Wapitis.'

The conversion of all four squadrons had been assisted by Flight Lieutenant Douglas Coxhead, a pilot with much experience of the Hawker line, who had completed a tour with 182 Squadron on Typhoons and started another with 222 Squadron on Tempest Vs: 'After testing and ferrying many of the Tempests from Drigh Road, I stayed on with each squadron to help aquaint them with its new aircraft. We lost some pilots here and there in India, but few Tempest IIs went down. It was rough country; one test-pilot force-landed twelve miles from base and started to walk back, and although we soon found his aircraft there was no sign of him. Later, ground searchers found a shoe; that was all. The Sind desert was no place to walk across at night. After that "Peewee" Judge went down with engine failure but was retrieved OK, having stayed in his

Left: Some Tempest IIs were repainted 'Aluminium' before handover to the IAF/PAF – as PR772 'OQ-R' of 5 Squadron seen here. (5 Squadron via P. H. T. Green)

Right: One of 33 Squadron's last Tempests, PR771 '5R-D', peels away to deliver a rocket attack on terrorist positions, Malaya 1951. (C. Thomas)

Far right: Flight Lieutenant Alex Shannon with one of the target-tugs he flew at Sylt. Note the clam-shell shutters on the carburettor air intake – peculiar to this mark of Tempest. (A. Shannon)

Left: Traces of the original camouflage are beginning to show through the 'Aluminium' paint scheme of this 33 Squadron Tempest II, PR533 '5R-V', taxiing at Kuala Lumpur in 1950. Spinner was blue, for 'B' Flight. (J. Macadam via P. H. T. Green)

Left: Tempest TT.5 SN290 'L' of Sylt APS sets out for another target-towing sortie. Among the 'silver' Tempests in the background can be seen a single camouflaged example – one of the two Mark VIs operated by this unit. In addition to the black and yellow stripes on their undersurfaces, Sylt Tempests had black codes and anti-glare panels, and red spinners. (A. Shannon)

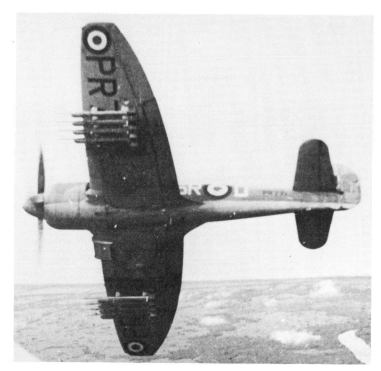

aircraft after a belly-landing. Later, after I had been posted to 152 Squadron as a flight commander, I led a demonstration for the Staff College at Quetta, where a buckled fairing meant that I had to fly all the way back at 190mph, with the under-carriage down. As a result, I ran out of fuel, and was forced to land at the old deserted strip at Tank, where fortunately there was an abandoned "Dak" from which I was able to drain some fuel. This was much to the delight of the local tribesmen, who seemed to think I was milking the beast! They didn't seem too keen to let me go so, as soon as I started the Tempest, with lots of smiling and waving, I wheeled it round and tore off without even fastening my straps!'

As more Tempests were assembled it was the turn of the Royal Indian Air Force squadrons to convert to the Hawker fighter-bomber, 3 Squadron commencing in September 1946 and 8 Squadron in November. With the RIAF squadrons preparing to take over, the RAF's days in India were numbered. First to go were 30 and 152 Squadrons, disbanding in December 1946 and January 1947 respectively. 20 Squadron disbanded on the last day of July 1947 and 5 Squadron followed the next day. During its last weeks 5 Squadron had acted as a conversion unit for RIAF pilots new to the Tempest. At Partition, on 15 August 1947, all Tempests (and many other RAF types) were handed over to the RIAF and the Royal Pakistan Air Force. Service with these Air Forces is covered later.

This was not to be the finale of the RAF Tempests in the Far East, however, for two years later the type made a return to this theatre in the hands of 33 Squadron which, instead of re-equipping with Vampires like the other BAFO Tempest II squadrons, had

been transferred to Singapore to strengthen the forces opposing the Communist guerrillas in Malaya – Operation 'Firedog'.

Disembarking from HMS *Ocean* at Seletar, the Squadron moved into nearby Changi to reassemble its aircraft; flying recommenced on 16 August 1947. This would be the Squadron's main base for the next seven months, although a detachment would be maintained up country at Kuala Lumpur during the early months of 1950. After a brief visit to Tengah, 33 Squadron left Singapore and settled at Butterworth, in Malaya, for its last year of operations with the Tempest. During this time regular strikes, mostly with cannon and RP, were flown against the elusive Communists. Using information from ground forces, photo-reconnaissance, and Intelligence sources, remote villages and jungle encampments were attacked, mainly with the aim of flushing out the terrorists and driving them into prepared ambushes. The campaign would last for several more years, but the last Tempest sortie was, appropriately enough, flown on the anniversary of D-Day, 6 June 1951. The very next day 'A' Flight began conversion to the De Havilland Hornet F.3, 'B' Flight having already done so earlier in the year. So, after seven years of varied front-line service, the majority of it overseas, the Tempest left the ranks of the RAF's operational units.

Tempests as Target Tugs

Simultaneously with the withdrawal of the last Sabre-engined Tempests from the Middle East, a new variant with this engine was entering service in Europe. From February 1950 to May 1952 eighty Tempest Vs, rebuilt as TT.5s left the conversion line at Langley for service with the RAF in the

UK and in Germany. At home TT.5s were spread among the Central Gunnery School, the Armament Practice Station (APS) at Acklington, and 226, 229 and 233 Operational Conversion Units; in Germany large numbers were operated by the APS at Sylt.* The intensive operations of this latter unit are described by Flight Lieutenant Alex Shannon, who ten years earlier had flown Typhoons with 257 and 197 Squadrons:

'The target drogue (or "flag", as the pilots called it) and its length of nylon cable were laid along the runway in the direction of take-off by a member of the ground staff, and attached to a device under the aircraft by him. At his signal the pilot took off and proceeded to the firing range. Here, flying at a predetermined height, the pilot pursued a course three miles distant from, and parallel with, the coastline, terminating about fifteen miles from the starting-point with a "dumbell" turn. He then flew a reciprocal course back to the starting-point, repeated the dumbell turn pattern and continued thus until the attacks by squadron pilots (four in an hour) had finished. On completion of the sortie the pilot flew to the dropping-zone at Hornum, where, flying low, he released the cable, allowing it and the flag to fall earthwards. Ground crew at the zone would then count the number of hits and telephone the result to Sylt.

The Target Towing Squadron comprised two flights. During the summer months pilots operated in shifts, from first light to one o'clock, then were free until one o'clock the following day, finishing at dusk. Normally three sorties were completed in each "stint". The flying was routine and was

*RAF Sylt also operated two Tempest VIs, the only Tempests of this mark to see service in Germany. Although not officially converted to target-tug standard, it is believed that they were used in this role.

regarded as a job of work to be done; there was little time for any other flying. An occasional air-test provided an opportunity to practise aerobatics, but, apart from that, it was all take off, fly to the range, drop the flag, land, have a game of darts, then take-off again. A wary eye had to be kept on the weather in spring and autumn, since a low cloud mass could precipitately roll in and blanket the airfield, when aircraft would be diverted to the satellite in Schleswig–Holstein.

Apart from the fact that the Tempest's cockpit was oily, and pilots' flying-boots and overalls quickly became contaminated and stained, the aircraft gave little trouble to the seasoned flyer. It trimmed easily into the repeated pattern of straight and level flight and performed the task it had to do admirably. It was, however, to the uninitiated, an aircraft whose motto could have been "nemo me impune lacessit", since it could, like its predecessor the Typhoon, ground-

loop savagely under the control of a heavy-handed pilot. Indeed there was a certain Wing Commander who, undaunted by its notorious record, got to the end of the runway, opened the throttle, ground-looped and returned to dispersal, never again to take on this mettlesome adversary! It was a sad day when a dozen or more assorted pilots flew the last Tempests to Aston Down on 19 October 1954, the Squadron having converted to Meteors. On arrival there the pilots saw "hundreds" of Tempests waiting to be demolished, I suppose the men in grey suits would say "written-off".'

The TT.5s were also withdrawn from Chivenor in December 1954, but continued in use across the Bristol Channel for a little longer. The very last examples were removed from service with 233 OCU at Pembrey in July 1955, when several high-ranking erstwhile Tempest pilots turned up to take the opportunity for a last flight in this great fighter.

Tempests in Foreign Service

When sufficient numbers of Tempest IIs became available in India, following the equipment of four RAF squadrons there, RIAF squadrons began conversion to the type. As already noted, the first unit to change its Spitfire VIIIs for the new aircraft was 3 Squadron at Kolar, commencing in September 1946; similar re-equipment was undertaken by 8 and 10 Squadrons before the end of the year. During the summer of 1947 4 Squadron, RIAF, returned from Japan where it had formed part of the British Commonwealth component of the Occupation Forces, flying Spitfire XIVs. On return this unit received Tempests, while three more Spitfire VIII squadrons, 1, 7, and 9, had all received these aircraft by the time independence was celebrated on 15 August 1947. Independence also brought the partition of the subcontinent into India and Pakistan. Preparatory to this event, the armed forces were divided pro-rata, 1 and 9

Left: 'WH' codes identify Acklington APS – one of the major Tempest TT.5 users; SN219 'WH-14' was in use from June 1950 to December 1952. Parts of this aircraft were used in 33 Squadron's composite Tempest rebuild, which now resides in the RAF Museum, Hendon. (E. Taylor)

Left: Tempest IIs awaiting delivery to the Indian Air Force. They are marked with the original style of roundel favoured by the IAF after Independence. (BAe)

Squadrons standing down so that 35 Tempests might be passed to the new Royal Pakistan Air Force. This left the RIAF with five squadrons of Tempests as the backbone of its air strength and it was not long before they were engaged in action. During October 1947 insurgent forces began crossing the border of the new state into the territories of Jammu and Kashmir; at once troops were air-lifted into the area, supported initially by a couple of Spitfires, but subsequently by 7 Squadron's Tempests. These played a decisive role in containing the insurgents, particularly during an action known as the Battle of Shelatung. Fighting was to continue for fifteen months before a ceasefire was finally agreed on 1 January 1949. Throughout this period the RIAF, and particularly its Tempests, were constantly and heavily involved. The original total of 124 ex-RAF Tempests had now been supplemented by a further 89 aircraft. These had been purchased by Hawker, from surplus RAF stocks at 20 MU Aston Down, refurbished and sold to India, deliveries taking place in 1949. Twenty more were acquired direct from RAF MUs in 1951.

In January 1950 India became a republic, the air force dropping its 'Royal' prefix. Strength of the IAF, which was soon to be modernized and increased in size, now included six operational fighter-bomber squadrons, 3, 4, 8, and 10 still flying Tempests, 7 Squadron having converted to Vampires in 1949. More of these were soon to follow to re-equip 3 and 8 Squadrons, while in May 1953 10 Squadron received two-seat night-fighter versions of the jet. Later in that year Dassault Ouragan jet fighter-bombers (known as Toofanis in India) were received to replace the remaining aged Tempests in 4 Squadron. Thereafter the Hawker fighters were usefully employed for several years in the advanced training role, before their final honourable retirement.

In Pakistan, too, the Tempest had seen valuable service, forming the equipment of 5 and 9 Squadrons of the RPAF from its formation in 1947. The aircraft were also soon in action, undertaking policing duties with guns, rockets and bombs against the incorrigible tribesmen of the North-West Frontier. From its small beginnings, the RPAF was steadily expanded, the fighter-bomber squadrons being built up to an establishment of sixteen aircraft each with the help of a further 24 refurbished aircraft from Hawker, which also allowed the formation of a third Tempest unit, 14 Squadron. Despite the acquisition of 21 more direct from the RAF in 1951/52 the Tempests' operational days were numbered and by 1953 all had been replaced by the Tempest II's 'younger brother' – the Hawker Fury FB.60. As in India, the remaining Tempests were retained for operational training, before being stored prior to their eventual disposal as scrap in 1958.

Right: Indian and Pakistani Tempests photographed in Cyprus during their delivery flights. HA635 appears to be managing with 45-gallon drop-tanks whereas the Pakistani aircraft has the more usual 90-gallon tanks. (J. D. Gibson and R. Hill)

Left: One of the IAF's last Tempest acquisitions, PR555, ex-'XL-Y' of 226 OCU, photographed at Bahrein in transit to its new owners, late in 1951. (K. Cumine)

Left: A sad sight at Chakeri in 1961 – lines of Tempests withdrawn from service and awaiting their fate. Most are in a 'silver' finish with black wingtips, rudders and rear fuselage bands. (F. Wilson via G. A. Jenks)

Below: Pakistani Tempests were delivered in a 'desert' scheme – Dark Earth and Mid-Stone upper surfaces with 'Azure' under surfaces. A128 has 90-gallon drop-tanks ready for the ferry flight (BAe)

CHAPTER FOURTEEN
Pilots' Notes

IN preceding chapters we have traced the development and operational history of the Typhoon and Tempest, and although pilots' accounts of incidents and operations have been used throughout, there remain many unanswered questions. What was it like to fly these aircraft for the first time, or on a first operational sortie? Was the reputation of 'one to sort the men from the boys' really deserved? How did this reputation affect morale? What were the most feared operations? These and similar questions can only be effectively answered by the pilots themselves.

The shortage of Typhoons in the operational squadrons during 1942 and 1943 precluded the formation of a Typhoon-equipped OTU. There was a brief attempt to provide such a unit in March 1943, when 59 OTU at Milfield began receiving Typhoons to supplement its Hurricanes. These were mostly 1As and early 1Bs and by the end of May seventeen were on charge, but by June the situation on the operational squadrons was judged so serious that even these war-weary specimens were reallocated, and the course finished on Hurricanes. It was not until April 1944 that 3 TEU began receiving Typhoons in large numbers, allowing conversion courses to be run for pilots who had completed their training on Hurricanes or who had previous operational experience on other types. Until then, the novice would not get a crack at the Typhoon until he joined an operational squadron. To ease the process most squadrons had one or two Hurricanes but it was still a big step to the Typhoon – half as heavy again and twice as powerful as the Hurricane.

Sergeant Phil Murton was a 19-year-old 'sprog' when he first saw a Typhoon while at Milfield in January 1943: 'It looked simply massive and rugged (which it proved to be) but the instruments and cockpit layout didn't seem to be all that different from those of the Hurricane – a few extra perhaps, but nothing untoward. Despite all the stories of tails dropping off and engine failures, most of us on the course dearly wanted a posting to a squadron equipped with these new and potent ground-attack aircraft – even in preference to the much-loved Spitfire (which we hadn't yet flown).' His wish was granted and a posting to 193 Squadron, then based at Harrowbeer near Plymouth, followed the end of his training.

Above: Flying Officer 'Phil' Murton with his 183 Squadron Typhoon, MN923 'HF-P', October 1944. (P. G. Murton)

'On the Squadron one was not allowed to solo the "Tiffie" too soon – one had to flog an old Hurricane II (complete with two dirty great long-range tanks) around the area to get used to the airfield and its environs. Harrowbeer itself consisted basically of one very much up-and-downhill runway (with a sandpit at the downhill end where, if necessary, one could retract one's undercarriage to avoid overshooting on to the main road) plus a short cross-runway which was rarely used except in very high winds.

On 29 May 1943 I was finally turned loose in the Tiffie and it really was as big and as powerful as it was cracked up to be – certainly, initially, somewhat frightening compared with the docile Hurricane. Taxiing was tricky due to the extremely high and long nose, and the brakes, which had to be used quite a lot to swing the aircraft for a forward view, were not all that efficient, tending to overheat and become rather useless.* Take-off had to be watched due to the inherent swing from the torque of the powerful engine and huge prop, but the power was strikingly efficient. Following take-off (and retracting the undercarriage MILES from the airfield!) a normal handling sortie was carried out to get the feel of the aircraft in most configurations. General handling was good, the controls were positive but a great deal of space was required (at least in those days for that type of aircraft) for aerobatics and spins – the latter were quite violent and frightening, but at least she came out in due course if the controls were operated correctly. The stories about the aircraft wallowing about the sky on the downwind leg, when the undercarriage was lowered, were quite true, and one felt, for a time at least, that the aircraft

*Larger brake drums were eventually fitted to Typhoons, greatly improving braking efficiency.

had control! Approach and landing were not too tricky apart from the complication of our relatively short runway (either uphill or downhill!) and not very good approach paths. Working up to operational standards took some time (unless I was awfully slow!) and it wasn't until early September that I flew my first operational sortie. This was preceded by getting to know the Typhoon thoroughly, formation flying, mock dog-fights and tail chases, night flying and the like, so that when one did go on ops one was really familiar with the aircraft in all aspects.'

The next major step for the fledgling Typhoon pilot was the first operational sortie; especially the first one over enemy territory, as recalled by Flight Sergeant Peter Baden: 'My previous experience was limited to some fifteen hours of convoy patrols and I was far from confident of my ability in air-fighting as I had been well trounced in an unexpected dogfight with a captured Fw 190 which I had encountered. Therefore I was a bit keyed-up when I was told I was to be No. 2 to the CO who was leading the Squadron. We flew to Tangmere where we were bombed up with 500-pounders and briefed for a dive-bombing attack on Poix aero-drome. Cover was to be given by two squadrons of Typhoons, as German fighters were expected. At this time "finger-four" had yet to be adopted and we used either line astern or line abreast, moving to echelon for the dive. The CO had chosen line abreast with himself on the extreme left, myself next and the rest strung across to the right of us.

Strapping in, closing up the canopy, start-ing up, taxiing out, all seemed to be happen-ing in a rush. We took off in stream on alternate sides of the runway, to avoid propwash and in case anyone swung to star-board, and then formed up at 1,000 feet, which seemed to take a while but gave me a chance to settle down. As we crossed the coast we dropped to about 50 feet and it was quite something to see in the sunshine, the sea quite blue with small waves, as I snatched glances to the right, a line of aircraft moving up and down and thunder-ing towards France in concert. I was quite enjoying it by now but thought that if the CO had to turn to starboard we would get in a Hell of a tangle.

Before I could see the enemy coast the CO radioed to increase revs for climbing and soon it was spread out in front of us. It was the first time that I had seen it and it seemed mysterious and threatening, and dark as there was a belt of cloud stretching inland. We crossed in without having to correct our heading; the CO had the reputa-tion of being an ace navigator. Unfortu-nately as we climbed we could see that we were heading for a large cloud so the CO put us in echelon starboard and told us to close

right up – to keep formation in cloud. He brushed the left side of it, I was in it, and when we came out the rest of the squadron had disappeared.

From then on things became chaotic. I opened out to about 200 yards off his star-board wing, that being the accepted position to give cross cover to the rear, and we con-tinued inland, on our own. With no R/T warning the CO turned to port and left me struggling to catch up. No sooner had I caught up than he made another turn, the other way, and so on with short intervals of straight and level, all in R/T silence. Most of this time I was either 200 feet above him, chasing with wide-open throttle, or a similar distance below with throttle closed trying to fall back in position. In the meantime there was agitated chatter on the R/T which seemed to indicate the presence of enemy aircraft, so I was frantically scanning the sky. Once I thought I saw a yellow 109 a few thousand feet above at 8 o'clock – probably the result of over-stressed imagination! I can remember wondering if the CO could see something behind that I couldn't, also why I had a trickling sensation on my back, chest and legs. The situation was unlike anything I had heard about or expected, almost like a nightmare, as I hadn't a clue what was happening or why, or what I ought to do, with the CO reeling about the sky like a drunken sailor.

Eventually we were over the Channel again and at last the CO used his R/T to tell me to jettison my bombs, which I thought was a bloody waste after going through all that. We landed back at Tangmere and I got out shaking with rage and exhaustion. My clothes were soaked with sweat, which

explained the trickling feeling; my battle-dress trousers were black where they were tucked into my boots. The CO forestalled insubordinate words from me by saying "Your formation was very good but you should have weaved in the opposite direc-tion instead of with me." So he had been weaving! If I'd only known I could have had a less strenuous ride by cutting corners, but we'd been told at OTU that this tactic was outmoded by more than a year! The follow-ing trips seemed like "milk-runs".'

The OTUs endeavoured to teach the latest operational techniques, but even when successful in this, they could not impart the urgency required in action. Pilot Officer Peter Brett of 183 Squadron found himself dive-bombing Guipavas airfield, near Brest, on his first trip: 'At that time we were going in quite high, about 12,000 feet, going into echelon formation just before we reached the target, peeling off and diving down to 6 or 8,000 feet where we would release the bombs. Being a new boy I was number five or seven down. The method of aiming was to point the aircraft at the target, start pul-ling out gently and as the target disappeared beneath the nose, release the bombs. Being my first op I just picked the middle of the

airfield and released the bombs as it disappeared, probably making two lovely holes in the middle of the grass. I then pulled out comfortably (I hadn't got the sense of urgency required in those early days!) without blacking-out, only to find myself at about 6,000 feet with the rest of the Squadron another 6,000 feet above me! Fortunately there were no enemy fighters and with fine pitch and full throttle I managed to catch up.'

Other pitfalls awaited the less experienced pilot. Jack Bridge, then a Flight Sergeant with 183 Squadron, ran into a bit of trouble which caused him to miss D-Day, much to his chagrin: 'On 29 May 1944 we took off from Thorney Island to attack RDF installations at Gravelines. In order to give us training in the techniques of landing on the tracking, which we were to shortly use in France, we landed at Newchurch before the operation and were to return there to refuel. In all the excitement of landing on this very short strip for the first time I found myself rolling extremely fast down the runway, and rapidly catching up with the chap in front. Too late I realized I had landed without flaps. Knowing the area was criss-crossed with dykes there seemed no future in trying to get off the deck again. I suppose it was probably the right decision because in no time at all, with brakes full on, I went full tilt into a dyke just off the end of the runway. This broke the back of the aircraft* and did nothing to endear me to the Wing Leader who happened to be with us that day (particularly as I had passed his aircraft on the runway and had probably missed him by inches!). On return to base the next day the Adjutant presented me with a rail ticket to Sheffield – the Wing Leader considered that three weeks in the RAF's equivalent of the Army's "glasshouse" might sharpen my reactions! After only a few days I was recalled to the Squadron because D-Day broke. I suppose I was lucky, but I think I lost some enthusiasm and was certainly thoroughly brassed-off for missing D-Day.'

Another Typhoon pilot was to visit this establishment a few weeks later, as recalled by Flight Lieutenant Pete Tickner, 181 Squadron, who also vividly describes action in Normandy: '"Gilbo" [Warrant Officer R. D. Gilbert, RAAF] was my No. 2, and was a great operator, much better than I. Discipline, however, was not his strong suit, and in a fit of boredom one day at Hurn, he got permission for an air-test and proceeded to put on the most fantastic air display ever – right over the field and at anything from 5,000 feet down to 5 feet. At the court-martial ATC insisted on punishment and he was sent on the Sheffield "naughty boys' course".'

*EK498 'HF-O' was subsequently repaired and (unusually) returned to 183 Squadron in October 1944, becoming 'HF-N'.

Meanwhile 181 Squadron had moved to France, but when Tickner returned to Hurn, to pick up a replacement aircraft, he was greeted with a disturbingly familiar sight: 'A Typhoon with Canadian squadron markings was knocking seven kinds of shit out of the control tower and performing the imperformable all over the sky – I knew it could be only one person! He had skipped after fourteen days of his sentence and spun the Canadian CO a yarn about getting his hand in as he was rejoining 181 Squadron in France! We smuggled him aboard the early morning mail "Dak" to B.2 – I was delighted to have him back as my No. 2. The next day we were on a cab-rank west of Caen and were called in to have a go at two silos which were being used as observation posts – we hit them and came out on the deck. As I overshot a north-facing slope I saw 20mm emplacements and took a dose in the radiator. I was trailing black and white smoke but the gauges were OK, and at that moment I saw a line of Tiger tanks half a mile ahead. We hit that lot and even now I can see a Polish idiot stand on a Sherman tank over to my left and wave to us. In the next instant there was a "chonk" and horrid silence as my engine seized. I stood it on its tail, jettisoned the hood, and a voice said "OK mate, where are you going now?" – Gilbo was in tight formation on my starboard side. It started to waffle so I dropped the nose, saw a field and pointed for it. It was too far and to my horror we dropped into one of those enormous French walled farmyards. Tanks either side of me, feet on the dashboard, flames round my arse, walls closed across in front of me. Someone had left a gateway! Bang! and I left the wings and tail behind. After about 100 yards it stopped – there was nothing left to burn. I dived over the side and collapsed a few yards away. I became aware that someone was going through my pockets and trying to steal my wristwatch – opened my eyes – two British Army muggers! I stood up and there was Gilbo, coming in wheels and flaps down. I waved wildly and he gave it the gun – just as well as he would have landed in a minefield. Later I asked him what he thought he was doing, "Well mate, I wasn't going to see you fry," was his reply. He was shot down and killed at Falaise, flying No. 2 to someone else.'

After the Invasion few Typhoon pilots needed to put into practice the air combat techniques which they had learned at OTU. Survival then depended more on the ability to make a difficult target for the Flak gunners. Flight Lieutenant Tommy Hall, RAAF, completed a tour with 175 Squadron, starting just before D-Day: 'If you could gain experience by graduating from "Blue 4" – last in to attack – then your chances of survival improved quite a lot. As soon as I had learnt the score I made a point of telling each new arrival, no matter what happened, never fly directly behind anybody else. Invariably the Flak gunners would undershoot the leading aircraft and anyone behind would cop the lot. Despite the advice I saw a lot hacked down this way, and it came about because the new chums would react that little bit slower and were always trying to regain the correct position, and in so doing would fly behind other aircraft. Even so, with all the advice and experience in the world, if you didn't have Lady Luck with you, you were always in trouble.'

Luck of course also played its part in the success of operations, which is well illustrated by this account by an anonymous 83 Group pilot: 'To hit a target with rockets a Typhoon pilot needed experience, skill, and a fair share of luck. I had only the last of these when our squadron took off to attack AFVs believed to be assembled at D---- in Holland. The army major who briefed us had shown touching faith in our ability. "Just knock out this armour in D---- square and you'll make our chaps' lives a lot easier." But there was almost ten/tenths cloud at 5,000 feet, just below our operational height. If we were fortunate enough to find D---- we would have very little time to pin-point the target, fire and leave room to pull out of a 60 degree dive.

Almost magically, bang over D----, a gap appeared in the cloud cover, just big enough to dive through. As we circled, preparing to attack, I vowed not to become so mesmerised by the target that I would forget to pull out of the dive and plough into the deck. Down we went in pairs, in line astern. As I broke cloud I thought I saw vehicles parked in the square. My rocket selection switch was at "salvo"; I pressed the button and let the whole lot go. Then I went into a steep climbing turn, anxious to be back above the cloud and out of the Flak. Just before I disappeared into cloud I saw dust and smoke rising from the ruins of what must have been a fairly large building. The squadron reformed and headed for base. I tried to push to the back of my mind that the large building had been a church tower. I had been brought up as a strict Nonconformist, so the thought of being responsible for the destruction of one of God's houses filled me with shame. There was a possibility that some other pilot had hit it . . .

I landed and taxied to dispersal. The Intelligence Officer was so keen to have my story that he was up on the wing before the prop had stopped. "You're the only one to have fired your rockets," he shouted. "You must have seen the armour." I tried to appear casual, unbuckling my straps slowly, and told him I couldn't be sure. He seemed very disappointed. At breakfast some days later the same man came and sat beside me. "You remember that attack on D---- a few days ago?" My eyes went up towards my

Left: Flight Lieutenant Pete Tickner in the cockpit of one of his five 'EL-Q's, B.6, Coulombs August 1944. (Captain P. E. Tickner)

forehead, which I hoped gave the impression that I was searching the recesses of my memory. "You will also remember that you were the only pilot to fire rockets on that particular op?" I reluctantly admitted that I was. "Well, the Army sent us their thanks. Seems we, that is you, destroyed a tower used by the Germans for artillery spotting. Pity it was a church tower." I felt myself redden. "Shame you didn't mention it at the time. It might have done you a bit of good." So there it was; I had to live with it.

After the war I took a teaching post in the North. Holidays were approaching and I was making polite conversation with a colleague whose leg I was prone to pull. I asked where he would spend his vacation. He told me that he had married a Dutch girl during the war and that every holiday she carted him off to see his in-laws . . . in D----. The memories and guilt came flooding back. "Tell me, have they rebuilt the church tower yet?" He became annoyed. "Every time I go to D---- they rope me in for another donation towards the restoration of that church tower. Some idiot of a Typhoon pilot knocked it down during the war." I had to confess sooner or later. "I did it," I said. He snorted, "It's not the sort of thing to be funny about" and strode away!'

One aspect of the Typhoon and Tempest's character which appealed to pilots was their impressive ability to safeguard the pilot in the event of a crash-landing. This resulted from the bulk of the Sabre engine and the resilience of the airframe, this latter factor also enabling both types to soak up a lot of damage and still get back to base. The Achilles' heel was the cooling system of the Sabre which, despite the addition, just before D-Day, of armour to protect the radiator, was always prone to fatal damage from Flak, debris or smallarms fire. Flying Officer Dennis Orriss of 247 Squadron had already been thankful for the Typhoon's toughness when he survived a catastrophic forced-landing near Eindhoven railway yards following an engine failure over the town; in April 1945 he was to test the Typhoon again in another unexpected arrival:

'On this occasion the volume and accuracy of the Flak was feeble, in fact more apologetic than vindictive in its attempt to deter our progress. On reflection I suppose that it was inevitable that my turn to collect some of the hot metal was overdue and I duly collected a small amount. A few minutes after the desultory barrage had occurred I noticed a film of moisture covering all my perspex; it could only be glycol. And it was not my imagination, the engine note did sound different . . . a quick glance at the temperature gauge confirmed my fears. I turned my aircraft on to a reciprocal course, at the same time calling the formation leader to inform him of my good reason for leaving. A quick "Good luck," and I was on my own.

I knew I had some way to go before crossing the 'bomb-line' on the way back, but although it was marked on my map it was not shown on the ground and I began searching for landmarks that would confirm I was over Allied territory. The engine was running rougher and rougher and the cockpit getting warmer and warmer, but I was still airborne and getting nearer to base with every minute. Open country with large treeless fields beckoned below, but just a few more miles I thought would certainly see me on the right side of that line between safety and capture. I pushed my luck along with the engine and finally had no choice, the engine stopped and small flames appeared from the exhausts.

My principal worry was the location rather than the execution of the landing, and then I was down, with the aircraft intact apart from propeller and flaps. Although the aircraft was now on fire, I got out and actually took my parachute with me before leaving in a hurry. I can't imagine why I took the time and trouble to take such an unwieldy object, but take it I did. I was reasonably sure I had reached the safety of our own lines but by no means certain. The aircraft was now blazing quite merrily and the cannon-shells were exploding in the heat. I left the scene if not at a run, certainly at a steady trot, hampered as I was by that bloody parachute. I could see no sign of rockets and assumed that they were still attached to the wings. If that were the case, then they were about to make their contribution to the action.

I was moving away from the Typhoon, sensibly in the opposite direction to the way it was pointing when suddenly, with an ear-splitting roar, all eight rockets left the wings and tore across the field. I had failed to notice that about two or three hundred yards ahead of the aircraft's nose stood a farmhouse. The noise was terrifying enough but the result was spectacular in the extreme – the house took the brunt of those eight charging rockets – and a huge cloud of dust, smoke, bricks and God knows what else, rose into the air as the rockets hit. The house disappeared from my petrified gaze to reappear moments later, about two feet lower and slightly askew.

I must admit that at the time I was rather more concerned for my own safety, but have since often wondered if there were any occupants. Moments later, however, I became aware that there was one person who had more than a passing interest in the outcome of my unwitting attack. He was approaching me in something of a haste, brandishing a lethal-looking farm implement. His attitude was hostile, his intent homicidal. Although his language was not clearly understandable, it was clear that he was German. I took action at last and drew the .38 revolver, with which the RAF in its wisdom had seen fit to issue us, and made a few warlike gestures of my own; he backed off. I shouldered my burden and started my walk to what I hoped might be forward elements of the British Army. This eventually materialized in the form of a khaki-clad figure on a bicycle!'

In the cut and thrust of operations on the Continent newcomers had to find their feet quickly. Paddy O'Brien arrived to join 257 Squadron at the end of 1944: 'They were very busy, they just sent me off for half an hour round the strip to familiarize myself with the local area and procedures, and then left me to my own devices. The next day I was allocated to one of the Flights and attended a briefing which wasn't anything like as detailed as I had expected. So off we went and at the end of that first day on the Squadron the CO came up to me and asked how I had got on. Had I had any trips? "Yes," I said, "I've had four!" He then wanted to know what I had done and I had to say "I don't know!"'

For a Typhoon pilot in Fighter Command a 'tour' was completed after 200 hours of operational flying, and many a pilot concealed his true total of operational hours in order to continue flying. When the squadrons were based in France, the length of the average sortie was reduced to such an extent that the tour was reckoned in sorties rather than hours. Although there was no hard and fast figure, like Bomber Command's 30 "ops", the guide-line was about 100. Some pilots were "screened" after 90 sorties, others managed to continue for 120 or even 150 without a rest. Many pilots, of course, never completed their tour; among the shortest tours on record was that of Flight Sergeant Barwise who joined 247 Squadron on 26 September 1944, arriving at 1400 hours. At 1725 he was airborne on his first trip and by 1745 he was missing, having last been seen weaving to avoid Flak near Schijdal; he was later reported PoW. Less fortunate was Sergeant Brown, who joined 181 Squadron shortly before the ceasefire and begged to be included in what promised to be 181's last operation of the war. It was his first and his last.

As Tommy Hall has indicated earlier, the chances of survival increased after the first few sorties, but, as we have seen throughout this book, Flak in particular was no respecter of experience. Many a veteran was brought down in the latter stages of his tour, although few can have been unluckier than Flight Lieutenant Jenvey of 440 Squadron who failed to return from his 98th sortie, which was already scheduled as his last. Some indication of the odds facing a 2nd TAF Typhoon pilot can be gathered from 439 Squadron's statistics at the end of April 1945. Of the 68 pilots who had served with

Above left: One of 83 GSU's early training aircraft, JR332 'S', c. April 1944. The two-tone spinner is a remnant of its previous service with 609 Squadron. Note the rack for small practice bombs fitted to the bomb carrier. (via E. Myall)

Above: Two 83 GSU instructors 'resting' between tours – Flying Officer 'Buzz' Leighton-Porter and Flight Lieutenant Ian Mallet. (A. Leighton-Porter)

Left: 83 GSU training aircraft later carried '7S' codes, as on RB509 'X', seen at its Dunsfold dispersal, early in 1945. (Air Commodore J. W. Frost)

Bottom left: Eventually enough Tempests were available to equip 83 GSU's training flight with a handful – NV718 '7S-F' arrived at Dunsfold in mid-February 1945. (Air Commodore J. W. Frost)

Top right: Like most training units, 3 TEU at Aston Down suffered its fair share of losses. On 16 November 1944 Flight Sergeant Haworth suffered an engine failure on take-off and made a wheels-up landing; he escaped with minor injuries but MN231 caught fire and was burnt out. (D. J. Coxhead)

Centre right: 3 Squadron of 59 OTU identified its Typhoons with '7L' codes and dark blue spinners, as seen on SW593 'C', at Acklington in May 1945. (Wing Commander S. J. Eaton)

Bottom right: When 59 OTU was disbanded most of its Typhoons went to 56 OTU at Milfield including SW593 (see above), which became 'HQ-11'. it was written-off in this spectacular accident, on 23 August 1945, when it left the runway and collided with SW638 'HQ-E' and SW571. (RAFM)

the Squadron since the beginning of 1944, 27 were still on strength, 26 had been killed and eight made prisoner; the remainder were posted off strength, mostly with wounds.

By the autumn of 1944, with full Typhoon courses available at 3 TEU Aston Down, the pilot training situation had changed; new Typhoon pilots arrived in a squadron with between 20 and 40 hours on Typhoons. Older hands converting from Spits or Mustangs might have to do with less, and this might take place at a Group Support Unit rather than an OTU. The two GSUs concerned with Typhoons, Nos. 83 and 84, were tasked with maintaining a stock of aircraft ready for immediate issue to the squadrons, and also a pool of pilots awaiting posting to operational units. To keep the latter in practice and to provide short conversion courses when necessary, the GSUs operated their own Training Flights from mid-1944. The instructors were mainly Typhoon pilots 'resting' between tours.

Pilot losses reached a peak in August 1944, with the climax of the battle for Normandy, and continued at a withering rate. In addition, many of the pilots who had started when the squadrons first equipped with Typhoons, reached the end of their tours in the autumn of 1944. By this time, with the end to the war still not in sight, it became evident that both Typhoon pilot and Typhoon aircraft shortages were in prospect. The latter was more easily solved by postponing the run-down of production which had been planned to facilitate Gloster Meteor manufacture, and by updating many of the early Typhoon airframes which had been held in storage since the Sabre problems early in 1943. The pilot shortage was tackled in two ways. First, two new training units were formed, 56 OTU with Typhoons and Tempests, and 59 OTU, a 'half' OTU with Typhoons only. To fill the gaps in 2nd TAF ranks until their graduates were available, a trawl for volunteers was made through other RAF fighter units. It is hardly surprising that the response was not overwhelming and the shortfall was made good, in best service tradition, by less willing 'volunteers', particularly from the Spitfire squadrons in Italy.

By January 1945 both new OTUs and 3 TEU, which had been renamed 55 OTU, were in full operation. However, continuing casualties and a shortage of instructors led to the premature disbandment of three 2nd TAF squadrons (as recorded earlier), their pilots being spread among the remaining units, thereby releasing tour-expired veterans to fill instructor posts at the OTUs. The new training units had just got into their stride when the war ended; 55 and 59 OTUs were disbanded forthwith, but 56 OTU continued until February 1946, giving it the distinction of being the last flying unit to operate the Typhoon.

The RAF was now without any Tempest training units, for 13 OTU, which had been the first unit to receive the Tempest II back in June 1945, also surrendered its Hawker fighters at this time. When the Middle East Tempest VI squadrons were about to form, some pilots, as mentioned earlier, received their introduction to the type, albeit on Mk IIs, courtesy of 54 Squadron. About the same time 226 OCU at Bentwaters received the first of several Tempests which it would operate, maintaining a flight of three or four Mk IIs alongside more numerous Vampires and Meteors. From late 1946 to late 1949 this was the only conversion facility available to pilots who had completed the latter stages of their training on Spitfires, before posting to a Tempest II or VI squadron. John Gibson was one such pilot who, having completed his course at 213 AFS Chivenor on Spitfires, arrived at Bentwaters in October 1948 for conversion to the Tempest, prior to his posting to 213 Squadron:

'The OCU was rather run-down, everyone seemed to be interested solely in their demob group, and the aircraft were in pretty poor condition. We had three allegedly serviceable Tempests available the first morning that we went out to fly them. On my first solo in the thing, when I closed the throttle on the downwind leg, it somehow got itself mixed up with the linkage for the supercharger gear. I was in "M" gear for low level, with the lever in "up" position, and somehow the throttle managed to push that lever back into "S" gear. The only way I was able to close the throttle was to hook one leg round the stick, hold the lever in "M" gear with one hand and operate the throttle with the other. So that one went unserviceable. Another chap took-off and a little bit of negative "G" after take-off caused a spurt of petrol to come up between his legs, up to nose level! Two down. We had been told in our briefing not to worry if the Centaurus sounded rough after the Merlins that we were used to . . . so when a third pilot took off for an hour's handling he was not too alarmed at the rough running. The Flight Commander who took the aircraft after him opened up for take-off and then promptly taxied back to dispersal. When the Flight Sergeant felt the "pots", two were cold! The previous pilot had done his first solo on 16 cylinders! So that was all three u/s on the first day. In a month I managed only seven and a quarter hours out of the ten we were supposed to do.

After the Spit it did seem to be a great lumbering chunk of metal. But when I had done about 40 hours on Tempests I loved them. Not because it was a particularly pleasant aeroplane to fly, but because when you were flying it you felt that if you could master it you had achieved something. It was always an aeroplane which you knew

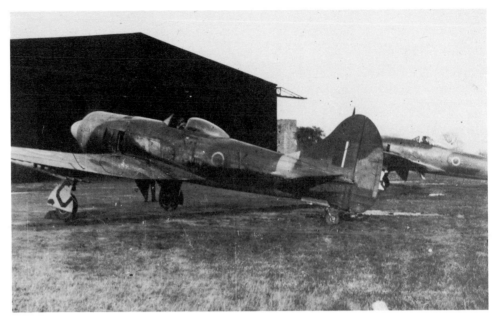

Above: Two Tempests of 226 OCU, Bentwaters in November 1948. The black codes, 'XL-Y', are difficult to see against the camouflage on the nearest aircraft, PR555, although they are more obvious in the photograph with P3 John Gibson, who describes his Bentwaters experiences below. (J. D. Gibson)

Top right: Squadron Leader 'Poppa' Ambrose in the cockpit of his 'EL-D', when commanding 181 Squadron. (Wing Commander H. Ambrose)

Centre right: Wing Commander E. D. Mackie with his 122 Wing Tempest, SN228 'EDM' (see also page 136). (Wing Commander E. D. Mackie)

Bottom right: 247 Squadron at B.78 Eindhoven in November 1944. Flying officer Dennis Orriss is at the extreme right of the bottom row.

that if you didn't keep your eyes on it, it would bite you. It was waiting for you to relax, and if you did it would have you!'

For pilots like Harry Pears, who had plenty of experience on Typhoons, adjusting to the Tempest was more straightforward: 'I liked the Typhoon right from the start, it was easy to handle and aerobat. It used up a lot of sky but was very responsive in all manoeuvres. The massive engine gave one a feeling of security which was well founded when the Flak began to fly! The Tempest V's thin, semi-elliptical wing improved handling without affecting the robust steadiness of its predecessor, and despite having the same engine power it was a much livelier aircraft. The Mk II with the Centaurus became a much smoother aircraft, and in my opinion the finest piston-engined ground-attack fighter of its day. It looked good on the ground and in the air and it was a superb fighting machine.'

Squadron Leader 'Poppa' Ambrose, one of the relatively small number of pilots who flew Typhoons, and Sabre- and Centaurus-Tempests extensively, was posted to command 41 Squadron in January 1946: 'I thought the Tempest V was an improvement on the Typhoon, although the benefits were difficult to identify at first as I felt so at home on the Typhoon, and the Tempest felt a little strange. Eventually I came to appreciate the Tempest for its improved control and stability and of course it was quite a bit faster. It was a good gun platform and was suitably stable as a rocket-firing aircraft – by using the gyro horizon you could almost guarantee to hit a tank twice out of four when practising on the range. We re-equipped with Tempest IIs in 1946 which turned out to be a very popular aeroplane, and an even better platform for rocket firing. It was not easy to land and we found that "wheeler" landings were advisable. In fact

we could manage formation landings with twelve aircraft on the runway simultaneously. A visiting Group Captain from HQ noted this with some horror and declared he would return to show us how to "three-point" a Tempest II. He duly arrived in an Auster a few days later, but ground-looped on landing, so we never did see his Tempest technique!'

Ronald Dennis, a New Zelander who flew Tempests with 56 Squadron: 'The aircraft – once you got used to its rather unforgiving nature – was an excellent combat machine. The engine loved tough handling and never objected to maximum revs or boost for extended periods. As a ground-attack machine it was a very stable gun platform, but due to its high acceleration in the dive and slightly nose-down attitude when in firing range of say, a locomotive, the pull-out had to be initiated good and early to avoid flying into the ground. All-round vision was very good and the controls light and responsive. One did not feel quite so much part of the machine as in a Spitfire, but that was partly due to the largeness of the aeroplane and cockpit. All my compatriots loved it – but it had to be handled with care on landing!'

While many ex-Spitfire pilots would never forget the exhilarating qualities of the little Supermarine fighter, many came to appreciate the more warlike advantages of the Hawker types. Among the Spitfire pilots who came to the Tempest late in their careers was another New Zealander, Wing Commander E. D. Mackie, who finished the war as Wing Leader of 122 Wing, with 21 aerial victories to his credit, all but the last 5 on Spitfires: 'The Spitfire was a great machine and after 805 hours on the various marks I grew really used to it, but it did not take me long to realize that the Tempest was ever so much superior in many ways, both as a fighter and a ground-attack machine. At the closing stages of the European conflict, I had the option of changing to the Meteor jet aircraft, but turned it down in favour of the tried and proven Tempest. The harder they were flown, the better they went, and despite their almost seven-ton weight they could be thrown around the sky like a piece of paper.'

To summarize these pilots' opinions, and those of many others consulted in the preparation of this book, it is apparent that, almost to a man, they enjoyed flying the Typhoon and had a great respect for its power and durability. It was not by any means the 'pilot's aeroplane' that the Spitfire was, but it was the aeroplane for the job that had to be done. When the Tempest came along it had all the Typhoon's qualities, but enhanced, and this lifted it into the top league of fighters, while maintaining the position of prime ground-attack aircraft established by its predecessor.

Postscript

AN Air Ministry census taken at the end of May 1945 revealed that there were no less than 1,149 Typhoons still in service; indeed, more than eighty of Glosters' last production contract remained to be delivered. However, as squadron after squadron surrendered its aircraft, those which required major inspection or repair work were scrapped, and the more serviceable examples went into storage at 5, 20 and 51 Maintenance Units. By the end of 1945, some 748 Typhoons remained, all but 74 in store.

Towards the end of 1946 it was decided that the Typhoons were no longer required, and wholesale scrapping took place. This left a mere handful of instructional airframes in use at Schools of Technical Training or ATC units, and these were gradually retired until, in 1955, the last known British survivor (a composite airframe with parts from DN502, MN282 and MN601) was delivered to 60 MU, Rufforth, and presumably suffered the same fate as so many of its predecessors.

Fortunately, one Typhoon had survived the massacre. In March 1944, in response to a USAAF requirement to investigate the Typhoon's potential as a fighter-bomber and to increase its fuel capacity, MN235 was delivered to Wright Field, Ohio. However, by this time, the Typhoon was in extensive use as a fighter-bomber and long-range tanks had been in service for six months! With just nine hours' flying time, MN235, which had been allocated the number FE-401 (FE for Foreign Experimental), was put into storage. It eventually became part of the Smithsonian Institution's collection, and in 1968 this organization came to an agreement with the RAF – the lone survivor in exchange for an example of its more numerous predecessor, the Hurricane. MN235 now resides in the RAF Museum at Hendon. The Imperial War Museum holds a Typhoon cockpit section, a relic of one of Halton's post-war instructional airframes, and three more are in private hands, undergoing restoration, but short of the discovery of an underwater wreck in good condition, or the miraculous survival of RB379 (delivered to the USSR in July 1945, in a rather belated response to a request for examples of modern Allied types), it seems that MN235 is destined to remain the only complete representative of its type.

When the Tempest was withdrawn from service, large numbers were held in store as part of the 'war reserve'. The Mk Vs which had not been converted to target-tugs were sold for scrap at 5 and 20 MUs in November 1950; many were purchased by Hawker, presumably for spares recovery. The Mk VIs survived a little longer but the majority were disposed of in two batches, from 6 MU to Hawker in May 1951 and from 20 MU to the Ministry of Supply in June 1953. It is believed that the latter were destined for use in weapon effect trials. As the Mk IIs were withdrawn from Germany most were sold to India and Pakistan, leaving few examples to be scrapped in the UK. When, in 1955, it was the turn of the TT.Mk 5 to leave the service, it was again Hawker and the Ministry of Supply which brought many of the redundant airframes.

The remains of a handful of Tempest TT.5s were still to be seen on International Alloys' dump at Aylesbury in 1961, and then suddenly the Tempest had all but gone from its homeland. Just one Mk II, LA607, the second prototype, and a single Mk V, 'SN219' survived. The former, which had been used for instructional purposes at Cranfield for many years, found a home in the Skyfame Museum at Staverton in 1966. The Mk V, marked as 'SN219', was in fact a composite airframe, its parts having been recovered from the Proof and Experimental Establishment, Shoeburyness, by 33 Squadron, and rebuilt to take part in the celebrations for the presentation of that unit's

Top left: Sole survivor – Typhoon MN235 in the RAF Museum at Hendon. (C. H. Thomas)

Below left: 'SN219' in 33 Squadron markings, during its spell as a 'gate-guardian' at RAF Middleton St. George, 1960.

Right: 'SN219', now painted as 'NV778', resides in the RAF Museum at Hendon, tail to tail with its predecessor, Typhoon MN235. (BAe)

Below and below right: Ex-Indian Air Force Tempest IIs awaiting restoration . . . to fly. (T. E. Stone)

standard in 1958. It then spent some years as a 'gate guardian' at Middleton St. George, before refurbishment for the RAF Museum, where it is now displayed. During this task evidence was found that suggested NV778 to be a more suitable identity than SN219, and the aircraft was repainted to reflect this discovery.

The RAF Museum also has in store the fuselage of another Tempest V, EJ693, which still carries its wartime 486 Squadron codes 'SA-I'. This aircraft had force-landed in Holland in October 1944, and somehow the fuselage was acquired by a technical school at Delft. Now it awaits an ambitious restoration, and possible mating to wings from an Indian Tempest II also in storage.

In 1985, the only Tempest in private ownership in the UK, LA602, was sold to American, Kermit Weeks, and it seemed that any chance of seeing the Hawker fighter in European skies again had gone. Most if not all of Pakistan's Tempests are believed to have been scrapped, but in India, in addition to a single example (HA623) in the IAF Museum, unknown numbers lingered on into the 1970s, in the humble role of airfield decoys. In 1977 eleven of these airframes (at Halwara and Jodphur) were put up for tender, and six of these were eventually reimported to the UK. By 1985 they were in the hands of Tangmere Flight, well known for its immaculate restoration of Spitfire T.9 ML407. The Tempests were missing pro-

pellers, spinners, canopies, rudders and had only two and a half tailplanes between them; the cockpits had been stripped of instruments and many controls. Various IAF serial numbers were visible on the wings, but the fuselages carried the serials HA457, '557, '564, '586, '591, and '604. At the time of writing (August 1987) one, HA591, had been restored to static display standard and re-exported, to the USA. More important, HA586 and HA604 have been selected by Tangmere Flight for rebuilding, and work on the latter has already commenced. Before the end of the decade, and after an absence of more than thirty years, the Tempest may once more howl through northern skies.

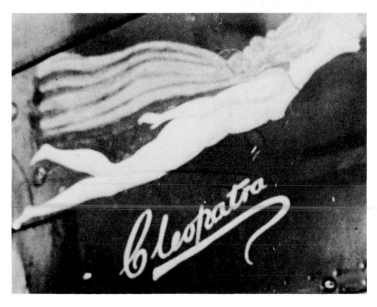

Top left: An aggressive Donald Duck armed with a red-hot poker adorned the radiator inspection panel on Squadron Leader D. M. Taylor's 195 Squadron Typhoon, EK273 'JE-DT' (see also page 46). (K. A. J. Trott)

Top centre: Flight Lieutenant Cedric Henman's 'Patoruzu II' – on a 175 Squadron aircraft (believed to be MN353 'HH-U'), at B.5, Le Fresne-Camilly August 1944. (Air Commodore J. E. Frost)

Top right: 'Zephyr Breezes' ('Zed for breezes'!) was the decoration on Flight Lieutenant Geoff Murphy's 'MR-Z', 245 Squadron, spring 1945. (G. Murphy)

Centre left: Flight Sergeant 'Buck' Feldman's R8895 'QO-E' of 3 Squadron sported 'Doity Goity' on the starboard cockpit door. (S. B. Feldman)

Above: Walt Disney's studio designed 438 Squadron's unofficial Wildcat badge, which appeared on many of their Typhoons in late 1944. (J. A. Lord)

Left: Another 195 Squadron Typhoon carried this apparently aquatic 'Cleopatra'. (K. A. J. Trott)

Appendices

A trio of 501 Squadron Tempest V Series 2 aircraft (EJ763
'SD-X', EJ599 'SD-W', EJ589 'SD-J') operating from Bradwell
Bay in October 1944. (RAFM/C. E. Brown)

Abbreviations used in the Appendices

A&AEE	Aircraft and Armament Experimental Establishment	FC	Flight Captain	nml	no man's land
a/c	aircraft	FIU	Fighter Interception Unit	nr	not repaired
acc	accident	f/l	force-landed	OCU	Operational Conversion Unit
ADF	Aircraft Delivery Flight	flg	flying	OFU	Overseas Ferry Unit
aeros	aerobatics	f/lk	fuel leak	ops	Operations
a/f	airfield	FLS	Fighter Leaders School	o/s	over-shot
AFDU	Air Fighting Development Unit	flt	flight	OTU	Operational Training Unit
APC	Armament Practice Camp	FP	Ferry Pool	(P)	probable
app	approach	FPP	Ferry Pilot Pool	(PoW)	prisoner of war
APS	Armament Practice Station	Fr	France	prac	practice
a/t	Allied territory	ftr	failed to return	psdb	presumed shot down by
b/c	balloon cable	FU	Ferry Unit	RAE	Royal Aircraft Establishment
BCW	BAFO Communications Wing	g/a	ground attack	rof	ran out of fuel
Bel	Belgium	GDC	Group Disbandment Centre	rnc	repair not completed
bfo	bomb fell off	GCI	Ground Control Interception	rpa	rocket attack
b/o	baled out	g/lk	glycol leak	RSU	Repair and Salvage Unit
cld	collided	Glst	Gloster Aircraft	RU	Repair Unit
cnk	cause not known	gnry	gunnery	r/w	railway
csd	crashed	Ger	Germany	(S)	safe
csu	constant speed unit	grd	ground	SC	Senior Commander
ct	caught	GSU	Group Support Unit	sdb	shot down by
dam	damaged	hbAA	hit by Allied AA fire	sdbF	shot down by Flak
dba	dive-bombing attack	hbd	hit by debris	Sect	Sector
dbf	damaged/destroyed by fire	hbF	hit by Flak	s/f	structural failure
det	detachment	hbsaf	hit by small arms fire	Spit(s)	Spitfire(s)
d/f	dogfight	h/f	hydraulic failure	StMg	RAF St. Mawgan
DFlt	Delivery Flight	htc	high-tension cable	t/a	taxiing accident
dila	damaged/destroyed in landing accident	Hwkr	Hawker Aircraft	tbto	tyre burst on take-off
Den	Denmark	(I)	Royal Indian Air Force	TEU	Tactical Exercise Unit
dtd	ditched	jett	jettisoned	TFU	Telecommunications Flying Unit
(E)	evaded capture	(K)	killed	t/o	take-off
e/a	enemy aircraft	L/C	Lieutenant-Commander	u/c	undercarriage
e/f	engine failure	ldg	landing	u/i	unidentified
e/fire	engine fire	lrt	long-range tank (fault/failure)	u/s	unserviceable
efto	engine failure on take-off	m	miles	vis	visibility
e/ftrs	enemy fighters	m/g	machine-gun	W	Wing
ELG	Emergency Landing Ground	met	mechanized enemy transport	w/o	written-off
e/t	enemy territory	mis	missing	w/u	wheels-up landing
ETPS	Empire Test Pilots' School	M/P	Master Pilot	wx	weather
expl	explosion/exploded	MU	Maintenance Unit	yd	yards
F?	possibly hit by Flak	Napr	Napier	?	possibly
		n/k	not known	☆	Bar
		NL	Netherlands		

1. Dimensions, Performance and Production

Dimensions and Performance

The performance figures below have been taken from manufacturers' test reports. The performance of individual aircraft varied to some degree and these figures should be taken as typical only. This factor may account for the variance between these figures and those measured by the A&AEE quoted in the main text. Tornadoes were fitted with a variety of 3-, 4- and 6-bladed De Havilland or Rotol propellers during the course of trials. Typhoons were fitted with 3- or 4-bladed De Havilland or Rotol propellers. If the latter were fitted, a slightly different spinner increased the aircraft's length by 1½ inches.

	Tornado Vulture	Tornado Centaurus	Typhoon Mk IB	Tempest Mk I	Tempest Mk II	Tempest Mk V	Tempest Mk VI
Wing span	41ft 11in	41ft 11in	41ft 7in	41ft 0in	41ft 0in	41ft 0in	41ft 0in
Wing area	283sq ft	283sq ft	278sq ft	302sq ft	302sq ft	302sq ft	302sq ft
Length	32ft 10in	32ft 10in	31ft 10in	34ft 2in	34ft 5in	33ft 8in	33ft 10½in
Height (tail down)	14ft 8in	14ft 8in	14ft 10in	15ft 10in	14ft 6in	16ft 1in	16ft 1in
Weight (empty)	8,377lb	–	8,690lb	8,950lb	8,900lb	9,000lb	9,150lb
Weight (loaded*)	10,668lb	10,320lb	11,780lb	11,300lb	11,800lb	11,400lb	11,560lb
Maximum speed	398mph at 23,000ft	402mph at 18,000ft	412mph at 19,000ft	466mph at 24,500ft	442mph at 15,200ft	426mph at 18,500ft	438mph at 17,800ft
Time to height	7.2 mins 20,000ft	8.4 mins 20,000ft	5.9 mins 15,000ft	4.25 mins 15,000ft	4.5 mins 15,000ft	5 mins 15,000ft	4.75 mins 15,000ft
Ceiling	34,900ft	32,800ft	34,000ft	39,000ft	37,500ft	36,500ft	38,000ft
Range	–	–	600 mls	770 mls	805 mls	740 mls	750 mls
Range with LR tanks	– –	– –	1,090 mls 2 × 45gal	– –	1,640 mls 2 × 90gal	1,530 mls 2 × 90gal	1,560 mls 2 × 90gal
Power-plant	Rolls-Royce Vulture Mk V	Bristol Centaurus CE 4S	Napier Sabre Mk IIA	Napier Sabre Mk IV	Bristol Centaurus Mk V	Napier Sabre Mk IIB	Napier Sabre Mk V
Max power	1,980hp	2,210hp	2,180hp	2,500hp	2,520hp	2,180hp	2,340hp
Propeller diameter	3-blade 13ft 3in	3/4-blade 12ft 9in	3/4-blade 14ft 0in	4-blade 14ft 0in	4-blade 12ft 9in	4-blade 14ft 0in	4-blade 14ft 0in

*'Loaded' means with full internal fuel load and fully armed, but with no external stores.

Typhoon and Tornado Orders and Production

Order	Built	
2	2	Typhoon prototypes built against Contract 815124/38 by Hawker Aircraft Ltd at Langley. P5212, P5216
2	2	Tornado prototypes built against Contract 815124/38 by Hawker Aircraft Ltd at Langley. P5219, P5224
1000	516*	Tornadoes ordered against Contract B12148/39 to be built by Hawker Aircraft Ltd. The contract was subsequently changed to 1000 Typhoons, though a further amendment called for 200 aircraft (R7936-R7975, R7992-R8036, R8049-R8091, R8105-R8150, R8172-R8197) to be built as Tornadoes after all, by A. V. Roe & Co. Of the latter, R7936-R7938 were to be prototypes, but only R7936 was completed. All 197 production aircraft were cancelled. Of the 800 Typhoons, 285 (R8232-R8261, R8275-R8309, R8325-R8364, R8377-R8410, R8425-R8468, R8484-R8525, R8539-R8572, R8590-R8615) were eventually cancelled and the remainder were built as IAs and IBs by Hawker Aircraft Ltd at Langley (R8198-R8200, R8220-R8231) and Gloster Aircraft Co at Hucclecote. R7576-R7599, R7613-R7655, R7672-R7721, R7738-R7775, R7792-R7829, R7845-R7890, R7913-R7923, R7936-R7975, R7992-R8036, R8049-R8091, R8105-R8150, R8172-R8197, R8198-R8200, R8220-R8231, R8232-R8261, R8275-R8309, R8325-R8364, R8377-R8410, R8425-R8468, R8484-R8525, R8539-R8572, R8590-R8615, R8630-R8663, R8680-R8722, R8737-R8781, R8799-R8845, R8861-R8900, R8923-R8947, R8966-R8981.
		*515 Typhoons and 1 Tornado.
200	–	Tornadoes ordered against Contract B97616/40 to be built by Cunliffe-Owen Ltd at Eastleigh. All were subsequently cancelled. X1056-X1090, X1103-X1117, X1166-X1195, X1220-X1264, X1297-X1326, X1343-X1387.
400	–	Tornadoes ordered against Contract ACFT/944/C.23(a) to be built by A. V. Roe & Co. All were subsequently cancelled. DM594-DM642, DM664-DM709, DM727-DM776, DM794-DM842, DM857-DM900, DM921-DM956, DM975-DM999, DN112-DN134, DN148-DN197, DN210-DN237.
300	300	Typhoon IBs built against Contract ACFT/943/C.23(a) by Gloster Aircraft Co at Hucclecote. DN241-DN279, DN293-DN341, DN356-DN389, DN404-DN453, DN467-DN512, DN529-DN562, DN576-DN623.
360	–	Tornadoes ordered against Contract ACFT/944/C.23(a) to be built by A. V. Roe & Co. All were subsequently cancelled. EG708-EG747, EG763-EG801, EG819-EG845, EG860-EG897, EG915-EG959, EG974-EG994, EH107-EH156, EH171-EH211, EH228-EH261, EH280-EH304.
570	–	Typhoons ordered against Contract B12148/39 to be built by Hawker Aircraft Ltd at Langley. The first 270 aircraft were subsequently cancelled and EJ504 onwards were built as Tempest Vs. EJ175-EJ222, EJ234-EJ283, EJ296-EJ334, EJ347-EJ392, EJ405-EJ454, EJ467-EJ504, EJ518-EJ560, EJ577-EJ611, EJ626-EJ672, EJ685-EJ723, EJ739-EJ788, EJ800-EJ846, EJ859-EJ896.
425	400	Typhoons ordered against Contract ACFT/943/C.23(a) to be built by Gloster Aircraft Co at Hucclecote. 25 aircraft (EK544-EK568) were subsequently cancelled. EJ899-EJ934, EJ946-EJ995, EK112-EK154, EK167-EK196, EK208-EK252, EK266-EK301, EK321-EK348, EK364-EK413, EK425-EK456, EK472-EK512, EK535-EK543, EK544-EK568.

Typhoon and Tornado Orders and Production

Order	Built	
1	1	Tornado (Centaurus) prototype built against Contract SB21392/C.23(a) by Hawker Aircraft Ltd at Langley. HG641.
2	–	Typhoon II prototypes ordered against Contract ACFT/1640/C.23(a) to be built by Hawker Aircraft Ltd at Langley. Both were completed as Tempests. HM595, HM599.
100	–	Typhoon IIs ordered against Contract ACFT/1876/C.23(a) to be built by Hawker Aircraft Ltd at Langley. All were completed as Tempest Vs. JN729-JN773, JN792-JN822, JN854-JN877.
600	600	Typhoon IBs built against Contract ACFT/943/C.23(a) by Gloster Aircraft Co at Hucclecote. JP361-JP408, JP425-JP447, JP480-JP516, JP532-JP552, JP576-JP614, JP648-JP689, JP723-JP756, JP784-JP802, JP836-JP861, JP897-JP941, JP961-JP976, JR125-JR152, JR183-JR223, JR237-JR266, JR289-JR338, JR360-JR392, JR426-JR449, JR492-JR535.
6	–	Typhoon (Centaurus) prototypes ordered against Contract ACFT/1986/C.23(a) to be built by Hawker Aircraft Ltd at Langley. LA594 and LA597 were subsequently cancelled and LA602 and LA607 were completed as Tempest II prototypes. LA610 and LA614 were subsequently intended to be completed as Tempest IIIs but the former became the Fury prototype and the latter was eventually cancelled. LA594, LA597, LA602, LA607, LA610, LA614.
800	800	Typhoon IBs built against Contract ACFT/943/C.23(a) by Gloster Aircraft Co at Hucclecote. MM951-MM995, MN113-MN156, MN169-MN213, MN229-MN269, MN282-MN325, MN339-MN381, MN396-MN436, MN449-MN496, MN513-MN556, MN569-MN608, MN623-MN667, MN680-MN720, MN735-MN779, MN791-MN823, MN851-MN896, MN912-MN956, MN968-MN999, MP113-MP158, MP172-MP203.
145	145	Typhoon IBs built against Contract ACFT/943/C.23(a) by Gloster Aircraft Co at Hucclecote. PD446-PD480, PD492-PD536, PD548-PD577, PD589-PD623.
255	255	Typhoon IBs built against Contract ACFT/943/C.23(a) by Gloster Aircraft Co at Hucclecote. RB192-RB235, RB248-RB289, RB303-RB347, RB361-RB408, RB423-RB459, RB474-RB512.
300	300	Typhoon IBs built against Contract ACFT/3864/C.23(a) by Gloster Aircraft Co at Hucclecote. SW386-SW428, SW443-SW478, SW493-SW537, SW551-SW596, SW620-SW668, SW681-SW716, SW728-SW772.
220	–	Typhoons ordered against Contract ACFT/3864/C.23(a) to be built by Gloster Aircraft Co at Hucclecote. All were subsequently cancelled. TR864-TR905, TR918-TR956, TR969-TR999, TS113-TS158, TS172-TS205, TS219-TS246.

Totals built: 3,317 Typhoons and 4 Tornadoes.

Tempest Orders and Production

Order	Built	
300	300	Tempest Vs built against Contract B12148/39 by Hawker Aircraft Ltd at Langley. This contract originally covered Tornado/Typhoon procurement but was subsequently amended several times. EJ504, EJ518-EJ560, EJ577-EJ611, EJ626-EJ672, EJ685-EJ723, EJ739-EJ788, EJ800-EJ846, EJ859-EJ896.
2	2	Prototypes built against Contract ACFT/1640/C.23(a) by Hawker Aircraft Ltd at Langley. One Tempest V prototype (HM595) and one Tempest I prototype (HM599), both having been ordered originally as Typhoon IIs. HM595, HM599.
100	100	Tempest Vs built against Contract ACFT/1876/C.23(a) by Hawker Aircraft Ltd at Langley. All were ordered originally as Typhoon IIs. JN729-JN773, JN792-JN822, JN854-JN877.
4	2	Prototypes ordered against Contract ACFT/1986/C.23(a) to be built by Hawker Aircraft Ltd at Langley. Originally part of a large order for Typhoon (Centaurus) prototypes, revised plans called for two Tempest II prototypes (LA602 and LA607) and two Tempest III prototypes (LA610 and LA614). LA614 was cancelled in Feb 1943 and LA610 completed as the Fury prototype. LA602, LA607, LA610, LA614.
300	50	Tempest Is ordered against Contract ACFT/2439/C.23(a) to be built by Gloster Aircraft Co. The order was subsequently transferred to Bristol Aeroplane Co where the first 50 aircraft (MW375-MW423, MW435) were built at Banwell as Tempest IIs against Contract ACFT/3210/C.23(a). MW436 onwards were cancelled. MW375-MW423, MW435-MW478, MW491-MW536, MW548-MW589, MW591-MW633, MW645-MW686, MW699-MW732.
503	100	Tempest IIs ordered against Contract ACFT/2438/C.23(a) to be built by Hawker Aircraft Ltd at Langley. Production was curtailed after 100 aircraft had been built, MW857 onwards having been cancelled 3 Mar 1943. MW735-MW778, MW790-MW835, MW847-MW888, MW900-MW945, MW957-MW999, MX112-MX156, MX168-MX212, MX225-MX268, MX280-MX326, MX339-MX389, MX399-MX448.
200	200	Tempest Vs built against Contract ACFT/1876/C.23(a) by Hawker Aircraft Ltd at Langley. NV639-NV682, NV695-NV736, NV749-NV793, NV917-NV948, NV960-NV996.
306	142	Tempest VIs ordered against Contract ACFT/1876/C.23(a) to be built by Hawker Aircraft Ltd at Langley. All were ordered originally as Tempest Is. Production was curtailed after 142 had been built, NX289 onwards having been cancelled. NV997-NV999, NX113-NX156, NX169-NX209, NX223-NX268, NX281-NX325, NX338-NX387, NX394-NX435, NX448-NX482.
300	–	Tempest IIs ordered against Contract ACFT/2439/C.23(a) to be built by Gloster Aircraft Co. The order was subsequently transferred to Bristol Aeroplane Co and then cancelled prior to commencement of production. PE885-PE927, PE939-PE966, PE978-PE999, PF112-PF158, PF171-PF213, PF225-PF266, PF280-PF319, PF333-PF367.
800	302	Tempest IIs ordered against Contract ACFT/2438/C.23(a) to be built by Hawker Aircraft Ltd at Langley. Production was terminated after 302 aircraft had been completed, PR922 onwards having been cancelled. PR525-PR567, PR581-PR623, PR645-PR689, PR713-PR758, PR771-PR815, PR830-PR876, PR889-PR928, PR941-PR967, PR979-PR999, PS115-PS157, PS173-PS215, PS229-PS273, PS287-PS329, PS342-PS387, PS408-PS449, PS463-PS507, PS520-PS563, PS579-PS625, PS637-PS681.
500	–	Tempest IIs ordered against Contract ACFT/2438/C.23(a) to be built by Hawker Aircraft Ltd. All were cancelled on 27 Feb 1945. RW400-RW443, RW456-RW496, RW510-RW539, RW553-RW589, RW602-RW648, RW663-RW698, RW713-RW758, RW771-RW813, RW825-RW860, RW873-RW915, RW928-RW959, RW975-RW999, RX113-RX152.
700	201	Tempest Vs ordered against Contract ACFT/1876/C.23(a) to be built by Hawker Aircraft Ltd at Langley. Production was terminated at SN355 after 201 aircraft had been completed, SN368 onwards having been cancelled. SN102-SN146, SN159-SN190, SN205-SN238, SN253-SN296, SN310-SN355, SN368-SN399, SN415-SN448, SN463-SN507, SN519-SN559, SN573-SN615, SN628-SN659, SN673-SN715, SN728-SN763, SN779-SN813, SN827-SN868, SN883-SN925, SN937-SN968, SN980-SN999, SP113-SP133.
30	–	Tempest IIs ordered against Contract ACFT/3210/C.23(a) to be built by Bristol Aeroplane Co at Banwell. All were subsequently cancelled. VA386-VA395, VA417-VA436.
9	–	Tempest VIs ordered against Contract ACFT/1876/C.23(a) to be built by Hawker Aircraft Ltd. This quantity had been transferred from ACFT/2438/C.23(a) 30 Nov 1945 only to be cancelled on 20 Mar 1946. VN763-VN771.
81	81	Tempest TT.5s ordered from Hawker Aircraft Ltd for conversion at Langley using surplus Tempest Vs. One prototype (SN329) was converted against Contract 6/ACFT/2074/CB.7(a) and was followed by 80 production conversions against Contract 6/ACFT/2485/CB.7(a). EJ580, EJ585, EJ599, EJ631, EJ643, EJ660, EJ663, EJ667, EJ669, EJ740, EJ744, EJ753, EJ758, EJ786, EJ801, EJ805, EJ807, EJ839, EJ846, EJ862, EJ875, EJ879, EJ880, JN807, JN871, NV645, NV661, NV664, NV665, NV669, NV671, NV699, NV704, NV711, NV723, NV725, NV762, NV778, NV780, NV781, NV793, NV917, NV922, NV923, NV928, NV937, NV940, NV960, NV962, NV965, NV974, NV975, NV978, NV992, NV994, NV996, SN127,

SN146, SN209, SN215, SN219, SN227, SN232, SN259, SN260, SN261, SN271, SN274, SN289, SN290, SN321, SN326, SN327, SN329, SN331, SN332, SN333, SN340, SN342, SN346, SN354.

Total built: 1,399 Tempests.

Indian Tempests

At Partition all the Tempest aircraft in India were handed over to the RIAF, with the exception of 35 aircraft which went to Pakistan. The following 124 Tempest IIs were officially handed over 25 Sept 1947. They were eventually given RIAF serials but none of the tie-ups is known.
MW405, MW406, MW407, MW410, MW411, MW412, MW413, MW414, MW419, MW420, MW421, MW435, PR527, PR529, PR536, PR539, PR540, PR541, PR543, PR544, PR545, PR546, PR548, PR551, PR552, PR553, PR556, PR557, PR558, PR559, PR562, PR564, PR567, PR584, PR585, PR590, PR591, PR592, PR593, PR594, PR595, PR597, PR598, PR600, PR601, PR602, PR603, PR605, PR606, PR607, PR609, PR610, PR612, PR614, PR617, PR618, PR619, PR620, PR621, PR647, PR651, PR652, PR653, PR655, PR658, PR660, PR664, PR666, PR668, PR671, PR675, PR677, PR678, PR681, PR684, PR688, PR713, PR714, PR717, PR719, PR721, PR722, PR725, PR727, PR728, PR729, PR730, PR731, PR732, PR734, PR735, PR739, PR740, PR741, PR747, PR748, PR750, PR751, PR752, PR773, PR775, PR780, PR783, PR787, PR789, PR791, PR794, PR795, PR801, PR804, PR808, PR813, PR814, PR815, PR830, PR835, PR836, PR837, PR840, PR842, PR843, PR849, PR863, PR868.
Of these, PR548, PR804 and PR836 were transferred in 'Category E' (written-off) condition.

In May 1948 Hawker Aircraft Ltd bought 113 Tempest IIs from surplus RAF stocks at 20 MU. Of these, 89 were sold to India after refurbishment with the following RIAF/RAF serial tie-ups.
HA547(PR874), HA548(PR907), HA549(PR893), HA550(PR902), HA551(PR869), HA552(PR890), HA553(MW385), HA554(MW764), HA555(MW751), HA556(MW831), HA557(MW404), HA558(MW854), HA559(MW847), HA560(MW851), HA561(MW743), HA562(MW770), HA563(MW808), HA564(MW376), HA565(MW748), HA566(MW742), HA567(MW760), HA568(MW377), HA569(MW817), HA570(MW807), HA571(MW819), HA572(MW824), HA573(MW761), HA574(MW739), HA575(MW403), HA576(MW853), HA577(MW773), HA578(MW830), HA579(MW777), HA580(MW758), HA581(MW402), HA582(MW856), HA583(MW823), HA584(MW752), HA585(MW392), HA586(MW763), HA587(MW745), HA588(MW398), HA589(MW395), HA590(MW382), HA591(MW810), HA592(MW387), HA593(MW850), HA594(MW762), HA595(MW386), HA596(MW396), HA597(MW754), HA598(MW809), HA599(MW822), HA600(MW746), HA601(MW750), HA602(MW759), HA603(MW793), HA604(MW401), HA605(MW814), HA606(MW796), HA607(MW775), HA608(MW795), HA609(MW768), HA610(MW797), HA611(MW397), HA612(MW829), HA613(MW400), HA614(MW791), HA615(MW769), HA616(MW756), HA617(PR525), HA618(MW855), HA619(MW852), HA620(MW390), HA621(MW828), HA622(MW741), HA623(MW848), HA624(MW767), HA625(MW389), HA626(MW391), HA627(MW378), HA628(MW380), HA629(MW771), HA630(MW381), HA631(MW383), HA632(MW379), HA633(MW399), HA634(MW393), HA635(MW388).

Once the Tempest II was withdrawn from use in the RAF, India was able to purchase 20 more aircraft. All were held by 20 MU at the time of purchase and were sold in two batches on 9 July 1951 and 29 Aug 1951
9 July 1951 Sale: PR659, PR676, PR736, PR743, PR745, PR746, PR756, PR774, PR851, PR856, PR867, PR901.
29 August 1951 Sale: PR555, PR663, PR683, PR733, PR758, PR777, PR779, PR834.
Known RIAF/RAF serial tie-ups for these aircraft are restricted to HA356(PR779), HA407(PR555), HA415(PR867) and HA465(PR901).

Total supplied to India: 233 Tempest IIs.

Pakistani Tempests

35 Tempest IIs were handed over to the RPAF at Partition. The official hand-over date was 25 Sept 1947 and all had previously been on RAF strength in India.
PR530, PR535, PR549, PR560, PR563, PR565, PR566, PR581, PR587, PR588, PR589, PR608, PR611, PR623, PR648, PR649, PR656, PR661, PR662, PR670, PR686, PR715, PR718, PR723, PR724, PR737, PR754, PR755, PR772, PR796, PR799, PR800, PR810, PR831, PR832.
Although RPAF/RAF serial tie-ups are not known for these aircraft, RPAF identities include A.107, A.109, A.120, A.121 and A.122.

Of the 113 Tempest IIs bought by Hawker Aircraft Ltd from surplus RAF stocks in May 1948, 24 were sold to Pakistan after refurbishment with the following RPAF/RAF serial tie-ups.
A.128(PR866), A.129(PR898), A.130(PR906), A.131(PR892), A.132(PR894), A.133(PR806), A.134(PR872), A.135(PR865), A.136(PR876), A.137(PR914), A.138(PR749), A.139(PR809), A.140(PR900), A.141(PR917), A.142(PR910), A.143(PR615), A.144(PR875), A.145(PR909), A.146(PR897), A.147(PR891), A.148(PR889), A.149(PR915), A.150(PR912), A.151(PR899).

Between 26 Nov 1951 and 11 Nov 1952 Pakistan was able to purchase 21 more Tempest IIs as the type became surplus to RAF requirements. RPAF/RAF serial tie-ups are not known for these aircraft.
MW408, PR528, PR531, PR542, PR550, PR613, PR673, PR685, PR771, PR784, PR803, PR805, PR847, PR860, PR871, PR873, PR896, PR903, PR905, PR913, PR919.

Total supplied to Pakistan: 80 Tempest IIs.

Research and Development Aircraft

In addition to the numerous aircraft retained by the engine and airframe manufacturers for trials, the following establishments used Typhoons and Tempests for trials as listed below.

Aircraft and Armament Experimental Establishment

Typhoon I
P5212	Performance and handling.
P5216	Performance and handling; camera-gun.
R7577	Rudder tab and handling.
R7579	Carbon monoxide contamination; flame damping.
R7614	Carbon monoxide contamination; cooling; sprung seat.
R7617	Weights and loading data; carbon monoxide contamination; crankshaft vibration; stability; night flying; rudder handling.
R7646	Gun heating; weights and loading data; handling and performance with 2 × 250lb and 2 × 500lb bombs; signal-discharger.
R7673	Spinning; flight attitude measurement.
R7700	Carbon monoxide contamination; radio; IFF; cooling; climb and speed; fuel consumption.
R7711	Cooling with mixed matrix radiator; oil cooler and tropical air cleaner.
R8762	Weights and loading data; handling and performance with 45-gallon drop-tanks, one 500lb bomb and one drop-tank, and with a single 500lb bomb; rudder handling.
R8809	Camera-gun installation.
R8889	Weights and loading data; cooling and handling of tropicalized aircraft.
DN340	Weights, loading and handling with 2 × 1,000lb bombs, 500lb anti-personnel bombs; 4-blade propeller; high-speed handling with bombs.
EK229	Handling with 'Tempest' tailplane, 3- and 4-blade propellers.
EK497	RP installations and performance.
JR210	'Rogue' aircraft tested for excessive engine vibration (also MN232, '319, '325)
JR307	Handling with M10 smoke tanks.
JR333	Handling with bubble canopy; gunsight vibration.
JR448	Handling with M10 smoke tanks.
MN290	Cooling with tropical air cleaner in temperate conditions.
MN466	Handling with 500lb, 1,000lb, smoke, and cluster bombs.
MN551	Handling with 2 × 1,000lb bombs.
MN861	Handling with 8 duplex (i.e., 16) RP; carriage of tier RP.
SW518	Handling with 2 × Mk VIII mines.
SW535	Bombing.

Tempest I
HM595	Handling and performance; position error and attitude.

Tempest V
JN730	Handling with 45-gallon drop-tanks; fuel consumption.
JN731	Weights and loading data; carbon monoxide contamination; handling; intake efficiency; IFF; gun heating; radio; C of G; fuel consumption; stability.
JN732	Empire Test Pilots' School (ETPS).
JN739	ETPS.
JN740	Mk III RP rails.
JN741	Spinning.
JN770	ETPS.
JN798	Weights and loading data; bombing.
JN799	Mk V cannon installation.
EJ592	Spring tab ailerons.
EJ723	Attitude correction.
EJ759	Engine cooling with tropical air cleaner (Khartoum).
EJ891	Bombing.
NV732	Gunnery.
NV773	Gunnery.
NV946	Zero-length RP launchers.
SN127	Mk TT.5, target stowage.
SN219	Smoke tanks.
SN329	Mk TT.5, type clearance and winch trials.

SN352 RP.
SN354 Handling; 47mm 'P' gun.

Tempest II
LA602 Handling and performance; weights and loading data; carbon monoxide contamination.
MW736 Gunnery, cockpit heating and ventilation; carbon monoxide contamination.
MW739 Intensive flying trials; 45-gallon drop-tanks.
MW741 Engine cooling; flame damping.
MW762 Spinning.
MW767 ETPS.
MW775 ETPS.
MW791 ETPS.
MW801 Engine cooling; weights and loading; position error; intensive flying trials, Khartoum (also MW802 to MW806 inclusive).
MW813 ETPS.
PR533 Handling with 1,000lb bombs.
PR550 Drop-tank jettison; handling with bomb-carriers; 'Window' launchers.
PR599 Intensive flying trials.
PR622 Modified flaps; armament; smoke tanks; ETPS.
PR806 Bombing.
PR903 Bombing.
PR918 ETPS.
PR919 ETPS.
PR920 ETPS.

Tempest VI
EJ841 Engine cooling.
NX115 Intensive flying trials.
NX119 Engine cooling and performance (Khartoum); weights and loading data.
NX133 Engine cooling.
NX288 Spinning; handling.

Royal Aircraft Establishment

Typhoon I
R7576 Carbon monoxide contamination; vibration; propeller governor; tail-wheel shimmy.
R7589 Rudder trim.
R7595 Carbon monoxide contamination.
R7617 Static vent; vibrograph; hydraulics.
R7632 Roll rate.
R7649 Carbon monoxide contamination.
R7698 'G' restrictions.
R7881 AI Mk VI radar.
R8635 Generator; homing.
R8688 Airframe stress; tailplane stress; propeller trials.
R8693 Stability.
R8709 Negative 'G'.
R8943 Propeller governor; cockpit ventilation.
DN340 Dive-bombing.
DN409 Carbon monoxide contamination and cockpit ventilation.
DN562 Rudder trials.
EK154 Bombing; smoke-generators; air cleaners.
EK327 Generator cooling; negative 'G'; vibrograph.
MM960 Dive-bombing sight.
MN519 Bombing.
MN708 Bombing.
MN943 Bombing; drag; buffeting.
PD615 Swing.
RB329 Icing; air cleaners.

Tempest V
EJ837 Dive recovery flaps.

Tempest II
MW767 Carbon monoxide contamination.

Air Fighting Development Unit

Typhoon I
R7580 Tactical trials.
R7581 Tactical trials.
R7595 Gun heating.
DN622 Comparison with Spitfire IX and Fw 190.
EK290 Bombing and RP.
JP443 Bombing and RP.
JP512 Comparison with Tempest V.
MN418 Dive-bombing.
MN433 Dive-bombing.
MN574 American 5-inch RP.

Tempest V
JN737 Tactical and comparative trials.
JN757 Tactical and comparative trials.
EJ529 Gunnery.

Fighter Interception Unit

Typhoon I
R7630 Turbinlite satellite trials.
R7651 Night-flying.
R7881 AI Mk VI radar-equipped night-fighter tactical trials.
MN236 'Abdullah' (radar homing) operational trials with 1320 Flt.
MN254 'Abdullah' trials. Later to 1320 Flt.
MN263 As for MN254.
MN296 As for MN236.

Tempest V
The following aircraft were used for the development of tactics and operations against the V-1 flying bombs, JN855, EJ524, '530, '531, '538, '553, '555, '556, '581, '587, '598.

△1

△4

△2   ▽3

△5   ▽6

2. Units

Front-line squadrons are listed below, in numerical order, with dates of equipment with Typhoon and/or Tempest aircraft.

Dates for the changeover of commanding officers are given to the nearest month only, as in many cases the new and old COs overlapped and it has not been possible to establish the exact date of transfer of command. If a squadron commander was not replaced immediately it was usual for the senior flight commander to act as CO; when this took place for a significant period, the acting CO has been included. Dates in brackets indicate that a CO was already in command prior to receipt of Typhoons or Tempests, or remained in command after re-equipment with another type.

Decorations are those awarded before or during the period of command. Many pilots later received further awards in recognition of their service with Typhoon or Tempest squadrons.

Movements between bases often took place over several days, with air and ground components sometimes moving on different dates; the dates quoted are for the movement of the major part of the air component.

Operational Squadrons

1 Squadron

First Typhoon received at Acklington 21 July 1942; fourteen more arrived in the next five days, replacing Hurricane IIs. First operation flown 4 Sept 1942. Last Typhoon operation 29 Mar 1944, Typhoons replaced by Spitfire IXs in early April 1944. Code-letters 'JX'.

S/L R. C. Wilkinson, DFM	July 42–May 43	Acklington	
S/L A. Zweigbergk	May 43–April 44	Biggin Hill	9 Feb 43
		Lympne	15 Mar 43
		Martlesham Heath	15 Feb 44
		North Weald	3 April 44

3 Squadron

First Typhoons received at Hunsdon 1 Feb 1943, replacing Hurricane IIs. Two Tempest Vs lent for experience at Manston 28 Feb 1944, conversion commencing at Bradwell Bay 7 Mar 1944. 150 Airfield/Wing Mar 1944. Last Typhoon operation 24 Mar 1944, first Tempest operation 23 April 1944. 122 Wing Sept 1944. 124 Wing Aug 1945. 135 Wing Sept 1945. 123 Wing Jan 1946. Re-equipped with Vampire F.1s from 10 April 1948, last Tempest flown to UK 21 June 1948. Code-letters 'QO', changing to 'JF' 5 June 1944, and 'J5' post-war.

Hunsdon		B.170	6 Oct 45	Wunstorf	21 Sept 46
West Malling	14 May 43	B.152	27 Oct 45	Sylt	23 Oct 46
Manston	11 June 43	Wunstorf	25 Jan 46	Wunstorf	27 Nov 46
Swanton Morley	28 Dec 43	Gatow	28 Mar 46	Gatow	5 Jan 47
Manston	14 Feb 44	Dedelstorf	7 May 46	Wunstorf	4 Feb 47
Bradwell Bay	6 Mar 44	Manston	2 June 46	(Gatow det. Oct 47)	
Ayr	6 April 44	Dedelstorf	13 June 46	Lübeck	6 Jan 48
Bradwell Bay	14 April 44	Manston	10 Sept 46	Wunstorf	25 Jan 48
Newchurch	28 April 44				
Matlaske	21 Sept 44	S/L L. F. de Soomer		(Feb 43)–Aug 43	
B.60	28 Sept 44	S/L S. R. Thomas, DFC, AFC		Aug 43–Sept 43	
B.80	1 Oct 44	S/L R. Hawkins, MC, AFC		Sept 43–Oct 43	
Warmwell	2 April 45	S/L A. S. Dredge, AFC		Oct 43–Aug 44	
B.112	18 April 45	S/L K. A. Wigglesworth, DFC		Aug 44–Sept 44	
B.152	27 April 45	S/L H. N. Sweetman, DFC		Sept 44–Jan 45	
B.160	21 June 45	S/L K. F. Thiele, DSC, DFC ☆		Jan 45–Feb 45	
B.156	18 July 45	S/L R. B. Cole, DFC☆		Feb 45–April 47	
B.158	8 Aug 45	F/L F. L. Latham		April 47–May 47	
B.155	5 Sept 45	S/L C. H. Macfie, DFC		May 47–(June 48)	

1. 1 Squadron, Typhoon IB EK176 'JX-K', Lympne, July 1943. (Public Archives of Canada)
2. 3 Squadron, Typhoon IB EJ922 'QO-F', 1943. (Leslie F. Whitfield via Charles W. Cain)
3. 3 Squadron, Tempest V SN212 'JF-T', B.112 Hopsten, April 1945. (RAFM/C. E. Brown)
4. 3 Squadron, Tempest V SN330 'J5-H', Squadron Leader Macfie's aircraft, August 1947 to April 1948. (Official)
5. 4 Squadron, Typhoon FR.IB EK427 'S', in open storage at 5 MU Kemble, March 1945. (IWM)
6. 5 Squadron, Tempest II PR656 'OQ-G', Risalpur, January 1947. (H. Pears)

4 Squadron

Partly equipped with Typhoon FR.IBs on loan from 268 Squadron, alongside main equipment of Spitfire XIs. First operation flown from B.70 11 Oct 1944; last Typhoon operation 2 Feb 1945. No squadron codes carried.

S/L W. Shepherd	(Dec 44–Feb 45)	B.70	
		B.77	23 Nov 44

5 Squadron

First Tempest IIs received 5 Mar 1946 at Bhopal, India, replacing Thunderbolts. Disbanded 1 Aug 1947. Codes 'OQ'.

Bhopal		(Miramshah det. Mar 47)			
Poona	1 June 46	Mauripur	1 July 47		
Risalpur	6 Jan 47	S/L L. H. Dawes, DFC			(Mar 46)–May 46
Peshawar	23 Jan 47	S/L F. Rothwell, DFC			June 46–Aug 47

6 Squadron

Tempest VIs replaced Mustangs at Nicosia, Cyprus, and were first flown 31 Dec 1946. 324 Wing June 1947. Re-equipment with Vampire FB.5 commenced 17 Sept 1949. Last Tempest sortie flown 12 Nov 1949. Code-letters 'JV'.

Nicosia		Khartoum	11 Feb 48	Nicosia	20 Jan 49
Shallufa	1 Sept 47	Fayid	5 May 48	Deversoir	4 Mar 49
Khartoum	30 Nov 47	Deversoir	30 Aug 48	Nicosia	24 Oct 49
Mogadishu	1 Feb 48	S/L C. K. Gray, DFC		(Dec 46)–Nov 47	
Khormaksar	7 Feb 48	S/L D. Crowley-Milling, DSO, DFC ☆		Nov 47–(Nov 49)	

8 Squadron

First Tempest VIs arrived at Khormaksar, Aden, 27 Mar 1947, replacing Mosquito FB.VIs. Conversion to Brigands commenced July 1949; the last Tempest was ferried back to UK 11 Mar 1950. Code-letters 'RT' were carried on the first four Tempests received, for a short period only.

S/L F. W. M. Jensen, DFC☆, AFC	(Mar 47)–April 49	Khormaksar
S/L A. M. S. Steedman, DFC	April 49–(Mar 50)	(Nairobi det. June 49)

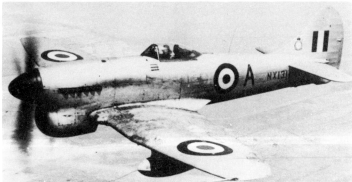

△7   ▽8

7. 6 Squadron, Tempest VI NX154 'JV-K', 1947/48. (via R. L. Ward)
8. 8 Squadron, Tempest VI NX131 'A', Squadron Leader Jensen's aircraft 1947–49. (Group Captain F. W. M. Jensen)

△1

△2

△3

△4

△5

△6　▽7

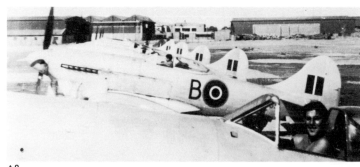

△8

△9

△10

△11

△12　▽13

16 Squadron

Reformed with Tempest Vs by renumbering 56 Squadron at Fassberg 1 April 1946, and continuing with 135 Wing. Re-equipment with Tempest IIs began Aug 1946. First Vampire FB.5s received Dec 1948 and the Tempests were last flown Jan 1949. Code-letters 'EG'.

Fassberg		(M. Wallop det. Jun/July 47)		(Lübeck det. July/Aug 48)	
Manston	1 June 46	Zeltweg	13 July 47	Manston	9 Sept 48
Fassberg	12 June 46	Fassberg	11 Aug 47	Gütersloh	19 Sept 48
Sylt	20 June 46	Gütersloh	2 Feb 48		
Fassberg	July 46	S/L M. P. Kilburn, DFC		April 46–April 46	
Gatow	4 Feb 47	S/L D. C. Usher, DFC, DFM		April 46–Jan 48	
Fassberg	20 Mar 47	S/L R. E. Mooney		Jan 48–June 48	
Ahlhorn	8 May 47	S/L L. A. Malins, DSO, DFC		June 48–Dec 48	
Fassberg	20 May 47	S/L L. H. Lambert, DFC		Dec 48–(Jan 49)	

20 Squadron

First Tempest IIs received at Agra, India, 19 May 1946, replacing Spitfire XIVs. Disbanded 31 July 1947. Code-letters 'HN'.

S/L A. A. Ritchie, AFC	June 46–Oct 46	Agra	
S/L R. A. Newbery, DFC ☆	Nov 46–July 47	(Kohat det. Aug 46)	
		(Miramshah det. Aug 46)	

26 Squadron

Reformed with Tempest Vs by renumbering 41 Squadron at Wunstorf 1 April 1946, continuing at first with 123 Wing, but transferring to 135 Wing by end of the month. First Tempest II arrived 19 June 1946, full conversion taking place the following month. Re-equipped with Vampire FB.5s from 20 April 1949, last Tempest returning to UK 6 May 1949. Code-letters 'XC'.

Wunstorf		Fassberg	20 May 47	Gatow	5 Dec 47
Fassberg	13 April 46	Zeltweg	10 July 47	Gütersloh	5 Jan 48
Gatow	8 May 46	Fassberg	11 Aug 47	Lübeck	7 June 48
Fassberg	23 June 46	Gütersloh	19 Nov 47	Gütersloh	5 July 48
Chivenor	24 Sept 46	S/L H. Ambrose, DFC		April 46–May 47	
Fassberg	23 Oct 46	S/L J. Brandt, DFC		May 47–Dec 47	
Sylt	– Jan 47	S/L A. D. Mitchell, DFC ☆ , AFC		Dec 47–June 48	
Fassberg	15 Feb 47	S/L J. W. Frost, DFC		June 48–Sept 48	
Ahlhorn	8 May 47	S/L J. F. Macphie		Sept 48–(May 49)	

30 Squadron

First Tempest IIs received at Bhopal, India, 4 Mar 1946, replacing Thunderbolts. Disbanded 1 Dec 1946. Code-letters 'RS'.

S/L T. H. Meyer	(Mar 46)–Aug 46	Bhopal	
S/L R. A. Newbery, DFC ☆	Aug 46–Nov 46	Agra	27 May 46

33 Squadron

First Tempest Vs received at Predannack 20 Dec 1944, replacing Spitfire IXs. 135 Wing Feb 1945. Re-equipped with Tempest IIs from Oct 1946. Left 135 Wing in Germany beginning of July 1949 for transit to Malaya on HMS *Ocean*. It was the last operational Tempest squadron in the RAF, the final sorties being flown 6 June 1951, re-equipment with Hornet F.3s having commenced the previous April. Code-letters '5R'.

Predannack		Lübeck	5 Jan 48	Changi	24 Oct 49
B.77	21 Feb 45	Gütersloh	12 Feb 48	Kai Tak	4 Nov 49
B.91	7 April 45	Gatow	28 April 48	Changi	16 Nov 49
B.109	22 April 45	Gütersloh	4 June 48	(Kuala Lumpur det. Jan/	
B.155	19 June 45	Seletar	7 Aug 49		April 50)
B.106	14 Sept 45	Changi	10 Aug 49	Tengah	17 Mar 50
B.170	17 Sept 45	Butterworth	10 Sept 49	Butterworth	30 Mar 50
B.155	7 Oct 45				
B.152	23 Oct 45	S/L I. G. S. Matthews, DFC		(Dec 44)–Mar 45	
Gatow	2 Jan 46	S/L A. W. Bower, DFC		Mar 45–June 46	
Fassberg	17 Feb 46	S/L R. N. G. Allen, DFC		June 46–June 48	
Sylt	31 Mar 46	S/L D. G. Smallwood, DSO, DFC		July 48–Sept 48	
Fassberg	8 May 46	S/L A. K. Furse, DFC		Sept 48–April 51	
Gütersloh	1 Dec 47	S/L C. C. F. Cooper		April 51–(June 51)	

39 Squadron

Reformed as a Tempest VI unit, pilots assembling at Manston June 1948 to convert to type and ferry their aircraft to Khartoum, Sudan, arriving 4 July 1948. Tempest flying ceased 28 Feb 1949, the squadron reforming on the next day as a Mosquito night-fighter unit. No squadron codes carried.

S/L A. M. S. Steedman, DFC	June 48–Feb 49	Khartoum	
		(Asmara det. Aug 48)	

41 Squadron

Received Tempest Vs in exchange for its Spitfire XIVs at Lübeck 13 Sept 1945, remaining with 124 Wing. 123 Wing Jan 1946. Renumbered 26 Squadron 1 April 1946. Code-letters 'EB'.

S/L J. B. Shepherd, DFC ☆	(Sept 45)–Jan 46	B.158	
S/L H. Ambrose, DFC	Jan 46–Mar 46	Wunstorf	1 Feb 46
		Sylt	1 Mar 46
		Wunstorf	23 Mar 46

54 Squadron

Reformed 15 Nov 1945 with Tempest IIs by renumbering 183 Squadron at Chilbolton. Reformed as a Vampire F.1 unit 11 Oct 1946, the Tempests being ferried to Aston Down three days later. Code-letters 'HF'.

Chilbolton		Odiham	27 Aug 46	Odiham	30 Sept 46
Odiham	28 June 46	Molesworth	5 Sept 46		
Acklington	9 Aug 46	S/L F. W. M. Jensen, DFC, AFC		(Nov 45)–Oct 46	

56 'Punjab' Squadron

The first front-line unit to receive Typhoons, deliveries commencing 11 Sept 1941 and replacing Hurricane IIs. First operation 30 May 1942. Part of the Duxford Wing until this was disbanded in Sept 1942. 150 Airfield/Wing April 1944. Last Typhoon operation 11 May 1944, re-equipment with Spitfire IXs having commenced in April 1944. First Tempest Vs received at Newchurch 24 June 1944 and first operation with these flown 2 July 1944. 122 Wing Sept 1945. 135 Wing Sept 1945. Renumbered 16 Squadron 1 April 1946. Code-letters 'US'.

Duxford		B.112	12 April 45	B.155	6 Sept 45
Snailwell	30 Mar 42	B.152	27 April 45	B.152	24 Oct 45
(Manston det. May/June 42)		Warmwell	8 May 45	Sylt	1 Jan 46
Matlaske	24 Aug 42	B.152	23 May 45	Fassberg	23 Jan 46
Manston	22 July 43	B.160	23 June 45	Gatow	28 Feb 46
Martlesham Heath	6 Aug 43	B.164	23 Aug 45	Fassberg	26 Mar 46
Manston	15 Aug 43				
Bradwell Bay	23 Aug 43	S/L P. P. Hanks, DFC		(Sept 41)–Dec 41	
Martlesham Heath	4 Oct 43	S/L H. S. L. Dundas, DFC		Dec 41–Nov 42	
Scorton	15 Feb 44	S/L A. C. Johnston		Nov 42–Jan 43	
Acklington	23 Feb 44	S/L T. H. V. Pheloung		Jan 43–June 43	
Scorton	7 Mar 44	S/L C. J. Donovan		June 43–Sept 43	
Ayr	7 April 44	S/L G. L. Sinclair, DFC ☆		Sept 43–May 44	
Newchurch	28 April 44	S/L A. R. Hall, DFC		May 44–Sept 44	
Matlaske	23 Sept 44	S/L D. V. C. Cotes-Preedy, DFC, GM		Sept 44–Feb 45	
B.60	28 Sept 44	S/L R. W. A. MacKichan, DFC ☆		Feb 45–May 45	
B.80	1 Oct 44	S/L M. P. Kilburn, DFC		May 45–Mar 46	

80 Squadron

Borrowed four Tempest Vs for familiarization at West Malling 9 Aug 1944, receiving further Tempests to replace its Spitfire IXs from 27 Aug 1944. First operation flown 30 Aug 1944. 125 Wing Oct 1944, 122 Wing Oct 1944, 124 Wing Sept 1945, 123 Wing Jan 1946. Tempests replaced by Spitfire F.24s Jan 1948. Code-letters 'W2'.

West Malling		B.158	6 Sept 45	Gatow	3 June 47
Manston	30 Aug 44	B.170	1 Nov 45	Wunstorf	19 July 47
Coltishall	20 Sept 44	B.158	16 Nov 45	Duxford	2 Sept 47
B.70	29 Sept 44	Wunstorf	31 Jan 46	Wunstorf	18 Sept 47
B.82	1 Oct 44	S/L R. L. Spurdle, DSO, DFC ☆		(Aug 44)–Jan 45	
B.80	7 Oct 44	S/L E. D. Mackie, DSO, DFC ☆		Jan 45–April 45	
B.112	16 April 45	Maj R. A. Henwick, DFC (SAAF)		April 45–Nov 45	
Warmwell	18 April 45	S/L A. H. B. Friendship, DFM ☆		Nov 45–May 46	
B.152	8 May 45	S/L H. E. Walmsley, DFC		May 46–Nov 47	
B.160	20 June 45	S/L R. A. Newbery, DFC ☆		Dec 47–(Jan 48)	

1. 16 Squadron, Tempest II PR733 'EG-X', Fassberg, 1947. (Wing Commander E. J. Shaw)

2. 20 Squadron, Tempest II PR652 'HN-S', Agra, May 1947. (D. W. Warne)

3. 26 Squadron, Tempest V SN345 'XC-K', Fassberg, May 1946. (Air Commodore J. W. Frost)

4. 26 Squadron, Tempest II PR757 'XC-B', Fassberg, August 1946. (Air Commodore J. W. Frost)

5. 30 Squadron, Tempest II PR652 'RS-S', Agra, 1946. (via A. S. Thomas)

6. 33 Squadron, Tempest V EJ886 '5R-N', awaiting overhaul at Langley, 1947. (C. H. Buck)

7. 33 Squadron, Tempest V PR689 '5R-E', visiting Thorney Island, 1948. (A. Fraser)

8. 39 Squadron, Tempest VI line-up at Khartoum, 1948, including NX285 'B'. (E. V. Walker via G. A. Jenks)

9. 41 Squadron, Tempest V 'EB-J' at Lübeck, late 1945, believed to be SN350. (J. Sobotnicki)

10. 54 Squadron, Tempest II MW833 'HF-H', about to be named 'Canadian DCMs', Chilbolton 1946. (Group Captain F. W. M. Jensen)

11. 56 Squadron, Typhoon IA R7648 'US-A', Squadron Leader Dundas's aircraft, Snailwell, summer 1942. (IWM)

12. 56 Squadron, Tempest V SN254 'US-T', Squadron Leader Kilburn's aircraft, Fassberg, late 1945. (A. Clark)

13. 80 Squadron, Tempest V SN355 'W2-A', Wunstorf, 1948 (the last Tempest V built). (P. Berry)

137 Squadron

Exchanged Hurricane IVs for Typhoons at Colerne 2 Jan 1944, flying its first operation with them 8 Feb 1944. 124 Wing Aug 1944. 125 Wing May 1945. Renumbered 174 Squadron at Warmwell 26 Aug 1945. Code-letters 'SF'.

Colerne		B.106	11 April 45	B.160	9 May 45
Fairwood Common	23 Jan 44	B.112	13 April 45	B.172	21 June 45
Lympne	4 Feb 44	B.120	17 April 45	B.158	11 July 45
Manston	1 April 44	B.156	30 April 45	Warmwell	20 Aug 45
B.6	13 Aug 44	B.118	7 May 45		
B.30	30 Aug 44	S/L J. R. Dennehey, DFC		(Jan 44)–April 44	
B.48	3 Sept 44	S/L G. Piltingsrud, DFC		April 44–Sept 44	
B.58	6 Sept 44	S/L E. T. Brough, DFC		Sept 44–Dec 44	
B.78	22 Sept 44	S/L R. G. V. Barraclough		Dec 44–Mar 45	
B.86	13 Jan 45	S/L D. Murray, DFC		Mar 45–Aug 45	

152 'Hyderabad' Squadron

First Tempest IIs received at Risalpur 22 July 1946, replacing Spitfire VIIIs and XIVs. Disbanded 31 Jan 1947. Code-letters 'UM'.

S/L G. B. Smither, DFC	(July 46)–Aug 46	Risalpur
S/L G. T. A. Douglas, DFC	Aug 46–Jan 47	

164 'Argentine-British' Squadron

First Typhoon flying took place at Twinwood Farm 9 Jan 1944, but it received a full complement of Typhoons to replace its Hurricane IVs on 1 Feb, when it took over 195 Squadron's aircraft at Fairlop, 136 Airfield. First operation flown 20 Mar 1944. 123 Airfield April 1944. 136 Airfield/Wing April 1944. 123 Wing July 1944. Fighter Command June 1945, re-equipping with Spitfire IXs at Turnhouse. Code-letters 'FJ'.

Twinwood Farm		B.23	3 Sept 44	B.77	28 Dec 44
Fairlop	13 Jan 44	B.35	6 Sept 44	A.84	1 Jan 45
Twinwood Farm	11 Feb 44	B.53	13 Sept 44	B.77	19 Jan 45
Acklington	8 Mar 44	B.67	30 Oct 44	B.91	21 Mar 45
Thorney Island	15 Mar 44	B.77	26 Nov 44	B.103	17 April 45
Llanbedr	11 April 44	Fairwood Common	17 Dec 44	B.116	26 May 45
Thorney Island	22 April 44	S/L H. A. B. Russell, DFC		(Jan 44)–May 44	
Funtington	17 June 44	S/L P. H. Beake, DFC		May 44–Aug 44	
Hurn	21 June 44	S/L I. D. Waddy, DFC		Aug 44–Aug 44	
B.8	17 July 44	S/L R. Van Lierde, DFC ☆		Aug 44–Jan 45	
B.7	20 July 44	S/L P. L. Bateman-Jones		Jan 45–(June 45)	

168 Squadron

Converted from reconnaissance Mustangs to Typhoons, the first arriving 23 Sept 1944, at B.66. 143 Wing Oct 1944. First operation flown 12 Oct 1944. Officially disbanded 26 Feb 1945 but last operation flown two days later. Code-letters 'QC'.

S/L L. H. Lambert, DFC	(Sept 44)–Feb 45	B.66
S/L E. C. H. Vernon-Jarvis, DFC	Feb 45–Feb 45	B.78 2 Oct 44

174 'Mauritius' Squadron

First Typhoons received at Gravesend 8 April 1943, replacing Hurricane IIs. 121 Airfield/Wing July 1943. First operation 14 July 1943. Disbanded 8 April 1945. Reformed with Typhoons by renumbering 137 Squadron at Warmwell 26 Aug 1945 but disbanded again 6 Sept 1945. Reformed again, with Tempest Vs, 9 Sept 1945 by renumbering 274 Squadron at Warmwell. 135 Wing Sept 1945. Disbanded 31 Mar 1946. Code-letters 'XP' on Typhoons, 'JJ' on Tempests.

Gravesend		B.70	17 Sept 44	Warmwell	26 Aug 45
Merston	12 July 43	B.80	30 Sept 44	Warmwell	9 Sept 45
Lydd	1 July 43	Warmwell	10 Nov 44	B.155	20 Sept 45
Westhampnett	10 Oct 43	B.80	21 Nov 44	Gatow	19 oct 45
Eastchurch	21 Jan 44	B.100	20 Mar 45	B.152	26 Nov 45
Westhampnett	4 Feb 44				
Holmsley South	1 April 44	S/L W. W. McConnell, DFC		(April 43)–Feb 44	
B.5	17 June 44	S/L W. Pitt-Brown, DFC		Feb 44–Aug 44	
B.2	19 June 44	S/L J. C. Melvill, AFC		Aug 44–Jan 45	
B.5	24 June 44	S/L D. T. N. Kelly		Jan 45–Mar 45	
B.24	27 Aug 44	S/L R. R. Monk, DFC		Mar 45–April 45	
B.42	1 Sept 44	S/L D. Murray, DFC		Aug 45–Sept 45	
B.50	4 Sept 44	S/L D. C. Usher, DFC, DFM		Sept 45–Mar 46	

175 Squadron

First Typhoons received at Colerne 10 April 1943, replacing Hurricane IIs. 124 Airfield May 1943. First operation flown 12 June 1943. 121 Airfield/Wing July 1943. Disbanded 30 Sept 1945. Code-letters 'HH'.

Colerne		B.50	4 Sept 44	B.110	11 April 45
Lasham	24 May 43	B.70	17 Sept 44	B.150	19 April 45
Appledram	2 June 43	B.80	30 Sept 44	Warmwell	28 May 45
Lydd	1 July 43	Warmwell	21 Nov 44	Manston	11 June 45
Westhampnett	9 Oct 43	B.80	4 Dec 44	B.164	16 June 45
Eastchurch	24 Feb 44	B.100	21 Mar 45	B.160	22 Aug 45
Westhampnett	8 Mar 44				
Holmsley South	1 April 44	S/L J. R. Pennington-Leigh, DFC		(April 43)–July 43	
B.3	20 June 44	S/L R. T. P. Davidson		July 43–Sept 43	
B.5	24 June 44	S/L M. R. Ingle-Finch, DFC, AFC		Sept 43–Oct 44	
B.24	28 Aug 44	S/L R. W. Campbell		Nov 44–Aug 45	
B.42	2 Sept 44	S/L A. Zweigbergk, DFC		Aug 45–Sept 45	

181 Squadron

Formed at Duxford as the first Typhoon bomber squadron, where its first aircraft were received 7 Sept 1942. First operation flown 28 Nov 1942. 124 Airfield/Wing April 1943. Disbanded 30 Sept 1945. Code-letters 'EL'.

Duxford		B.30	30 Aug 44	B.120	18 April 45
Snailwell	10 Dec 42	B.48	3 Sept 44	B.156	1 May 45
Cranfield	1 Mar 43	B.58	6 Sept 44	B.158	7 May 45
Snailwell	8 Mar 43	B.78	22 Sept 44	B.160	6 July 45
Gravesend	24 Mar 43	Warmwell	12 Jan 45	Warmwell	21 July 45
Lasham	5 April 43	B.86	3 Feb 45	B.160	3 Aug 45
Appledram	2 June 43	B.106	11 April 45	B.166	5 Sept 45
New Romney	2 July 43	B.112	13 April 45	B.164	8 Sept 45
Merston	8 Oct 43	S/L D. Crowley-Milling, DFC ☆		Sept 42–Aug 43	
Odiham	31 Dec 43	S/L F. W. M. Jensen, DFC, AFC		Aug 43–Oct 43	
Merston	13 Jan 44	S/L J. G. Keep, DFC		Oct 43–May 44	
Eastchurch	6 Feb 44	S/L C. D. North-Lewis, DFC		May 44–Aug 44	
Merston	21 Feb 44	S/L A. E. S. Vincent, DFC		Aug 44–Nov 44	
Hurn	1 April 44	S/L W. H. B. Short, DFC		Dec 44–Dec 44	
B.6	20 June 44	S/L D. R. Crawford		Dec 44–Feb 45	
Hurn	22 June 44	S/L H. Ambrose, DFC		Feb 45–Aug 45	
B.6	27 June 44	F/L D. G. Brandreth, DFC		Aug 45–Sept 45	

182 Squadron

Formed at Martlesham Heath where their first Typhoon was received 12 Sept 1942. First operation flown 3 Jan 1943. 124 Airfield/Wing April 1943. Disbanded 30 Sept 1945. Code-letters 'XM'.

Martlesham Heath		Merston	21 Jan 44	B.86	21 Feb 45
Sawbridgeworth	7 Dec 42	Hurn	1 April 44	B.106	11 April 45
Snailwell	17 Jan 43	B.6	20 June 44	B.112	13 April 45
Sawbridgeworth	20 Jan 43	Holmsley South	22 June 44	B.120	17 April 45
Martlesham Heath	30 Jan 43	B.6	3 July 44	B.156	1 May 45
Middle Wallop	1 Mar 43	B.30	30 Aug 44	B.158	7 May 45
Zeals	12 Mar 43	B.48	3 Sept 44	B.160	11 July 45
Middle Wallop	13 Mar 43	B.58	6 Sept 44	Warmwell	5 Aug 45
Fairlop	5 April 43	B.78	22 Sept 44	B.160	19 Aug 45
Lasham	29 April 43	B.86	13 Jan 45	B.166	5 Sept 45
Appledram	2 June 43	Warmwell	3 Feb 45	B.164	8 Sept 45
New Romney	2 July 43	S/L T. P. Pugh, DFC		Sept 43–Aug 43	
Wigtown	18 Sept 43	S/L D. R. Walker		Aug 43–Oct 43	
New Romney	22 Sept 43	S/L M. E. Reid		Oct 43–April 44	
Merston	12 Oct 43	Maj D. H. Barlow		April 44–July 44	
Odiham	31 Dec 43	S/L G. J. Gray, DFC		Aug 44–Mar 45	
Eastchurch	5 Jan 44	S/L J. D. Derry, DFC		Mar 45–Sept 45	

4. 168 Squadron, Typhoon IB EK140 'QC-K', B.78, Eindhoven, December 1944. (RAFM/C. E. Brown)

5. 174 Squadron, Typhoon IB JR252 'XP-M', August 1944. (IWM)

6. 174 Squadron, Tempest V NV772 'JJ-E', Fassberg, early 1946. (P. May)

7. 175 Squadron, Typhoon IB SW399 'HH-K', B.164, Schleswig, July 1945. (W. J. Lincoln)

8. 181 Squadron, Typhoon IB RB395 'EL-P', B.158, Lübeck, June 1945. (P. Riley)

9. 182 Squadron, Typhoon IB R8981 'XM-X', Fairlop, April 1943. (L. Woodhouse)

△1

△2

△3 ▽4

△5

△6

△7

△8 ▽9

△1

△2

△3

△4   ▽5

△6

△7

△8   ▽9

183 'Gold Coast' Squadron

Formed at Church Fenton, where their first Typhoons were received 1 Nov 1942. First operation flown 5 April 1943. 124 Airfield May 1943 (only). 136 Airfield/Wing April 1944. 123 Wing July 1944. Typhoons left at Milfield 16 June 1945. Re-equipped with Spitfire IXs at Chilbolton 17 June 1945 pending conversion to Tempest IIs, which took place Aug 1945, the first squadron to be so equipped. Renumbered 54 Squadron 15 Nov 1945. Code-letters 'HF'.

Church Fenton		Hurn	22 June 44	B.77	19 Jan 45
Cranfield	1 Mar 43	Eastchurch	14 July 44	B.91	21 Mar 45
Snailwell	8 Mar 43	B.7	25 July 44	B.103	17 April 45
Church Fenton	12 Mar 43	B.23	3 Sept 44	B.116	27 April 45
Colerne	26 Mar 43	B.35	6 Sept 44	Milfield	16 June 45
Gatwick	8 April 43	B.53	11 Sept 44	Chilbolton	17 June 45
Lasham	3 May 43	B.67	29 Oct 44	Fairwood Common 9 Oct 45	
Colerne	30 May 43	B.77	25 Nov 44	Chilbolton	Nov 45
Harrowbeer	5 June 43	A.84	1 Jan 45		
Tangmere	4 Aug 43	S/L A. V. Gowers, DFC		Nov 42–Oct 43	
Perranporth	18 Sept 43	S/L W. Dring, DFC		Oct 43–April 44	
Predannack	13 Oct 43	S/L F. H. Scarlett		April 44–July 44	
Tangmere	1 Feb 44	S/L R. W. Mulliner, DFC		July 44–Jan 45	
Manston	15 Mar 44	S/L H. M. Mason		Jan 45–Feb 45	
Thorney Island	1 April 44	S/L J. R. Cullen, DFC		Feb 45–Oct 45	
Funtington	18 June 44	S/L F. W. M. Jensen, DFC,AFC		Oct 45–Nov 45	

184 Squadron

Typhoons collected at Redhill 5 Mar 1944, to replace Hurricane IVs. 129 Airfield/Wing April 1944. First operation flown 28 April 1944. 121 Wing July 1944. Disbanded 10 Sept 1945. Code-letters 'BR'.

Redhill		B.42	2 Sept 44	B.110	11 April 45
Odiham	7 Mar 44	B.50	4 Sept 44	B.150	19 April 45
Eastchurch	11 Mar 44	B.70	17 Sept 44	Warmwell	7 May 45
Odiham	3 April 44	B.80	30 Sept 44	B.164	28 May 45
Westhampnett	23 April 44	Warmwell	4 Dec 44	B.160	2 Aug 45
Holmsley South	13 May 44	B.80	18 Dec 44	B.166	5 Sept 45
Westhampnett	20 May 44	B.100	21 Mar 45		
Holmsley South	17 June 44	S/L J. Rose, DFC		(Mar 44)–July 44	
B.10	27 June 44	S/L J. W. Wilson, DFC		July 44–Oct 44	
B.5	14 July 44	S/L W. B. Edwards, DFC		Oct 44–Nov 44	
B.24	28 Aug 44	S/L W. Smith, DFC		Nov 44–Sept 45	

193 'Fellowship of the Bellows' Squadron

Formed at Harrowbeer where its first Typhoons were received 22 Jan 1943. First operation flown 1 April 1943. 136 Airfield Feb 1944. 146 Airfield/Wing April 1944. Disbanded 31 Aug 1945. Code-letters 'DP'.

Harrowbeer		Manston	8 Sept 44	B.89	8 Feb 45
Gravesend	17 Aug 43	B.51	11 Sept 44	B.105	16 April 45
Harrowbeer	18 Sept 43	Fairwood Common	18 Sept 44	B.111	30 April 45
Fairlop	20 Feb 44	B.70	6 Oct 44	R.16	8 June 45
Thorney Island	15 Mar 44	S/L G. W. Petre		(Jan 43)–Feb 44	
Llanbedr	6 April 44	S/L D. G. Ross, DFC		Feb 44–June 44	
Needs Oar Point	11 April 44	S/L J. C. Button		June 44–Aug 44	
Hurn	3 July 44	S/L J. M. G. Plamondon, DFC		Aug 44–Nov 44	
B.15	11 July 44	S/L C. D. Erasmus, DFC		Nov 44–Mar 45	
B.3	15 July 44	S/L D. M. Taylor, DFC		April 45–Aug 45	

195 Squadron

Formed at Hutton Cranswick where their first Typhoon was delivered 27 Nov 1942. First operations flown May 1943. 136 Airfield Oct 1943. Last operation flown 29 Jan 1944. Typhoons transferred to 164 Squadron 1 Feb 1944. Disbanded 15 Feb 1944. Code-letters 'JE'.

Hutton Cranswick		Coltishall	21 Aug 43	Fairlop	21 Sept 43
Woodvale	12 Feb 43				
Ludham	13 May 43	S/L D. M. Taylor		Nov 42–Jan 44	
Matlaske	31 July 43	S/L C. A. Harris		Jan 44–Feb 44	

197 Squadron

Formed at Turnhouse, but soon moved to Drem where its first Typhoon was received 28 Nov 1942. First operation flown 31 Jan 1943. Tangmere Wing Mar 1943. 146 Airfield/Wing April 1944. Disbanded 31 Aug 1945. Code-letters 'OV'.

Drem		B.70	11 Dec 44	B.111	30 April 45
Tangmere	28 Mar 43	B.89	8 Feb 45	R.16	8 June 45
Manston	15 Mar 44	B.105	16 April 45		
Tangmere	1 April 44	S/L L. O. Prevot, DFC		Nov 42–June 43	
Needs Oar Point	10 April 44	S/L A. H. Corkett		June 43–July 43	
Hurn	3 July 44	S/L M. P. C. Holmes, DFC		June 43–Jan 44	
B.3	17 July 44	S/L D. M. Taylor		Jan 44–July 44	
Manston	2 Sept 44	S/L A. H. Smith, DFC		July 44–Dec 44	
B.51	11 Sept 44	S/L R. C. Curwen, DFC		Jan 45–Feb 45	
B.70	2 Oct 44	S/L K. J. Harding, DFC		Feb 45–Aug 45	
Fairwood Common	25 Nov 44	S/L R. E. G. Sheward		Aug 45–Aug 45	

198 Squadron

Formed at Digby with Typhoons 8 Dec 1942. First operation flown 16 Feb 1943. 123 Airfield/Wing Mar 1944. Officially disbanded 15 Sept 1945, Typhoons flown to Lasham 20 Sept 1945 and left there. Code-letters 'TP'.

Drem		B.7	19 July 44	B.77	26 Nov 44
Ouston	23 Jan 43	B.23	3 Sept 44	A.84	31 Dec 44
Acklington	9 Feb 43	B.35	6 Sept 44	B.77	19 Jan 45
Manston	24 Mar 43	B.53	11 Sept 44	B.91	21 Mar 45
Woodvale	15 May 43	B.67	30 Oct 44	B.103	17 April 45
Martlesham Heath	15 June 43	Fairwood Common	6 Nov 44	B.116	27 May 45
Bradwell Bay	19 Aug 43	B.67	21 Nov 44		
Manston	23 Aug 43	S/L J. W. Villa, DFC ☆		Dec 42–May 43	
Tangmere	17 Mar 44	S/L J. Manak		May 43–Aug 43	
Llanbedr	30 Mar 44	S/L J. M. Bryan, DFC ☆		Aug 43–Nov 43	
Thorney Island	6 April 44	S/L J. R. Baldwin, DSO, DFC ☆		Nov 43–April 44	
Llanbedr	22 April 44	S/L J. M. Bryan, DFC ☆		April 44–May 44	
Thorney Island	30 April 44	S/L J. Niblett, DFC		May 44–June 44	
Funtington	18 June 44	S/L I. J. Davies, DFC		June 44–June 44	
Hurn	22 June 44	S/L Y. P. E. H. Ezanno, CdeG		June 44–Oct 44	
B.5	8 July 44	S/L A. W. Ridler		Oct 44–Dec 44	
B.10	11 July 44	S/L N. J. Durrant, DFC		Dec 44–Sept 45	

213 'Ceylon' Squadron

First Tempest VIs received at Nicosia 21 Jan 1947, replacing Mustang IVs. 324 Wing June 1947. Re-equipped with Vampires, commencing 12 Nov 1949; the last Tempests flown out Feb 1950. Code-letters 'AK'.

Nicosia		Deversoir	21 April 49	(Asmara det. July 49)	
Shallufa	3 Sept 47	Khartoum	15 July 49	Deversoir	4 Aug 49
Khartoum	22 Oct 47				
(Asmara det. Mar/May 48)		S/L D. C. Colebrook		(Jan 47)–Jan 48	
Mogadishu	17 May 48	F/L H. E. A. Douglas-Reid		Jan 48–April 48	
Deversoir	21 Oct 48	S/L P. J. Kelley, DFC		April 48–April 49	
Nicosia	4 Mar 49	S/L D. J. A. Roe, DSO, DFC		April 49–(Feb 50)	

222 'Natal' Squadron

Exchanged Spitfire IXs for Tempest Vs at Predannack, commencing 18 Dec 1944, returning to 135 Wing when conversion was complete. Left the Tempests at Weston Zoyland 23 Oct 1945 and re-equipped with Meteors at Molesworth the next day. Code-letters 'ZD'.

Predannack		Manston	3 Sept 45	Chilbolton	10 Sept 45
B.77	21 Feb 45	Weston Zoyland	5 Sept 45	Weston Zoyland	15 Sept 45
B.91	7 April 45				
B.109	29 April 45	S/L H. C. Rigby, DFC ☆		(Dec 44)–Jan 45	
Fairwood Common	3 June 45	S/L E. B. Lyons, DFC		Jan 45–May 45	
B.155	25 June 45	S/L R. M. Mathieson		May 45–Oct 45	

1. 183 Squadron, Typhoon IB DN275 'HF-B', May 1943. (IWM)
2. 183 Squadron, Tempest II MW774 'HF-X', Chilbolton, late 1945. (Group Captain F. W. M. Jensen)
3. 184 Squadron, Typhoon IB MN851 'BR-H', B.5 Le Fresne-Camilly, August 1944. (IWM)
4. 193 Squadron, Typhoon IB MN982 'DP-X', B.70 Deurne, December 1944. (via A. J. Cranston)
5. 195 Squadron, Typhoon IB EJ910 'JE-E', Ludham, summer 1943. (K. A. J. Trott)
6. 197 Squadron, Typhoon IB RB255 'OV-M', R.16, Hildesheim, July 1945. (K. F. C. Bowman)
7. 198 Squadron, Typhoon IB MN526 'TP-V', B.10, Plumetot, July 1944. (IWM)
8. 213 Squadron, Tempest VI NX229 'AK-R', Deversoir, 1948. (via A. S. Thomas)
9. 222 Squadron, Tempest V NV933 'ZD-W', B.109, Quackenbrück, 19 May 1945. (D. J. Coxhead)

△1

△2

△3

△4   ▽5

△6

△7

△8

△9   ▽10

1. 245 Squadron, Typhoon IB MN740 'MR-U', landing at B.5, Le Fresne-Camilly, at the height of the Falaise operations, 18 August 1944. 'MR-U' was usually flown by Flying Officer John Golley, who has described his experiences in *The Day of the Typhoon*, PSL, 1986. (IWM)

2. 247 Squadron, Typhoon IB EK140 'ZY-X', B.158, Lübeck, July 1945. (J. Dick)

3. 247 Squadron, Tempest II believed to be MW756 'ZY-B', Chilbolton, September 1945. (Wing Commander R. P. Beamont).

245 'Northern Rhodesia' Squadron

First Typhoons arrived at Charmy Down 31 Dec 1942, replacing Hurricane IIs. First operation flown 9 Feb 1943. 121 Airfield/Wing June 1943. Disbanded 10 Aug 1945. Code-letters 'MR'.

Charmy Down		B.5	27 June 44	B.80	6 Jan 45
Peterhead	29 Jan 43	B.24	28 Aug 44	B.100	21 Mar 45
Gravesend	31 Mar 43	B.42	2 Sept 44	B.110	11 April 45
Fairlop	28 May 43	B.50	4 Sept 44	B.150	19 April 45
Selsey	1 June 43	B.70	17 Sept 44	B.164	28 May 45
Lydd	30 June 43	B.80	1 Oct 44	Warmwell	16 June 45
Westhampnett	10 Oct 43	Warmwell	24 Dec 44	B.164	3 July 45
Holmsley South	30 April 44				
Eastchurch	12 May 44	S/L S. S. Horden		(Dec 42)–Sept 43	
Holmsley South	22 May 44	S/L J. R. Collins, DFC ☆		Sept 43–Aug 44	
B.5	20 June 44	F/L W. B. Edwards, DFC		Aug 44–Oct 44	
Holmsley South	22 June 44	S/L A. Zweigbergk, DFC		Oct 44–Aug 45	

247 'China-British' Squadron

First Typhoons received at High Ercall 9 Jan 1943, replacing Hurricane IIs. First operation flown 5 April 1943. 121 Airfield May 1943 (only). 124 Airfield/Wing July 1943. Began re-equipping with Tempest IIs at Chilbolton at end of Aug 1945, last Typhoon ferried to Aston Down 27 Nov 1945. Tempests exchanged for Vampire F.1s, the first squadron to be so equipped, April 1946. Code-letters 'ZY'.

High Ercall		B.6	27 June 44	B.106	12 April 45
Middle Wallop	1 Mar 43	B.30	30 Aug 44	B.112	13 April 45
Fairlop	1 April 43	B.48	3 Sept 44	B.120	18 April 45
Gravesend	28 May 43	B.58	6 Sept 44	B.156	2 May 45
Bradwell Bay	4 June 43	B.78	22 Sept 44	B.158	6 May 45
New Romney	10 July 43	B.86	13 Jan 45	Chilbolton	20 Aug 45
Attlebridge	7 Aug 43	Warmwell	21 Feb 45	Fairwood Common	8 Jan 46
New Romney	13 Aug 43	B.86	7 Mar 45	Chilbolton	16 Feb 46
Merston	11 Oct 43	S/L J. C. Melvill		(Jan 43)–Aug 43	
Odiham	31 Dec 43	S/L E. Haabjoern, DFC		Aug 43–Jan 44	
Merston	13 Jan 44	S/L R. J. McNair, DFC		Jan 44–Aug 44	
Eastchurch	4 April 44	S/L B. G. Stapleton, DFC		Aug 44–Dec 44	
Hurn	24 April 44	F/L B. T. Tatham		Dec 44–Jan 45	
B.6	20 June 44	S/L J. H. Bryant, DFC		Jan 45–Dec 45	
Hurn	22 June 44	S/L C. Scott-Vos, DFC		Dec 45–(April 46)	

249 'Gold Coast' Squadron

Tempest VIs received at Habbaniya 23 Dec 1946, replacing Mosquitoes. 324 Wing Mar 1949. Tempests replaced by Vampires commencing 9 Jan 1950, the last Tempests departing for UK Mar 1950. Code-letters 'GN'.

S/L J. I. Kilmartin, DFC	(Dec 46)–Nov 47	Habbaniya	
S/L P. F. Steib, DFC	Dec 47–Oct 48	Deversoir	29 Mar 49
S/L J. R. Baldwin, DSO, DFC ☆ , AFC	Jan 49–Feb 49	Nicosia	28 June 49
S/L C. Scott-Vos, DFC	Feb 49–Mar 50	Deversoir	8 Aug 49

257 'Burma' Squadron

First Typhoons received at High Ercall 22 July 1942, replacing Hurricane IIs. First operation flown 5 Aug 1942. 146 Airfield/Wing April 1944. Disbanded 5 Mar 1945. Code-letters 'FM'.

High Ercall		B.23	6 Sept 44	B.70	2 Oct 44
Exeter	21 Sept 43	B.51	11 Sept 44	B.89	8 Feb 45
Warmwell	8 Jan 43				
Gravesend	12 Aug 43	S/L P. G. Wykeham-Barnes, DFC ☆		(July 42)–Sept 42	
Warmwell	17 Sept 43	S/L G. A. Brown, DFC		Sept 42–April 43	
Beaulieu	20 Jan 44	S/L C. L. C. Roberts		April 43–May 43	
Tangmere	31 Jan 44	S/L P. H. Lee		May 43–July 43	
Needs Oar Point	10 April 44	S/L R. H. Fokes, DFC, DFM ☆		July 43–June 44	
Hurn	2 July 44	S/L W. C. Ahrens		June 44–July 44	
B.3	15 July 44	S/L W. J. Johnston, DFC ☆		July 44–Oct 44	
Fairwood Common	11 Aug 44	S/L D. P. Jenkins, DFC		Oct 44–Jan 45	
B.3	30 Aug 44	S/L A. G. Todd, DFC		Jan 45–Mar 45	

263 'Fellowship of the Bellows' Squadron

First six Typhoons delivered 2 Dec 1943 at Warmwell; 13 more received later in the month, replacing Whirlwinds. First operation 1 Feb 1944. 146 Wing Aug 1944. Disbanded 28 Aug 1945. Code-letters 'HE'.

Warmwell		B.3	6 Aug 44	B.89	10 Feb 45
Ibsley	5 Dec 43	Manston	6 Sept 44	B.105	16 April 45
Fairwood Common	5 Jan 44	B.51	11 Sept 44	B.111	30 April 45
Beaulieu	23 Jan 44	B.70	2 Oct 44	R.16	8 June 45
Warmwell	6 Mar 44	Fairwood Common	13 Jan 45		
Harrowbeer	19 Mar 44	S/L G. B. Warnes, DSO, DFC		Dec 43–Feb 44	
Bolt Head	19 June 44	S/L H. A. C. Gonay		Feb 44–June 44	
Hurn	10 July 44	S/L R. D. Rutter, DFC		June 44–Jan 45	
Eastchurch	23 July 44	S/L M. T. S. Rumbold, DFC		Jan 45–Aug 45	

266 'Rhodesia' Squadron

First Typhoon received at Duxford 6 Jan 1942, first equipping 'B' Flight; an 'A' Flight detachment continued with Spitfire Vs at Coltishall until May 1942. Flew the first ever Typhoon operation – a 'Scramble' – 28 May 1942. Duxford Wing June–Sept 1942. 146 Airfield/Wing April 1944. Disbanded 31 July 1945. Code-letters 'UO', changing to 'ZH' April 1942.

Duxford		B.3	17 July 44	B.70	2 Oct 44
Warmwell	21 Sept 42	B.23	6 Sept 44	B.89	8 Feb 45
Exeter	2 Jan 43	Manston	8 Sept 44	B.105	16 April 45
Gravesend	7 Sept 43	Tangmere	9 Sept 44	Fairwood Common	27 April 45
Exeter	10 Sept 43	Manston	10 Sept 44	B.111	4 June 45
Bolt Head	7 Mar 44	B.51	11 Sept 44	R.16	8 June 45
Harrowbeer	12 Mar 44				
Acklington	15 Mar 44	S/L C. L. Green, DFC		(Jan 42)–July 43	
Tangmere	22 Mar 44	S/L A. S. MacIntyre		July 43–Aug 43	
Needs Oar Point	10 April 44	S/L P. W. Lefevre, DFC		Aug 43–Feb 44	
Snaith	27 April 44	S/L J. W. E. Holmes, DFC, AFC		Mar 44–July 44	
Needs Oar Point	6 May 44	S/L J. D. Wright		July 44–Oct 44	
Eastchurch	29 June 44	S/L J. H. Deall		Oct 44–Mar 45	
Hurn	13 July 44	S/L R. E. G. Sheward		Mar 45–July 45	

268 Squadron

Received first of several standard Typhoons for training 2 July 1944 at Odiham, prior to partial equipment with Typhoon FR.IBs, to operate alongside its Mustang Is. First Typhoon operation 8 Aug 1944 and last 19 Nov 1944. Typhoons passed to 4 Squadron and replaced by Mustang IIs. No squadron code-letters carried.

Odiham		B.31	5 Sept 44	B.61	27 Sept 44
B.10	10 Aug 44	B.43	11 Sept 44	B.70	11 Oct 44
B.4	13 Aug 44	S/L A. S. Mann, DFC		(July 44)–(Nov 44)	
B.27	1 Sept 44				

274 Squadron

Exchanged Spitfire IXs for Tempest Vs at West Malling 7 Aug 1944 and first operational sorties flown five days later. 125 Wing Oct 1944. 122 Wing Oct 1944. 135 Wing Mar 1945. Renumbered 174 Squadron at Warmwell 7 Sept 1945. Code-letters 'JJ'.

West Malling		B.155	20 June 45	Warmwell	3 Sept 45
Manston	23 Aug 44	S/L J. F. Edwards, DFC, DFM		(Aug 44)–Aug 44	
Coltishall	20 Sept 44	S/L M. G. Barnett, DFC		Aug 44–Sept 44	
B.70	29 Sept 44	S/L J. R. Heap, DFC		Sept 44–Nov 44	
B.82	2 Oct 44	S/L A. H. Baird, DFC		Nov 44–Feb 45	
B.80	7 Oct 44	S/L D. C. Fairbanks, DFC ☆		Feb 45–Feb 45	
B.91	17 Mar 45	S/L W. J. Hibbert		Mar 45–April 45	
B.109	20 April 45	S/L D. C. Usher, DFC, DFM		April 45–Sept 45	

438 'Wildcat' Squadron RCAF

Formed by renumbering 118 Squadron RCAF. First Typhoons received 30 Jan 1944, at Ayr, replacing temporary equipment of Hurricane IVs. 143 Airfield/Wing. First operation flown 20 Mar 1944. Disbanded 26 Aug 1945. Code-letter 'F3'.

Ayr		B.100	3 April 45	B.150	21 April 45
Hurn	18 Mar 44	B.110	12 April 45	B.166	29 May 45
Funtington	2 April 44				
Hurn	19 April 44	S/L F. G. Grant, DFC		(Jan 44)–July 44	
B.9	27 June 44	S/L J. R. Beirnes, DFC		July 44–Oct 44	
B.24	31 Aug 44	S/L R. F. Reid		Oct 44–Dec 44	
B.48	3 Sept 44	F/L P. Wilson		Dec 44–Jan 45	
B.58	6 Sept 44	S/L J. E. Hogg, DFC		Jan 45–Mar 45	
B.78	25 Sept 44	S/L J. R. Beirnes, DFC		April 45–June 45	
Warmwell	19 Mar 45	S/L P. Bissky		June 45–Aug 45	

4. 249 Squadron, Tempest VI NX142 'GN-G', Habbaniya, 1948. (K. L. Chapman)

5. 257 Squadron, Typhoon IB MM955 'FM-N', Tangmere, March 1944. (D. P. Jenkins)

6. 263 Squadron, Typhoon IB RB305 'HE-S', B.89, Mill, February 1945. (R. E. G. Sheward)

7. 266 Squadron, Typhoon IB RB478 'ZH-Q', Squadron Leader Sheward's aircraft, B.89, Mill, March 1945. (R. E. G. Sheward)

8. One of several standard Typhoon IBs issued to 268 Squadron for type conversion, prior to equiping with Typhoon FR.IBs. (via Chris Ashworth)

9. 274 Squadron, Tempest V line-up at B.155, Dedelstorf, summer 1945, including SN135 'JJ-R'. (via S. B. Feldman)

10. 438 Squadron, Typhoon IB RB433 'F3-P', B.166, Flensburg, summer 1945. (J. A. Lord)

439 'Westmount' Squadron RCAF

Formed by renumbering 123 Squadron RCAF. Received Typhoons at Ayr commencing 29 Jan 1944. 143 Airfield/Wing. First operation flown 27 Mar 1944. Disbanded 26 Aug 1945. Code-letters '5V'.

Ayr		B.58	6 Sept 44	Warmwell	3 April 45
Hurn	18 Mar 44	B.78	25 Sept 44	B.150	22 April 45
Funtington	2 April 44	B.100	30 Mar 45	B.166	29 May 45
Hurn	19 April 44				
Hutton Cranswick	11 May 44	S/L W. M. Smith		(Jan 44)–Mar 44	
Hurn	20 May 44	S/L H. H. Norsworthy, DFC		Mar 44–Sept 44	
B.9	27 June 44	S/L K. J. Fiset, DFC		Sept 44–Dec 44	
B.24	31 Aug 44	S/L R. G. Crosby		Dec 44–Jan 45	
B.48	3 Sept 44	S/L J. H. Beatty, DFC		Jan 45–Aug 45	

440 'City of Ottawa' Squadron RCAF

Formed by renumbering 111 Squadron RCAF. Typhoon flying commenced at Ayr 25 Feb 1944. 143 Airfield/Wing. First operation 30 Mar 1944. Disbanded 26 Aug 1945. Code-letters 'I8'.

Ayr		B.100	30 Mar 45	Warmwell	23 April 45
Hurn	18 Mar 44	B.110	11 April 45	B.150	8 May 45
Funtington	3 April 44	B.150	20 April 45	B.166	29 May 45
Hurn	20 April 44				
B.9	27 June 44	S/L W. H. Pentland, DFC		(Feb 44)–Oct 44	
B.24	31 Aug 44	S/L A. E. Monson, DFC		Oct 44–Dec 44	
B.48	3 Sept 44	S/L H. O. Gooding, DFC		Dec 44–Mar 45	
B.58	6 Sept 44	S/L R. E. Coffey, DFC		Mar 45–July 45	
B.78	26 Sept 44	S/L A. E. Monson, DFC		Aug 45–Aug 45	

486 Squadron RNZAF

First Typhoons received at Wittering 30 July 1942, replacing Hurricane IIs. First operation flown 25 Aug 1942. Received five Tempest Vs Jan 1944 but these were transferred to 3 Squadron the following month. Full re-equipment with Tempest Vs took place at Castle Camps April 1944; a detachment at Bradwell Bay flew the last Typhoon sorties 14 April 1944. 150 Airfield/Wing April 1944. 122 Wing Sept 1944. 124 Wing July 1945. Tempests handed over to 41 Squadron 14 Sept 45 and officially disbanded 12 Oct 1945. Code-letters 'SA'.

Wittering		Beaulieu	31 Jan 44	Castle Camps	29 Mar 44
North Weald	27 Sept 42	Drem	28 Feb 44	Newchurch	30 April 44
West Malling	10 Oct 42	Castle Camps	13 Mar 44	Matlaske	19 Sept 44
Tangmere	30 Oct 42	Ayr	21 Mar 44	B.60	28 Sept 44

B.80	1 Oct 44	S/L C. L. C. Roberts	(July 42)–April 43
B.118	11 April 45	S/L D. J. Scott, DFC ☆	April 43–Sept 43
B.150	26 April 45	S/L I. D. Waddy	Sept 43–Jan 44
B.118	6 May 45	S/L J. H. Iremonger	Jan 44–Dec 44
B.160	8 May 45	S/L A. E. Umbers, DFC	Dec 44–Feb 45
B.172	20 June 45	S/L K. G. Taylor-Cannon, DFC	Feb 45–April 45
B.158	6 July 45	S/L W. E. Schrader, DFC	April 45–May 45
B.166	8 Sept 45	S/L C. J. Sheddan, DFC	May 45–(Sept 45)

501 'County of Gloucester' Squadron

First Tempest Vs received at Westhampnett 18 July 1944, replacing Spitfire IXs. First operations flown 2 Aug 1944. Remained with ADGB. Disbanded 20 April 1945. Code-letters 'SD'.

S/L M. G. Barnett	(July 44)–Aug 44	Westhampnett	
S/L J. Berry, DFC	Aug 44–Oct 44	Manston	2 Aug 44
S/L A. Parker-Rees, DFC	Oct 44–April 45	Bradwell Bay	23 Sept 44
		Hunsdon	3 Mar 45

609 'West Riding' Squadron

First Typhoons received at Duxford 10 April 1942, replacing Spitfire Vs. Duxford Wing June–Sept 1942. First operation 30 July 1942. 123 Airfield Mar 1944. 146 Airfield Mar 1944. 123 Airfield/Wing April 1944. Officially disbanded 15 Sept 1945, Typhoons flown to Lasham and left there 20 Sept 1945. Code-letters 'PR'.

Duxford		B.35	6 Sept 44	B.91	21 Mar 45
Bourn	26 Aug 42	B.53	11 Sept 44	B.103	17 April 45
Duxford	30 Aug 42	B.67	30 Oct 44	B.116	27 May 45
Biggin Hill	18 Sept 42	B.77	26 Nov 44	Lasham	2 June 45
Manston	2 Nov 42	A.84	31 Dec 44	Fairwood Common	4 June 45
Matlaske	22 July 43	B.77	19 Jan 45	B.116	23 June 45
Lympne	18 Aug 43	S/L G. K. Gilroy, DFC ☆		(April 42)–June 42	
Manston	14 Sept 43	S/L P. H. M. Richey, DFC		June 42–Oct 42	
Fairwood Common	6 Feb 44	S/L R. P. Beamont, DFC ☆		Oct 42–May 43	
Manston	20 Feb 44	S/L A. Ingle, AFC		May 43–Aug 43	
Tangmere	16 Mar 44	S/L P. G.Thornton-Brown		Aug 43–Dec 43	
Acklington	21 Mar 44	S/L J. C. Wells, DFC		Dec 43–June 44	
Thorney Island	1 April 44	S/L L. E. J. M. Geerts, DFC		June 44– Aug 44	
B.2	18 June 44	S/L R. A. Lallemant, DFC ☆		Aug 44–Sept 44	
Hurn	22 June 44	S/L T. Y. Wallace, DFM		Sept 44–Nov 44	
B.10	1 July 44	S/L C. J. G Demoulin, DFC		Nov 44–Dec 44	
B.7	19 July 44	S/L E. R. A. Roberts, DFC		Dec 44–Mar 45	
B.23	3 Sept 44	S/L W. F Stark, DFC ☆		Mar 45–Sept 45	

△1

△3 ▽4

▽2

Miscellaneous Units

1320 Flight

Formed at Holmsley South 8 May 1944, with FIU personnel and four specially equipped Typhoons, for brief operational trials of 'Abdullah'. Disbanded 14 June 1944.

Fighter Interception Unit

Received the Typhoon NF.IB at Ford, for trials June 1943. Two uneventful defensive patrols over London Nov 1943. To Wittering 4 April 1944, where several Typhoons were flown on 'Abdullah' trials. First Tempest V received 22 June 1944 and two days later a detachment was formed at Newchurch to operate by night against V-1 flying bombs. Pilots and aircraft absorbed by 501 Squadron at Manston 10 Aug 1944. Tempests carried code-letters 'ZQ'.

Squadrons using small numbers of Typhoons or Tempests in non-operational roles

170 Squadron: Two Typhoons on charge at Snailwell from April to June 1943; probably for development of tactics and/or assessment in the FR role.
186 Squadron: First Typhoons received at Ayr 15 Nov 1943, replacing Hurricane IVs. To Tain 7 Jan 1944, but re-equipped with Spitfire VBs before becoming operational. Code-letters 'AP'.
268 Squadron: Three Typhoons on charge from Feb to July 1943 (as for 170 Squadron).
287 Squadron: An anti-aircraft co-operation squadron which operated Tempest V (mainly Series 1) aircraft, alongside several other types, from Nov 1944 to June 1946. Gatwick, to Redhill Jan 1945, to Hornchurch May 1945, to Bradwell Bay June 1945, to West Malling Sept 1945. Code-letters 'KZ'.
349 Squadron: Began conversion from Spitfire IXs to Tempest Vs at Predannack 24 Feb 1945. Owing to a shortage of Tempests, several Typhoons were utilized, but conversion was eventually abandoned 14 April 1945.
350 Squadron: Three Typhoons on charge Sept and Oct 1945, use not known.

---

1. 439 Squadron, Typhoon IB RB402 '5V-P', B.100, Goch, April 1945. (Public Archives of Canada)
2. 440 Squadron, Typhoon IB RB389 'I8-P', B.100, Goch, April 1945. (Public Archives of Canada)
3. 486 Squadron, Typhoon IB JP853 'SA-K', flown by Flight Lieutenant Frank Murphy, November 1943. (IWM)
4. 486 Squadron, Tempest V EJ627 'SA-E', B.80, Gilze-Rijen, October 1944. (IWM)
5. 501 Squadron, Tempest V EJ555 'SD-Y', Bradwell Bay, late 1944. (ATP)
6. 609 Squadron, Typhoon IB R7855 'PR-D', Manston, early 1943. (R. A. Lallemant)

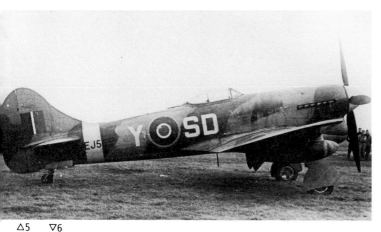

△5 ▽6

400 Squadron RCAF: Two Typhoons on charge from Feb to Nov 1943 (as for 170 Squadron). Also evaluation of the Typhoon FR.IB trials aircraft (JR207) from Jan to Mar 1944.
451 Squadron RAAF: Received three tropicalized Typhoons, for extended trials, at Idku, Egypt, June 1943. A detachment operated the Typhoons at LG.106, El Daba, from 13 July 1943 until the trials were completed 20 Oct 1943.
485 Squadron RNZAF: Began conversion from Spitfire IXs to Tempest Vs at Predannack Feb 1945. First Tempest flown 28 Feb, but this type was withdrawn early in March and replaced by Typhoons, as a temporary measure. However, conversion was abandoned April 1945, the last Typhoon flying having taken place on the 10th.
542 Squadron: One Typhoon FR.IB (production prototype MN315) on charge Sept and Oct 1945.
778 Squadron FAA: One Typhoon issued to this Naval flight trials unit at Arbroath 5 Feb 1943, but it was written-off in an accident after only one week.

Training Units

1 Combat Training Wing: Formed from 56 OTU (Hurricanes) in Oct 1943, it had two Typhoons on charge Nov 1943 to Jan 1944. Later renamed 1 Tactical Exercise Unit.
3 Tactical Exercise Unit: Formed by renumbering 4 TEU at Annan 28 Mar 1944. Only two Typhoons at this time, but in April the unit's Hurricanes were replaced by Typhoons. A detachment for Typhoon conversion was formed at Great Orton 7 April 1944 and moved to Honiley 10 May 1944. The complete unit moved to Aston Down 14 July 1944, with Chedworth as a satellite. Renamed 55 OTU 15 Dec 1944. Code-letters, 1 Squadron 'UW' and 'ZX'; 2 Squadron 'EH' and 'PA'.
4 Tactical Exercise Unit: Formed at Annan 26 Jan 1944 by renaming 55 OTU. Main equipment was Hurricanes but two Typhoons were on charge. Renumbered 3 TEU 28 Mar 1944.
13 Operational Training Unit: Small numbers of Tempest IIs operated from June 1945 to Feb 1946 (main equipment Mosquitoes), at Harwell, moving to Middleton St. George 22 July 1945. Code-letters 'FV' and 'SL'.
55 Operational Training Unit: Two Typhoons on charge from Nov 1943 at Annan (main equipment Hurricanes). Renamed 4 TEU 26 Jan 1944. Reformed by renaming 3 TEU at Aston Down on 15 Dec 1944, with an establishment which included 107 Typhoons. Satellite at Chedworth. Training ceased 29 May 1945, unit was disbanded 14 June 1945. Code-letters as for 3 TEU.
56 Operational Training Unit: Reformed at Milfield 15 Dec 1944, with an establishment which included 53 Typhoons and 54 Tempests. Satellite at Brunton. It was the last flying unit still (partly) equipped with Typhoons when it was disbanded 14 Feb 1946. Code-letters, 1 Squadron 'GF'; 2 Squadron 'FE'; X Squadron 'HQ'; Brunton 'OD'.
59 Operational Training Unit: Began receiving Typhoons to replace its Hurricanes 10 Mar 1943, at Milfield. 21 had been received by June 1943, when they were relinquished to operational squadrons. Reformed as a 'half OTU' 26 Feb 1945, with an establishment which included 54 Typhoons. Code-letters in 1943 'MF'; in 1945, 1 Squadron '4Q'; 2 Squadron '1I'; 3 Squadron '7L'.
83 Group Support Unit: This unit was responsible for the maintenance of a pool of aircraft and pilots to provide replacements to the 83 Group squadrons. A Training Flight, which provided type conversion and continuation training, included Typhoons and later Tempests among its equipment. Single code-letters carried at first, but from mid-1944 '7S' codes were used. Formed at Redhill 1 Mar 1944, to Bognor 25 June 1944, Thorney Island 25 Sept 1944, Westhampnett 3 Nov 1944, Dunsfold 22 Sept 1945. Renamed 83 Group Disbandment Centre 1 Aug 1945, and moved to Lasham 24 Oct 1945.
84 Group Support Unit: Role as for 83 GSU. No code-letters carried, but aircraft were numbered; known examples include Typhoons in the '40's and Tempests in the '60's. In early 1945 some sorties were made by trainees, against the German garrisons at Dunkirk, as an introduction to operations. Formed at Aston Down 14 Feb 1944, to Thruxton 13 July 1944, Lasham 27 Nov 1944. Renamed 84 Group Disbandment Centre 1 Aug 1945.
226 Operational Conversion Unit: Operated small numbers of Tempest IIs (coded 'XL') Sept 1946 to June 1949, at Bentwaters. Three Tempest TT.5s in use Oct/Nov 1950.
229 Operational Conversion Unit: Operated Tempest TT.5s at Chivenor June 1952 to Dec 1954. Code-letters 'RS', with numbers in the range '20' to '40'.
233 Operational Conversion Unit: Operated Tempest TT.5s at Pembrey Oct 1952 to July 1955. It was the last unit to fly Tempests in the RAF.
Acklington Armament Practice Camp (later Station): Operated Tempest TT.5s Mar 1950 to Jan 1953. Code-letters 'WH' and numerals between '1' and '20'.
Sylt Armament Practice Camp (later Station): Operated Tempest TT.5s May 1950 to Oct 1954. Single code-letters carried.
Central Gunnery School: Operated Tempest TT.5s at Leconfield Mar 1950 to July 1952. Code-letters 'FJU'.
Fighter Leaders School: Formed at Milfield 18 Jan 1944 with five squadrons of Typhoons and Spitfires. Code-letters 'HK', 'MF' and 'RL'. To Wittering to become part of the CFE 27 Dec 1944.
Central Fighter Establishment: Typhoons were used by the Fighter Leaders School, within the CFE, until Aug 1945, when they had been replaced by Tempest Vs. The Typhoons carried code-letters 'MF' and numerals in the range '1' to '23'. Also operated was a Typhoon stripped of paint and polished, and known as the 'Silver Bullet'. The Tempests were coded 'MF' with letters rather than numbers, and continued in use until mid-1947. Other sections within the CFE used Tempest IIs and Vs coded 'GO' and 'RE'.

Miscellaneous Units

The following units used single or very small numbers of Typhoons or Tempests:

14 and 18 Armament Practice Camps
1 and 3 Armament Practice Stations
Air-Sea Warfare Development Unit
Air Transport Tactical Development Unit
BAFO Communications Wing
Bombing Trials Unit
Coastal Command Development Unit
Central Flying School
2nd TAF Communications Squadron
84 and 85 Group Communications Squadrons

5 Ferry Pool
1, 15 and 16 Ferry Units
1689 Flight
Gunnery Research Unit
Handling Squadron
Torpedo Development Unit
Telecommunications Flying Unit
Telecommunications Research Establishment
Station Flights at Acklington, Bradwell Bay, Chilbolton, Gatow, Lübeck, Manston, Middle Wallop, Swinderby and Sylt.

The use of Typhoons and Tempests by AAEE (including ETPS), AFDU, FIU and RAE is covered in a separate appendix.

Wing Formations including Typhoon and Tempest Squadrons

Listed below are the main Wing formations which included Typhoon and Tempest squadrons among their constituent units. Many of the mobile Wings began life as 'Airfields', but, as described in the main text, they were renamed 'Wings', retaining their original numbers; for the sake of simplicity they are listed here as Wings.

In 1943 and post-war, mixed Wings were common, but squadrons flying aircraft types other than Typhoons or Tempests are not included here. Bases are also not listed, but may be found by reference to the individual squadron histories in the appropriate appendix. Bracketed dates indicate service with the Wing prior to or after the Typhoon/Tempest period.

16 Wing

Controlled 121 and 124 Airfields July 1943 to April 1944, when it was disbanded, the Airfields being absorbed by 22 Sector.

Commanding Officers

W/C D. E. Gillam, DSO, DFC, AFC	July 43
G/C H. de C. A. Woodhouse, DFC, AFC	Aug 43–April 44

20 Wing (later Sector)

Controlled 123, 136 and 146 Airfields Mar 1944 to July 1944 when it was disbanded.

Commanding Officers

G/C C. E. St. J. Beamish, DFC	Mar 44
G/C D. E. Gillam, DSO, DFC ☆, AFC	April 44–July 44

22 Wing (later Sector)

Controlled 143 and 144 (Spitfire) Airfields from Jan 1944. 144 Airfield replaced by 121 and 124 Airfields April 1944. Disbanded July 1944.

Commanding Officer

G/C P. Y. Davoud, DSO, DFC	Jan 44–July 44

121 Wing

Commanding Officers

W/C later G/C C. S. Morice, DSO, MC	(May 43)–Dec 44
G/C G. Jones, DSO, DFC	Dec 44–April 45
G/C R. P. R. Powell, DFC ☆	April 45–Aug 45
G/C P. G. Jameson, DSO, DFC	Sept 45

Wing Commanders, Flying

W/C D. Crowley-Milling, DFC ☆	Aug 43–Sept 43
W/C R. T. P. Davidson, DFC	Sept 43–Jan 44
W/C C. L. Green, DFC	Jan 44–Aug 44
W/C W. Pitt-Brown, DFC	Aug 44–Oct 44
W/C M. T. Judd, DFC, AFC	Nov 44–Jan 45
W/C J. G. Keep, DFC	Feb 45–Sept 45

Squadrons

247 Squadron	May 43
245 Squadron	May 43–Aug 45
174 Squadron	July 43–April 45
175 Squadron	July 43–Sept 45
184 Squadron	July 44–Sept 45

122 Wing

Commanding Officers

G/C P. G. Jameson, DSO, DFC	(Sept 44)–Sept 45

Wing Commanders, Flying

W/C R. P. Beamont, DSO, DFC ☆	Sept 44–Oct 44
W/C J. B. Wray, DFC	Oct 44–Jan 45
W/C R. E. P. Brooker, DSO, DFC	Jan 45–April 45
W/C E. D. Mackie, DSO, DFC ☆	April 45–Sept 45

Squadrons

3 Squadron	Sept 44–Aug 45
56 Squadron	Sept 44–Aug 45
486 Squadron	Sept 44–May 45
80 Squadron	Oct 44–June 45
274 Squadron	Oct 44–Mar 45

123 Wing

Commanding Officers

W/C later G/C D. J. Scott, DSO, OBE, DFC ☆	Mar 44–Feb 45
G/C J. R. Baldwin, DSO, DFC ☆	Feb 45–Dec 45
G/C P. G. Jameson, DSO, DFC	Dec 45–Mar 46
G/C R. P. R. Powell, DFC ☆☆	Mar 46–Aug 46
G/C R. A. T. Stowell, OBE, DFC	Aug 46–(June 48)

Wing Commanders, Flying

W/C R. E. P. Brooker, DFC ☆	May 44–July 44
W/C W. Dring, DSO, DFC	July 44–Jan 45
W/C J. C. Button, DSO, DFC	Jan 45–Sept 47
W/C P. P. Hanks, DSO, DFC	Sept 47–(June 48)

Squadrons

183 Squadron	Mar 44–April 44
198 Squadron	Mar 44–Sept 45
609 Squadron	Mar 44–Sept 45
197 Squadron	Mar 44–April 45
164 Squadron	July 44–June 45
183 Squadron	July 44–June 45
3 Squadron	Jan 46–(June 48)
41 Squadron	Jan 46–Mar 46
80 Squadron	Jan 46–Jan 48

124 Wing

Commanding Officers

W/C L. A. Lynn, DFC	April 43–July 43
W/C V. E. Maxwell	July 43–Aug 43
W/C B. G. Carroll	Sept 43–July 44
G/C C. H. Appleton, CBE, DSO, DFC	July 44–Aug 44
G/C C. L. Green, DSO, DFC	Aug 44–Dec 44
G/C E. R. Bitmead, DFC	Jan 45–July 45
G/C J. E. Johnson, DSO ☆☆, DFC ☆	July 45–(Jan 46)

Wing Commanders, Flying

W/C D. E. Gillam, DSO, DFC, AFC	July 43–Aug 43
W/C A. Ingle, DFC, AFC	Aug 43–Sept 43
W/C D. R. Walker, DFC	Oct 43–Jan 44
W/C E. Haabjoern, DFC	Jan 44–Aug 44
W/C C. D. North-Lewis, DSO, DFC ☆	Aug 44–April 45
W/C G. F. H. Webb, DFC	April 45–May 45
W/C M. R. Ingle-Finch, DFC, AFC	May 45–(Jan 46)

Squadrons

181 Squadron	April 43–Sept 45
182 Squadron	April 43–Sept 45
175 Squadron	May 43–June 43
247 Squadron	July 43–Aug 45
137 Squadron	Aug 44–May 45
486 Squadron	July 45–Sept 45
3 Squadron	Aug 45–Sept 45
80 Squadron	Aug 45–Jan 46
41 Squadron	Sept 45–Jan 46

129 Wing

Commanding Officer

W/C D. C. S. Macdonald, DFC	(April 44)–July 44

Squadron

184 Squadron	April 44–July 44

135 Wing

Commanding Officers

G/C P. R. Walker, DSO, DFC	Nov 45
G/C H. L. Maxwell, CBE, DSO	Nov 45–Mar 46
G/C J. E. Johnson, DSO ☆☆, DFC ☆☆	Mar 46–May 46
G/C H. P. Broad, CBE, DFC	May 46–Aug 46
G/C M. F. D. Williams, DSO	Aug 46
G/C L. F. Sinclair, GC, CB, CBE, DSO	May 48

Wing Commanders, Flying

W/C H. M. Mason	Feb 45–Feb 46
W/C R. Deacon-Elliot, DFC	Feb 46–April 46
W/C M. R. Ingle-Finch, DFC, AFC	May 46–June 46
W/C R. Deacon-Elliot, DFC	June 46–Aug 46
W/C J. W. E. Holmes, DFC	Aug 46–July 47
W/C F. R. Carey, DFC ☆☆, AFC, DFM	Aug 47–Feb 49

Squadrons

33 Squadron	Feb 45–July 49
222 Squadron	Feb 45–Sept 45
274 Squadron	Mar 45–Sept 45
3 Squadron	Sept 45–Jan 46
56 Squadron	Sept 45–Mar 46
174 Squadron	Sept 45–Mar 46
16 Squadron	April 46–(Jan 49)
26 Squadron	April 46–(May 49)

136 Wing

Commanding Officer

W/C J. M. Bryan, DFC ☆	May 44–June 44

Squadrons

195 Squadron	Oct 43–Feb 44
164 Squadron	(Feb 44)–July 44
193 Squadron	Feb 44–April 44
183 Squadron	April 44–July 44
266 Squadron	May 44–July 44
263 Squadron	July 44

143 Wing

Commanding Officers

W/C F. W. Hillock	Jan 44–July 44
G/C P. Y. Davoud, DSO, DFC	July 44–Dec 44
W/C A. D. Nesbitt, DFC	Jan 45–Sept 45

Wing Commanders, Flying

W/C R. Marples, DFC	Jan 44
W/C R. T. P. Davidson, DFC	Jan 44–May 44
W/C M. T. Judd, DFC, AFC	May 44–Oct 44
W/C F. G. Grant, DSO, DFC	Oct 44–Sept 45

Squadrons

438 Squadron	(Jan 44)–Aug 45
439 Squadron	(Jan 44)–Aug 45
440 Squadron	(Feb 44)–Aug 45
168 Squadron	Oct 44–Feb 45

146 Wing

Commanding Officers

W/C D. E. Gillam, DSO, DFC ☆ , AFC	Feb 44–Mar 44
W/C E. W. W. Ellis	Mar 44–July 44
G/C D. E. Gillam, DSO ☆☆ , DFC ☆ , AFC	July 44–Feb 45
G/C J. C. Wells, DFC ☆☆ , CdeG	Feb 45–Aug 45

Wing Commanders, Flying

W/C E. R. Baker, DFC ☆	April 44–June 44
W/C J. R. Baldwin, DSO ☆☆ , DFC ☆	June 44–Nov 44
W/C J. C. Wells, DFC ☆ , CdeG	Nov 44–Feb 45
W/C J. H. Deall, DSO, DFC	Feb 45–Aug 45

Squadrons

183 Squadron	Feb 44–Mar 44
197 Squadron	Feb 44–Mar 44
257 Squadron	Feb 44–Mar 45
266 Squadron	Mar 44–July 45
609 Squadron	Mar 44
193 Squadron	April 44–Aug 45
197 Squadron	April 44–Aug 45
263 Squadron	July 44–Aug 45

150 Wing

Commanding Officer

W/C R. F. Aitken, AFC	Mar 44–(Sept 44)

Wing Commander, Flying

W/C R. P. Beamont, DSO, DFC ☆	April 44–Sept 44

Squadrons

3 Squadron	Mar 44–Sept 44
56 Squadron	April 44–Sept 44
486 Squadron	April 44–Sept 44

324 Wing

Commanding Officers

G/C S. S. Murray, OBE	June 47–Jan 48
G/C A. F. Anderson, DSO, DFC	Jan 48–(Mar 50)

Wing Commander, Flying

W/C W. D. Blackwood, OBE, DFC	Mar 49–(Mar 50)

Squadrons

6 Squadron	June 47–(Nov 49)
213 Squadron	June 47–(Feb 50)
249 Squadron	Mar 49–(Mar 50)

Operational Service Chart: Typhoons

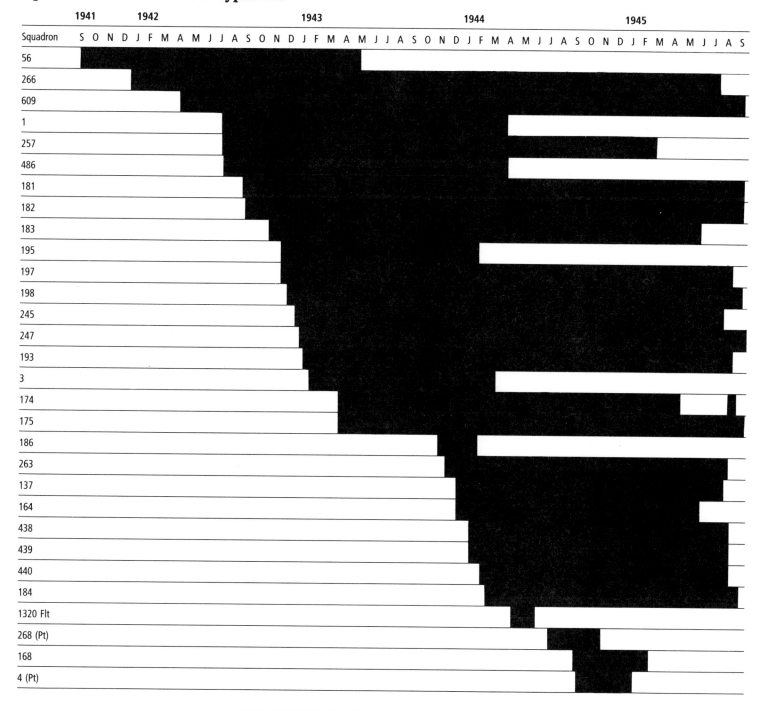

Operational Service Chart: Tempests

A M J J A S O N D

Mark VI

Mark II

Mark II

Mark II

Mark II

ark II

Mark II

Mark II

Mark II

Numbered Airfields

Airfields which were used by Typhoons/Tempests or are mentioned in the appendices or text and were allocated a code are listed below. Sometimes the names reflect the airfield's position between two villages or towns. Alternate names are given where known.

B.2	Bazenville, Fr	B.77	Gilze-Rijen, NL
B.3	St-Croix, Fr	B.78	Eindhoven, NL
B.4	Beny-sur-Mer, Fr	B.80	Volkel, NL
B.5	Le Fresne-Camilly, Fr	B.82	Grave, NL
B.6	Coulombs, Fr	B.86	Helmond, NL
B.7	Martragny, Fr	B.88	Heesch, NL
B.8	Sommervieu, Fr	B.89	Mill, NL
B.9	Lantheuil, Fr	B.91	Kluis, NL
B.10	Plumetot, Fr	B.100	Goch, Ger
B.14	Amblie, Fr	B.103	Plantlunne, Ger
B.15	Ryes, Fr	B.105	Drope, Ger
B.23	Morainville, Fr	B.106	Twente/Enschede, NL
B.24	St-André de l'Eure, Fr	B.108	Rheine, Ger
B.26	Illiers l'Evêque, Fr	B.109	Quackenbrück, Ger
B.27	Boisney, Fr	B.110	Achmer/Osnabrück, Ger
B.30	Creton, Fr	B.111	Ahlhorn, Ger
B.31	Fresnoy Folney/Londonières, Fr	B.112	Hopsten, Ger
B.35	Baromesnil, Fr	B.116	Wunstorf, Ger
B.42	Beauvais-Tille, Fr	B.118	Celle, Ger
B.43	Fort Rouge, Fr	B.120	Langenhagen, Ger
B.48	Amiens-Glisy, Fr	B.150	Hustedt/Schwerin, Ger
B.50	Vitry-en-Artois, Fr	B.152	Fassberg, Ger
B.51	Lille-Vendeville, Fr	B.154	Soltau/Schneverdingen, Ger
B.53	Merville, Fr	B.155	Dedelstorf, Ger
B.55	Coutrai/Wevelgem, Bel	B.156	Lüneburg, Ger
B.56	Evère, Bel	B.158	Lübeck, Ger
B.58	Melsbroek, Bel	B.160	Kastrup, Den
B.60	Grimbergen, Bel	B.164	Schleswig, Ger
B.61	St-Denis Westrem, Bel	B.166	Flensburg, Ger
B.64	Diest, Bel	B.170	Sylt/Westerland, Ger
B.66	Schaffen/Blankenberge/Diest, Bel	B.172	Husum, Ger
B.67	Ursel, Bel	A.84	Chievres, Bel
B.70	Deurne/Antwerp, Bel	R.16	Hildesheim, Ger

181 Squadron, July 1943

609 Squadron, June 1943

3. Claims

Enemy aircraft claimed as destroyed or probably destroyed by Typhoon pilots

Date	Type	No.	Sqn	Pilot	Aircraft		Location	Identity of Victim where known
9 Aug 42	Ju 88	1	266	P/O N. J. Lucas	R7696	ZH-C	50 m off Cromer	
				P/O I. M. Munro	R7822	ZH-H		
13 Aug 42	Me 210	1	266	F/L A. C. Johnston	R7819	ZH-S	E Cromer	VN+AV of ErpGr 210, WNr 184; Lt H. Manger KIA, Uffz E. Rudolph PoW
19 Aug 42	Do 217	1	266	F/L R. H. L. Dawson	R7815	ZH-S	E Le Tréport	KG 2 lost sixteen Do 217s with seven damaged against RAF claims for 33 destroyed, eight probables and 46 damaged
19 Aug 42	Do 217	1(P)	266	P/O I. M. Munro	R7822	ZH-H	Near Le Tréport	
19 Aug 42	Fw 190	1(P)	266	F/L A. C. Johnston	R7819	ZH-S	N Le Tréport	
6 Sept 42	Me 210	1	1	P/O T. G. B. Bridges	R7923		Robin Hood's Bay	2H+HA of 16/KG 6, WNr 2321; Oblt Walter Maurer, or Fw Rudolf Jansen PoW
6 Sept 42	Me 210	1	1	P/O D. P. Perrin	R7922		2 m SW Redcar	2H+CA or, of 16/KG 6, WNr 2342; Fw Heinrich Mörgen Ogfr Edouard Czerny KIA
14 Sept 42	Ju 88	1	56	F/O M. R. Ingle-Finch	R7846	US-R	40 m E Cromer	
				P/O W. E. Coombes	R7629	US-P		
28 Sept 42	Ju 88	1	257	F/S A. J. Addington	R8658	FM-P	24 m SW Bridport	
17 Oct 42	Fw 190	1	486	P/O G. G. Thomas			9 m S Hastings	'Schwarz 14' of 10(Jabo)/JG 26, WNr 2403; Fw Klaus Niesel
				Sgt A. N. Sames				
3 Nov 42	Fw 190	1	257	F/O G. F. Ball	R8872	FM-R	35 m W Guernsey	'Schwarz 3' of III/JG 2, WNr 2150; Lt H. Hennenig
3 Nov 42	Fw 190	1	257	P/O P. G. Scotchmer	R8652	FM-V	35 m W Guernsey	
5 Dec 42	Fw 190	1(P)	609	F/S A. Haddon	R8810	PR-R	Off Dover	
15 Dec 42	Fw 190	1	609	F/S A. Haddon	R8715	PR-J	Off Ramsgate	
16 Dec 42	Fw 190	1	609	Sgt T. S. Turek	R7849	PR-U	N Boulogne	
17 Dec 42	Bf 109	1	486	F/S F. Murphy	R8744	SA-M	3 m S St. Catherine's Point	Bf 109F-4s of 4(F)/123; '7+', WNr 10246, Lt H. Raucheisen; '1+', WNr 10189, Oblt H. Rück
17 Dec 42	Bf 109	1	486	Sgt K. G. Taylor-Cannon	R8684	SA-B	3 m S St. Catherine's Point	
18 Dec 42	Do 217	1	486	F/O G. G. Thomas	R8681	SA-E	10 m SE Shoreham	F8+RI of II/KG 40, WNr 4384; 4 crew MIA
19 Dec 42	Fw 190	1	609	F/O R. A. Lallemant	R7855	PR-D	Off Deal	10(Jabo)/JG 26, WNr 0712; Oblt Kurt Müller
19 Dec 42	Fw 190	1(P)	609	F/S A. Haddon	R8715	PR-J	Off Deal	
19 Dec 42	Fw 190	1	486	Sgt A. N. Sames	R8660	SA-T	30 m S Shoreham	'3+' of 3(F)/122, WNr 395; Fw P. Gellert
20 Dec 42	Fw 190	1	609	Sg T. S. Turek	R8837		Off Dungeness	
	Fw 190	1(P)	609	Sgt T. S. Turek	R8837		Off Dungeness	
22 Dec 42	Do 217	1	486	F/O A. E. Umbers	R8697	SA-Z	15 m S Selsey	2/KG 2 or 4/KG 40 (both units lost one Do 217)
				F/S C. N. Gall	R8699	SA-S		
24 Dec 42	Bf 109	1	486	F/O G. G. Thomas	R8781	SA-H	30 m SSE St. Catherine's Point	Both 4(F)/123; Bf 109F-1 '22+', WNr 14135; Fw A. Ripplinger; Bf 109G-1, '19+', WNr 14133; Lt B. Frank
24 Dec 42	Bf 109	1	486	F/S F. Murphy	R8744	SA-M	30 m SSE St. Catherine's Point	
10 Jan 43	Fw 190	1	266	F/O J. Small	R8937	ZH-L	500 yd off Teignmouth	10(Jabo)/JG 2, WNr 5424, Fw J. Bitter
17 Jan 43	Bf 109	1	486	Sgt K. Taylor-Cannon	R8781	SA-H	40 m SE St. Catherine's Point	'4+' of 4(F)/123, WNr 10190; Uffz E. Lank
20 Jan 43	Bf 109	3	609	F/O J. R. Baldwin	DN360	PR-A	E Manston	Spitfires also claim five Bf 109s and five Fw 190s AA claims two Fw 190s. Losses by Luftwaffe three Jabos and six fighters mainly from JG 26
20 Jan 43	Fw 190	1	609	F/L J. A. Atkinson	R8810	PR-R	15 m SE Dover	
20 Jan 43	Fw 190	1	609	F/O R. A. Lallemant	R7855	PR-D	Off Dymchurch	
20 Jan 43	Fw 190	1	609	F/O R. Van Lierde	R8838	PR-N	S Dover	
21 Jan 43	Fw 190	1	609	F/O P. J. Nankivell	R8838	PR-N	E Deal	
26 Jan 43	Fw 190	1	266	F/O C. R. M. Bell	R8772		Off Start Point	'7' of 10(Jabo)/JG 2, WNr 5680; Fw K. Blaas
5 Feb 43	Fw 190	1	609	F/O P. J. Nankivell	DN305	PR-M	S Eastbourne	'Schwarz 1' of 10(Jabo)/JG 26, WNr 2435; Uffz Herbert Buttner
10 Feb 43	Bf 109	1	609	F/L J. C. Wells	R8810	PR-R	Off St. Margaret's Bay	Possibly Fw 190A-4 'Brun 14' of I/JG 2, WNr 5655; Uffz N. Leber
14 Feb 43	Fw 190	2	609	F/O R. A. Lallemant	R7855	PR-D	Off Calais	
	Fw 190	1(P)	609	F/O R. A. Lallemant	R7855	PR-D	Off Calais	
14 Feb 43	Fw 190	1	609	F/O A. Polek	R8899	PR-X	Off Calais	III/JG 2 lose three Fw 190s
	Fw 190	1(P)	609	F/O A. Polek	R8899	PR-X	Off Calais	
14 Feb 43	Fw 190	1	609	F/O J. M. Selys	R8888	PR-Y	Off Calais	
14 Feb 43	Fw 190	1	609	F/O R. H. Payne	R7845	PR-H	Off Calais	
16 Feb 43	Ju 88	1	486	F/S F. Murphy	DN428	SA-L	30 m SE St. Catherine's Point	Ju 88D-1 4N+MH of 1(F)/123, WNr 1243; four crew MIA
26 Feb 43	Fw 190	1	609	F/L J. A. Atkinson	DN360	PR-A	Off Boulogne	8/JG 26, WNr 0674; Lt Hermann Thiessen
26 Feb 43	Fw 190	1	266	S/L C. L. Green	EJ924	ZH-G	50 m S Exmouth	WNr 0725, Fw H. Rohne, and WNr 2588, Uffz K. Pressler, both of 10(Jabo)/JG 2
26 Feb 43	Fw 190	1	266	S/L C. L. Green	EJ924	ZH-G	50 m S Exmouth	
				Sgt R. K. Thompson	R8772			
1 Mar 43	Fw 190	1	486	F/S W. B. Tyerman	DN303	SA-P	4 m S Bognor	'11' of 10(Jabo)/JG 2, WNr 1106; Uffz E. Laepple
3 Mar 43	Fw 190	1	609	F/O J. R. Baldwin	R8940	PR-V	Off Cap Gris Nez	
3 Mar 43	Fw 190	1(P)	609	F/O J. M. Selys	R8715	PR-J	Cap Gris Nez	
12 Mar 43	Fw 190	1	609	F/S L. W. F. Stark	DN406	PR-F	Off Dunkirk	'Schwarz 12' of 10(Jabo)/JG 54, WNr 0829, Fw Emil Boesch
13 Mar 43	Fw 190	1	1	F/L L. S. B. Scott	DN585		SW Beachy Head	

Date	Type	No.	Sqn	Pilot	Aircraft		Location	Identity of Victim where known
13 Mar 43	Fw 190	1	1	Sgt R. W. Hornall	R7922		SW Beachy Head	
13 Mar 43	Fw 190	1	266	F/L J. H. Deall	EJ932	ZH-N	20 m S Start Point	'Weiss E', WNr 47153; E. Ziegler, and
13 Mar 43	Fw 190	1	266	F/L J. H. Deall	EJ932	ZH-N	20 m S Start Point	'Weiss B', WNr 52356; Fw H. Schern,
				Sgt D. S. Eadie	EJ917			both of 5/SKG 10
14 Mar 43	Fw 190	1	486	F/S R. H. Fitzgibbon	R8744	SA-M	40 m S Beachy Head	'Gelbe 9' of 5(F)/123, WNr 5346; Fw D. Sahre
26 Mar 43	Ju 52	1	609	F/O R. Van Lierde	DN298	PR-O	Ath, Belgium	
7 April 43	Bf 109	1	257	F/O P. F. Steib	R8685	FM-E	30 m S Isle of Wight	
7 April 43	Do 217	1(P)	609	Sgt T. D. L. Leslie	R7849	PR-U	Cap Gris Nez	
9 April 43	Fw 190	1	1	Sgt R. W. Hornall	R7919	JX-R	Off Cap Gris Nez	Probably 10(Jabo)/JG 54, Lt Otto-August Backhaus
9 April 43	Fw 190	1(P)	486	S/L D. J. Scott	EJ928		Off Etretat	
				F/L H. N. Sweetman	R8881	SA-R		Spitfires also claim two and AA one; losses were:
				F/L A. E. Umbers	EJ969	SA-A		10(Jabo)/JG 54 Uffz Karl Heck; 6/JG 26 Ofw Kurt
				F/O I. D. Waddy	R8684	SA-B		Kruska; 5/JG 26 Uffz Horst-Günther Winter
9 April 43	Fw 190	1	609	F/L E. Haabjoern	DN360	PR-A	Strait of Dover	
14 April 43	Bf 109	1	486	S/L D. J. Scott	DN596	SA-I	Off Pointe de Barfleur	Uffz Detlef Walter
				F/S R. H. Fitzgibbon	R8781	SA-H		
14 April 43	Bf 109	1	257	F/O C. W. Henman	R8680	FM-I	S Portland	
14 April 43	Bf 109	1(P)	257	P/O S. J. Khin	R8661	FM-J	S Portland	
16 April 43	Bf 109	1	486	Shared by 8 pilots			Le Havre	
16 April 43	Bf 109	1(P)	197	F/L R. J. Hyde	DN264	OV-G	Off Fécamp	
16 April 43	Fw 190	1(P)	197	F/O J. Turton	DN363	OV-B	Off Fécamp	
29 April 43	Bf 109	1	486	F/O A. H. Smith	DN428	SA-L	20 m S Isle of Wight	Bf 109G-4s of 4(F)/123; '7+', WNr 14773;
29 April 43	Bf 109	1	486	P/O F. Murphy	EJ969	SA-A	20 m S Isle of Wight	Lt E. Senzbach; '2+'. WNr 14764, Fw W. Quante
14 May 43	He 111	1	609	F/O R. Van Lierde	DN547	PR-S	NW Blankenberge	
15 May 43	Bf 109	1	195	Sgt R. Hough	DN389	JE-F	N Southwold	
23 May 43	Fw 190	1	1	F/S W. H. Ramsey	R8752	JX-L	29 m S Rye	AA also claimed three Fw 190s; II/SKG 10 lost two Fw 190s
25 May 43	Fw 190	1	486	S/L D. J. Scott	EJ928		30 m S Brighton	Spitfires also claim five Fw 190s and AA four in two raids; SKG 10 lost four Fw 190s
30 May 43	Fw 190	1	257	F/S B. C. J. Calnan	DN276	FM-C	Guernsey	Spitfires also claim four Fw 190s; SKG10 lost 2
1 June 43	Fw 190	2	609	F/L J. C. Wells	DN586	PR-N	Off Broadstairs	Only known loss 'R' of II/SKG 10, WNr 52524,
1 June 43	Fw 190	3	609	F/O I. J. Davies	DN367	PR-E	Off Broadstairs	Uffz O. Zügenrücher
24 June 43	Fw 190	1	486	S/L D. J. Scott	EJ981	SA-F	Off Somme estuary	
24 June 43	Fw 190	1	486	F/L A. E. Umbers	EK119	SA-H	Off Somme estuary	
15 July 43	Fw 190	1	486	S/L D. J. Scott	EJ981	SA-F	Off Le Havre	
				P/O R. H. Fitzgibbon	DN332	SA-D		
15 July 43	Fw 190	1	486	P/O A. N. Sames	R8699	SA-S	Off Le Havre	
15 July 43	Fw 190	1(P)	486	F/L A. E. Umbers	EJ973	SA-B	Off Le Havre	
15 July 43	Fw 190	1(P)	486	P/O F. Murphy	DN369	SA-C	Off Le Havre	
23 July 43	Bf 109	1(P)	198	F/O A. R. F. Jonas			12 m SE Dunkirk	
30 July 43	Bf 109	1	609	F/L E. Haabjoern	EK321		Zandvoort	
30 July 43	Bf 109	1	609	F/O R. Van Lierde	EK187		Zandvoort	
15 Aug 43	Fw 190	1	266	F/S D. Erasmus	EJ917		Guipavas	
28 Aug 43	Fw 190	1	609	S/L P. G. Thornton-Brown	JP582	PR-N	S Verneuil	
28 Aug 43	Fw 190	1	609	F/L J. R. Baldwin	JP583	PR-A	S Verneuil	
11 Sept 43	Hs 126	1	609	P/O T. D. L. Leslie	JP678	PR-O	Juvincourt	
14 Sept 43	Bf 109	1	197	P/O W. C. Ahrens	JP546	OV-D	40 m S St. Catherine's Point	'12+' of 4(F)/123, WNr 19194; Oblt F. Wittmer
				F/S R. Shelton	DN325	OV-C		
3 Oct 43	Fw 190	1	183	F/L W. Dring	JP402	HF-P	Channel	
3 Oct 43	Fw 190	1	183	F/O J. E. Mitchell	JP427		Channel	
4 Oct 43	Bf 109	1	609	F/L J. R. Baldwin	JP909		Juvincourt/Laon	
4 Oct 43	Bf 109	1	609	Sgt L. L. Henrion	JP662	PR-L	Juvincourt/Laon	
4 Oct 43	Bf 110	1	609	F/O C. J. C. Demoulin	JP851	PR-Q	Florennes	
5 Oct 43	Fi 156	1	247	F/L C. E. Brayshaw	JP910	ZY-H	Boissets	
5 Oct 43	Fi 156	1	247	F/O P. A. Chappell	JP581	ZY-V	Boissets	
5 Oct 43	Ju 88	1	609	F/L R. Van Lierde	JP909		Laon/Soissons	
5 Oct 43	Ju 88	1	609	P/O L. W. F. Stark	JP659	PR-S	S Soissons	
7 Oct 43	Fw 190	1	198	S/L J. M. Bryan		TP-X	SE Thielt	
				F/L V. Fittall	JP727	TP-Y		
15 Oct 43	Fw 190	1	266	F/O N. J. Lucas	JP906	ZH-L	40 m SSE Start Point	Fw 190A-4 'Schwarz 11', WNr 694; Oblt V. Klein,
15 Oct 43	Fw 190	1	266	F/O N. J. Lucas	JP906	ZH-L	40 m SSE Start Point	and Fw 190A-3 'Schwarz 9', WNr 367;
				Sgt D. Drummond	EJ934	ZH-C		Oblt H. Sell, both of NAGr 13
15 Oct 43	Fw 190	1	257	F/O S. J. Khin	JP447	FM-C	Poulmic	
				F/S D. C. J. Calnan	JP799			
16 Oct 43	Ju 88	1	609	S/L P. G. Thornton-Brown	R8845		Brétigny	
				F/L J. R. Baldwin	JP909			
16 Oct 43	Ju 88	1	609	S/L P. G. Thornton-Brown	R8845		Brétigny	
				F/L L. E. Smith	JP924			
16 Oct 43	Me 410	1	609	F/L L. E. Smith	JP924		Brétigny	
				P/O C. F. J. Detal	JP917			
21 Oct 43	Fw 190	1	1	F/O J. W. Wiley	JP961	JX-U	15 m off St-Aubin	
				F/S J. D. Fairburn	JP795			
1 Nov 43	Ju 52	1	197	P/O E. O'Callaghan	JP844	OV-F	Forêt l'Evêque	
2 Nov 43	Ju 88	1	609	P/O L. W. F. Stark	JP659	PR-S	15 m NE Paris	
2 Nov 43	Bu 133	1	609	P/O G. L. C. F. Jaspis	JP924		15 m NE Paris	
2 Nov 43	Fw 190	1(P)	198	F/O W. G. Eagle		TP-E	Off Le Tréport	

Date	Type	No.	Sqn	Pilot	Aircraft		Location	Identity of Victim where known
30 Nov 43	Fw 190	1	198	S/L J. M. Bryan		TP-X	Deelen	
30 Nov 43	Fw 190	1	198	F/L V. Fittall	JP670	TP-V	Deelen	
30 Nov 43	Fw 190	1	198	F/O C. R. Abbott		TP-G	Deelen	
30 Nov 43	Fw 190	1	198	F/O J. F. Williams		TP-J	Deelen	
30 Nov 43	Ju 188	1	198	F/L V. Smith		TP-D	8 m NE Deelen	
30 Nov 43	Bf 110	1	609	F/L R. Van Lierde	JR378		Hasselt, Belgium	
1 Dec 43	Ju 52	1	266	F/O S. J. P. Blackwell	JP906	ZH-L	NW Ile de Groix	
1 Dec 43	Ju 88	1	193	F/O J. A. Pressland(½)	JR211	DP-L	Cap Chèvre	
			266	F/O J. D. Miller(¼)	JR135			
				F/L J. H. Deall(¼)	JP856			
1 Dec 43	Ju 88	1	266	S/L P. W. Lefevre	JP846	ZH-G	Ile de Groix	
				F/O S. J. P. Blackwell	JP906	ZH-L		
				F/O W. V. Mollet	JR289	ZH-C		
				F/S I. O. Hulley	JP934			
1 Dec 43	Bf 109	1	609	W/O G. K. E. Martin	JP909		Brussels	
1 Dec 43	Fw 190	1	198	S/L J. R. Baldwin		TP-X	Harskamp, Arnhem	
1 Dec 43	Fw 190	1(P)	198	F/S J. Stanley	JP727	TP-Y	Near Arnhem	
4 Dec 43	Do 217	1	198	S/L J. R. Baldwin		TP-X	Eindhoven	
4 Dec 43	Do 217	1	198	F/L V. Fittall	JP670	TP-V	Eindhoven	
				F/O C. R. Abbott		TP-E		
4 Dec 43	Do 217	1	198	F/O K. F. C. Bowman	JP727	TP-Y	Eindhoven	
				F/O J. F. H. Williams		TP-J		
4 Dec 43	Do 217	1	198	F/O H. Freeman	JP666	TP-N	Eindhoven	
				F/O J. MacDonald	JR371	TP-R		
4 Dec 43	Do 217	1	609	S/L P. G. Thornton-Brown	R8845		Eindhoven	
4 Dec 43	Do 217	1	609	S/L P. G. Thornton-Brown	R8845		Eindhoven	
				F/O A. S. Ross	JR364	PR-G		
4 Dec 43	Do 217	1	609	F/O A. S. Ross	JR364	PR-G	Eindhoven	
4 Dec 43	Do 217	1	609	F/O A. S. Ross	JR364	PR-G	Eindhoven	
				Sgt L. L. Henrion	JP909			
4 Dec 43	Do 217	1	609	F/O L. E. J. M. Geerts	JR312	PR-D	Eindhoven	
4 Dec 43	Do 217	2	609	P/O C. F. J. Detal	JP851	PR-Q	Eindhoven	
25 Dec 43	Fw 200	1	183	S/L W. Dring	JR128	HF-S	Kerlin Bastard	
				F/L R. Hartley	JR145	HF-A		
				F/O C. N. Walley	JR183	HF-W		
30 Dec 43	Ju 52	1	266	F/O N. J. Lucas	JP969	ZH-D	10 m W Ile de Groix	
				F/O W. V. Mollet		ZH-L		
2 Jan 44	Fw 190	1	609	F/O L. E. J. M. Geerts	JR429	PR-D	40 m W Charleville	
2 Jan 44	Fw 190	1	198	S/L J. R. Baldwin		TP-Z	W Paris	
2 Jan 44	Bu 131	1	198	F/L R. Dall		TP-P	Paris	
				F/L J. Scambler		TP-W		
2 Jan 44	Me 210	1	198	F/L J. Niblett		TP-H	St-Quentin	
				F/O P. D. L. Roper		TP-A		
3 Jan 44	Bf 109	1	198	F/L R. Curtis			Compiègne	
3 Jan 44	Fw 190	1	609	F/O C. F. J. Detal	JP851	PR-Q	Cambray/Epinoy	
4 Jan 44	Do 217	1	609	F/L I. J. Davies	JR379	PR-A	Gilze-Rijen	
4 Jan 44	Do 217	1	609	F/O C. F. J. Detal	JP976		Gilze-Rijen	
4 Jan 44	Do 217	1	609	F/O W. F. Watts	JR312		Gilze-Rijen	I/KG 2 lost four Do 217s
4 Jan 44	Do 217	1	609	F/O L. E. J. M. Geerts	JR429	PR-D	Gilze-Rijen	
				F/L L. W. F. Stark	JP659	PR-S		
4 Jan 44	Do 217	1	198	F/S J. S. Fraser-Petherbridge			Gilze-Rijen	
8 Jan 44	Twin Eng	1	121W	W/C R. T. P. Davidson			Soissons	
			245	P/O K. J. A. Dickie				
8 Jan 44	Ju 88	1(P)	174	F/L F. A. Grantham	JR241		Villaroche	
				F/S G. J. Steel	JR133			
10 Jan 44	Ju 88	1	609	F/O G. L. C. F. Jaspis	JP976		Melsbroek	
13 Jan 44	Ju 88	1	198	F/L R. Dall		TP-P	4 m W St-Léger	
13 Jan 44	Ju 88	1	198	F/O J. MacDonald	JR371	TP-R	N La Roche Guyon	
13 Jan 44	Ju 88	1	198	F/O G. Plamondon		TP-W	3 m E Septeuil	
13 Jan 44	Ar 96	1	198	F/L R. Dall		TP-P	Near St-Cyr en Arthies	
				F/O J. MacDonald	JR371	TP-R		
				F/O G. Plamondon		TP-W		
				W/O J. Allan		TP-T		
13 Jan 44	Goeland	1	198	S/L J. R. Baldwin		TP-Z	15 m S Poix	
13 Jan 44	Goeland	1	198	S/L J. M. Bryan		TP-C	Poix	
13 Jan 44	Bf 109	1	198	F/L J. Niblett		TP-H	Near Rosières	
13 Jan 44	Bf 109	1	198	S/L J. M. Bryan		TP-C	Near Rosières	
				F/O H. Freeman		TP-G		
21 Jan 44	Bf 109	1	198	F/L G. E. Cassie			Lannion airfield	
				F/O J. A. Inglis				
21 Jan 44	Bf 109	1	266	S/L P. W. Lefevre	JP846	ZH-G	Lannion airfield	
23 Jan 44	Fw 190	1	266	S/L P. W. Lefevre	JP846	ZH-G	2 m SE Gael airfield	
				F/L J. H. Deall	JP856			
				F/L A. V. Sanders	JP962			
				P/O G. M. R. Eastwood	JP934			
24 Jan 44	Bf 109	3	198	F/O W. G. Eagle			30 m N Ameland	

Date	Type	No.	Sqn	Pilot	Aircraft		Location	Identity of Victim where known
27 Jan 44	Goeland	1	609	P/O L. W. F. Stark	JP659	PR-S	SSE Brussels	
27 Jan 44	Bf 109	1	609	F/O C. F. J. Detal	JR443	PR-M	Brussels	
27 Jan 44	Bf 110	1	609	F/O C. F. J. Detal	JR443	PR-M	Evère	
29 Jan 44	Fw 200	1	124W	W/C E. Haabjoern	JR449	EH	E Châteaudun	
			247	F/O A. S. Aitchison	JP649	ZY-Z		
				F/O K. B. Sellick	JR521	ZY-B		
				P/O R. S. Colquhoun	JP785	ZY-X		
29 Jan 44	Do 217	1	257	F/O J. N. P. Arkle	JP507	FM-M	Fécamp	
				F/O T. Clift				
				F/O D. A. Porter	JP975	FM-P		
				W/O J. Wood	JR151	FM-K		
29 Jan 44	Bu 131	1	257	F/O J. N. P. Arkle	JP507	FM-M	Paris	
29 Jan 44	Bu 131	1	257	W/O J. Wood	JR151	FM-K	Paris	
30 Jan 44	Fw 190	2	198	S/L J. R. Baldwin			Rouen/La Roche	
30 Jan 44	Fw 190	2	198	F/L J. Niblett			Rouen/La Roche	
30 Jan 44	Fw 190	2	198	F/O J. F. Williams			Rouen/La Roche	III/JG 2 lost four Fw 190s; Stab/JG 2 lost Hpt Fritz
30 Jan 44	Fw 190	2	198	W/O J. Stanley			Rouen/La Roche	Edelmann 10/JG 2 lost Hpt Bernhard Scheikbier
30 Jan 44	Fw 190	1	198	F/S R. C. A. Crouch			Rouen/La Roche	
	Fw 190	1(P)	198	F/S R. C. A. Crouch			Rouen/La Roche	
30 Jan 44	Fw 190	2	609	F/O C. J. G. Demoulin	JR379	PR-A	S Gisors	
30 Jan 44	Fw 190	1	609	P/O L. W. F. Stark	JR429	PR-D	S Gisors	
8 Feb 44	Fw 190	1	Hwbr	W/C E. R. Baker			Gael	
8 Feb 44	Fw 190	1	193	F/L P. H. Beake			Gael	
9 Feb 44	Do 24	1	266	F/O N. J. Lucas	JP925	ZH-J	Near Evreux	
				F/O J. D. Miller	JP941			
9 Feb 44	Bf 109	1	266	P/O D. Erasmus	JP938		SE Chartres	
10 Feb 44	Fw 190	1	Hwbr	W/C E. R. Baker	JP941		Brétigny	
10 Feb 44	Do 217	1	Hwbr	W/C E. R. Baker	JP941		Brétigny	
10 Feb 44	Ju 88	1	266	F/L J. H. Deall	JR135		Brétigny	
10 Feb 44	Yale	3	266	F/O D. McGibbon	JP512		Villacoublay	
12 Feb 44	Do 217	1	263	S/L G. B. Warnes	JR440		5 m S Gael	
12 Feb 44	LeO 451	1	198	F/L J. Niblett			Near Arras	
12 Feb 44	LeO 451	1	198	F/O H. Freeman			Near Arras	
13 Feb 44	Bf 109	1	263	S/L G. B. Warnes	JR389	HE-K	NW Chartres	
24 Feb 44	LeO 451	1	3	P/O R. Dryland	JR314		Near Louvain	
				F/S R. W. Cole	JP534			
				F/S R. W. Pottinger	JP744			
26 Feb 44	Bf 110	1	198	F/L R. A. Lallemant			Off Dunkirk	Ofw. Helmut Vincke of IV/NJG1
				F/O G. E. A. Hardy				
26 Feb 44	Ju 88	1	609	F/O G. L. C. F. Jaspis	MN231		Near Fruges	
26 Feb 44	Fi 156	1	245	F/L J. W. H. Wilson			10 m NW Laval	
				F/O D. Maxwell				
29 Feb 44	Ju 188	1	609	Shared by 6 pilots			Villaroche	
29 Feb 44	Ju 188	1	609	Shared by 5 pilots			Villaroche	
16 Mar 44	Ju 188	1	175	P/O W. Cross	JR319		Villaroche	
16 Mar 44	Bf 108	1	175	F/L H. Davies			S Fontainebleau	
16 Mar 44	Ar 96	1	174	F/L F. A. Grantham	JR310		N Etampes	
16 Mar 44	Ar 96	1	174	P/O G. J. Steel	JP451		N Etampes	
				W/O R. C. Hayes	JP608			
31 Mar 44	Me 410	1	263	F/L G. G. Racine	MN170		Morlaix	
6 April 44	Ju 88	1	266	P/O G. M. R. Eastwood	MN150		Rennes	
				F/S J. O. Hulley	MN234			
18 April 44	Me 410	1	263	F/S J. Thould			S Brétigny	
18 April 44	Do 217	1	263	F/L J. Rutter			NW Villaroche	
				F/O J. H. Purkis				
				P/O F. Green				
				F/S W. A. Handley				
18 April 44	Ju 188	½	266	F/L A. V. Sanders	MM953		Southampton estuary	Ju 188E-1 Z6+EM of 2/KG 66, WNr 260523
				F/S D. H. Dodd	JR183			
				(shared with AA Command)				
29 April 44	LeO 451	1	193	F/L A. S. Ross			Near Lisieux	
			257	F/O D. A. Porter	MN381			
				P/O B. J. Spragg	MN492			
18 May 44	Bf 109	1	136W	W/C J. M. Bryan	MN415		Pontoise/Gisors	
			183	F/L F. H. Pollock	MN265			
18 May 44	Bf 109	1	183	F/L F. H. Pollock	MN265		Pontoise/Gisors	
			164	F/L A. G. Todd	MN177	FJ-T		
				F/S L. Plows	EJ958	FJ-C		
29 May 44	Bf 109	2	183	F/O A. R. Taylor	JR390	HF-U	40 m S Isle of Wight	
6 June 44	Fw 190	1	164	S/L P. H. Beake	DN432	FJ-F	8 m E Caen	
6 June 44	Fw 190	1	164	Shared by Squadron			Bayeux area	
8 June 44	Bf 109	1	164	F/L A. G. Todd	MN130	FJ-Y	10-15 m S Caen	
				F/S R. J. M. Wilson	MN419			
23 June 44	Bf 109	1	609	F/L E. R. A. Roberts	MN322		Lisieux-Evreux	
23 June 44	Bf 109	1(P)	609	F/O R. S. Royston	JP659		Lisieux-Evreux	
29 June 44	Bf 109	2	146W	W/C J. R. Baldwin			Near Conches	

Date	Type	No.	Sqn	Pilot	Aircraft		Location	Identity of Victim where known
29 June 44	Bf 109	1	193	F/L A. S. Smith			Near Conches	
29 June 44	Bf 109	1	193	F/O W. M. J. Bulleid			Near Conches	
29 June 44	Bf 109	1	193	F/S G. A. Gough			Near Conches	
11 July 44	Bf 109	1	198	F/L G. Plamondon	MN546	TP-S	W Caen	
13 July 44	Bf 109	1	146W	W/C J. R. Baldwin			S Lisieux	} I/JG 5 Lt Dieter Sachse
13 July 44	Bf 109	1	257	F/S A. Shannon		FM-H	S Lisieux	
13 July 44	Bf 109	1(P)	257	F/S M. E. Marriot		FM-J	S Lisieux	
19 July 44	Bf 109	1	266	P/O I. H. Forrester	MN361		3 m N Lisieux	I/JG 5
25 Sept 44	Fw 190	1(P)	182	F/L E. T. Brough			Near Kleve	
26 Sept 44	Bf 109	1(P)	175	F/L H. Ambrose	MN358	HH-U	Arnhem-Apeldoorn	
26 Sept 44	Ju 88	1	439	F/O J. H. Stitt	MN379	5V-E	N Arnhem	
27 Sept 44	Bf 109	1	438	F/O H. G. Upham	PD476	F3-E	E Nijmegen	
5 Dec 44	Bf 109	1	182	S/L G. J. Gray			15 m S Münster	
				F/S R. Lockyer				
8 Dec 44	Fw 190	1	181	F/L H. R. Isachsen			W Dummer See	
25 Dec 44	Fw 190	1	193	F/O W. M. J. Bulleid			Coesfeld	
27 Dec 44	Fw 190	1	182	S/L G. J. Gray			4 m E St-Vith	
				Lt J. I. A. Watt				
27 Dec 44	Fw 190	1	440	F/L D. E. Jenvey			5 m SE St-Vith	
29 Dec 44	Fw 190	1	168	Shared by 7 pilots			SW Steinfurt	
29 Dec 44	Fw 190	1	439	F/O R. H. Laurence	RB233		8 m NW Coesfeld	
29 Dec 44	Bf 109	1	439	F/O R. H. Laurence	RB233		8 m NW Coesfeld	
31 Dec 44	Fw 190	1	137	P/O R. A. Egley	MN198	SF-L	NW Osnabrück	
31 Dec 44	Fw 190	1	247	F/O T. R. Jackson	JP538	ZY-H	Petershagen	
1 Jan 45	Fw 190	1	168	F/L H. P. Gibbons	MN486	QC-D	Eindhoven	
1 Jan 45	Fw 190	1	198	F/L F. B. Lawless	MN951	TP-A	Euskirchen	
1 Jan 45	Fw 190	2	439	F/O A. H. Fraser	RB281		Near Deurne	
1 Jan 45	Fw 190	1	439	F/O R. H. Laurence	RB233		Near Deurne	
	Fw 190	1(P)	439	F/O R. H. Laurence	RB233		Near Deurne	
14 Jan 45	Bf 109	1	184	W/O A. J. Cosgrove	JR525	BR-M	SW Münster	
22 Jan 45	Bf 109	1	168	F/L E. C. H Vernon-Jarvis	JP920		S Münster	
23 Jan 45	Ju 188	1	168	S/L L. H. Lambert	MN265		Twente	
				F/O J. B. C. Catterns	EK140	QC-K		
				F/O P. B. Noble	RB376			
14 Feb 45	Bf 109	1	193	F/L J. H. Hilton			NE Grave	
				F/O R. W. G. Austin				
				W/O K. R. Goodhew				
14 Feb 45	Me 262	1	439	F/L L. C. Shaver	MN144		20 m N Coesfeld	} 9K+BN, Oblt Hans-Georg Richter, and 9K+HN,
14 Feb 45	Me 262	1	439	F/O A. H. Fraser	RB281		20 m N Coesfeld	Fw Werner Witzmann, both of 5/KG(J)51
22 Feb 45	Ju 88	1	182	F/L T. Entwistle			NNE Hamm	
				F/L D. Murray				
				F/O W. J. Boots				
				F/O I. Ladely				
1 Mar 45	Bf 109	1(P)	245	P/O R. N. M. Brown			Bocholt area	
				F/S J. E. Adam				
26 April 45	Me 262	1	263	F/L W. J. Fowler			2 m NE Niebull	
				P/O J. W. Shellard				
				W/O H. Barrie				
2 May 45	Ju 188	1	181	F/L B. N. E. Ford-Coates			Near Eutin	
				Sgt C. J. Boon				
2 May 45	Ju 188	1*	182	S/L J. Derry			Lübeck	
2 May 45	e/a	1	184	P/O J. H. Whaley	RB408		S Lübeck	
2 May 45	Fw 44	1	439	F/L J. H. Cook	RB477		Near Schönberg	
2 May 45	Fi 156	1	439	F/L J. O. Gray	SW524		Near Schönberg	
3 May 45	Bv 138	1	193	Shared by 12 pilots			Off Fehmarn	

*This Ju 188 was taking off from an airfield; it is not known if it was airborne.

Enemy aircraft claimed as destroyed or probably destroyed by Tempest pilots

Date	Type	No.	Sqn	Pilot	Aircraft		Location	Identity of Victim where known
8 June 44	Bf 109	1	150W	W/C R. P. Beamont	JN751	R-B	N Rouen	
8 June 44	Bf 109	1	3	F/L A. R. Moore	JN753		N Rouen	
8 June 44	Bf 109	1	3	P/O G. A. Whitman	JN743	JF-P	N Rouen	
29 Sept 44	Fw 190	1	56	S/L D. V. C. Cotes-Preedy	EJ721	US-C	Emmerich area	
29 Sept 44	Fw 190*	1	56	F/L A. R. Moore	EJ741	US-M	Emmerich area	
29 Sept 44	Fw 190	2	56	F/O D. E. Ness	EJ533	US-E	Emmerich area	
29 Sept 44	Fw 190	1(P)	56	F/O J. J. Payton	EJ578	US-I	Emmerich area	
30 Sept 44	Bf 109	1	486	F/L S. S. Williams	EJ715		Didam	
2 Oct 44	Fw 190	1	122W	W/C R. P. Beamont	EJ578	US-I	Nijmegen area	

*Later down-graded to 'Probable' and shared with P/O K. Watts (EJ522, US-F).

Date	Type	No.	Sqn	Pilot	Aircraft		Location	Identity of Victim where known
6 Oct 44	Fw 190	1	56	P/O A. S. Miller	EJ522	US-F	N Nijmegen	
6 Oct 44	Fw 190	1	56	F/S L. Jackson	JN867	US-H	N Nijmegen	
13 Oct 44	Me 262	1	3	P/O R. W. Cole	JN868		Grave	9K+FL of I/KG(J) 51, Uffz Edmund Delatowski
3 Nov 44	Me 262†	1(P)	122W	W/C J. B. Wray	EJ750	JBW	Venraj-Geldern	Believed to be from 3/Kdo Nowotny, Uffz Willi Banzhoff, which was lost to fighters
19 Nov 44	Me 262	1(P)	486	F/L K. G. Taylor-Cannon	JN858		Rheine	
				P/O O. D. Eagleson	EJ828			
26 Nov 44	Ju 188	1	486	F/L K. G. Taylor-Cannon	EJ606		Münster area	
				F/L S. S. Williams	EJ577			
26 Nov 44	Ju 188	1(P)	486	P/O J. Steedman	JN869		Münster area	
28 Nov 44	He 219	1	56	F/L A. R. Moore	EJ536	US-B	Münster area	I/NJG 1, Lt Kurt Fischer
28 Nov 44	He 219‡	1(P)	56	Shared by 5 pilots			Münster area	
3 Dec 44	Me 262	1	80	F/O J. W. Garland	EJ722		4 m S Rheine	9K+BH of I/KG(J) 51, Oblt Joachim Valet
8 Dec 44	Fw 190	1	56	F/O K. Watts	EJ522	US-F	N Rheine	
8 Dec 44	Bf 109	1	80	F/L J. M. Weston	EJ713	W2-K	Bielefeld area	
11 Dec 44	Bf 109	1	56	S/L P. R. St. Quintin	EJ700	US-O	Near Rheine	
11 Dec 44	Bf 109	1	56	P/O H. Shaw	EJ548	US-G	Near Rheine	
14 Dec 44	Bf 109	1	56	F/L J. D. Ross	EJ780	US-D	S Rheine	
14 Dec 44	Bf 109	1	56	F/O D. E. Ness	EJ552	US-A	S Rheine	
14 Dec 44	Bf 109	1	56	P/O H. Shaw	EJ548	US-G	S Rheine	
17 Dec 44	Me 262	1	122W	W/C J. B. Wray	EJ750	JBW	Near Wesel	9K+BP of II/KG(J) 51, Lt Wolfgang Lübke
17 Dec 44	Bf 109	1	3	F/S M. J. A. Rose	EJ777		Scahle	
17 Dec 44	Bf 109	1	56	F/L A. R. Moore	EJ778	US-M	NE Münster	
17 Dec 44	Bf 109	1	56	F/L A. R. Moore	EJ778	US-M	Grave	} Believed to be aircraft of II/JG 27
				F/L J. D. Ross	JN864	US-E		
17 Dec 44	He 219	1	56	F/L J. D. Ross	EJ804	US-I	Münster airfield	I/NJG 1
				P/O H. Shaw	EJ548	US-G		
17 Dec 44	Bf 109	1	56	F/L J. D. Ross	JN864	US-E	Grave	}
				P/O H. Shaw	EJ548	US-G		
17 Dec 44	Bf 109	1	56	F/O K. Watts	EJ522	US-F	Grave	} Believed to be from JG 27
				F/S L. Jackson	EJ804	US-I		
17 Dec 44	Bf 109	1	56	F/S J. A. Bosely	EJ692	US-R	NE Münster	}
17 Dec 44	Bf 109	1	274	F/L W. J. Hibbert	EJ648		10 m SE Emmerich	} Believed to be aircraft of III/JG 3
17 Dec 44	Bf 109	2	274	F/L D. C. Fairbanks	EJ762		Burgsteinfurt & Dingen	}
24 Dec 44	Bf 109	1	3	F/L K. A. Thiele	JN817	JF-W	S Malmédy	}
24 Dec 44	Fw 190	1	3	F/O R. Dryland	EJ747		S Malmédy	} Believed to be from IV/JG 54
24 Dec 44	Fw 190	1	274	S/L E. D. Mackie	EJ688		Eindhoven	}
25 Dec 44	Me 262	1	486	F/O J. H. Stafford	EJ625		Aachen area	
				P/O R. D. Bremner	JN803	SA-D		
27 Dec 44	Fw 190	1	80	F/L R. W. A. MacKichen	EJ705	W2-X	5 m NW Rheine	
27 Dec 44	Fw 190	1	80	F/O D. S. Angier	EJ695		5 m NW Rheine	}
27 Dec 44	Fw 190	1	80	F/O J. W. Garland	EJ667		5 m NW Rheine	14/JG 54; four pilots KIA
27 Dec 44	Fw 190	1	80	W/O G. W. Dopson	EJ641		5 m NW Rheine	}
27 Dec 44	Bf 109	1	274	F/L J. Malloy	EJ781		Near Eusenkirchen	} Aircraft of II/JG 27
27 Dec 44	Bf 109	1	274	W/O E. Twigg	EJ707		7 m NE Düren	}
27 Dec 44	Fw 190	1	486	F/L E. W. Tanner	EJ541		Münster area	}
27 Dec 44	Fw 190	1	486	F/L K. G. Taylor-Cannon	EJ828		Münster area	
27 Dec 44	Fw 190	1	486	F/O K. A. Smith	EJ771		Münster area	10/JG 54 lost four
27 Dec 44	Fw 190	1	486	P/O S. J. Short	JN808	SA-N	Münster area	
27 Dec 44	Bf 109	1(P)	486	F/L E. W. Tanner	EJ541		Münster area	}
29 Dec 44	Fw 190	1	56	F/O W. R. MacLaren	EJ692	US-R	S Dummer See	}
29 Dec 44	Fw 190	1	56	F/O V. L. Turner	EJ579	US-Z	S Dummer See	Believed to be aircraft from 12/JG 54 and 7/JG
29 Dec 44	Fw 190	2	56	F/O J. J. Payton	EJ536	US-B	S Dummer See	}
29 Dec 44	Bf 109	1	3	F/L K. A. Thiele	JN817	JF-W	N Rheine	13/JG 27
1 Jan 45	Bf 109	1	3	F/O D. J. Butcher	EJ719		N Helmond	
				W/O D. R. Worley	EJ765	JF-T		
1 Jan 45	Bf 109	1	3	F/S M. J. A. Rose	EJ827		N Helmond	
1 Jan 45	Bf 109	1	56	F/O D. E. Ness	EJ536	US-B	Helmond area	
				P/O H. Shaw	EJ548	US-G		
1 Jan 45	Fw 190	2	80	F/O J. W. Garland	EJ774	W2-B	15 m N Münster	
1 Jan 45	Fw 190	2	486	S/L A. E. Umbers	EJ577		Helmond	
1 Jan 45	Fw 190	1	486	F/O W. A. L. Trott	EJ606		Venlo	
1 Jan 45	Fw 190	1	486	P/O J. G. Hooper	EJ750		Venlo	
1 Jan 45	Fw 190	1	486	P/O C. J. Sheddon	EJ748	SA-I	N Venlo	
4 Jan 45	Fw 190	1	3	F/L D. C. Fairbanks	EJ777		13 m NE Hengelo	Possibly from II/JG 26
4 Jan 45	Bf 109	1	56	F/L J. H. Ryan	EJ780	US-D	5 m S Osnabrück	
4 Jan 45	Bf 109	1	56	F/O D. E. Ness	EJ544	US-J	5 m S Osnabrück	
4 Jan 45	Fw 190	1	80	P/O N. J. Rankin	EJ633	W2-B	12 m NE Rheine	}
				F/S L. B. Crook	EJ830			Possibly from II/JG 26
4 Jan 45	Fw 190	1	80	F/O G. A. Bush	EJ691		12 m NE Rheine	}
14 Jan 45	Fw 190	1	3	F/L D. C. Fairbanks	EJ690		SW Gütersloh	
14 Jan 45	Bf 109	1	3	F/L D. C. Fairbanks	EJ690		SW Paderborn	
14 Jan 45	Fw 190	1	56	F/L J. H. Ryan	EJ544	US-J	SW Gütersloh	}
				P/O J. E. Hughes	EJ772	US-T		} IV/JG 3
14 Jan 45	Fw 190	1	56	F/O J. J. Payton	EJ548	US-G	SW Gütersloh	}

†Later down-graded to 'Damaged', despite possible actual loss. ‡Later down-graded to 'Damaged', which German records confirm to have been the case.

Date	Type	No.	Sqn	Pilot	Aircraft		Location	Identity of Victim where known
14 Jan 45	He 219	1	274	F/L H. A. Crafts	EJ762		4 m E Hamm	
14 Jan 45	Bf 109	1	486	F/O C. J. MacDonald	EJ755	SA-A	3 m N Münster	
14 Jan 45	Bf 109	1	486	W/O J. E. Wood	EJ748	SA-I	E Münster	
22 Jan 45	Bf 109	1	56	F/O W. R. MacLaren	EJ721	US-C	Neede area	
23 Jan 45	Fw 190	1	3	F/L J. S. B. Wright	EJ654	JF-N	10 m W Gütersloh	
23 Jan 45	Fw 190	1	3	F/O H. W. Longley	EJ700		10 m W Gütersloh	
23 Jan 45	Fw 190	2	3	F/O B. M. Vassiliades	EJ660		10 m W Gütersloh	
23 Jan 45	Me 262	1	56	F/L F. L. MacLeod	EJ663	US-S	Paderborn area	
				F/O R. V. Dennis	EJ778	US-M		
23 Jan 45	Fw 190	1	56	F/O W. R. MacLaren	EJ708	US-W	10 m NW Rheine	
23 Jan 45	Fw 190	1	56	F/O J. J. Payton	EJ804	US-I	10 m NW Rheine	
23 Jan 45	Bf 109	1	56	F/O V. L. Turner	EJ778	US-M	10 m NW Rheine	
23 Jan 45	Bf 109	1	80	S/L E. D. Mackie	EJ740		Bramsche	
23 Jan 45	Bf 109	1	80	F/L L. R. G. Smith	EJ705	W2-X	1 m NE Lengerich	
23 Jan 45	Bf 109	1	80	F/L D. Price	EJ663		Bramsche	
				P/O F. A. Lang	EJ705	W2-X		
23 Jan 45	Bf 109	1	80	F/L R. J. Holland	EJ665		10 m NE Achmer	
				F/O R. H. Anders	EJ640			
23 Jan 45	Fw 190	1	80	F/L A. Seager	EJ740		SW Gütersloh	
	Fw 190	1(P)	80	F/L A. Seager	EJ740		SW Gütersloh	
23 Jan 45	Fw 190	1	80	F/S L. B. Crook	EJ713	W2-K	E Bohmte	
23 Jan 45	Bf 109	1	80	F/S L. B. Crook	EJ713	W2-K	SW Gütersloh	
23 Jan 45	Bf 109	2	274	F/L G. Mann	EJ762		Gütersloh area	
23 Jan 45	Fw 190	1	274	F/L L. A. Wood	EJ814		Gütersloh area	
23 Jan 45	Fw 190	1	274	F/O C. G. Scriven	EJ771		Gütersloh area	
23 Jan 45	Bf 109	1	486	S/L A. E. Umbers	NV715		Rheine	
23 Jan 45	Bf 109	1	486	F/O J. H. Stafford	EJ706		Rheine	
				W/O A. H. Bailey	EJ750			
23 Jan 45	Fw 190	1(P)	486	F/O R. J. Danzey	NV715		Minden area	
24 Jan 45	Bf 109	1	80	F/L R. J. Holland	JN870	W2-F	2 m S Rheine	
24 Jan 45	Bf 109	1	80	F/L D. L. Price	EJ669		2 m S Rheine	
1 Feb 45	Fw 190	1	274	F/L W. J. Hibbert	NV722		Rheine area	
2 Feb 45	Bf 109	1	3	F/L J. S. B. Wright	EJ654	JF-N	Soltau	
2 Feb 45	Do 217	1	486	F/O R. D. Bremner	NV719	SA-E	S Paderborn	
				F/O J. H. Stafford	EJ523			
				P/O C. J. Sheddan	NV652	SA-K		
8 Feb 45	Fw 190	1	80	P/O R. S. E. Verran	EJ691		20 m SE Bremen	
8 Feb 45	Bf 109	1	274	F/O W. F. Mossing	EJ784		Rheine	⎫
8 Feb 45	Bf 109	1	274	F/O W. S. J. Stark	EJ751		NW Rheine	⎬ II/JG 27 lost two Bf 109s
8 Feb 45	Bf 109	1	274	F/O T. R. Sutherland	EJ764	JJ-E	NW Rheine	⎭
11 Feb 45	Me 262	1	274	S/L D. C. Fairbanks	NV645		Rheine airfield	Ar 234B of 1(F)/123, Hpt Hans Felden
14 Feb 45	Bf 109	1	80	P/O N. J. Rankin	EJ705	W2-X	10 m E Celle	
16 Feb 45	Bf 109	2	274	S/L D. C. Fairbanks	NV645		NE Hildesheim	
16 Feb 45	Bf 109	1	274	F/O W. F. Mossing	EJ801		NE Hildesheim	
21 Feb 45	Ju 88	1	274	F/L W. J. Hibbert	EJ771		S Steinhuder Lake	
22 Feb 45	Bf 109*	1	122W	W/C R. E. P. Brooker			Rheine area	
22 Feb 45	Fw 190	1	56	S/L P. R. St. Quintin	EJ708	US-W	Cloppenburg area	
22 Feb 45	Fw 190	2	274	S/L D. C. Fairbanks	EJ648		Rheine airfield	Fw 190Ds of III/JG 54
22 Feb 45	Bf 109	1	486	F/L J. H. Stafford	NV791	SA-L	S Münster	
22 Feb 45	Bf 109	1	486	F/O A. R. Evans	EJ714	SA-W	S Münster	
24 Feb 45	Fw 190	1	274	S/L D. C. Fairbanks	NV943		Plantlunne	
24 Feb 45	Ju 88	1	274	F/L R. C. Kennedy	NV639		5 m E Plantlunne	
				F/O W. F. Mossing	EJ801			
24 Feb 45	Bf 109	1	486	S/L K. G. Taylor-Cannon	NV706	SA-F	NE Bramsche	
24 Feb 45	Bf 109	1	486	F/L N. J. Powell	NV763	SA-U	NE Bramsche	
25 Feb 45	Bf 109	1	33	S/L I. G. S. Matthew	NV678		SW Rheine	⎫ I/JG 27
25 Feb 45	Bf 109	2	33	F/L C. L. Luckhoff	EJ880	5R-R	S Rheine	⎭
25 Feb 45	Bf 109	1	56	F/L F. L. MacLeod	EJ579	US-Z	15 m W Münster	⎫ Believed to be from 1/JG 27, including
25 Feb 45	Bf 109	1	56	F/O R. V. Dennis	EJ526	US-N	15 m W Münster	⎭ Oblt Max Winkler
25 Feb 45	Bf 109	1	222	F/L A. W. Bower	EJ886		S Rheine	I/JG 27
28 Feb 45	Si 204	1	3	F/L H. K. Hughes	NV923	JF-F	S Hildesheim	
				F/L J. A. McCairns	NV703			
28 Feb 45	Bf 109	1(P)	3	F/L H. K. Hughes	NV923	JF-F	S Hildesheim	
				F/L J. A. McCairns	NV703			
2 Mar 45	Fw 190	1	3	S/L R. B. Cole	NV775		Rheine area	
2 Mar 45	Bf 109	1	222	F/L V. W. Berg	EJ873	ZD-R	E Lingen	⎫
2 Mar 45	Bf 109	1	222	F/L L. McAuliffe	NV670	ZD-X	5 m E Lingen	⎬ IV/JG 27
2 Mar 45	Bf 109	1	222	F/O H. E. Turney	NV674	ZD-V	E Lingen	⎪
2 Mar 45	Bf109	1	222	F/L G. W. Varley	EJ882	ZD-E	5 m E Lingen	⎭
2 Mar 45	Ar 234	1	222	F/L G. W. Varley	EJ882	ZD-E	5 m E Lingen	Fl+QT of 9/KG(J) 76, Lt Eberhard Rögele
5 Mar 45	Bf 109	1	274	F/L P. H. Clostermann	EJ893	JJ-W	Hengelo area	
7 Mar 45	Fw 190	1	3	F/O B. M. Vassiliades	EJ755		Rheine area	
7 Mar 45	Fw 190	1	56	F/L J. J. Payton	EJ780	US-D	Twente-Rheine	
7 Mar 45	Bf 109	1	56	F/O V. L. Turner	EJ761	US-P	Twente-Rheine	
7 Mar 45	Fw 190	1	80	S/L E. D. Mackie	NV700		N Rheine	

*Apparently later down-graded to 'Damaged'.

Date	Type	No.	Sqn	Pilot	Aircraft		Location	Identity of Victim where known
14 Mar 45	Ar 234	1	222	F/L L. McAuliffe	NV774		N Quakenbrück	
				F/O D. G. C. McCleland	NV670	ZD-X		
22 Mar 45	Fw 190	1	56	F/L J. T. Hodges	EJ804	US-M	Hesepe area	
22 Mar 45	Fw 190	1	56	F/L G. B. Milne	NV786	US-E	Hesepe area	
22 Mar 45	Fw 190	1	56	F/O V. L. Turner	NV728	US-X	Hesepe area	
22 Mar 45	Fw 190	1	56	Sgt P. C. Brown	NV970	US-O	Hesepe area	Aircraft from II/JG 26, which lost three pilots KIA
22 Mar 45	Fw 190	1	80	F/L R. C. Cooper	NV983		Hesepe area	
22 Mar 45	Fw 190	1	80	F/O G. A. Bush	NV938		Hesepe area	
25 Mar 45	Bf 109	1	80	F/O W. R. Sheaf	EJ649	W2-Y	NE Wesel	
25 Mar 45	Bf 109	1	222	F/L R. P. Dashwood	NV939	ZD-H	Beckum	
25 Mar 45	Fw 190	1	222	F/L G. F. J. Jongbloed	NV972		2 m NE Haselunne	III/JG 54
25 Mar 45	Bf 109	1	222	F/L H. E. Turney	NV984	ZD-L	3 m E Beckum	
25 Mar 45	Fw 190	1	222	F/L G. W. Varley	NV757		SW Quackenbrück	III/JG 54
25 Mar 45	Fw 190	1	222	F/O W. Donald	NV756		SW Quackenbrück	
25 Mar 45	Bf 109	1	222	F/O G. W. Marshall	NV972		4 m E Beckum	
25 Mar 45	Bf 109	1	222	F/L W. G. Mart	SN187		Beckum	
				F/L H. E. Turney	NV984	ZD-L		
				F/O R. H. Reid	NV760			
26 Mar 45	Fw 190	1	33	S/L A. W. Bower	EJ886	5R-N	10 m SE Münster	III/JG 54, Ogfr Hansen and Uffz Flakowski
				F/S C. P. Nisbet	SN163			
26 Mar 45	Fw 190	1	33	F/O R. H. Brown	NV682		10 m SE Münster	
28 Mar 45	Bf 109	1(P)	80	F/L A. Seager	SN130		Osnabrück	
28 Mar 45	Bf 109	1(P)	80	P/O G. W. Dopson	EJ663		Osnabrück	
31 Mar 45	Ju 188	1	80	F/O K. Burton	EJ549	W2-S	W Dummer See	
				F/O G. A. Bush	NV982			
				F/L R. C. Cooper	SN139	W2-N		
				P/O G. W. Dopson	NV945			
2 April 45	Fw 190	1	56	F/L P. H. Clostermann	NV968	US-G	Vechta	
6 April 45	Fw 190	2	56	S/L R. W. A. MacKichan	NV974	US-K	Stolzenau area	
6 April 45	Fw 190	1	56	F/L J. J. Payton	NV987	US-R	Stolzenau area	
6 April 45	Fw 190	1	80	F/L R. C. Cooper	NV983		Hoya	
6 April 45	Fw 190	1	80	F/O L. Smith	SN139	W2-N	Hoya	
6 April 45	Ju 87	2	486	F/O C. J. Sheddan	EJ711	SA-Q	Stolzenau	
9 April 45	Bf 108	2	80	S/L E. D. Mackie	NV700		Fassberg	Camera-gun film identifies these as Ar 96 trainers
9 April 45	Bf 108	1	80	F/O W. R. Sheaf	NV938		Fassberg	
10 April 45	Fw 190	1	486	F/L W. E. Schrader	SN129	SA-M	Nienburg	
12 April 45	Fw 190	1	33	Capt E. D. Thompson	SN180	5R-V	Hamburg	
12 April 45	Fw 190	1	33	F/O D. J. ter Beek	NV754		Hamburg	Believed to be aircraft of I/JG 26
12 April 45	Fw 190	1	33	F/S P. W. C. Watton	NV783		Hamburg	
12 April 45	Fw 190	1	56	F/O D. E. Ness	NV963	US-C	5 m E Fassberg	
12 April 45	Ju 88	1	274	F/L J. D. Morrison	SN159		NE Fassberg	
				F/L D. M. Nichols	EJ876			
12 April 45	Fw 190	1	486	F/L J. H. Stafford	SN129	SA-M	E Ludwigslust	
14 April 45	Fw 190	1	486	F/O C. J. Sheddan	SN129	SA-M	N Ludwigslust	
14 April 45	Fw 190*	1	486	W/O W. J. Shaw	NV753	SA-J	Ludwigslust	
15 April 45	Ar 234†	1	56	F/L N. D. Cox	NV968	US-G	Kaltenkirchen airfield	
				F/L J. A. McCairns	NV786	US-E		
15 April 45	Fw 190	1	80	S/L E. D. Mackie	SN189		10 m SW Uelzen	
				Sgt W. F. Turner	NV700			
15 April 45	Fw 190	1	80	F/L A. Seager	SN172		8 m NW Celle	
15 April 45	Fw 190	1	486	F/L A. I. Ross	SN176	SA-N	SE Uelzen	
15 April 45	Fw 190	2	486	F/L W. E. Schrader	NV969	SA-A	SE Uelzen	
15 April 45	Fw 190	1	486	F/O A. R. Evans	NV988	SA-Y	Uelzen	
15 April 45	Fw 190	1	486	F/O B. J. O'Connor	SN129	SA-M	Uelzen	
15 April 45	Fw 190	1	486	W/O R. J. Atkinson	EJ739		Uelzen	
15 April 45	Fw 190	1	486	W/O G. Maddaford	EJ888		SE Uelzen	
15 April 45	Fw 190	1	486	F/S R. A. Melles	NV753	SA-J	Uelzen	
16 April 45	Ju 88‡	1	56	F/L F. L. MacLeod	NV927	US-Z	Neustadt airfield	
				F/O W. M. Wallis	EJ804	US-M		
16 April 45	Fw 190	1	80	F/L M. P. Kilburn	NV991		Pritzwalk area	
16 April 45	Fw 190	1	80	F/L R. B. Prickett	NV790		Pritzwalk area	
16 April 45	Fw 190	1	486	F/L C. J. Sheddan	SN129	SA-M	Neustadt	
				W/O W. J. Shaw	NV753	SA-J		
16 April 45	Fw 190	1	486	F/L W. E. Schrader	NV969	SA-A	Ludwigslust	
16 April 45	Fw 190	1	486	F/O J. W. Reid	EJ651		Ludwigslust	
17 April 45	Fw 190	1	80	Capt R. A. Henwick	NV964		Grevesmühlen	Believed to be aircraft from I/JG 26
17 April 45	Fw 190	1	80	F/O R. S. E. Verran	EJ691		4 m S Lübeck	
17 April 45	Ju 88	1	274	F/L R. C. Stockburn	SN179		Schleswig	
				Sgt J. Wilson	EJ893	JJ-W		
19 April 45	e/a	1	222	F/O G. Walkington	SN185		Husum	Believed to be He 162 of I/JG 1
20 April 45	Fw 190	2	3	F/L P. H. Clostermann	NV994	JF-E	Hamburg area	
21 April 45	Bf 109	1	486	S/L W. E. Schrader	NV969	SA-A	2 m W Schwerin	
21 April 45	Fw 190	1	486	F/O A. R. Evans	SN136		NE Wismar	Possibly from II/JG 26
23 April 45	Ju 188	1	274	F/S A. C. Inglis	EJ781		Eggebeck airfield	

*This claim was subsequently disallowed. †Although identified and credited as an Ar 234 by HQ, 2nd TAF, this claim was originally submitted for an Me 262. ‡Apparently this claim was subsequently credited by HQ, 2nd TAF as an He 111 'Damaged'.

Date	Type	No.	Sqn	Pilot	Aircraft		Location	Identity of Victim where known
23 April 45	Fw 190	2	274	F/S A. C. Inglis	EJ781		Eggebeck airfield	
25 April 45	Me 262	1	486	F/O K. A. Smith	EJ711	SA-Q	Lübeck airfield	
28 April 45	Ju 352*	1	486	F/L J. W. Reid	EJ697		W Plon	
				F/O O. D. Eagleson	SN136			
29 April 45	Bf 109	2	486	S/L W. E. Schrader	NV969	SA-A	Lauenburg area	
29 April 45	Fw 190	1	486	S/L W. E. Schrader	NV969	SA-A	Lauenburg area	
29 April 45	Bf 109	1	486	S/L W. E. Schrader	NV969	SA-A	Lauenburg area	Includes seven Fw 190s of 12/SG 151; Lt Ernst
				W/O N. D. Howard	EJ659			Orzegowski baled out; Fw Erhard baled out;
29 April 45	Fw 190	1	486	F/O J. W. Reid	EJ659		S Ratzeburg	Ogfr Fricke KIA, all in the Lauenburg area.
29 April 45	Fw 190	1	486	F/O O. D. Eagleson	SN176	SA-N	Lauenburg area	Possibly includes at least three Fw 190Ds of I and
29 April 45	Fw 190	1	486	F/O C. J. MacDonald	SN176	SA-N	S Ratzenburg	II/JG 26 – possibly the combat south of Ratzenburg
29 April 45	Fw 190	1	486	W/O J. R. Duncan	JN802	SA-Y	S Ratzenburg	
29 April 45	Fw 190	1	486	F/O A. R. Evans	SN136		Lauenburg	
29 April 45	Bf 109	1(P)	486	F/O A. R. Evans	SN136		S Bergedorf	
29 April 45	Fw 190	1	486	F/O C. S. Kennedy	JN802	SA-Y	Lauenburg area	
30 April 45	Bf 109	1(P)	3	S/L R. B. Cole	NV749		SW Lauenburg	
30 April 45	Fw 190	1	3	F/O J. T. Adams	SN212	JF-T	SW Lauenburg	
30 April 45	Ju 352	1	56	F/S A. M. L. Kennaugh	NV974	US-K	W Wismar	
				Sgt N. Willis	NV963	US-A		
1 May 45	Ju 88	1	3	F/L H. L. Longley	SN189	JF-R	Schwerin	
1 May 45	He 111	1	56	F/S A. M. L. Kennaugh	NV970	US-O	Schwerin	
				Sgt N. Willis	EJ804	US-M		
1 May 45	Bf 109	1	486	S/L W. E. Schrader	SN136		Bad Segeberg	
2 May 45	Fw 190	1	56	F/L R. V. Garton	NV987	US-R	NE Eutin	
2 May 45	Fi 156	1	56	F/L R. V. Garton	NV987	US-R	NE Eutin	
2 May 45	Fw 190	1	56	F/L F. L. MacLeod	NV927	US-Z	NE Eutin	
				Sgt N. Willis	SN137	US-B		
2 May 45	Fw 190	1	56	F/L J. Sowerbutts	NV965	US-S	NE Eutin	
2 May 45	Bv 138	1	56	W/O A. J. Brocklehurst	SN140	US-N	Eutin area	
				P/O P. F. Woodfall	SN137	US-B		
2 May 45	Ju 52W	1	56	F/S P. Tullie	EJ601	US-T	N Neustadt	
2 May 45	Fi 156	1	56	Sgt G. J. Swindells	NV987	US-R	5 m W Gruber	
2 May 45	e/a	1	486	S/L C. J. Sheddan	SN129	SA-M	Heiligenhafen	Described as a 4-engined flying-boat
				F/O D. J. Thomson	EJ659			
2 May 45	Fw 44	1	486	F/O O. D. Eagleson	SN176	SA-N	SE Schwerin	
2 May 45	Fi 156	1	486	F/O O. D. Eagleson	SN176	SA-N	SE Schwerin	
2 May 45	Fw 190	1	486	P/O W. J. Shaw	NV753	SA-J	S Neumünster	
				W/O N. D. Howard	EJ739			
2 May 45	Fi 156	1	486	P/O W. J. Shaw	NV753	SA-J	W Plon	
				W/O N. D. Howard	EJ739			
3 May 45	Fw 44	1	3	F/L H. K. Hughes	SN221		Kiel	
3 May 45	Fi 156	1	3	F/L H. K. Hughes	SN221		Schleswig	
3 May 45	Fi 156	1	3	F/L H. W. Longley	NV937	JF-J	Plon	
				W/O D. G. Saunders	SN166			
3 May 45	Fw 190	1	56	W/O A. J. Brocklehurst	SN140	US-N	12 m NE Lübeck	
3 May 45	Do 217	1	274	F/L J. A. Houlton	SN181		40 m SW Kiel	
3 May 45	Ju 88	1	486	F/L C. J. MacDonald	SN176	SA-N	NE Tegel	
3 May 45	Ju 88	1	486	W/O J. R. Duncan	JN802	SA-Y	NE Tegel	

*This claim was credited as a Ju 52.

The following aircraft are also believed to have been victims of Tempests:

10 Dec 44 Me 262 claimed as 'Damaged' by F/S L. Jackson, 56 Squadron (EJ522 US-F) – believed to be 9K + FL of I/KG(J) 51, Lt Walter Roth, lost in action on this date.

25 Dec 44 Ar 234 claimed as 'Damaged' by P/O R. S. E. Verran, 80 Squadron (EJ740), was Fl + DT of III/KG(J) 76, Lt Alfred Frank, which crash-landed in German-occupied Holland due to the damage inflicted and was written-off.

2 Mar 45 Ar 234, one of two claimed 'Damaged' by 222 Squadron (one by W/O T. B. Hannan, NV695 ZD-B, in the morning, or one shared by F/L G. W. Varley, EJ882 ZD-E and F/O R. A. Carson, NV670 ZD-X, in the afternoon) was Fl + ET of 9/KG(J) 76, Oblt Arthur Stark, which crash-landed at Lippstadt and was written-off.

11 April 45 Me 262 took off from Fassberg during a strafing attack by 222 Squadron, was seen to climb to 2,000 feet, on fire, and the pilot baled out; it may have been hit during the strafing by S/L E. B. Lyons (SN165 ZD-H).

Top Scoring Pilots

Most Successful Pilots in Aerial Combat, Flying Typhoons, 1942–45

	Nationality	Units	Individual Victories	Shared Victories	Destroyed on Ground	Probables
G/C J. R. Baldwin, DSO, DFC ✩	Brit	609, 198, 146 Wing	15	1(½)		
F/O C. F. J. Detal*	Belg	609	6	1(½)	1	
S/L R. Van Lierde, DFC✩†	Belg	609, 164	6		1	
S/L L. W. F. Stark, DFC ✩	Brit	609, 263, 164	5	1(½)	1	
S/L R. A. Lallemant, DFC	Belg	609, 198	4	1(½)	1	1
S/L J. Niblett, DFC*	Brit	198	4	1(½)	1	
P/O F. Murphy, DFC	NZ	486	4			1
F/L I. J. Davies, DFC	Brit	609	4			

*Killed on active service. †Also claimed forty V-1s while flying Tempests with 3 Squadron.

Most Successful Pilots in Aerial Combat, Flying Typhoons and Tempests

	Nationality	Units	Individual Victories: Typhoon	Tempest	Shared Victories: Typhoon	Tempest	Probables: Typhoon	Tempest	Shared Probables: Typhoon	Tempest	V-1s
S/L K. G. Taylor-Cannon, DFC ☆	NZ	486	2	2		1(½)					
S/L A. E. Umbers*	NZ	486	1	3	1(½)			2	1(½)		28

*Killed in Action.

Most Successful Pilots in Aerial Combat, Flying Tempests, June 1944–May 1945

	Nationality	Units	Individual Victories	Shared Victories	Destroyed on Ground	Shared on Ground	Probables	V-1s	Previous Victories
S/L D. C. Fairbanks, DFC ☆ ☆	US	3, 274	11 or 12		1	1		1	1
S/L W. E. Schrader, DFC ☆	NZ	486	9 .	1(½)	2				2½
F/L J. J. Payton, DFC	Brit	56	6				1	1	
W/C E. D. Mackie, DSO, DFC ☆	NZ	274, 80, 122 Wing	5	1(½)	3	2			16
F/O D. E. Ness, DFC	Can	56	5	1(½)				5	
S/L C. J. Sheddan, DFC	NZ	486	4	3(½, ½, ⅓)				7½	
F/L P. H. Clostermann, DFC ☆	Fr	274, 56, 3	4		App. 7				10
F/O A. R. Evans, DFC	NZ	486	4				1		
F/O J. Garland, DFC	Brit	80	4						
F/O V. L. Turner, DFC	Aus	56	4					2	
F/L A. R. Moore, DFC ☆	Brit	3, 56	3	1(½)				½	21½

Breakdown of Claims by Unit and Type: Typhoons

Unit	Bf 109	Fw 190	Do 217	Ju 88	Me 210/410	Bf 110	Me 262	Ju 188	Ju 52	Goeland	LeO 451	Bu 131	Bu 133	Fi 156	Yale	He 111	Hs 126	Fw 200	Ar 96	Fw 44	Do 24	Bv 138	Bf 108	u/i	Total
609	11:1*	28:6	11:1	7:0	1:0	3:0	–	2:0	1:0	1:0	–	–	1:0	–	–	1:0	1:0	–	–	–	–	–	–	–	68:8
198	7:1	19:3	5:0	3:0	1:0	1:0	–	1:0	–	1:0	–	–	–	–	–	–	–	–	1:0	–	–	–	–	–	39:4
266	3:0	10:1	1:1	4½:0	1:0	–	–	½:0	1:0	–	–	–	–	3:0	–	–	–	–	–	–	1:0	–	–	1:0	23:2
486	9:0	9:3	2:0	1:0	1:0	–	–	–	–	–	–	–	–	–	–	–	–	–	–	–	–	–	–	–	22:3
257	3:2	4:0	1:0	1:0	–	–	–	–	–	–	½:0	2:0	–	–	–	–	–	–	–	–	–	–	–	–	11½:2
439	1:0	4:1	–	1:0	–	–	2:0	–	–	–	–	–	1:0	–	–	–	–	–	1:0	–	–	–	–	–	10:1
193	5:0	2:0	–	½:0	–	–	–	–	–	–	½:0	–	–	–	–	–	–	–	–	–	1:0	–	–	–	9:0
1	–	5:0	–	–	2:0	–	–	–	–	–	–	–	–	–	–	–	–	–	–	–	–	–	–	–	7:0
183	3:0	2:0	–	–	–	–	–	–	–	–	–	–	–	–	–	–	–	1:0	–	–	–	–	–	–	6:0
263	1:0	–	2:0	–	2:0	–	1:0	–	–	–	–	–	–	–	–	–	–	–	–	–	–	–	–	–	6:0
168	1:0	2:0	–	–	–	–	–	1:0	–	–	–	–	–	–	–	–	–	–	–	–	–	–	–	–	4:0
182	1:0	1:1	–	1:0	–	–	–	1:0	–	–	–	–	–	–	–	–	–	–	–	–	–	–	–	–	4:1
164	1½:0	2:0	–	–	–	–	–	–	–	–	–	–	–	–	–	–	–	–	–	–	–	–	–	–	3½:0
247	–	1:0	–	–	–	–	–	–	–	–	–	–	–	–	2:0	–	–	½:0	–	–	–	–	–	–	3½:0
197	1:1	0:1	–	–	–	–	–	–	1:0	–	–	–	–	–	–	–	–	–	–	–	–	–	–	–	2:2
174	–	–	–	0:1	–	–	–	–	–	–	–	–	–	–	–	–	–	–	2:0	–	–	–	–	–	2:1
175	0:1	–	–	–	–	–	–	1:0	–	–	–	–	–	–	–	–	–	–	–	–	–	1:0	–	–	2:1
181	–	1:0	–	–	–	–	–	1:0	–	–	–	–	–	–	–	–	–	–	–	–	–	–	–	–	2:0
184	1:1	–	–	–	–	–	–	–	–	–	–	–	–	–	–	–	–	–	–	–	–	–	–	1:0	2:1
245	0:1	–	–	–	–	–	–	–	–	–	–	–	1:0	–	–	–	–	–	–	–	–	–	–	½:0	1½:1
3	–	–	–	–	–	–	–	–	–	–	1:0	–	–	–	–	–	–	–	–	–	–	–	–	–	1:0
56	–	–	–	1:0	–	–	–	–	–	–	–	–	–	–	–	–	–	–	–	–	–	–	–	–	1:0
137	–	1:0	–	–	–	–	–	–	–	–	–	–	–	–	–	–	–	–	–	–	–	–	–	–	1:0
195	1:0	–	–	–	–	–	–	–	–	–	–	–	–	–	–	–	–	–	–	–	–	–	–	–	1:0
438	1:0	–	–	–	–	–	–	–	–	–	–	–	–	–	–	–	–	–	–	–	–	–	–	–	1:0
440	–	1:0	–	–	–	–	–	–	–	–	–	–	–	–	–	–	–	–	–	–	–	–	–	–	1:0
Wg Cdrs	3½:0	2:0	1:0	–	–	–	–	–	–	–	–	–	–	–	–	–	–	½:0	–	–	–	–	½:0	–	7½:0
Totals:	54:8	94:16	23:2	20:1	8:0	4:0	3:0	7½:0	3:0	2:0	2:0	2:0	1:0	4:0	3:0	1:0	1:0	2:0	3:0	1:0	1:0	1:0	1:0	2:0	246½:27

*11:1 = 11 destroyed: 1 probable.

Breakdown of Claims by Unit and Type: Tempests

Unit	Bf 109	Fw 190	Me 262	Ar 234	He 219	Ju 88	Ju 188	Ju 52	Ju 352	He 111	Do 217	Fi 156	Bv 138	Ju 87	Fw 44	Ar 96	Si 204	u/i	Totals
486	14:2	33:1	2:1	–	–	2:0	1:1	–	1:0	–	–	2:0	–	2:0	1:0	–	–	1:0	59:5
56	18:0	30:1	1:0	1:0	2:1	1:0	–	1:0	1:0	1:0	1:0	1:0	1:0	–	–	–	–	–	59:2
80	10:2	22:1	1:0	–	–	–	1:0	–	–	–	–	–	–	–	–	3:0	–	–	37:3
274	14:0	9:0	1:0	–	1:0	4:0	1:0	–	–	–	1:0	–	–	–	–	–	–	–	31:0
3	9:2	12:0	1:0	–	–	1:0	–	–	–	–	2:0	–	–	–	1:0	–	1:0	–	27:2
222	9:0	3:0	–	2:0	–	–	–	–	–	–	–	–	–	–	–	–	–	1:0	15:0
33	3:0	5:0	–	–	–	–	–	–	–	–	–	–	–	–	–	–	–	–	8:0
Wg Cdrs	2:0	1:0	1:1	–	–	–	–	–	–	–	–	–	–	–	–	–	–	–	4:1
Totals:	79:6	115:3	7:2	3:0	3:1	8:0	3:1	1:0	2:0	1:0	2:0	5:0	1:0	2:0	2:0	3:0	1:0	2:0	240:13

Tempest Pilots Claiming 5 or more V-1 'Diver' Flying Bombs Shot Down

Wing Commander R. P. Beamont has advised that personal totals were not always accurately kept, although Unit and Wing Intelligence Officers subsequently sought to produce final listings. Totals quoted in decoration citations and personal logbooks do not always tally with those that can be arrived at from the (often incomplete) notations in Operational Record Books (F.540 and F.541); subsequent confirmations, assessment of shares with other units and commands, etc., also resulted in changes. Where totals differ, the alternative given in brackets is that gleaned from squadron diaries – the primary source.

	Nationality	Score	Squadrons		Nationality	Score	Squadrons
S/L J. Berry, DFC ✩✩	Brit	60⅓	FIU (52½), 501	W/O B. J. O'Connor, DFC	NZ	8½	486
S/L R. Van Lierde, DFC ✩	Belg	40 (36½)	3	F/O R. C. Deleuze	Fr	8	501
W/C R. P. Beamont, DSO, DFC ✩	Brit	32 (30)	150 Wing	W/O J. G. Hooper, DFC	NZ	8	486
F/L A. E. Umbers, DFC ✩✩	NZ	28 (15½)	3	W/O W. A. Kalka	NZ	8	486
F/O R. Clapperton, DFC	Brit	22	3	P/O K. A. Smith	NZ	8 (12)	486
F/S R. W. Cole, DFC	Brit	21⅔ (20½)	3	W/O J. H. Stafford, DFC	NZ	8	486
F/L A. R. Moore, DFC ✩	Brit	21½ (22½)	3	F/O S. S. Williams	NZ	8	486
F/S O. D. Eagleson, DFC	NZ	21 (20)	486	F/S B. M. Hall	NZ	7½	486
P/O R. Dryland, DFC	Brit	21 (15⅚)	3	W/O C. J. Sheddan, DFC	NZ	7½	486
F/O R. J. Cammock, DFC	NZ	20½	486	P/O R. B. Bremner	NZ	7	486
P/O K. Slade-Betts, DFC	Brit	20 (19)	3	F/O W. A. Hart, DFC	NZ	7	486
S/L J. H. McCaw	NZ	19½	486	F/O B. F. Miller (USAAF)	US	7	FIU (2), 501 (5)
P/O H. R. Wingate	Brit	17½ (18½)	3	F/O W. L. Miller	NZ	7	486
F/O J. R. Cullen, DFC	NZ	16	486	S/L A. S. Dredge, DSO	Brit	6 (5)	3
F/S M. J. A. Rose, DFC	Brit	12 (11)	3	P/O K. McCarthy	NZ	6	486
F/O R. E. Barckley, DFC	Brit	12 (11½)	3	P/O W. A. L. Trott, DFC	NZ	6	486
F/L L. R. J. Robb	Brit	12	FIU (9), 501 (3)	P/O L. G. Everson	Brit	5½ (6½)	3
F/S H. G. Bailey	Brit	11½	3	F/S J. K. Foster	Brit	5½	3
P/O R. J. Dansey, DFC	NZ	11	486	S/L A. R. Hall	Brit	5½	56
F/L H. N. Sweetman, DFC	NZ	10½	486	F/O H. M. Mason	NZ	5½	486
F/O E. L. Williams, DFC ✩ *	Brit	10	FIU (6), 501 (7)	F/O W. R. MacLaren	Brit	5½	56
P/O F. B. Lawless	NZ	10	486	F/S R. Pottinger	Brit	5½	3
P/O S. B. Feldman, DFC	US	9¾	3	F/S G. H. Wylde	Brit	5½	56
F/S H. Shaw	Brit	9½	56	F/L G. A. Whitman	Brit	5¼ (6¼)	3
F/L C. B. Thornton	Brit	9	FIU (6), 501 (3)	F/L G. L. Bonham	Brit	5	501
F/S D. V. MacKerras	Brit	8⅚ (9⅚)	3	F/O D. E. Ness, DFC	Can	5 (4)	56
P/O M. F. Edwards	Brit	8¾	3	F/L N. J. Powell	NZ	5	486
				F/S S. J. Short	NZ	5	486

*F/L E. L. Williams was a successful night-fighter pilot; he claimed five further V-1s while flying Mosquitoes with 605 Squadron for a personal total of fifteen.

Top left: The pilot of R7847 'ZH-N' of 266 Squadron was unable to retract the undercarriage when the engine failed on short finals for Ibsley. (F. Ziegler via C. Goss)

Left: Wearing the short-lived white-nose recognition markings, DN269 overshot the runway at Staverton and turned over. (RAFM)

Above: On 8 December 1942 R7846 'US-R' of 56 Squadron caught the slipstream of the preceding aircraft and in the ensuing spin the cockpit door came open. The pilot was unable to recover and baled out. (RAFM)

4. Losses

Included in the following list are all known incidents which involved the loss of a Typhoon or Tempest aircraft or its pilot. In many instances, particularly in the case of older airframes, or when the type was approaching obsolescence, aircraft which were reparable under normal circumstances were reduced to spares or scrapped; these have been included. There were, of course, many other crash-landings, or examples of severe battle damage, where the aircraft was repaired; these are not included.

The list has been compiled using all known official records available to researchers, plus additional material from private sources, notably pilots' flying log books. Many of the serial numbers quoted are not the same as those given for specific incidents in the Squadron Operations Record Books, some of which have proved notoriously unreliable in this respect. In these cases very careful cross-checks have been made and it is believed that this list reflects the true situation.

Space economies have made abbreviations necessary (see page 164); it should be remembered that behind many of these brief and bland statements lie stories of the utmost drama, involving injury or sacrifice. Pilot casualties have been categorized as killed (K), prisoner of war (PoW); many others were injured to a greater or lesser extent, but these are not identified in the tables. In addition, those who evaded capture are denoted by (E), and those who, in the last weeks of the war, were posted missing but are known to have been safe, either as an evader or a PoW, are marked (S). Units denoted by a number only are squadrons except those with four-digit numbers, which are flights.

Every effort has been made to check spellings of names and locations, but having detected many errors in the original sources it is quite possible that more remain to be discovered. Where it has not been possible to give a location for an incident, the intended target is given in brackets.

Typhoons

Date	Unit	Aircraft	Pilot	Circumstances
1 Nov 41	56	R7592 US-L	P/O J. F. Deck (K)	CO fumes, csd E. Harling
14 Feb 42	266	R7642	P/O G. S. Sherwood	e/f f/l Bottisham
8 Mar 42	266	R7637	P/O C. E. Lees (K)	spun in 400 yds E Duxford
27 Mar 42	Glst	R7625	n/k	csd on test
24 April 42	266	R7654	P/O N. N. Allen (K)	flew into grd Gt. Casterton
11 May 42	A&AEE	R7614	W/C M. G. Stevenson	csd on t/o Boscombe Down
28 May 42	609	R7647	P/O J. M. P. De Selys	e/f b/o near Ely
1 June 42	56	R7678	P/O R. H. Deugo	sdb Spits off Dover
1 June 42	56	R8199 US-E	Sgt K. M. Stuart-Turner (K)	sdb Spits off Dover
4 June 42	266	R7655	P/O J. J. R. McNamara	e/f f/l E Duxford
10 June 42	609	R7628	P/O R. Van Lierde	w/u Duxford
13 June 42	266	R7618	Sgt E. H. E. Welby (K)	csd in bad vis Welney
22 June 42	8MU	R7590	S/C M. V. S. Boucher	dila Little Rissington
26 June 42	609	R7710	F/L F. X. E. De Spirlet (K)	cld R7817 on t/o Duxford
26 June 42	609	R7817	P/O R. A. Lallemant	cld R7710 on t/o Duxford
29 June 42	266	R7672 ZH-X	P/O J. R. D. Menelaws	e/f f/l Duxford
29 July 42	257	R8633	P/O W. R. McDunnough (K)	s/f csd 2 m SW High Ercall
30 July 42	609	R7816	P/O H. L. Gilbert	e/f f/l Catwater Farm, Cambs
30 July 42	56	R7853 US-X	Lt E. Haabjoern	sdb Spits 10 m off Dungeness
1 Aug 42	609	R7883 PR-E	F/O R. E. J. Wilmet	h/f w/u Duxford
11 Aug 42	Hwkr	R7692	Mr K. G. Seth-Smith (K)	s/f csd Staines
18 Aug 42	56	R7644 US-B	Sgt J. S. Jones (K)	s/f csd near Spalding
19 Aug 42	266	R7813	P/O W. R. Smithyman (K)	last seen N Le Tréport
19 Aug 42	266	R7815 ZH-E	F/O R. N. L. Dawson (K)	sdb Spits 20 m S Dungeness
24 Aug 42	56	R7585	P/O R. H. Deugo	dila Duxford
26 Aug 42	Napr	R7694	n/k	csd on test
27 Aug 42	56	R7633 US-C	F/L A. V. Gowers	e/f f/l Oulton
28 Aug 42	56	R7648 US-T	F/S W. I. Mouat	dila Matlaske
29 Aug 42	9FPP	R7820	F/C L. D. Moss	dila Brockworth
5 Sept 42	1	R8690	Sgt A. E. Pearce	e/f f/l 4 m NE Longtown
15 Sept 42	266	R7645 ZH-B	P/O J. L. Spence (K)	e/f b/o 25 m off Cherbourg
15 Sept 42	266	R7847 ZH-N	Sgt S. N. J. P. Blackwell	e/f f/l Ibsley
16 Sept 42	266	R7814	–	hit by Spit Warmwell
20 Sept 42	56	R7652 US-W	Sgt F. W. Woodfall	dila Matlaske
27 Sept 42	181	R7676	F/L A. G. H. Lindsell (K)	spun in, Duxford
29 Sept 42	257	R8711 FM-X	P/O D. R. Kenward	hit GCI on app Bolt Head
30 Sept 42	182	R7629	P/O F. D. Cotton	dila Martlesham Heath
1 Oct 42	56	R7711 US-M	P/O N. A. Wright	dila Coltishall
2 Oct 42	486	R8683	P/O R. I. Phillips (K)	mis over Channel (Le Havre)
12 Oct 42	266	R8864	P/O J. D. Miller	dila at night Warmwell
16 Oct 42	486	R8698	Sgt D. B. Clark	e/f csd Battle
21 Oct 42	1	R7861	P/O P. N. Dobie (K)	cld? R7867 4 m off Amble
21 Oct 42	1	R7867	Mr P. E. G. Sayer[1] (K)	cld? R7861 4 m off Amble
23 Oct 42	609	R8812 PR-K	P/O R. Dopere (K)	csd in bad vis Battle
24 Oct 42	266	R7695 ZH-Z	Sgt P. D. Audley (K)	s/f csd Glanvilles Wooton
25 Oct 42	486	R8814	F/S J. Pearce (K)	e/f spun in, Willesborough
27 Oct 42	266	R8823	Sgt N. Borland	dila Warmwell
31 Oct 42	609	R7708 PR-V	P/O R. H. Payne	hbAA dtd Pegwell Bay
31 Oct 42	486	R8701	F/O L. V. Weir (K)	csd 6 m S Selsey Bill cnk
31 Oct 42	486	R8801	P/O R. J. Dale	dila Tangmere
4 Nov 42	56	R7702 US-N	Sgt J. R. Isherwood	e/f f/l Matlaske
5 Nov 42	609	R7818	F/S S. H. Spallin (K)	hit b/c csd Dover Harbour
8 Nov 42	266	R7819 ZH-S	Sgt D. C. Borland	e/f w/u Warmwell
9 Nov 42	1	R7868	P/O T. G. Bridges	hit by R8630 on grd Acklington
13 Nov 42	182	R7691	S/L T. P. Pugh	tbto csd Martlesham Heath
21 Nov 42	1	R7862	F/O C. H. Watson	e/f f/l near Charterhall
21 Nov 42	5FPP	DN251	F/C W. Mason (K)	csd in bad vis Banbury, Shropshire
24 Nov 42	486	R7866	Sgt L. Walker	e/f f/l Durrington
28 Nov 42	266	R7687 ZH-Q	P/O G. G. Osborne (K)	csd near Rufus Stone
29 Nov 42	257	R8650 FM-N	P/O J. F. McEwan	dila Exeter
8 Dec 42	56	R7846 US-R	P/O N. A. Wright	b/o in spin Fordham
15 Dec 42	609	R7689 PR-B	F/O H. D. F. Amor (K)	sdb Fw190 off Ramsgate
15 Dec 42	257	R8663 FM-C	Sgt J. C. Mumford	e/f f/l Chilframe
18 Dec 42	486	R8800	Sgt R. W. Penny (K)	sdb Do217 10 m SE Shoreham
20 Dec 42	9FPP	DN269	P/O J. M. Cathey	dila Staverton
20 Dec 42	195	DN302	Sgt T. Webster	dila Hutton Cranswick
22 Dec 42	257	R8872 FM-R	Sgt G. A. Butt	e/f f/l near Exeter
23 Dec 42	609	R8837	Sgt A. P. N. Davies (K)	csd 15 m S S. Foreland, cnk
8 Jan 43	486	R8941	Sgt P. C. Fisher	dila Tangmere
9 Jan 43	56	R7679 US-N	P/O O. Pavla	e/f f/l Saxthorpe
11 Jan 43	266	R8802	F/L J. C. Thompson (PoW)	g/lk F? f/l near Guicamp
13 Jan 43	56	R8865 US-T	F/O A. G. H. Rouse (K)	sdbF Kijkduin, 's

Date	Unit	Aircraft	Pilot	Circumstances
				Gravenhage (claimed by Flak as Hurricane, SW Den Haag 0946 hrs)
13 Jan 43	56	R8876 US-M	S/L A. C. Johnston (PoW)	sdbF NE Haarlem (claimed as Hurricane by Flak NE Haarlem 0956 hrs)
13 Jan 43	245	DN532	P/O C. G. Kennerley (K)	s/f csd 2 m S Calne
15 Jan 43	18MU	R8226	F/L F. M. Paul	e/f f/l Craigs Marsh
17 Jan 43	56	R7854	Sgt F. A. Sullivan (K)	s/f csd Brinton
17 Jan 43	245	DN312	P/O D. H. Gross	e/f f/l Beach-Bitton
18 Jan 43	609	R8815 PR-C	F/O R. A. Lallemant	e/f f/l Swingate
18 Jan 43	609	R8898 PR-F	F/O G. Evans	t/a Bradwell Bay
20 Jan 43	56	R8822	P/O B. G. McKenzie	cld DN433 csd Blickling
20 Jan 43	56	DN433	P/O D. J. Coleman (K)	cld R8822 csd Blickling
22 Jan 43	182	R8839 XM-S	F/S B. F. Gilland	tbto csd Ridgewell
23 Jan 43	195	DN306	Sgt R. A. Hough	e/f f/l Maltby le Marsh
24 Jan 43	257	R8637 FM-D	P/O T. Clift	dila Zeals
24 Jan 43	197	DN365	P/O A. S. N. Gould (K)	csd in bad vis Lochwinnoch?
27 Jan 43	183	DN243	F/L W. Dring	dila Sherburn-in-Elmet
28 Jan 43	197	DN364	Sgt C. F. Beechey (K)	s/f csd E. Linton
2 Feb 43	266	R7821	Sgt E. V. Horne (K)	csd Morebath
3 Feb 43	266	R7686 ZH-E	F/O C. R. M. Bell (K)	e/f dtd 15 m S Torquay
4 Feb 43	193	DN510	P/O A. W. Kilpatrick	s/f csd Meavy
7 Feb 43	266	R7800 ZH-K	S/L C. L. Green	e/f f/l Bolt Head
7 Feb 43	609	R8838 PR-N	F/O P. J. Nankivell (K)	sdb Fw190 S Dixmude
7 Feb 43	266	DN359	–	hit by DN262 on ground Exeter
9 Feb 43	1	DN241	Sgt E. Crowley	dila Southend
12 Feb 43	778[2]	DN419	n/k	n/k
13 Feb 43	266	R7715 ZH-R	Sgt J. Hawarth	e/f w/u Exeter
13 Feb 43	1	R7864 JX-Y	Sgt R. W. Hornall	e/f f/l Danehill
13 Feb 43	182	R8221	F/O S. A. McMane	hit b/c f/l 4 m S Salisbury
14 Feb 43	609	R7872 PR-S	Sgt J. Wiseman (K)	sdb Fw190s off Cap Gris Nez
14 Feb 43	609	DN294 PR-O	F/S A. Haddon (K)	sdb Fw190s off Cap Gris Nez
14 Feb 43	183	DN297	F/L W. Dring	dila Church Fenton
14 Feb 43	197	DN313	P/O R. Bokobza (K)	csd 4 m S East Fortune
14 Feb 43	197	DN366	Sgt J. Bowler (K)	csd E Ferresay
15 Feb 43	193	DN310	P/O R. B. Dunsmuir (K)	spun in, Kingston Halt
16 Feb 43	DFlt	DN422	F/L M. J. Gray	csd on t/o Sawbridgeworth
16 Feb 43	198	DN439	W/O W. L. Mount	csd on t/o Acklington
18 Feb 43	195	EJ909	Sgt J. Lindsey	e/f f/l near Woodvale
19 Feb 43	181	R8880	F/L P. S. C. Lovelace (K)	lost in fog off Hook of Holland
20 Feb 43	266	R8743 ZH-B	F/O F. M. Furber	e/f dtd 15 m SE Torquay
21 Feb 43	183	DN278	Sgt D. A. Napier	e/f f/l Barkston
21 Feb 43	245	DN468 MR-D	Sgt K. J. A. Dickie	t/a Peterhead
24 Feb 43	486	R8682 SA-A	F/S R. H. Fitzgibbon	tbto hit Lanc R5665 Tangmere
24 Feb 43	486	R8816 SA-J	F/S E. Preston	csd avoiding R8682 Tangmere
24 Feb 43	56	DN411	Sgt K. Jenner (K)	spun in off Winterton
25 Feb 43	195	R8760	Sgt G. W. Dopson	comp-air bottle expl in flt
25 Feb 43	193	DN470	F/S E. A. MacKay	dila Harrowbeer
26 Feb 43	198	R7653	F/S W. Freitag	f/l csd Acklington throttle u/s f/l
28 Feb 43	266	R8772	Sgt C. W. Baillie	Whimple

Date	Unit	Aircraft	Pilot	Circumstances
28 Feb 43	257	DN295 FM-T	F/L C. M. Burfield (K)	e/f csd 5 m E Colerne
1 Mar 43	486	R8706 SA-U	Sgt M. O. Jorgensen	e/f f/l Sidlesham
1 Mar 43	247	DN445	Sgt J. H. Berry	efto f/l near High Ercall
6 Mar 43	1	R8942	Sgt H. R. Frazer (K)	cld DN615 csd Benenden
6 Mar 43	1	DN615	P/O G. C. Whitmore (K)	cld R8942 csd Glassenbury
6 Mar 43	182	R8842	F/O N. Snowdon	e/f f/l 2 m SW Andover
7 Mar 43	182	DN247	S/L T. P. Pugh	t/a Middle Wallop
7 Mar 43	183	DN271 HF-M	Sgt T. Narishkin (K)	csd near Weston Turville
8 Mar 43	257	EJ916 FM-M	F/L R. S. Miller (K)	csd on t/o Warmwell
9 Mar 43	181	R8742 EL-A	Sgt G. R. Hadley	e/f w/u Cheddington
9 Mar 43	609	R8810 PR-R	S/L R. P. Beamont	e/f f/l near Deal
9 Mar 43	6FPP	DN446	Cpt G. N. Wickner	e/f w/u Henlow
9 Mar 43	195	DN474	Sgt F. H. Jones	csd on app Woodvale
9 Mar 43	609	DN481	Sgt N. Booth (K)	s/f csd near Ash
11 Mar 43	198	R8935 TP-R	Sgt K. F. C. Bowman	e/f f/l Radcliffe
11 Mar 43	183	DN405 HF-T	F/L W. Dring	e/f f/l Slapton
14 Mar 43	486	R8744 SA-M	F/S R. H. Fitzgibbon	rof f/l Tarring Neville
15 Mar 43	56	DN374 US-A	S/L T. H. V. Pheloung	hbF b/o 35 m off Happisburgh
19 Mar 43	1	DN335	P/O C. H. Watson	dila Lympne
19 Mar 43	247	DN444	Sgt Q. M. Shippee (K)	spun in, Madeley
21 Mar 43	266	DN486 ZH-M	Sgt C. W. Baillie	rof f/l near Bovey Tracey
24 Mar 43	486	EJ956 SA-I	F/S W. Mawson (PoW)	hbF f/l Cany-Barville
25 Mar 43	609	DN560	F/O J. R. Baldwin	sdb Fw190 off Ramsgate
27 Mar 43	182	DN602	Sgt R. L. H. Dench	e/f f/l Blandford Camp
29 Mar 43	1	R7876	F/O C. L. Bolster (K)	psdb e/a 40 m S Beachy Head
29 Mar 43	609	R8888 PR-Y	Sgt H. W. Jackson (K)	e/f csd near Manston
1 April 43	198	DN299	Sgt C. J. R. Ansell (K)	e/f csd 5 m SW Dover
1 April 43	609	DN619	W/O T. W. Barker (K)	sdbF near Dunkirk
3 April 43	195	DN440 JE-T	Sgt G. R. Simpson	e/f f/l Mona
3 April 43	247	DN534 ZY-E	F/S D. Archibald (K)	dtd 7 m S Portland
5 April 43	266	R7882	Sgt D. C. Borland	dila Exeter
6 April 43	609	DN416 PR-P	Sgt E. J. Van Zuylen (K)	e/f dtd SE Dover
8 April 43	195	DN336 JE-N	F/O Z. Nantwich	f/l w/u Woodvale
9 April 43	195	DN424	Sgt W. A. Dixon (K)	cld r/w signal Burscough
10 April 43	56	R7714	Sgt F. Nettleton (PoW)	sdbF off Ijmuiden
10 April 43	56	R8799 US-P	P/O R. S. Birks (K)	e/f csd 40 m off Yarmouth
10 April 43	197	DN309 OV-W	Sgt D. H. Clennel (K)	sdbF Aire
12 April 43	56	R7739	F/O V. G. Poulter (K)	spun in, 3 m E Oulton
13 April 43	175	EJ947	F/O K. N. Wilson	dila Colerne
15 April 43	266	R8861	Sgt D. S. Peters (K)	csd in sea 3 m S Bolt Hd, cnk
15 April 43	247	DN431 ZY-V	F/S R. R. Campbell (K)	sdb Fw190s? (Triqueville)
15 April 43	56	DN489 US-F	F/O C. T. Stimpson	hbF off Holland nr
16 April 43	609	R7855 PR-D	Sgt R. W. Aitken-Quack	dila Manston
16 April 43	182	R8834 XM-M	F/O N. Snowdon (K)	sdbF Triqueville
16 April 43	486	R8881 SA-R	F/L H. N. Sweetman	f/l after d/f Selsey
16 April 43	195	DN373 JE-J	P/O W. McGurgan (K)	e/f f/l near Warton
16 April 43	175	EK138	Sgt H. E. Hare	dila Filton
17 April 43	266	R8811 ZH-D	Sgt G. M. R. Eastwood	sdb Spit 4 m ESE Exeter
17 April 43	56	DN478 US-U	F/O E. N. Cluderay (K)	e/f b/o 90 m NE Cromer
17 April 43	174	DN504	–	t/a Gravesend

Date	Unit	Aircraft	Pilot	Circumstances
17 April 43	245	DN507 MR-?	F/L R. J. McNair	t/a Gravesend
18 April 43	59OTU	R8867	W/C F. Aitkens	tbto csd Milfield
18 April 43	182	R8930	F/O A. Lowey	hbF csd near Fairlop
18 April 43	197	DN376	P/O M. L. Soors	e/f f/l near Tangmere
22 April 43	197	DN545 OV-J	Sgt E. H. Fletcher (K)	spun in, Bognor Regis
23 April 43	56	DN317 US-C	P/O L. Cramer	dila Matlaske
25 April 43	182	R8924 XM-E	F/O D. I. Vize (K)	sdbF Hesdin
27 April 43	56	R8873 US-W	Sgt D. A. Hind	e/f f/l 2 m SW Matlaske
28 April 43	1	R8634 JX-P	Sgt H. Bletcher	e/f f/l Pevensey
28 April 43	56	R8825 US-Y	Sgt A. P. McNicol	cld DN265 f/l N. Walsham
28 April 43	182	R8893 XM-M	Sgt H. D. Houghton (K)	csd in low attack Hardelot
28 April 43	56	DN265 US-B	Sgt D. Driscoll (K)	s/f csd Buxton-Lamas
28 April 43	3	DN609	Sgt E. K. Ticklepenny	e/f f/l Laindon
30 April 43	609	R8883 PR-K	P/O M. L. Van Neste (K)	csd in sea 3 m ESE Dover cnk
30 April 43	266	R8937 ZH-L	Sgt A. G. Henderson	e/f f/l near Topsham
2 May 43	1DFlt	R7624	F/S K. K. Cox	e/f f/l 1 m W Ouston
2 May 43	56	R8721 US-X	W/O J. K. Allen	dila Matlaske
2 May 43	182	DN261 XM-L	P/O W. H. Else	e/f f/l 4 m S Basingstoke
3 May 43	197	DN537 OV-S	Sgt E. S. Lavery	e/f f/l near Tangmere
3 May 43	266	EJ932 ZH-N	F/O I. Munroe (K)	s/f csd 4 m S Exeter
4 May 43	174	EK186 XP-A	F/O J. W. Reynolds (K)	s/f csd near Redhill
5 May 43	197	DN388	P/O G. S. M. Pearson	efto w/u Tangmere
7 May 43	245	DN311 MR-A	F/S J. D. Flyn	e/f w/u West Malling
7 May 43	197	DN407 OV-Q	Sgt J. R. Hill (K)	spun in, Patcham
11 May 43	197	DN473 OV-E	P/O H. M. S. Patullo	e/f b/o 5 m SE Selsey Bill
13 May 43	182	R8931 XM-X	F/L E. R. Baker	hbF f/l near Ford
14 May 43	183	R8944	P/O G. Berrisford (PoW)	rof dtd? near Cherbourg
14 May 43	245	DN599 MR-D	F/O R. H. Milnes	e/f b/o 5 m E Winterton-on-Sea
15 May 43	195	DN389 JE-F	Sgt R. A. Hough	dam by Bf109 off Southwold
16 May 43	486	EJ969 SA-A	F/O A. A. Brown (K)	hbF b/o off Le Havre
16 May 43	195	EK214 JE-DT	Sgt G. M. Carr	e/f w/u Ludham
17 May 43	A&AEE	R8809	G/C H. A. Purvis	e/f f/l Oaklands Hill
17 May 43	197	DN333 OV-K	F/S W. C. Laing	tbto w/u Tangmere
18 May 43	3	R8835 QO-M	F/O L. G. Gill (K)	sdb Bf109s SSW Abbeville
18 May 43	3	R8879 QO-D	Sgt V. Bailey (K)	sdb Bf109s (Poix)
18 May 43	3	R8979 QO-N	F/O D. R. Hall (K)	sdbF Metigny
18 May 43	3	DN246 QO-A	F/S F. K. Whitall (K)	sdb Bf109s (Poix)
18 May 43	3	DN598 QO-Z	F/O R. Inwood (K)	sdb Bf109s (Poix)

Date	Unit	Aircraft	Pilot	Circumstances
				(7 claims for the above aircraft submitted by I/JG27 – Hpt Steinmann (1), Lt Wünsch (2), Oblt von Lieres (1), Uffz Schanz (1), Uffz Döring (1), Uffz Wiese (1))
18 May 43	247	EJ977 ZY-H	F/O A. H. Burton (K)	s/f csd Fairlop
18 May 43	175	EK171 HH-Z	Sgt O. R. Kelstick	e/f csd Weston-super-Mare
19 May 43	1	R7863	P/O E. A. Glover (PoW)	sdbF near St-Omer
20 May 43	59OTU	R8709	F/L M. C. Knight (K)	efto csd near Milfield
21 May 43	RAE	R8635	F/L L. A. Martin	e/f f/l Meadfoot Bay
22 May 43	18MU	EK216	W/O H. J. Marson	e/f f/l near Dalbeattie
23 May 43	197	DN559 OV-Y	–	hit by R8227 on t/o Tangmere
26 May 43	198	DN438	P/O R. R. Walters (K)	csd in sea off St. Anne's
28 May 43	247	DN430 ZY-B	F/L C. E. Brayshaw	tbto csd Fairlop
29 May 43	486	DN303 SA-X	F/S D. Bennet	e/f F? f/l St. Helens, IoW
1 June 43	609	DN360 PR-A	F/L E. Haabjoern	hbF off Dutch coast w/u Manston
2 June 43	1	R8752 JX-L	F/S W. H. Ramsey	hbF w/u Lympne
2 June 43	181	R8877	Sgt K. Doan	e/f f/l near Appledram
2 June 43	3	EK227 QO-D	F/O R. E. Barckley (E)	sdbF N Menin
9 June 43	3	DN409 QO-O	F/O B. S. Lumsden	efto w/u Manston
10 June 43	609	DN582 PR-P	Sgt R. J. Bryan	e/f f/l N. Foreland
10 June 43	198	EK142	Sgt R. E. Broad	csd on t/o Martlesham Heath
12 June 43	198	DN587	P/O G. R. Abbot	e/f b/o off Harwich
13 June 43	59OTU	R7580	Sgt A. V. Jones (K)	spun in near Milfield
13 June 43	182	R8928 XM-H	Sgt D. H. Castle	tbto w/u Manston
15 June 43	59OTU	DN557	Sgt R. J. Mclean	efto csd Milfield
16 June 43	1	R7919 JX-R	F/L L. S. B. Scott	dam by Fw190 dila Lympne (claimed by Lt Hoppe II/JG26 mid-Channel 0530 hrs)
16 June 43	3	DN498 QO-C	Sgt E. K. Ticklepenny	hbF dtd 10 m N Cap Gris Nez
16 June 43	1	DN585	P/O S. P. Dennis (PoW)	sdb Fw190 near Douai (claimed by Lt Kehl II/JG26 SE Arras 0534 hrs)
17 June 43	59OTU	R7621	Sgt R. Street	dila Milfield
17 June 43	266	R7915 ZH-E	F/O H. A. Cooper	e/f b/o 25 m SE Start Point
17 June 43	182	DN484	W/O D. K. Lovell	e/f f/l near Findon
18 June 43	3	EK167 QO-D	P/O W. H. Moore (K)	ftr Brugge

Below: On 18 April 1943 Flying Officer Alan Lowey nursed his Flak-damaged Typhoon back from France only to suffer an engine failure in the circuit at Fairlop; he was thrown clear, unharmed, when R8930 stalled and crashed on the airfield boundary. (D. J. Coxhead)

Below: R8825 'US-Y' of 56 Squadron was an indirect victim of structural failure when it was struck by pieces of DN265 which broke up during a formation flight on 28 April 1943. The pilot of DN265 was killed, but R8825's baled out successfully. (RAFM)

Date	Unit	Aircraft	Pilot	Circumstances
19 June 43	266	R7829 ZH-A	P/O R. K. Thompson	e/f w/u Exeter
19 June 43	245	DN293 MR-C	P/O K. Clift (K)	spun in, Pagham Harbour
19 June 43	175	EK184	P/O G. D. Cockbone (K)	ftr (Dieppe)
20 June 43	198	DN435	Sgt J. Blackie (K)	csd Little Bealings
20 June 43	56	EK174 US-C	S/L T. H. V. Pheloung (K)	sdbF csd 15 m W Den Haag
21 June 43	266	EJ931	P/O N. V. Borland	e/f b/o 12 m S Berry Head
21 June 43	182	EK195	W/O J. A. Allen	hbF near Les Hayons nr
26 June 43	59OTU	R7630	Sgt K. V. Bailey	dila Milfield
26 June 43	182	R8931 XM-N	F/S H. W. J. Henry	dila Appledram
27 June 43	3	EJ964 QO-G	Sgt E. K. Ticklepenny (K)	hit b/c csd Dover Harbour
29 June 43	3	EJ961 QO-H	P/O R. M. Purdon (K)	sdbF Dunkirk
1 July 43	3	R8946 QO-L	F/O A. T. Little (K)	sdb Fw190s off Hook of Holland
1 July 43	197	DN357 OV-Q	S/L A. H. Corkett (PoW)	e/f b/o near Poix
1 July 43	175	DN408	F/S O. R. Kelsick	hbF Poix b/o over Channel
1 July 43	266	DN479	F/O D. McGibbon	e/f w/u Exeter
1 July 43	3	DN589 QO-A	P/O C. G. Benjamin (K)	sdb Fw190s off Hook of Holland
1 July 43	3	EJ970 QO-M	Sgt F. Lawrence (PoW)	sdb Fw190s off Hook of Holland (4 claims for the 3 Sqn aircraft above by Lt Wurmheller and Ofw Knappe of III/JG2, and Hpt Bühligen and an unknown pilot of II/JG2)
3 July 43	195	DN315 JE-A	F/S T. H. McGovern	hbF Bergen nr
3 July 43	56	JP392	F/S R. G. Gravett (K)	sdbF near Leiden (claimed by Flak at 1253 hrs)
6 July 43	56	DN447 US-V	F/S J. K. Clusas (K)	sdb Fw190s off Yarmouth
6 July 43	1	EJ982	P/O C. H. Watson	csd on t/o Lympne
6 July 43	195[3]	EK273 JE-DT	W/C A. C. Rabagliati (K)	hbF b/o 60 m off Yarmouth
7 July 43	3	EK217 QO-N	Sgt G. A. Whitman	dila Tangmere
7 July 43	183	JP404	F/O E. Gottowt (K)	spun in near Harrowbeer
8 July 43	3	DN253 QO-T	F/O J. L. Foster	dila at night Manston
8 July 43	609	DN586 PR-N	F/O I. J. Davies	efto w/u Manston
8 July 43	247	EK224 ZY-B	F/O R. W. Lornie (K)	sdbF 4 m SE Vlissingen (claimed by Flak SE Vlissingen 1643 hrs)
8 July 43	195	JP405 JE-B	F/S F. S. Vause (K)	csd Potter Heigham
9 July 43	266	R8804 ZH-J	F/O F. M. Furber (PoW)	hbF dtd off St-Brieuc
10 July 43	245	JP432 MR-?	S/L S. S. Horden	e/f f/l near New Romney
11 July 43	198	EJ966	P/O W. I. Mouat (PoW)	sdb Bf109s Zaffelare
13 July 43	Napr	EJ984	n/k	csd on test
13 July 43	183	JP388	F/S G. F. Gillman	dam by Fw190 dila Harrowbeer
15 July 43	181	R8866	P/O E. A. Haddock (PoW)	ftr (Poix)
15 July 43	1	EK228	P/O J. M. Chalifour (K)	s/f csd Paddlesworth
16 July 43	56	DN535 US-M	F/S C. C. Harborne	dila Matlaske
18 July 43	197	DN371 OV-I	Sgt L. S. Clark	e/f b/o 1 m off Newhaven
20 July 43	198	JP486	F/L R. H. Deugo (K)	sdbF Ypres-Menin
23 July 43	197	JP426 OV-Q	P/O G. K. Hignell (K)	ftr last seen near Yvetot
24 July 43	195	EJ921 JE-N	Sgt F. H. Jones	hit sea csd 18 m off Great Yarmouth
26 July 43	247	DN338 ZY-S	F/O R. F. Murray	e/f f/l 1 m SW New Romney
28 July 43	245	DN591 MR-K	F/S T. H. Gray	e/f f/l 1 m SW Eythorne
28 July 43	183	JP393	F/S R. N. Foster	tbto w/u Harrowbeer
30 July 43	266	R8638 ZH-O	F/O H. A. Cooper	e/f f/l csd Portreath
30 July 43	181	R8833 EL-D	F/O N. R. Maxwell (K)	sdb Bf109 in Channel (Poix)
30 July 43	174	DN580	F/O A. C. Dunning (PoW)	cld EK134 csd Furnes
30 July 43	174	EK134	F/O V. J. Markey (K)	cld DN580 csd Avekapelle
30 July 43	181	JP493 EL-A	F/L W. O. Peacock	dam by Bf109 csd Merston
31 July 43	182	EJ957	F/L W. H. Bewg	e/f f/l near Woodchurch
31 July 43	247	JP545 ZY-V	F/S C. D. McIntosh (K)	sdbF off Gravelines
2 Aug 43	182	EK395	S/L T. P. Pugh (K)	sdbF Dunkirk harbour
3 Aug 43	486	R8697 SA-Z	F/O C. N. Gall	cld DN611 on ground Tangmere
3 Aug 43	486	DN611 SA-U	–	hit by R8697 Tangmere
3 Aug 43	266	JP399	P/O R. K. Thompson (K)	sdb Fw190s near Guipavas
6 Aug 43	195	DN361 JE-M	W/O S. W. Stanley	e/f f/l Plumstead
8 Aug 43	609	JP390 PR-J	F/L L. E. Smith	hbF dtd 100 yd off Deal
11 Aug 43	175	DN263 HH-F	F/S J. J. Rowlands	tbto w/u Detling
11 Aug 43	197	JP533 OV-V	P/O G. S. M. Pearson (K)	sdbF near Ghent
12 Aug 43	56	EJ953	S/L C. J. Donovan	efto f/l near Martlesham Heath w/u Rearsby
15 Aug 43	59OTU	R8652	F/S Groux	
15 Aug 43	266	R8767	F/O F. B. Biddulph (K)	d/f spun in, Channel (Guipavas)
15 Aug 43	266	DN296 ZH-K	F/O J. Small (K)	sdb Fw190? near Guipavas
15 Aug 43	182	JP403	Sgt A. B. E. Rutherford	e/f f/l 1 m SW New Romney
15 Aug 43	247	JP487 ZY-Y	F/L A. W. Robertson (K)	cld JP505 csd New Romney
15 Aug 43	266	JP492	S/L A. S. MacIntyre (K)	sdb Fw190 Guipavas
15 Aug 43	247	JP505 ZY-R	Sgt E. S. McCuaig (K)	cld JP487 csd New Romney
16 Aug 43	3	EJ950 QO-X	F/O J. M. P. de Selys (K)	s/f csd on app Manston
16 Aug 43	1	EK176 JX-K	F/O L. J. Wood (K)	e/f csd 2 m SE Lydd
16 Aug 43	198	JP442	F/O A. J. Houston	dila Lympne
16 Aug 43	174	JP444	F/L J. R. Sterne (K)	sdbF Amiens-Glisy
16 Aug 43	195	JP549	P/O D. J. Webster (K)	csd 1 m N Bergen a/f
16 Aug 43	175	JP577 HH-T	Sgt H. E. R. Merlin (E)	hbF f/l (Amiens-Glisy)
17 Aug 43	182	DN553	F/L W. H. Bewg (K)	sdb Fw190 (Lille) (claimed by Ofw Heitmann III/JG26)
18 Aug 43	3	JP586	F/O R. Schwarz	w/u Manston
19 Aug 43	182	R8927 EL-R[4]	F/O M. I. Fraleigh (K)	ftr (Amiens)
19 Aug 43	182	JP400 XM-U	F/L G. F. Ball (PoW)	sdbF (Amiens)
19 Aug 43	174	JP550	P/O E. O'Callaghan	hbF b/o 8 m off Le Touquet
19 Aug 43	182	JP552	F/S R. L. H. Dench (E)	sdb Fw190 near Amiens (claims for the 182 Sqn aircraft above were submitted by II/JG26 – Lt Hoppe (2), Lt Heinemann (1))
23 Aug 43	1	R7856	P/O H. Gray (K)	spun in, 3 m NW Tangmere
25 Aug 43	174	EK369	F/O S. W. Burney	dila Lydd
25 Aug 43	245	JP481	F/S K. J. A. Dickie (K)	w/u Lydd
28 Aug 43	198	JP516 TP-O	F/L L. S. B. Scott (PoW)	sdbF 2 m SW Breskens (claimed by Flak SW

Date	Unit	Aircraft		Pilot	Circumstances
28 Aug 43	198	JP613	TP-N	S/L J. Manak (PoW)	Breskens 1958 hrs) hbF dtd 3 m W Knocke (claimed by Flak W Vlissingen 1959 hrs)
2 Sept 43	175	JP387	HH-N	F/O K. N. Wilson	tbto w/u Detling
2 Sept 43	198	JP591	TP-R	F/S R. T. Osborne (PoW)	hbF dtd off Vlissingen (claimed by Flak W of Vlissingen 1052 hrs)
4 Sept 43	609	EK321		Sgt F. J. Bryan	dila Lympne
4 Sept 43	195	JP587	JE-M	F/S I. R. MacMillian (K)	spun in, Coltishall
5 Sept 43	3	JP585		S/L S. R. Thomas (PoW)	hbF f/l N Sluis (sdb 2nd Battalion of Infantry Regiment 743, pilot set fire to aircraft)
6 Sept 43	486	EK119	SA-H	P/O R. H. Fitzgibbon (K)	s/f csd off Berneval
7 Sept 43	266	EJ917		Sgt I. O. Hulley	e/f f/l Lidshott Common
8 Sept 43	175	JP379	HH-N	F/S N. J. Scott	efto w/u Lydd
9 Sept 43	174	JP484		F/O B. F. Proddow	e/f f/l near Lydd
9 Sept 43	56	JP595	US-C	F/O A. C. Leigh	hbF b/o 4 m off Cap Gris Nez
10 Sept 43	198	JP508	TP-F	F/S H. Donaghy (PoW)	sdbF N Sluis (claimed by Flak, 1322 hrs, between Hazegraf and Retranchement)
11 Sept 43	124W	JP436	AI-16	W/C A. Ingle (PoW)	sdb Fw190s near Beauvais
11 Sept 43	175	JP536		F/S R. O'Hara-Murray (K)	sdb Fw190s Quincampoix (3 claims for the above aircraft by II/JG26 – Lt Hoppe, Fw Crump, Hpt Naumann)
11 Sept 43	609	JP678	PR-O	P/O J. Leslie (K)	ftr (Sissonne a/f)
13 Sept 43	609	R8224		W/O R. E. Bavington	wing overstressed in dive
13 Sept 43	3	DN623	QO-U	F/S C. Chrisford (PoW)	csd near Dordrecht cnk
13 Sept 43	257	EJ927	FM-Y	F/S R. Gittus	tbto w/u Gravesend
13 Sept 43	3	EJ989	QO-S	F/O J. M. Downs (PoW)	hbF b/o Overflakkee (claimed by 4th 'Scharfrichter' with m/g guns, 5 m NW Sluis)
13 Sept 43	3	JP594		Sgt G. A. Whitman	dtd on ASR flight
15 Sept 43	56	JP657		F/O S. M. McGregor	tbto w/u Bradwell Bay
16 Sept 43	486	EJ976	SA-V	F/S D. Bennet (K)	sdbF near Le Havre
16 Sept 43	486	EK225		F/S M. O. Jorgensen (K)	sdbF off Le Havre
16 Sept 43	486	JP485	SA-M	P/O N. E. Preston (K)	sdbF off Le Havre
17 Sept 43	3	JP724		F/L G. L. Sinclair	dila at night Manston
20 Sept 43	198	JP723		F/S R. F. Broad (K)	sdbF Vladslo cnk
20 Sept 43	198	JP735		F/L A. Houston (PoW)	sdbF E Dixmude
20 Sept 43	609	JP745	PR-L	P/O T. S. Turek	hbF dtd off Dieppe
23 Sept 43	266	EJ901		F/O N. J. Lucas	e/f F? b/o 33 m S Lizard
24 Sept 43	245	R7880	MR-B	F/O E. A. Bater	tbto csd Lydd
24 Sept 43	486	EJ915		F/S H. C. Saward (PoW)	sdb e/a SW Trouville
24 Sept 43	182	JP391	XM-G	P/O D. H. Castle	dila New Romney
24 Sept 43	197	JP502	OV-B	F/S R. M. Allan	rof f/l near Tangmere
24 Sept 43	247	JP653	ZY-E	F/L C. E. Brayshaw	e/f dtd off Dymchurch
25 Sept 43	181	R8875	EL-N	Sgt K. G. Joachim	tbto w/u Detling
25 Sept 43	3	JP439	QO-L	P/O J. de Callatay (K)	sdbF 2 m NE Middelburg (claimed by 10th Battery Luftwaffe Felddivision 19 at 1119 hrs)
26 Sept 43	609	JP543	PR-A	F/O C. J. G. Demoulin	e/f b/o over Channel
27 Sept 43	56	EK189	US-T	F/S G. Plumb	tbto w/u Bradwell Bay
27 Sept 43	198	JP837	TP-P	Sgt J. A. Colvin (PoW)	hbF b/o Schouwen
27 Sept 43	198	JP840		P/O B. F. Gilland (PoW)	hbF b/o Schouwen (the 2 aircraft above were claimed by Flak from Naval ship, Zierikzee 0850 hrs)
30 Sept 43	181	JP603		F/O L. P. Alexander (K)	spun in, Brasted
3 Oct 43	486	JP676	SA-J	F/S C. J. Sheddan	hbF dtd off Barfleur
4 Oct 43	245	JP434		F/O O. B. James (K)	sdb e/a? csd near Evreux
4 Oct 43	245	JP668	MR-F	F/S J. D. Flyn (K)	sdb e/a? csd near Hautot-sur-mer
4 Oct 43	247	JP729		F/O J. B. Watchorn (K)	e/f f/l New Romney
4 Oct 43	609	JP750		P/O J. M. J. Gueffen (PoW)	sdbF near Poix
4 Oct 43	3	JP755		F/L G. L. Sinclair (PoW)	hbF f/l Overflakkee (claimed by unknown German fighter at Herkingen, Overflakkee 1215 hrs)
4 Oct 43	198	JP791	TP-C	S/L C. C. F. Cooper (PoW)	hbF b/o NW Klundert (sdb 6th Group of 665 Light Luftwaffe Flak, W Klundert 1130 hrs)
5 Oct 43	3	JP514		F/O J. L. Foster (K)	sdb Fw190s Wevelgem cnk (claimed by Fw Wiegand, I/JG26)
5 Oct 43	174	JP547		F/S E. G. Boucher (E)	g/lk F? f/l near Montreuil
5 Oct 43	247	JP581	ZY-V	F/O P. A. Chappell (K)	sdb Bf109s? csd near Ablis
5 Oct 43	3	JP733	QO-H	S/L R. Hawkins (K)	sdbF Evergem
5 Oct 43	3	JP911		W/O J. A. La Roque (K)	sdbF near Ghent
6 Oct 43	175	JP731		F/O G. E. Adamac (K)	spun in, Brooklands
9 Oct 43	486	JP863	SA-D	F/S K. McCarthy	dila Lympne
14 Oct 43	183	JP383		F/O K. H. Ridley	tbto csd Predannack
15 Oct 43	181	JP539		Sgt L. P. Dean	e/f f/l near Shripney
16 Oct 43	197	JP374	OV-P	F/S L. C. Morris (K)	spun in, Hambrook
16 Oct 43	257	JP490	FM-P	–	hit by JP788 on gnd Warmwell
16 Oct 43	257	JP788		F/S R. Gittus	hbF cld JP490 on gnd Warmwell
17 Oct 43	182	JP609	XM-A	F/O W. H. Else	e/f b/o W Mayfield
20 Oct 43	181	JP489	EL-B	F/O J. H. Bryant	b/o in spin near Westhampnett
21 Oct 43	245	JP905	MR-A	F/O E. A. Bater (K)	e/f b/o 1 m off Hastings
22 Oct 43	197	JP797	OV-M	F/S J. C. Adey (K)	sdbF off Le Havre
24 Oct 43	183	JP368		F/O D. N. Munrowd	hbF w/u Warmwell
24 Oct 43	183	JP396		S/L A. V. Gowers (K)	sdbF off Cherbourg
24 Oct 43	183	JP428	HF-N	F/O P. W. B. Timms (PoW)	sdbF Cherbourg
24 Oct 43	183	JP542		F/O C. E. Rawson (K)	sdbF Cherbourg
25 Oct 43	181	JP435	EL-V	F/O E. H. Collins (PoW)	hbF f/l near Caen
25 Oct 43	181	JP513	EL-F	S/L F. W. M. Jensen (PoW)	hbF f/l near Caen
25 Oct 43	181	JP590	EL-C	F/O W. R. King (K)	sdbF Caen
26 Oct 43	193	JP497	DP-L	F/O J. A. Inglis	e/f w/u Harrowbeer
26 Oct 43	175	JP740		F/S G. A. Shanks (K)	e/f? csd in mid-Channel
31 Oct 43	257	JP732	FM-N	F/S R. Gittus (K)	hbF? last seen SW Pleneuf
1 Nov 43	197	JP665	OV-I	F/S J. L. Richards (K)	sdbF 8 m SW Caumont
2 Nov 43	183	JR184		F/O A. S. Palmer (K)	hbF csd 5 m W Camaret

Date	Unit	Aircraft		Pilot	Circumstances
3 Nov 43	56	JP754	US-N	P/O P. M. Wooldridge (K)	hbF b/o 5 m N 'S Gravenhage
4 Nov 43	183	JP897		F/S C. E. Waddington	dila Predannack
5 Nov 43	197	JP844	OV-F	F/S L. S. Clarke	rof f/l near Newport
7 Nov 43	195	EJ980	JE-M	P/O G. R. Simpson (PoW)	rof dtd 6 m N Merdijk
7 Nov 43	183	JP431	HF-T	F/S W. F. Tollsworth	e/f f/l Weeks St. Mary
7 Nov 43	257	JP447	FM-C	F/O M. J. Coombe (K)	e/f 20 m S St. Catherine's Point
7 Nov 43	56	JP728	US-G	F/O L. M. Sullivan (K)	efto csd Martlesham Heath
10 Nov 43	247	JP544	ZY-D	F/O H. L. Van Zuilecom (K)	bfo expl csd near Ford
10 Nov 43	197	JP588	OV-V	F/O M. L. Soors (K)	ftr night Intruder (Poix)
10 Nov 43	486	JP914		P/O W. B. Tyerman (K)	ftr night Intruder (Koxyde)
10 Nov 43	3	JP926		F/L R. M. Walmesly (K)	sdbF Cap Gris Nez
11 Nov 43	183	JP386	HF-R	F/S L. D. Harding (K)	sdbF 3 m S St-Mathieu
11 Nov 43	247	JP675	ZY-R	F/O G. W. Waugh (K)	bfo on landing expl Merston
12 Nov 43	181	JP930		F/O D. W. Steeper (K)	F? csd 5 m E Formerie
13 Nov 43	181	JP597		F/L W. O. Peacock (K)	F? csd in sea S Shoreham
13 Nov 43	181	JP737		Sgt I. S. Paterson (K)	hbF b/o (Paris)
13 Nov 43	181	JP965	EL-S	F/O P. L. Green (K)	ftr (Paris)
13 Nov 43	56	JR216	US-N	F/O N. A. Wright (PoW)	hbF f/l 2 m S 'S Gravenhage
15 Nov 43	183	JP932		F/S C. E. Waddington (K)	sdbF 5 m SW St-Mathieu
17 Nov 43	609	JR147		F/S R. O. Ellis (PoW)	ftr (Rouen)
17 Nov 43	609	JR191		Sgt G. L. Watelet (E)	ftr (Rouen)
19 Nov 43	174	EJ993		F/O R. W. Wheeler (K)	dtd 20 m NW Le Havre
20 Nov 43	486	EJ981	SA-E	F/S N. J. Helean	e/f f/l Eartham
20 Nov 43	197	EK141	OV-X	–	dbf in hangar Tangmere[5]
20 Nov 43	56	EK209	US-P	F/O R. R. Amey (K)	hbF csd Witnesham
20 Nov 43	486	JP501	SA-R	–	dbf in hangar Tangmere[5]
20 Nov 43	197	JP680	OV-S	–	dbf in hangar Tangmere[5]
20 Nov 43	197	JP787	OV-K	–	dbf in hangar Tangmere[5]
20 Nov 43	486	JP853	SA-K	–	dbf in hangar Tangmere[5]
20 Nov 43	197	JP970	OV-L	–	dbf in hangar Tangmere[5]
25 Nov 43	198	JP509	TP-A	F/O A. R. F. Jones (K)	F? csd 8 m off Ventnor
25 Nov 43	1	JP592		F/O J. W. Wiley (K)	sdbF near Cherbourg
25 Nov 43	186	JR200		F/S I. E. Mathieson (K)	cld Spit AD239 Heathfield
30 Nov 43	183	JR187	HF-N	P/O M. H. W. N. Gee	dila Predannack
1 Dec 43	266	JP906	ZH-L	F/O S. J. Blackwell (E)	sdb Ju88 W Cap Chèvre
1 Dec 43	609	JP924		F/S R. W. Aitken-Quack (PoW)	sdb e/a near Brussels (claimed by Uffz Guttmann, II/JG26, S Valenciennes 1315 hrs)
1 Dec 43	193	JR211	DP-L	F/O J. A. Pressland	g/lk b/o 30 m S Land's End
3 Dec 43	609	JP748		Sgt J. A. A. Zegers	e/f f/l Dungeness
7 Dec 43	1	EK113		W/O J. D. Fairburn (K)	csd in bad vis 1 m N Hawkinge
12 Dec 43	1	JP795		–	e/fire on gnd Lympne
15 Dec 43	182	JP912		F/O C. G. Richards (K)	ftr (Londinières)
18 Dec 43	197	JP967	OV-F	Sgt E. O'Callaghan (K)	csd in bad vis 6 m NW Tangmere
20 Dec 43	182	JP605	XM-W	F/S R. Wilkinson (PoW)	cld JP725 csd Berck
20 Dec 43	198	JR316		F/L V. Smith (K)	csd W Dreumel cnk
21 Dec 43	69	R8845		S/L P. G. Thornton-Brown (K)	sdb P47s near Doullens
21 Dec 43	609	JP674	PR-D	F/O C. W. Miller (K)	sdb P47s near Doullens
21 Dec 43	486	JP845	SA-H	F/S N. J. A. Helean (E)	F? f/l 12 m SW Abbeville
21 Dec 43	1	JR144		F/S S. D. Cunningham (K)	e/f last seen 13 m off Dover
21 Dec 43	266	JR221		F/S R. McElroy	e/f f/l W Tavistock
22 Dec 43	1	JP961	JX-U	W/O F. J. Wyatt (PoW)	ftr ('Noball' St-Pol-Hesdin)
22 Dec 43	1	JR237		P/O J. W. Sutherland (PoW)	ftr ('Noball' St-Pol-Hesdin)
23 Dec 43	245	JP801		F/O W. F. Freshwater	hbF f/l near Hawkinge
24 Dec 43	263	JR203		F/O K. J. F. Funnell (K)	csd near Wimborne
26 Dec 43	263	JR239		F/O D. E. G. Mogg (K)	csd in bad vis S Shaftesbury
29 Dec 43	186	JR218		P/O D. Kelley (K)	cld JR313 csd near Beith
29 Dec 43	186	JR313		W/O S. R. Shaw (K)	cld JR218 csd near Beith
30 Dec 43	486	JP532	SA-T	F/O R. A. Peters (K)	dtd 8 m S Worthing cnk
30 Dec 43	245	JP593		W/O R. P. A. McKillop (K)	e/f b/o 15 m W Le Touquet
30 Dec 43	198	JP670	TP-V	S/L J. H. Chrystall	e/f f/l near Sandwich
31 Dec 43	198	JP652	TP-T	F/O W. R. Widdess (K)	cld JP727 csd mid-Channel
31 Dec 43	198	JP727	TP-Y	F/O K, Johnson (K)	cld JP652 csd mid-Channel
31 Dec 43	257	JP742	FM-R	F/O M. H. Yi (K)	dtd off St-Brieuc cnk
1 Jan 44	183	JR213	HF-B	F/L R. Hartley (K)	spun in, Chywood Farm, Cornwall
3 Jan 44	609	JP425	PR-B	Sgt J. A. A. Zegers (K)	sdb Fw190 near Bapaume (claimed by Uffz Guttmann, II/JG26, E Doullens 1340 hrs)
3 Jan 44	56	JP446	US-U	F/O R. G. Crosby (E)	ftr ('Noball' Bois-Rempre)
3 Jan 44	56	JP915	US-K	F/O S. M. McGregor (PoW)	hbF f/l near Forêt d'Hesdin
3 Jan 44	197	JR150	OV-M	F/S N. F. Miles (K)	sdbF Ligecourt
3 Jan 44	198	JR523		F/O H. H. Mackenzie (K)	ftr (Compiegne)
4 Jan 44	175	JP376	HH-H	P/O H. E. Hare (PoW)	hbF b/o near Bois-Carré
4 Jan 44	245	JR238		F/O K. W. Sim (E)	g/lk F? f/l (Yvrencheux)
4 Jan 44	609	JR374		F/O D. J. C. Daix (K)	e/f F? dtd mid-Channel
5 Jan 44	3	JP756		P/O C. A. Tidy	e/f f/l Manor Farm, Norfolk
5 Jan 44	247	JP850	ZY-E	F/O A. S. Aitchison	e/f f/l Itchel Manor, Odiham
6 Jan 44	193	EJ902		P/O R. G. McLeod (K)	sdbF near Cherbourg
6 Jan 44	175	JR190		F/S G. L. Renshaw (PoW)	ftr 'Noball' near Dieppe
7 Jan 44	174	JP600	XP-K	F/O J. F. Cobbett (K)	cld JR373 over Béthune
7 Jan 44	174	JR373		F/S R. V. Smith (PoW)	cld JP600 over Béthune
7 Jan 44	20MU	JR426		F/L W. B. H. Statham	f/l 2 m SW Stonehouse
7 Jan 44	193	JR436		F/L J. Crabb (K)	sdb Fw190s 2 m NE Guernsey
8 Jan 44	245	JP971	MR-E	F/S W. N. Waudby (E)	sdb Ju88 S Evreux
10 Jan 44	245	JP852		P/O J. P. Bassett (K)	sdbF SE Londinières
10 Jan 44	195	JP935		F/S L. J. Warner (K)	hbF ditched 3 m off Fr coast
13 Jan 44	198	JR435	TP-E	P/O M. Laman (K)	sdbF Juvincourt

Date	Unit	Aircraft	Pilot	Circumstances
14 Jan 44	247	JR196 ZY-P	F/O C. C. Heathcote (K)	e/f F? csd 10 m S St-Valéry
14 Jan 44	486	JR329 SA-R	F/O G. Philp (K)	sdbF S Paris
14 Jan 44	609	JR375	P/O J. G. McLaughlin (E)	e/f f/l E Helmond
14 Jan 44	183	JR383 HF-Y	F/L A. G. McAdam (K)	sdbF ('Noball' Cherbourg)
20 Jan 44	198	JR361 TP-Y	F/L R. O. Curtis (K)	hbF crashed near St-Omer
21 Jan 44	183	JR369	Sgt E. F. Bush (K)	dtd 36 m N Batz cnk
24 Jan 44	174	JP576	F/S H. S. Brown	dila Eastchurch nr
24 Jan 44	197	JR529	S/L M. P. C. Holmes (K)	F? csd 3 m NNE Buchy
25 Jan 44	181	JP968 EL-Y	F/O L. R. Allen (K)	spun in, attacking 'Noball' Fr
26 Jan 44	1	EK139	F/S H. Bletcher	efto Lympne crashed in wood
28 Jan 44	183	JP402 HF-P	F/S R. G. Phillips (K)	dtd 25 m N Brest cnk
29 Jan 44	257	JP491 FM-E	F/L P. G. Scotchmer (PoW)	hbF f/l near Cap d'Antifer
29 Jan 44	1	JP498	F/S L. E. Watson (K)	last seen W Amiens
29 Jan 44	609	JP662	P/O L. L. Henrion (K)	Missing near Walcheren
29 Jan 44	193	JP784	F/O J. A. Inglis	e/f f/l Powerstock
29 Jan 44	257	JP799	F/O S. H. James (PoW)	Missing near Cap d'Antifer
29 Jan 44	183	JP973 HF-E	F/S S. W. Smith (K)	ftr (Guipavas a/f)
29 Jan 44	198	JR518	F/O D. W. J. Reynolds (PoW)	csd NW Malines cnk
29 Jan 44	183	MM970	F/L S. J. Lovell (K)	sdbf Guipavas a/f
30 Jan 44	1	JP841	W/O J. W. McKenzie	e/f undershot Lympne
31 Jan 44	183	MM964	F/O R. N. Foster (K)	sdbF Kerlin Bastard a/f
1 Feb 44	186	JR131	F/L F. H. Sproule	e/f w/u Tain
1 Feb 44	186	JR335	P/O H. R. D. Patton (K)	spun into sea off Cromarty
2 Feb 44	609	EK121 PR-F	F/O J. A. Stewart	dila Manston
2 Feb 44	174	JP658	P/O J. R. R. Boyer (K)	csd in bad vis 1 m E Brighton
3 Feb 44	247	JP927 ZY-D	F/O R. Walker-Lutz	e/f dtd 2 m S Selsey
3 Feb 44	3	JR188	W/O J. C. M. Earle (K)	e/f dtd 30 m W Overflakkee
4 Feb 44	193	JP902	Sgt J. R. King-Meggat (K)	bfo expl csd N Cap de la Hague
5 Feb 44	56	EJ962 US-R	F/O H. R. Harling	e/f csd 8 m off Orfordness
5 Feb 44	175	JP369 HH-P	F/S D. A. Slack (PoW)	missing near Clermont
5 Feb 44	175	JP385	P/O C. Tucker (PoW)	hbF f/l near Evreux
5 Feb 44	263	JR251	F/O N. P. Blacklock (K)	missing F? off Cap de la Hague
6 Feb 44	266	JP846 ZH-G	S/L P. W. Lefevre (K)	sdbF off Aber-Vrac'h
6 Feb 44	245	JR323	F/O R. L. Hawkins (K)	sdbF near Cherbourg
7 Feb 44	198	JP747	F/S A. B. Kirkwood (K)	sdbF near Poix
7 Feb 44	198	JR242	F/O J. A. MacDonald (K)	sdbF near Poix
8 Feb 44	3	JP684	F/S N. J. Cook	dtd 30 m off Lowestoft
8 Feb 44	183	MN183	F/L R. B. Lord (PoW)	sdbF near Crécy
9 Feb 44	56	JR442 US-W	F/O F. Cueto (K)	F? b/o 5 m S Dungeness
10 Feb 44	198	R8894	W/O J. Stanley (PoW)	hbF last seen near Boulogne
10 Feb 44	486	JP689 SA-P	F/S W. J. Swinton (PoW)	missing 25 m NE Chartres
11 Feb 44	183	JR260	P/O J. de B. Holland (K)	dtd 18 m S St. Catherine's Point (possibly the aircraft claimed by Fw Wiegand, I/JG26, NW Calais)
12 Feb 44	137	MM974 SF-R	P/O J. W. T. Purdy (K)	e/f last seen Ardouval
13 Feb 44	263	JR215	F/S G. Williams (K)	sdbF near Etampes
13 Feb 44	263	JR309	P/O W. E. Watkins (E)	hbF b/o near Rambouillet
14 Feb 44	174	JP548	F/O B. F. Proddow (E)	e/f f/l Fr SE Marigny
14 Feb 44	247	JP649 ZY-Z	F/O A. S. Aitchison (K)	csd Châteaudun cnk
14 Feb 44	174	MM962	S/L W. W. McConnell (PoW)	f/lk f/l 3m NW Percy
15 Feb 44	247	JP381 ZY-F	F/S C. E. B. Eckel (E)	e/f b/o 1 m S Flers
15 Feb 44	266	JP925 ZH-J	F/S D. Drummond (K)	sdbF Morlaix a/f
15 Feb 44	266	JP941	F/O J. D. Miller (K)	sdbF Morlaix a/f
15 Feb 44	266	JR387	F/O W. V. Mollet (E)	sdbF Morlaix a/f
17 Feb 44	439	MN213	–	set on fire by heater Ayr
18 Feb 44	175	JP429 HH-A	W/O H. Taylor (K)	csd on t/o Westhampnett
18 Feb 44	174	JP793	F/S H. S. Brown (K)	last seen 20 m SSE Beachy Head
18 Feb 44	174	JR133	F/O J. E. Renaud (PoW)	sdb Fw190 near Amiens (claimed by Lt Radener, II/JG26, N Amiens 1210 hrs)
20 Feb 44	439	R8971	F/O E. L. Dixon (K)	csd near New Cumnock
21 Feb 44	266	JP962	F/S H. W. Paul	e/f f/l near Harrowbeer
21 Feb 44	247	JR258	F/L C. E. Brayshaw (K)	hbF csd in sea 10 m N Cabourg
21 Feb 44	182	JR370	F/L P. J. McGuire (K)	sdbF Beaumont a/f
22 Feb 44	263	JR302	F/O R. B. Tuff (K)	b/o 8 m NW Guernsey
22 Feb 44	263	JR304	F/O R. C. Hunter (K)	last seen 8 m NW Guernsey
22 Feb 44	263	MN249	S/L G. B. Warnes (K)	dtd 8 m NW Guernsey cnk
23 Feb 44	3	EK370 QO-C	F/S J. Fudala (K)	sdbF Zeebrugge
25 Feb 44	1	JP611	F/O W. Smith	e/f f/l near Acklington
25 Feb 44	257	JP936 FM-Z[6]	W/O H. S. McGill (K)	f/l near Seaford
26 Feb 44	181	JP739 EL-R	F/L D. E. De La Hoyde	prop hit sea f/l near Merston
28 Feb 44	247	JP730 ZY-M	W/O P. S. W. Daniel (K)	e/f b/o 3 m N Sark
29 Feb 44	3	JP921 QO-P	F/L E. Wardsinski (E)	hbF f/l near Volkel
29 Feb 44	609	MN211	F/O M. H. Shelton (K)	sdbF near Douai
1 Mar 44	257	JP507 FM-M	F/L K. A. Buckley (K)	csd West Harting
2 Mar 44	164	EK175	F/S L. E. Bignall (K)	s/f csd near Twinwood Farm, Bedfordshire
2 Mar 44	1	JP483	W/O N. D. Howard (E)	e/f f/l Tergnier
2 Mar 44	257	JR295 FM-C	P/O P. A. Shardlow (PoW)	e/f f/l 10 m E Le Touquet
2 Mar 44	193	JR430	F/O M. Soble	e/f f/l near Detling
2 Mar 44	266	MN259	F/L T. W. Healy (K)	hit tree on ops dtd mid-Channel
5 Mar 44	56	MN123	F/O O. D. Hill (K)	missing off NE coast at night
6 Mar 44	174	JP836	F/O J. A. Irwin (K)	e/f b/o mid-Channel
6 Mar 44	198	MN137 TP-X	F/L P. D. L. Roper	e/f w/u at night West Malling
6 Mar 44	3	MN188	P/O C. A. Tidy (E)	sdb Bf109s near Poix (claimed by Maj Mietusch, III/JG26, NE Amiens 1305 hrs)
9 Mar 44	198	JR447	F/O W. Parkes (K)	hit trees on ops dila Lydd
11 Mar 44	257	JR151 FM-K	P/O N. Carter (PoW)	sdbF near Barfleur
12 Mar 44	263	MN129	P/O G. N. Smith (K)	csd near Warmwell
13 Mar 44	486	JR146 SA-M	W/O H. W. Williams (K)	e/f csd 3 m S Downham Market
14 Mar 44	4DFlt	JR199	F/L P. F. Sewell	e/f f/l 1 m E Tangmere
16 Mar 44	257	JP510	P/O J. B. Wood (PoW)	e/f F? last seen E Fécam
16 Mar 44	245	JR143	F/O C. E. Austin (K)	sdbF S Etampes
16 Mar 44	175	JR319	P/O W. Cross (PoW)	hbF at Villaroche f/l in Fr

Date	Unit	Aircraft	Pilot	Circumstances	Date	Unit	Aircraft	Pilot	Circumstances
18 Mar 44	439	JR439	P/O K. O. Mitchell (K)	csd Little Water of Fleet, Scotland	9 May 44	266	MM981ZH-J	F/O C. W. Baillie (PoW)	ftr last seen near Dieppe
19 Mar 44	3	JP857	F/S S. Domanski	efto csd Bradwell Bay	9 May 44	124W	MN406 EH	W/C E. H. Haabjoern	e/f b/o 40 m E N. Foreland
20 Mar 44	245	JP972	P/O N. W. Crabtree (K)	sdbF ('Noball' Croisette)	9 May 44	266	MN483	Sgt A. D. McMurdon (PoW)	g/lk last seen W Rouen
21 Mar 44	183	MN247[7]	F/L P. E. Raw (K)	sdbF near Nijmegen	11 May 44	609	MN496	F/O P. L. Soesman (K)	hbF b/o 20 m WNW Fécamp
22 Mar 44	3	R8895 QO-E	F/S R. W. Pottinger	e/f dtd N Bradwell Bay	11 May 44	609	MN544	F/L R. L. Wood (K)	sdbF Cap d'Antifer
22 Mar 44	184	MN149	F/S D. B. Smith	efto w/u Eastchurch	13 May 44	609	MN155	F/S L. P. Fidgin (K)	sdbF S Rouen
23 Mar 44	1	EK245	F/O H. T. Jackson (K)	e/f dtd 7 m NE Orfordness	13 May 44	609	MN414	F/O J. A. Stewart (PoW)	hbF b/o Fleury
23 Mar 44	609	MN140	F/O C. F. J. Detal (K)	spun in, Acklington	19 May 44	175	JR136 HH-E	F/S J. R. Gerrard	e/f f/l Hursley
24 Mar 44	245	JP798 MR-S	P/O D. F. Martin	csd on t/o 1 m S Westhampnett	19 May 44	266	MM953	F/S A. O. Holland (K)	hbF csd 40 m S IoW
24 Mar 44	A&AEE	JR448	F/O D. Grundy (K)	csd 1 m S Grately	21 May 44	137	JR433	F/L H. C. Knight (K)	sdb e/a 10 m SW Brugge
25 Mar 44	137	MM972SF-F	F/O B. W. Gutteridge	e/f f/l SW Dymchurch	21 May 44	184	MN252 BR-T	P/O R. G. Worthington (PoW)	ftr last seen Walcheren
26 Mar 44	193	EK132	W/O P. J. Thomas (K)	F? csd near Beauvoir	21 May 44	137	MN312	F/O A. Hawker (K)	hbF csd off Ostend
26 Mar 44	A&AEE	JR307	S/L H. N. Fowler (K)	s/f csd 3 m N Tarrant Rushton	21 May 44	263	MN545	F/L D. P. M. Bell (K)	hbF csd 10 m off Cap Frehel
27 Mar 44	183	MN120[7]	F/O R. M. Coutts (K)	spun in, Joiners Farm, Kent	22 May 44	440	MN489 I8-N	F/O A. A. Watkins	hbF b/o 5 m off Arromanches
31 Mar 44	263	MN170	F/L G. G. Racine (E)	dam by Me410 b/o NW Morlaix	22 May 44	124W	MN542 EH	W/C E. H. Haabjoern	hbF b/o 3 m off Dieppe
31 Mar 44	183	MN246[7]	F/O E. W. Harbutt	e/f f/l near Faversham	23 May 44	183	EK268	F/O J. Ralph (K)	sdbF off Cap d'Antifer
1 April 44	137	MN145 SF-B	P/O J. W. Carter (K)	ftr (Dunkirk Vlissingen)	23 May 44	83GSU	JR206	F/S R. A. Kerr	csd near Chilam
4 April 44	439	JR324	P/O A. C. Clarke	dila Funtington	23 May 44	181	JR381 EL-Z	S/L J. G. Keep	hbF dtd 10 m off Cherbourg
5 April 44	486	JP839 SA-V	F/S A. G. Turner (K)	spun in, SW Croxton	23 May 44	84GSU	MM971	W/O A. E. James	e/f csd near Charfield
9 April 44	257	JR139	W/O F. T. Norton (PoW)	sdbF Bouzincourt	23 May 44	123W	MN143 RL-7[8]	W/C R. E. P. Brooker	e/f b/o 25 m S Beachy Head
9 April 44	266	MN181	Sgt D. Shepherd (E)	e/f F? f/l near Beaumont	23 May 44	137	MN474	S/L J. Brandt (E)	sdbF 2 m E Aire
10 April 44	439	JR264 5V-H	P/O P. J. Elfner (K)	missing dtd? near Beachy Head	23 May 44	440	MN637	F/O F. J. Crowley	hbF b/o off Cherbourg
12 April 44	257	JP546	F/O W. W. Kistler	w/u Needs Oar Point	24 May 44	175	JR311	P/O S. S. Finlayson (K)	s/f csd Le Havre
22 April 44	1FPP	JP686	1/O L. Curtis	e/f csd near Langley	24 May 44	198	JR527 TP-M	F/S L. Vallely (K)	sdbF Jobourg
24 April 44	174	MM967	F/L W. D. D. Montgomery	e/f f/l Hinton Admiral	24 May 44	257	MN367 FM-Y	F/O M. F. Cullen (PoW)	hbF f/l Picquigny
24 April 44	137	MN117	F/O D. J. N Kelly	csd on t/o Manston	24 May 44	198	MN410 TP-G	F/O H. Freeman (K)	sdbF Jobourg
27 April 44	263	MN250	F/S J. W. Shellard	hbF Morlaix w/u Harrowbeer	24 May 44	197	MN458 OV-N	F/O H. W. Coles (K)	hbF csd off Pte de la Percée
27 April 44	245	MN480	F/S J. D. Clark (K)	csd in sea Leysdown range	24 May 44	439	MN516 5V-W	S/L H. H. Norsworthy	e/f f/l 4 m SE Horsham
28 April 44	245	JP660 MR-S	F/O L. E. Reynolds	e/f f/l Isle of Sheppey	25 May 44	184	MN233 BR-Y	W/O G. C. Polkey (K)	hbF csd Gisors
28 April 44	182	JR293 XM-C	F/O I. M. Briscoe (K)	F? csd near Ile St-Marcouf	25 May 44	137	MN469	W/O A. Witham (K)	sdbF 1 m off Ostend
28 April 44	198	MN436 TP-S	F/O M. Broadhurst (K)	spun into sea off Llanbedr	27 May 44	440	MN342	F/O N. Stusiak (K)	spun in, W Bransgore
29 April 44	137	MN180 SF-Q	W/O A. W. Emslie	rof f/l near Predannack	28 May 44	263	EK211	F/S J. D. Pringle (K)	hit church csd Yelverton
2 May 44	183	MN465 HF-C	F/O N. T. Glenn (K)	csd in sea 11 m S Selsey Bill	28 May 44	164	JR515 FJ-L	S/L H. A. B. Russell (PoW)	hbF b/o Torcy
3 May 44	56	MM969US-U	F/O T. G. Atkinson (K)	ftr weather recce (Dieppe)	29 May 44	175	JR534 HH-Y	F/O P. J. Spellman	dila Holmsley South
4 May 44	440	MN431 I8-K	F/O W. D. Peacock (K)	hit b/c csd Eastleigh	30 May 44	175	JP931	F/O J. M. Cowie (K)	sdbF near Hardelot
5 May 44	137	MM980	F/S R. J. Eastabrook (K)	sdbF off 'S Gravenhage	30 May 44	609	JR386	F/O J. D. Thorogood (E)	hbF b/o 15 m NW Formerie
7 May 44	175	JR257 HH-W	F/O G. J. Clermont (K)	e/f csd 3 m N Emsworth	2 June 44	198	MN192 TP-H	S/L J. Niblett (K)	sdbF Dieppe
7 May 44	193	MN350	F/S R. O. Cvylenburg	e/f f/l Broadstairs	2 June 44	245	MN355	Sgt D. J. Lush (K)	hbF b/o 8 m NNW Cherbourg
7 May 44	184	JR494 BR-B	F/O J. R. Best	e/f F? b/o mid-Channel	5 June 44	3TEU	R7822	W/O J. S. Gilbert (K)	e/fire csd Low Newton
8 May 44	247	JP488 ZY-J	F/O J. Brown (K)	cld JP661 csd Ferndown	5 June 44	439	MN210 5V-U	F/L J. W. Saville (K)	sdbF St. Peter Port
8 May 44	56	JR504 US-D	F/S F. S. Blinkhorn	e/f dtd 5 m off Dover	5 June 44	175	MN456	W/O J. H. Pugh (K)	hbF b/o 15 m off Cherbourg
8 May 44	438	MM957F3-N	W/C R. T. P. Davidson (E)	e/f F? f/l near Béthune	5 June 44	193	MN761	S/L D. G. Ross (K)	hbF b/o 15 m SE IoW
8 May 44	245	MN302	W/O S. T. Bennet	f/l near Holmsley South	5 June 44	245	n/k[9]	F/L W. E. Reynolds	e/f? b/o 30 m off Cherbourg
					5 June 44	245	n/k[9]	F/O W. Smith	hbF b/o 30 m off Cherbourg
					6 June 44	183	R8973 HF-P	F/O A. R. Taylor (K)	sdb Bf109s S Caen
					6 June 44	266	DN562	Sgt E. H. Downe	hbd b/o 5 m NW Caen
					6 June 44	181	JP604 EL-W	F/S G. J. Howard (K)	sdbF near Caen
					6 June 44	440	MN428 I8-G	F/O L. R. Allman (K)	sdbF Falaise – Condé

Date	Unit	Aircraft	Pilot	Circumstances
6 June 44	183	MN432	F/L R. W. Evans (K)	sdb Bf109s S Caen
6 June 44	164	MN454	F/O A. E. Roberts (K)	sdb Fw190s NE Caen
6 June 44	183	MN478	F/O M. H. Gee (K)	sdb Bf109s Vieux
6 June 44	609	MN697	W/O G. Martin (E)	hbF b/o SE Caen
7 June 44	198	JP503 TP-F	W/O G. J. Stokes (K)	F? csd near Lisieux
7 June 44	184	JP656	F/S J. J. Rowland (K)	sdbF Mézidon
7 June 44	181	JR244 EL-Q	P/O G. E. Rendle (K)	e/f b/o 20 m S IoW
7 June 44	245	JR289	F/L L. J. Greenhalgh (K)	sdbF 3 m N Thury-Harcourt
7 June 44	245	MN121	F/S E. E. G. Noakes (E)	lrt f/l 40 m SW Caen
7 June 44	20Sect	MN125 SA-Q[10]	F/L P. D. L. Roper (E)	sdbF near Villers-Bocage
7 June 44	440	MN257 I8-D	F/O R. W. Doidge (E)	hbF b/o S Caen
7 June 44	266	MN264	Sgt P. K. Mitchell (E)	hbF f/l near St-Aubin
7 June 44	440	MN307	F/O W. J. Mahagan (K)	sdbF S Caen
7 June 44	245	MN377 MR-B	F/O K. J. A. Dickie (E)	hbF f/l 5 m NNE Falaise
7 June 44	197	MN423 OV-S	F/O D. E. F. Potter (K)	ftr last seen 5 m SE St-Lô
7 June 44	183	MN461 HF-M	F/L F. H. Pollock (PoW)	e/f F? last seen SE Le Havre (possibly the aircraft claimed by Oblt Saar, IV/JG27, NE Caen 1753 hrs)
7 June 44	263	MN515	F/O L. Parent (K)	sdbF St-Malô
7 June 44	440	MN548 I8-F	F/O S. V. Garside (K)	sdbF S Caen
7 June 44	184	MN642	F/S L. Tidbury (PoW)	sdbF Mézidon
7 June 44	184	MN667	F/L F. E. Holland (E)	sdbF Mézidon
8 June 44	198	JP655 TP-P	F/S J. Milne (K)	e/f F? csd N Caen
8 June 44	266	MN297	F/O H. C. Ballance	F? b/o 40 m N Caen (possibly one of the above claimed by Lt Becker, IV/JG27, SE Caen 1307 hrs)
9 June 44	83GSU	DN381	F/S J. J. Alston (K)	spun in, SE Mark Cross
9 June 44	263	MN449	F/O W. W. Heaton (K)	ftr St-Lô cnk
10 June 44	413RSU	MN305	Sgt D. White	efto f/l near Thorney Island
10 June 44	136W	MN415	W/C J. M. Bryan (K)	sdbF 2 m SE Falaise
10 June 44	193	MN522	F/S G. A. Gough	hbF f/l beachhead ELG
11 June 44	193	MN700	F/L A. S. Ross (E)	sdbF E Falaise
11 June 44	83GSU	MN876	F/O D. S. Green (K)	presumed dtd off Dungeness cnk
12 June 44	174	MM968	F/L L. McNeill (K)	hbF b/o 4 m off Biville
12 June 44	440	MN115	F/L J. G. Gohl (K)	hbF b/o 2 m S Christchurch
12 June 44	193	MN258 DP-P	F/O J. A. Inglis (K)	hit htc csd Potigny
12 June 44	438	MN346 F3-X	F/L P. Wilson	hbF b/o off Fr coast
12 June 44	257	MN372 FM-A	S/L R. H. Fokes (K)	sdbF 8 m S Caen
12 June 44	438	MN538 F3-N	F/O T. A. Bugg	hbF b/o off Fr coast
12 June 44	266	MN741	F/L R. W. Nesbitt (K)	sdbF S Caen
13 June 44	197	MN495 OV-E	F/S M. C. Richards (K)	ftr (Caen)
14 June 44	198	JR512 TP-J	F/S C. S. Stratford	hbF f/l N Carentan
14 June 44	198	MN649 TP-R	P/O R. C. A. Crouch (K)	hbF csd Montebourg
14 June 44	193	MN656	F/O E. Statters	e/f f/l 4 m W Bayeux
14 June 44	263	MN661	S/L H. A. C. Gonay (K)	hbF csd Grantez
14 June 44	183	MN742	F/L J. W. Scambler (PoW)	sdbF b/o 10 m SW Caen
15 June 44	198	MN175 TP-U	F/S E. L. Bartley (K)	sdbF Duclair
15 June 44	263	MN292 HE-Z	F/O W. K. Windeller (K)	e/f f/l SE Launceston
15 June 44	439	MN417	F/O J. W. Ross (PoW)	hbF b/o 1 m N Caen
15 June 44	175	MN481	W/O O. D. Leitch (K)	e/f? b/o S IoW
15 June 44	245	MN490	F/L J. S. Slaney (PoW)	sdfF Caen – Falaise
16 June 44	181	MN200	F/L G. J. Jones (K)	sdbF Normandy
16 June 44	438	MN298 F3-A	F/O R. C. Getty (E)	sdb Bf109s near Lisieux
16 June 44	146W	MN754	W/C E. R. Baker (K)	sdbF 3 m W Caen
17 June 44	193	EJ912	W/O S. F. G. Walker	e/f f/l near Wantage
17 June 44	197	MN269 OV-W	P/O J. Watson (K)	sdbF S Caen
17 June 44	257	MN416 FM-N	F/L W. W. Kistler (PoW)	ftr last seen 3 m SW Caen
17 June 44	247	MN809	F/O W. F. Anderson (K)	hbF b/o Missy-Bougy
18 June 44	198	MN132 TP-K	P/O D. W. Mason (K)	last seen SW Caen
18 June 44	198	MN314 TP-Z	F/O R. Armstrong (PoW)	sdbF S Caen
18 June 44	247	MN710 ZY-N	F/L B. T. Tatham	cld MN704 on t/o B.6
20 June 44	84GSU	MN488	F/O J. R. Campbell (K)	dila Aston Down
20 June 44	198	MN815 TP-Y	P/O J. S. Fraser-Petherbridge (K)	ftr (SW Lisieux)
21 June 44	257	MN857	F/S W. B. Whitmore	e/f dtd off Keyhaven
22 June 44	198	JR197 TP-T	S/L I. J. Davies (K)	sdbF near Cherbourg
22 June 44	181	MN648 EL-Z	–	dam by shell fire B.6
22 June 44	257	MN820 FM-E	F/S G. Turton (K)	hbF f/l (Argentan)
22 June 44	164	MN852 FJ-K	F/L M. P. Davies	f/l in a/t Fr cnk
23 June 44	198	EK218 TP-X	F/S P. S. Barton (K)	e/f F? dtd S IoW
23 June 44	440	MN171 I8-E	F/O R. G. Hattie	hbF b/o near Juvigny
23 June 44	263	MN300	F/S I. D. M. Dunlop	hbF b/o 35 m off Bolt Head
23 June 44	439	MN663	F/O R. A. Brown	hbF b/o mid-Channel
24 June 44	263	MN296	F/S J. Charlton (K)	sdbF off St-Malô
24 June 44	263	MN524	W/O A. J. Ryan (K)	sdbF St-Malô
24 June 44	183	MN576 HF-E	F/O K. C. Matthews (PoW)	hbd f/l e/t (S Bernay)
24 June 44	197	MN629 OV-Z	P/O R. H. Jones	hbF f/l in a/t Fr
25 June 44	193	MN760	F/S K. G. Hodnett (K)	csd in sea S Needles
25 June 44	181	MN814	F/O E. Hursey (K)	spun in near Ringwood
27 June 44	197	MN750	P/O P. A. Taylor (K)	e/f csd near Fawley
27 June 44	439	MN776	F/O B. P. Swingler	e/f f/l near B.5
27 June 44	609	MN818	F/O R. H. Holmes (K)	sdb Fw190 near Laval
27 June 44	438	MN746 F3-X	F/L L. E. Park (K)	sdbF near Caen
28 June 44	181	JR334	F/O W. H. B. Short	hbF f/l in a/t Fr
29 June 44	609	MN339	F/O G. A. Rowland (K)	ftr (St-Maske-Couches) (possibly the aircraft claimed by Lt Heckmann, II/JG1)
3 July 44	263	MN527 HE-X	F/L L. W. F. Stark (E)	hbF b/o near Kerpert
3 July 44	183	MN657 HF-M	F/L E. Harbutt	hbF b/o S St. Catherine's Point
5 July 44	3TEU	MN127	F/S L. H. Johnson (K)	csd near Stoneleigh
5 July 44	197	MN854 OV-E	P/O L. S. Clark (K)	missing in bad wx off Fr coast
6 July 44	247	JP786 ZY-A	–	hit by MN821 B.6
6 July 44	247	MN303 ZY-W	–	hit by MN821 B.6
6 July 44	164	MN368	Sgt G. M. Fisher (K)	csd 15 m off Cabourg cnk
6 July 44	137	MN468	W/O A. W. Emslie	e/f f/l near Manston
6 July 44	164	MN605 FJ-P	F/S G. D. Fowell (K)	missing off Cabourg
6 July 44	257	MN766 FM-L	F/S R. R. Blair (K)	hbd b/o near Livarot
6 July 44	247	MN795 ZY-G	–	hit by MN821 B.6
6 July 44	181	MN821 EL-H	F/L J. K. Allison	hbF csd B.6
7 July 44	263	MN865	F/O J. A. Hodgson (K)	sdbF off Lanmeur
8 July 44	182	JP934 XM-C	–	bombed on B.6
8 July 44	439	MN464 5V-N	F/O F. M. Thomas (K)	hbF csd on app B.4
9 July 44	257	JR330 FM-K	F/S K. E. Button	dila B.3
9 July 44	175	JR502 HH-Z	F/S R. C. Dale (K)	ftr (S St-Lô)
9 July 44	137	MN556 SF-E	W/O A. W. Emslie	dila Manston
11 July 44	609	R8972	F/S L. E. Bliss (K)	sdbF near Hottot
11 July 44	182	MN373 XM-K	F/O B. McBean	hbF f/l 2 m E Cully

Date	Unit	Aircraft	Pilot	Circumstances
12 July 44	183	MN806 HF-T	S/L F. H. Scarlett (K)	sdbF Cap d'Antifer
13 July 44	197	MN209 OV-A	F/O K. A. J. Trott (PoW)	cld Bf109 near Pont-l'Evêque
13 July 44	257	MN405 FM-J	F/S M. E. Marriot (E)	sdb Bf109 near Cormeilles (the two aircraft above were lost in a combat with I/JG5 who made three claims – Hpt Weissenberger (2) and Lt Mors (1); the third aircraft may have been that flown by F/O J. Rook, 197 Sqn – MN860 OV-G, badly damaged but repaired)
13 July 44	245	MN748	F/L W. E. Reynolds (K)	ftr (la Forge-à-Cambro)
14 July 44	1ADF	JR127	W/O Wlodarski (K)	spun in near Aston Down
15 July 44	247	MN808 ZY-J	W/O D. L. Burke (K)	ftr last seen near Esquay
15 July 44	247	MN812 ZY-B	F/L G. C. Robinson (K)	hbF last seen near Evrecy
16 July 44	440	MN703 I8-L	W/O C. J. McConvey (K)	csd on t/o bombs expl B.9
16 July 44	257	MN713 FM-X	F/S W. H. Ewan (E)	e/f F? b/o 2 m S St-Lô
16 July 44	257	MN879 FM-A	S/L W. C. Ahrens (K)	hbd? b/o E Caen
17 July 44	440	MN715	F/O R. G. Hattie	hbF b/o a/t (Maltot)
18 July 44	198	EK187 TP-K	F/S L. W. Sellman	hbF NE Caen b/o a/t
18 July 44	175	MN185 HH-H[11]	F/O F. M. Botting (PoW)	hbF f/l near Caen
18 July 44	439	MN574	F/O J. Kalen (K)	sdbF Mesnil-Frémentel
18 July 44	247	MN597 ZY-E	Sgt S. R. Ryen (K)	e/f csd B.14
18 July 44	440	MN644	W/O R. A. Watson	hbF b/o near Frémentel
18 July 44	438	MN707 F3-E	F/L R. M. McKenzie (K)	sdbF (Orne bridge)
18 July 44	193	MN743	F/L E. B. Wallace (PoW)	hbF b/o S Caen
18 July 44	182	MN762	Cpt G. H. Kaufman (K)	sdbF near Troarn
18 July 44	182	MN771	F/L A. C. Flood (PoW)	hbF f/l near Douville
19 July 44	266	JR303	P/O J. H. Meyer (K)	sdb Bf109s N Lisieux
19 July 44	266	MN133	F/S J. C. Harrold (K)	sdb Bf109s N Lisieux
19 July 44	181	MN179	F/L K. F. Gear	hbF csd B.6
19 July 44	266	MN751	F/S R. McElroy (K)	sdb Bf109s N Lisieux (the three 266 Sqn aircraft above were claimed by I/JG5 – Hpt Weissenberger (3), Lt Mors (2), Lt Lehner (1), near Lisieux and NW Cormeilles)
20 July 44	438	n/k F3-F	F/O A. B. Newsome	hbF b/o a/t Fr
24 July 44	3TEU	JP847	2Lt S. H. E. Capstick-Dale (K)	spun in, West Hanney
25 July 44	247	JR290 ZY-O	F/S L. B. Morgan (K)	ftr (May-sur-Orne)
25 July 44	182	JR300 XM-U	W/O H. C. B. Tallalla (K)	ftr last seen Fontenay
25 July 44	181	MN186 EL-Q	F/L P. E. Tickner	hbF f/l S Caen
25 July 44	198	MN293 TP-D	F/L G. Sheppard	hbF f/l Cuverville
25 July 44	266	MN624	F/L R. N. G. Allen (PoW)	csd near Thury-Harcourt cnk
25 July 44	182	MN891 XM-Q	Maj D. H. Barlow (PoW)	hbF b/o Bretteville-le-Rabet
26 July 44	164	JR446 FJ-K	F/S A. H. Rowley	hbF f/l near Caen
26 July 44	440	MN369	F/L D. C. Stults	hbF b/o Rocquancourt
26 July 44	440	MN403 I8-J	F/S N. L. Gordon	hbF b/o N Caen
26 July 44	174	MN525 XP-B	F/O W. C. Vatcher (K)	sdbF St-Pierre-sur-Dives
26 July 44	440	MN709 I8-B	S/L W. H. Pentland	e/f f/l bombs on Carpiquet
26 July 44	257	MN919 FM-Q	F/L J. F. Williams (K)	sdbF 10 m E Caen
27 July 44	609	JP843	F/S P. M. Price (K)	ftr F? (Tilly-la-Campagne)
27 July 44	137	MN156	F/O R. A. Johnstone (K)	cld MN596 csd Denton Court
27 July 44	609	MN494 PR-Z	P/O J. D. Buchanan (K)	hbd? csd Tilly-la-Compagne
27 July 44	137	MN596	F/S A. R. Hack (K)	cld MN156 csd Denton Court
28 July 44	84GSU	JP939	F/O G. F. De Bueger	e/f csd near Thruxton
28 July 44	266	MN361	P/O I. H. Forrester (K)	e/f csd SE Bayeux
29 July 44	609	JP407	F/S R. Ashworth (K)	sdbF near Laigle
29 July 44	174	JP671 XP-R	F/S H. J. Somerville (K)	F? csd N Gavray
30 July 44	175	DN267 HH-P	W/O K. M. Hopley (K)	sdbF Aunay-sur-Odon
30 July 44	184	JP495	F/L H. M. Laflamme (K)	sdbF S Aunay-sur-Odon
30 July 44	440	MN793 I8-Z	F/O J. Lippert (K)	sdb e/a? csd Grainville
31 July 44	183	JP909	F/S D. J. Campbell	csd on t/o B.7
31 July 44	198	JP963 TP-C	F/L J. Champion (K)	tbto csd B.7
31 July 44	183	JR445	F/S T. W. Stokoe (K)	csd 2 m W B.7
31 July 44	609	MN239	F/S R. K. Adam (K)	sdbF near Viessoix
1 Aug 44	181	JP650 EL-Y	F/O J. H. F. Kenny (PoW)	F? csd Courvaudon
2 Aug 44	181	JP430 EL-E	F/O R. A. Crane (PoW)	sdbF SW Pont-d'Ouilly
2 Aug 44	184	MN948	F/L D. L. Stevenson	e/f w/u B.5
3 Aug 44	438	MN321 F3-G	F/O D. K. Moores (K)	sdbF 3 m N Henonville
3 Aug 44	609	MN322 PR-F	F/O P. H. M. Cooreman	hbF b/o a/t Fr
4 Aug 44	137	JR511	P/O J. C. Holder (K)	sdbF off Colynsplaat
4 Aug 44	3TEU	MN286	W/O R. A. Richardson	e/f w/u Aston Down
4 Aug 44	181	JP651 EL-L	F/S C. Pole	hbF b/o near Vendes
5 Aug 44	174	JP500 XP-V	P/O E. G. Boucher (K)	hbF b/o NE Condé
5 Aug 44	3TEU	JR516	Sgt N. J. Brightwell (K)	ct fire csd Tibberton
6 Aug 44	245	JR135 MR-V	F/O T. L. Jeffreys	hbF 2 m W Villers-Bocage
7 Aug 44	107MU	R8891	F/O F. R. Barker (K)	csd 28 m E Cairo
7 Aug 44	174	JR377	P/O G. J. Steele	hbF b/o NW Lessay
7 Aug 44	266	MN400	F/S H. Wheeler	hbF f/l a/t Fr
7 Aug 44	245	MN459 MR-R	F/L R. G. F. Lee	sdbF Mesnil-Tove
7 Aug 44	193	MN535 DP-A	F/O A. W. Kilpatrick (E)	hbF f/l near Vire
7 Aug 44	184	MN718 BR-T	F/L L. Parker (E)	hbF b/o E Mortain
7 Aug 44	245	MN770 MR-N	F/O R. E. Temple (K)	sdbF near Gavray
7 Aug 44	257	MN927 FM-C	F/O J. A. Smith	efto csd B.3
8 Aug 44	83GSU	JP785	F/S J. A. D. Meechan[12]	e/f b/o mid-Channel ftr (Gavray)
8 Aug 44	247	JP792 ZY-O	P/O R. B. Hemmings (K)	
8 Aug 44	439	JR521	F/O I. W. Smith	F? f/l St-Germain d'Ectot
8 Aug 44	440	MN313	F/L C. W. Hicks (K)	sdbF N Ussy
9 Aug 44	268	JP389	F/L F. G. Barber	tbto csd B.10
9 Aug 44	198	JR256 TP-I	F/S R. A. Thursby (K)	sdbF Ste-Marguerite-de-Viette
9 Aug 44	266	MN600	F/S P. C. Green (E)	F? f/l 10 m NE Falaise
9 Aug 44	183	MN638 HF-O	W/O W. F. Tollworthy (K)	sdbF SE Falaise
9 Aug 44	182	MN694	F/O W. J. Kasubeck (K)	missing W Clecy
10 Aug 44	174	JP541 XP-Y	F/S E. W. J. Taylor (K)	ftr (Sassy)
10 Aug 44	198	JR306 TP-O	F/L MacLennan	hbF b/o near Potigny
10 Aug 44	245	JR499 MR-V	F/O G. Murphy	hbF w/u B.5
10 Aug 44	193	MN887 DP-O	W/O J. MacCartney (K)	hbF last seen near Argentan
11 Aug 44	245	MN993	S/L J. R. Collins (K)	hbF b/o SSW Bourguebus
12 Aug 44	197	DN274 OV-S	F/L D. A. Backhouse (PoW)	hbF b/o NW Falaise
12 Aug 44	439	MN310 5V-U	F/O R. O. Moen (K)	hbF csd St-Pierre-la-Vieille

Date	Unit	Aircraft	Pilot	Circumstances
12 Aug 44	439	MN553 5V-K	F/O E. J. Allen (K)	sdbF near le Pont de Vere
12 Aug 44	609	MN630 PR-B	F/L T. Y. Wallace	hit by JR379 at B.7
12 Aug 44	438	MN687 F3-S	F/L T. A. Bugg (K)	sdbF Le Mesnil-Villemont
12 Aug 44	124W	MN928 ZY-G	G/C C. H. Appleton (K)	sdbF near Flers
12 Aug 44	440	MP122	F/O J. F. Dewar (K)	sdbF near Condé-sur-Noireau
13 Aug 44	84GSU	EK243	P/O A. M. R. G. Paquot (K)	csd Studland Bay
13 Aug 44	440	MN720	F/O R. E. M. McCurdy (K)	sdbF near Flers
13 Aug 44	198	MN813 TP-R	F/L N. G. Pye	hbF b/o a/t Fr
13 Aug 44	184	MN864 BR-Y	Lt J. Schlebusch (E)	hbd? f/l Habloville
13 Aug 44	247	MN867 ZY-Y	P/O A. Younger (PoW)	missing near Ménil-Hermei
14 Aug 44	609	JP966	P/O R. G. Grant (PoW)	ftr (Falaise-Trun)
14 Aug 44	175	JR388 HH-T	F/L C. W. C. Henman (PoW)	g/lk F? b/o near Falaise
14 Aug 44	175	MN138 HH-X	F/O P. S. G. Moran (K)	sdbF near Bernay
14 Aug 44	174	MN577 XP-S	F/L F. A. Grantham (K)[13]	hbF b/o near Sentilly
14 Aug 44	164	MN885	F/L A. E. Napier (K)	F? csd W Falaise
15 Aug 44	609	JP659	W/O F. L. Taylor (K)	ftr (Falaise-Trun)
15 Aug 44	266	MN184	F/S H. Wheeler (E)	sdbF S Falaise
15 Aug 44	438	MN426 F3-H	F/O W. H. Morrison (K)	hit tree csd near Trun
15 Aug 44	193	MN602	F/L W. A. Switzer (PoW)	sdbF near Argentan
16 Aug 44	263	MN878	F/L J. B. Purkis (E)	sdbF near Bernay
17 Aug 44	183	R8970 HF-P	F/S R. Gibson (E)	sdb Bf109s Le Neubourg
17 Aug 44	183	JP681 HF-M	F/L G. C. Campbell-Brown (K)	sdb Bf109s Le Neubourg
17 Aug 44	183	JP789 HF-V	W/O W. A. J. Carragher (PoW)	sdb Bf109s Le Neubourg
17 Aug 44	245	JP898	Lt W. A. Gale (K)	F? csd Ticheville
17 Aug 44	183	JR148	W/O G. F. Humphrey (K)	sdb Bf109s Le Neuborg
17 Aug 44	FLS	MN114	F/L P. H. B. Unwin	e/f hit trees on app Milfield
17 Aug 44	184	MN255 BR-D	P/O R. Downing (PoW)	sdb Fw190s NE Livarot
17 Aug 44	197	MN341 OV-L	F/S D. J. A. W. Price (K)	sdbF or e/a Vimoutiers
17 Aug 44	266	MN680	F/S W. R. Love (K)	sdb Fw190s near Livarot
17 Aug 44	245	MP137	F/L A. E. Miron (K)	hbF csd Les Autels (the 183 Sqn aircraft above correspond to claims by III/JG27 – Obgfr Tissat (1), Obfw Gromotka (1), Fw Arnold (1), Lt Fadschild (1). Claims by Maj Düllberg of III./JG27 and Fw Söldner of I/JG2 may relate to the 184 and 266 Sqn losses)
18 Aug 44	247	R7820 ZY-J	P/O A. E. Diggins (K)	sdbF Vimoutiers
18 Aug 44	198	R8966 TP-B	P/O J. Allen	hbF b/o near B.7
18 Aug 44	182	JP427	F/L A. J. Hay (K)	sdbF near Orbec
18 Aug 44	245	JP445	F/S L. A. Ryan (K)	ftr (E Vimoutiers)
18 Aug 44	84GSU	JP664	F/O R. C. Beaumont (K)	csd Piddletrenthide
18 Aug 44	609	JR125	F/L M. L. Carrick (K)	F? csd S Trun
18 Aug 44	181	JR128	F/O W. Grey (PoW)	hbF b/o E Livarot
18 Aug 44	137	MN126 SF-X	F/L M. Wood (K)	sdbF (Vimoutiers)
18 Aug 44	184	MN131	F/L D. H. Gross (K)	missing WSW Trun
18 Aug 44	438	MN347 F3-Z	F/O G. H. Sharpe (K)	spun in near Orbec
18 Aug 44	197	MN463 OV-M	F/S L. S. Bell (K)	missing near Vimoutiers
18 Aug 44	438	MN579 F3-J	F/L G. P. Edington (PoW)	hbF b/o near Roiville
18 Aug 44	183	MN595	F/O R. D. Ackers (K)	sdbF S Falaise
18 Aug 44	184	MN623	F/O R. J. Currie (K)	sdbF WSW Trun
18 Aug 44	245	MN915	Lt P. Clulow (E)	missing S Trun
18 Aug 44	440	MN929	F/O J. S. Colville (K)	sdbF near Vimoutiers
18 Aug 44	175	MN990	F/L H. Davies	hbF f/l a/t (Vimoutiers)
18 Aug 44	247	MP144 ZY-G	F/L R. Guthrie (K)	sdbF near Vimoutiers
19 Aug 44	609	JP975	P/O J. K. Stellin (K)	ftr (Orbec)
19 Aug 44	245	JR429 MR-A	F/L W. B. Edwards	hbF f/l 4 m SE Trun
19 Aug 44	181	MM961EL-Q	F/S C. Pole (PoW)	hbF b/o 2 m E Vimoutiers
19 Aug 44	198	MN119 TP-F	F/L S. G. J. Lane (PoW)	sdbF near Vimoutiers
19 Aug 44	440	MN154	F/O R. H. Milne (PoW)	missing near Le Sap
19 Aug 44	182	MN288	Lt R. G. Jennings (K)	sdbF 3 m NE Vimoutiers
19 Aug 44	439	MN401 5V-G	P/O R. A. Porrit (K)	ftr last seen SE Vimoutiers
19 Aug 44	198	MN877 TP-Y	F/S F. Bonnet (K)	missing (Vimoutiers)
19 Aug 44	182	MN913	F/O C. C. Leigh (E)	sdbF near Vimoutiers
19 Aug 44	181	MN920 EL-T	W/O R. D. Gilbert (K)	csd E Vimoutiers cnk
19 Aug 44	439	PD448	F/L W. K. Scharff (K)	sdbF S Ticheville
20 Aug 44	198	MN719 TP-J	P/O J. T. N. Frost (K)	hbF f/l near Vimoutiers
22 Aug 44	198	JR253 TP-H	W/O C. E. Stratford (K)	hbF csd near Cormeilles
23 Aug 44	257	MN492	F/L D. P. Jenkins	f/l Llanglennith beach
24 Aug 44	84GSU	EK439	F/L P. W. Lear (K)	csd near Odiham
24 Aug 44	263	MP153	F/L H. M. Proctor (K)	sdbF near Quillebeuf
25 Aug 44	3TEU	MN207	F/S C. S. Cameron (K)	e/f csd Clyffe Pypard
25 Aug 44	263	MN477 HE-T	P/O S. D. Thyagarajan (K)	hbF csd E Pont-Audemer
25 Aug 44	164	MN588	F/O G. R. Trafford (K)	missing N Rouen
25 Aug 44	164	MN711 FJ-Z	F/S R. A. E. White (K)	sdbF N Rouen
25 Aug 44	263	MN883 HE-J	F/O A. W. Campbell (K)	hbF csd Theillement
25 Aug 44	164	PD457	S/L I. D. Waddy (PoW)	missing N Rouen
26 Aug 44	609	MN142	F/L R. J. H. Roelandt (K)	sdbF E Rouen
26 Aug 44	182	MN714 XM-F	F/S A. Bales	e/f f/l 5 m SE Evreux
27 Aug 44	175	JR223	P/O B. L. J. Foley (PoW)	missing near Rouen
27 Aug 44	137	MN803 SF-V	F/O I. C. Hutcheson (K)	hbF b/o W Rouen
28 Aug 44	83GSU	R8897 7S-V	F/L A. C. Jonas (K)	s/f csd near Milford
29 Aug 44	3TEU	JR301	W/O J. N. Philpott (K)	e/f csd N Kewstoke
31 Aug 44	174	MN608 XP-D	F/L H. R. H. F. Irwin	F? f/l near Albert
3 Sept 44	3TEU	MM958	F/S R. W. Ainsley	e/f f/l near Stratton
3 Sept 44	440	MN764	F/O J. Campbell	dila B.26
5 Sept 44	257	MP121 FM-O	F/L W. F. Watts (PoW)	hbF last seen Oosterschelde
6 Sept 44	257	JR219	F/O F. J. Broad	hit by MN947 Manston
6 Sept 44	257	MN947	F/O W. B. Richardson (K)	tbto hit JR219 Manston
7 Sept 44	3TEU	JP537	P/O R. W. Keller	e/f f/l SW Witney
8 Sept 44	182	EK289	W/O T. W. Coburn (K)	sdbF SW Aeltre
8 Sept 44	181	MN994	F/L G. F. Stooks (PoW)	e/f F? f/l (Venlo, NL-Wesel)
9 Sept 44	440	MN817	F/S N. L. Gordon	g/lk F? f/l NE Brussels
9 Sept 44	439	MP152	F/O G. W. Hewson (PoW)	hbF b/o E Vlissingen
10 Sept 44	3TEU	EK179 PA-I	F/O A. J. Lord	e/f w/u Aston Down
10 Sept 44	263	JP933	F/O F. S. Le Gear (K)	F? missing (Dutch Islands)
10 Sept 44	184	MN590 BR-?	P/O J. F. Sellors (E)	sdbF Westerschelde
10 Sept 44	174	MN753	W/C W. Pitt-Brown	hbF b/o Lille-Ghent
10 Sept 44	440	MN796	F/O F. J. Crowley	e/f f/l near B.58
10 Sept 44	198	MP116 TP-T	F/L D. Palmer-Perrin (K)	tbto csd B.35
11 Sept 44	182	MN472 XM-Z	F/O P. J. Spellman (E)	ftr (Breda-Dordrecht)
11 Sept 44	175	MN983	F/L W. J. Moore (E)	sdbF Terneuzen
11 Sept 44	83GSU	MP202	F/S E. N. A. Lush	s/f csd 1 m NE Bognor

Date	Unit	Aircraft	Pilot	Circumstances
13 Sept 44	197	MP198 OV-K	F/O M. D. Reid (K)	sdbF near Boulogne
13 Sept 44	164	PD515	F/O G. C. T. Deas (E)	hbd? b/o near Roosendaal
14 Sept 44	198	JR384	P/O H. F. R. Goblet	f/l Llangennith beach
14 Sept 44	609	PD505	S/L R. A. Lallemant	e/fire w/u B.53
18 Sept 44	198	JP482 TP-D	F/O J. T. Boundy (K)	hbF csd N Cap Gris Nez
20 Sept 44	137	PD551 SF-U	Sgt A. H. O. Butler (K)	e/fire csd Rethy
21 Sept 44	247	JP842	F/O R. Walker-Lutz (K)	csd 3 m N Arnhem cnk
22 Sept 44	181	JP800 EL-R	F/O T. I. Pervin (K)	F? f/l E B.78
22 Sept 44	181	MN241	P/O D. R. Shearburn (K)	sdbF Erp, NL
22 Sept 44	247	JR208 ZY-C	F/S J. A. D. Meechan	e/f F? f/l S Helmond rnc
23 Sept 44	137	MN421 SF-D	W/O T. J. Pike	dila B.78 nr
23 Sept 44	182	MN664 XM-H	F/S A. Bales	dila B.78
23 Sept 44	175	MN986 HH-T	–	dest by shell-fire B.70
24 Sept 44	137	MN955	S/L G. Piltingsrud (K)	sdb Fw190s near Kalkar
24 Sept 44	247	MN973 ZY-O	F/S I. A. Lloyd (K)	sdbF Kevelaer
24 Sept 44	439	PD465	F/O R. W. Vokey (K)	csd 3 m N Oosterhout cnk (claims by Lt Ellenrieder, I/JG26, NW Geilenkirchen, and two RP Typhoons by II Jagdkorps, N Venlo)
26 Sept 44	247	MM973	F/S F. Barwise (PoW)	sdbF near Schijndel
26 Sept 44	183	MN130 HF-V	F/L R. U. Williams (K)	hbF b/o off Dunkirk
26 Sept 44	175	MN582 HH-A	F/S W. R. S. Hurrell (K)	sdb Bf109s Apeldoorn (claim by Lt Klaffenbach, III/JG4)
27 Sept 44	3TEU	JP904	F/L R. A. Yates	e/f f/l Ashburton
27 Sept 44	175	MN717 HH-N	F/O N. J. Scott (PoW)	hbF b/o e/t (Ruhr)
27 Sept 44	439	PD458	W/O W. A. Gray (K)	sdbF near Geldern
28 Sept 44	438	JR497 F3-F	F/O A. H. Vickers (PoW)	hbF b/o S Papenbeek
28 Sept 44	137	MN169 SF-Z	P/O H. T. Nicholls (PoW)	hbF b/o near Kassel
28 Sept 44	439	MN375	F/O M. J. A. Cote	rof b/o Luxemburg
28 Sept 44	609	MN954	F/L J. N. C. Vandaele (K)	hbF b/o near Rotterdam
28 Sept 44	247	MN998 ZY-F	P/O B. F. Lee (K)	s/f csd 3 m SE Boxtel
28 Sept 44	137	MP125 SF-M	F/O D. W. Guttridge (K)	sdbF near Kassel
29 Sept 44	181	R8843	F/L T. F. Rosser (PoW)	hbF f/l S Goch
29 Sept 44	182	MN599	F/S T. S. Edwards (K)	ftr (Huizen)
29 Sept 44	438	PD479 F3-Q	F/O J. E. Cornelison (K)	sdb Bf109s E Nijmegen (claim by Uffz Utz, II/JG27, Arnhem 1117 hrs)
30 Sept 44	FLS	R8967	F/O S. Lloyd	e/f f/l near Lowick
30 Sept 44	137	MN627 SF-N	W/O M. J. Whitby	f/l 2m SW Nijmegen cnk
1 Oct 44	183	JP856 HF-H	F/S E. M. Denny	e/f f/l 5 m S Antwerp
2 Oct 44	439	MN379 5V-E	P/O W. G. McBride	hbF f/l nml (NE Geldern)
2 Oct 44	266	MN493 ZH-O	S/L J. D. Wright (PoW)	hbd f/l NW Rotterdam
2 Oct 44	198	MN880 TP-Q	W/O S. Barnes (K)	csd on t/o B.53
5 Oct 44	197	JR366 OV-T	F/O H. F. Wakeman (K)	sdbF near Ederveen
5 Oct 44	439	MN765	F/O R. A. Johns (K)	hbF csd Speelberg
6 Oct 44	175	MN376 HH-S	W/O I. W. Cain (K)	hbF b/o S Nijmegen
6 Oct 44	182	MN592	P/O N. G. Sievwright	e/f f/l S B.80 rnc
6 Oct 44	440	MN805 I8-D	F/L C. S. Aistrop (K)	ftr last seen Geldern
6 Oct 44	266	MN866 ZH-J	W/O A. W. Paul (K)	hbF b/o near Hook of Holland
7 Oct 44	440	MN641 I8-J	S/L W. H. Pentland (K)	sdbF SW Hamminkeln
7 Oct 44	184	MN779 BR-R	F/L J. P. Jessel	tbto csd B.80
7 Oct 44	164	MN862	W/O J. B. Teather (K)	ftr (Aardenburg)
7 Oct 44	438	MP135 F3-G	F/L A. B. Newsome (K)	sdbF S Coesfeld
8 Oct 44	257	JR365 FM-E	W/O J. R. Powell (K)	sdbF S Bergen op Zoom
11 Oct 44	245	JP661	W/O E. Hughes	tbto csd B.80
11 Oct 44	137	JP663	F/O R. S. Wilson (PoW)	F? f/l 2 m S Zaltbommel
12 Oct 44	247	DN252 ZY-N	W/O S. R. Thomas	hbF f/l 2 m S Gemert
12 Oct 44	193	MN529	F/S R. A. Pratt (K)	sdbF near Breskens
12 Oct 44	182	PD477	W/O F. W. Cuthbertson (E)	hbF f/l near Oostnun
13 Oct 44	247	EK223	W/O K. H. Brown	hbF f/l a/t
13 Oct 44	245	JP589 MR-T	F/S J. Darlington	tbto w/u B.80
13 Oct 44	263	MN476	P/O J. Thould (K)	sdbF SE Hoogstraten
13 Oct 44	181	MN640 EL-C	F/L R.D. W. McKenzie (K)	sdbF Amersfoort
13 Oct 44	197	MN921 OV-S	F/O W. B. T. Smiley (PoW)	hbF f/l near Hensden
14 Oct 44	263	R8923 HE-U	F/L D. F. Evans (K)	F? cld MN769 csd S Oostburg
14 Oct 44	263	MN769 HE-B	F/O A. Barr (K)	cld R8923 csd S Oostburg
18 Oct 44	84GSU	JR201	F/S L. S. Brookes	e/f f/l Kent
18 Oct 44	182	MN248	P/O S. T. Byer (K)	hbF f/l near Venraj
18 Oct 44	245	MN319 MR-Z	F/S J. Darlington (K)	hbF csd E Horst
18 Oct 44	438	MN555 F3-Z	F/O V. E. McMann (PoW)	e/f F? 3 m S Rheden
18 Oct 44	197	MP157	P/O F. J. Vance (K)	sdbF near Korteven
18 Oct 44	266	PD513	F/L D. McGibbon (PoW)	hbF b/o N Venlo
19 Oct 44	83GSU	JR367	F/S D. V. Oram	e/f f/l N Louvain
19 Oct 44	184	MN851 BR-H	F/O R. A. Gaskin (K)	F? csd near Neukirchen
20 Oct 44	440	PD469	F/O R. W. Doidge (K)	sdbF near Nijverdal
21 Oct 44	266	JP441	F/S R. A. Cambrook (K)	sdbF SW Breskens
21 Oct 44	197	MP143 OV-G	P/O R. H. Jones	hbF b/o a/t NL
22 Oct 44	439	MP136	F/O R. V. Smith (E)	sdbF b/o 's Hertogenbosch
24 Oct 44	247	JP688 ZY-R	F/L P. Langston (K)	ftr last seen Loon op Zand
24 Oct 44	263	MN295 HE-S	F/L A. L. S. Hallet (PoW)	hbF b/o 2 m SE Zaltbommel
24 Oct 44	175	PD494 HH-T	F/O R. W. Clarke (K)	hbF b/o 2 m E Megan
28 Oct 44	174	MN153 XP-T	W/O W. F. Morely	hbF b/o St. Antonis
28 Oct 44	182	MN204	W/O K. Lewis (K)	sdb Fw190s near Venlo (claims by Maj Hackl (1), Lt Vogt (1), II/JG26, Venlo-Kempen 1325 hrs)
28 Oct 44	193	MN767 DP-C	S/L J. M. G. Plamondon	hbF f/l near Merxem
28 Oct 44	439	MN870 5V-P	F/O M. P. Laycock (K)	sdbF 4 m W Deventer
28 Oct 44	197	PD460	F/O G. G. Mahaffy	hbF f/l near Dunkirk
29 Oct 44	609	JP494	F/S F. S. Hammond	hbF f/l near Brugge
29 Oct 44	247	JR202 ZY-N	W/O K. H. Brown	F? f/l near Eindhoven
29 Oct 44	247	JR249	W/O S. L. Williams	tbto w/u B.78
29 Oct 44	609	MN268	W/O T. F. Annear	e/f f/l Estaires
29 Oct 44	440	MN352	S/L A. E. Monson	hbF b/o S Geldrop
29 Oct 44	137	MN995 SF-X	F/O E. Ashworth	F? b/o near Roermond
2 Nov 44	182	MN699	F/L P. H. Strong (K)	sdbF near Weert
3 Nov 44	439	JR500 5V-X	F/O R. N. MacDonald (K)	stalled and csd near B.78
3 Nov 44	198	MN702 TP-F	F/O J. L. Allan (K)	hbF f/l Zuid Beveland
4 Nov 44	181	DN549 EL-C	P/O E. C. Jarvis	hbF f/l E Geldrop
4 Nov 44	247	EK135	W/O S. R. Thomas	e/f f/l 7 m NE Louvain
4 Nov 44	247	PD603	F/O D. Wallace (K)	sdbF Apeldoorn
6 Nov 44	439	MN345	F/O J. A. Brown (PoW)	hbd? g/lk b/o W Deventer

Date	Unit	Aircraft	Pilot	Circumstances
6 Nov 44	438	PD475 F3-G	F/O R. G. Crosby	e/f f/l 1 m NE B.78
7 Nov 44	263	PD506	F/O A. G. Davies (E)	hbF f/l SW Zwolle
8 Nov 44	247	EK133 ZY-L	F/O D. C. Orriss	efto f/l near B.78
8 Nov 44	164	MP174 FJ-X	F/L C. J. G. Demoulin	e/f f/l S Wavre
9 Nov 44	247	JP937	F/O W. Osborne (K)	e/f csd Niewchirken
10 Nov 44	FLS	EJ995	F/O A. B. E. Rutherford (K)	expl csd Goswick ranges
10 Nov 44	3TEU	EK151	F/O D. H. Cumming	efto w/u Aston Down
11 Nov 44	263	MN196	W/O J. Quigley	tbto bomb expl B.70
11 Nov 44	609	MN205	S/L T. Y. Wallace (K)	sdbF off Dunkirk
11 Nov 44	439	MN547	F/O J. G. Fraser (E)	F? f/l 8 m S Sneek
11 Nov 44	440	MP124	F/O F. J. Crowley (K)	sdbF SE Staphorst
16 Nov 44	174	JP602	F/O J. G. Penfield	e/f f/l 3 m NW Weymouth
16 Nov 44	3TEU	MN231	F/S B. S. Haworth	efto w/u Aston Down
18 Nov 44	4	EK429	F/L R. M. Cowell (PoW)	hbF f/l E Kessel
18 Nov 44	137	MN191 SF-P	F/O N. J. M. Manfred (K)	ftr (E Sittard)
18 Nov 44	440	MN475	F/O R. J. Reilly (K)	hbF csd N Wassenburg
18 Nov 44	438	MP131 F3-J	F/O N. E. Dawber	hbF b/o 4 m SSE Arnhem
18 Nov 44	263	PD566	F/L J. Arkle (K)	sdbF S Roermond
19 Nov 44	137	JR207 SF-B	F/O M. J. B. Cole	F? f/l SSW Geilenkirchen
19 Nov 44	439	MN357	F/O R. A. Hiltz	hbF f/l 3 m N Maeseik
19 Nov 44	440	MN801	F/O J. M. Cordick (K)	hbF csd 2 m E Goch
19 Nov 44	266	MN807 ZH-G	F/S J. N. Laing (E)	hbd? f/l 4 m SSE Leerdam
19 Nov 44	183	PD516	F/O J. A. Hollingworth (K)	csd in RP attack NNE Ede
19 Nov 44	257	PD526 FM-F	F/O F. H. Broad (K)	F? csd SE Zwolle
19 Nov 44	439	PD607	F/O J. G. Martin (K)	hbF b/o 10 m NE Roermond
21 Nov 44	175	JP666 HH-W	F/O J. D. Wood	e/f f/l West Wellow
21 Nov 44	439	MN124	F/O R. A. Hiltz (K)	hbF b/o E Rhede
21 Nov 44	137	MN533 SF-E	F/O J. R. Baldwin	tbto w/u B.78
21 Nov 44	197	MN752 OV-D	F/L E. K. Necklen (K)	cld MN881 csd Amersfoort
21 Nov 44	197	MN881 OV-R	P/O C. B. Hall (K)	cld MN752 csd Amersfoort
21 Nov 44	440	PD523	F/O J. L. Duncan (PoW)	hbF f/l NE Horst
25 Nov 44	193	MN912	F/O G. E. Langille (K)	sdbF SW Voorthuizen
26 Nov 44	168	JP677 QC-P	F/L J. K. Brown	f/l Brighton beach cnk
28 Nov 44	198	JP900 TP-O	F/L D. G. Colebrook (PoW)	hbF last seen S Utrecht
28 Nov 44	193	MN763	F/L J. H. Hilton	csd on t/o B.70
28 Nov 44	184	MP146 BR-W	Sgt J. Thomson (K)	F? csd S Coesfeld
28 Nov 44	440	MP183	F/O A. Frombolo (PoW)	hbF b/o 2 m NNW Papenbeek
29 Nov 44	247	MN647 ZY-S	F/O A. C. McWhirter (PoW)	e/f F? f/l e/t NL
29 Nov 44	182	MN970	F/O A. J. Whitamore (PoW)	hbF f/l SW Rheydt
29 Nov 44	182	PD552	F/L W. M. Weeks (K)	hbF csd 5 m N B.78
3 Dec 44	184	JR310 BR-K	P/O J. C. Richardson (K)	csd in bad wx Shorncliffe
3 Dec 44	184	MN136	F/L C. G. Haddow (K)	csd in bad wx Shorncliffe
3 Dec 44	439	MN348	F/L W. L. Saunders (K)	sdbF Buldern (possibly the aircraft claimed by Lt Günther, I./JG26)
3 Dec 44	184	MN889	F/O W. T. O'Brien (K)	csd in bad wx Shorncliffe
4 Dec 44	164	MN237 FJ-O	F/L N. L. Merret	hbF f/l a/t (Tiel)
5 Dec 44	137	MN586 SF-G	F/O J. Gates (PoW)	hbF b/o N Dinslaken
5 Dec 44	247	MP126 ZY-Y	F/O F. K. Wiersum (PoW)	hbF f/l near Bocholt
5 Dec 44	609	PD470	S/L C. J. G. Demoulin (PoW)	hbF b/o Ede
5 Dec 44	137	PD609	W/O W. A. Flett	e/f f/l near B.56
7 Dec 44	198	JR338	–	hangar collapsed B.77
8 Dec 44	198	JR248 TP-P	F/O M. A. Milich (K)	ftr (Hoevelaken)
8 Dec 44	247	MM951 ZY-V	F/S J. Coull (K)	sdbF near Lette
8 Dec 44	440	MN251* I8-T	P/O A. E. Sugden (K)	o/s B.78 into canal
8 Dec 44	198	MN291 TP-S	Lt P. H. A. Brisdoux (K)	sdbF near Hoevelaken
8 Dec 44	181	MN888	F/O H. K. Lyle (K)	ftr last seen Dummer See
8 Dec 44	175	MP176 HH-Y	P/O G. B. Swift	rof w/u B.80
9 Dec 44	609	MN150	F/S R. J. Portheous (K)	ftr in bad wx N Gorinchem
10 Dec 44	164	MN284	W/O J. R. K. Black	e/f b/o 1 m NW Beers
11 Dec 44	198	JR245 TP-N	F/L O. H. Oden (K)	sdbF NE Zaltbommel
11 Dec 44	164	JR507 FJ-W	F/L N. L. Merrett (PoW)[14]	sdbF W Utrecht
11 Dec 44	257	MN652 FM-Y	F/O R. Logan	e/f b/o Goirle
15 Dec 44	83GSU	DN592	F/S P. Tullie	efto csd Tangmere
15 Dec 44	182	MN798 XM-Y	F/O J. A. Patterson	hbF csd near Halst
15 Dec 44	439	PD478	F/L C. A. Lambert (K)	hbF f/l NW Haltern
23 Dec 44	247	MP189	S/L B. G. Stapleton (PoW)	hbd? f/l E Duren
24 Dec 44	247	JP583	F/O H. Stevenson (K)	sdbF Poteau
24 Dec 44	168	JP919	F/O D. G. Dickson (PoW)	hbF last seen SE Malmédy
24 Dec 44	181	MN317 EL-H	F/L J. A. Donfox	dila B.64
24 Dec 44	440	MN453	F/O C. F. Harwood (K)	sdbF SE Schleiden
24 Dec 44	197	MN634 OV-R	P/O D. I. McFee (PoW)	sdb Fw190s near Gronau
24 Dec 44	440	MN665	F/O D. H. Cumming (K)	sdb Fw190 SE Eindhoven
24 Dec 44	193	MN705	P/O N. I. Freakley (K)	ftr after d/f E Enschede
24 Dec 44	439	MN894	F/L K. F. Sage (K)	sdbF near Mayen

*This aircraft was subsequently retrieved and repaired.

Below: While escorting a VIP back from the Continent on 26 November 1944, Flight Lieutenant J. K. Brown of 168 Squadron made a forced-landing in JP677 'QC-P' on Brighton beach. (via A. Saunders)

Below: MN251 'I8-F' of 440 Squadron just after recovery from the canal near Eindhoven by 403 R&SU. The pilot had been drowned when the Typhoon failed to get airborne, overshot the runway, and turned over in the canal. (A. Burden)

Date	Unit	Aircraft	Pilot	Circumstances
24 Dec 44	257	MN931 FM-S	P/O A. B. Campbell (K)	sdbF W Utrecht
24 Dec 44	438	MP178 F3-H	W/O R. F. Breen (K)	sdbF near Bullange
24 Dec 44	438	MP186 F3-V	F/O D. J. Washburn (K)	sdbF NW Dahlem
24 Dec 44	197	MP196 OV-G	W/O H. W. Read (K)	sdb Fw190s near Gronau
24 Dec 44	440	PD462	F/O W. T. Dunkeld (K)	sdb Fw190 SE Eindhoven
24 Dec 44	439	PD492	F/S W. A. Wright (K)	sdb P.47s 4 m SE Duren
24 Dec 44	263	RB335	F/L L. Unwin (K)	sdbF near Barneveld
25 Dec 44	175	JP918 HH-Y	W/O H. E. R. Merlin	hbF f/l near Malmédy
25 Dec 44	266	MN206	F/S P. C. Green (K)	F? csd near Winterswijk
25 Dec 44	440	MP149 I8-P	F/O H. J. Hardy	hbF b/o near B.78
25 Dec 44	266	MP180 ZH-K	F/O D. S. Eadie (PoW)	sdb e/a near Dortmund
26 Dec 44	168	EJ946	F/O V. O. Gilbert (K)	ftr (Prum)
26 Dec 44	137	JP504 SF-E	W/O W. A. Flett (K)	hbF csd W Schleiden
26 Dec 44	439	MN482	F/O W. Kubicki	dila B.78
26 Dec 44	263	MP132	F/L D. J. Turner (K)	sdbF N Deventer
26 Dec 44	124W	MP156 CG	G/C C. L. Green (PoW)	hbF b/o W St-Vith
26 Dec 44	439	PD459	F/O J. D. Sweeney	hbF csd on landing B.78
26 Dec 44	174	RB308	W/O K. E. Love	rof f/l near Ypres
27 Dec 44	174	JP499	F/O J. M. Harbidge	F? g/lk f/l near Malmédy
27 Dec 44	184	JR493 BR-B	Lt A. N. Fisher (PoW)	cld MN318 b/o W Ahrdorf
27 Dec 44	137	MN234 SF-T	P/O N. F. Swift (PoW)	F? last seen 10 m E St-Vith
27 Dec 44	184	MN318 BR-T	Lt A. E. Collet (K)	cld JR493 csd W Ahrdorf
27 Dec 44	184	MN682	W/O J. S. Marshall	F? csu fail b/o W Schleiden
27 Dec 44	439	MP145	F/O B. E. Bell (PoW)	hbF b/o NW St-Vith
27 Dec 44	181	MP191 EL-P	S/L W. H. B. Short (K)	cld u/i a/c SW St-Vith
29 Dec 44	168	JR332	F/L E. Gibbons (K)	sdb Fw190s SW Steinfurt
29 Dec 44	247	MN253	F/O G. M. Hill	efto w/u B.78
29 Dec 44	247	MN356 ZY-J	F/L E. A. McGee	hbF (Osnabrück) nr
29 Dec 44	168	MN639 QC-S	F/L R. F. Plant (PoW)	sdb e/a SW Steinfurt
29 Dec 44	439	MN791	W/O S. A. Church (PoW)	sdb Fw190 S Coesfeld
29 Dec 44	175	PD532 HH-H	F/L M. De Kerdrel (K)	sdbF SE Steinfurt
29 Dec 44	137	RB194	F/O J. L. Crossley (PoW)	hbF f/l NE Sulingen
29 Dec 44	440	RB201	F/L D. E. Jenvey (K)	hbF f/l near Gronau
31 Dec 44	182	MN262	F/O J. A. Patterson (K)	sdbF (St-Vith)
31 Dec 44	247	MN399 ZY-M	W/O R. G. McGregor (K)	sdb Fw190 W Steinhuder Lake
31 Dec 44	182	MN540	F/L T. Entwistle	hbF f/l near St-Vith
31 Dec 44	137	MN660 SF-K	P/O J. A. D. Shemeld (K)	sdbF near Hunteburg
31 Dec 44	181	MN690	Cpt H. R. Isachsen (PoW)	hbF b/o Vielsalm
31 Dec 44	197	PD471 OV-S	F/O R. H. Jones (K)	hbF csd near Aalburg
31 Dec 44	247	PD612 ZY-K	W/O W. H. A. Lye (PoW)	hbF csd S Münster
31 Dec 44	182	RB196	P/O N. G. Sievwright (K)	sdbF (St-Vith)
31 Dec 44	197	RB321 ---A[15]	S/L A. H. Smith (PoW)	hbF f/l 2 m SW Culemborg
1 Jan 45	181	EK172 EL-H	–	destroyed in air raid B.78
1 Jan 45	183	EK497 HF-E	F/O D. Webber (K)	sdb P.51 near Y.29 Asche
1 Jan 45	182	JP397 XM-S	–	damaged in air raid B.78 rnc
1 Jan 45	182	JP654 XM-P	–	destroyed in air raid B.78
1 Jan 45	137	JR261 SF-Z	F/S L. A. V. Burrows (K)	damaged in air raid B.78 rnc
1 Jan 45	182	JR328	–	destroyed in air raid B.78
1 Jan 45	440	JR530 I8-Y	–	damaged in air raid B.78 rnc
1 Jan 45	168	MN486 QC-D	F/L H. P. Gibbons (K)	sdb e/a B.78
1 Jan 45	440	MN569	–	destroyed in air raid B.78
1 Jan 45	439	MN589	F/O S. Angelini (K)	sdb e/a near Rips (shot down by Ofw G. Schmidt, 15./JG3, who was also shot down moments later)
1 Jan 45	438	MN607	–	destroyed in air raid B.78
1 Jan 45	182	MN768 XM-T	–	destroyed in air raid B.78
1 Jan 45	438	MN816	–	destroyed in air raid B.78
1 Jan 45	182	MN823 XM-W	–	damaged in air raid B.78 rnc
1 Jan 45	439	MN869	–	destroyed in air raid B.78
1 Jan 45	440	MN940 I8-M	–	destroyed in air raid B.78
1 Jan 45	440	MN984	–	destroyed in air raid B.78
1 Jan 45	440	MP139 I8-W	–	destroyed in air raid B.78
1 Jan 45	438	MP177 F3-F	–	destroyed in air raid B.78
1 Jan 45	438	PD503 F3-R	F/O R. W. Keller (K)	destroyed in air raid B.78
1 Jan 45	438	PD556 F3-Q	F/L P. Wilson (K)	destroyed in air raid B.78
1 Jan 45	440	PD595	–	destroyed in air raid B.78
1 Jan 45	440	PD621	–	destroyed in air raid B.78
1 Jan 45	440	RB192	–	destroyed in air raid B.78
1 Jan 45	143W	RB205 FGG	–	destroyed in air raid B.78
1 Jan 45	193	RB218	F/L A. S. Smith (K)	sdbF W Zuilichem
1 Jan 45	439	RB257 5V-S	–	damaged in air raid B.78 rnc
2 Jan 45	247	MP201 ZY-O	W/O S. G. Jones	hit by RB209 B.78
2 Jan 45	168	RB209	F/L J. B. Stubbs (K)	cld MP201 on t/o B.78
5 Jan 45	257	MN868 FM-W	P/O G. D. Jones (K)	e/f f/l NE Brecht
5 Jan 45	257	PD454 FM-T	F/O B. J. Spragg	e/f f/l near B.58
7 Jan 45	1FP	RB313	2/O A. J. Murray	e/f f/l 6 m SE Ghent
13 Jan 45	123W	MN598[16]	W/C W. Dring (K)	csd on landing A.84
13 Jan 45	56OTU	RB210	F/L R. W. Hall (K)	csd in bad wx N Charlton
14 Jan 45	247	R8688 ZY-X	F/S D. C. Horn (K)	sdb P.47s csd 3 m SW Ewijk
14 Jan 45	55OTU	JP916	W/O W. L. Lang	e/f f/l 2 m E Aston Down
14 Jan 45	182	PD450	W/O R. Sockyer	efto w/u B.86
14 Jan 45	184	RB200 BR-K	F/L I. G. Handyside (PoW)	hbF f/l N Bocholt
14 Jan 45	439	RB204	F/L M. J. A. Cote (E)	hbF f/l Deventer
14 Jan 45	174	RB331	F/O G. B. Chapman (PoW)	sdb P.47 b/o E Haltern
15 Jan 45	56OTU	EJ965	Sgt H. G. Evans	e/f f/l 2 m N Wooler
17 Jan 45	55OTU	MN938	W/O H. C. Blizard (K)	e/f f/l 2 m W Malmesbury
20 Jan 45	257	MN696 FM-R	W/O K. E. Button (K)	csd in bad wx SW Utrecht
20 Jan 45	438	PD446 F3-Z	F/L E. J. D. McKay	hbF f/l N B.78
20 Jan 45	257	PD598 FM-T	P/O W. E. Whitmore (E)	missing in bad wx SE Utecht
20 Jan 45	266	RB260	F/O N. V. Borland	dila B.70
20 Jan 45	439	RB317	F/O J. D. Sweeney (PoW)	hbF f/l Arnhem
20 Jan 45	257	RB319 FM-V	F/L M. Y. Lao (K)	csd in bad wx SW Utrecht
21 Jan 45	440	PD601	F/O P. H. Kearse (K)	sdbF Montfoort
21 Jan 45	438	RB397	F/O P. G. Macklem	hit by PD592 taxiing B.78

Date	Unit	Aircraft	Pilot	Circumstances
22 Jan 45	439	MN424	F/O W. Kubicki	e/f f/l NW Eersel
22 Jan 45	438	MP128 F3-X	F/O F. R. F. Skelly (K)	sdbF NW Montfoort
22 Jan 45	439	MP134	S/L R. G. Crosby (E)	sdbF Uetterath
22 Jan 45	168	RB361	F/O W. G. Huddart (K)	ftr last seen NE Haltern
23 Jan 45	184	MN485 BR-G	Cpt A. F. Green	hbF f/l N Baexem rnc
23 Jan 45	440	RB325	F/L H. Byers (K)	sdbF Dremmen
23 Jan 45	438	RB333 F3-R	F/O I. J. V. Wallace (K)	sdbF S Geldern
24 Jan 45	56OTU	JP551	–	e/fire on start up Milfield
24 Jan 45	183	MN452 HF-W	F/O P. W. D'Albenas (E)	ftr last seen N Meppel
24 Jan 45	440	MN626 I8-B	P/O I. L. Gunnarson	e/f f/l SW Venlo
24 Jan 45	257	PD464 FM-V	F/O J. D. Lunn (K)	sdbF SW Utrecht
24 Jan 45	247	PD495 ZY-B	F/O M. J. Cheyney (PoW)	F? e/f f/l SE Borken
24 Jan 45	193	PD509 DP-R	W/O A. G. Randall	rof w/u B.70
28 Jan 45	83GSU	JP685	F/L J. W. Wilson	dila Westhampnett
29 Jan 45	413RSU	RB271	F/L G. E. Cassie	e/f dila B.70
31 Jan 45	193	RB404	–	e/fire on start up B.70
1 Feb 45	182	RB276	F/L W. J. L. S. Lowes (K)	e/f f/l 7 m N Hasselt
1 Feb 45	56OTU	RB343	P/O N. L. Gordon (K)	efto csd Milfield
2 Feb 45	168	MN265	F/O T. Lowe (E)	F? e/f f/l N Paderborn
2 Feb 45	175	MN358 HH-U	F/O B. S. Lyons (K)	sdbF NE Venlo
2 Feb 45	440	PD493 I8-F	F/O G. L. Passmore (K)	sdbF near Legden
3 Feb 45	55OTU	JP382	F/L C. T. H. McIntosh (K)	e/f csd near Chepstow
3 Feb 45	247	MN471 ZY-G	F/L E. A. Magee (PoW)	e/f f/l 15 m SE Münster
3 Feb 45	440	PD497	F/O J. F. Warrell (K)	spun in, NW Bocholt cnk
3 Feb 45	137	RB252 SF-T	F/S A. V. Crory (K)	ftr last seen Roermond
3 Feb 45	168	RB270	S/L E. C. H. Vernon-Jarvis (K)	sdbF near Dorenthe
4 Feb 45	83GSU	RB501	W/O J. Cunningham	e/f f/l near Cranleigh
6 Feb 45	181	PD561	S/L D. R. Crawford (K)	sdbF near Wietzen
8 Feb 45	56OTU	EK541	F/O E. P. Robey	e/f dila Milfield
8 Feb 45	198	MN344 TP-Q	F/L G. S. Chalmers	hbF f/l on fire B.86
8 Feb 45	609	MN360	F/O J. De Bruyn	hit tree b/o near Handel
8 Feb 45	174	MN570	F/O J. M. Harbidge	efto f/l Volkel
8 Feb 45	183	RB280 HF-W	F/L A. R. Cocks (PoW)	hbF b/o 2 m N Boxmeer
8 Feb 45	174	RB385	F/L R. F. Sweeting	e/f w/u B.80
9 Feb 45	83GSU	MN704	F/O J. N. Beattie (K)	e/f on app csd SE Dunsfold
10 Feb 45	197	PD447 OV-F	P/O D. E. Tapson (PoW)	ftr (Kalkar)
10 Feb 45	439	PD564	W/O B. Propas	e/f dila B.86
11 Feb 45	413RSU	PD616	–	destroyed by V-1 B.70
11 Feb 45	181	RB364	F/O K. Goddard (PoW)	hbF b/o SW Soest
13 Feb 45	55OTU	EJ951	W/O W. A. E. Corbett	e/f f/l N Elberton
13 Feb 45	164	EJ967 FJ-C	F/S C. L. Mouzon	hbF b/o near Kleve
13 Feb 45	181	JP672 EL-U	F/O D. W. D. Guest (K)	hit htc csd W Meschede
13 Feb 45	164	JR141	W/O A. M. Elston (PoW)	sdbF near Kleve
13 Feb 45	55OTU	JR318	Sgt P. W. Johnson	e/f f/l 2 m E Whitfield
13 Feb 45	56OTU	JR385	P/O A. E. Feney	e/f f/l W Longformacus
13 Feb 45	181	RB392	W/O W. A. J. Graham (PoW)	ftr last seen Werl
14 Feb 45	198	EJ958 TP-U	F/S A. W. Britton	efto f/l near B.77
14 Feb 45	56OTU	EK348	Sgt D. T. Donovan	e/f f/l near Wooler
14 Feb 45	198	JP669 TP-S	P/O L. W. Sellman (K)	hbF csd SE Goch
14 Feb 45	175	MN308	P/O R. P. Townsend (PoW)	hbF b/o 5 m S Goch
14 Feb 45	164	MN794 FJ-E	P/O I. A. S. Moore (K)	ftr last seen SE Kleve
14 Feb 45	263	PD467	W/O C. G. Points (K)	sdbF Wetten
14 Feb 45	263	PD550	F/O G. F. Gillman	dila B.89
14 Feb 45	438	RB226 F3-H	F/O F. A. Nixon (S)	F? csd S Geldern
14 Feb 45	609	RB311	F/L R. K. Gibson (K)	sdbF S Kleve
15 Feb 45	184	MN924 BR-X	W/O J. S. Marshall	b/o in bad wx E Louvain
16 Feb 45	198	MN467	F/O L. F. Bastin	e/f f/l near B.77
16 Feb 45	198	MN487 TP-R	W/O J. D. Cambell (K)	ftr last seen near Goch
21 Feb 45	184	JP535	F/L K. A. Creamer (PoW)	F? g/lk NE Soest
21 Feb 45	245	MN536	F/O H. S. Young (K)	hbF f/l near Vreden
21 Feb 45	184	MN749 BR-W	F/O W. D. Ross (K)	F? csd SW Bocholt
21 Feb 45	438	PD476 F3-E	W/O G. R. Errington (PoW)	hbF b/o NE Piershil
21 Feb 45	164	PD511	F/L W. K. Merret	hbF b/o W Kalkar
22 Feb 45	183	JR296 HF-V	F/L A. G. Hill (K)	sdbF near Marienbaum
22 Feb 45	257	MN420 FM-L	W/O W. H. Ewan	e/f dila B.89
22 Feb 45	183	MN941	Cpt A. Lens (K)	sdbF E Udem
22 Feb 45	439	MP151	F/L B. P. Swingler (K)	sdbF near Haldern
23 Feb 45	182	JP922	P/O J. A. Howard (K)	sdbF 3 m N Moers
23 Feb 45	182	MN422	F/S R. F. Whicker	efto f/l 3 m SSE Helmond
24 Feb 45	193	EK236	W/O J. A. Merryshaw	hbF b/o near Breda
24 Feb 45	183	JP682 HF-O	F/L G. H. Borham (K)	ftr last seen Geldern
24 Feb 45	181	JR438 EL-W	Sgt A. P. Mann (K)	hbF csd NE Lengerich
24 Feb 45	198	JR528 TP-Z	W/O J. M. Roberts (K)	sdbF E Weeze
24 Feb 45	175	MN534 HH-W	P/O G. B. Swift (PoW)	hbd? b/o near Dulmen
24 Feb 45	174	MN977	P/O R. B. T. Adams (K)	F? csd 6 m N Osnabrück
24 Feb 45	440	PD592	F/O J. Flintoft (PoW)	hbF f/l near Enschede
24 Feb 45	174	RB362	F/L B. F. Proddow (PoW)	F? g/lk f/l near Emmerich
25 Feb 45	609	MN178	F/O J. D. F. Wathieu (S)	sdbF near Weeze
25 Feb 45	184	MN972 BR-D	F/L N. Snelson (PoW)	F? e/f b/o 4 m N Rees
25 Feb 45	174	RB282	F/L H. Knight (PoW)	F? g/lk b/o NE Ahaus
26 Feb 45	164	JP367 FJ-J	–	damaged by V-1 B.77 rnc
27 Feb 45	175	JR376	W/O R. W. Ashman (K)	csd in bad wx N Altenhagen
28 Feb 45	182	R7771	W/O F. W. Cuthbertson (K)	hbF f/l near Lohne
28 Feb 45	183	EK498 HF-N	W/O J. H. P. W. Crowther (PoW)	sdbF W Xanten
28 Feb 45	55OTU	MP118	Sgt J. D. Austin	e/f f/l Charndon
28 Feb 45	266	RB253	P/O Shephard (PoW)	hbF b/o SW Xanten
28 Feb 45	440	RB338	F/O W. R. Gibbs (K)	sdbF E Goch
28 Feb 45	182	SW415	F/L J. H. Taylor (K)	hbF f/l near Lohne
1 Mar 45	183	JP969 HF-S	W/O D. A. Blair	tbto dila B.77 rnc
2 Mar 45	439	MN144	F/L L. C. Shaver (K)	sdbF NE Dulmen
2 Mar 45	198	MN354 TP-K	W/O W. A. Livesley (K)	sdb P.51s NW Neuss
2 Mar 45	440	MN380	F/L W. J. McCarthy	dila B.78
2 Mar 45	438	RB285 F3-Z	F/L D. J. Heard (PoW)	sdbF near Appelhülsen
3 Mar 45	609	EK380	P/O T. H. R. Goblet (PoW)	sdbF Xanten
3 Mar 45	197	MP113 OV-V	F/S R. J. Farmiloe	e/f f/l 3 m SE Volkel
5 Mar 45	55OTU	MP114	F/S P. Livingstone	hit by JR443 taxiing Aston Down
6 Mar 45	174	MN810	–	e/fire on start up B.80
7 Mar 45	245	JP936	F/L H. T. Mossip (K)	hit htc csd SW Soest
8 Mar 45	247	MN606 ZY-T	W/O M. G. Croft	dila B.64; rnc
8 Mar 45	56OTU	MP187	P/O R. F. D. Smith (K)	spun in near Kettleburn
9 Mar 45	193	RB381	S/L C. D. Erasmus (K)	hbd? csd Raalte
9 Mar 45	609	SW447	S/L E. R. A. Roberts (PoW)	hbF f/l SW Achthuizen
10 Mar 45	184	MN997 BR-Z	Sgt A. A. V. Maxwell	t/a B.80
10 Mar 45	609	PD449	W/O G. M. Reynolds	e/f dila B.77
12 Mar 45	55OTU	JR212	Sgt F. Gill (K)	csd in R. Severn
16 Mar 45	Napr	JP940	n/k	csd on trials
18 Mar 45	55OTU	MN146	Sgt L. Clayton	dila Chedworth
18 Mar 45	193	MP193 DP-K	W/O N. D. Samuels (K)	hbF f/l NE Arnhem
18 Mar 45	609	PD519	W/O G. M. Reynolds	tbto csd B.77 rnc
19 Mar 45	609	JP858	W/O F. S. Hammond (PoW)	e/f f/l NE Deventer
19 Mar 45	263	JR362	W/O R. A. Richardson (PoW)	hbF b/o NE Deventer

Date	Unit	Aircraft	Pilot	Circumstances
19 Mar 45	175	RB214 HH-B	S/L M. Savage (K)	spun in, NW Hamm cnk
19 Mar 45	247	RB480	F/L T. H. McGovern (PoW)	hbF f/l near Appelhülsen
20 Mar 45	550TU	JP433	F/S J. A. Mason (K)	cld Anson on app Aston Down
22 Mar 45	184	MN301 BR-Y	Sgt P. T. Hall	dila B.100
22 Mar 45	439	PD451 5V-A	F/O A. W. Saunders	dila B.78
22 Mar 45	193	RB500	F/L G. H. Hilton	w/u B.89
23 Mar 45	245	MN371 MR-J	F/O G. F. Putt	dila B.100 rnc
23 Mar 45	438	MP138	S/L J. E. Hogg (K)	csd in sea off Portland
24 Mar 45	184	MM956	W/O W. Green	dila B.100 rnc
24 Mar 45	184	MN359	Lt D. Quick	hbF f/l 3 m SE Haldern
24 Mar 45	183	MN747	F/S N. L. Lancaster	dila B.91 rnc
24 Mar 45	440	MN777 I8-J	F/O A. M. Scott	tbto csd B.78 rnc
24 Mar 45	174	MN917	W/O K. Bodden	d/f[17] rof f/l N Venlo rnc
24 Mar 45	439	MN936	F/O W. Anderson (K)	hbF last seen Dingden
24 Mar 45	247	MP120 ZY-A	F/O C. G. Monk	hbF f/l 6 m NW Wesel
24 Mar 45	193	PD597	F/L J. Harrison	hbF b/o near Wesel
24 Mar 45	124W	RB208 KN-L	W/C C. D. North-Lewis (E)	hbF f/l Gravel Is, Wesel
24 Mar 45	137	RB376	F/O R. A. Egley (K)	hbF b/o S Brünen
24 Mar 45	247	RB378 ZY-J	F/L J. D. Compton	hbF f/l 4 m NW Kleve
24 Mar 45	245	SW456	W/O R. L. Thomas	e/fire f/l N Kalkar
24 Mar 45	266	SW465 ZH-Z	F/L R. G. Miller	e/f f/l NE Udem
25 Mar 45	245	EJ971	F/O G. A. Clissold (E)	hbF b/o E Dingden
25 Mar 45	175	JP614 HH-H	n/k	battle damage cnk
25 Mar 45	550TU	MN236	W/O R. Thompson (K)	e/f csd Aston Down
25 Mar 45	245	MN470	n/k	hbF near Wesel rnc
25 Mar 45	182	MP172	F/L D. K. Lovell	hbF f/l 10 m E B.86
25 Mar 45	247	RB225 ZY-V	S/L J. H. Bryant	hbF b/o B.86
25 Mar 45	182	RB289	F/L H. G. Kinsey (PoW)	hbF f/l near Mechelen
25 Mar 45	247	RB314	n/k	Flak damage rnc
25 Mar 45	181	RB341 EL-R	Sgt J. Hodgson	dila B.78 rnc
25 Mar 45	247	RB344 ZY-B	F/L D. Compton	hbF b/o near B.86
26 Mar 45	137	JP736	P/O J. W. C. Collins	hbF f/l a/t (Brünen)
26 Mar 45	590TU	JP851	F/L W. H. P. Leray	e/f f/l Goswick Sands
26 Mar 45	181	JR337 EL-W	F/S E. D. Milliken	e/f f/l 1 m NE B.86
26 Mar 45	266	PD501	F/S P. J. Culligan (K)	tbto csd B.89
26 Mar 45	175	RB440 HH-R	W/O P. Wyper	hbF b/o a/t (Isselburg)
26 Mar 45	137	RB454	F/S J. A. Pennant	hbF b/o a/t (Brünen)
27 Mar 45	560TU	EK364	P/O G. A. Sullivan (K)	s/f csd Ilderton
27 Mar 45	560TU	MN532	P/O R. E. Bellis (K)	csd in bad wx Stoney Hill
28 Mar 45	245	JR246	W/O W. George	e/f f/l SE Kempen
28 Mar 45	182	SW418	W/O A. H. Lethaby	hbF f/l B.78 rnc
30 Mar 45	175	EK382 HH-T	F/L C. A. B. Slack (K)	csd in rpa NW Telgte
30 Mar 45	182	JP752	F/S L. S. Phillips	hbF f/l SE Dingden
30 Mar 45	247	MM979 ZY-O	Sgt B. V. Clinton (K)	hbF last seen Zutphen
30 Mar 45	439	RB435	F/L W. G. Davies (K)	sdbF 4 m S Lengerich
30 Mar 45	182	RB505	F/O P. J. Spellman	hbF f/l NW Wettringen
30 Mar 45	174	SW495	P/O F. C. Johnson (PoW)	F? f/l near Gronau
31 Mar 45	247	JP443	F/L D. H. Rutter	F? f/l Holten-Lochem
31 Mar 45	181	MN775 EL-N	W/O S. Ainsley	hbF f/l S Enschede
31 Mar 45	181	MN875 EL-B	F/S D. D. J. Carter (K)	sdbF 4 m SSW Enschede
31 Mar 45	175	RB287	Sgt A. G. Mitchell (K)	csd S Wuppertal cnk
1 April 45	183	DN248 HF-K	W/O D. P. Drummond (K)	sdbF Hardenberg
1 April 45	137	EK128	Sgt P. A. Langley	hbF f/l NW Rheine
1 April 45	183	MN419 HF-G	F/S T. P. Ward	battle damage cnk rnc
1 April 45	181	MN819	F/S H. W. M. Desmond (E)	F? e/f f/l E Nordhorn
1 April 45	266	PD473 ZH-E	F/O E. H. Donne (K)	sdbF Lonneker
1 April 45	137	RB193 SF-U	Sgt F. A. Edwards (K)	sdbF E Münster
1 April 45	193	RB373	F/O A. C. Smith (PoW)	sdbF NE Almelo
1 April 45	174	RB396 XP-W	F/L C. W. House	hbF f/l NE Denekamp
1 April 45	247	SW408	P/O E. W. P Thomas (E)	hbF b/o 4 m NW Ensberen
1 April 45	247	SW425	F/O T. R. Jackson (PoW)	hbF f/l near Meppen
1 April 45	183	SW476	W/O S. B. Lang (PoW)	ftr last seen E Zutphen
2 April 45	439	MN581	F/O D. G. Cleghorn (PoW)	F? e/f f/l 9 m N Nordhorn
2 April 45	198	MN573 TP-H	W/O M. Ryan	e/f f/l near B.89
2 April 45	438	MN758 F3-M	W/O W. J. Kinsella	e/f w/u Warmwell rnc
3 April 45	349	EK240	F/S N. Leroy	e/f b/o off Predannack
3 April 45	183	MN365	F/S W. E. Barber	e/f csd on app B.91
3 April 45	174	RB487	Lt L. F. Higgins (K)	csd 6 m W Rheine cnk
4 April 45	181	MM990	F/S J. O. Jones (K)	csd NE Ibbenburen cnk
4 April 45	175	MN773 HH-C	W/O A. G. T. Muttock (K)	hbF b/o SW Varenrode
4 April 45	137	MN863	F/O J. R. Nixon	hbF f/l 2 m N Kleve
4 April 45	438	MP181 F3-F	W/O W. J. Kinsella (K)	sdb Bf109s W Diepholz
4 April 45	438	RB217 F3-J	F/L E. J. McAlpine (K)	sdb Bf109s W Diepholz
5 April 45	175	JR308 HH-D	F/S R. Robinson	lrt hit fuselage rnc
5 April 45	247	MN585 ZY-H	Sgt A. W. Brooks	dila B.86 rnc
5 April 45	247	SW445	F/S W. G. Morgans (PoW)	hbF f/l S Hopsten
5 April 45	247	SW526	F/L D. H. Rutter (K)	ftr last seen NE Cloppenburg
5 April 45	181	SW552	F/L R. F. Galbraith (K)	sdbF N Furstenau
6 April 45	175	JR517 HH-U	W/O K. W. Patrick	F? e/f f/l SE Greven
7 April 45	175	JP753 HH-S	F/O R. J. H. Ansley	dila B.100 rnc
7 April 45	198	JR222 TP-J	W/O A. W. Britton	tbto csd B.91
7 April 45	245	MN362	Sgt C. M. Brocklehurst	dila B.100 rnc
7 April 45	550TU	MP127	Sgt C. C. Latimer (K)	cld RB486 csd W Woolaston
7 April 45	263	RB438	W/O R. W. Ainsley	hbF b/o NW Naarden
8 April 45	263	RB479	F/L E. J. Whitfield	hbF b/o a/t (Deventer)
8 April 45	175	SW506 HH-R	Sgt D. Melville	dila B.80
9 April 45	266	RB267	W/O N. V. Phillips (E)	e/f f/l SW Eemshaven
9 April 45	1FP	RB322	1/O A. E. Boyes	t/a Odiham
9 April 45	164	SW523	S/L P. Bateman-Jones	hbF f/l B.88
10 April 45	164	MN853 FJ-J	W/O D. W. McCulloch (K)	hbAA csd NE Lingen
10 April 45	198	PD605 TP-U	F/L W. R. Wardle	e/fire on start-up B.91
10 April 45	193	RB274	W/O A. G. Randall (K)	hit htc csd 3 m E Arnhem
10 April 45	182	SW427	Sgt I. Cameron	dila B.86
11 April 45	245	R8230	F/L I. G. Campbell (S)	hbF f/l NE Loningen
11 April 45	198	DN341 TP-F	F/O F. G. Williams	hbF f/l SE Zwolle
11 April 45	550TU	JP578 PA-P	F/S R. A. Smith	tbto w/u Aston Down rnc
11 April 45	182	MN693	Sgt R. A. Nash	dila B.106 rnc
11 April 45	266	PD528	F/O D. Dodd (PoW)	F? f/l e/t (Groningen)
11 April 45	247	RB306	Sgt J. Dick	dila B.106 rnc
11 April 45	164	SW410 FJ-E	F/L A. P. Hammond-Hunt	e/fire on start-up B.91 rnc
11 April 45	181	SW467	F/O W. H. Ironside	efto csd B.106 rnc
12 April 45	247	DN588 ZY-G	F/O D. C. Orriss	hbF f/l near Bawinkel
12 April 45	137	JR444	W/O R. S. Knight-Clarke (K)	hbF csd near Kampe
12 April 45	181	MP203	F/L R. A. Done (K)	sdbF NW Otersen

Date	Unit	Aircraft	Pilot	Circumstances
12 April 45	609	PD593	F/L J. D. Inches	hbF b/o W Friesoythe
12 April 45	197	RB228 OV-B	F/L T. Clift (PoW)	e/f f/l NE Hesei
12 April 45	197	RB251 OV-G	F/L G. R. Gibbings (PoW)	hbd b/o SE Barssel
12 April 45	182	SW391	F/L E. G. Hutchin (K)	hbF f/l E Walle
13 April 45	609	MN434	P/O H. M. Rendall (K)	cld RB250 csd Grave
13 April 45	198	PD508 TP-T	F/O L. J. Bastin	e/f b/o Beers
13 April 45	609	RB250	F/S H. E. DeBlommaert (K)	cld MN434 csd Grave
13 April 45	193	RB279	W/O K. R. Goodhew	hbF b/o a/t (Kampen)
13 April 45	175	SW475	F/L L. H. Parker (K)	F? csd N Langwedel
14 April 45	438	MM989 F3-R	F/S G. S. Livingstone (K)	spun in near B110 cnk
14 April 45	137	MP154	F/S J. A. H. G. Pennant (K)	hbF csd near Verden
16 April 45	609	JR294	Sgt A. R. A. Deschamps	hbF f/l SE Kampe rnc
16 April 45	184	MN232 BR-A	F/L D. L. Stevenson	F? w/u B.80 rnc
16 April 45	193	MN886 DP-E	W/O W. L. Wheeler	cld MN982 landing B.89 rnc
16 April 45	193	MN895	P/O J. Quigley	dila B.89 rnc
16 April 45	193	MN982 DP-X	F/O J. Fishwick	cld MN886 landing B.89 rnc
16 April 45	245	MN988	W/O G. A. Lomas	hbF f/l near Minden
16 April 45	438	MP192 F3-J	F/O J. K. Brown (PoW)	F? e/f last seen near Wumme
16 April 45	193	RB346	F/S O. L. Pratt (E)	hbF f/l SW Apeldoorn
17 April 45	247	R8932 ZY-X	F/O L. R. Barnes	e/f landing B.110 rnc
17 April 45	55OTU	DN442	F/S P. I. Watts	t/a Aston Down rnc
17 April 45	83GSU	DN495	F/S W. G. Wood	csd on t/o Dunsfold
17 April 45	84GSU	MN230 40	F/S W. A. Webster	dila Lasham
17 April 45	245	MN633	F/O F. J. Pearson	F? f/l a/t (Uelzen)
17 April 45	263	MN706	F/L N. P. C. Woodward (K)	sdbF off Harderwijk
17 April 45	439	RB387	F/O F. M. Hallford	dila Warmwell rnc
17 April 45	263	RB398	F/O C. J. Devey	tbto csd B.105 rnc
18 April 45	FLS	JP726 MF-10	F/L L. P. Boucher	dila Yeovilton rnc
18 April 45	193	RB482	F/O B. Lenson	hbd b/o a/t (Scharrel)
19 April 45	245	JR189	W/O H. Stephenson	csd on t/o B.110
19 April 45	182	SW412	F/O L. K. Jackson (K)	sdbF Bleckwedel
20 April 45	181	RB233	W/O B. J. Calnan (PoW)	hbF b/o S Schwazenbeck
21 April 45	440	SW452	W/C F. G. Grant	u/c dam in dive B.150 rnc
23 April 45	55OTU	DN260	Sgt B. K. Feekery	e/f dila Aston Down
23 April 45	55OTU	EK212	Sgt G. Blythe	efto csd Aston Down rnc
23 April 45	609	PD572 PR-D	W/O S. E. Smith (K)	hbF b/o near Nieuwolde
23 April 45	438	RB342 F3-Q	P/O T. Hartnett (K)	ftr last seen SW Lüneberg
23 April 45	266	RB423 ZH-S	F/O N. Borland (K)	hbF csd NE Leer
23 April 45	198	SW472 TP-K	P/O R. T. Casey (K)	sdbF N Bremen
23 April 45	439	SW525	F/L J. H. McCullough (PoW)	hbF f/l 12 m SE Ratzeburg
25 April 45	247	JP511	W/O T. W. Mooney	dila B.110
25 April 45	164	JR363	F/L M. E. Jones (S)	hbd? f/l S Neumünster
25 April 45	184	MN294 BR-V	P/O W. H. Gilman (K)	F? csd NW Schwarzenbeck
25 April 45	164	MN896 FJ-F	F/O R. J. M. Wilson	hbd f/l a/t (Neumünster)
25 April 45	438	RB323 F3-V	F/O T. M. Jones (K)	hbF csd SE Bovenau
26 April 45	181	EJ963	Sgt G. Dawson	dila B.120
26 April 45	263	RB215	P/O D. E. Morgan (PoW)	hbF f/l Niebull
26 April 45	164	RB264 FJ-C	F/O W. T. Lawston (PoW)	hbF b/o Wilhelmshaven
26 April 45	438	RB429 F3-X	F/O E. D. Brydon (K)	hit trees csd SW Gnissau
26 April 45	247	SW513	W/O G. E. T. Lawley	e/f f/l 5 m SW Boizenburg
26 April 45	198	SW520 TP-F	F/O W. G. Ford	dila B.103

Above: On 11 May 1945 Squadron Leader Kelly borrowed Squadron Leader Campbell's 175 Squadron Typhoon, SW450 'HH-L', to renew his acquaintance with the type. When the engine failed he made a forced-landing on ground newly cleared of timber – the stumps tore the Typhoon to pieces but he escaped without serious injury. (R. W. Campbell)

Date	Unit	Aircraft	Pilot	Circumstances
27 April 45	55OTU	EK232 ZX-J	F/L W. R. Richmond	e/f f/l Cerne Abbas rnc
29 April 45	182	EK114	Sgt I. Cameron	F? f/l N Rehrhof
2 May 45	55OTU	MN147	W/O J. C. Bayliss	dila Aston Down
2 May 45	124W	SW530	W/C G. F. H. Webb (K)	sdbF N Gleschendorf
3 May 45	247	DN551	Sgt A. W. Brooks (K)	sdbF NE Kiel
3 May 45	181	JP838	F/S J. A. Brown (K)	hbF last seen NE Kiel
3 May 45	197	MP190 OV-J	P/O L. S. Brookes (S)	hbF f/l near Neustadt
3 May 45	198	PD466 TP-S	P/O J. E. N. C. Scoon	e/f f/l S Eimke
3 May 45	198	PD618 TP-U	F/S P. W. W. Millard (E)	e/f f/l SW Neustadt
3 May 45	439	SW443	F/O G. F. Burden (K)	sdbF near Pinneberg
4 May 45	175	RB492 HH-J	W/O C. E. Swales	w/u B.150
4 May 45	183	SW454	S/L J. R. Cullen	hbF f/l Fehmarn Is
5 May 45	182	EJ910	–	ct fire in hangar B.156
7 May 45	56OTU	MN546	P/O J. H. Fraser	e/f f/l Ayton
8 May 45	609	SW497 PR-G	F/S N. F. Dixon	e/f f/l NE Meppen
11 May 45	175	SW450 HH-L	S/L D. T. W. Kelly	e/f f/l N Celle
12 May 45	197	MN343	F/O W. H. Setterfield	e/f f/l Hildesheim
13 May 45	55OTU	DN561	F/L W. Bolton	lrt trouble f/l Farnham
13 May 45	183	MN681 HF-L	W/O A. F. Storr	e/f w/u B.108
14 May 45	438	RB446	Sgt A. G. Wilks	efto w/u B.166
16 May 45	84GSU	MN860	F/S D. R. E. Ray	lrt e/f f/l N Wokingham
17 May 45	184	EK220 BR-H	F/O A. W. A. Scott	tbto w/u Warmwell
18 May 45	83GSU	JR531 7S-V	F/O T. T. Hall	efto w/u Dunsfold
18 May 45	FLS	MN433 MF-14	Maj Van der Spay	hbd f/l W. Wittering nr
18 May 45	59OTU	MN944	W/O J. J. Spencer	e/f f/l N Warkworth
18 May 45	184	PD496 BR-N	F/L B. N. Byrne	e/f f/l Chesilfield
22 May 45	FLS	JR434	Lt F. S. Rader[25] (K)	csd NW Selsey
25 May 45	83GSU	MN135 7S-Q	Sgt W. R. Pearson	dila Lasham
25 May 45	193	MN968	F/O J. Fishwick (K)	e/f csd Havekost
25 May 45	266	MP140 ZH-R	F/O G. Henderson	efto Fairwood Common rnc
27 May 45	164	JP362	F/O R. L. Chaseling	dila B.116
27 May 45	183	RB453	F/O T. J. Lee-Warner	e/f w/u B.116
28 May 45	184	EJ926	F/O R. S. Bruce (K)	e/f f/l in trees Petershagen
28 May 45	245	PD613	F/S E. H. Knight (K)	dila B.154
29 May 45	83GSU	EJ907 7S-P	W/O H. T. Laurie	e/f f/l near Petworth
29 May 45	263	MN323	W/O L. J. Miller	dila B.111 rnc
29 May 45	438	MN325	F/S R. S. Guerd	w/u B.166
30 May 45	DeH-	SW519	F/L W. G. Eagle (K)	s/f csd near Brockenhurst
1 June 45	438	SW393	S/L J. R. Beirnes (K)	e/f csd near Schelde
1 June 45	184	SW413 BR-W	–	ct fire on ground run B.164
2 June 45	263	PD480	W/O E. J. H. Rodgers	dila B.111
2 June 45	263	SW584	S/L M. T. S. Rumbold	e/f f/l 8 m NE Twente

Date	Unit	Aircraft	Pilot	Circumstances
13 June 45	FLS	MN974	F/L A. W. Kilpatrick	efto w/u Tangmere
16 June 45	247	MN688	Sgt D. E. H. Murrels (K)	csd 5 m WNW Bad Segeberg
22 June 45	439	MP117	W/O R. J. Roach	w/u B.160
23 June 45	137	SW426 SF-V	F/S J. H. Nutter (K)	csd in sea S Langeland
24 June 45	198	JP579 TP-E	F/S J. Taylor	dila B.116
26 June 45	83GSU	EK432	F/L J. L. Lewis (K)	s/f csd Dunsfold
26 June 45	266	MN739 ZH-U	–	e/fire on start up R.16
30 June 45	182	RB366	F/O W. J. Boots (K)	cld SW407 B.172
30 June 45	137	SW561	S/L D. Murray	e/f w/u Vaerlose
5 July 45	609	JR440	F/S N. F. Dixon	h/f dila B.58
8 July 45	266	MN353 ZH-J	P/O P. K. Mitchell	e/f f/l NE Hildesheim
8 July 45	440	RB485 I8-E	F/L H. T. C. Taylor	h/f w/u R.56
18 July 45	181	SW386	F/L J. F. L. Sinclair (K)	s/f csd B.160
20 July 45	56OTU	MN975	F/S F. R. Jeyes (K)	e/f csd Cornhill Farm, Northumberland
24 July 45	181	SW536	–	dam by jack Manston rnc
25 July 45	181	MN311 EL-N	Sgt J. D. Austin	dila Christchurch
26 July 45	197	PD468 OV-W	F/S W. A. Webster	e/f f/l NW Hanover
27 July 45	83GSU	RB444	–	hit by SN258 Dunsfold rnc
29 July 45	439	MN691	–	e/fire on start up B.166
1 Aug 45	137	MM966	P/O J. A. Cunningham	tbto w/u B.158
3 Aug 45	184	MN141 BR-E	Sgt J. M. Kennedy	t/a B.160
8 Aug 45	FLS	EK208	–	hit by Wellington Tangmere
8 Aug 45	609	MN658	F/L E. R. Carruthers (K)	csd in bad wx E Schedehausen
10 Aug 45	182	MP200 XM-X	F/L T. H. Catchpole	dila Warmwell
11 Aug 45	182	MP147	W/O A. W. A. P. Wilson	tbto w/u Warmwell
11 Aug 45	182	RB256	P/O A. H. Letensly (K)	csd in RP dive Chesil Beach
11 Aug 45	137	SW510	F/L C. Peirson-Jones	e/f f/l 1 m NW Haveghorst
14 Aug 45	181	SW504	F/L J. Entwistle	e/f f/l near B.160
15 Aug 45	245	RB269	P/O K. D. Bodden	dila B.106
20 Aug 45	184	JR194	W/O C. de B. Newcomb	efto f/l near B.160
22 Aug 45	609	JP375	W/O R. Dutton	e/f f/l near B.116
23 Aug 45	56OTU	SW571	–	hit by SW638 Milfield
23 Aug 45	56OTU	SW593 HQ-11	–	hit by SW638 Milfield
23 Aug 45	56OTU	SW638 HQ-E	Sgt H. W. J. Garrett	dila Milfield
26 Aug 45	174	PD611	F/L C. Stone	dila Warmwell
30 Aug 45	174	JR510	F/L R. O. Westlake	tbto csd Warmwell
4 Sept 45	181	JR265 EL-A	Sgt J. D. Austin	efto csd B.160
8 Sept 45	151RU	RB220	–	e/fire on start up B.55
11 Sept 45	198	JR298 TP-N	F/S P. A. Campbell	e/f w/u B.116
12 Sept 45	174	MN306	W/O E. H. Philips	e/f f/l NW Oldenburg
13 Sept 45	181	MN999	F/O R. D. Cole (K)	spun in, 8 m NE Schleswig
13 Sept 45	247	RB504	F/L R. D. Sheret	w/u West Malling
19 Sept 45	Napr	MP141	F/L Covington	e/f w/u Heston
20 Sept 45	56OTU	MN113	F/O G. H. Wylde	dila Milfield
20 Sept 45	609	SW392	F/S T. L. Kerr	t/a B.116
21 Sept 45	83GDC	RB310	P/O K. D. Bodden	efto f/l near Dunsfold
19 Oct 45	Lt.St.	JR390	G/C J. R. Jeudivine (K)	spun in, Little Staughton
30 Oct 45	56OTU	SW573	Sgt A. Greenwood (K)	csd in bad wx Lowick
22 Nov 45	56OTU	SW632	Sgt J. W. Coales	hit grd f/l Goswick
29 Nov 45	84GDC	RB363	F/S D. R. Ray	t/a Breighton
15 Dec 45	1APS	RB265	F/L Pawson-Jones	dila Fairwood Common
14 Jan 46	56OTU	SW635	–	e/fire on start up Milfield
11 Feb 46	151RU	PD604	–	w/o after accident on grd

Below: JR265 'EL-A' of 181 Squadron had an engine failure while getting airborne from B.160 Kastrup, and Sergeant Austin was injured in the ensuing crash. (A. C. Schaefer)

Tempests

Date	Unit	Aircraft	Pilot	Circumstances
20 Jan 44	Hwkr	JN747	n/k	csd before delivery
26 April 44	3	JN733 QO-A	W/O F. M. Read	e/f f/l near Bradwell Bay
27 April 44	486	JN792 SA-H	F/O H. M. Mason	e/f w/u Castle Camps
1 May 44	486	JN771	P/O J. G. Wilson	e/f f/l Staple
17 May 44	3	JN762	F/S H. J. Bailey	dila Deanland
23 May 44	Napr	JN814	n/k	csd on test
27 May 44	3	JN736	F/O T. Zurakowski (K)	ftr Cap Gris Nez-Ostend
27 May 44	3	JN749	F/S J. L. Mannion (K)	ftr Cap Gris Nez-Ostend
31 May 44	3	JN748	F/S S. B. Feldman	e/f f/l 1 m W Lydd
10 June 44	486	JN772	P/O F. B. Lawless	e/f dtd off Dungeness
22 June 44	486	JN806	F/O T. M. Fenton	dila Newchurch
28 June 44	486	JN804	F/S R. J. Wright (K)	V-1 exp csd Jevington
28 June 44	486	JN859	P/O F. B. Lawless	V-1 exp f/l NE Rye
30 June 44	486	JN810	W/O S. J. Short	hbAA csd ldg Newchurch
1 July 44	3	JN765 JF-K	F/O G. E. Kosh (K)	csd chasing V-1 SW Rye
1 July 44	486	JN773	F/O K. McCarthy	e/f f/l Battle
3 July 44	3	JN752 JF-S	F/S S. Domanski (K)	hbAA csd Playden
3 July 44	486	JN811	F/O W. L. Miller	e/f b/o Horsmonden
4 July 44	486	JN820	P/O S. S. Williams	dila Newchurch
5 July 44	486	JN854 SA-G	W/O C. J. Sheddan	e/f f/l Netherfield
5 July 44	FIU	EJ531	S/L E. G. Daniel (K)	e/f b/o 5 m S Dungeness
7 July 44	56	JN857 US-L	F/S G. H. Wylde	e/f dtd S Hastings
12 July 44	56	EJ559 US-L	F/L J. G. Mansfield	hbAA f/l near Ripe
17 July 44	FIU	EJ581	F/L A. D. Wagner (K)	csd Sellindge
18 July 44	3	JN745	F/S R. W. Pottinger	dila Newchurch
18 July 44	FIU	EJ530	W/C C. H. Hartley	cld Mosquito csd Burwash
20 July 44	486	EJ527	W/O S. J. Short	e/f f/l Laughton

Date	Unit	Aircraft	Pilot	Circumstances
23 July 44	486	JN758	P/O W. A. L. Trott	e/f f/l near Polegate
24 July 44	486	JN809 SA-M	W/O W. A. Kalka	e/f f/l near Willingdon
24 July 44	486	JN860	F/L N. J. Powell	e/f f/l near Snargate
26 July 44	RAE	JN735	L/C E. M. Brown	e/fire b/o Headley Park
27 July 44	56	EJ545 US-Z	F/L R. K. Dean	e/f f/l Kent
29 July 44	56	EJ532 US-H	F/S A. C. Drew (K)	csd in bad vis Rise Place, Kent
31 July 44	486	EJ586	F/S A. A. Wilson (K)	cld Spitfire csd Hooe
6 Aug 44	3	JN759	F/S D. J. Mackerras (K)	spun in, Ninfield
10 Aug 44	486	JN866 SA-U	F/O R. J. Cammock	e/f f/l Catsfield
13 Aug 44	274	EJ637	F/S R. W. Ryman (K)	csd in bad vis NW Elham
17 Aug 44	486	JN805	F/S J. W. Waddel (K)	csd in bad vis Woodchurch
21 Aug 44	501	EJ602 SD-P	F/L C. B. Thornton (K)	csd in bad vis Woodnesboro
23 Aug 44	n/k	EJ702	n/k	w/o before delivery cnk
25 Aug 44	486	EJ635	F/L E. W. Tanner	dila Newchurch
5 Sept 44	56	JN816 US-W	F/O R. V. Dennis	e/f f/l near Brookland
10 Sept 44	3	EJ540	F/S C. W. Orwin (PoW)	e/f dtd SW Den Haag
10 Sept 44	274	EJ642	F/L J. A. Malloy	hbF dtd in Channel
13 Sept 44	56	EJ534 US-O	P/O J. Harvey	e/f csd on app Brenzett
13 Sept 44	3	JN818	S/L K. A. Wigglesworth (K)	hbd? csd near Den Haag
14 Sept 44	80	EJ670	W/O H. F. Ross	hbF b/o over Channel
16 Sept 44	80	EJ662	P/O W. E. Maloney (K)	sdbF E Arnhem
17 Sept 44	80	EJ519	W/O P. L. Godfrey (K)	sdbF off Walcharen
17 Sept 44	80	EJ657	F/L E. E. O. Irish	e/f b/o 1 m E Manston
18 Sept 44	80	EJ583	F/O R. H. Hanney (K)	csd Strijen cnk
18 Sept 44	80	EJ668[18]	F/O P. S. Haw (K)	hbF b/o 20 m W Hook of Holland
23 Sept 44	501	EJ603 SD-M	F/O G. Wild	e/f b/o 3 m off Colchester
25 Sept 44	501	EJ590 SD-L	F/L G. L. Bonham (K)	csd bad vis Spitfield Barn, Essex
25 Sept 44	80	EJ650	F/O J. E. Wiltshire (PoW)	hbF b/o Steenbergen
25 Sept 44	3	EJ652	F/O W. Davies (K)	e/fire csd 70 m E Great Yarmouth
25 Sept 44	80	EJ664[18]	W/O S. A. Williams (K)	hbF Steenbergen csd N. Sea
27 Sept 44	274	EJ611	F/S W. L. F. Randall (PoW)	hbF f/l SW Zwolle
29 Sept 44	3	EJ504	F/O R. H. Clapperton (PoW)	hbF b/o 2 m SE Kranenburg
29 Sept 44	501	EJ626 SD-E	F/O O. P. Faraday (K)	e/f csd St. Osyth
30 Sept 44	274	EJ629	F/S N. G. G. Carn (K)	sdbF S Arnhem
1 Oct 44	3	JN812 JF-M	W/O F. M. Reid (K)	hbF csd near Volkel
2 Oct 44	501	EJ600 SD-F	S/L J. Berry (K)	sdbF Veendam
3 Oct 44	486	EJ693[19] SA-I	P/O B. M. Hall	e/f F? f/l near B.60
5 Oct 44	274	EJ709	F/O G. T. Kinnell	F? f/l 5 m SW Wageningen
6 Oct 44	80	JN794	–	hit by Mosquito Coltishall
6 Oct 44	486	JN863	F/O R. J. Cammock (K)	sdbF E Deventer
6 Oct 44	274	EJ628	F/L G. G. G. Walkington	dila B.82
7 Oct 44	486	EJ535	F/O W. A. Hart (PoW)	hbF b/o 2 m SW Kevelaer
7 Oct 44	274	EJ655	F/O J. M. Mears (PoW)	sdb Fw190 near Zwolle (claimed by Obl Heilmann, III/JG54)
7 Oct 44	486	EJ704 SA-M	W/O A. H. Bailey	e/f f/l Langsraat
11 Oct 44	274	EJ604	W/O F. A. Wilks (K)	spun in, near Grave
12 Oct 44	122W	EJ710 JF-L[20]	W/C R. P. Beamont (PoW)	hbF f/l 8 m SE Bocholt
13 Oct 44	80	EJ671 W2-P	–	hit by AA fragments parked B.80
14 Oct 44	56	EJ742 US-T	F/O W. R. MacLaren	e/f f/l SE B.80
2 Nov 44	3	EJ766 JF-Z	F/O D. J. Butcher	dam by Fw190 near Achmer nr
5 Nov 44	56	EJ718 US-B	P/O A. S. Miller (K)	hbF b/o Venlo
5 Nov 44	3	EJ743	F/S L. G. Everson	wing wrinkled in dive rnc
7 Nov 44	274	EJ632	F/S R. C. Cole (PoW)	sdb Fw190 N Münster
14 Nov 44	501	EJ551 SD-S	F/O J. A. L. Johnson	e/f b/o 1 m E Standon
20 Nov 44	3	EJ658	F/O C. A. Tidy	efto csd into Spits B.80
21 Nov 44	274	EJ802	S/L J. R. Heap (K)	efto csd NE B.80
26 Nov 44	56	EJ800 US-D	P/O C. J. Mills	efto csd B.80
26 Nov 44	3	JN822	P/O R. W. Cole (PoW)	hbF b/o 15 m SE Rheine
29 Nov 44	3	EJ723	F/L E. M. Sparrow	e/f f/l 3 m SE Nijmegen
29 Nov 44	419RSU	EJ782	F/O C. Steele	e/f dila B.80
8 Dec 44	274	EJ597	Maj J. Vaissier	efto csd B.80
8 Dec 44	A&AEE	EJ759	F/L A. R. Majcherczyk	dila Cairo West
8 Dec 44	3	JN815	W/O J. L. R. Torpy	efto csd B.80
11 Dec 44	274	EJ634	F/O F. W. Trench (PoW)	e/f F? b/o 3 m E Arnhem
13 Dec 44	Hwkr	NV751	n/k	w/o before delivery
17 Dec 44	80	EJ746	Lt J. B. Gilhaus (K)	sdbF near Raesfeld
17 Dec 44	80	EJ788	F/L J. M. Weston (PoW)	ftr (Bielefeld)
22 Dec 44	486	EJ715	F/L S. S. Williams (K)	sdbF near Vreden
24 Dec 44	3	EJ747	F/O R. Dryland (E)	hbF f/l S Malmédy
26 Dec 44	486	EJ716	F/O C. J. MacDonald	cld JN869 b/o W Liège
26 Dec 44	486	JN869	P/O B. J. O'Connor	cld EJ716 f/l near Liège
27 Dec 44	486	EJ627 SA-E	F/O B. M. Hall (K)	sdb Fw190 near Münster (claimed by Lt P. Crump, 10/JG54)
28 Dec 44	33	EJ881	W/O N. E. M. MacDonald (K)	e/f csd 3 m SE Helston
29 Dec 44	56	EJ522 US-F	F/O K. Watts (K)	sdb Fw190s S Dummer See
29 Dec 44	56	EJ552 US-A	F/S L. Jackson (K)	sdb Fw190 S Dummer See (both the above aircraft claimed by III/JG54)
29 Dec 44	3	EJ803	F/L M. F. Edwards (K)	sdb Bf109s N Rheine
29 Dec 44	3	JN803	F/O K. G. Slade-Betts (K)	sdb Bf109s N Rheine (both the above aircraft claimed by IV/JG27)
1 Jan 45	3	EJ719 JF-R	P/O R. W. Pottinger (PoW)	hbF b/o near Dulmen
13 Jan 45	486	EJ606	P/O W. A. Kalka	hbAA b/o near Euskirchen
13 Jan 45	274	EJ639	F/L J. A. Malloy (K)	dived in, W Hamm cnk
13 Jan 45	486	EJ752 SA-H	F/L L. J. Appleton	hbAA f/l near Euskirchen
13 Jan 45	80	EJ774 W2-B	F/O A. W. D. McLachlan (PoW)	hbF f/l S Stavelot
13 Jan 45	486	EJ577	S/L A. E. Umbers	hbAA f/l near Euskirchen
14 Jan 45	56OTU	JN819	Sgt P. C. Brown	dila Milfield
14 Jan 45	222	NV649	F/L R. J. Floyd (K)	csd in sea 25 m S Lizard cnk
16 Jan 45	56	EJ548 US-G	P/O H. Shaw (PoW)	hbd f/l 3 m SE Doetinchem
19 Jan 45	287	JN796	W/O R. J. Cowan	e/f f/l Kent
20 Jan 45	56	EJ741 US-O	P/O J. S. Ferguson (K)	sdbF 10 m W Enschede
27 Jan 45	80	EJ644	–	cockpit fire on ground B.80
28 Jan 45	80	EJ699	n/k	dam in action nr

Date	Unit	Aircraft	Pilot	Circumstances
1 Feb 45	274	EJ762	F/L G. J. Bruce (PoW)	e/f F? f/l near Krefeld
1 Feb 45	3	NV681	F/O D. J. Butcher (PoW)	e/f f/l near Winterswijk
2 Feb 45	486	EJ787 SA-L	P/O G. J. Hooper (E)	hbF f/l S Kirchdorf
2 Feb 45	56	JN808 US-G	Sgt J. K. Holden (K)	sdbF SE Hildesheim
2 Feb 45	80	NV657	S/L E. D. Mackie	e/f f/l 2 m N St-Antonis
3 Feb 45	287	JN769	F/S A. Lewis	tbto csd North Weald
6 Feb 45	3	EJ654 JF-N	F/L J. S. B. Wright (PoW)	hbF b/o SW Seesen
6 Feb 45	56	NV659 US-E	F/L J. D. Ross (E)	hbF b/o (Paderborn)
8 Feb 45	486	EJ750	F/L W. L. Miller (E)	hbF f/l near Verden
8 Feb 45	274	EJ783 JJ-N	S/L A. H. Baird (K)	sdb Bf109s near Rheine (claimed by JG27)
8 Feb 45	3	EJ895	F/L R. W. Jones (PoW)	e/f f/l SW Apeldoorn
8 Feb 45	3	NV676	F/L J. W. Garland (PoW)	hbF b/o SE Rheine
10 Feb 45	274	EJ751	F/L J. Woolfries (PoW)	hbF f/l 9 m NE Arnhem
10 Feb 45	3	NV644	S/L K. F. Thiele (PoW)	hbF b/o E Dorsten
10 Feb 45	3	NV656	P/O M. J. A. Rose (E)	hbF f/l W Paderborn
12 Feb 45	560TU	EJ819	F/O L. Smith	csd on t/o Milfield
13 Feb 45	274	EJ764 JJ-E	F/O R. E. Mooney	dam by flak nr
13 Feb 45	222	NV648	F/L R. P. Dashwood	e/f b/o SW Constantine
14 Feb 45	80	EJ695	F/O D. S. Angier (K)	hbF last seen S Brunswick
14 Feb 45	80	EJ776	F/O C. F. Royds (K)	cld Bf109 b/o E Celle
14 Feb 45	3	EJ812	P/O R. S. Adcock (E)	hbF Quackenbrück a/f b/o
14 Feb 45	486	NV715	S/L A. E. Umbers (K)	sdbF near Meppen
21 Feb 45	274	EJ687	F/O C. J. Day (PoW)	F? f/l near Halle
22 Feb 45	56	EJ544 US-J	F/L W. J. Green (PoW)	hbF[21] last seen Cloppenburg
22 Feb 45	3	EJ653	P/O H. J. Bailey (PoW)	sdb Fw190s near Rheine (claimed by Lt Söffing, I/JG26)
22 Feb 45	80	NV921	F/S L. B. Crook (K)	hbF f/l S Ruthen
23 Feb 45	222	NV765	–	destroyed by V-1 B.77
24 Feb 45	274	NV705	F/L L. A. Wood (PoW)	e/f f/l E Enschede
25 Feb 45	486	EJ523	W/O R. C. Macpherson (PoW)	e/f f/l near Wennigsen
25 Feb 45	274	EJ775	F/L R. G. Deleuze (K)	e/f last seen near Hamm
25 Feb 45	33	EJ868	F/O A. Harmon (PoW)	sdb Bf109 S Rheine (claimed by I/JG27)
25 Feb 45	80	NV646	F/L D. L. Price (PoW)	sdbF NW Bielefeld
28 Feb 45	274	EJ771	F/O J. B. Spence (PoW)	psdb Fw190s NE Osnabrück
28 Feb 45	560TU	EJ867	F/O B. S. McGregor (K)	csd Langloch Farm, Lanarkshire
28 Feb 45	222	NV680	F/L A. A. McIntyre (K)	sdbF 10 m NE Nijmegen
28 Feb 45	3	NV776	F/L R. F. Humphries (K)	hbF last seen Hildesheim
28 Feb 45	274	NV943	S/L D. C. Fairbanks (PoW)	sdb Fw190 NE Osnabrück
2 Mar 45	80	EJ691	Cpt O. Ullestad (E)	sdb Bf109 SW Rheine
4 Mar 45	560TU	NV924	F/O P. N. Bernhart (K)	csd in bad vis near Lowick
11 Mar 45	80	EJ705 W2-X	F/O F. A. Lang	e/fire on start up B.80 nr
13 Mar 45	560TU	EJ842	Sgt T. Warren	e/f f/l Goswick
14 Mar 45	274	EJ876	F/O G. E. Trayhurn	e/fire b/o 3 m W Emmerich
14 Mar 45	222	NV782 ZD-H	F/L W. G. Mart	e/f dila B.77
15 Mar 45	222	NV792	–	e/fire on start up B.77 nr
15 Mar 45	56	SN133	W/O J. F. Alexander (K)	w/u csd B.80
16 Mar 45	560TU	NV733	F/O I. W. McKenow	e/f f/l Duddo Farm, Northumberland
17 Mar 45	222	EJ873 ZD-R	W/O G. S. Catford (K)	missing in cloud Bramsche
17 Mar 45	222	NV710	F/L L. McAuliffe (K)	missing in cloud Zutphen
17 Mar 45	3	NV929 JF-T	P/O L. G. Everson	e/f f/l 1 m NW Goch
18 Mar 45	501	EJ591 SD-Z	W/O E. L. Wojczynski	dila Hunsdon
24 Mar 45	274	NV920	F/L J. B. Stark (K)	ftr (Plantlunne a/f) (possibly the aircraft claimed by Maj E. Rudorffer, II/JG7, near Wesel)
24 Mar 45	274	NV942	F/L R. C. Kennedy (K)	sdbF Plantlunne a/f
24 Mar 45	80	NV966	S/L J. A. Gibson	hbF f/l 6 m SE Helmond
25 Mar 45	3	EJ755	F/O B. M. Vassiliades (K)	hbF blew up
25 Mar 45	3	EJ757	P/O T. H. McCulloch (PoW)	hbF f/l near Bocholt
25 Mar 45	222	EJ871 ZD-D	F/O R. H. Davidson	e/f f/l B.100 nr
25 Mar 45	486	NV981	F/O W. A. Kalka (K)	hbF b/o 3 m NW Grave
25 Mar 45	80	SN138	F/O W. H. Long (K)	sdbF SE Bocholt
26 Mar 45	56	EJ708 US-W	F/L W. R. MacLaren (K)	sdbF NE Dorsten
26 Mar 45	33	NV720	W/O C. A. Ligtenstein (PoW)	sdb Fw190 b/o S Münster (claimed by Oblt H. Dortenmann, III/JG54)
26 Mar 45	486	NV932 SA-U	P/O A. H. Bailey (K)	hbF csd 3 m S Xanten
28 Mar 45	274	EJ887	F/O D. L. Boyd (S)	hbF b/o in e/t (Münster)
28 Mar 45	56	NV973 US-B	Sgt S. A. Sheppard (K)	ftr (Hanover-Osnabrück)
28 Mar 45	3	SN143	P/O D. R. Worley	hbF (Embeck-Minden) rnc
30 Mar 45	80	NV766	F/O N. J. Rankin (K)	sdbF E Vechta
31 Mar 45	3	NV979	Sgt H. R. Butt (K)	sdb e/ftrs NE Damme
2 April 45	3	NV777	Sgt W. Campbell	e/f f/l near B.56
2 April 45	80	NV982	F/O R. J. H Holland (K)	hbF ftr (Rheine-Hanover)
2 April 45	80	SN139 W2-N	P/O H. A. Horsey (K)	e/f F? E Friesoythe ftr
3 April 45	56	EJ526 US-N	W/O W. M. D. Tuck (E)	e/f csd S Diepholz
3 April 45	56	NV728 US-X	Sgt P. C. Brown (S)	e/f f/l E Friesoythe
3 April 45	274	NV990	F/L J. C. Ward	e/f f/l 2 m SW Hengelo
4 April 45	56	EJ546 US-B	W/O R. R. Hales (K)	F? last seen S Bremen
4 April 45	274	NV660	F/O P. A. Halliwell (K)	csd in g/a (Bremen) last seen
4 April 45	222	NV698	F/O W. Donald (K)	Oldenburg (3 Tempests claimed by I/JG26 E Diepholz, inc. one by Lt Söffing)
6 April 45	56	EJ761 US-V	W/O L. W. Freeman	hbF f/l near Helmond
6 April 45	56	NV667 US-A	W/O D. C. H. Rex	hbF f/l near B.102
6 April 45	222	NV750 ZD-P	F/O R. H. Davidson (K)	spun in, NW Nijmegen
7 April 45	1FPP	MW757	F/C A. C. Irwin	dila Henlow
8 April 45	151RU	EJ778	G/C H. L. Messita	e/f dila B.55
9 April 45	560TU	EJ845	F/L I. W. Smith (K)	csd on t/o Brunton
9 April 45	274	SN142	P/O W. B. Weir (K)	sdbF (Emden-Oldenburg)
11 April 45	56	EJ640 US-T	W/O D. Hutchinson	dila B.80
12 April 45	80	EJ714	F/O W. R. Sheaf	f/l w/u B.112
12 April 45	33	NV783	F/S P. C. Walton (E)	sdb Fw190s b/o W Uelzen
12 April 45	33	NV919	Sgt J. Staines (K)	sdb Fw190s W Uelzen
12 April 45	33	SN180 5R-V	Cpt E. D. Thompson	dam by Fw190 Uelzen w/o (6 Tempests claimed

Date	Unit	Aircraft	Pilot	Circumstances
				by I/JG26, inc. Oblt Dortenmann (2) and Lt Söffing (1))
13 April 45	56OTU	EJ542	F/O G. W. R. Ford (K)	csd in bad vis Lamberton
13 April 45	486	EJ864	F/S W. J. K. Hart	rof f/l NE Horstel
13 April 45	486	SN184 SA-F	S/L K. G. Taylor-Cannon (K)	hbF b/o NW Dömitz
14 April 45	486	SN141	W/O O. J. Mitchell (K)	psdb Bf109s E Ludwigslust
15 April 45	80	NV719 W2-E	W/O A. M. Rollo (PoW)	hbF/Fw190 f/l N Ludwigslust
15 April 45	486	NV988 SA-Y	F/O A. R. Evans	e/f near Uelzen b/o in a/t
16 April 45	122W	NV641 B	W/C R. E. P. Brooker (K)	sdb Fw190s near Wittenberge
16 April 45	80	NV983	Sgt W. F. Turner (K)	sdb Fw190s near Neuruppin
17 April 45	80	NV991	F/O L. Smith (K)	sdb Fw190 S Lübeck (3 Tempests claimed by I/JG26, inc. Oblt Dortenmann (1) and Lt Söffing (1))
19 April 45	83GSU	EJ689	F/L Latham	dila Dunsfold
19 April 45	56OTU	EJ877	F/O D. H. N. Reid	e/f f/l Fenwick
19 April 45	222	EJ883	F/L C. G. F. Deck (K)	sdbF Neumunster a/f
19 April 45	33	SN190 5R-B	F/L R. A. McPhie (PoW)	hbF f/l N Freetz
21 April 45	3	EJ610	F/L B. C. McKenzie (K)	hbF last seen E Hamburg (possibly the aircraft claimed by II/JG26 NW Perleberg)
22 April 45	80	NV789	F/L L. Y. J. Friend	e/f f/l near Warmwell
23 April 45	274	EJ781	F/S A. C. Inglis (E)	sdbF Eggebaek a/f
23 April 45	222	NV695 ZD-B	W/O J. A. G. Samirande	dila B.109
23 April 45	33	SN173	F/S C. Peters (PoW)	hbF f/l 8 m SW Schleswig
24 April 45	222	EJ875	F/O J. G. Wilson (S)	hbF Ratzeburg f/l a/t
24 April 45	486	NV651 SA-R	F/S W. W. May (PoW)	hbF b/o near Hamburg
24 April 45	33	NV731	F/S J. E. Fraser (K)	hbF csd Königsmoor
24 April 45	33	NV754	F/O D. J. ter Beek (PoW)	hbF b/o near Schönberg
24 April 45	56	NV980 US-J	P/O D. C. H. Rex (S)	hbsaf f/l near Pritzwalk
24 April 45	56	SN131 US-P	F/L J. J. Payton (PoW)	hbsaf f/l W Pritzwalk
25 April 45	33	SN163	W/O H. M. Thomas (PoW)	hbF f/l near Krautsand
26 April 45	56OTU	EJ560	F/S A. E. Gunn	dila Milfield
26 April 45	486	NV967	F/O K. A. Smith (S)	hbF f/l N Uithiele
27 April 45	486	EJ584	F/S R. A. Melles (PoW)	hbF b/o N Hamburg
29 April 45	3	NV663 JF-S	W/O A. Crowe (S)	F? f/l N Gresse (claimed by Lt Söffing, I/JG26, W Lanenburg)
30 April 45	3	EJ598 JF-W	F/O S. T. Worbey (K)	psdbF (Schwerin a/f)
30 April 45	3	NV936	P/O D. R. Worley (K)	sdbF Schwerin a/f
1 May 45	56OTU	EJ822	F/L J. H. Flynn	e/f f/l near Berwick
1 May 45	222	SN205	F/L J. L. Lawson	e/f f/l 6 m N Stade
2 May 45	486	NV722	F/O O. D. Eagleson (E)	hbF f/l near Lübeck
3 May 45	486	EJ550	F/O C. E. Blee	hbF f/l near Stade
3 May 45	486	NV791 SA-L	P/O J. E. Wood	hbF f/l SW Kiel
3 May 45	3	SN189 JF-R	F/L J. Bone (K)	F? csd near Kiel
4 May 45	486	JN877 SA-X	F/O M. Austin (PoW)	F? f/l W Barsinghausen (probably the aircraft claimed as a Typhoon by Lt R. Schmitt, I/JG1 (He 162))
7 May 45	56OTU	EJ661 HQ-P	W/O D. E. Sheppard	e/f f/l Bolsden Hall, Northumberland
12 May 45	3	EJ588 JF-N	F/L W. R. Robertson (K)	cld SN166 N Rotenburg
12 May 45	56OTU	EJ685	F/L F. W. Mossing (K)	cld NV759 csd Ford
12 May 45	56OTU	NV759 GF-N	F/S C. W. Powell (K)	cld EJ685 csd Doddington
12 May 45	222	NV985	F/O D. G. C. McLelland	dila Grossenbrode
12 May 45	3	SN166	Sgt W. Campbell (K)	cld EJ588 N Rotenburg
18 May 45	287	JN751	F/S P. C. A. Redstone (K)	csd in bad wx I of Sheppey
18 May 45	56OTU	NV643	W/O B. S. Pollard (K)	stalled csd Coldingham
18 May 45	56OTU	NV712	F/O H. R. Wingate	efto csd Milfield
19 May 45	222	NV933 ZD-W	F/S F. Salter	dila B.109
23 May 45	3FP	NV666	F/O R. Jackson	missing Aston Down-Kirkbride
28 May 45	33	SN164	F/S C. P. Nisbet	e/f f/l E Eickeloh
6 June 45	274	EJ525 JJ-K	n/k	dam in flying acc nr dila B.120
10 June 45	56	EJ593	F/S G. J. Swindells	dila B.120
19 June 45	486	NV969 SA-Z	F/O O. D. Eagleson	b/o over sea S Copenhagen cnk
25 June 45	56OTU	EJ763	Sgt M. R. A. Harries	dila Milfield
25 June 45	13MU	MW753	F/O M. S. Hewitt (K)	csd in aeros Meppershall
26 June 45	56OTU	EJ811 GF-A	F/S A. Herbert	e/f f/l near Milfield
4 July 45	A&AEE	MW806 6	F/L E. Statters	dila Khartoum
4 July 45	274	NV976	F/L R. C. Topley	e/f f/l 1 m NNW B.168
4 July 45	33	SN160	F/L R. J. Dall (K)	csd in aeros R.16
4 July 45	274	SN181	W/O H. D. Parker	e/f f/l S Lüneburg
5 July 45	1FP	MW827	I/O D. Ramsay	efto f/l near White Waltham
11 July 45	56	NV927	P/O A. M. L. Kennaugh	e/f b/o over sea SE Hoorn
25 July 45	A&AEE	NV946	S/L L. Gregory (K)	csd in rpa Enford Range
27 July 45	15FU	MW792	F/L I. Tuckson	dila Filton
5 Aug 45	A&AEE	MW801 1	F/L H. A. Curry	e/f b/o near Marble Arch, Libya
20 Aug 45	82MU	PR538	F/L G. L. Farquharson	e/f f/l near Lichfield
27 Aug 45	486	EJ659	P/O W. J. Shaw	hit pole low flg f/l N B.158
31 Aug 45	56OTU	EJ808	F/O A. B. Mattock	dila Milfield
8 Sept 45	174	NV977	F/O P. A. Sutherland	e/f f/l near Warmwell
10 Sept 45	15FU	MW825	P/O J. M. Harris (K)	e/f csd near Filton
11 Sept 45	80	SN218 W2-J	F/O A. J. Taylor	e/f f/l w/u B.158
18 Sept 45	3	NV718	F/O R. E. Pendle (K)	csd in g/a practice B.155
26 Sept 45	33	SN225	Sgt R. Ellis (K)	csd in g/a practice Sylt
8 Oct 45	56OTU	SN110 HQ-2	F/O R. W. Pottinger	hit by tractor Milfield

Below: On 26 April 1945, 56 OTU instructor, Flight Sergeant 'Ben' Gunn, returned to Milfield low on fuel only to find the main runway blocked. Obliged to land on the short runway, out of wind, he attempted to raise the undercarriage to avoid overshooting. Unfortunately the wheels refused to come up and two and a half somersaults later, having crossed the main road in front of a rather surprised bus driver, he stepped out of the remains of EJ560! (A. E. Gunn)

Date	Unit	Aircraft	Pilot	Circumstances
10 Oct 45	174	EJ595 JJ-F	F/O K. R. Pullan (K)	csd in aeros near Eldingen
16 Oct 45	80	NV703	F/O R. C. Rudkin (K)	csd low flg 12 m ENE B.118
17 Oct 45	80	NV970	F/O R. S. E. Verran (K)	dived in, Kostorf cnk
18 Oct 45	41	NV763	W/O P. E. Wheatley	e/f f/l 1 m S Dahme
5 Nov 45	183	MW747	W/O W. G. Barber	t/a Fairwood Common
10 Nov 45	3	NV724 JF-E	F/L C. E. Hall	u/c collapsed Fassberg
15 Nov 45	287	JN763	W/O R. B. Farmiloe (K)	csd in aeros near Harlow
26 Nov 45	54	MW778	F/O L. Richardson (K)	csd in bad wx Chatford
26 Nov 45	54	MW799	F/S F. Blakey (K)	csd in bad wx Mungry Lodge, Wiltshire
26 Nov 45	54	MW811	W/O P. Cobb (K)	csd in bad wx Pill Heath
27 Nov 45	56OTU	NV709	F/O R. G. Marshall (K)	s/f in dive csd Birgham
27 Nov 45	56	SN208	Sgt G. V. Parker	flaps dam in flight nr
30 Nov 45	56OTU	EJ834	Sgt P. G. Hickson	e/f f/l Fogorig Farm, Borders
30 Nov 45	41	EJ888	F/S W. G. Gordon	efto csd B.158
30 Nov 45	174	NV642	W/O M. A. Lush	e/f f/l near Weyhausen
3 Dec 45	56	NV963 US-A	W/O A. G. Bain	e/f f/l Bannetze
19 Dec 45	80	SN337	F/O R. A. Wheeler (K)	spun in, Binnensee
29 Dec 45	33	SN116	W/O N. T. Beckwith (K)	hit trees csd N B.118
4 Jan 46	287	JN797	Sgt S. G. Brooks	t/a West Malling nr
8 Jan 46	56	EJ690	W/O W. Y. Kinsman	csd on t/o B.170
22 Jan 46	41	NV640	S/L J. B. Shepherd (K)	efto csd B.116
29 Jan 46	56OTU	EJ859	F/L V. Parker (K)	csd in aeros Felkington
15 Feb 46	247	MW794	W/O Cowin	dila Fairwood Common
16 Feb 46	1APS	NV787	W/C A. Eyre (K)	e/f f/l in woods near St. Athan
4 Mar 46	56	EJ538	W/O W. Y. Kinsman	e/f dila Gatow
8 Mar 46	56OTU	EJ666	W/O J. Alves	f/l near Hirwaun
12 Mar 46	287	JN766	W/O O. Cocuran	efto csd West Malling
14 Mar 46	5	PR616	W/O R. Shanks	dila Bhopal nr
14 Mar 46	33	SN231	F/S G. H. Curtis (K)	csd in bad wx near Springe
30 Mar 46	3	NV948 J5-P	F/S P. N. Mawhood	e/f w/u Gatow
2 April 46	5	PR654	F/O J. Rixon	dila Bhopal nr
9 April 46	287	JN795	W/O E. F. G. Newman	e/f w/u West Malling nr
4 May 46	33	NV697	F/S W. A. Hickey	e/f f/l Holkenhaven
16 May 46	54	MW772	F/L A. L. S. Stooke-Hallet (K)	cld MW816[22] csd Chilbolton
16 May 46	54	MW812	F/S L. F. Oman (K)	cld MW772 csd Chilbolton
27 June 46	3	SN222	F/S J. W. Coates (K)	csd in bad wx Schwagstorf
11 July 46	54	MW818	W/O E. J. Gardiner	dila Odiham
3 Aug 46	5	PR650 OQ-S	F/L H. Pears	f/l in bad wx 26 m NW Poona
6 Sept 46	BCW	SN103	F/L R. W. Bunyan	e/f f/l Bergen
9 Sept 46	Napr	EJ823	Mr G. A. Reston	e/f f/l near Luton
13 Sept 46	152	PR604 UM-X	P2 J. Pitt-Lewis	e/f b/o Hauelign
14 Sept 46	3	SN221	P/O E. R. Campbell	cld SN334 f/l Margate
14 Sept 46	3	SN334	W/O E. C. Cruse (K)	cld SN221 csd Ramsgate
7 Oct 46	26	PR679	F/S H. Doyle	dila Aston Down
10 Oct 46	30	PR583	F/S J. P. Whyte	cld PR672 f/l 30 m SE Agra
10 Oct 46	30	PR672	W/O R. T. W. Hewetson	cld PR583 b/o 30 m SE Agra
11 Oct 46	320MU	PR547	F/L B. M. Byrne	e/f f/l 10 m NE Dabeji
21 Oct 46	322MU	PR526	F/L A. C. Bird	e/fire f/l N Kanpur
25 Oct 46	33	SN210 5R-V	F/L G. F. Wheeler	e/f on start up Fassberg nr
15 Nov 46	5	PR720 OQ-A	P2 Cover	dila Poona
2 Dec 46	20	PR841	F/S J. Birnie	dila Agra
9 Dec 46	80	SN226	S/L H. A. Walmsley	e/f f/l Deek
20 Dec 46	StMg	NX145	F/L G. J. James	e/f f/l 6 m E Launceston
17 Jan 47	16	PR792	F/O Bishop	dila Fassberg
17 Feb 47	20	PR582	W/O R. T. W. Hewetson	hbd near Agra nr
20 Feb 47	3(I)	PR532	F/O Khans	e/f f/l 8 m E Yelahanka
25 Feb 47	1FU	NX255	F/O D. W. D. Sturgeon	e/f b/o off Benghazi
18 Mar 47	5	PR716	P/O Pennington	dila Miramshah
18 Mar 47	16	PR667	W/O A. Mackay	e/f f/l near Gatow
28 Mar 47	TFU	PR802	F/O J. W. Patterson	dila Defford
17 April 47	5	PR680	F/O Davison	dila Miramshah
6 May 47	6	NX251	F/L Walker	e/f f/l near Nicosia
14 May 47	3(I)	PR836	S/L M. K. Misra	dila Risalpur
16 May 47	20	PR807	F/O R. D. Thornton (K)	csd 25 m W Agra cnk
11 June 47	5	PR646	S/L Pandit[23]	csd on t/o Peshawar
18 June 47	3(I)	PR596	F/L R. Singh	dila Miramshah
18 June 47	80	SN216	P2 A. R. Warrior	e/f f/l Brandenburg
20 June 47	3(I)	PR855	F/L R. Singh	dila Miramshah
21 June 47	16	PR839	P2 P. G. Hickson (K)	csd in bad wx 1 m NE Gemert
26 June 47	10(I)	PR804	P/O S. R. Bose	e/f f/l near Chakeri
6 July 47	3(I)	PR586	F/O G. H. King	dila Miramshah

▽1

▽2

Date	Unit	Aircraft	Pilot	Circumstances
16 July 47	8	NX198	F/O F. G. Tanner (K)	csd in rpa N Khormaksar
24 July 47	2(I)	PR548	P/O H. S. Bedi	dila Poona
26 July 47	2(I)	PR534	F/L D. B. Rai (K)	csd in hills near Poona
9 Aug 47	26	MW422 XC-H	P1 J. Westwell	e/f f/l near Zeltweg
14 Aug 47	6	NX149	F/L D. O. Luke	e/f b/o Voroklini
26 Aug 47	33	PR781	P2 W. A. Hickey	e/fire csd Fassberg
1 Sept 47	213	NX181	F/L A. E. Johnston	dila Nicosia
8 Sept 47	109MU	NX190	F/O E. W. Ginger	h/f w/u Khormaksar
15 Sept 47	213	NX192	W/O R. G. Leeson	e/f w/u El Firdan
19 Sept 47	6	NX195	P2 D. V. Cooper	e/f w/u 1 m NW Fayid
27 Oct 47	6	NX194	F/O M. A. D'Arcy	e/f csd on app Shallufa
4 Nov 47	226OCU	PR657	P2 J. F. James (K)	csu failure csd Bentwaters
26 Nov 47	6	NX266	F/O M. W. Reid	e/f f/l 5 m S Khartoum
18 Dec 47	26	PR665	F/O F. Mandeville	dila Gatow
29 Dec 47	3	NV989 J5-F	P1 W. R. Irving	e/f f/l w/u Calais a/f

Date	Unit	Aircraft	Pilot	Circumstances
30 Dec 47	26	MW417 XC-R	P3 W. K. Sewell	e/fire f/l 1 m W Spandau
14 Jan 48	3	SN339 J5-P	F/L J. M. Wardlow (K)	csd in rpa off Neustadt
16 Jan 48	16	PR778	F/O N. C. Davison (K)	e/f csd Ruhlegen
7 Feb 48	6	NX257 JV-Z	F/L G. D. Sutcliffe	g/lk f/l near Ferfer
12 April 48	8	NX140	F/L J. A. Wilson	g/lk f/l 36 m NNW Khormaksar
31 May 48	26	PR687	P2 T. J. H. Doyle (K)	csd in rpa Haustenbeck range
1 June 48	213	NX180 AK-D	P2 J. P. Crighton (K)	csd low flg Harmil Is
16 Aug 48	8	NX148	P2 J. Sutton	dila Khormaksar
20 Aug 48	8	NX244	P2 Bowyer (K)	csd in rpa Awabil
24 Aug 48	249	NX209	P2 C. Peters (K)	stalled csd 14 m SE Habbaniya
11 Sept 48	109MU	NX187	F/O Vracaric	dila Fayid
17 Sept 48	213	NX253	P2 M. A. R. Heald	dila Eastleigh
12 Oct 48	26	PR861	P4 R. J. Turnbull (K)	hit htc csd 8 m W Minden
16 Nov 48	249	NX142	F/O D. M. Scrimgeour	hbd f/l near Habbaniya
4 Dec 48	226OCU	PR846	P4 M. A. Mole	dila Bentwaters
6 Dec 48	33	PR798 5R-G	F/L R. W. Bunyan	h/f b/o SW Dummer See
9 Dec 48	26	PR738	P4 C. Randle	csd on t/o Gütersloh
18 Dec 48	1FU	NX223	P2 D. V. Cooper	e/f f/l near Orange
5 Jan 49	26	PR674	P4 J. J. Sycamore (K)	csd low flg 8 m S Melle
7 Jan 49	213	NX207	P/O D. C. Tattersfield (K)	sdb Israeli Spits Sinai
7 Jan 49	39	NX287	F/O C. C. Davidson (K)	s/f in dive csd SE Khartoum
24 Jan 49	39	NX247 H	P3 R. Watson	cld NX264 on t/o Khartoum
24 Jan 49	39	NX264 G	F/O A. Twigg	cld NX247 on t/o Khartoum
28 Jan 49	BCW	PR848	W/C A. D. Grace	dila Buckeburg
11 Feb 49	6	NX134 JV-T	F/L D. O. Luke	dila Nicosia
21 Feb 49	6	NX254	G/C A. F. Anderson	e/f f/l Abu Zenim
11 Mar 49	26	PR793	F/O C. R. Percival (K)	csd bad wx Ems-Weser Canal
14 Mar 49	249	NX141	P3 J. Haton	e/f f/l 30 m SW Habbaniya
22 Mar 49	26	PR862	P2 J. J. H. Penny	e/f b/o 2 m S Gütersloh
23 Mar 49	8	NX228	P4 A. E. Staves (K)	csd in rpa off Khormaksar
8 April 49	33	PR689 5R-E	P2 E. E.Tyrer	e/f f/l 2 m E Lienen
19 May 49	249	NX150 GN-H	F/O D. G. L. Heywood	dila Deversoir
26 May 49	8	NX156	F/O R. A. W. Stobart	e/f f/l near Khormaksar
2 June 49	6	NX261 JV-B	P2 Z. T. Kozlowski	dila Deversoir
20 June 49	226OCU	PR811	P4 G. N. G. Bowtle	e/f w/u Bentwaters

1. PR716 'OQ-A' of 5 Squadron was written-off after a landing accident at Miramshah on 18 March 1947. (H. Pears)

2. Flight Lieutenant 'Tug' Wilson of 8 Squadron was forced to land in the desert north of Aden when NX140 had a glycol leak on 12 April 1948. (Group Captain F. W. M. Jensen)

3 and 4. NX247 'H' and NX264 'G' of 39 Squadron met on the runway at Khartoum on 24 January 1949, each sustaining fatal damage. (via D. Howley/R. L. Ward)

5. On 22 June 1949, NX239 'G' of 213 Squadron burnt out after a drop-tank caught fire during a landing accident at Deversoir. (J. D. Gibson)

△3 ▽4

▽5

Date	Unit	Aircraft		Pilot	Circumstances
22 June 49	6	NX239	G	P4 G. T. Lovett	dila Deversoir
5 July 49	249	NX268		W/C R. Deacon-Elliot	hbd f/l Morphou Bay
8 Aug 49	213	NX249	Q	F/O G. Mott	efto csd Fayid
24 Aug 49	107MU	NX132		F/O D. A. Hagragan	e/f w/u Habbaniya
2 Sept 49	33	PR753		P/O J. D. Evans	dila Changi
7 Sept 49	213	NX248		P2 V. R. Strobel (K)	csd in rpa Abu Sultan range
17 Sept 49	1689	SN328		P3 A. D. Liquorish	e/f w/u Aston Down
23 Sept 49	249	NX233	W	P3 R. Watson	dila Deversoir
29 Sept 49	107MU	NX282		P2 K. A. Dingley	e/f f/l W Kasfareet
29 Sept 49	213	NX229	R	P3 J. D. Gibson	h/f dila Deversoir
30 Sept 49	33	PR853	5R-K	P/O D. T. Parfitt	e/f f/l near Changi
18 Oct 49	249	NX126	A	P3 G. A. Hunt	dila Deversoir
29 Oct 49	249	NX182	Q	P2 R. E. Maxwell	cld NX281[24] w/u Kabrit
4 Nov 49	Napr	NX235		Mr A. Sutcliffe (K)	csd in aeros Luton
15 Nov 49	33	PR726	5R-S	P3 C. Randle	dila Changi
15 Dec 49	20MU	EJ641		F/L F. E. C. Underhill	dila Langley
25 Dec 49	OFU	NX128		F/L E. L. Jacobs	e/f f/l Auny
20 Jan 50	33	MW423	5R-G	P2 C. Thomas	w/u Changi
10 Feb 50	249	NX252	O	P2 R. Watson (K)	e/f csd Deversoir
24 Mar 50	1FP	NX129		P1 D. F. Smith	e/f f/l W Wroughton
24 July 50	33	PR786	5R-U	P1 H. E. A. Hurn (K)	e/f csd 1 m N Khan Itan
28 July 50	33	PR921	5R-F	F/O A. Twigg	h/f w/u Butterworth
13 Sept 50	33	PR742	5R-K	F/L J. P. Langer	e/f w/u Butterworth
24 Oct 50	33	PR788	5R-A	F/O G. J. Swindells	dila Butterworth
16 Nov 50	33	PR895	5R-F	F/O G. J. Swindells (K)	csd on ldg Butterworth
30 Nov 50	226OCU	EJ862		F/L D. A. Maddox	e/f f/l Saffron Walden
9 Jan 51	1689	NX127		F/S A. L. Steel (K)	spun in, Hallen
28 Feb 51	33	PR782	5R-R	F/O J. F. Wilson	dila Butterworth
6 June 51	APS	JN807	WH-18	Sgt C. T. Wilson	e/f f/l near Acklington
30 April 52	Sylt	NV960		F/L D. McDonald	dila Sylt
4 June 52	Sylt	SN329		F/S W. M. Scott	e/f f/l near Sylt
10 July 52	Sylt	SN209		P/O Easterbrook	e/f f/l near Sylt
6 Nov 52	Sylt	JN871		F/O R. Eames	efto csd Sylt
10 Dec 52	233OCU	NV965		F/S S. Piatkowski	e/f csd in f/l Templeton
5 Jan 53	Sylt	SN346		F/L D. W. Jaques (K)	dila Sylt
26 Mar 53	Sylt	NV974	Y	F/O W. A. Howe	e/f f/l SE Utersum
8 May 53	Sylt	NX151		F/L W. H. N. Sloan (K)	hit trees csd S Oldenburg
13 July 53	Sylt	SN327		F/L T. B. Watt	e/f f/l S Hornum lighthouse
6 Aug 53	Sylt	EJ758	B	M/P T. A. Barnett	e/f dtd 1m S Morsum
10 Aug 53	Sylt	EJ786		F/O J. D. MacCarthy	e/f w/u Sylt
17 Aug 53	Sylt	NV975		M/P T. A. Barnett	dam by m/g fire from Sabre nr
1 Nov 53	Sylt	SN289		F/L G. B. Smither (K)	e/f dtd 3 m NW Westerland
8 June 54	Sylt	NV665		M/P I. P. Morris	h/f w/u Sylt
25 June 54	Sylt	NV661		F/S E. J. Ledwidge	e/f dtd 2 m ENE Sylt
6 Sept 54	Sylt	EJ839		F/L A. Shannon	hit by cannon-shell in wing nr
21 Oct 54	229OCU	EJ663	RS-23	Sgt J. MacKenzie	e/f dila Chivenor

Notes

1. P. E. G. Sayer was the Gloster Chief Test-Pilot on a visit to 1 Squadron.
2. 778 Squadron, Fleet Air Arm – the unit which undertook service trials of new Naval aircraft types. The significance of the allocation of a Typhoon to this unit is not known.
3. Wing Commander Rabagliati was Wing Commander Flying, Coltishall, and usually flew a Spitfire; he had borrowed Squadron Leader Don Taylor's aircraft, 'JE-DT', for this ill-fated sortie.
4. 'EL-R' R8927 was a 181 Squadron aircraft on loan to 182 Squadron.
5. These six Typhoons, plus three Spitfires and two Lysanders, were destroyed when a 10 Squadron Halifax II, HX181, crashed into the servicing hangar while attempting to land at Tangmere. Despite valiant efforts by station personnel, the crew perished.
6. This aircraft was repaired and later saw service with 245 Squadron.
7. These three aircraft actually belonged to 198 Squadron; 183 and 198 Squadrons exchanged aircraft for the period 15 March–1 April 1944.
8. 'RL-7' were Fighter Leader School codes – Wing Commander Brooker had brought his aircraft with him on posting to 123 Wing.
9. One of these two aircraft was MN552, the other remains unidentified.
10. Although still carrying 486 Squadron codes, this aircraft belonged to 20 Sector HQ Flight, and was usually flown by Group Captain Gillam.
11. This aircraft was retrieved after the German retreat and subsquently repaired. It later saw service with 55 OTU.
12. Flight Sergeant Meechan was a 247 Squadron pilot ferrying an 83 GSU aircraft.
13. Flight Lieutenant Grantham baled out safely and evaded capture, but was killed on 16 August 1944, attempting to pass through the German lines.
14. Flight Lieutenant Merret was taken prisoner of war, but was later killed in captivity.
15. This was a new aircraft and had not yet had the squadron letters (OV) applied.
16. This aircraft was subsequently repaired and later saw service with 182 Squadron.
17. The dogfight was with (unidentified) Allied fighters.
18. Although the two 80 Squadron Tempests lost on 18 and 25 September 1944 are given various identities by different sources, EJ668 and EJ664 are believed to be correct. However, it has so far proved impossible to determine which of the two aircraft was lost on which day.
19. The fuselage of this aircraft was in use as a training aid at a Delft technical school for many years. It now resides in the RAF Museum's store, still wearing its 486 Squadron codes.
20. Wing Commander Beamont was flying a 3 Squadron aircraft on this occasion, rather than his usual 'RPB' (which had replaced his earlier 'RB' JN751).
21. Flight Lieutenant Green was also attacked by a P-51.
22. MW816 landed safely.
23. Squadron Leader Pandit was one of the 10 Squadron (RIAF) pilots converting to Tempests with 5 Squadron (RAF).
24. NX281 landed safely.
25. Detached from 61st Fighter Squadron, 56 Fighter Group USAAF 'to fly the Typhoon in all its aspects'.

Below: The pilot of Tempest TT.5 SN346 was killed when it turned over on landing at Sylt on 5 January 1953. (via R. L. Ward)

Index

Numbers in *italic* refer to illustrations.
Names of units, personnel and places mentioned in the appendices
covering losses of Typhoons and Tempests are not listed here unless they
are also mentioned in the main text of the book.

2. Index of Units

3. Index of Places

Locations marked thus * can be found on one or other of the maps included in the book.

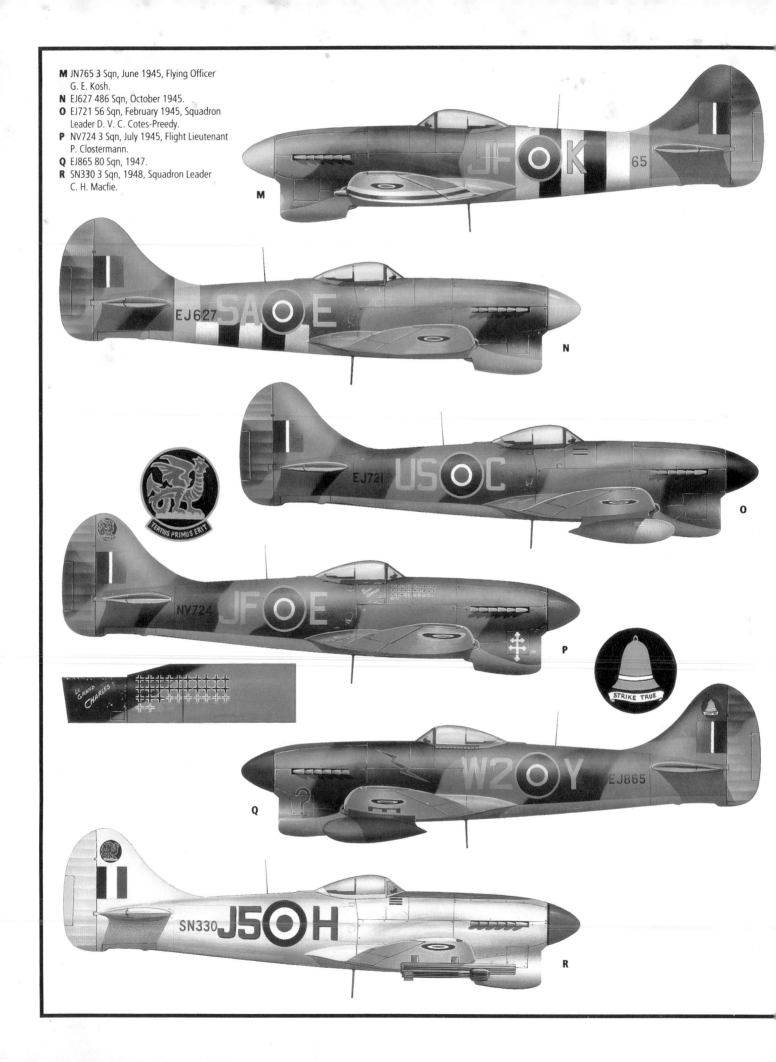

M JN765 3 Sqn, June 1945, Flying Officer G. E. Kosh.

N EJ627 486 Sqn, October 1945.

O EJ721 56 Sqn, February 1945, Squadron Leader D. V. C. Cotes-Preedy.

P NV724 3 Sqn, July 1945, Flight Lieutenant P. Clostermann.

Q EJ865 80 Sqn, 1947.

R SN330 3 Sqn, 1948, Squadron Leader C. H. Macfie.